FROM SLAVERY TO FREEDOM

Also by Seymour Drescher

TOCQUEVILLE AND ENGLAND

TOCQUEVILLE AND BEAUMONT ON SOCIAL REFORM (*editor*)

DILEMMAS OF DEMOCRACY: Tocqueville and Modernization

CAPITALISM AND ANTISLAVERY

ECONOCIDE: British Slavery in the Era of Abolition

THE ABOLITION OF SLAVERY AND THE AFTERMATH OF EMANCIPATION IN BRAZIL (*with Rebecca J. Scott et al.*)

ANTISLAVERY, RELIGION AND REFORM (*editor with Christine Bolt*)

POLITICAL SYMBOLISM IN MODERN EUROPE (*editor with D. Sabean and A. Sharlin*)

THE MEANING OF FREEDOM (*editor with Frank McGlynn*)

A HISTORICAL GUIDE TO WORLD SLAVERY (*editor with Stanley L. Engerman*)

From Slavery to Freedom

Comparative Studies in the Rise and Fall of Atlantic Slavery

Seymour Drescher

Foreword by Stanley L. Engerman

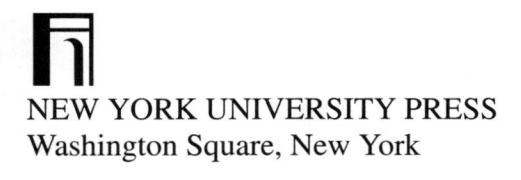

NEW YORK UNIVERSITY PRESS
Washington Square, New York

© Seymour Drescher 1999
Foreword © Stanley L. Engerman 1999

For details of original publication of different chapters,
please see the Acknowledgements on p. xxv.

All rights reserved

First published in the U.S.A. in 1999 by
NEW YORK UNIVERSITY PRESS
Washington Square
New York, N.Y. 10003

This book is printed on paper suitable for recycling and
made from fully managed and sustained forest sources.

Library of Congress Cataloging-in-Publication Data
Drescher, Seymour.
From slavery to freedom : comparative studies in the rise and fall
of Atlantic slavery / Seymour Drescher ; foreword by Stanley L.
Engerman.
p. cm.
Includes bibliographical references and index.
ISBN 0–8147–1918–X (cloth : alk. paper)
1. Slavery—Great Britain—History.   2. Slavery—United States—
History.   3. Slave-trade—Great Britain—History.   4. Slave-trade—
United States—History.   5. Great Britain—Politics and government.
6. Great Britain—Race relations.   7. United States—Politics and
government.   8. United States—Race relations.   I. Title.
HT1161.D74   1999
306.3'62'0941—dc21   98–37693
                                                                             CIP

Printed in Great Britain

To my grandchildren
Atalya, Eliana, Matthew and Yasmin

Contents

List of Tables and Figures	ix
Foreword by Stanley L. Engerman	xi
Preface	xxiii
Acknowledgements	xxv

Part I

Introduction   1

1. Capitalism and Abolition: Values and Forces in Britain, 1783–1814 (1976)   5
2. Two Variants of Anti-Slavery: Religious Organization and Social Mobilization in Britain and France, 1780–1870 (1980)   35
3. Public Opinion and the Destruction of British Colonial Slavery (1982)   57
4. The Decline Thesis of British Slavery since *Econocide* (1986)   87

Part II

Introduction   117

5. Brazilian Abolition in Comparative Perspective (1988)   119
6. British Way, French Way: Opinion Building and Revolution in the Second French Slave Emancipation (1991)   158
7. The Long Goodbye: Dutch Capitalism and Antislavery in Comparative Perspective (1994)   196
8. Servile Insurrection and John Brown's Body in Europe (1993)   235

Part III

Introduction 273

9 The Ending of the Slave Trade and the
Evolution of European Scientific Racism (1990) 275

10 The Atlantic Slave Trade and the Holocaust:
A Comparative Analysis (1996) 312

11 The Role of Jews in the Transatlantic
Slave Trade (1993) 339

12 Eric Williams: British Capitalism and
British Slavery (1987) 355

13 *Capitalism and Slavery* after Fifty Years (1997) 379

14 Free Labor vs Slave Labor: The British and
Caribbean Cases (1999) 399

Index 445

List of Tables and Figures

Tables

2.1 Anti-slavery petitions and religious affiliation, 1788–1833 — 39

2.2 Anti-slavery and English evangelical denominations, ca 1833 — 40

3.1 Averages of prices per slave sold for debt in Jamaica, 1808–27 — 79

4.1 British West Indian shares of British trade, 1763–83 — 92

4.2 British percentage of area shares' contributions to increased exports, 1700–1 to 1804–6 — 96

4.3 Slave-grown share of British imports, 1784–6 to 1814–16 — 103

4.4 Percentage of received slaves re-exported from Jamica by five-year intervals, 1713–87 — 106

4.5 Re-exports of sugar compared to 'British'/foreign sugar ratios, 1765–1818 — 113

5.1 Distribution of foreigners, United States and Brazil, 1860 and 1872 — 126

5.2 Percentage of the labor force in selected urban areas — 127

6.1 Resolutions in favor of emancipation presented by Conseils-Généraux of French departments, 1835–47 — 173

Figures

2.1 Methodist and New Dissenting membership and Abolitionist petitions, 1750–1914 — 38

3.1	Petitions to legislatures of Britain and France, 1831–48	61
3.2	Three petition campaigns, 1829–47	62
3.3	Trade of the slave colonies of Britain and France, as a percentage of the total trade of each	77
4.1	British West Indian trade, 1722–1822	91

Foreword

In an academic career that spans nearly four decades, Seymour Drescher has written mainly on two topics – the views of Alexis de Tocqueville and the nature of British antislavery viewed in comparative perspective. The transition between these topics had been rather gradual. His first book, *Tocqueville and England*, was focused on the year 1835, just after the British abolition of slavery and the first year of the apprenticeship that was part of the emancipation agreement, but neither was discussed, nor even barely mentioned. The transition between topics began with his second book, *Dilemmas of Democracy*, which includes a chapter on French antislavery, with some discussion of Tocqueville's imaginative *Report on Abolition of Slavery in French Colonies* prepared for the French legislature and of other contemporaries describing the movement. Tocqueville's *Report* included a rather perceptive remark on the importance of public opinion for British abolition, in contrast with its relative unimportance for the French. For the next three decades Drescher has drawn upon, as well as extended, Tocqueville's conjecture, and since 1976 he has published two books, co-edited three volumes, and written more than twenty essays on abolition and its aftermath. The first of these books drew heavily upon economic data and coined a new word to describe the ending of slavery that was not due to economic failure, but which indeed caused the economic decline – econocide. Subsequently there was a turn to more ideological factors to explain the demise of the slave system in the European colonial areas.

This volume, therefore, includes less than half of Drescher's writings on British abolition, but they indicate why Drescher has become one of the major contributors to the discussion of slavery and abolition in the past several decades. These studies have greatly enriched our understanding of the abolition process, even if disagreements remain to be reconciled. Moreover, these studies have made quite significant contributions to British, American, European, and African history, more generally. The leading scholars of slavery and antislavery in the modern world include, among others, Drescher,

David Brion Davis, Roger Anstey, David Eltis, Robert Fogel, and Howard Temperley. These have presented varying interpretations and often reach different conclusions, but they have usefully posed relevant questions and their analyses no longer look at slavery in isolation, but in its relation to religion, politics, culture, and economic behavior and attitudes. At times, perhaps, slavery may seem to swallow up everything else in the time period studied but, at the least, it is no longer regarded as an unusual or peculiar institution divorced from more modern or acceptable parts of life.

The case of England has long been studied as the central model for the ending of the slave trade and slavery in the modern world. England was by no means the first to end the slave trade. An earlier ending occurred in Denmark, while the United States had earlier indicated an ending that was to occur in the same year as that in England (1808). Nor was Britain the first to regulate the structure of the slave trade, the Portuguese doing so more than one century before Dolben's Act of 1788. And while the legal slave trade for most nations ended about one decade after that of the British, despite British attempts at naval suppression, an illegal slave trade to Brazil and Cuba continued for more than half a century. Nor was England the first nation to end slavery (for the approximately 700 000 slaves in its Empire); predecessors included the gradual emancipation of the slaves of the northern states of the United States (where slave populations totaled less than 50 000 at this time), via legislation and other measures, beginning between 1777 and 1804; St Domingue, as the result of revolution achieving freedom by 1804 (freeing about 500 000 slaves); and even the other French colonies in 1796 (though these had reinstituted slavery by 1804). And while the English slave emancipation may have helped accelerate emancipation elsewhere, such responses were not immediate, occurring in the Swedish colony only in 1847; in the French and Danish colonies in 1848; in the Dutch colonies in 1863; in the United States in 1865; in Puerto Rico in 1873, in Cuba in 1886, and in Brazil in 1888, with most of independent South and Central America having undergone abolition by the 1850s. Strictly, the first abolition of slavery in Europe occurred with the ending of enslavement of one's own nationals as well as of other white Europeans. This movement was generally accomplished by the fourteenth century, sometimes resulting in serfdom, sometimes free labor. Indeed, in some European regions it may have been that neither slavery nor serfdom had ever existed. Even with the legal elimination of slavery in New World colonies and independent nations, slavery persisted in parts of Africa and Asia, and in some areas continued into the second half of the twentieth century.

The British case, however, was the one example of a major, public dispute over whether or not to end the slave trade and then slavery, and the debates included both parliamentary and extra-parliamentary components. It was a political debate, as was necessary given the need for parliamentary legislation to influence and change these institutions, and also a public debate, with an extended pamphlet literature as well as numerous newspaper editorials, magazine articles, and public meetings on both sides to influence the population. The public attention began soon after the Somerset decision of 1772, and led the similar type of widespread writings and discussions in the United States by about half a century. Moreover, with the debates on slave trade regulation, the abolition of the slave trade, the ending of slavery, and the termination of apprenticeship, the British had a larger and more extensive public record regarding slavery than did other countries. And with the agreements at the Congress of Vienna in 1815, the British tried to use public opinion and diplomacy to lead a world-wide movement to end the slave trade.

There are several aspects of the abolition of slavery that need be highlighted for further discussion. First, in the most studied of cases – of European colonies and then independent settlements in the New World – abolition of Negro slavery took place in, by historical standards, a relatively short time, about 120 years. In this same period serfdom was ended for whites throughout Europe, another major shift from coerced to free labor. Thus the dramatic change in labor institutions at this time was broader than the ending of slavery, reflecting a rise in new ideas about the role of labor in economic society. Second, British abolition of the slave trade and slavery occurred during a period of rather dramatic economic and changes, the Industrial Revolution, with economic modernization, economic expansion outside Europe, and the onset of industrialization. Given on the one hand that the magnitude of change was greater for the British than for the Dutch and that British industrialization preceded that of others, and that, on the other, there was an earlier abolition for Britain relative to the other Western Europe nations, a linking of the two events might seem obvious, with the changing pattern of British industrialization being seen as leading to the economically-based ending of both the slave trade and slavery.

This is the historical background to the issues with which Drescher is concerned in these essays. To better understand the nature of his contributions, and those of others, it will be useful to describe its historiographic background, and to see how the debate has evolved over the past half-century, particularly after the beginnings of the modern study of the slave trade and slavery with the publication in 1944 of *Capitalism and Slavery* by Eric Williams. Prior to Williams' book the literature, mainly by English historians, tended to provide only minimal treatment of slavery in the British colonies, and slavery was not regarded as a central aspect of British society. Abolition, when discussed, was most frequently regarded as a noble act, undertaken for religious or other motives, but one seemingly independent of any economic concerns, either in the colonies or in the metropolis. There was, as Drescher notes, some belief in economic motives in accounting for the ending of slavery. Adam Smith was suggestive in his explanation of the ending of slave ownership by the Quakers in Pennsylvania – it could not have been important for them. Later historians, such as Lowell Ragatz, were not optimistic about the continued economic future of British West Indian slavery. They argued that, in some relatively short time, slavery's unprofitability would somehow bring about its ending, although it was not argued how this would be implemented by the members of the planting class.

The major revisions in the study of British slavery and abolition were to come with the detailed historical writings of Eric Williams. Prior to becoming the first prime minister of independent Trinidad and Tobago, Williams had written several books on Caribbean history, based on a mixture of West Indian nationalism and Marxism. Williams' *Capitalism and Slavery* is notable for its arguments on two issues. First, Williams argued that not only did British New World slavery rise and expand during the period of the Industrial Revolution, but that slavery and the slave trade generated the incomes that facilitated industrial growth, since they permitted an expansion of foreign trade, as well as contributing to new economic developments in England. This hypothesis is given rather mixed reviews these days, but is not a central concern of Drescher's, although the issue is touched on in Chapter 13 on *Capitalism and Slavery*, and elsewhere.

Second, and more relevant to these collected essays, is Williams' hypothesis concerning British abolition, which he sees as occurring after the successful accomplishment of the Industrial Revolution. Williams links together several changes in the economics and politics of the British West Indies, providing an economic motivation for the ending first of the slave trade and then of slavery. He argues that at the start of the abolition debate in England the sugar economy of the British West Indies had entered a severe decline, in part because of the loss of the food-provisioning mainland colonies in the Revolutionary War, reducing food availability and raising its costs. Further, the interests of the empire shifted eastward to India, reflecting the declining importance of the West Indies, when the thirteen mainland colonies became independent. The desire to maintain the Navigation Acts kept the price of sugar high to English consumers. Within England, with the growing dominance of industrial capitalism relative to merchant capitalism, there was a shift in the relative political power reflecting these economic interests. To Williams the combination of lower profits that reduced the incomes to the British, and the political power shifts, made it possible to end the slave trade and slavery based on economic, not moral or ideological reasons.

Part of the favorable reception of the two Williams' arguments is due to the fact that he had historical timing on his side. Slavery was developing at the time the expansion of British industrialization and abolition occurred at a time when British industrialization continued to grow. This sense of appropriate timing gives great plausibility to Williams' contentions, and the simultaneity of events in both cases makes for belief in what seems a strong, persuasive argument.

Tracing direct links between the relevant events of the time and abolition, however, is not so clear, and there have been a number of quite different interpretations proposed, consistent with the chronology and timing. These are, of course, not all mutually exclusive, nor is the history summarized below exhaustive, but they do suggest the types of data needed to sort out and evaluate them. While the categorization of motives is not exact, explanations have been based on economic, political, and ideological factors. Each of these, in turn, has several different variants.

The simplest of the economic arguments is that slavery had declined in profitability, leading to its ending either voluntarily by planters or by metropolitan legislation, now that abolition was less costly and more advantageous to the home country. Even if still profitable, however, the growth elsewhere in the British economy could have made the slave-based areas less important in terms of trade and/or incomes, to the metropolis, and continuation of slavery less essential for sustained growth. Or, the continued profitability of the sugar islands could have been based upon mercantilistic regulations that raised the price of sugar for British consumers, and the emergence of a shift to a belief in free trade to encourage exports may have made this form of protection no longer desirable. Thus even if an economic interpretation of abolition is advocated it would be consistent with quite different possible interpretations of the state of the West Indian and of the British economies.

Those explanations based on political elements similarly include several different variants. It might be the declining power of the West India interest in Parliament, or some shift in political importance from the West Indies to the East Indies, or from mercantilism to freer trade, or else a shift due to factors not directly related to slavery but mainly internal political reasons within Britain. Alternatively, the key change may have been in the increased responsiveness of parliamentary representatives to the role of public opinion and the wishes of the electorate on certain key issues of interest to extra-parliamentary advocates.

Finally, changes in beliefs and attitudes may have given rise to an antislavery ideology. New moralities that influenced either the public or the parliamentary voting may have led to an attack on black slavery in various parts of the world. The source of this new morality might have reflected an emerging religious sensibility or else a more secular development responding, perhaps, to changes in British society at the time. And these secular or religious developments might have first arisen among the middle or upper classes, or else from among the working classes and artisans most directly affected by the new economy in Britain. The impetus for abolition, it could be argued, was due either to the new, modernizing sectors or else to those sectors that were left behind in the backwash of progress. Or maybe it was the ideology accompanying the market economy that led to a different attitude toward human relations. Or, perhaps, the basic ideological change was seen in the need felt by the upper classes and industrialists to displace onto slavery the possible concerns of the laboring classes with their own difficulties. In each of these possible scenarios, however, it is necessary to link changing ideology with specific actions in the political sphere, with possible new developments in attitudes towards the workings of the political system. The changing nature of public discourse, the new role of public petitions to parliament, and the growing responsiveness of politicians to such influences, suggest a number of possible influences.

Thus the number of (not mutually exclusive) scenarios indicates that even if there is full agreement as to the timing of the process leading to abolition, there remain a considerable number of alternative explanations, with quite different implications for understanding British society. With the growth in relevant empirical data some of these explanations are seen to be less plausible, or inconsistent with certain key facts or with the beliefs of individuals at the time, and the ensuing analysis will be more complex and less monocausal than before.

Somewhat similar debates about abolition have arisen for other societies as well, some highlighting similarities with the British case, others pointing to major differences in economic, political, and ideological developments. But, as judged by the historical writing, nowhere else apart from the United States did antislavery attract the political and subsequent intellectual attention that it has in England. In none of the European colonies was slavery declining when it was legislatively ended, suggesting that to end slavery required some political or ideological changes affecting society. A major difference was in the political systems, with a probably more democratic-type political system in England than in most other countries. And, as

Drescher has highlighted, in England there was a great role of public opinion, manifest in petitions by the members of the working class, to influence legislative bodies.

Where exactly, then, has Drescher made his important contributions to the study of antislavery in England and elsewhere? In his book *Econocide* his major contribution was in drawing together a considerable amount of economic data to argue that, rather than slavery's decline leading to abolition, it was abolition of the slave trade that preceded, by several decades, a decline in the West Indian economy. Of particular importance, he pointed also to the regulations limiting the westward expansion of slavery in the Caribbean, and the role that this movement had played in sustaining slavery's profitability. Thus for those who had argued that economic decline would mean the end of slavery, the timing of the ending of the slave trade and slavery appears to have happened too soon. This aspect of Drescher's work has been generally (though by no means universally) accepted, but the weight of evidence presented by most other scholars is consistent with the absence of an absolute decline of the British West Indies prior to abolition (Chapters 12 and 13).

Drescher's most original contribution to the study of antislavery has been his attention to the role of petitions after the 1780s, petitions that served to rally working-class support for the antislavery movement (Chapters 2 and 3). Also noteworthy is the source of signatures for these petitions – the artisans and working-class radicals of the expanding industrial cities of England. And although there were some large-scale religious networks of evangelical protestants in those areas, Drescher argues for a more secular motivation by the petitioners. Thus, to Drescher, the emergence of antislavery is seen to be correlated, as others might suggest, with economic modernization and early industrialization, but with a rather different key set of actors than most of the previous historians working on the topic. The input of the working classes into a widespread movement fought on economic, political, and cultural grounds, with many and diverse arguments utilized, adds a new aspect to the historiographic debates.

Raising these questions regarding actors and motives has marked a new turn in antislavery studies, one of several that has emerged in recent decades. Several issues remain, discussed but perhaps not fully resolved by Drescher and by others. Why did the working-class movement start when it did, and why did it take its particular form? Was it an ideological shift or a change in political mechanisms? Why did the working classes appear more concerned with the difficulties of the slaves than with their own social and economic problems? To what extent did they understand the conceptual relationship between criticizing slavery and attacking capitalism, and did they believe that antislavery would provide an important wedge for future use? These are not new questions, but since Drescher's studies they have taken on a new interest and relevance.

Drescher's studies of British abolition raise other important questions. Not only was Britain the country with the most active antislavery movement but, unlike most others, the antislavery interests persisted, albeit with diminished intensity, through the period of apprenticeship, through the struggles in the United States and, indeed, through today, attacking evils similar to enslavement. Such persistence was lacking elsewhere in Europe. Drescher's discussion of the debates regarding British abolition suggests a limited role of racism and, as he points out subsequently, a virulent pattern of racism did not develop until the late nineteenth century, influenced, in part, by what some considered the undesired outcomes of the emancipation process. At no time, however, was there any substantive discussion of aiding West Indian blacks by bringing them to England. Nor was there much advocacy of granting them political independence.

Another important contribution made by Drescher to the study of abolition is his work in placing the British experience in comparative perspective, focusing on some different questions than do other scholars also making comparisons of slavery and antislavery (Chapters 1 and 4). England is the first major case of widespread agitation on this issue, about a decade or so before similar movements in the United States. Because these antislavery changes must be filtered through a legislative process, attention must be paid to the British political system. France, whose colonies at one time had almost as many slaves as those of the British, had a much more limited antislavery movement both inside of and outside of the political sphere (Chapter 6). There were relatively few petitions, and religious movements were insignificant for most of the first half of the nineteenth century. Public concern, even after the St Domingue uprising, and the ending and restart of slavery elsewhere, was minor, and this limited attention permitted the French to subsequently receive compensation from the freed ex-slaves of Haiti. In explaining this difference, Drescher focuses on the differences in the political systems in France and in England, leading to different sources of public pressure. A similar set of issues occurred in the Dutch case, with its rather belated concern with antislavery and its limited discussions of plans to end slavery in its colonies (Chapter 7). Being an early modernizer, some may have expected an earlier antislavery movement in the Netherlands, although perhaps it was the greater concern with its East Indian colonies that helped divert Dutch attention. In any event, Drescher has pointed out that the rise of capitalism in the Netherlands did not necessarily give rise to a significant antislavery ideology and movement.

With the exception of Brazil (Chapter 5), Drescher presents less detail on the Iberian nations and their emancipations, but these generally fit into the argument of British uniqueness. After achieving independence, most of the South American nations ended slavery, but with little public debate on antislavery legislation. Slaves played a rather smaller role in these economies and these nations had fewer ties to the world market than did the Spanish Caribbean colonies, whose later abolition was via Spanish legislation, with only some relatively minor agitation based on the slavery issue in either the colonies or the metropolis. Brazil, independent after 1822, had, as Drescher points out, some greater amount of political debate than did Spain, primarily in the last decades before the Law of the Free Womb (1871) and then emancipation (1888), but it, too, had no large-scale political movement or discussion of this issue, and despite the presence of a population about one-third ex-slaves, the movement ended when slavery ceased.

The US case was perhaps the one most similar to that of England, with heated political debates and large-scale public activities, although unlike the British, the US had a more active and extensive proslavery movement. Both proslavery and antislavery groups generated physical violence, not just moral debates. Drescher does not here deal specifically with this comparison, but his discussion of images of John Brown (Chapter 8) raises some significant questions for the study of abolitions. The issue of the willingness to compromise in ending slavery in the British colonies, by payment of cash compensation and the allowance of a period of forced labor called apprenticeship, differed quite dramatically from the US case, which ended up with almost as many war dead as slaves freed by the British three decades earlier. Brown clearly saw a moral issue that demanded immediate, not gradual emancipation, and if that emancipation could not be accomplished peacefully, war was deemed an acceptable means to the desired ends. Any US emancipation would be costly, because of the relatively large contribution of slaves to US as well as southern wealth. With the complications of being an independent nation composed of two sections with relatively equal political power, no doubt an adjustment such as was possible for the British empire could not occur for the United States. Among the independent nations in the Americas, the United States alone had a Civil War in which slavery was the central cause. And, unlike most of these other nations, the antislavery movement of the United States continued into the post-slavery era.

In addition to his important work on British abolition in comparative perspective, Drescher has contributed to other aspects of the study of slavery and antislavery. He has written on two new questions arising from the present stage of black–Jewish relations in the United States, the role of the Jews in the transatlantic slave trade, and the comparative barbarism of two great moral evils, the slave trade and the Holocaust (Chapters 11 and 10). His work on scientific racism discusses the varying impacts of slavery, emancipation, and of the European movement into Africa in determining European racial ideas (Chapter 9). Several recent essays have dealt with the economics and ideology of the shift from slave to free labor, discussing their uses in the antislavery debate and also, later, in the aftermath of emancipation (Chapter 14). Drescher argues that none of the major critics of slavery presented any empirical evidence that free labor could produce more plantation crops than slave labor. The expectations of greater output from free labor, due to its provisions of greater incentives, led to some disappointment with black economic performance in those societies that had earlier been based on slave labor. This failure led, on the one hand, to some reintroduction of coerced labor, via laws regulating land and labor, and increased flows of indentured workers from Asia and elsewhere, and, on the other, a perception of black failure that fed into the emerging scientific racism of the late nineteenth century. These issues of the economic patterns under slavery and emancipation are, however, discussed in more detail in Drescher's introductory essay, written with Frank McGlynn, to the edited volume *The Meaning of Freedom*.

The value of Drescher's work has been in the long time-span covered and in its wide geographic scope. His new looks at old questions, and the asking of new questions, have provided other scholars with new interpretations with which to study slavery and abolition. The innovative and thoroughly researched essays collected here have done much to advance scholarly discussion of these topics, and to sharpen our understanding of the past.

STANLEY L. ENGERMAN

Preface

The essays brought together here first appeared in scholarly journals or as chapters in collective volumes. Their republication has allowed me to make a small number of changes. Studies that were once cited as works in progress have been updated to reflect their ultimate status as published works. Keith Povey's careful re-editing has also resulted in the correction of minor typographical errors in the originals. I have refrained from updating other data or altering my original arguments in any way.

In the course of twenty-five years of writing and discussion, a scholar inevitably amasses an enormous debt to colleagues. Fortunately, I have had the opportunity to acknowledge their aid in individual articles and chapters. I must take this opportunity, however, to reiterate my gratitude to those who played a special role in this body of work taken as a whole. Twenty-two years ago, in *Econocide*, I noted that Stanley Engerman had been an indefatigable and consistently helpful critic, reading that study at its earliest and latest stages. A decade later, in *Capitalism and Antislavery*, I reiterated that he had read every draft of the typescript. In the case of this volume, he has already long since commented on drafts and revisions of almost every entry. It is appropriate that he also have his last word in the Foreword.

I must also evoke the memory of my first colleague in the history of slavery, Roger Anstey, of the University of Kent. Roger helped to organize the 1974 conference in Liverpool where I made my initial presentation on the subject, now the first essay in this volume. He was far more than a colleague. When Roger died in 1979, Christine Bolt and I dedicated to his memory the collection in which this volume's second essay appears. I take this opportunity to repeat my acknowledgment to him in *Econocide*:

> In the recounting of my variegated debts there is one friend whom I would have had to mention under every rubric. When I first arrived in England, Roger Anstey literally laid before me the feast of his unfinished manuscript, his years

of research, his scholarly experience and contacts. We spent hours, sometimes days together in interchange over the course of three years. His home more than once afforded me a cherished family away from family in the delightful Kentish countryside. Roger has read every draft of this study, and whatever divergences of interpretation are apparent in our works, the impact of his findings will be evident throughout.

Roger cast a shadow far beyond that first work. In 1984, I had the privilege of delivering the second of the Anstey Memorial lectures, published as *Capitalism and Antislavery*, in 1986. In losing Roger, history is even repeating itself, first as tragedy and then as folklore. Just ten years after the publication of *Capitalism and Antislavery*, I attended a conference in Trinidad, in honor of Eric Williams, Roger's scholarly adversary. A Jamaican historian informed me that I was reportedly responsible for Roger's death. In shock, I replied that such a charge was beyond the realm of possibility. When Roger died of heart failure in January 1979, 1 was teaching at my university three thousand miles away. 'Ah,' he said, 'but *Econocide* was found upon his chest.'

So generational an exercise as this series of essays inevitably stimulates multi-generational reflection. My teacher and friend George Mosse receives his due only tangentially in these pages, where my historical interests briefly intrude into his own area of expertise. Yet, no graduate student could ever have had better fortune than to share the exhilaration that was George Mosse's seminar; no aspiring young scholar could have been more challenged to sustained effort than I was by the relentless tide of George Mosse's own work; and no sexagenarian, standing amazed by the restless energy of his globetrotting octogenarian mentor, would dare to dream of pausing for a breath in ours, the world's most satisfying preoccupation. I can only be thankful that my wife Ruth appeared on the horizon of my life just in time to keep George's example in comparative human perspective.

In this same multi-generational spirit, I dedicate this work to my grandchildren, the cohort of a new generation.

SEYMOUR DRESCHER

Acknowledgements

The author and publishers acknowledge with thanks permission from the following to reproduce copyright material:

The Historical Society of Lancashire and Cheshire: Chapter 1, from R. Anstey and P. E. H. Hair (eds), *Liverpool, the African Slave Trade, and Abolition*, Occasional Series, 2 (1976).

William Dawson: Chapter 2, from C. Bolt and S. Drescher (eds), *Anti-Slavery, Religion and Reform: Essays in memory of Roger Anstey* (1980).

Frank Cass: Chapter 4, from *Slavery and Abolition*, 7(1) (May 1986); Chapter 11, from *Immigrants and Minorities*, 12(2) (July 1993); Chapter 13, from *Slavery and Abolition*, 18(3) (December 1997).

Duke University Press: Chapter 5, from *The Hispanic American Historical Review*, 68(3) (August 1988).

The American Historical Association: Chapter 6, from *The American Historical Review*, 96(3) (June 1991); and Chapter 7, from *The American Historical Review*, 99(1) (February 1994).

The Organization of American Historians (Indiana University): Chapter 8, from *The Journal of American History*, 80(2) (September 1993).

The Social Science History Association: Chapter 9, from *Social Science History*, 14(3) (Fall 1990).

Westview Press, Inc.: Chapter 10, from Alan S. Rosenbaum (ed.), *Is the Holocaust Unique? Perspectives on comparative genocide* (1996).

Wesleyan University: Chapter 12, from *History and Theory: Studies in the Philosophy of History*, 26(2) (1987).

Stanford University Press: Chapter 14, from *The Terms of Labor* Stanley L. Engerman (ed.) (stemming from a conference sponsored by the Center for the History of Freedom, Washington University, St Louis) (1999).

Part I

For almost a century and a half the demise of the British slave system was dominated by a variant of the 'Whig' interpretation of history. First elaborated in Thomas Clarkson's narrative of British slave trade abolition in 1808, the story's status as the icon of moral progress was enshrined in William E. H. Lecky's famous dictum: 'the unweary, unostentatious, and inglorious crusade of England against slavery may probably be regarded as among the three or four perfectly virtuous pages in the history of nations' (*A History of European Morals* (1869), 1, p. 153).

In almost all of its variants the principal agents of the process were a small band of 'Saints', who progressively opened the eyes of their countrymen and of the world to the iniquity of a once widely sanctioned institution (Chapters 1–3). For a century after the abolition of British colonial slavery (1834) British historians added an imperial postscript to this core theme of moral progress. In this way, Britain's subsequent expansions in Africa and Asia derived *prima facie* legitimacy from its stance against slavery.

More skeptical historians occasionally introduced elements of economic and political contingency to round out this essentially humanitarian story. Lecky himself invoked Britain's short-term strategic interest to limit the competition of newly acquired sugar islands and tropical frontiers during the Napoleonic wars. Lowell Ragatz emphasized the declining and uncompetitive economic position of the British planter class from the last third of the eighteenth century. Further, if more incidental challenges to the humanitarian school were offered by Continental Europeans, or by colonial historians like the Trinidad-born, C. L. R. James (*The Black Jacobins*, 1938). None of these dissenting voices managed to seriously erode the idealistic frame of reference that dominated both academic and popular histories of British antislavery. The narrative of the metropolitan turn against slavery largely remained a variation of Lecky's judgement.

In 1944, Eric Williams' *Capitalism and Slavery* initiated a major challenge to the humanitarian school. To the next generation of historians, Williams' assertion of the primacy of economic motives and forces gained increasing recognition as a necessary frame of reference in explaining the ending of British slavery (Chapter 4). By 1966, David Brion Davis' Pulitzer Prize-winning *The Problem of Slavery in Western Culture* could note, without fear of dissent, that Britain's disenchantment with the slave trade came 'only when her own Caribbean colonies were on the decline'. However exaggerated one might find Williams' 'sweeping thesis' in other respects, it was thus more difficult 'to get around the simple fact that no country thought of abolishing the slave trade until its economic value had considerably declined' (p. 153 and n. 56). Even those, like Roger Anstey, who were most hostile to Williams' caustic devaluation of humanitarian idealism, accepted his 'decline' thesis as an unassailable fact. Anstey even insisted that if Williams had erred in this respect, it was that he had *understated* the decadence of the British Caribbean plantation system before the rise of British abolitionism (see Roger T. Anstey, 'A Re-interpretation of the Abolition of the British Slave Trade, 1806–1807', *English Historical Review*, 87 (1972), pp. 304–22).

Capitalism and Slavery had effectively contributed to two major changes in the historiography of slavery by the early 1970s. It had decisively reinforced the historiographical perception that the value and viability of British slavery deteriorated before the emergence of British antislavery. To this extent, the book also successfully inverted the relative casual significance of economic change and moral outrage in the abolition of the British Atlantic slave trade in 1806–7, and in the rise of British emancipationism after 1815. Williams had achieved this inversion without recourse to any important shift in the traditional cast of collective actors before 1815: planters, merchants, parliamentary, and abolitionist Saints.

The chapters in Part I of this volume challenge both the Williams' decline thesis and the traditional cast of agents. They adumbrate my pivotal arguments in *Econocide* (1977), that slavery's decline did not occur during the final quarter of the eighteenth century nor, *pace* Williams as a consequence of the American Revolution. Both the emergence of political abolitionism, in 1787–92, and the abolition of the British slave trade in 1806–7, occurred against a background of slave expansion, and at the peak of slavery's value to British imperial political economy.

Within a decade of *Econocide*, the main current of antislavery historiography was already running strongly against *Capitalism and Slavery*. In 1988, David Brion Davis concluded that a historiographical revolution against Williams' decline thesis had already occurred. The 1988 edition of *The Problem of Slavery in Western Culture* dropped its casual reference to the 'simple fact' of British slavery's decline prior to slave trade abolition. A decade later the overwhelming majority of historians of abolition concurred (see S. Drescher '*Capitalism and Slavery* after Fifty Years', *Slavery and Abolition*, 18 (December 1997), pp. 212–27). By 1997, in a judgement that cut across the ideological spectrum, Robin Blackburn consigned Williams' decline thesis to a superseded historiography (see Blackburn, *The Making of New World Slavery: From the Baroque to the Modern 1492–1800* (London/New York, 1997), 577n.

Two of the essays in Part I (Chapters 1 and 2) also suggest a less elitist and less economistic explanation for the emergence and success of British antislavery. They focus attention on the dynamic interaction of religion and politics in early industrial Britain. In terms of its capacity for engendering mass religious and political mobilizations, antislavery is compared with its more ephemeral French counterpart and suggests a preliminary distinction between Anglo–American and Continental 'models' of antislavery.

1 Capitalism and Abolition: Values and Forces in Britain, 1783–1814 (1976)*

ABOLITION AND THE HISTORIANS

The abolition of the British slave trade has been rightly regarded as one of the most dramatic alterations in British imperial policy. In 1783 the Prime Minister's response to the first Quaker petition for abolition was a statement combining sympathy with a categoric denial of its practicality. Since it would be next to impossible to induce every nation to give it up for ever, Lord North said, it was unnecessary for parliament to consider forcing British subjects to do so. Thirty years later, the balance of policy had altered beyond recognition. In 1814, when other European powers were preparing to return in force to the slave trade on the African coast, not a single M.P. even suggested the possibility of a concomitant revival of the British trade. Britain's policy, seven years after her abolition acts, was clearly set. The elimination of what had been deemed in 1783 'necessary to almost every nation in Europe'[1] was now to be urged, if not forced, on every nation in Europe. This change of attitude in government and parliament was paralleled by a change throughout the country. In 1783, the Quaker petition had entered parliament alone and isolated. In 1814, abolitionist opinion concerning the slave trade reverberated in hundreds of petitions signed by hundreds of thousands of British citizens.[2] The most dramatic shift in opinion actually occurred within an even shorter time span. In 1787, the question of abolition had never been moved in either legislative body; but by 1792, the House of Commons had voted

---

* Chapter 9 in R. Anstey and P. E. H. Hair (eds), *Liverpool, the African Slave Trade, and Abolition*, The Historical Society of Lancashire and Cheshire, *Occasional Series*, 2 (1976), pp. 167–95.

overwhelmingly for the gradual abolition of the slave trade. Within five short years abolitionism had moved from political non-existence to the threshold of victory, even though the threshold was not finally crossed until fifteen years later. Thus an element of Britain's political economy which was considered to be of well-nigh vital significance in 1787 lost all ability to influence policy by 1814.

The question as to why this occurred at these dates has been one of the most puzzling and fascinating in the historiography of modern imperial slavery. There have been essentially two types of explanations offered, sometimes in combination. Both are as old as abolition itself. They are what might be called the 'moral' and the 'material' approaches to the problem. According to the first, the slave trade was destroyed because of its negative moral value. it was essentially and inevitably an institutionalised criminal system of kidnapping and murder. However, many other activities of society, pursued for profit, have similarly been branded as violent, destructive and immoral, without the decay of these activities resulting. The accusation of dehumanisation levelled against slavery has also been applied to almost all forms of economic interaction. In practice, what is 'moral' and what is 'material' is historically and socially determined; and the line between the two shifts from century to century. We need to explain why that line changed its position in the period under discussion, in relation to slavery.

The historiographic tradition which stemmed from the abolitionist movement almost entirely ignored this problem. Evolving within a framework which presumed providential or historical movement in a given progressive direction, the 'moral' school considered its task complete when it had identified the agencies through which the flow of progress made itself manifest. In other words, the history of abolition was largely a history of the abolitionists written in their own terms. From Thomas Clarkson's *History of Abolition* onwards the story was essentially an essay in intellectual or moral chronology.[3] The historian had only to identify the spreading sparks of consciousness along the road, and the moments at which a critical mass was reached which ignited the conscience of a nation. The obstacles to progress were those which rose from the misguided identification of self-interest with slavery.

The story of abolition was thus a triumph of changing consciousness over unchanging economic interests damned by moral progress. British abolition was a revolution in the moral economy of the British people, and incidentally a justification of the empire.

The alternative or 'material' approach has treated abolition as principally an outcome of shifting economic interest relationships within the Empire. In these writings, the fate of the slave trade becomes a function of the relation of slavery to the evolving economic interests of the metropolis. Beneath the shifting pattern of changes in moral values at the end of the eighteenth century lies a sharper pattern of dramatic economic change. In its starkest form, in Eric Williams' *Capitalism and Slavery*, abolitionism is the façade behind which emerged a new political economy based on industrial capitalism.[4] Abolition is seen as the ideological superstructure of a shift in the balance of economic power from those interests which favoured slavery to those interests which opposed it. The end of the slave trade is a tale of triumphant economic supersession.

Most recent accounts of abolition attempt to harmonise these two allegedly linked sources of abolitionist success. The supposition is that the influences of economic interest and the influences of evolving moral values were mutually reinforcing. Generally the writers accept the thesis that the slave economy was no longer integrated with the British imperial economy at the end of the eighteenth century, and that this speeded the demise of the trade. The planters of Jamaica, the traders of Liverpool, Glasglow, and London, the manufacturers of Manchester and Birmingham, that is, all who clung to the African trade, had somehow or other lost touch with the prevailing economic trends of the empire and the metropolis. Part of an archaic and inefficient mode of production, slavery and the African slave trade had become obstacles to the progress of the British imperial economy and the political empire which rested on it.[5]

I propose to review these general premises, which have dominated almost all interpretations of abolition. My first task will be to examine the assumption that the West Indian slavery in general, and the Atlantic slave trade in particular, were anachronisms in the general economic evolution of the British Empire.

My second task will be to examine the assumption that the interests of the American planters and British slave merchants clashed with the prevailing norms of political economy which guided government policy during the debate over abolition between 1783 and 1807. Finally, I will turn to the question of the relationship between the moral values implied by abolition and the body of social and moral values in British society around 1800, to see whether it is possible to suggest more likely explanations of the strength and timing of abolition.

CONTINUITY OF ECONOMIC DEVELOPMENT

Over the past four decades a broad consensus has prevailed regarding the economic background to the abolition of the British slave trade. Here we need only outline the main features. Lowell Ragatz and Eric Williams developed a theory of the decline of British slavery after 1763, which was incorporated into almost every subsequent history of abolition. They argued that abolition was preceded by a sharp decline in the value of slavery, hence of the slave trade, to the imperial economy. The decline is asserted to have occurred at almost every measurable level. The British sugar colonies were supposedly past their period of regular growth, and in various phases of stagnation. The planters were beset by limited and marginal resources for expansion, soil exhaustion, rising costs for their provisions and labour, falling prices for their sugar, and chronic disequilibrium between sugar production and the market. In the international setting, the British slave islands were faced with rising competition from non-British rivals. In so far as the British slave trade helped to sustain these rivals, its disappearance would presumably have been a differential gain to the British slave system between 1787 and 1807.[6]

I have shown elsewhere that the economic standing of slavery in the British Caribbean was altogether different from that indicated by Ragatz and Williams, and the accounts which follow them. Over the whole period from 1783 to 1807, the British slave system enlarged its frontier, its supply of virgin soil, its relative proportion of British trade, its imports and exports, its share of world sugar and coffee production, and its overall size, both absolutely and relative to other colonial systems. Short periods of severe profit squeeze for the planters were balanced by others of windfall profits. And the slave trade was, of course, a major ingredient in the continuing expansion of the slave system. In other words, the British colonial slave system after 1783 was doing what it had done before, and doing it even better. Abolitionism came not on the heels of trends adverse to slavery but in the face of propitious ones.[7]

A second false assumption concerning the economic background to abolition is that economic change in Britain severely diminished the value of the British slave system to the metropolis. At the supply end, the period before the Seven Years' War is correctly represented as an age in which sugar was the great commercial crop of slavery. But after 1763 (it is argued) cotton began to gain on sugar, and presumably cotton colonies gained in importance in relation to sugar ones. What is overlooked in this assessment is that down to 1800, the slave West Indies were not only Britain's chief source of sugar but also its chief source of cotton. The rise of abolitionism, and its first major triumphs, occurred during the climax of the 'West Indian' decade of British cotton supply. While Britain's non-slave sources of cotton remained of minor importance, slave labour, both imperial and foreign, continued to be the main support of the metropolitan cotton industry. As a customer for British goods, the slave system was likewise a dynamic element between 1783 and 1807. Thus, in any way in which the figures could be and were measured by contemporaries, the British slave system was outdoing itself between 1783 and 1806. Wartime acquisition of territories meant that an even larger proportion of the British slave trade henceforth completed its trade cycle within the boundaries of the formal Empire.[8]

British slavery patently declined after, not before, the abolition of the British slave trade. Therefore abolition itself may be justly described as *the* economic turning point for British slavery. The significance of abolition and the problems of its causation are not reduced but intensified by examination of the statistics of British slavery in the pre-abolition decades.

CONTINUITY IN THE IMPERIAL POLITICAL ECONOMY

The alleged decline of British slavery at the level of performance represents only one aspect of the prevailing explanation. Even more fundamentally, it is argued that abolition is related to a change in the economic ideology of empire. Abolition is treated as part of the transition from an old empire, dominated by mercantilism, to a new one, dominated by the principles of *laissez-faire*. As a major constituent of both the old imperial system and general mercantilist policy, slavery should have lost support as the two concepts lost ground.[9] This is another way of identifying slavery as a retarding element in the development of empire.

The terms 'old imperial system' and 'mercantilist policy' are of course retrospective labels. Contemporaries had no idea that they were living in what was to be regarded much later as a transitional period, and little idea how their actions would accord with, or diverge from, long-term trends. Close scrutiny of the documents makes it impossible to describe the development of the British Empire from 1775 to 1815 in a way that does not allow slavery a continuing and growing role. The imperial losses of 1775–83 involved a far larger proportion of free than slave labour. The West Indies emerged from the American war of independence as the most important constituent of Britain's settler empire. There was no visible 'swing' to the East, or revulsion from empire in general.[10] With the outbreak of war again in 1793, much more British blood and treasure was spilled in the acquisition of new territories in the West Indies than in corresponding acquisitions in Asia or Africa. The territories gained between 1793 and 1806 included a preponderance of slave-labour areas. In terms of hemispheres it would be possible to argue for a swing to the West (or at least a continuation of a swing to the West) between 1787 and 1807. But it would be more accurate to say that Britain was expanding in both hemispheres in the period of abolitionist agitation. British governments saw no need to make a commercial choice between West and East, between slave and free economies.[11]

Equally significant is the fact that Britain was not swinging towards *laissez-faire* after 1783. A study of the decisions on the

West India carrying trade in 1784, the Irish commercial propositions in 1785, the Navigation Act of 1786, the Anglo–French treaty in 1787, and the Free Port Acts of 1787 and 1792, affords no evidence of a pre-war general shift, or even drift, towards the dissolution of the protectionist framework. John Ehrman's richly documented studies of British commercial policies in the peace-time decade after 1783 show how thickly the departments formulating commercial policy were seeded with men of a protectionist and cautious bent.[12] Charles Jenkinson (later Lord Hawkesbury, and still later the first Earl of Liverpool) was president of the Committee of Trade from 1784. He placed an unambiguous stamp on imperial commercial policy. It was the stamp of a protectionist, anxious to husband British resources and nurture British trade after the trauma of American independence. George Chalmers, chief clerk at the same Committee of Trade, and Thomas Irving, Inspector-General at the Customs, were both in favour of preserving the general framework of the navigation system. While this outlook brought them into conflict with the planters over an issue like the exclusion of American carriers from the British West Indian trade, they were equally forthright in defending both sellers and buyers of slaves against the encroachments of the abolitionists. These 'protectionists' in the administration also favoured the liberalising propensities of the West Indians themselves on the Free Port question after 1787. William Pitt, the most influential member of the government for almost the whole period of the abolitionist campaign, was not prepared to risk the 'navigation system' for the principle of free trade. He was convinced of the value of extended reciprocity in order to expand trade, but his assessment of the acceptable risks was fairly circumscribed. Even his first bold, though unsuccessful, move for a freer trade with Ireland was made in order to fortify the internal links of empire, rather than as a step towards global free trade. Pitt's pragmatism was rendered even more cautious by the defeat of his move.

Behind such hesitation after 1783 lay not just the heavy hand of the old landed and securities-owning classes, but that of the rising industrial entrepreneurs as well. A class which would one day speak boldly for free trade still frequently ran for the cover of the protectionist system. Thus not only Josiah

Wedgwood, speaking for the pottery industry, but even the representatives of the burgeoning cotton industry appealed vociferously (and successfully) to the Committee of Trade for restrictions on the importation of Indian cottons. It was only when economic interests were seriously divided, as with the Anglo–French treaty of 1787, or when they overwhelmingly favoured a move, as with the West Indian Free Port Bills of 1787 and 1792, that the government had leeway to move in the direction of freer trade.[13]

Thus, as far as economic policy was concerned, the post-1783 ship of state was a vessel confined to tacking between fairly narrow options. Lower barriers with France were matched by new restrictions on American shipping, and a *status quo* victory on the Irish trade. The Free Port bills of 1787 were a loosening up of the West India trade. But they were not a radical departure in policy. The Free Port system had first been introduced a decade before the American war of independence, without any dismantling of the protectionist empire. The renewal of the system in 1787 took place less than a year after the government had strengthened the central fortress of protection by a new Navigation Act. Jenkinson, in moving this bill, alluded to the popularity of protection, its antiquity, and its utility. Not a voice in parliament, so far as we know, was raised in objection in 1786 either to the bill or to the system.[14]

The renewal of the Navigation Acts in 1786 was thus a central element of the post-war economic planning: 'If proper means could be devised to secure the navigation trade to Great Britain, though we lost a dominion, we might almost be said to have gained an empire.'[15] Britain carried conventional commercial policy in conventional legislative form into the era of abolitionism. The Free Port Acts were no more than a traditional attempt to extend Britain's trade to foreign colonial systems without Britain bearing the costs and risks of empire, or relinquishing the benefits of protection in the British colonial sector. Moreover, they were designed not only to insure the easy passage of British manufactures to, and cotton from, the foreign colonies, but to enhance the re-export of British-carried slaves to the foreign colonies.[16] Thus, on the very eve of the first abolitionist campaign, one of the two significant moves toward liberalised trade was intimately bound up with the extension, not diminution, of the commerce in human beings.

Certain aspects of this policy are central to our discussion. First, British commercial policy after 1783 was cautious, calculating, and experimental. There was no dramatic or even perceptible swing to the East, or towards free trade, or towards what has come to be called the imperialism of free trade. In restricting the American trade to the West Indies, the government was not cashing West Indian chips for Canadian, Indian, or metropolitan ones. It was testing the extent to which the Navigation Acts system could tolerate limited short-term losses to the West Indian producers in order to promote other economic interests within the protectionist framework. The government tested and evaluated the resiliency of the trade restrictions year by year. When the system responded well, legislation made adjustments permanent. The consensus on economic policy, when it existed, was to treat everything in the framework of conservative pragmatism, giving up nothing from the past without very good cause. In 1787, the slave trade and slavery were treated no differently from other enterprises.

The second important aspect is the continuity of imperial commercial policy beyond American Independence. Not only were the personnel and interests working through the Board of Trade not likely to demand any dramatic shift in policy, but the machinery of administration remained such that no new philosophy of empire or imperial commerce could emerge.[17] The 'national advantage' was still viewed in the old framework. Adam Smith himself called the expectation of total free trade utopian. Furthermore, the continuity of protectionism held good not only for the peacetime abolitionist period (1788–92), but for the very war years in which abolition was a central issue in British politics. If the Smithian assertion that the West Indies distorted the flow of British capital was disputable when the abolitionist movement began, it was even more dubious in 1806, when the British colonies were forced to buy dearer and sell cheaper than they would have done under free trade. There is some disagreement as to when in the nineteenth century the interests of non-colonial trade began to preponderate over those of the formal empire in determining Britain's general commercial policy. There is firm agreement, however, that free-trade principles did not begin to influence colonial policy until after 1807.[18] Accounts of the long-run swing to *laissez-faire* after 1775 date the beginnings of real movement no earlier than the 1820s. The clear reason for this is that from 1792 to 1815 economic survival absorbed British energies. Abolition therefore triumphed after fifteen years of almost unbroken warfare, climaxed, precisely in 1806–7, by acts against British trade throughout Europe and the United States. It would be impossible to imagine a worse moment for implementing policies based on open market assumptions, or for linking abolition to the claims of *laissez-faire*.[19]

Any historiographical explanation which relies on a general tide of anti-mercantilism to explain the rise and triumph of abolition is therefore vitiated from the start by the demonstrable weakness of that principle in the formulation of imperial commercial policy between 1783 and 1815.[20] But apart from considerations of the relative strength of free-trade principles after 1783, recent historians of abolition have erroneously identified British slavery and the slave trade wholly with mercantilism and protectionism. Much of the system was indeed part of the 'protected' sector of British imperial trade. The sugar trade, the West Indian merchants and shippers, and the British exporters to the West Indies, were all 'protected' interests.[21] However, the slave-related enterprise which most clearly operated in a competitive context was the British African slave trade. Until restricted by a political decision in 1806, well over half of the slaves transported in British vessels eventually wound up in foreign or conquered colonies. The outports had been identified with *laissez-faire* in Africa for generations. It was the slave-merchants of Liverpool and Bristol who in 1749 petitioned for the 'free and open' trade to Africa which was then accepted by parliament.[22] The investment of Liverpool and London in the slave system was increasingly diversified beyond the British colonies. The Free Port system had been designed to increase that diversification. At the outbreak of the French wars, a significant amount of British capital was already sunk in the foreign West Indies colonies and a further £15 million found its way to Guiana alone by 1802. British-bought African slaves moved into foreign colonies in the same vessels as British manufactures. The former helped to expand the market for the latter, with gains for British capital at both ends.

A REVOLUTION IN SOCIAL VALUES?

The crucial change in attitudes towards the slave trade occurred neither because the West Indian slave system became economically redundant, nor because of the triumph of free market ideology. It occurred when certain non-commercial judgements on the slave trade gained ground and prevailed. This was not so much an intellectual revolution as a revolution in public and parliamentary opinion.

Considerations which weighed against property in people had been evident long before abolition became a political issue. From antiquity, writers had felt the need for rationalisations of slavery. It was an institution which paradoxically reduced human beings to the level of livestock, yet required the stock to respond like rational creatures in order to be of maximum value. The modern psychological basis for abolition, based on sympathetic identification of free Europeans with enslaved Africans, and on the legalistic reduction of the slave trade to mere theft and kidnapping, had already appeared in the Germantown Pennsylvania petition a full century before mass petitioning began in Britain. Further, the linkage of slavery with communities plagued by devaluation of work, by violence, and by fear, had led to an abortive attempt to prevent its establishment in Georgia in the 1730s. The disadvantages of slave-based societies were already fully elaborated at the beginning of the eighteenth century.[23] As the northern American colonies seemed more normal, racially and economically, they were seen by those who reckoned in non-economic terms as the more healthy element of the empire in America.[24] In contrast, the social and political characteristics of the slave colonies, and especially the sugar islands, had developed long before 1776 in complete opposition to those of the metropolitan community: rule by a narrow absentee oligarchy, the legal exclusion of three-quarters of the population from British due process, the total concentration of economic resources on export staples, the stagnation of local institutions, exemplified in religious, cultural and welfare organisations. Slave societies made inferior communities.

Even the details of the horrors of the African slave trade itself were widely available long before the rise of abolitionism, and as early as 1665 Richard Baxter made a complete and unequivocal condemnation of the slave-trader. While the planter's position might be redeemed if he cared for the souls of his slaves, those who went as 'pirates', to 'catch up poor Negroes, or people of another land, that never forfeited life or liberty, and to make them slaves, and sell them, [carried out] one of the worst kinds of thefts in the world, and such persons are to be taken as the common enemies of mankind'.[25] Thus, at the very founding of the British slave empire, traditional acceptance of the slave trade had already been attacked by a major British theologian. Veteran members of parliament were also familiar with both the nature and the magnitude of the slave trade long before 1788. The slave trade and slavery were defended from the outset principally because of the wealth and power they produced, not because of any argument that they embodied contemporary social or moral values. Plantation slavery could never draw psychological sustenance from identification with any motives more lofty than mere dreams of avarice.[26] At the end, as at the beginning of the eighteenth century, the value of the Caribbean islands, in metropolitan eyes, was their cash value. The vital question remains, why was this not enough to protect the system at the end of the century as at the beginning? And the question is sharpened by the fact that their cash value was greater in 1800 than in 1700, absolutely and relatively.

SLAVERY AND FREE LABOUR IN BRITAIN

An answer might be sought in the evolving pattern and status of metropolitan labour. It has been asserted that colonial slavery and the African slave trade could be more easily maintained in the seventeenth century than later because of increasing social stratification in Britain itself. That is, the metropolitan sanction for slavery could be expected to change in tandem with the evolving relation of British labour to British society. This line of explanation poses difficulties.

Whatever the limitations placed on the personal freedom of the labourer in Stuart England, servitude, no matter how involuntary, was not perpetual slavery. Englishmen understood and emphasised the distinction. They never applied the status of slavery to members of their own ethnic group anywhere in the empire. Furthermore, even before the consolidation of the British slave system, the metropolitan trend was against personal bondage and against property rights in Englishmen. The last recorded case involving villeinage was heard in 1618, the plaintiff being declared free. By the early eighteenth century, 'liberty' was being increasingly used in a legal sense not as a special privilege but as one's right to do as one wished, unless restrained by law from specific actions.[27] It seems unlikely that scholarship will be able to correlate the steps in the consolidation and dismantling of the British slave system with secular trends in the legal status of metropolitan labour.

If the legal position of the metropolitan working classes affords no clear linkage with evolving attitudes towards slavery, it is also difficult to construct an argument on the basis of the position of Africans in the metropolis. The attack on the intrusion of slave law into England involved no systematic attack on slavery. Before and after the Somerset case the question of property rights in African slaves was clouded with ambiguity.[28] In 1693 a judicial decision acknowledged that a man could have property in Negroes in England. But a few years later another decision reasserted the proposition that English soil frees – an assertion which was then virtually ignored for over half a century. No doubt the loss of the Somerset case in 1772 was a clear setback for the slaveholders. It strengthened the ideological principle that labour in England was part of the contractual, not the proprietary, zone of the capitalist market. Yet the victory was neither total nor clear-cut. The Lord Chief Justice's decision did not, as some abolitionists asserted, abolish slavery in England. Runaway slaves continued to be advertised for and purchased, long after the Somerset decision.[29] The decision was sought in order to prevent forcible repatriation of a slave, and it was not the result of any urgent need of non-slaveholding capitalists for African labour in England. Granville Sharp astutely proved that since the price offered for a literate Negro in London was half what he could be sold for in the West Indies, even excluding the charge for 'freight', there was obviously no market rationale for bringing such persons to Britain. Moreover, since 'the English labourer is not able, with hard work, to earn more than what will barely provide him his necessary food and coarse or ragged cloathing', slaves were a conspicuous luxury article within the metropolis.[30] The free black population in England represented neither a large body of workers nor any set of specialised skills in great demand. Far from being an indispensable sector of the labour force, it was considered, by friend and foe alike, as a demoralised and largely unemployed sector of the London poor.[31] The decision of 1772 probably had a deterrent effect on the importation of slaves into Britain. There was thus no struggle within British society between the need for fluid labour and the need for proprietary security.

This line of argument, however, implicitly strengthened the market argument for overseas slavery and the slave trade. While it might have deterred slaveholders from bringing slaves to Britain without taking additional precautions beyond their Common Law rights as 'proprietors', their right to own human beings overseas remained entirely unchallenged. Indeed it was affirmed by Somerset's counsel during the proceedings, and again in the Knight case in Scotland. Slaves continued to be reckoned as capital in all entrepreneurial and governmental estimates. David Davis points out that Justice Mansfield's decision had to balance the needs of a domestic ideology, wedded to the idea of free labour, against commercial and imperial interests. In terms of our search for the weight carried by commercial and non-commercial values, this is significant in itself. The cutting edge against slavery within Britain came from domestic Common Law, which often ran counter to mercantile practices, and not from international trade law, which was more attuned to those practices. In other words, restriction came from a legal tradition largely insulated from the new inter-continental capitalism.[32] Further, the Somerset decision was more than a balancing out of a domestic ideology of voluntarism and free labour against a commercial overseas interest. Foreshadowing the controversy over the slave trade, it was a clash between specific capitalist interests on the one hand, and diffused domestic public opinion on the other.

Public opinion weighed against the proprietary principle. Even before 1772 the London courtroom crowd was more hostile than the Chief Justice to extending the principle of property to human beings. Mansfield at first expressed his fear of coming to a decision in the Somerset case on the ground that if he declared for Somerset, 15 000 blacks in England might be declared free. A large sum of capital would simply vanish. 'Good God!' commented one outraged newspaper, 'is this the language of an English Judge? ... *Fiat Justicia, ruat Coelum* – Dastardly Braggard!'[33] But the same day the same newspaper announced, without comment, the arrival of the slaver *Polly Duncomb* at Virginia, with 434 slaves. Whether public hostility could be directed so as to operate in the direction of abolition of the Atlantic slave trade was still an open question. In 1787, as in 1677, Negroes were recorded as 'goods and commodities' in commercial legislation. Not until 1788 did they even acquire the status of cargo requiring special regulation in transit.

Finally, it is uncertain whether the decision in 1772 speeded or retarded the further extension of the abolitionist movement. By deterring planters from importing 'insecure' capital into England, and by portending a reduction of the black presence in England, it may have helped to defer consideration of the larger question, at least until a new wave of black refugees arrived from America after 1783.[34] The Somerset case was necessarily argued within the circumscribed boundaries of the Common Law, and the decision underlined a division between Britain and the colonial world which lay at the very heart of the controversy over property rights in humans. For some, the crucial question emerged: to what extent were the norms of metropolitan behaviour to be followed in the colonies? But the slave-merchants apparently slept just as easily after the Mansfield decision as they had before it. As late as 1786 they freely provided Wilberforce with information on the details of their activity.

PERCEPTUAL CHANGE OF 'BEYOND THE LINE'

Two decisive changes had to occur before British society turned against the slave trade. The first was a gradual shift in the perception of the relation of Britain to the overseas world. The second was a dramatic extension of public power to individuals whose opinions on slavery had never before been counted. European-controlled overseas slavery was related to the fact that for almost two centuries after the discoveries beyond the Atlantic, the world to south and west remained another planet for all but a handful of Europeans. Immanuel Wallerstein convincingly argues that the capitalist economy which began in Europe in the sixteenth century, encouraged different modes of labour control in different zones of development. Slavery was adopted overseas because it was a 'pre-eminently capitalist institution', which could be geared to capitalist expansion. And Africa was an eminently suitable source of labour because it lay outside the mainstream of the international economy, so that Europe could feel unconcerned about the economic consequences of wide-scale removal of manpower from this supply region.[35]

The overseas territories at first lay beyond the line, not only in international treaties, but socially and even biologically. The tropical world was especially associated with violence, death, and dramatic changes of fortune. Lawbreakers beyond the line might return as respected heroes or gentlemen at home. Exoticism therefore created a moral penumbra permitting sharp differences in behaviour on the part of men in England and the same men in the outside world. The descriptive term 'trade' was likewise expanded to include piracy, pillage, and smuggling. As long as the activity was exercised on remote outsiders, aliens, or enemies, a wide range of behaviour was acceptable. Thus, the dissonance of slavery with domestic practice was mediated by racial and geographical distance. Having neither the power nor the leisure to transform the world, British overseas adventurers and settlers took the rules as they found them. In Africa people were regularly sold, and in the Americas they were eagerly bought. The norms of Africa and America, being profitable, were very acceptable. The British who remained at home had little choice or concern about the rules of overseas behaviour. As late as the middle of the eighteenth century even philosophers hostile to slavery in principle paid homage to the requirements of economic survival in exotic and frontier lands. Montesquieu's influential chapter on slavery in the *Spirit of the Laws* was very significantly located in the section of the book on climate, not in those dealing with trade, war, or liberty, where they would have seemed just as relevant. He clearly wanted to keep slavery out of Europe, and to justify it, in so far as he did, only to the degree that the public good or production in the tropics required coerced labour. Montesquieu's later influence on anti-slavery developed in direct proportion to the extent that his climatological emphasis was ignored.[36]

However, the dividing line became less clearly demarcated during the eighteenth century. European norms of international law, of personal security, and of economic activity, were gradually extended to the settled colonies. American colonies ceased to be considered exclusively as a frontier, and began to be thought of as normal societies, to be judged accordingly. Africa likewise became gradually identified, not only with the barbarities of human sale and sacrifice, of unlimited sexuality, and idolatry, but with ordered and highly developed agricultural communities. By the 1780s some British even began to seriously consider Middle Africa as a possible location of European settlements.[37]

This change must not be exaggerated. In the first place the images of a normal society infiltrated, but did not displace, the more exotic images of frontier and barbarous lands. Right up to and beyond the triumph of abolition, travellers to Africa continued to disseminate pictures of a barbaric, unchanging, and indolent continent; pictures which contributed to the empirical argument for the slave trade as a form of necessary adoption by Europeans to African society. Moreover, the emerging contrary picture of 'normal' societies in Africa in one respect tended to strengthen the argument for the legitimacy of the slave trade. According to the prevailing interpretations of international law, the internal sanctioning of enslavement by African laws legitimised purchases by Europeans.[38] The merchants of Liverpool did not insist that all Africans were born to be slaves, or that they lacked the essential qualities of humans (or even the developed capacities of capitalists). By the 1780s these merchants were actually attempting to educate selected Africans in Liverpool, so as to strengthen their trade contacts and stabilise their sources of supply.

Nevertheless, as the concept that one was beyond the pale of civilised humanity in Asia, Africa, or America came to be eroded, and as Britain came to see herself as mistress of the world's seas and the centre of a single global empire, the exportation of British metropolitan norms of human relations began to seem more feasible. In this sense, Britain's naval hegemony after 1760 marked a clear erosion of earlier perceptions. With their overwhelming victory in the Seven Years' War, the British no longer viewed non-European populations almost exclusively in relation to scattered and insecure overseas settlers, who had to define their own relations to the native populations on three unpoliced continents. As metropolitan control tightened, one result was the revolt of the thirteen American colonies. Another was the beginnings of an imperial rather than a local policy towards native populations. By 1788 the policy of defensive non-intervention in native and colonial relations was over, even if the initial manifestations of the change were still haphazard and uncertain.[39]

The difference between the pre- and post-Seven Years' War periods lay not in the decline of the commercial ethos but in the assertion of non-commercial standards alongside it. It was especially evident after 1775 that attempts to maximise trade and revenue at all costs could endanger dominion and lose it. However, this did not mean that abolition of the slave trade flowed logically from a new conception of empire. On the contrary, the slave trade might conceivably have been the last sector to feel the impact of the redefinition of imperial welfare. In 1788, Africa was a continent without British colonies. Senegambia had been abandoned to its African merchants and to the French. War, brutality and social violence in Africa still had least impact on the peace and security of the empire. Yet, paradoxically, the beginnings of what one historian has called the concept of 'trusteeship' developed first towards that continent where the internal fate of non-Europeans was not in British hands. It was not imperial security that recommended African slaves to legislative action. Since the beings who were first defended by the abolitionists were black Africans, enslaved beyond the limits of the empire, the abolitionists were creating a new category of essential human rights, enforceable within a concrete legal system. The abolitionist standard was here that of humanity in the purest and broadest sense of the word.

We can only skirt the difficult problem of the relation between change in the perception of the overseas world and the general evolution of European philosophy and religion. The impact of that evolution on effective attitudes towards the slave trade is difficult to measure. Until recently, most studies, following the Clarkson tradition, confined themselves to simply enumerating the opinions against slavery: opinions in favour of the *status quo* have not yet been adequately studied and may prove even more difficult to weigh. For our purposes it is necessary to distinguish between academic philosophical and theological treatises on the one hand, and more popular and more urgent writings, often calling for action, on the other. The studies of David Davis and Roger Anstey have amply demonstrated a shift towards anti-slavery among the leading western European writers during the eighteenth century. Davis sensitively traces the major trend and its accompanying ambivalences within the Anglo–French intellectual community, moving from a posture which provided little basis for criticising the burgeoning colonial slave economies, to a point, around 1770, when evangelicals and philosophers were coming from their new perspective to 'sense that American slavery might symbolise all the forces that threatened the true destiny of man'. Anstey has meticulously sought to uncover the dynamic element in evangelical psychology which, when not otherwise inhibited by powerful countervailing pressures within slave societies themselves, placed anti-slavery high on the agenda of social action. Duncan Rice's study of Scottish anti-slavery motivation in the eighteenth and nineteenth centuries also suggests that the effective shift in attitudes coincided with the evangelical, rather than with the earlier philosophical phase of the movement.[40]

Enlightenment themes of progress and individual happiness, and the religious revivals emphasising individual responsibility and collective providential progress, may have helped to break down the moral line between Europe and the external world. They may have made it increasingly difficult to rationalise the idea of human beings as mere instruments of other human beings. But the Enlightenment also circulated ideas which could serve the defenders of slavery.[41] The extent to which the balance of attitudes shifted in favour of an active abolitionist policy remains unclear. Perhaps the most one can say is that, at the level of social theory, almost all major writers after 1770 emphasised the anomalous situation of colonial slavery under free Europe, rather than the anomalous situation of the world beyond Europe. Freedom and progress were increasingly accepted by leading thinkers, in Britain at least, as the normal trend of European evolution. Without having any immediate practical purpose, the philosophers probably reflected the views of the broader audience for whom they acted. On the other hand, until the late 1780s all practical questions related to the slave trade were deferentially left to the 'interests'. Slave-trading, like coal-mining, might be judged a harsh and dangerous activity, but as long as it was linked to the wealth and power of the nation on the one hand, and to competitive necessity on the other, the gap between moral judgement and practical action remained as wide as ever.[42] And as long as the principal interlocutors remained the Council for Trade, the colonial bureaucracy, and the slave interests, the slave-traders were effectively insulated from the slowly changing moral milieu around them.

PUBLIC OPINION: ECONOMICS AND THE MISTS OF FANATICISM

Before the 1770s the slave trade, like any other trade, was the province of those groups who were most directly interested in it. A few hundred well-placed individuals in British society were in a unique position to influence policy. It was considered to be their right to be in continuous dialogue with the political machinery of colonial governance, via petitions, memorials, and private correspondence. However, slavery's special place in the British Empire could be observed clearly in the Somerset case. It was symptomatic that one of the traditional clichés of British justice, public silence on a matter still before the bar, was completely disregarded. Either because of its extraordinary status, or because of its obvious ideological implications, slavery called forth an extensive newspaper correspondence. Before 1788, however, there was no way of measuring broad public sentiment on the slave trade, or estimating how many felt that they had the right to an opinion on the slave trade. For example, on the contemporary question of serfdom in the Scottish coal mines, the opinions of those not directly interested were neither sought nor offered.[43]

The disinterested were apparently also the uninterested. In 1787, the slave trade likewise stood officially where it had stood a century before, a necessarily unpleasant, but a necessary and profitable economic venture. The decisive moment of advance occurred in the winter of 1787–8. A moral debate carried on by occasional pamphlets, or in corners of major philosophical works, suddenly became a mass concern and a political question. Petitions flowed into parliament from all parts of the country.[44] The country's leading minister placed it on the legislative agenda. For the first time in history the British African trade was subjected to regulations not designed to maximise the profits of investors but to protect, if only minimally, the health and comfort of the 'goods'. By 1792 an even larger wave of mass petitions and respectable parliamentary support had elicited a resolution by the House of Commons calling for the total abolition of the slave trade. Within these few years abolition had moved from a political impossibility to a political imperative. And the traditional ground rules for legislating on economic matters, by leaving it to the interplay of direct interests, were ignored.

It was only when the shocking figures on the mortality and brutality of the trade were taken up by the major figures in parliament, and backed by very large numbers of local meetings called to petition for abolition, that the slave-merchants of Liverpool belatedly took alarm. They were eventually able to undermine the effectiveness, or at least question the implications of many abolitionist statistics. They were able to match the abolitionist political leadership with support of their own from the very peak of the British political and social pyramid. But they were not able to reverse the public decision against them which had occurred at the outset. There is strong evidence which cannot be detailed here, that despite their sustained role in the economic life of Liverpool between 1788 and 1806 the slave-merchants became morally isolated in, and even within, the confines of their own city. Their propaganda counter-attack was initially dispersed over several fronts, moral, patriotic, and traditionalist, in an attempt to recapture public opinion.[45] During the next two decades the whole panoply of non-economic rationalisations was slowly abandoned. But the principal weapon in their armoury, the principal defence of their trade, was an appeal to the ethos of capitalism.

At the end, in 1806–7, this was virtually their sole defence. While the planters could plead the injury to an imperial community caused by abolition, the petitions of Liverpool and Manchester in 1806–7 were pure capitalist documents. In the eyes of the Liverpool petitioners, the abolition bill of 1806 meant only the diminution of the value of their capital in the West Indies, and the destruction of a legitimate enterprise in Africa. The bill violated an established principle of the British constitution, the defence of property. It ran counter to the unchallenged commercial policy of government, by diminishing the established trade of the kingdom, especially in wartime, 'since it is evidently for the public good, during a war which demands all our resources, to augment our mercantile and colonial industry (in every quarter), our productive Capital, our Returns, our Exports and Imports, by every means ...' Abolition would instead benefit the foreign capital remaining in the trade.[46] The Manchester petition followed the same lines. Britain's prosperity and wealth, 'the subject of astonishment and admiration to all surrounding Nations', and her independence, confronting French-ruled Europe, were based on the encouragement of private property and individual industry, the extension of manufactures and the freedom to export them anywhere. Uninhibited export to all places that 'offered an advantageous market' was a principle accepted by all governments and all political economists, whatever their orientation. British policy was to set no limits on the 'enterprising genius of the people', especially in the face of an increasing threat of continental blockade. Every one of these capitalist precepts was being violated by the abolition bills.[47]

In all the arguments from Liverpool, Manchester, Glasgow and London, capitalists were not mobilised against countervailing capitalists with countervailing interests. There were no rival capitalists in the petition lists of 1788, or of 1792, 1794, 1806 and 1807. The sharp rapier of capitalist ideology was mobilised against enemies who refused to fight on the battlefields of capitalist interest, political economy, or commercial policy. Ironically, in the light of subsequent interpretations, which laid stress solely on the power of the market ethic, the slave interest found itself increasingly isolated from the rest of the country. In a kind of paradigmatic leap, the political nation decided that the area covered by capitalist ground-rules no longer extended to the buying and selling of human beings. The form of labour that fitted the market model most perfectly was legislated out of the market.[48] Henceforth, British capital could buy and use (under increasing restrictions) only slaves already in British ownership.

What so baffled the defenders of the trade between 1787 and 1807 was that the old capitalist arguments were not refuted, except in a vague and unempirical way. They were side-stepped by a premise of radical novelty. Those connected with the slave system felt they, and not their opponents, had been faithful to the economic heritage of the nation. Yet Britain had decided to alter the boundaries of economic endeavour in a way which left them outside the bounds of respectable trade, and 'beyond the line' of acceptability. They were criticised and even ostracised for clinging to a criminal system, for associating respectable commercial towns with criminality, and for damaging the good name of trade by lowering their standards to those of uncivilised Africa. The accusation hurt precisely because the slave-traders considered themselves especially well-deserving members of the merchant class.

The new metaphysical correlation of property with non-human objects, and of contract with men, achieved a major victory against an entrenched economic interest in 1792. Until 1807 the slave-traders fought a desperate rear-guard action, clinging doggedly to their definition of capital. They knew their enemies were not 'interests' but 'fanatics', people who denied that the term 'trade' could be applied to dealings involving slaves and slavery, and who confusingly refused to consider economic and utilitarian arguments as final. They felt the anguish of members of a society which had formerly encouraged them to specialise in a respectable and profitable activity, and which had now reversed the rules, radically devaluing their skills and experience. They shared the frustration of the Jamaica planters who, on the eve of abolition, were prepared to argue for the trade on the rational premises of political economy – only to find none would listen.[49] The astonishment of the slave interests about the 'mists of fanaticism' that engulfed them has been subtly re-echoed by later generations of historians quite unsympathetic to either the slavers' cause or their plight. But attempts to ignore or proscribe these mists, or to rationalise them as 'capitalism in disguise', have only increased the problem of explaining the victory of fanaticism. The reason is that the fanatics were not mists but myriads, not spectres but masses. It was not a specific political economy or commercial polity which prevailed in the matter of abolition, but a more stringent definition of human relations both in and out of the market place. What stood in support of the slave trade was over a hundred years of colonial development, an almost limitless conception of the primacy of property, and a relatively narrow-based capitalist investment. What stood against it was a century of domestic social and political development, an expanding conception of human identity, and an ideological appeal which was far broader and more durable than that of the slave-traders.

Because it hung on the single thread of capital alone, the allegiance to the slave trade virtually died with abolition. It never called forth that bitter strain of nostalgia which lingers for institutions prized for their own sakes or their ideals. No better illustration exists of capitalism's great capacity for total conversion. Liverpool suffered from the loss of one of its main channels of trade for a few years after 1807. But even before the end of the war with Napoleon the readjustment had been made, the ships and sailors redeployed. Overlooking the irony that the redeployment had been largely from the African to the American slave zone, Liverpool had complied with the new law of the empire. In 1814 Liverpool was offered a supreme opportunity to demonstrate its allegiance to the new definition of the limits of the market. The Anglo–French Treaty of Paris, allowing France to reopen its slave trade for five years, called forth an unprecedented storm of petitioning througout Britain. Special joy was exhibited everywhere else when Liverpool, weaned from the trade for a mere seven years, joined in with a monster petition of tens of thousands of signatures. Yet the Liverpool petition meeting showed the residual clash of the capitalist and abolitionist value systems. The opening speaker, John Gladstone, advocated a new theme of commercial interest to lend support to the appeals to humanity and justice. Not only would France benefit by the lack of competition in Africa, he noted, but it would thereby win the European market for tropical staples, restoring the pre-war British inferiority on the Continent. Roscoe, the Liverpool humanitarian, strongly objected to introducing economic interests into the discussion. He insisted that this would not only dilute the pure strain of humanitarian agitation, but it would reintroduce the calculus of means and ends into the question. If Britain began to think again in terms of economic policy, it might be equally expedient to revive the trade for Britain too. Roscoe therefore successfully moved that the Liverpool resolution restrict its rationale to humanity, as the rest of the country had done.[50] Roscoe chose to overlook the point that the British slave interest might have cogently argued that Britain should either demand immediate French abolition, which it was not open to Britain to enforce, or else consider British restoration, which was within British capacity. The slave interest instead spoke as if only French abolition was possible. Nothing could better demonstrate how total and inevitable British abolition seemed in 1814, even to Liverpool merchants. Henceforth one could argue the logic of capitalist interest only inasmuch as it respected the policy of abolition. By 1814 the norms of British capitalism had been redefined.

Nineteenth-century capitalism would, of course, ingeniously invent or re-discover forms of semi-slavery for areas of scarce labour 'beyond the line'.[51] But the battle over the treatment of labour as a pure commodity was over in Britain before the industrial revolution finally took hold. The slave trade was rapidly assimilated to piracy as a form of economic behaviour. The ideal of the globe as an open area for unrestrained British acquisitiveness had met its first internal check. If the political nation was not yet prepared to declare that citizens of the empire could no longer possess proprietary interests in men, it had nevertheless declared a total ban on the re-enforcement of those interests from sources outside the empire. Precisely because slavery at the beginning of the nineteenth century was still fully viable and still profitably integrated with the British commercial system, abolition marked a clear-cut shift in the institutionalised values of British society.

NOTES

Place of publication is London, unless otherwise stated.
1. Cobbett's *Parliamentary History* (hereafter *Parl. History*), 22 (1783), pp. 1026–7, speech of Lord North, 17.6.1783.

2. Betty Fladeland, 'Abolitionist Pressures on the Concert of Europe, 1814–1822', *Journal of Modern History*, 38 (1966), pp. 335–73, on pp. 358–9.
3. Thomas Clarkson, *The History of the rise, progress and accomplishment of the abolition of the African slave-trade by the British Parliament* (1808).
4. See Eric Williams, *Capitalism and Slavery* (Chapel Hill, 1944; reprinted New York, 1966). The thesis is repeated in the same author's *From Columbus to Castro: The History of the Caribbean, 1492–1969* (New York, 1970), pp. 280–1.
5. See David B. Davis, *The Problem of Slavery in Western Culture* (Ithaca, 1966), pp. 153, 160–4; D. B. Davis, *The Problem of Slavery in the Age of Revolution, 1770–1823* (Ithaca, 1975), pp. 52–6; Patrick Richardson, *Empire and Slavery* (New York, 1972), p. 87; E. V. Goveia, *Slave Society in the British Leeward Islands at the end of the Eighteenth Century*, (New Haven, 1965), pp. 335–6; Jack Gratus, *The Great White Lie* (New York, 1973), p. 14; Howard Temperley, *British anti-slavery 1833–1870* (1972), appendix on Williams, pp. 273–4; C. Duncan Rice, *The Rise and Fall of Black Slavery* (New York, 1975), ch. 4. The most assertive recent rendition of Williams' economic thesis may be found in Michael Craton, *Sinews of Empire: A short history of British slavery* (New York, 1974), p. xiii, and ch. 5, especially pp. 239–42. For the fullest statements of the decline thesis, see Williams, *From Columbus to Castro*, pp. 226 ff.; *Capitalism and Slavery*, pp. 120–7. Works which do not support this theory of senescence before abolition are Glyndwr Williams, *The Expansion of Europe in the Eighteenth Century: Overseas rivalry, discovery and exploration* (1966), pp. 278–9; J. H. Parry, *Trade and Dominion, the European Overseas Empires in the Eighteenth Century* (1971), pp. 277–80, 318–25; and Roger Anstey, *The Atlantic Slave trade and British Abolition 1760–1810* (1975), p. 52 note 33.
6. See Lowell J. Ragatz, *The Fall of the Planter Class in the British Caribbean 1763–1833* (New York, 1928), *passim*; Williams, *Capitalism and Slavery*, chs. 6–9; Williams, *From Columbus to Castro*, chs. 15–17; Davis, *The Problem of Slavery in Western Culture*, pp. 157–9, 160–4; Davis, *The Problem of Slavery in the Age of Revolution*, pp. 52–7; Rice, *The Rise and Fall*, pp. 155–8; Ricardson, *Empire and Slavery*, pp. 60–3; Craton, *Sinews of Empire*, pp. 262–4.
7. See S. Drescher, 'Le "Declin" du système esclavagiste britannique et l'abolition de la traite', *Annales* (1976), pp. 414–35.
8. S. Drescher, *Econocide: British slavery in the era of abolition* (Pittsburgh, 1977), chs. 4, 5.
9. See Williams, *Capitalism and Slavery*, pp. 135–42, and the work cited in note 7. It should be noted that the identification of the West Indies with the old, or 'mercantilist' empire, is a tradition that precedes Williams and is not confined to adherents of his interpretation. See also the essay of J. F. Rees, 'Mercantilism and the Colonies', in *The Cambridge History of the British Empire*, 1 (1929), pp. 561–602; also 2 (1940), Preface, p. vi. Vol. 1, running to 1783, is called *The Old Empire*; Vol. 2, running from 1783, is called *The New Empire*. The 'old' empire, because of the American split, was radically 'defective' (1, p. 783); slavery tied to the old empire, was among the radical defects (1, p. 819). On the Seven Years' War and

the American Revolution as the boundary lines between the old and new empires, see also R. Coupland, *The American Revolution and the British Empire* (1930); Vincent T. Harlow, *The Founding of the Second British Empire 1763–1793* (1952), 1, pp. 3–4. On the close connection between declining slavery and mercantilism, see also Klaus E. Knorr, *British Colonial Theories 1570–1850* (Toronto, 1944), pp. 156–7, 212–17, 317–18; D. A. Farnie, 'The Commerical Empire of the Atlantic 1607–1783', *Economic History Review* 15 (1962), pp. 205–18; and Judith B. Williams, *British Commery Policy and Trade Expansion, 1750–1850* (1972), p. 6.

10. See Peter Marshall, 'The First and Second British Empires: A question of demarcation', *History*, 49 (1964), pp. 13–23. Parry, *Trade and Dominion*, pp. 277–80; and especially John Ehrman, *The Younger Pitt: The years of acclaim* (New York, 1969), p. 332.
11. *Ibid.*, p. 335.
12. *Ibid.*, ch. XII; see also J. Ehrman, *The British Government and Commercial Negotiations with Europe, 1783–1793* (1962), ch. 8. The West India Committee voted *not* to petition against the liberalising Anglo–French treaty of 1787: Duke University Library, Stephen Fuller Letterbook, 28.2.1787.
13. Ehrman, *The Younger Pitt*, pp. 208–10, 338–9, 382–3; Arthur Redford, *Manchester Merchants and Foreign Trade, 1792–1858* (Manchester, 1934), pp. 1–14, 126–7; Drescher, *Econocide*, ch. 4. On the manufacturing interest and the Free Port system, see Frances Armytage, *The Free Port System in the British West Indies* (1953), ch. 5.
14. See Duke University Library, Stephen Fuller Letterbook, 1786–90, letters of 28.2.1786; Ehrman, *The Younger Pitt*, p. 341. Jenkinson claimed, and the claim went unchallenged, that the Act of 1786 was the only important trade measure to pass unanimously in the course of half a century. See also Ralph Davis, 'The Rise of Protection in England 1689–1786', *Economic History Review*, 19 (1966), pp. 306–17. The end of the seventeenth century was not 'when the turn towards free trade began; they were the years when protection began', and the dismantling process began only in the second quarter of the nineteenth century (p. 306).
15. See *Parl. History*, 25 (1785–6), p. 1373, speech of Jenkinson, 11.4.1786.
16. H. C. Bell, 'British Commercial Policy in the West Indies, 1783–93', *English History Review*, 31 (1916), pp. 429–41; Ehrman, *The British Government and Commerical Negotiations*, p. 117.
17. See D. L. Mackay, 'Direction and Purpose in British Imperial Policy, 1783–1807', *Historical Journal*, 18 (1974), pp. 487–501.
18. See J. Gallagher and R. Robinson, 'The Imperialism of Free Trade', *Economic History Review*, 6 (1953), pp. 1–15; D. C. M. Platt, 'The imperialism of Free Trade: Some reservations', *ibid.*, 21 (1968), pp. 296–307, and 'Further objections to an 'Imperialism of Free Trade', 1830–60', *ibid.*, 26 (1973), pp. 77–91.
19. Eli F. Heckscher, *The Continental System: An economic interpretation* (1922), reprinted 1964), pp. 51–148; Williams, *British Commercial Policy*, p. 445; François Crouzet, *L'économie Britannique et le blocus continentale* (Paris, 1958), II, p. 827.
20. B. Semmel, *The Rise of Free Trade imperialism, 1750–1850* (1970), p. 44.
21. See Rees, 'Mercantilism and the Colonies', pp. 581–91.

22. *Parl. History*, 14 (1747–53), pp. 565–6, April 1749.
23. See Davis, *The Problem of Slavery in Western Culture*, chs. 1 and 5, and pp. 308–9.
24. Richard Koebner, *Empire* (1961), p. 218.
25. The passage by Baxter, quoted from his *Chapters from a Christian Directory*, was written in 1664–5 and published in 1673: see Davis, *The Problem of Slavery in Western Culture*, p. 338 and note. So unequivocal were Baxter's strictures on the trade that they could be printed without exegesis in an abolitionist broadside a century later. And as early as 1743, John Wesley's *General Rules* for his followers specifically prohibited engaging in the purchase of humans with intent to enslave them: see Donald G. Mathews, *Slavery and Methodism, A Chapter in American Morality 1780–1845* (Princeton, 1965), pp. 5–6. See also Douglas Grant, *The Fortunate Slave: An illustration of African slavery in the early eighteenth century* (1968), *passim*. On Stanley's speech (15.2.1773), see *Parl. History*, 17 (1771–4), p. 732.
26. Richard S. Dunn, *Sugar and Slaves: The rise of the planter class in the English West Indies, 1624–1713* (Chapel Hill, 1972). p. 340.
27. See Charles Wilson, *England's Apprenticeship 1603–1763* (1965), p. xi; and David Ogg, *England in the Reigns of James II and William III* (1955), p. 54.
28. *Ibid.*, pp. 73–4; F. D. Shyllon, *Black Slaves in Britain* (1974), chs. 3–10; James Walvin, *Black and White: The negro and English society 1555–1945* (1973), pp. 120–8.
29. *Ibid.*, p. 128.
30. Granville Sharp, *A representation of the dangerous tendency to tolerate slavery* (1769), pp. 51, 75–6. Much of Sharp's very effective plea for the illegality of slavery in England rested on the accurate assumption that Negro slavery was both alien and novel to the metropolis, pp. 39, 81, 92, 133–4, 153–4, 161. See also Shyllon, *Black Slaves*, p. 179; Davis, *The Problem of Slavery in the Age of Revolution*, p. 474 and note.
31. Walvin, *Black and White*, pp. 144–5.
32. Davis, *The Problem of Slavery in the Age of Revolution*, p. 483. Davis asserts that it was a serious mistake for slaveholders to appeal to villeinage precedents in the Somerset case. As he indicates, these precedents made the slaveholders vulnerable by confusing the distinction between property and personal service rights. It must be recalled, however, that Granville Sharp had already made so strong a case against certain property claims in the Jonathan Strong case that the owners had dropped the case, see Shyllon, *Black Slaves*, pp. 38–9.
33. *Public Advertiser*, 13.6.1772; Shyllon, *Black Slaves*, p. 9; Davis, *The Problem of Slavery in the Age of Revolution*, pp. 497–8; Walvin, *Black and White*, p. 120.
34. *Ibid.*, ch. 4.
35. I. Wallerstein, *The Modern World-system: Capitalist agriculture and the origins of the European world-economy in the sixteenth century* (New York, 1974), pp. 87–8. See also Fernand Braudel, *Capitalism and Material Life 1400–1800* (English translation, New York, 1974), pp. 371–2, 443.
36. C. L. de Secondat de Montesquieu, *De l'Esprit des loix* (1950–5, Paris edition), liv. 15, chs. 7–8, pp. 222–3, and 416; Dunn, *Sugar and Slaves*, ch. I; Winthrop D. Jordan, *White over Black: American attitudes toward the*

Values and Forces in Britain, 1783–1814   33

Negro, 1550–1812 (Baltimore, 1969), ch. 2; M. I. Finley, article on 'Slavery' in *International Encyclopedia of the Social Sciences*, 14 (1968), pp. 307–13. On the adaptive quality of European overseas economic activity, see K. G. Davies, *The Royal African Trading Company* (1957), pp. 3–4.

37. Philip Curtin, *The Image of Africa* (Madison, 1964), p. 4.
38. See Davis, *The Problem of Slavery in Western Culture*, pp. 108–18.
39. See Koebner, *Empire*, pp. 86, 105–19, 157–65, 219–20; Cecil Headlam, 'Imperial Reconstruction', in *Cambridge History of the British Empire*, 1, pp. 634–45; G. R. Mellor, *British Imperial Trusteeship, 1783–1850* (n.d.), ch. 1; Parry, *Trade and Dominion*, p. 17. In a sense abolition also represented a technical rationalisation of commerical law within the British empire. The breakdown of the 'line' may also be noted in Edmund Burke's indictment of Warren Hastings, to the effect that a British governor in India ought to rule 'as much as possible in a spirit of the laws of this country', quoted in C. P. Courtney, *Montesquieu and Burke* (1963), p. 183.
40. See Davis, *The Problem of Slavery in Western Culture*, Part III; Anstey, *The Atlantic Slave Trade and British Abolition*, chs. 5, 7–9; Walvin, *Black and White*, pp. iv, ix, and xi; C. Duncan Rice, 'The Problem of Anti-Slavery Motives: Three cases of Scottish concern', pp. 6–10, MSS kindly sent to me by the author.
41. Cf. P. D. Curtin, *The Image of Africa* (Madison, 1964), pp. 41–8.
42. See Baron F. Duckham, 'Serfdom in Eighteenth-century Scotland', *History*, 54 (1969), pp. 178–97.
43. *Ibid*.
44. See E. M. Hunt, 'The North of England Agitation for the Abolition of the Slave Trade, 1780–1800', MA thesis, University of Manchester, 1959; James Walvin, 'How Popular was Abolition? Popular dissent and the Negro Question 1787–1833', unpublished paper kindly lent by the author.
45. See F. E. Sanderson, 'The Liverpool Delegates and Sir William Dolben's Bill', *The Historical Society of Lancashire and Cheshire*, 124 (1973), pp. 57–84; and Davis, *The Problem of Slavery in the Age of Revolution*, pp. 541–51.
46. House of Lords Record Office, MSS, Slave trade 6.5.1806, 'Petition from Merchants, Ship Owners and Manufacturers on behalf of themselves and others in the town and port of Liverpool interested in the Slave Trade'.
47. House of Lords Record Office, 13.5.1806, petition of 'the Town and Neighborhood of Manchester'; 7.5.1806, petition of 'London Merchants and Manufacturers Trading with Africa'; and the petitions from London and Liverpool, 2.2.1807.
48. The new note had been sounded just before the debate on abolition began. It was not in the demonstration of a utilitarian argument for the abolition of the commerce in human beings, but in a rejection of utility as an argument: see *Parl. History*, 26 (1786–7), p. 520. For those who wish to correlate abolition and liberalised trade policy, we may note that this argument came first in a speech *denouncing* the Anglo–French commercial treaty of 1787.
49. 'Whether tried on the Principles of the mercantile System, or on those of the Economists, as developed to the English Reader in the Writings

of Mr. Hume and Doctor Adam Smith, this important Commerce [the Afro-West Indian trade] will be found equally beneficial ... Yet in Place of cherishing this Source of National Prosperity, in place of extending and encouraging a Market which no Despot can shut against her, will it hereafter meet Belief, when the Mists of Fanaticism shall be dissipated, that at a Moment when all Intercourse with her was proscribed in the most opulent and commercial States of Europe, and both Force and Artifice were being employed to exclude her from the others, when Great Britain was preparing to meet the mightiest Host that ever had been arrayed against her, and was engaged in a Contest for national Existence, of which her youngest son might not see the Termination, her Statesmen adopted Measures more fatal to her Prosperity, than all that the rancorous Hatred or insidious Guile of her arch Enemy could have accomplished or hoped, and by Laws and Regulations, withholding from the West India Colonies a necessary Supply of Labourers ... finally accomplished the overthrow of these once flourishing Islands, and, by their Fall, ruined the Manufactures, withered the Commerce and subverted the Naval strength of the empire?': *PP*, 1805, x, *Papers respecting the Slave Trade*, pp. 673–4, from *Report of a Committee of the House of Assembly of Jamaica, appointed to inquire into the Proceedings of the Imperial Parliament relative to the Slave Trade, 23.11.1804*, and printed for the Commons 25.2.1805.
50. See *Cowdroy's Manchester Gazette*, 16.7.1814.
51. See Johnson U. J. Asiegbu, *Slavery and the Politics of Liberation, 1787–1861: A study of liberated African emigration and British anti-slavery policy* (1969); W. Kloosterboer, *Involuntary Labour since the Abolition of Slavery: A survey of compulsory labour throughout the world* (Leiden, 1960), chs. 1, 3; E. W. Docker, *The Blackbirders: The recruiting of South Seas labour for Queensland, 1863–1907* (Sydney, 1970), *passim*. It must be stressed that the preceding analysis has not been designed to discount all economic interpretations of abolition. What is challenged is any interpretation which maintains that abolition flowed logically from the central tendency of British capitalism in 1800 to maximise both returns to the capitalist and the exploitation of labour power at the contemporary level of technology. Either one must analyse abolition as an extra or counter-economic process, or one must acknowledge that a major element of welfare economics was already incorporated into British society in 1800. The mere identification of such welfare elements is not enough. One must be able to trace the social and institutional linkage between abolition and other related welfare movements. We may still conclude that abolition was imposed on British capitalists, within British capitalist society.

2 Two Variants of Anti-Slavery: Religious Organization and Social Mobilization in Britain and France, 1780–1870 (1980)*

Dealing with its international aspects, histories of abolition tend to concentrate primarily on its Anglo–American dimension as a mutually reinforcing 'connection', rather than as a subject for comparative national analysis.[1] In this context other European colonial powers are treated as peripheral. French anti-slavery is duly accorded recognition in the intellectual history of pre-abolitionism, and a brief dramatic role in the French Revolutionary era. Thereafter French abolitionists disappear into oblivion, or remain in the unfolding drama as modest members of the chorus.

One might begin by broadly contrasting an 'Anglo–American' and a 'Continental' model of abolitionism. The distinguishing characteristic of the Anglo–American variant was its relatively broad appeal. It had the characteristics of what we think of as a social movement.[2] It attempted to bring public pressure to bear on reluctant or hostile economic interests and agencies of government. At critical moments it used mass propaganda, petitions, public meetings, lawsuits and boycotts, presenting anti-slavery action as a moral and political imperative. Its adherents achieved, at least occasionally, a reputation for fanaticism. Organizationally, it tended to be decentralized in structure and rooted in local communities. It usually aimed

---

*Chapter 2 in C. Bolt and S. Drescher (eds), *Anti-Slavery, Religion and Reform: Essays in Memory of Roger Anstey* (Folkstone and Hamden: William Dawson, 1980), pp. 43–63.

at inclusiveness, welcoming participants who were otherwise excluded by sex, religion, race, class or locality, from the ordinary political process. Europe had one example of this variant – Britain.

The 'Continental' variants generally had the opposite characteristics. They were usually confined to a very small political or cultural elite. They generally were reluctant or unable to seek mass recruitment. Efforts were concentrated on plans of abolition submitted to government, and on elaborate post-emancipation social control. They often attempted to act as brokers between governments and external pressure groups, including British abolitionists and their own colonial interests. Debate was confined to one or two localities, the capital, and/or the chief commercial center. Continental abolitionism, in other words, preferred to work quietly from within. It rarely achieved the status of fanaticism, even in the eyes of enemies. The 'Continental' variant tended to be not only limited in participation but enjoyed a brief existence. A movement would typically emerge in response to external pressures and last only until the abolition of a single slave trade or slave system. With the partial exception of France, Continental abolitionist societies remained satellites of their British counterpart, and failed to capture any mass following on their own soil.

French abolition is a particularly interesting and partly anomalous case of the Continental variety. At the outset it looked very much like its British counterpart. The abolitionist climate of philosophical opinion which inclined heavily against colonial slavery from 1760 to 1790 was as much a Franco–Anglo–American enterprise, as the subsequent movement was predominantly Anglo–American. If only momentarily, France was the first metropolitan nation to declare slavery abolished throughout its sphere of influence in 1794. But after 1800 abolitionism either lacked formal organization, or was confined to a small group in the capital.[3] It had become a 'Continental' movement. For the next three-quarters of a century French manifestations of popular support for antislavery were either aborted by larger revolutionary events, or nipped in the bud by repression. France also had the unenviable distinction of having restored slavery and the slave trade in 1802. Her later abolitionist acts were, like the original, always decreed in the wake of political revolution, and without reference to organized domestic pressure.

The primary purpose of this essay is to broadly compare the relation of religious activity in Britain and France in regard to political abolition. Our hypothesis is that such religious activity was decisively bounded by more general political and social developments. It explicitly does not assume that the particular theological stance of specific religious groups made the critical difference in the timing or intensity of the abolitionist movements at a national level, although the possibility of such a correlation is by no means ruled out. Predominantly Protestant Holland, Denmark and Sweden, for example, were even more clearly Continental cases than was predominantly Catholic France. Nor do we assume that religious networks were the only channels for social change. The press, itinerant propagandists, public meetings at taverns and halls, and the petition were effective alternative or complementary means of mobilizing communal opinion. Over the period 1780–1870 as a whole, however, religious organization remained a primary form of cosmopolitan social organization, linking communities to the larger national and international world. Thus, the response of religious organizations of each society to the social potential of abolitionism seems an excellent place to study metropolitan association for overseas reform.

I

Religious networks were especially significant in the development of British abolitionism. Interlocking specialized antislavery societies did not appear until late in the history of anti-slavery. Other institutions which were important in political mobilization, such as newspapers and public houses, could not match religious institutions in ubiquity and international connections. Once launched by the resources and personnel of the Quaker international, Anglo–American abolitionism was quickly identified with the evangelical wing of Protestantism, even in institutions where it was not dominant, as in the Anglican church, or regions where anti-slavery was soon overwhelmed by a powerful countervailing force, as in the American South.[4]

English anti-slavery and evangelical non-conformity seem to have peaked together (see Figure 2.1). The most dynamic period of nonconformist growth coincides almost exactly with

Figure 2.1 Methodist and New Dissenting membership and Abolitionist petitions, 1750–1914

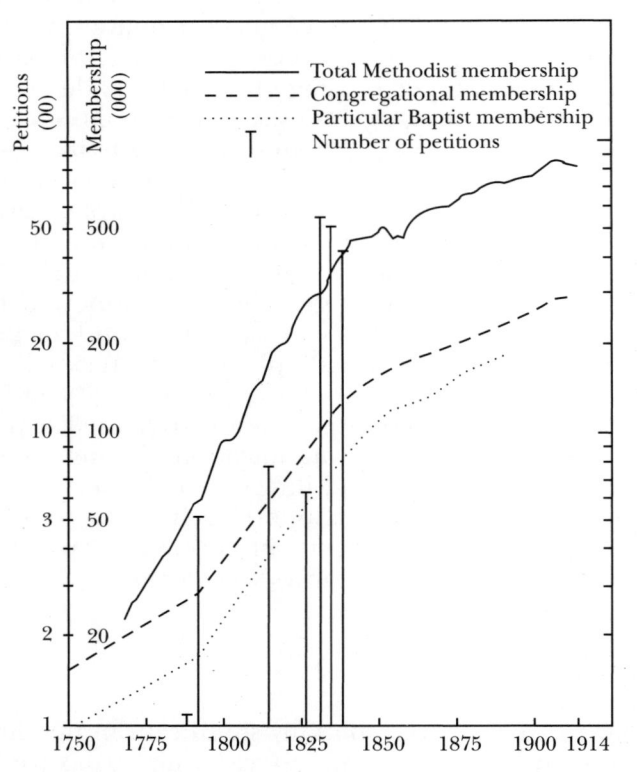

Sources: Nonconformist membership, A. D. Gilbert, *Religion and Society in Industrial England: Church, Chapel and social change, 1740–1914* (1976), Figure 2.1, p. 38; abolitionist petitions, *Journals of the House of Commons*, 1788–1838.

the dynamic period of anti-slavery. In strictly institutional terms, however, evangelical nonconformity latched on to, rather than independently launched the anti-slavery movement. In its formative period, abolition appealed to a broad spectrum among the politically mobilized, ranging from theological rationalists and Unitarians to Quakers and artisanal radicals. If evangelicals participated actively in the earlier petition campaigns they participated as members of geographical rather than religious communities. Table 2.1 shows

Table 2.1 Anti-slavery petitions and religious affiliation, 1788–1833

Date	Total petitions	Established churches* (%)	Dissent (%)
1788	108	23	2
1792	509	14	1
1814	774	1	3
1824	509	3	6
1826	634	7	7
1831	5484	3	72
1833	5020	N.A.	56
	Total signatures		
1833	1 309 931	N.A.	27

Note: N.A. – Not available.
*Including all petitions in which ministers of the Established churches appear as sponsors of petitions, but not in petitions indicating only that the document originated in a particular parish. The percentage for 1831 is uncertain owing to obscurities in the classification of petitions in the House Journal that year.
Sources: Journals of the House of Commons, 1788–1831; Anti-slavery Reporter, 1831; First Report from the Select Committee on Public Petitions (1833).

that it was only toward the climax of anti-slavery in 1830–3, that denominationalism rivaled location as an indicator of the origin of such petitions.

The relevant parliamentary committee was so impressed with the nonconformist component of the climactic anti-slavery petition, that it published a unique appendix to its report in 1833, aggregating the signatures of nonconformity by denomination (Table 2.2). Earlier, evangelical identity apparently merged sufficiently with community affiliation to lend a peculiarly pan-denominational image to anti-slavery. Moreover, although well over half of the petitions of 1833 were explicitly affiliated with non-denominational organizations, Table 2.1 shows that only 27 per cent of the total signatures were submitted under specifically nonconformist banners.

Table 2.2 Anti-slavery and English evangelical denominations, ca 1833

Denomination	(1)* Estimated membership	(2) Anti-slavery petition signatures (1832–3)	(3) % of (2) in (1)
Wesleyan Methodist	(1831–6) 241 000	229 426	95.2
Other Methodist	(1831–6) 62 500	7 166	11.5
Congregational	(1800–38) 112 500	26 430	23.5
Baptist, Particular, General, and New Connexion	(1800–30–38) 87 800	34 650	39.5
Total	503 800	297 672	59.1

Note: *Column (1) is calculated on the basis of enclosed estimates.
Sources: Column (1), A. D. Gilbert, *Religion and Society in Industrial England: Church, Chapel and Social Change 1740–1914* (1976), pp. 31, 37; (2), *First Report from the Select Committee on Public Petitions* (1833).

Another aspect of British religious development is salient in accounting for the sustained strength of programs for overseas social change. The peak period of mass abolitionism in Britain also coincided with an expansion of the Anglo–American religious network to full planetary dimensions. The take-off of British abolitionism coincided almost exactly with the revival of the British missionary movement. After 1790, the British-sponsored religious networks in Africa and the West Indies were responsive to increasingly abolitionist pressures at home.[5] Missionaries could appeal more directly to their metropolitan sources of support than ever before. This linkage also allowed the development of a religious relationship between slaves and missionaries well before emancipation. Conversely British missionaries after 1790 were less dependent upon the metropolitan state church or on the colonial elite for financial support than their predecessors.

In the first half-century of abolitionism the British dominated the Protestant missionary movement as thoroughly as its imperial navy dominated the oceans, and far more thoroughly than its trade dominated the world's commercial networks. Of the missionary establishments created outside the United States by European Protestants or their descendants in the formative generation (1790–1820), 22 were British, 5 were American, and 1 was Dutch. During the next thirty years, of 72 new missions, 26 were British, 28 were American and 17 were Continental. (America's great surge came in the 1820s, as her abolitionist movement was entering a new phase.) Of the Continental establishments, only the two sponsored by French Protestants came from nations with slave colonies, and none originated in the Netherlands.

This is not to say that evangelical expansion automatically entailed a resolutely abolitionist posture. Before 1790 the fate of religious missions to slave colonies demonstrated the opposite. Until the fate of American slavery was decided, evangelical Christianity temporized with slavery. The history of the international 'Evangelical Alliance' abundantly illustrated this. But if slaveholding American Protestants were long powerful enough to prevent international movements for evangelical unity from becoming organs of abolitionism, the thickening network of religious communication kept the question at the forefront of Protestant politics. Anti-slavery advocates clearly played a role in evangelical ideology and organization, sometimes to the disadvantage of British religious initiatives (the international Evangelical Alliance controversy, for example), which was absent from other religious organizations with similar international dimensions.[7]

Religious organizations in France never achieved the same prominence in anti-slavery. If the dynamism of missionary activism may be taken as an indicator of the potential linkage of overseas to domestic change, French activity indicates a low level of metropolitan interest both before and after the Great Revolution of 1789. For more than sixty years, coinciding with the development of Anglo–American anti-slavery, the whole European Catholic missionary enterprise was virtually paralyzed. The monarchical attack on the Jesuits in the 1760s and 1770s entailed the recall or displacement of hundreds of French colonial missionaries. The French Revolution shattered the resources of the Church. The old French empire and the broader missionary effort disintegrated together. In many areas the entire Catholic overseas network was abandoned for decades. In others, such as the French Antilles, with only one priest to 10 000 souls, only the free population received the attentions of the clergy. Effectively, until the second third of the nineteenth century, Catholic mobilization for abolitionist or missionary enterprise moved in the opposite direction from Anglo–American development, and until the last third, lagged far behind.[8]

From its foundation in 1788 to its demise in the early 1790s, the French antislavery society, the *Amis des Noirs*, did not seek to use religious organizations or their personnel to mobilize French opinion. The French Revolution shook the Catholic Church to its roots, and it had to make its peace with a post-revolutionary government which had already restored slavery and required civil subservience in exchange for its protection. A restored Church, which identified the abolitionist Abbé Grégoire with all the sufferings and apostacies of its revolutionary martyrdom, was unlikely to raise another abolitionist to take up the mantel of the Constitutional Bishop of Blois. The first concern of the Church was its own survival in a post-revolutionary society where the trauma of the Jacobin terror at home had been re-inforced by the trauma of the Haitian revolution overseas.

In addition to its obligations as a state-supported religion, Catholicism was also deeply embedded in the colonial status quo.[9] Its clerical training center, Saint-Sulpice, maintained the accommodating doctrine of the legitimacy of slavery, and a passive role towards the issue of emancipation. Equally, those Catholic periodicals most clearly subordinated to the hierarchy also tended to defend a passive and pastoral role for the clergy in the colonies.[10]

The embryonic theological hostility to slavery which appeared in France at the outbreak of the French Revolution appears to have found no sequel in nineteenth-century France. Like the Protestant denominations which established deep roots in slave systems, French Catholicism continued to maintain its traditional compromise with the institution.[11] Hesitant to embrace anti-slavery because of its linkage with an anti-clerical revolution, the French Church found its performance measured against more a progressive Protestantism in Britain and a more radical secularism in France. Until the eve of the second emancipation in 1848, calls for clerical participation in the movement received little encouragement from the French hierarchy.

If the clergy hesitated to become identified with the French campaign for emancipation from a general wariness of political agitation, nineteenth-century conditions offered few incentives for international Catholic pressures in favor of anti-slavery. Catholicism was linked to an institutional network which discouraged any radical transformations in attitudes or in social structures. In the first half of the nineteenth century the Papacy was closely bound to metropolitan forces of order which sanctioned various forms of bound labor within and without Europe. Neither the Central Europe of the Holy Alliance, nor Iberia were likely sources of pressure against the status quo. Indeed, Rome was busily restricting attempts to atune theology to libertarian values.[12] Even in the Americas the balance of social pressures and immigration patterns weighed against an anti-slavery stance by Catholics. The largest concentration of Catholics in the South, the French of Louisiana, adhered to the slave system. In the North, the bulk of the burgeoning Irish Catholic immigration before the Civil War was not mobilized for anti-slavery.[13]

One major campaign with a highly visible, if quantitively indeterminate, Catholic presence, was the Anti-slavery Address to Irish Americans, signed by 60 000–70 000 people in Ireland in 1841–2. Neither the intended recipients, nor the American Catholic hierarchy gave the Address a favorable reception, despite the well-publicized adhesion of Daniel O'Connell, Father Theodore Mathews, and many Irish priests. Equally significant, this attempt by Irish abolitionists to convert their fellow countrymen was not repeated with coreligionists on the Continent. When an appeal was addressed to the French clergy very shortly after the Irish Address, it took the form of a private letter by a Catholic abolitionist to the archbishop of Paris. The potential of massive international pressure was never realized.

One cannot, however, explain the relative quietism of French Catholicism towards abolition simply in terms of French Revolutionary demoralization, or international affiliation. French Catholicism had certainly achieved some internal stability as early as the First Empire, and despite occasional threats was not again subjected to a sustained institutional attack before 1870. Moreover, in its broader context, European Catholicism did renew its overseas mission, especially after 1830. France again became Europe's principal Catholic exponent of overseas religious, as well as economic and political expansion. The central Catholic missionary periodical the *Annales de la propagation de la foi*, was founded in France in 1825. In 1847, on the eve of the second French emancipation, 178 000 copies circulated, of which 55 per cent went to French subscribers alone. By contrast, the other Catholic slave powers accounted for less than 2 per cent of the subscribers.[14]

Therefore, while France lagged behind Britain in its depth of international penetration and religious investment in overseas activity, there was no lack of means in France for converting concern with religious conversion abroad into a concern for overseas social transformation. There are other, more proximate, indicators that French Catholicism was becoming available for political mobilization, especially after 1830. In the absence of a Catholic religious organization dedicated to popular mobilization, it was still possible to use other means to galvanize religious support for anti-slavery. The July Monarchy witnessed an enormous expansion of newspaper circulation. Like its secular counterparts, the Catholic lay press began to demand a role in the articulation of opinion, breaking with the accommodating posture of the hierarchy *vis-à-vis* the state. The most successful example was Louis Veuillot's *L'Univers*.[15] Veuillot was eager to employ the technique of the mass petition as well as of popular journalism. In 1847, while a handful of French abolitionists were accumulating less than 11 000 signatures for emancipation, Veuillot was able to elicit almost 90 000 in favor of proclerical legislation. *L'Univers* was also the most anti-slavery Catholic newspaper in France. By the end of the year it was clear that *L'Univers* would support plans for a new, broadly based campaign.[16] There were equally obvious signs that the French clergy could be drawn into the anti-slavery network. In the petition campaign of 1846–7, during an assembly of the clergy of Paris, a French abolitionist collected 800 signatures, the first substantial intrusion of the Catholic clergy into the anti-slavery cause. For a few months before the February Revolution of 1848 it appeared as though splintered groups of abolitionists were on the verge of forming a national movement. Notables, urban radicals, metropolitan *hommes de couleur*, and men identified with religious opinion began to coordinate their efforts for the first time. Catholics figured prominently in abolitionist plans. The Archbishop of Paris indicated his approval of Catholic involvement. Abbé Dupanloup, a leader of liberal Catholicism, promised to help gather 20 000 clerical signatures. *L'Univers* publicized the activities of the special bureau created to launch the 1848 campaign and to create pressure 'from below'.[17]

The events of February 1848 snapped the still frail abolitionist alliance. Once again emancipation became the work of Parisian revolutionaries acting by decree. At the popular level the only abolitionist group visible was the radical *Club des Amis des Noirs*, formed in Paris in the wake of the revolution.[18] The only petitions on slavery which reached the Emancipation Committee from beyond the capital were those of Chambers of Commerce, pleading for compensation, delay, or guarantees of order and labor.[19] Emancipation was decreed in the name of the Provisional Government, before it handed over power to the socially and fiscally more conservative Constituent Assembly. Despite flickerings of a national appeal, abolitionism never became linked with mass Catholic support or organization.

Before assessing the historical context of this disjuncture, it may be useful to consider the role of Protestants in French abolitionism. The Protestant clergy were excluded from the state-supported French missionary enterprise both before and after the Revolution. A minor branch of world Protestantism, its overseas missionary effort was meager. The Paris Evangelical Mission Society succeeded in establishing only one overseas post before 1845, and only in a British sphere of influence.[20] In terms of its own economic resources and the persistent policy of subordination to the French state, on which it was heavily dependent, French Protestantism had little of the dynamic which made slavery so significant an organizational issue in Britain.

French Protestants were more visibly involved in abolitionism than their French Catholic counterparts during the Constitutional Monarchy in France (1815–48). The *Société de la Morale Chrétienne*, the only French organization with an abolitionist committee during the Bourbon restoration, was disproportionately Protestant. For most of the period of the July Monarchy, however, independent Protestant involvement in abolition leaned heavily on English information and initiatives. The July Monarchy was especially receptive to the integration of the French Protestant elite into the highest echelons of power and respectability. It was relatively cautious about the opportunity to organize a mass appeal around the question of abolition.[21] At least one section of French Protestant journalism consistently urged British-style abolitionism campaigns throughout the July Monarchy, a suggestion just as consistently ignored by abolitionist notables.[22]

On the eve of the Revolution of 1848, and encouraged by the British, French Protestants showed clear signs of becoming activists. The campaign was, in fact, initiated by a provincial Protestant and a mulatto from the Antilles.[23] Some communities began to submit abolitionist petitions to the Chamber of Deputies, with their pastors heading the lists.[24] In relative terms, French Protestants were therefore probably over-represented among the provincial localities which responded to the campaign. Constituting about 2 per cent of the French population, they accounted for about 10 per cent of the abolitionist petition in 1847. Protestant ministers also made up about 10 per cent of the total clerical support.[25]

French Protestant anti-slavery, like all other varieties, disappeared in the wake of the February Revolution. Protestants were probably always represented among the abolitionists, but French Protestants were closer to their Catholic and Protestant counter-parts on the Continent than to the British in terms of broad involvement in abolitionist activity. Given the inhibitions of a small, minority sect, it is the situation of French Catholicism which was the more significant determinant of the national pattern.

II

In all metropolitan countries abolitionism declined as a popular issue following the elimination of the institution in their respective colonial areas. Yet, here too, we have British and

Continental variants. British anti-slavery remained a relatively salient issue for a generation after emancipation. It was manifested not only in the continuance of specialized organizations for international abolition, but in the continuance of institutional involvement with freedmen. A large scale metropolitan religious and educational effort continued in the British colonies and the African continent, and issues raised by slavery in the United States were continuously debated before interested and contributing British audiences. The British post-emancipation movement was also still capable of launching campaigns which involved tens and hundreds of thousands of signatories.

In France, emancipation was equivalent to the total suspension of abolitionism as an organized movement. The radical Parisian *Amis des Noirs* of 1848 was a victim of the general reaction against associations. The elite anti-slavery society looked forward to its own demise even before the emancipation decree.[26] The combination of apathy and governmental hostility to political associations after the presidential coup of December 1851 discouraged even a nominal institutional revival until the imperial liberalization of the mid-1860s.[27]

The religious shoots that had appeared towards the end of the July Monarchy withered. The ties between popular Catholic journalism and anti-slavery seem to have disappeared. Veuillot swungs sharply over to the traditional view that abolitionism was the tool of British liberalism. When Imperial France embarked on a barely disguised renewal of the African slave trade in the late 1850s, *L'Univers* was as vitriolic as the conservative French press in denouncing British abolitionist complaints as the Anglo–Protestant complement to revolutionary subversion in Europe. Imperial policy was defended against 'comedies of philanthropism' and 'Negrophilia'.[28]

The American Civil War produced a final opportunity to arouse flagging European concern with the question of slavery in the Americas. Interest was heightened and vastly complicated by the high stakes of international power politics, and the acute suffering which prevailed in the textile districts of both France and Britain.[29] In Britain this took the form of a vigorous press war, public meetings, and petitions on behalf of both belligerents.[30] In the British political campaign revolving around the American conflict, the division between the Establishment and nonconformity was even more striking than in the previous generation. Of ninety-four petitions submitted to Parliament against recognition of Confederate independence in 1863, twenty (21 per cent) were sent in on behalf of nonconforming congregations. None were headed up by the Anglican clergy. On the opposite side during the following year, seventeen (21 per cent) of the eighty petitions in favor of British action to terminate hostilities were presented on behalf of the 'Clergy and Laity' of various communities. No nonconformist congregation subscribed to what would have amounted to *de facto* recognition of Southern independence, with slavery. More significantly, however, the combined number of signatures accumulated in both campaigns amounted to less than 30 000. The conflict over slavery had ceased to be a major concern of either the religious or the political community.

In France, because of the imperial restrictions, journalistic commentary was more muted, and public activity almost non-existent. On this occasion, even so, there were signs of attempts to use the religious network to increase the domestic salience of the struggle. After the Emancipation Proclamation some French Bishops urged their flocks to pray for American slaves. The *Annales de la propagation de la foi* took the optimistic position that emancipation might lead to a reactive expansion of Catholicism among ex-slaves of Protestant masters. But these were editorial glosses on events rather than attempts to initiate or influence political or religious policy.[31]

In France the two most important attempts at public mobilization related to emancipation came at the end of the war. The first was a campaign for a commemorative medal to be presented to Lincoln's widow. It gathered 40 000 subscribers before the government became alarmed over the domestic political implications. But its sponsors were overwhelmingly radical and secular.[32] The second venture was a fund-raising drive on behalf of the American freedmen. A parallel campaign in Britain yielded up to $800 000 in cash and goods (more, notes Howard Temperley, than all British contributions for antislavery since British colonial emancipation). The French campaign yielded approximately $10 000. This sum certainly also exceeded the total of private French contributions to antislavery activity after 1848.[33] Despite wartime musings about the conversion of ex-slaves, potential Catholic contributors in France could hardly have been less wary than their Anglican counterparts about stinting their own modest missions to fund relief and education under the aegis of nonconformist agencies in a Protestant cultural area. French aid to the American freedmen seemed to be the same pale reflection of the larger British effort. The movement, which before emancipation obtained a hundred British signatures for every French one, collected eighty dollars in Britain for every dollar contributed in France for Freedman's Aid.

However, the reaction to the American Civil War was not just one more demonstration of an excitable British evangelical revival pulling along a French satellite movement. The conflict's initially ambiguous implication for slavery was more than matched by divisions in British Protestant opinion on the appropriate position towards the belligerents. It was French ministers who took a collective initiative in favor of the North, a move only subsequently endorsed by sympathetic British clergymen. The Freedman's Aid appeal also reopened opportunities for personal participation in France which had been foreclosed by the aborted abolitionism of the late 1840s. For the first time French women openly assumed roles of organizational leadership.[34]

The British movement, despite its relative generosity, was showing clear signs of a hardening of the anti-slavery arteries. Its successes were calculated more in terms of contributions than individual participation. A few wealthy supporters could determine the relative 'enthusiasm' of a region, whilst those areas of Britain which had suffered from the Northern blockade of their cotton supply could not even be canvassed. The first mass petition campaign triggered in Manchester, in 1787, must have included a majority of signatures from the lower middle and working classes. Eighty years later, the Freedman's Aid campaign could not even be properly organized among a resentful Manchester working class.[35] Popular apathy was for the first time contrasted with Continental initiative. The same document which proposed the termination of the Freedman's Aid movement in 1868 announced that it was still waiting to realize a penny subscription from working men, following the example set by artisans of Paris, by the Swiss peasants and, partially, by Birmingham.[36] The fund-raising campaign failed to evoke a response from even those who had not been embittered by the economic consequences of the conflict. Nonconformity, flourishing and unassailably respectable, was no longer interested in a sustained campaign in favor of ex-slaves. Britain now converged towards the Continental variant of prestigious committees. British anti-slavery, which the old agitator, George Thompson had hoped to rekindle from the heat of the American conflict, was, in more than one sense, liquidated in a post-war charity subscription.

Here we note a final irony in anti-slavery's potential as a vehicle for mobilization in France. Although the French working class contribution to American freedmen was fragmentary, this may have been due to a more general absence of religious or alternative modes of class mediating organizations. In the France of 1865 anti-slavery had not been converted into a charity appropriated by large subscribers. There were no aging and wealthy veterans of French abolition at hand to capitalize on the past commitment of millions to the glory of their participation. While the unexpected paucity of the workers' response surprised and disappointed the veteran canvassers in Britain, its unexpected extension in France took its inexperienced female organizers by equal surprise. Working class contributions came in without any central planning or canvassing. Only at the end of the campaign did upper class organizers realize, with regret, quite how large a reservoir of sympathy might have been at their disposal. One donation of 1000 francs represented the combined contribution of 10 000 workers. It is unclear whether the female organizers of the French Freedman's Aid drive were aware of the equally unheeded opportunity twenty-one years before, when thousands of workers of Paris and Lyon had launched the first mass petition for emancipation on the Continent. Certainly they were unaware of the contrast between the artisans of Grenoble who had celebrated Grégoire's electoral victory in Isère forty-five years before, and the Liberal notables who had then voted for his exclusion from the Chamber of Deputies. To British abolitionists, the campaign gave pointed notice of diverging class perceptions at the end of a long crusade. To the French it was a glimpse of a cause which might have linked them to at least a portion of the working class.

III

In religious perspective British anti-slavery movements, in their heyday, paid homage to the increasing power of nonconformist values and modes of association. They provided the basis for a cross-class and cross-national appeal to a common standard of human rights. In their independence from state support and subordination they were also more flexible channels for the rapid mobilization of public opinion against a traditional economic institution than the established religious and political organizations of unreformed Britain. Although anti-slavery became increasingly denominational towards 1830, and elicited a counterpoint of class-oriented anti-evangelical criticism, this far from unanimous dissent from below was lacking in the formative period, when the movement claimed the adhesion of Painite deists no less than Clapham saints.[37] Moreover, given both the extraordinary mobilization of Wesleyan Methodists for anti-slavery in 1833 (Table 2.2), and the occupational structure of Wesleyan and other evangelical nonconformists (Table 2.3), it is apparent that artisanal

Table 2.3 Occupational structure of nonconformity with high participation in anti-slavery petitions (sample 1830–7)

Occupation	English society (%)	Wesleyans (%)	Baptists and Congregationalists (%)
Aristocracy	1.4	0	0
Merchants	2.2	1.7	5.4
Merchants/ Manufacturers	6.2	5.8	8.2
Tradesmen	14.0	5.5	7.1
Artisans	23.5	62.7	63.0
Laborers	17.0	9.5	3.9
Miners, etc.	2.5	7.6	2.1
Others	33.2	7.2	10.3

Source: A. D. Gilbert, *Religion and Society in Industrial England: Church, Chapel, and Social Change 1740–1914* (1976), pp. 63, 67.

England continued to support the movement at its climax. In cross-cultural terms the significant fact remains that an unprecedented and unparalleled proportion of the nation adhered to a common cause for so long, and shaped a synthesis of political and religious action around the question of slavery which proved difficult to export beyond its zone of origin.

As Halévy long ago noted, the French religious system lacked this burgeoning dissenting and evangelical network. Its religious organizations were economically dependent upon a state generally hostile to associational agitation. Revolutions and threats of revolution caused the surviving elite of both state and church to be wary of mass action for virtually the whole period during which slavery was an unresolved issue in French politics. From the second decade of the nineteenth century, abolitionism in France was also vulnerable to associations with British colonial supremacy, Anglophile Protestantism and secular radicalism. Non-revolutionary British citizens validated their imperial and economic hegemony with a socio-religious crusade, and mythologized their incremental abolition as a testimony to their moral progress. Their French counterparts were left to poke among the shards of their past to make what they could of unsuccessful emancipations unsuccessful restorations, and imperial humiliations.

Historians cannot overlook the significance of this temporal priority and divergence in the emergence of abolitionism. By 1814 the evangelical William Wilberforce became a national hero precisely because he was an abolitionist saint. It is hardly possible to imagine anyone else who could, with impunity, condemn a treaty which sealed the greatest military triumph in his country's history. At the same moment his closest French abolitionist counterpart, Abbé Grégoire, lived frozen in ostracism, stigmatized as the incendiary of two worlds. His very existence inhibited the organization of another abolitionist society. The belated hero of French emancipation was to be the unbeliever Victor Schoelcher. But in 1814, the difference between the voice of abolition in Britain and France was not *vox Dei*, but *vox populi*. Behind the words of Wilberforce flowed the greatest wave of petitions in his country's history. This was the tide in the affairs of 'men and brothers', that swept the British evangelical to glory in the name of God and humanity.

NOTES

Place of publication is London, unless otherwise stated.

1. See for example, Christine Bolt, *The Anti-Slavery Movement and Reconstruction: A study in Anglo–American co-operation, 1833–77* (1969); and Betty Fladeland, *Men and Brothers: Anglo–American anti-slavery co-operation* (Urbana, 1972). For some explicitly comparative analyses, see E. Genovese, *The World the Slaveholders Made* (New York, 1969), part I; Howard Temperley, 'British and American Abolitionist Compared' in *The Anti-Slavery Vanguard*, ed. M. Duberman (Princeton, 1965); David Davis, *The Problem of Slavery in the Age of Revolution, 1770–1823* (Ithaca, 1975). Toward the end of the eighteenth century, abolitionism emerged as only one of a large number of social reform movements. They aimed at effective political action at the regional, national and, in the case of abolition, at the international level. This rapid thickening of large-scale associational activity outside traditional authority networks was a counterpart to economic development. Abolitionism was thus an aspect of what Karl Deutsch calls 'social mobilization', a process in which major social and economic patterns are broken, and people become more available for new patterns of action. In domestic terms British, although not French, abolitionism served as a very early vehicle both for the formulation of new values and for the transformation of old forms of political pressure into novel contexts. For lack of space, in this essay we are confining the comparison of social mobilization in Britain and France primarily to religious organization.
2. For recent descriptions of the development of British abolitionism in addition to the accounts of Rice, Temperley and Davis, above, see especially Roger Anstey, *The Atlantic Slave Trade and British Abolition, 1760–1810* (1975), part four; Peter F. Dixon, 'The Politics of Emancipation: The movement for the abolition of slavery in the British West Indies, 1807–1833,' D. Phil. Oxford (1971); Howard Temperley, *British Anti-Slavery, 1833–70* (1972).
3. See Gabriel Debien, *Les Colons de Saint-Domingue et la Revolution: Essai sur le club Massiac* (Paris, 1953); Yves Debbasch, *Couleur et liberté* (Paris, 1967); Valerie Quinney, 'The Committee on Colonies of the French Constituent Assembly, 1789–1971,' Ph.D. dissertation, University of Wisconsin (1967); Ruth F. Necheles, *The Abbé Grégoire 1788–1831: The odyssey of an egalitarian* (Westport, 1971); D. P. Resnick, 'Political Economy and French anti-slavery: The case of J.-B. Say', *Proceedings of the 3rd Annual Meeting of the Western Society for French History* (1976), pp. 179–86; S. Drescher, *Dilemmas of Democracy: Tocqueville and modernization* (Pittsburgh, 1968), ch. 6.
4. On the abortive anti-slavery impulse in the slave South, see especially Donald G. Matthews, *Religion in the Old South* (Chicago, 1977), ch. 2.
5. See Stiv Jacobson, *Am I Not A Man and a Brother? British Missionaries and the abolition of the slave trade and slavery, 1786–1838* (Uppsala, 1972); and G. R. Mellor, *British Imperial Trusteeship 1783–1850* (1951).

6. See *The Encyclopedia of Missions*, ed. H. O. Dwight *et al.* (New York, 1904), Appendices II and VI.
7. A French Protestant newspaper sarcastically asked whether an English 'Evangelical Alliance', which refused to excommunicate orthodox proprietors of slaves and excluded Quakers, could be a model for unity (*Le Lien* (1847), p. 76). On region as a source of anti-slavery controversy, see Fladeland, *Men and Brothers*, pp. 364–70.
8. S. Delacroix (ed.), *Histoire Universelle des Missions Catholiques*, 4 vols. (Paris, n.d.), III, pp. 14–15, chs. 1–3.
9. Antoine Gisler, *L'Esclavage aux Antilles Françaises (XVIIe–XIXe siècle): Contribution au problème de l'esclavage* (Friburg, 1965), part 3, 'Les Missionnaires'. On the extraordinary degree of clerical creolization in the colonies, see the letter of the Prefect Apostolique, Castelli, to Baron Mackau, July 10, 1841 (Archives Nationales (hereafter A. N.)), Archives privées, Fonds Mackau, 156 API.
10. On abolitionist complaints about institutional passivity *vis-à-vis* colonial pressures or emancipation see *Rhodes House Anti-Slavery Papers* (hereafter *RHASSP*), G/103 (France), letter of Ismabert to Scoble, 19 January 1843, *L'Abolitioniste francais*, T. III (1846), pp. 71, 107–122, 270; on defenses of accommodation, see *La Tribune sacrée* vols. 5–6 (February 1846), pp. 145–51; *L'Ami de la Religion* (1846), p. 413; *Revue Catholique IV* (July 1839), p. 374 and *V* (July 1840), pp. 357–63; and above all a letter from Leguay, replying to an attack on the seminary of Saint-Esprit by Ledru-Rollin in the Chamber of Deputies (*L'Ami de la Religion* (April 1847), p. 287. His reply clearly shows that almost halfway through the century, anti-slavery still evoked Grégoire, unorthodoxy, and fanaticism.
11. Necheles, *The Abbé Grégoire*, pp. 205–7, 229, 235–6, 243; John Francis Maxwell, *Slavery in the Catholic Church: The History of the Catholic Teaching Concerning the Moral Legitimacy of the Institution of Slavery* (London, 1975), pp. 98–102; L. Swidler, 'Liberal Catholicism: A lesson from the past', *Cross currents*, 21 (1971), 25–37.
12. *Ibid.* The Clergy are described as conspicuous by their absence in the late-blossoming Spanish abolitionist movement of the 1860s. (See A. F. Corwin, *Spain and the Abolition of Slavery in Cuba, 1817–86* (Austin and London, 1967), pp. 166–71).
13. Gilbert Osofsky, 'Abolitionists, Irish immigrants and the dilemmas of Romantic Nationalism', *American Historical Review*, 80(4), (October 1975), 889–912; Joseph M. Hernon, *Celts, Catholics and Copperheads: Ireland views the American Civil War* (Columbus, 1968), ch. 4. For the conspicuous place given to Irish clerical adhesions, see Garrison's newspaper, *The Liberator*, 8 October 1841, 18 March 1842. I have not been able to discover any estimate of the number of Catholics who signed the address. An even greater number of Irish signatures was collected during the campaign to curtail Negro Apprenticeship in 1837–8, but the disproportionately Protestant areas of the country were geographically over-represented. By the late 1840s Irish nationalism was increasingly hostile to the American abolitionists (Hernon, *Celts*, 62). On the appeal to the French hierarchy see the letter of Richard Madden, to Msgr. Affre, Archbishop of Paris, 17 March 1842,

Archevêché de Paris, Archives historiques, Direction des Oeuvres, 4KII, Dossier: 'Pour l'abolition de l'esclavage'.
14. Delacroix, *Histoire Universelle*, III, pp. 66–7.
15. Anita Rasi May, 'The challenge of the French Catholic Press to Episcopal authority, 1842–60: A crisis of modernization', Ph.D. dissertation, University of Pittsburgh (1970), pp. 113 ff.
16. See *L'Univers*, 16 September 1847. *L'Univers* clearly encouraged clerical campainging in favor of abolition and thought anti-slavery activism could be transfered to the education question (*Ibid*., 25 April 1847).
17. *Ibid*., 30 October 1847. On the role of Dupanloup and the attitude of the Archbishop, see *RHASSP*, C13/111 Letter of Bissette to Scoble, 27 April 1847. The outspoken defenders of slavery in the Chambers interpreted the signs of clerical defection from 'benevolent neutrality' as indicating a very dangerous trend in French opinion. See Bibliothèque Nationale, N.A. fr 3631, Schoelcher collection, 'compte de M. Jollivet avec pièces à l'Appui', letters of Jollivet, delegate of Martinique, 29 January and 29 October 1847, and letter of Jabrun, delegate of Guadeloupe, 14 September 1847; and A. N. Archives Outre-Mer, Généralités 173 (1388), letter of Reiset and Jabrun, 29 June 1847. By the end of 1847 about 30 000 signatures had been gathered for the 1848 petition drive.
18. A. N. C942, Enquête sur les evenements de mai et juin 1848, dr. 4, 'Club des Amis des Noirs'.
19. A. N. Archives Outre-Mer, Généralités; 153 (1284), dr: 'Abolition de l'esclavage, 1848'.
20. Dwight, *Encyclopedia of Missions*, p. 571, 'Paris Evangelical Mission Society'; *Le Lien* (17 July 1847), p. 86.
21. Serge Daget, 'L'Abolition de la traite des Noirs en France de 1814 à 1831', *Cahiers d'Etudes Africaines*, XI (41), 14–58. By the July Monarchy, *Morale Chrétienne* was restricting itself to merely occasional reporting on abolitionist activity elsewhere. The more activist *Le Semeur* characterized it as moribund in 1833. On the lack of incentive for mass agitation during a 'golden age' of French Protestantism, see André-Jean Tudesq, *Les Grands Notables en France (1840–9): Etude historique d'une psychologie sociale*, 2 vols. (Paris, 1964), I, pp. 124, 443–7; II, pp. 834–8. On the role of the British in the petition campaign of 1846–7, see Temperley, *British Anti-Slavery*, pp. 185–9.
22. *Le Semeur*, 1831–48.
23. See *RHASSP*, C13/110–129, letters from Bissette to Scoble, January 1847 to January 1848.
24. A. N. Archives Outre-Mer, SA 197 (1489), petitions of 1847, in 48 cahiers.
25. Professor Serge Daget kindly furnished me with information on the percentage of Protestant signatures. The figure on Protestant clerical signers is in *Le Lien* (17 July 1847) p. 105. At the beginning of 1848 the petitions which began to reach the Chamber of Peers were again disproportionately Protestant, as revealed in the presence of Pastors as the clerical representative. See AN CC 475 (645).
26. A. N. Archives Outre-Mer, Généralités, 153 (1276): Dutrône, on behalf of the French Abolition Society, to V. Schoelcher, of the Provisional Government's Emancipation Committee, 23 March 1848.

27. In 1853 a former leader of the defunct French society informed the British that there was no hope of reviving the association to promote abolition in America and Cuba. (*RHASSP*, G/103, Isambert to Scoble, 15 June 1853).
28. *L' Univers*, 7 July, 24 September, 3 November, 8 December, 1858.
29. See Mary Ellison, *Support for Secession: Lancashire and the American Civil War* (Chicago, 1972); Lynn M. Case, *French Opinion on the United States and Mexico 1860–7* (1936, 1969) *passim*; Fladeland, *Men and Brothers*, ch. 16; Royden Harrison, 'British Labor and American Slavery', *Science and Society*, 25 (1961), 291–319.
30. D. Jordan and E. J. Pratt, *Europe and the American Civil War* (Boston, 1931), especially chs. 6 and 7, and E. D. Adams *Great Britain and the American Civil War*, 2 vols. (New York, 1924), II, chs. 14–15.
31. Serge Gavronsky, *The French Liberal Opposition and the American Civil War* (New York, 1968), p. 186.
32. *Ibid.*, pp. 241–2.
33. See Bolt, *The Anti-Slavery Movement*, p. 113, and Temperley, *British Anti-Slavery*, pp. 258–61.
34. *Le Lien*, 16 December 1865 (summary of the Freedmen's Aid campaign). The 10 000 contributors were from the Mulhouse working class. Workers of Paris, and Lyon were also prominently mentioned. 'The fact is', wrote the reporter, 'that we went to them less than they came to us ... It seemed to us more natural to address ourselves preferably those who possess ... [but] in certain cases, the sympathy roused is much more important than the gift received. I hasten to compensate for this gap in our publicity, and to herein declare the number of adhesions which came from where we least expected it'. The French Freedmen's Aid Campaign received 86 500 francs, held two major public meetings, and included Catholics, Protestants, Jews, and Freemasons, finally achieving that ecumenical image which had been lacking in prior anti-slavery movements although Protestants were again over-represented in the leadership at the first public meeting in the Salle Herz in Paris (See *Le Lien*, 11 November 1865.) During the war, the circular address in favor of the North was signed by almost 800 French pastors, and subsequently by 4000 English clergymen.
35. See Bolt, *The Anti-Slavery Movement*, pp. 64–73, and Ellison, *Support For Secession*. The sympathies of a large part of the Manchester business community had also been with the South during the war.
36. Bolt, *The Anti-Slavery Movement*, pp. 67, 109–10, on the general apathy among all classes.
37. On the mixture of adhesion and antagonism towards the anti-slavery movement at the time of emancipation, see for example, *The Poor Man's Guardian*, 18 October 1831, 25 February, 9 June, 17 November, 1 December, 1832, 2 March 1833; *The Poor Man's Advocate*, 4 February, 4 August, 1 December, 1832; *The Working Man's Friend*, 26 Jannuary, 2 February 1833; *The Chronicler of the Times*, 12 January 1833. The extent of this class-orientated analysis was pointed out to me by Patricia Hollis of the University of East Anglia.

3 Public Opinion and the Destruction of British Colonial Slavery (1982)*

Embedded in most histories of the abolition of British imperial slavery is what one might call a downward flowing model. From Thomas Clarkson's graphic figure of abolitionism as a converging system of leading moralists, in 1808, to David Brion Davis's hypothesis of anti-slavery as an expression of the hegemony of the British ruling class, in 1975, the emphasis has been on how leading members of cultural, political or economic sectors of society generated and directed the force which ultimately destroyed the British slave trade and slavery.[1] In individual accounts saints are pitted against slave-driving planters and merchants, or statesmen and political economists join forces against imperial slave interests, but attention centres on leading economic interests, on clusters of intellectuals or philosophers, on lines of division in Cabinets and Parliament. When historians have introduced the larger public into the story, it is generally and briefly treated as a 'mass sentiment', consciously or unconsciously worked on by élites for good or ill.[2]

This model of the movement of public opinion is by no means purely a retrospective imposition by later historians. Indeed most contemporary chroniclers of British anti-slavery adopted a similar perspective. Historians continue to be concerned with economic profitability and interests, with the ideology of the anti-slavery leadership and with the proceedings of the British Parliament. Most recently, both Roger Anstey's major finished study on the abolition of the slave trade and his unfortunately fragmentary chapters on subsequent emancipation are

---

*Chapter 1 in J. Walvin (ed.), *Slavery and British Society 1776–1846* (London: Macmillan, 1982), pp. 22–48, 216–21.

organised in terms of the stages of parliamentary action.³ There have been brief forays which look more closely at 'popular' aspects of abolition,⁴ but there has as yet been no attempt to define the kinds of questions that must be systematically raised or the data that should be looked at in order to comprehend the role of public mobilisation in the destruction of the British imperial slave system.

This essay will ask a number of questions about mass abolitionism in Britain. A first set of questions is directed towards the relationship of the movement to the broader social and political setting:

(1) How extensive was mass mobilisation against slavery in an international context?
(2) How extension was abolitionism in relation to other contemporary issues in Britain for which there were similar attempts at pressure from without?
(3) To what extent should this movement be looked upon as an extension of a parallel religious mobilisation – the rise of evangelical nonconformity in Britain?
(4) To what extent should 'mass' public abolitionism be considered a class rather than a mass movement?

A second set is directed towards results:

(1) How important was the role of public opinion in determining the timing or outcome of emancipation?
(2) How does public opinion relate to other considerations, notably the economy or social conditions in the West Indies?
(3) What impact might it have had on the fiscal constraints of the British Government?

A brief essay cannot definitively address all these questions but it can indicate those answers which seem most plausible, or challenge assumptions which have hitherto seemed acceptable beyond question.

It is important first to clarify the relative significance of British mass anti-slavery in spatial and temporal perspective. The British movement formed part of an international movement which emerged in the 1780s.⁵ Anti-slavery took institutionalised form in countries on both sides of the Atlantic, from Germany to Brazil. On the north-eastern side of the Atlantic, however, the period of institutional mobilisation was much briefer in time and much narrower in appeal. Abolitionism became an identifiable massive movement only in the United Kingdom, with minor reverberations in France, first at the very end of the *ancien régime* and again at the end of the July Monarchy.[6]

In Britain mass anti-slavery definitively emerged at the end of the 1780s and reached peaks in the campaigns for abolition of the slave trade (1788, 1792 and 1814), for emancipation (1823, 1830 and 1833), and for the end of Negro apprenticeship (1838). It then ebbed and fragmented, with a final lower-level revival during and immediately after the American Civil War.[7] It survived as a minor lobby into the twentieth century. Outside Parliament the movement took the form of massive propaganda, petition and subscription campaigns intended to make the issue a priority item on both the public and parliamentary agendas. During the principal peaks of agitation, local accounts of petitioning rallies would often casually note that the gatherings or numbers of signatories were the largest in a generation or in recorded memory. Although brawls and broken heads were exceptional,[8] enough emotion was aroused to generate angry heckling at public meetings and disruption of related functions such as the auctions in Britain of West Indian estates.

British anti-slavery was organised on the basis of a national network which became increasingly formal and durable with each successive campaign. Beginning as a single committee of individuals in 1787, and relying heavily on the Quaker connection, it gradually evolved into a movement of well-defined local associations. Over 200 existed in 1814, 800 in the mid-twenties, and 1300 at the climax of emancipation.[9] Moreover, after 1806 the abolitionist network lay in reserve, ready to apply either discreet or highly visible pressure on the legislature. This reservoir of abolitionist power as well as the periodic upsurges were used to prod ministers and ordinary MPs on specific issues. Correspondingly, when, after about 1840, anti-slavery was no longer able to invoke such a united national constituency, the power of the abolitionist leadership was severely reduced.[10]

As a comparative indicator of public opinion, we will focus on the petitions which were the rallying point of all the major campaigns between 1787 and 1838, except 1806-7. They signified more than the mere deposition of a number of signatures before Parliament. Almost all petitions were the end product of extensive expenditures of energy, ingenuity, material resources, organisation, propaganda and public discussion. Almost all petitions resulted from public meetings called for that specific purpose. The number of petitions, as well as of signatures, was important because each particular one enabled the MPs presenting them to Parliament repeatedly to draw attention to the issue before an abolition bill was discussed and put to a vote.

In cases of exceptionally numerous petitioners, an MP could also place their number in the parliamentary record. He might also dramatically impress the legislature with the size or weight of the sheets, sewn together like great scrolls. When a number of strong men were required to haul a single petition into Parliament the visual impact of volume and weight was added to number. When soaring numbers of petitions finally caused the Commons to tabulate officially the weekly flood of signatures in 1833 (precisely at the peak of the emancipation campaign), newspapers gave a running account of the number of signatures piling up for each subject.[11] By the 1830s, then, petitions were regarded as an imprecise but none the less tangible indicator of public feeling about social problems. The canvassing, gathering and presentation of these requests for parliamentary action had developed into an elaborate ceremony for the creation and expression of public opinion and became a symbol of the people mobilised. The abolitionist petitions were, in fact, the single most important embodiment of that phenomenon in the fifty years between 1788 and 1838.

The process of gathering petitions therefore implied far more than the mere exercise of the right to have individual names placed on the tables of the two Houses. It required the existence of the complex political and social network which could foster the easy circulation of political literature and agitators throughout society, and of associations capable of well-timed agitation on the broad scale. The vastly different levels on which such mobilisation might occur is shown by comparing Britain and France. In Figure 3.1, column (2) represents the total number of petitions submitted to the French legislature in the ten years before the emancipation of French colonial slaves in 1848. Petitioning the legislature in France was quite legal, but there were severe restrictions on the press and on political organisation. Column (3) represents the number of

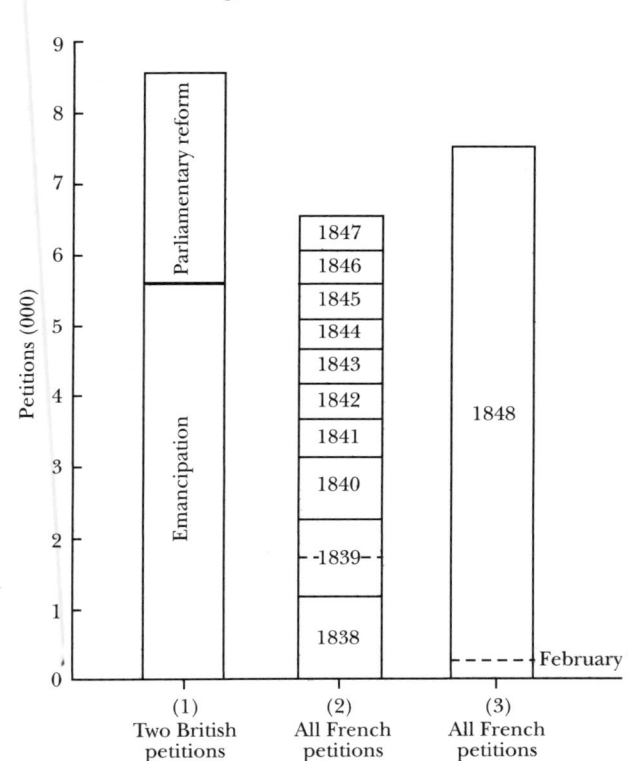

Figure 3.1   Petitions to legislatures of Britain and France, 1831–48

	(1) Two British petitions (1831)	(2) All French petitions (1838–47)	(3) All French petitions (1848)

Bar (1): Parliamentary reform (upper portion to ~8.5); Emancipation (lower portion to ~5.7).
Bar (2) stacked years from bottom to top: 1838, 1839, 1840, 1841, 1842, 1843, 1844, 1845, 1846, 1847.
Bar (3): 1848 (to ~7.5), with dashed line marked "February".
Y-axis: Petitions (000), 0 to 9.

Sources: Column (1) *Journals of the House of Commons*, 1830–1; columns (2) and (3), Archives Nationales, series C Register of Petitions, 1838–48.

petitions presented when political association became easier after the revolution of 1848.[12] A comparison with England (column (1)) is equally revealing. The number of petitions submitted to the House of Commons for just two major public issues during the single session 1830–1 easily exceeded the total number of petitions presented to the French Chamber of Deputies in the last ten years of the July Monarchy.

The emergence of public abolitionist petitions was a major example of the wider use of public petitions to Parliament in the 1780s.[13] British anti-slavery reached an early peak in 1792, just before the Government's disillusionment with popular politics. After the imposition of legal restrictions, mass petitioning practically disappeared for more than a decade.[14] In this respect the rhythm of the anti-slavery movement developed in tandem with egalitarian and liberalising trends in general. But the anti-slavery petitions also seem to have held a special place in comparative national mobilisations which deserves emphasis. Figure 3.2 shows that in pre-1848 France,

Figure 3.2 Three petition campaigns, 1829–47

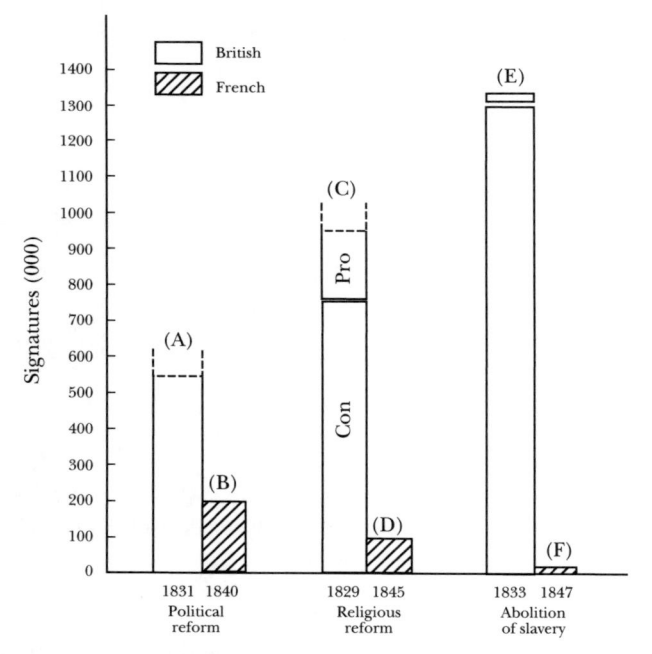

Sources: Columns (A) and (C) represent approximate figures tallied from statements in *Hansards Parliamentary Debates*, concerning the numbers signing individual petitions. The figures for some smaller petitioning areas were not announced. Column (E) comes from the official tally of the Select Petition Committee of Parliament, Columns (B) and (D) are derived from Tudesq, *Les Grands Notables*, I, p. 517 and II, p. 701. Column (F) comes from *L'Abolitioniste Française*, and Archives Nationales, Section Outre-Mer, SA 197 (1489), petition of 1847 in 48 cahiers.

modification of the electoral franchise attracted far greater numbers of signers than even the peak level for slave emancipation before 1848. Across the Channel, however, anti-slavery in Britain (1833) probably attracted more signatures than either parliamentary reform (1830–1) or Catholic emancipation (1829), despite the fact that the latter was treated as a quasi-public opinion poll in many areas of Britain.[15] British colonial emancipation successfully competed with the most popular of domestic issues of a peculiarly volatile political period.

Even more clearly, anti-slavery was strikingly more popular in Britain than in France in the period just prior to their respective emancipations. More than one British male in five over the age of fifteen probably signed the anti-slavery petitions of 1814 and of 1833. In France less than one man in a thousand did so in 1847.[16] Even at its relatively modest beginning, in 1787, British abolitionism outpolled French popular abolitionism at its height, in 1847. The first British mass petition against the slave trade was launched in Manchester at the end of 1787. This city, with fewer than 50 000 souls (including women and children), mustered about 10 700 signatures against the trade. Just sixty years later, the entire French petition campaign of 1846–7 accumulated just over 10 700 signatures, out of a population of thirty-five million.[17]

If one looks at petition mobilisation over the long run the performance of British abolition is equally striking. During the entire half-century between the first and last campaigns against the British imperial slave system, abolitionist petitions consistently surpassed those from other campaigns. In the seed time of parliamentary public petitioning in the 1780s,[18] the first slave trade campaign attracted more petitions than any other. In the 1790s the slave trade campaign of 1792 was again at the top, as was the one in 1814 against the revival of the international trade. In the twenties, anti-slavery again demonstrated its attractive powers, although it was not as spectacularly ahead of a host of competitive issues, and was momentarily outpaced by the Catholic emancipation campaigns at the very end of the decade. In the 1830s anti-slavery regained its pre-eminence as a petition issue.

Another distinguishing characteristic of anti-slavery was the imbalance in opinion mobilised for and against change. On most other issues involving civil, political, religious or economic reforms between 1780 and 1838 it was possible for the opponents of change to mobilise respectable, and sometimes superior, numbers of counter-petitions or signatures. The differential on anti-slavery was greater than on most major issues at the climax of their respective campaigns. On Catholic emancipation in 1829, for example, the proportion of signatures against reform in Britain (excluding Ireland) was something in the order of five to one.[19] In 1833 the proportion in favour of immediate emancipation against all alternatives was over seventy-five to one. In such terms it seems safe to say that slave emancipation, in 1833, had as much claim to being a national opinion as any other identifiable political issue.

Anti-slavery reached its climax in the 1830s, sending over 4000 petitions to Parliament during three separate sessions, a feat unequalled by any other national movement. In terms of signatures, only the first Chartist petition at the very end of the 1830s came close to matching anti-slavery in total numbers. In signatures *per capita*, the abolitionist campaigns of both 1814 and 1833 probably represented peaks or near peaks of mobilisation in the period before 1840, and were possibly not surpassed even by the spectacular campaigns of Chartism or the Anti-Corn Law League in the following decade.

Traditional accounts are correct in their outlines of the climactic campaigns of 1830–3. The abolitionist intention to place immediate emancipation high on the political agenda of the first reformed Parliament in 1833 was also a resounding success. During the election of 1832 anti-slavery managed to impose itself on political discourse. An extensive survey of campaign rallies and acceptance speeches shows an almost universal acknowledgment that emancipation was one of the items requiring the attention of the reformed Parliament, even where explicit reservations were made regarding the need for social order or the claims of vested property rights.[20] An apparent betrayal of anti-slavery commitments, like that of the Methodist 'Pope' Jabez Bunting in voting for a 'West Indian' at Liverpool, was an occasion for scathing comment.[21] By 1832 the abolitionist movement felt powerful enough to weigh prior legislative reliability as well as verbal promises. They demanded pledges by candidates to support immediate emancipation.

'Schedules' of reliables and unreliables (denounced as proscription lists by the opposition) were published in order to focus attention and force clarification of individual positions. Local anti-slavery associations backed candidates who supported emancipation across the political spectrum. They thereby strengthened the role of advanced pledging and of legislative responsiveness to direct constituent pressure over a traditional emphasis on the independent function of the elected MP.[22]

Symptomatic of the way anti-slavery intruded on political behaviour in the electoral process of 1832 was the election at Salford. The candidate who took the 'immediacy' pledge won the election. Even more interesting was the concession speech of the defeated candidate, Garnett. He insisted that he would have voted for emancipation, but having been approached late in the campaign, he did not want to look as though he was pledging only to gain votes.[23] If candidates associated with anti-slavery by birthright, like the Whig Thomas B. Macaulay, rested on their ancestral oars, they might find themselves excoriated from both the right and left as really being soft in their commitment to emancipation. Anti-slavery banners and hecklers were often noted in newspaper accounts of the verbal battles at the hustings. The list of 163 pledged candidates published by the central agitational anti-slavery organ (*The Tourist*) therefore considerably under-states the numbers of candidates who were belatedly forced to add at least a precise reference to the need for immediate emancipation in the 1832 campaign,[24] and could no longer evade the issue through silence.[25] In a sample of dozens of campaign accounts I have found few contenders who simply avoided slavery, or who even claimed that it was not a paramount issue before the new Parliament.

The speeches to the electorate in 1832 reflected the influence of an earlier mobilisation. The ground work had been prepared by a host of speakers touring the country from 1830 onwards to focus interest on the problem of colonial slavery. One part of this effort was the centrally co-ordinated campaign of paid agents who systematically visited the major population centres throughout the Kingdom. Anti-slavery agents required a local network to work most effectively at local and regional meetings. Lecturers with personal experience of slavery, especially colonial missionaries, systematically transformed colonial persecution into metropolitan sympathy. As a result, politicians took the resulting anti-slavery public with particular seriousness by 1832. When abolitionist agent George Thompson came to give his immediate emancipation lecture in Sheffield, all the local parliamentary candidates either attended or sent regrets which were read to the meeting. At Bradford, all three contenders appeared at the main anti-slavery rally.[26]

Because of the disproportion between pro- and anti-emancipation audiences in Britain itself, even the West Indian efforts at counter-lecturing could be converted into occasions for pro-abolitionist mass demonstrations. George Thompson claimed to have spoken to 750 000 listeners when he passed through Manchester in 1832. In the same city the West Indian agent found himself confronted by a heckling phalanx who reduced his lecture to a splintered liturgy of statements and responsive hoots and hisses. Newspapers hostile either to anti-slavery or to its rough open-air tactics reacted with a mixture of wonder and disgust at the behaviour of people who were so obviously 'respectably attired'. Even in Liverpool, where West Indian capital was heavily over-represented, thousands attended lectures on slavery and many were turned away.[27] The lecture campaigns of 1830–3 were intended to generate a clear message of common anti-slavery sentiment to audiences throughout the country, and to forge a temporal national solidarity around the principle of emancipation.

Accounts of the abolitionist campaigns almost always conveyed the impression that, in gathering and signing, the public was playing a unique role in precipitating changes in parliamentary opinion and in the legislative process. On the part of the opposition the reproof that popular passions were inflamed was implicit acknowledgement that the movement was both popular and passionate. On the other side, abolitionists invoked symbolism linking divine and popular inspiration: 'For the *vox populi erit vox Dei*, the voice of a united people shall be as the voice of God', declared the *Sheffield Iris*. 'What arguments could be urged for staying execution upon the sentence ... by the *vox populi vox Dei* ... that slavery shall be no more', asked the *Manchester and Salford Advertiser*.[28] Hostile conservative opinion might consider the demand for anti-slavery pledges as a test for public office to be 'unparalleled affrontery', but radicals, even when later embittered by the 'perversion' of compensation for planters and apprenticeship rather than unconditional emancipation for ex-slaves, saw petitions as an eminently useful tactic for forcing Governments at least to confront grievances.[29]

The perception of 'forcing attention' was accurate. None of the Governments between 1792 and 1837 could claim full credit for taking the initiative in dismantling the overseas slave system, although the ministers of 1806–7 came closer than others in that respect. Concerning the breadth of pressure from without, anti-slavery continually broke new ground. As early as the 1780s it appears that a good deal of care was taken by organisers to ensure authenticity in order to avoid parliamentary devaluation through fraudulent adhesions. Women began to petition *en masse* at the beginning of the 1830s and anti-slavery was in the vanguard. In 1833 a single petition of 187,000 'ladies of England – a huge featherbed of a petition' – was hauled into Parliament by four sturdy Members.[30] The impact of the movement created new precedents in governmental public relations. When anti-slavery delegates meeting in London were given a mass audience with the Colonial Secretary in order to lobby collectively for changes in the emancipation bill, the *Manchester Guardian* could not recall any previous case in which 'such a body of delegates have been admitted to the presence of ministers'.[31]

Anti-slavery also assimilated agitational styles from radical and working-class rallies. The hostile reporter of the *Manchester Courier* wrote of one such major meeting: 'I was *astonished* to see so many well-dressed professing Christians keep such a continual noise of applause, while the cause of the suffering negroes was trifled with and the sacred language of revelation was prostituted'.[32] At the height of the agitation over emancipation so impressive was the breadth of public opinion that contemporaries projected popular abolitionist opinion back into the early eighteenth century.[33] None the less, if one considers numbers of signatures, petitions or public meetings as measures of 'popularity' it is impossible to identify anti-slavery as less than one of the most extensive movements of national opinion in the first half of the nineteenth century.

So much for the voice of the people. But what of the voice of God? We have dealt with popular abolitionism only in terms of other single issues at the national and international level, but historians have seen abolitionism as intimately linked to the religious development of Britain, from the initial eighteenth-century Quaker impetus and the leadership of the Clapham 'Saints', to it nonconformist climax in the 1830s. A number of recent works reflecting on this aspect of the British anti-slavery crusade see it as an indication of the triumph of the spiritual over the material, and more specifically as the result of the mobilisation of one variety of British Protestantism. For Edith Hurwitz this mobilisation occurred both in theological and in liturgical terms: 'Antislavery thought cannot be divorced from the general body of Protestant theology. Antislavery societies and Antislavery meetings followed the Protestant congregationalist community–organisational pattern.'[34] Hurwitz rightly focuses on the theological transference of evangelical symbols to the issue of black slavery, as well as on the mobilisation of religious fervour into the goals, techniques and indeed the cadences of anti-slavery reform. In her view, the formation of anti-slavery societies and petition meetings derived from Protestant organisation and evangelical dissent.

There is a general chronological correlation between the burgeoning of British anti-slavery and the rise of evangelical nonconformity.[35] Although Thomas Clarkson emphasised the significance of the Quakers rather than the new nonconformity in the early organisation of the movement, the more one moves toward the climax of anti-slavery in the early 1830s, the more clearly the evangelical ties appear. From contemporary evaluation we also have the testimony of the agitator-general, George Stephen that his campaign was aimed at the 'religious' public. Indeed, to Stephen, it was self-evident 'that if the religious world could be induced to enter upon the subject ... viewing it simply as a question between God and man, the battle was won'.[36] Stephen's strategy was to insist on the link with the Christian imperative as a response to all nuances of opposition argument. From the opposition, a resentful linking of anti-slavery and nonconformity was equally emphatic. The tendency of those commentators relying on these sources is therefore to see anti-slavery as an extension of the British nonconformist revival.

Viewed in broad international perspective this seems to be a fair general statement of the historical nexus. This has already been the subject of extensive analysis. It must be remembered that the same Protestant–evangelical revival in the American South took religious organisations and theology in quite a different direction in relation to slavery.[37] Moreover, although anti-slavery was usually heavily dependent on denominational support for funding and organisation in Britain, this does not demonstrate that anti-slavery was merely an offshoot of the nonconformist religious revival. In the initial phase of the movement the focus of abolitionist organisation was communal not denominational. The local civic centre and the tavern were far more frequently the venue of meetings and petitions than either church or chapel. One cannot ignore the vigorous support for early anti-slavery by a popular secular radicalism which was driven to the periphery, but not out of the picture, by the conservative reaction of the 1790s. The democratic tradition of Yorkshire proudly dated its contribution back *beyond* Wilberforce to David Hartley, who made the first parliamentary motion denouncing colonial slavery in the 1770s. It was, in fact, only toward the end of the 1820s that nonconformity began to play its overshadowing role in the anti-slavery movement.[38] In the famous Yorkshire 'slave trade' election of 1807, only one of twenty-four dissenting clergy voted for Wilberforce, although the Methodists already gave him disproportionate support. As for the latter, as late as 1819, when Wilberforce canvassed the Methodists (who had objected to the Jamaica slave laws in 1809) on further anti-slavery initiatives, he found that they were 'for leaving to their masters all improvements in the condition of the slaves', and postponed immediate action.[39] The pressure of countervailing forces on Methodist conservatives was manifest as late as the controversial vote of Jabez Bunting in 1832, mentioned above.

Even at the height of the nonconformist presence in 1830–3, however, the pattern of religious support reached well beyond organised nonconformity. If the Wesleyan Methodists began moving away from earlier political quietism over the issue of slavery, and if the Baptists rigorously organised petitions and revived the early abolitionist tactic of boycotting slave-grown sugar, even the anti-Claphamite Anglican *Record* published model petitions and faithfully recorded those Anglican gentry or clergy who attended petition rallies.[40] Anti-slavery therefore demonstrated an appeal well beyond the boundaries of nonconformity. Contrary to Hurwitz's assessment, the pattern of petitioning in Parliament was not 'by denomination in a given local community' even in the 1830s.[41] The denominational effect was indeed strong enough to receive special note by the parliamentary report on public petitions. However, the same report showed that communal petitioning continued to be the predominant source of affiliated signatures. Denominations collectively accounted for 56 per cent of the 5000-plus anti-slavery petitions in 1833, but they accounted for less than 27 per cent of the signatures.[42] Only after 1840 did it become more exclusively identified with nonconformity. In the British public debate on policy in the American Civil War, what denominational petitioning occurred in favour of the North after Lincoln's Emancipation Proclamation was exclusively nonconformist. A less explicit religious identification with a pro-southern interventionist position, on the other hand, was Anglican. By then, however, the mass base of anti-slavery was rapidly vanishing.[43]

To consider anti-slavery in general as merely an extension of nonconformity is therefore to designate a part as the whole. In this context we can appropriately compare the petitions and signatures mobilised for anti-slavery with those accumulated on behalf of contemporary religious issues. In the late 1780s and early 1790s those who sought a repeal of the Text and Corporation Act clearly could not match abolitionism in mass support.[44] Two decades later, neither the petitions against Sidmouth's attempt to restrict nonconformity, nor those submitted in favour of Wilberforce's evangelical project for India, could approach the scope of the 1814 petition campaign against the slave trade clause in the treaty with France. Finally, if anti-slavery attracted more signatures in 1833 than the Catholic emancipation petition on both sides combined, it even more easily surpassed all religious issues dear to evangelical nonconformity.[45] Allowing for a large evangelical role in the organisation and rhetoric of the movement at its climax, anti-slavery's attraction of more than twice as many signatures as any nonconformist petition campaign in the 1830s impels us to think of abolitionism as far more than a spin-off of the evangelical revival.

Beyond the evidence from petitions, the more strictly religious issues usually met with far more indifference and hostility than anti-slavery mobilisations. A meeting for stricter observance of the sabbath in Manchester in the wake of an anti-slavery rally was swamped by its opponents. This pleased the *Manchester Guardian* which hoped that such a result would reduce the growing number of 'promiscuous' public meetings. Now that the poor had felt the itch for public meetings 'the more intelligent and respectable classes' might be less disposed to attend.[46] At its most popular phase in 1833, anti-slavery was clearly attracting radical as well as evangelical support. The organ of the Anglican evangelicals began to denounce the popular movement as an ungodly alliance between Dissenters and contaminated radicals.[47]

This also raises the problem of class affiliation and anti-slavery. When socially characterised, anti-slavery is usually assumed to be a political movement directed by the ruling class, or a portion thereof, in Parliament, and expressive of the sentiment of the rising middle class in the country at large.[48] As in the case of the religious connection, the writings of the abolitionists themselves tend to encourage this conclusion. George Stephen, whose *Antislavery Recollections* have given historians the most detailed retrospective insight into the motivations of the organisation of popular agitation in 1832–3, explicitly designated the 'provincial respectability', not the saints of religious communities, as the prime target for the great final push.[49] The propaganda organ of his agency, *The Tourist*, for all its clear defence of the 'Rights of Man',[50] was directed more at the buyers than the sellers of manual labour, at farmers and landowners rather than agricultural workers.

Closer analysis of anti-slavery support gives us a somewhat different view. Even those historians who emphasise the middle-class evangelical nature of the anti-slavery constituency by 1830, concede that in its earlier period there was a vociferous source of support for anti-slavery which few would regard as middle class. The widely recognised abolitionist participation of English popular radicalism in the 1790s, outlined by James Walvin among others, casts doubt on any equation of middle class and abolitionism for the early period of political mobilisation. Popular radicalism gave unequivocal support for one of the earliest of the protest movements of the early 1790s to come to fruition – the abolition of the slave trade.[51]

On the other hand, during the early 1830s, there is also a good deal of evidence of radical working-class hostility to abolitionism.[52] Yet it does not appear that anti-slavery had lost its working-class constituency. The quantitative evidence is indirect and partial but worthy of attention. We have clear evidence from at least one large denomination, Wesleyan Methodism, which accounted for about one-sixth of the signatures on the 1833 petition. The great majority of that denomination's signatories must have been artisans and labourers.[53]

But we also have other direct evidence of working-class loyalty to anti-slavery which was sufficient to convert its most inveterate populist enemy. In 1832, just after the passage of the Reform Act, William Cobbett announced his conversion to emancipation at a Manchester campaign rally.[54] Cobbett had been one of England's most virulent Negrophobes. He also detested both Wilberforce and evangelicalism. His motivation in changing sides during his campaign is therefore of some interest. Cobbett was not speaking in Yorkshire, whose citizens he had more than once written off as religious fanatics. Nor was Cobbett's Manchester audience George Stephen's target, the newly enfranchised 'respectable' middle-class voter. It was a rally of the working-class population of the city. Perhaps Cobbett recalled his unsuccessful election campaign at Preston, in 1826, when he was singled out for his hostility towards emancipation, and for his description of blacks as 'degraded brutes'.[55] This time Cobbett pledged himself to support emancipation precisely because his working-class audience favoured such a position. At the Oldham hustings in another part of industrial Lancashire a few months later, he received support from the anti-slavery movement.[56]

It is equally significant that Cobbett had not relinquished his view that black slaves in the islands lived more comfortably and worked less arduously than many whites in England. While all of the radicals who claimed to represent the working class did not support emancipation, and some actually interrupted anti-slavery meetings with interjections about the proper relationship between charity at home and abroad, they were apparently not able to carry the rank and file of the industrial North along with them.

There was, however, at least a fraction of working-class sentiment which deeply resented the priority given by some abolitionist leaders to relief of suffering abroad. There seem to have been few cases in which a militant working-class contingent, or at least militant radical spokesmen, actually attempted to deflect or disrupt anti-slavery petition meetings in 1832–3, but there may also have been enough resentment in other cases to prevent petitions from being launched by public meeting. The Tory and anti-abolitionist *Leicester Herald* hinted that its local abolitionists avoided such a meeting for fear that radicals would move an amendment 'upon the present state of the white slaves in this country'.

The fears were not groundless. In the wake of the dismay over parliamentary action on compensation and apprenticeship the Blackburn working-men's Political Union condemned the activity of abolitionists as misleading the people. In two other recorded instances, however, this approach was over-ruled. After a disrupted anti-slavery meeting in Birmingham, its Political Union voted by three to one to send a petition to Parliament in favour of emancipation. And in Bolton, where an anti-slavery meeting had been disrupted in the name of the working class, the local operatives denied both that the speaker was an operative or that he spoke for their community.[57]

The older antagonistic tradition of Cobbett remained a staple but equivocal attitude of some of the radical working-class spokesmen into the mid-thirties. At a rally in Preston, a radical could casually invoke the pro-slavery symbolism of the sleek, well-clothed and lazy black, whose problems could be tabled pending the emancipation of white workers without bread or votes. In the next breath, however, the same speaker denounced slavery both at 'home and abroad', to the cheers of his audience.[58] Even the most radical anti-abolitionist MPs found colonial anti-slavery to be a popular political symbol. Orator Henry Hunt, hostile to anti-slavery to the bitter end of his electoral defeat in 1832, had cheerfully adopted its symbolism to attack opponents on the hustings who could be linked with the 'groans and anguish of poor creatures whose colour was their only crime'.[59]

Other segments of the working class were apparently less ambivalent. Although George Stephen's agency committee may have decided that influential 'respectability' was their principal target, the Methodist and Baptist petition campaigns obviously had far broader aims. The agitation, even among the unenfranchised, did not stop with the acquisition of their signatures. When the compensation clauses of the Government brought an angry backlash among both radical middle- and working-class spokesmen, a special campaign to maintain support for emancipation was conducted among the Methodist poor.[60] Working-class anti-slavery was neither ignored nor taken for granted.

Given the support for anti-slavery among other politically mobilised working-class groups in America and France, it would be odd if English urban artisans had completely abandoned a component of the democratic ideology they forged at the end of the eighteenth century. And there is evidence that they not only did not break with their anti-slavery tradition but, even after emigration, were most likely to be among the working-class supporters of American abolitionism as well. This evidence further reinforces the conviction that abolitionism had deep and continuing roots in British artisanry.[61]

Having indicated the range of anti-slavery support in the early nineteenth century, it remains to examine the impact of anti-slavery opinion on the outcome. To some extent the answer will depend on the frame of reference.[62] The record of petition campaigns without some other source of leverage was never very encouraging in terms of immediate success. Consider only the three campaigns in Figure 3.2, or the great Chartist petition at the end of the 1830s. Catholic emancipation passed in spite of the fact that a clear majority of the petitioners came out against it.[63] Parliamentary reform passed before slave emancipation although abolitionism produced twice as many petitions in the session of 1830–1.[64] And Chartism, in 1839, emerged from its first national campaign without so much as a symbolic gesture from Parliament in return for its massive effort.[65] In each of the successful cases one must also consider phenomena extraneous to the public opinion campaign which might have played a decisive role in the precise timing of the outcome. The revolutionary potential of the Irish Catholics in 1829, of the political militants in 1832, and of the West Indian slaves in 1831 can be brought into each political equation in order to argue that something 'extra', even in extra-parliamentary agitation, was necessary to push Parliament to the point of implementing radical legislation, however large the harvest of petitions. The general record of parliamentary responsiveness to non-violent mass requests which also threatened major interests was otherwise rather poor in the short term.

Viewed even in this light, however, the relative success of anti-slavery petitions in achieving some quick positive response from above is impressive. In 1788 the first regulatory bill on the slave trade was passed in the wake of the first large-scale demand for action. In 1792 the House of Commons reversed its almost two to one rejection of the previous year and resolved on the abolition of the trade in 1796, although its will to implement that vote dissolved with the fear of domestic social upheaval. The petition of 1814 apparently was accepted by the Government as a major restatement of national priorities,[66] and induced it to increase dramatically international pressure on the slave trade. The Government's sponsorship of an emancipation bill in May 1833, shortly after the King's opening speech had neglected even to mention colonial slavery, came not in direct response to the immediate threat of either metropolitan or slave violence, but on the heels of an unprecedented levy of signatures that issue. Finally, the Government made an about-face on resistance to ending the apprenticeship system after the petition campaign of 1838. Of all the major abolitionist campaigns, only the petitions of 1830–1, when anti-slavery was overshadowed by the constitutional crisis, failed to obtain at least a major symbolic response. It is possible, by looking at the details and compromises of each governmental act, to minimise the role of public opinion. But this is to view public opinion as an instrument for producing details of legislation. Only rarely could public opinion operate in this way and almost never on major questions. Rather than taking the perspective of the parliamentary product, inevitably filtered through very complex stages, we might again profitably consider the impact of public opinion in the broader geographical and temporal perspective of the first section of this essay.

Compared with France, where anti-slavery opinion was never massively mobilised, British abolition was far more cumulative and consistent. Even in the fervour of the early phases of the revolution of 1789 the French National Assembly refused to consider any limitations on the expansion of their colonial slave system. The impetus to the revolutionary emancipation decree of 1794 came almost entirely from colonial developments, including the threat of imminent British conquest and the most massive slave uprising in the history of black slavery.[67] Nor was there any outcry when France revived the slave trade after the peace treaties with Britain in 1802 and 1814. The identification of the British Government with international abolition in the wake of the 1814 petition was far more persistent and determined than that of any other power. Continental action against slavery in general consistently lagged behind Britain's initiatives.

We can consider a few of the implications of this lag, by testing the possible link of popular mobilisation with economic interest theories of abolition. One of the favourite alternative explanations of the timing of emancipation of British colonial slaves emphasises changing economic interests. The argument usually focuses either on the long-term declining value of slave colonies as trading partners before emancipation, or the short-term market situation for British slave-grown products at the time of legislation.[68] Neither the relative nor absolute value of Britain's slave colonies, in terms of invested capital or as trading partners, declined during the crusade against the slave trade 1787–1815. There was a measurable relative decline in some respects between 1815 and emancipation, but the West Indies were no negligible entity even in 1833. Edward Stanley pointedly opened the Government's motion on emancipation by first alluding to 'this question of unparalleled importance – involving a greater amount of property – affecting the happiness and the well-being of a larger proportion of individuals than was ever before brought forward'.[69] Stanley was referring to British commerce, shipping, revenue and capital including the slaves in the West Indies. Although the imperial trading significance of the British West Indies and declined, partly as a consequence of prior abolitionist legislation, it still compared favourably with that of its still unthreatened French counterpart. Figure 3.3 shows the relative importance of the slave colonies of Britain and France as trading partners of their respective metropolises. If one were to measure the slave colonial trade as a percentage of national product rather than of total trade alone, the differential between the British and French colonies would be more than two and a half times greater in favour of the British than is shown in the table. On the eve of their respective emancipations Britain's total trade

Figure 3.3 Trade of the slave colonies of Britain* and France in the generation before their respective emancipations, as a percentage of the total trade (including re-exports) of each (data display corrected from an error in the original version)

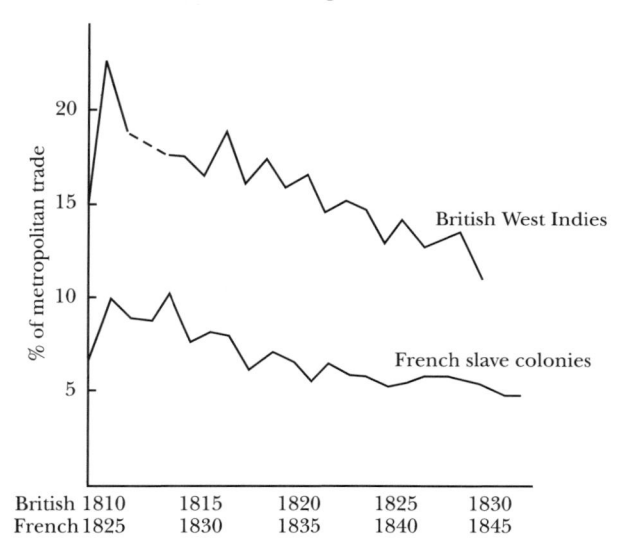

Note: *This does not include the British trade with colonies using slave labour in the Eastern hemisphere. The value of the trade of the Cape Colony and Ceylon might theoretically be added to the British figure.
Sources: For the British system: B. R. Mitchell and P. Deane, *Abstract of British Historical Statistics* (Cambridge, 1962), pp. 309–11; *Parliamentary Papers* (1831–2), XX; for the French system: *Statistique de la France*, Imprimerie royale, 1835–47 (tables of colonial commerce).

sector accounted for 18 per cent of its national product. The trade sector accounted for only 7 per cent of the French national product. I have used the less dramatic indicator because contemporaries tended to measure the significance of regional trades in terms of the more accessible figures on overseas trade rather than proportions of national product.

Beyond the significance of slave agriculture as a source of trade lay the crucial question of compensation for legal property in persons.[70] Every European Government was committed to the general sanctity of private property and considered some form of compensation necessary to the erstwhile proprietor.[71] This premise represented the major practical stumbling block to metropolitan emancipation. For parsimonious politicians everywhere, the cost of compensation of itself constituted a capital incentive for indefinitely postponing action. The longer the implementation of emancipation could be delayed after a declaration of intention to emancipate, the lower the price of slaves (and so compensation costs) might fall in anticipation.[72] Correspondingly, if the British public had subverted confidence in slave property its proprietors reasoned that compensation should be calculated largely on the pre-agitation slave market. The Government might accept the premise that the metropolis had undermined confidence in slave capital but it rejected the conclusion. Wary as ministers might be about equating the voice of the people with the word of God, for purposes of liability popular agitation became an act of God. It is important to bear in mind the reluctance of Members of Parliament to disburse large sums of money for which the taxpayer received no certain return beyond the assurance that the juridical status of some inhabitants of the tropical empire was to change.

Since there were more than three times as many British as French colonial slaves, the potential fiscal burden of emancipation in that regard alone was considerably heavier for the British taxpayer than for the French.[73] At the best compensation rate per slave imagined by a Royal commission in France[74] before 1848, the cost of indemnity per British citizen would have been over seven times that of each metropolitan French citizen. Even taking into account the higher productivity of British labour in 1831, each British subject would have paid between five and six times as much as his or her French counterpart, at the best compensation price which the metropolitan élites thought it reasonable to offer slave owners.[75] The French Government dragged its feet despite the knowledge that slave compensation would cost only one third as much, and would represent even less of a burden *per capita*. As it turned out, after emancipation the French Republic allowed its colonists only 60 per cent of the sum contemplated before the Revolution of 1848. The delayed French emancipation therefore ultimately cost the French a quarter as much as the British with a corresponding reduction of *per capita* costs.

Insulated from great public pressure for emancipation, French colonial policy moved in a very different direction. The pacification of Algeria, which proceeded during the period of most intense debate over French emancipation in the 1840s, cost France far more than the projected compensation to the French colonial planters.[76]

The weight of public opinion also needs to be viewed in less narrow terms than its immediate effect on the implementation of legislation. The psychological impact of even symbolic parliamentary reaction to petitioning could be quite profound. The West Indian response to the impact of British public opinion was significant even when a tide of petitions was seemingly channelled into a vague resolution for gradual emancipation in 1823. Table 3.1 shows the five-year average prices of public sales of slaves in Jamaica from the abolition of the African slave trade in 1808 until just before the emancipation mobilisation of the 1830s. From 1808 until 1822 the average price of slaves remained unusually high, presumably in response to the inevitable consequences of the end of the African supply.[77] After 1823 the average price dropped sharply, apparently responding to the clear knell of metropolitan opinion.

One must also carefully consider the role of colonial slaves themselves in discussing the impact of public opinion on the emancipation process. Historians often treat the large slave

Table 3.1 Averages of prices per slave sold for debt in Jamaica, 1808–27

Period	Number of slaves sold	Price (£)	Price per slave (£)
1808–11	4452	341 414	76.7
1812–15	5546	402 753	72.6
1816–19	4158	334 886	80.5
1820–3*	4064	317 588	78.1
1824–7	4441	225 760	50.8

Note: *The emancipation compensation figure was computed upon average sale prices of all slaves for the decade following 1822.
Source: Parliamentary Papers (1828), XXVI, pp. 25–9.

uprising in Jamaica immediately preceeding emancipation simply as an external catalyst of the legislation which followed. It is necessary to recall that far more extensive and successful instances of colonial slave resistance did not alter metropolitan determination to preserve the institution. The greatest and most successful slave uprising in history on St Domingue did not deter France from twice restoring its colonial slave empire thereafter. Yet the much less extensive uprising on Jamaica in 1831, perhaps because of its brutal suppression, resulted in the intensification of metropolitan pressures for immediate emancipation. In European imperial terms slave rebellions were not confined to the British colonies before 1833. In assessing the role of the Jamaica uprising of 1831, the prior roles of the abolition of the slave trade and of the increasing communication of abolitionist sentiment to the colonies after 1815 must be taken into account.[78] British public opinion was as communicable to the slave cabins as to the Houses of Parliament, and the nonconformist network of anti-slavery stretched from the working-class chapels of Britain to those of the West Indies.[79]

The long-term impact of opinion is therefore as important as short-term results measured in parliamentary motions and votes at any given moment. Anti-slavery opinion could hardly be regarded by those in or out of power as an isolated wave in an otherwise placid sea of indifference. It was seen as persistent and cumulative. As Francis Jeffrey wrote of the reform agitation of 1830: 'True the cry for reform has formerly subsided; but has it not always revived; and, at every revival, been echoed from a wider circle, and in a louder tone?'[80] Jeffrey articulated the conviction which lay beneath all of these activities, that public opinion was a social force which had to prevail in the long run. Ten years before emancipation, the Baptist magazine urged the people of the Kingdom to press the issue on the legislature in a similar temporal perspective. If it were simply universal enough, 'though for a time ... unsuccessful ... the voice of the people could not continually be lifted up in vain'.[81] During the 1830s no other cause could begin to approach the number of petitions submitted to Parliament against slavery and black apprenticeship. Foreigners noted with awe that a British MP could cover the floor of the Commons with these petitions, boasting with the assurance of an Inca ruler that he would fill the whole chamber the next time around if Parliament did not act on those before it.[82]

Anti-slavery involved far more than a downward flow of ideology from élites to a nascent capitalist or evangelical middle class. The movement was, of course, 'shallow' in the sense that there was never, on the European side of the Atlantic, any attempt to intensify the voice of the people by even the hint of an appeal to civil discord. In developing a whole range of agitational techniques and symbolic forms, it primarily expanded the tactics and the social base of non-violent public opinion. It ventured beyond the printed word to the famous mass-produced scheme of the packed slave ship which hung on walls all over Britain. The Wedgwood cameo of the kneeling slave allowed women and children to join the movement through wearing of emblems whether or not they could sign petitions. The abolitionists initiated the selective commodity boycott of slave sugar to strengthen commitment, and symbolically to strengthen the sense of collective dedication through a dietary taboo. The variety of techniques used to develop a common consciousness was almost endless. Carlisle weavers who saw a fellow worker dressed up 'as an ethiopian in collars and chains' could identify immediately with the victims of overseas slavery.[83] Displays of whips, chains and so on created a dramatic and palpable sense of social distance between the audience and the merchants and planters who used the hardware of slavery as their ordinary instruments of production and trade. Anti-slavery agitators knew the value of having black lecturers as well as persecuted missionaries giving personal testimony in preparation for electoral and petition campaigns. Popular mobilisation thus aimed not just at arousing the attention of ministers and Members of Parliament, but at forging an alliance which would link innumerable and disparate individuals, including people who had no direct previous role in the national political process. With the exception of a small intellectual counter-tradition, abolitionism institutionalised from one basic symbol a shared activity, a shared vision of the future and, ultimately, a myth of national achievement with more than a grain of truth.

NOTES

The research for this essay was undertaken during a Guggenheim Fellowship in 1977–8. I wish to express my gratitude to the Rockefeller Foundation's Bellagio Study and Conference Centre, for the residency, during the summer of 1980, in which this essay was written and to James Walvin for his helpful editorial suggestions.
Place of publication is London, unless otherwise stated.

1. See *inter alia*: Thomas Clarkson, *History of the Rise, Progress and Accomplishment of the Abolition of the African Slave-trade by the British Parliament*, 2 vols (1808); David Brion Davis, *The Problem of Slavery in Western Culture* (Ithaca, 1966) and *The Problem of Slavery in the Age of Revolution, 1770–1823* (Ithaca, 1975). For recent trends see Roger Anstey's 'The Historical Debate on the Abolition of the British Slave Trade', in R. Anstey and P. E. H. Hair (eds), *Liverpool, the African Slave Trade, and Abolition* (Liverpool, 1976), pp. 157–66.
2. S. Drescher, 'Capitalism and the Decline of Slavery: The British case in Comparative Perspective', in Vera Rubin and Arthur Tuden (eds), *Comparative Perspectives on Slavery in New World Plantation Societies*, of the *Annals of the New York Academy of Sciences* (1977), pp. 132–42.
3. Roger Anstey, *The Atlantic Slave Trade and British Abolition 1760–1810* (Atlantic Highlands, 1975). Five very rough draft chapters to Anstey's sequel to the above volume were completed before his untimely death. Although they are too incomplete for separate publication, they are the product of extensive research and contain important insights on a broad variety of themes relating to anti-slavery between 1823 and 1833. I will refer to them as Anstey, 'Emancipation' (MS.).
4. James Walvin, 'The Rise of British Popular Sentiment for Abolition 1787–1832', in Christine Bolt and Seymour Drescher (eds), *Anti-Slavery, Religion and Reform* (Folkestone and Hamden, 1980), pp. 149–62; Walvin, 'The Impact of Slavery in British Radical Politics: 1787–1838', in Rubin and Tuden (eds), *Comparative Perspectives*, pp. 343–55; Howard Temperley, 'Anti-Slavery', in Patricia Hollis (ed.), *Pressure from Without in Early Victorian England* (1974), pp. 27–51; E. M. Hunt, 'The North of England Agitation for the Abolition of the slave trade, 1780–1800' (University of Manchester, MA thesis, 1959).
5. For the early period to 1807 see Anstey, *The Atlantic Slave Trade*; for the period from then to emancipation, see P. F. Dixon, 'The Politics of Emancipation: the Movement for the Abolition of Slavery in the British West Indies, 1807–1833' (Oxford, D. Phil., 1970); for the post-emancipation era, see H. Temperley, *British Antislavery 1833–1870* (1972).
6. S. Drescher, 'Two Variants of Anti-slavery: Religious Organization and Social Mobilization in Britain and France, 1780–1870', in Bolt and Drescher (eds), *Anti-Slavery*, pp. 43–63; see also chapter 2 in this volume.
7. Temperley, *British Antislavery*, Epilogue.
8. *The Record*, 14 October 1830.
9. Dixon, 'The Politics of Emancipation', p. 213; Anstey 'Emancipation', ch. 5.

10. Temperley, *British Antislavery*, esp. chs. 7 and 8.
11. See, for example, the *Manchester Times*, 4 May 1833.
12. On the difficulties of organising a national petition, see the account of the reform petition of 1793 in Albert Goodwin, *The Friends of Liberty: The English democratic movement in the age of the French Revolution* (Cambridge, Mass., 1979), pp. 279–80.
13. John A. Phillips, 'The Political Nation, Political Awareness, and Popular Participation in Late Eighteenth Century England' in MSS., kindly provided by the author.
14. See E. P. Thompson, *The Making of the English Working Class* (1968); Gwyn A. Williams, *Artisans and Sansculottes* (1969).
15. On the Catholic emancipation petitions, see G. I. T. Machin, *The Catholic Question in English Politics 1820 to 1830* (Oxford, 1964), pp. 144–9.
16. The adult male population over fifteen for each country was estimated using figures from B. R. Mitchell and P. Deane, *Abstract of British Historical Statistics* (Cambridge, 1962), p. 11, and B. R. Mitchell, *European Historical Statistics* (New York, 1975), pp. 20, 24, 35, 52 and 53.
17. See Drescher, 'Two Variants', p. 52.
18. See Peter Fraser, 'Public Petitioning and Parliament before 1832', *History*, XLVI (1961), pp. 195–211.
19. From an estimate compiled from *PD* (1829).
20. I have checked campaign speeches in *The Times*, and checked more closely from newspapers in the industrial North, including Manchester, Salford, Preston, Leeds, Bolton, Sheffield, Halifax, Blackburn, Carlisle, Whitehaven, Liverpool, Bradford, Stamford, Nottingham, Birmingham and Leicester.
21. *Leeds Intelligencer*, 24 January 1833; *The Christian Advocate*, 29 December 1832.
22. Stephen, *Antislavery Recollections*, letter XI.
23. *Manchester Courier*, 15 December 1832.
24. *The Tourist*, 19 December 1832.
25. On political symbolism and the control of discourse see Seymour Drescher, David Sabean and Allan Sharlin (eds), *Political Symbolism in Modern Europe*, Introduction (New Brunswick, USA., 1982).
26. Stephen, *Antislavery Recollections*, letters X and XI.
27. *Liverpool Courier*, 5 September 1832; *Manchester and Salford Advertiser*, 18 August 1832.
28. *Sheffield Iris*, 29 January 1833; *Manchester and Salford Advertiser*, 18 August 1832.
29. *Manchester Courier*, 29 September 1832; *Manchester and Salford Advertiser*, 9 July 1833.
30. Stephen, *Antislavery Recollections*, p. 196.
31. 27 April 1833.
32. 18 August 1832, emphasis in the original.
33. *The Baptist Magazine*, January 1833, p. 3.
34. Edith F. Hurwitz, *Politics and the Public Conscience: Slave emancipation and the abolitionist movement in Britain* (1973), p. 44. Roger Anstey's *Atlantic Slave Trade* emphasises the primacy of the evangelical impulse in the launching of abolitionism although he allows for a conjuncture of interests and

idealism in accounting for at least one abolitionist victory, the termination of the British foreign slave trade in 1806: *ibid.*, ch. 8.
35. Drescher, 'Two Variants', pp. 45–9.
36. Stephen, *Antislavery Recollections*, p. 160.
37. Donald G. Mathews, 'Religion and Slavery: The case of the South', in Bolt and Drescher, *Anti-Slavery*, pp. 207–32.
38. See the historical squibb on anti-slavery in the *Sheffield Iris*, 29 January 1833. Anstey refers to the growing role of the Methodists in anti-slavery in the 1820s in his 'Emancipation', ch. 1, p. 6, and at greater length in the very incomplete second chapter: 'The Methodist Paradox and Slavery Emancipation'.
39. Dixon, 'The Politics of Emancipation', p. 118.
40. See *Minutes of the Methodist Conferences, 1825–1837*, esp. VI, pp. 51, 514–15; VII, pp. 67, 175; *The Baptist Magazine*, XXII (1830), 343, 480–4, 524; (1833), pp. 10–12, 226–9; *The Record*, 14 October 1830.
41. Hurwitz, *Politics and the Public Conscience*, p. 44.
42. Drescher, 'Two Variants', p. 47. *The Record*, 1 November 1830, claimed 6000 petitions from the Methodists alone.
43. Drescher, 'Two Variants', pp. 54–7.
44. G. M. Ditchfield, 'Repeal, Abolition and Reform: A study in the interaction of reforming movements in the Parliament of 1790–6', in Bolt and Drescher, *Anti-Slavery*, pp. 101–18.
45. The chief religious petition issues in the 1830s were: the admission of dissenters to the universities, sabbath enforcement, and the abolition of church-rates.
46. 9 March 1833.
47. *The Record*, 10, 16, 23 and 27 January and 4 July 1833.
48. See *inter alia*: Hurwitz, *Politics and the Public Conscience*, pp. 48, 79 and 81 (although there is a later statement that all strata supported emancipation, p. 83); D. B. Davis, *The Problem of Slavery*, vol. II, pp. 357, 361–5, 385, 421 and 450; Dixon, 'The Politics of Emancipation', pp. 208–11; Williams, *Capitalism and Slavery*, p. 181; Patricia Hollis, 'Anti-Slavery and British Working-Class Radicalism', in Bolt and Drescher, *Anti-Slavery*, pp. 294–313. Howard Temperley, following E. M. Hunt, emphasises the fact that the constituency of popular abolitionism in the early period at least 'drew its support from a broad range of social classes'; see his 'Anti-Slavery' in Hollis (ed.), *Pressure from Without*, p. 33.
49. Stephen, *Antislavery Recollections*, pp. 158–9.
50. Vol. I, no. 1, 17 September 1832.
51. See n. 4 above.
52. Hollis, 'Anti-Slavery and British Working-Class Radicalism', pp. 294–302.
53. Drescher, 'Two Variants', pp. 48 and 58, Tables 2 and 3.
54. *Manchester Guardian*, 8 September 1832.
55. Dixon, 'The Politics of Emancipation', p. 230 and note.
56. *Manchester Courier*, 16 December 1832.
57. On Blackburn see Hollis, 'Anti-Slavery and British Working-Class Radicalism', p. 302. On the motivation of the Leicester abolitionists,

see the *Leicester Herald*, 10 April 1833. On the Birmingham Political Union's petition see the *Birmingham Journal*, 20 April 1833. At a Nottingham rally the *Nottingham Review* (7 December 1832) observed 'a more complete admixture of classes' than it had witnessed for sometime.

58. *The Times*, 1 June 1826.
59. *Preston Chronicle*, 15 December 1832.
60. *Manchester Times*, 22 June 1833.
61. On French working-class petitioning see Augustin Cochin, *The Results of Emancipation*, tr. M. L. Booth (Boston, 1863), p. 73; and Drescher, 'Two Variants', pp. 57 and 63, n. 34. On the English tradition in American working-class abolitionism in the 1830s, see John B. Jentz, 'Artisans, Evangelicals, and the City: A social history of the labor and Abolitionist movements in Jacksonian New York' (City University of New York, Ph.D., 1977), pp. 208 and 217. See also Eric Foner, 'Abolitionism and the Labor Movement in Antebellum America', in Bolt and Drescher, *Anti-Slavery*, pp. 254–71.
62. For example, Reginald Coupland, *The British Anti-slavery Movement* (1935, 1966), p. 111; E. M. Howse, *Saints in Politics: The Clapham Sect and the growth of freedom* (London, 1953), ch. 8, esp. p. 179; Anstey, *The Atlantic Slave Trade*, pt 4. On Anstey's general model of the limited scope of the popular phase, see 'The Pattern of British Abolitionism in the Eighteenth and nineteenth Centuries' in Bolt and Drescher, *Anti-Slavery*, pp. 19–42.
63. Machin, *The Catholic Question in English Politics*, pp. 144–8.
64. Figure 3.1 and Roger Anstey, 'Emancipation', draft ch. 3, 'Reform and Anti-Slavery, 1830–32', 4th and 5th pages.
65. John Cannon, *Parliamentary Reform, 1640–1832* (Cambridge, 1973), p. 214 n; J. T. Ward, *Chartism* (1973), pp. 113–17.
66. Diplomatic note of Castlereagh to the Spanish Ambassador, in Chester New, *The Life of Henry Brougham to 1830* (Oxford, 1961), p. 138.
67. C. L. R. James, *The Black Jacobins*; Augustin Cochin, *L'Abolition de l'esclavage*, 2 vols (Paris, 1961) I, ch. 1.
68. For the decline thesis in general, see S. Drescher, *Econocide*, ch. 1; for the period after 1815 see W. L. Burn, *Emancipation and Apprenticeship in the British West Indies* (1937, rpt 1970), pp. 51–2 and 73.
69. PD, 3rd ser., XVII (1833), cols 1193–4. The West Indians were able to muster well over 1800 signatures against Stanley's plan, and 'no city meeting was ever more numerously attended, or more zealously watched, than the assemblage of the West Indian body', in responding to the plan (*The Times*, 28 May 1833).
70. See Stanley Engerman, 'Some Considerations Relating to Property Rights in Man', *Journal of Economic History*, 33 (March 1973), pp. 43–64.
71. It was with the West Indians, not with the abolitionists, that continuous negotiations took place once it was determined that an emancipation bill would be introduced. See *CO* 318/116 and *Grey Papers*, 3rd Earl, Box 147, item 53, printed minutes of proceedings between Government and West Indians 16 January–2 May 1833, cited in Anstey's 'Emancipation', ch. 5, n. 55.

72. In France, the cost of compensation was the principal barrier to emancipation during the July Monarchy. See S. Drescher (ed.), *Tocqueville and Beaumont on Social Reform* (New York, 1968), p. 172.
73. On the eve of their emancipation the number of French colonial slaves was estimated at 250 000, of British at over 770 000.
74. Report of a committee on slavery, named on 26 March 1840, and presided over by the duc de Broglie, who wrote the report.
75. The productivity *per capita* in Britain and France was estimated from J. Marczewski, *Introduction à l'histoire quantitative* (Geneva, 1965), pp. 134 and 135.
76. See Adolphe Gueroult, *De la Question coloniale en 1842. Les colonies francaises et le sucre de betterave* (Paris, 1842).
77. *PD*, new series, IX (15 May 1823), cols 257–360. The West Indian estates themselves were described as unsaleable by 1831: *Report of the Select Committee on the Commercial State of the West Indies* (evidence), question nos. 69, 282, 752, 848 and 989 (*PP* 1831–2, XX). The Committee report itself emphasised abolitionist initiatives as a principal, if irremediable, cause of West Indian distress (pp. 5–6 of the *Report*).
78. B. W. Higman argues convincingly that the Jamaican slave revolt was an unforseen consequence of the abolition of the British slave trade in 1807, in his *Slave Population and Economy in Jamaica, 1807–1834* (Cambridge, 1976), pp. 231–2.
79. Dixon ('Politics of Emancipation', p. 203) characterises the revolts as setbacks to abolition, except as failures. One must, however, separate the impact of a long-term series of pressures from individual events. Anstey, ('Emancipation', 3rd ch., 21st p.) also remarks in passing on the negative impact of the Jamaica uprising itself until the results of the repression began to be known. Other accounts treat the uprising itself as more central, the 'decisive factor' in the abolition process. See W. A. Green, *British Slave Emancipation: The sugar colonies and the great experiment 1830–1865* (Oxford, 1976), p. 112.
80. Francis Jeffrey, 10 October 1831, quoted in Cannon, *Parliamentary Reform*, p. 245.
81. *The Baptist Magazine for 1823*, 15, 283.
82. Dixon ('The Politics of Emancipation', p. 341) concludes, 'and it was indeed the strength of opinion that ended slavery'.
83. *Ibid.*, pp. 341–2. The abolitionists were themselves frequently astonished at the explosions of popular excitement during the anti-slavery campaigns. See Z. Macaulay to Lord Brougham, 13 May 1833, Private, Brougham, MSS. 10544 reprinted (but, according to Anstey, wrongly dated), in M. J. Knutsford, *Life & Times of Macaulay* (1900) p. 70.

4 The Decline Thesis of British Slavery since *Econocide* (1986)*

PART ONE: THE DECLINE THESIS AND ITS OPPONENTS

Appearing in 1944, *Capitalism and Slavery* was a comprehensive attempt to explain the rise and fall of British colonial slavery in relation to the evolution of European world-capitalism.[1] In dealing with the final stages of slavery, Eric Williams developed a two-pronged argument linking its demise to changes in the British imperial economy. The first prong related to changes in the structure of economic relationships between the metropolis and the colonies. Down to the American Revolutionary War, concluded Williams, British slavery, including the Atlantic slave trade, was a growing and complementary element of the imperial economy. The slave system provided an ever-increasing amount of tropical staples, a protected market for British manufactures, and a source of British metropolitan capital. In a number of ways, the slave economy thus helped to fuel the industrial revolution. Williams' second prong related to political economy, to an economic ideology designated as mercantilism. It sustained the multiple linkages of the system by assuming the need for a protected imperial zone in which British manufactures, trade and maritime skills could develop.

For Williams, the American War dramatically changed the economic and ideological relationship which had sustained the slave system. British colonial production, under increasing competition from its French counterpart, ceased to provide what was needed by the empire amply or cheaply enough. In *Capitalism and Slavery*, 1776 began the 'uninterrupted decline' of the British West Indies both as a producer of British staples, as a consumer of British industrial output and as a contributor

---

***Slavery and Abolition*, 7(1) (May 1986), pp. 3–24. ©1986 Frank Cass & Co. Ltd.

to British capital. The very capitalism that had been nurtured by slavery now destroyed the fetter on its own further development. At precisely the same moment a new political economy was adumbrated, in Adam Smith's *Wealth of Nations*. It viewed protected colonial trade as a brake on the creation of national wealth. The demise of slavery was thus perfectly congruent with the rise of *laissez-faire*.[2]

At a less global level *Capitalism and Slavery* also provided a detailed set of rigorous economic motivations for the short-run successes and failures of British abolition. The failure of the British West Indies to recover its rate of profitability after the American war combined with the growth of alternative staple sources to set the stage for the rise of abolitionism in the 1780s. The St Domingue revolution momentarily stemmed the tide, but colonial overproduction induced abolition of the slave trade in 1806–7 and emancipation in 1833. All of this was set against the background of a continuous decline in West Indian profits, the imperial significance of British slavery and its metropolitan economic supports. One by one those interests which had once supported slavery turned against it.[3] Each and every tightening of the noose could be explained by reference to the interplay of economic patterns and motives. *Capitalism and Slavery* also contained two interesting but basically post-scriptural chapters on the roles of the abolitionist 'Saints' and the colonial slaves but the main story was carried along the path of its putative economic determinants.

In the three decades following the appearance of *Capitalism and Slavery* a number of objections were raised to some of Williams' short-run interpretations. Its major structural elements, however, remained deeply entrenched in the historiography of British antislavery: the rise of abolitionism was closely correlated with the rise of *laissez-faire* and the decline of the British West Indies. One of these elements rested on a tradition of British imperial history which divided an 'old' mercantilist from a 'new' *laissez-faire* empire by the American Revolution. The other element rested on the work of a number of historians of the Caribbean, above all Lowell Ragatz's *Fall of the Planter Class in the British West Indies, 1763–1833*. The striking novelty of *Capitalism and Slavery* lay in Williams' vigorous fusion of these two historiographical streams.

The Decline Thesis since Econocide 89

In approaching the discussion of Williams' most famous work during the past decade one should begin by observing that the systematic discussion of *Capitalism and Slavery* is itself little more than a decade old. Apart from Roger Anstey's initial foray in the *Economic History Review* (1968), *Capitalism and Slavery* was either praised in passing or summarily dismissed, both without extended analysis. It therefore percolated, rather than flowed, into historiographical discourse for reasons which would make an interesting study in its own right.[4] By the mid-1970s, the Williams decline theory was being described by some historians as the new orthodoxy.

A major challenge appeared with the publication of two works. In 1975 *The Atlantic Slave Trade and British Abolition*, by Roger Anstey, attacked some of Williams' short-run interpretations, especially the motives for British abolition in 1806–7. In *Econocide* (1977) I challenged both the long- and short-term premises of *Capitalism and Slavery*. With the same data used both by contemporary actors and by Williams to show the 'amazing value' of the British West Indies before 1775, I found no decline in the value of the British slave system until well after the abolition of the slave trade.[5] There was in other words a disjuncture between the dramatic rise of political abolitionism and the economic value of its target. *Econocide* also took sharp issue with the premise that there was a major shift in the political economy of the British Empire following the American Revolution. Here too, I found that the change required by the Williams' thesis was not tangibly operative until *at least* three-quarters of the age of British abolitionism (1788–1838) had expired, if then. The thrust of *Econocide*'s attack was quite clear. If British slavery was economically expanding at the moment that its growth was decisively inhibited by political action, its economic decline was contingent upon, not determinative of, abolitionism. Economic decline may well have eased the later stages of destruction. Likewise, a structural change in imperial political economy could not have been determinant at the beginning or the middle of the abolition process. One might even question whether it was clearly so at the end, in 1833. Some of *Econocide*'s subordinate arguments will be considered at the appropriate place. The basic point is that *Econocide* challenged the validity of these two givens in the explanation of British abolition. It neither precluded hypotheses based on indirect economic arguments nor urged a reversion to the old humanitarian narrative of the victory of the Saints.

PART TWO: AFTER '*ECONOCIDE*': DEFENDERS OF THE DECLINE THEORY

In dealing with the Williams' decline thesis since *Econocide* one initial difficulty presents itself. There have been few further extended discussions of the Williams' thesis. In this sense the discussion of the critique of the Williams' thesis has been almost as slow in getting off the ground as Williams' original critique of the 'Coupland' tradition. One extended essay on the status of the question was published by Stanley Engerman and David Eltis in 1980.[6] Another was produced by Cecil Gutzmore for the Hull Sesquicentennial in 1983.[7] A much lengthier critique of *Econocide*, by Selwyn Carrington, appeared, with an appended reply, in June 1984.[8] Otherwise the decline theory has been discussed more casually in books, essays, and introductions to other collective enterprises. For our purposes, one valuable vein of discussion can also be assayed – reviews and review essays on *Econocide*. To their authors my procedure might be viewed as sacrilege or, at the very least, as hitting well below the intellect. Scholars never expect to have what they say in reviews held against them. Yet the large number of reviews offer a very broad sampling of the general reaction to the issues raised by *Econocide*. There is already some precedent for using the reviews. Walter E. Minchinton's essay, 'Williams and Drescher: Abolition and Emancipation', in the September 1983 issue of *Slavery and Abolition*, extensively quotes from the most critical ones. I will therefore use them to highlight typical reactions, including areas of agreement, disagreement, and designated directions for future orientation.

One may logically begin with the decline theory. *Capitalism and Slavery* posited that the British Caribbean had attained an 'amazing value' for Britain on the eve of American independence. Its value depreciated from 1776 on. Williams' empirical demonstration was founded on the data of British overseas trade, drawn from official records from 1697 to 1773, as compiled by Sir Charles Whitworth.[9] It should be noted that Williams broadly and explicitly included both the African and foreign slave trades sectors in his accounting system.[10] He also compared the British Afro-Caribbean system to others. *Econocide*'s first major step was to carry Williams' systemic analysis of 1697–1773 forward half a century, using the same data-base and 'filling in' the void in the Williams' account for the period between the Declaration of Independence and Waterloo.[11]

The central indicator used by both *Capitalism and Slavery* and *Econocide* as a measure of value is conceptually important in another respect. It was the one measure most available to, and overwhelmingly used by, contemporaries in the political debate over abolition. Its use therefore avoids severe epistemological problems which arise from employing measures of value which were either unclear to contemporaries or not central to their arguments. I must return to this problem below. *Econocide* portrayed the impact of the trade data graphically by superimposing the Williams 'rising' years (until the early 1770s) with the putative 'decline' period thereafter (see Figure 4.1).[12] One might easily perform similar operations in tabular form. Table 4.1 shows the British West Indian percentage of British

Figure 4.1 British West Indian trade, 1722–1822

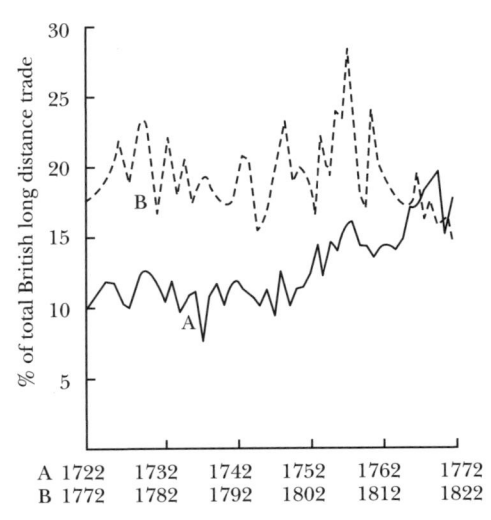

Source: Mitchell and Deane, *Abstract of British Historical Statistics* (Cambridge, 1962), pp. 309–11, 'Overseas Trade'.

Table 4.1 British West Indian shares of British trade (imports, exports and re-exports) for various 'pivotal' years 1763–83

Years	(%)	Years	(%)
Pivot of 1763 (Ragatz)		*Prior–equivalent period*	
1763–92	18.30	1728–62	11.99
1763–97	18.24	1723–62	11.88
1763–1802	18.69	1718–92	11.70
1763–1807	19.08	1713–62	11.62
Pivot of 1776 (Williams)			
1777–1806	19.36	1737–76	14.50
1777–1811	19.82	1732–76	14.16
1777–1816	19.46	1727–76	13.96
1777–1821	18.97	1722–76	13.76
Pivot of Peace of Versailles			
1783–1807	19.42	1758–82	17.54
1783–1812	19.76	1753–82	17.04
1783–1817	19.36	1748–82	16.36
1783–1822	18.71	1743–82	15.82

Source: Mitchell and Deane, *Abstract*, pp. 309–11.

overseas trade using key pivotal years ranging from 1763 to 1783. In each case the period *after* exceeds the share of the period *before* the pivotal date, both for the medium and the long term. To judge from the general reception of *Econocide*, most scholars have accepted the idea that the systematic extension of the Williams' data-base requires some revision of *Capitalism and Slavery*'s argument in its classical format of '1776 and all that'.[13]

One statistical demolition did not of course end the discussion. One way of responding to any given data series is to extend it. Perhaps the Williams' data-base doesn't work for the fifty years after 1763 or 1776, but what if we use Ragatz's 'falling planters' of 1763–1833 or Williams' 'rising free-traders' of 1776–1846?[14] Isn't decline visible toward the end? The answer is yes, but the point also strikes me as wide of the original mark. *Econocide*'s own first table shows that by 1828–32 the British West Indies was relatively back where it had been in the mid-eighteenth century. (One might still be tempted to say that Britain's slave system had, at long last, declined only to the point where it was as valuable as in its Ragatzian 'golden age'.) Such a line of argument already grants the basic point of the original argument against the Williams' thesis no matter how deeply or steeply the slave system declined after the abolition of the slave trade. It is clear that thereafter the limits to the value of antislavery were political rather than economic. It is also difficult to see how any scholar inclined toward economic determinism can much take comfort in the observation that the 'real' decline in West Indian fortunes was political.[15] The unique strength of *Capitalism and Slavery* resides in the affirmation of a conjuncture between economic and political change. No correlation, no thesis.

Econocide did not suppose that all political limitations on the slave system were ineffectual until the moment of emancipation. That seemed irrelevant. Lengthening the frame of reference to 1833 or even to 1983 does not alter the basic Williams hypothesis – that economic decline induced the abolitionist–capitalist attack in 1788–92, or the victory in 1806–7. The relationship between imperial economic policy in the final stages of abolition and apprenticeship may therefore be treated quite independently of the crucial policy decision to limit its further growth. Even beyond this the Williams' scenario faces other difficulties which have not yet been faced by those who see the period 1823–46 as a saving remnant for *Capitalism and Slavery*. The final 'stage' of the Williams decline theory is based on the following argument. By 1833 a Parliament had been elected in Britain which, said Williams, 'was perfectly responsive to the needs and aspirations of British capitalists'.[16] Hence, British capitalism destroyed slavery as a first step in the destruction of the West Indian Monopoly (p. 169). Yet the fact is that emancipation was not coordinated with a step against West Indian monopoly but with one which gave it a new lease on life.

If the protection of British slave sugar produced resentment after the Napoleonic wars, whether from East Indian or consumer interests, relief was clearly no priority in Parliament during the debates over emancipation and apprenticeship between 1823 and 1838. As late as 1841 the government was defeated in the Commons when it attempted to reduce the protection accorded to British colonial sugar. Therefore it seems that by 1833 either a Parliament had been elected which was not 'perfectly responsive' to the aspirations of the capitalists, or the capitalists in 1833 did *not* aspire to antimonopoly, or emancipation was not taken as a step toward the end of West Indian monopoly, or Parliament aspired more to destroy slavery than West Indian monopoly. From Williams' account I do not believe it is possible to sustain the sequence of his argument.

Alongside the role of the slave system as an imperial trading partner, *Capitalism and Slavery* stressed a second aspect of economic development – the putative profit decline of the West Indian planters. Here Williams challenged the economic viability of the British plantation system after the American Revolutionary War. He stressed not only the 'monopoly' character of the West Indies, 'but that it was so unprofitable that for this reason alone its destruction was inevitable'.[17] *Capitalism and Slavery* therefore argued for a sharp fall in Jamaica profits after 1774. Since the link between unprofitability and destruction is made so forcefully at the general level recent scholars have rightly introduced more detailed and systematic analysis to this aspect of the Ragatz and Williams' decline thesis.

It should be pointed out that there is a difference between the rate of plantation profits to the planters or African merchants, and the value of their system to the Empire. The happiness of the planters over their profit conditions was no more central to their utility to the metropolis than the happiness of the slaves over their working conditions.

In any event, the viability of slavery to the planters may have been less impaired by the abolition of the slave trade than was slavery's relative significance in the trade system. On this question J. R. Ward has done much to systematically demonstrate that the West Indian colonies as a whole were operating at a profit down to the eve of emancipation. His data seem to indicate that profit rates were as high or higher after the American War as before, and that, at least until 1820, an average return of 10 per cent was as characteristic of the period following as for the period before the American War, at least down to 1820. Ward also seems to agree that the Ragatzean picture of progressive decrepitude has to be modified.[18]

Econocide was also criticized for insufficient attention to the issue of shifting patterns of capital investment in the slave property of the British West Indies.[19] Using Caribbean slave population growth as an index of capital growth, it would appear that capital investment was increasing at a more rapid rate between 1790–1805 than between 1750–70. The capital value of the British slave empire more than doubled between 1785 and 1815 (including conquered areas). The £15m sunk by British investors into Demerara alone between the British conquest in 1796 and its temporary return to the Dutch in 1802 served as a standing reminder to abolitionists concerning the prospects of slavery as a field for investment before the abolition of the slave trade.

Scholarly attention has also been recently focused on the significance of British slavery in accounting for the growth of British exports before and during the industrial revolution.[20] In this context François Crouzet estimates that the West Indies accounted for 18 per cent of the increase of British exports from 1700–1 to 1772–3. Until the end of the century the West Indies actually increased its share. Considering the three decades 1783–1812 as a whole the West Indies and Latin America (also served by the African slave trade) contributed more to Britain's cumulated additional exports (official values) than any area except the United States. Table 4.2 shows that the West Indies steadily maintained its relative role in British export growth until the abolition of the slave trade as other areas rose or fell dramatically. Africa's independent role fell as did that of North America and, most dramatically, the export trade east of the Cape of Good Hope.

These are measures which can be placed alongside the trade figures. For some supporters of a 1776+ decline theory, however, the use of trade figures to measure the long-range value of British slavery to the British imperial economy was spurious and beside the point. The same would apparently hold for both planter profits and capital accumulation rates. They were all amassed under protective barriers. For some reviewers, the central shift in the abolitionist victory lies not at all in the trade series but in a decisive shift of the *measurement* of value which presumably occurred under the aegis of a shifting political economy from mercantilism to *laissez-faire*. For Barbara Solow, as for Mary Turner and Elsa Goveia, *the* major long-run fact of British slave production is that the British consumer paid more for eighteenth-century British sugar than his or her Continental counterpart paid for non-British, and especially French, sugar. Fundamentally, this is a cost-accounting argument, using the world market as the basic measure of value.

Table 4.2 British percentage of area shares' contributions to increased exports, 1700–1 to 1804–6

Area	(Official values) 1700–1 to 1772–3 (1)	(Current values) 1784–6 to 1804–6 (2)	Manufacturing exports only 1784–6 to 1804–6 (3)
West Indies	18.2	21.1	22.3
Latin America		4.0	4.3
Africa	7.8	2.5	2.6
Ireland, etc.	14.6	10.1	8.0
East Indies	13.5		
Asia (incl. China)		3.2	2.8
Europe Continental	4.2	30.3	28.7
North America	41.8	28.3	30.7
Other		0.4	

Sources: Column (1), François Crouzet, 'Toward an Export Economy: British exports during the Industrial Revolution', *Explorations in Economic History*, 17 (1980) pp. 48–93, p. 72; columns (2) and (3), Ralph Davis, *The Industrial Revolution and British Overseas Trade* (Leicester, 1978), p. 89.

If British importers were paying a higher price for their muscovado than was warranted by the world market the value of the sugar colonies was deceptive. Noel Deerr accounts for this in terms of a qualitative difference between British and French muscovado,[21] but the fact remains that for most of the eighteenth century British plantation sugar did not compete effectively on the Continental market except in war years, when French sugars were bottled up by the British navy and privateers.

Whether or not it was Williams' principal line of attack, this point, acknowledged by *Econocide*, was part of an effort to resuscitate the decline thesis. This, says Barbara Solow, 'is the decline that matters'. Fair enough – let us give the price-competitive argument the attention it deserves. The single major problem with the 'mercantilist sugar' argument is the same one that attaches generically to a whole set of parallel longrange indictments concerning the efficiency of the British slave system – absenteeism, indebtedness, white flight, demographic deficiency, soil exhaustion, etc. All of these 'disabilities' were identified on both sides of the ocean more than half a century before 1790 without inciting either to abolitionism or abolition.[22] So it is with French sugar. The condition did not, as Solow speculates, begin as early as the 1760s. It was definitively recognized at least as early as the 1730s, using, of course, the same import, export and re-export data used for the volume of trade measures in *Capitalism and Slavery* and *Econocide*. The planters and their friends complained of it, their North American enemies gloated over it, their own allies pled it every time there was an internal squabble over redistribution of mercantilist burdens – whether in the 1730s or the 1780s.

Without too much difficulty one could push the perception back still further. The comparative cheapness of foreign sugar was in fact emphasized by the West Indian planters as early as the Peace of Utrecht.[23] How then could such a hoary fact induce abolition? The neo-decliners claim that a new stimulus to recognition of this fact burst through in the 1780s and held fast thereafter. Why? Various 'candidate' catalysts are offered. Williams himself had offered booming St Domingue after 1783. The American Revolution left the British sugar planters 'face to face with their French rivals'.[24] *Econocide* showed that the relationship remained 'back to back', as it had for half a century before. Each system served separate markets, and Jamaican sugar was actually expanding faster than that of St Domingue on the eve of abolitionist take-off in the late 1780s. *Econocide* therefore claimed that before 1790 'British planters did not seriously challenge their French rivals and that the metropolis did not seriously challenge the planter monopoly'. Therefore the British planters I concluded 'nestled comfortably in the arms' of their own protected market.[25] The neo-decliners disagree. Mary Turner's catalysts are the fall of the Bastille and the French Revolution. Solow's are Adam Smith in 1776 and Pitt's condemnation of the slave trade in 1791. All of these catalysts were followed (Solow's within a few hours) by Parliament's thumping *rejection* of abolition by a vote of almost two to one.

There is another more fundamental fact of sugar prices, however, which argues against the cheap sugar argument for abolition. Abolition scored its first symbolic victory in 1792, and its second substantive victory in 1806–7, after a decade in which world market sugar prices actually moved in favour of the British consumer.[26] It was precisely in 1791 that British sugar once again massively re-entered the Continental market. (As for emancipation, Howard Temperley has also argued that, in the period prior to 1833, a large proportion of the West Indian crop was sold on the world market, which determined its price.[27]) The biggest price gap between the British and the world market reopened as a consequence, not a cause of the advent of a free labour market after apprenticeship. Moreover, the market price economic interpretation of abolition must also account for the reason why planters' spokesmen were more open to *laissez-faire* on both the carrying and marketing of their sugar at the time of the abolition of the slave trade than was the British Parliament which controlled their destinies. In 1807 the British Government served up the Orders-in-Council and protectionism all around. Economists might wish to do another estimate of the value of the Sugar Colonies to Great Britain for the period 1790–1807 to see whether the abolitionists attacked and won during the precise period when, by cost-accounting criteria, the metropolis was a loss to the Colonies, not vice versa. In the first decade of the nineteenth century, British *per capita* consumption of sugar was probably at its all-time peak for the entire era of British colonial slavery.

If a neo-classical cheap sugar model has difficulty enough in addressing the timing of abolitionism it gets into even more difficulty in accounting for the targets. If Smithian antimonopoly sentiment was a source of antagonism to British slavery after 1788, why was the first target that segment of the slave economy (the African slave trade) which did so much of its business in successful competition in the world market? And why was abolitionism's second target (1805) the premier British *cotton* colony (Demerara) whose produce received absolutely no protection whatever in the metropolitan market? Neo-classical economism may wind up with as many facts to explain away as its Marxian predecessor.

Finally, the classical approach must respond to the same epistemological problem as historians who regard trade figures as more central indicators (than planter profit) of value.

Empirically, the trade figures were primarily used by contemporary policy makers in abolition debates. The abolitionists pointed to potential alternative sources of British trade, but until well after slave trade ended the abolitionists always had to point toward the bush rather than the hand. Over the course of the 50 years from 1783 to emancipation the abolitionists were always more speculative customer-counters than their opponents.

This approach to decline strikes me as deriving from a broader historical misconception. It assumes, with Williams, that there was a political swing away from mercantilism in the generation after the publication of *Wealth of Nations* and the Peace of Versailles. As P. J. Cain and A. G. Hopkins have argued, there was no widespread conversion to *laissez-faire* after 1776. There were merely sectoral adjustments for specific targets of opportunity within the old framework.[29] The French Wars gave added impetus to the arguments for strengthening the empire rather than lowering barriers to free competition. The burdens of war, not of the consumer, were the main concern of British governments in the decades before abolition. The ever-ascending proportion of the retail price of sugar determined by fixed rate duties amply demonstrates this. The great shift in the balance of economic power and priorities came during the 30 years after the fall of Napoleon. The Cain–Hopkins reassessment coincides with that of *Econocide* rather than with those theories requiring more of a *laissez-faire* 'spirit of '76'.

In addition to its neo-classical defenders, the decline thesis has also found new supporters within the mercantilist frame of reference which was less explicitly but in fact more frequently employed by *Capitalism and Slavery*. Given the stubborn persistence of the mercantilist perspective in Britain, indeed its reaffirmation less than two years before political abolition was placed on the parliamentary agenda, it has been re-argued that the very interests united by mercantilism before 1775 were instrumental in undermining the West India interest. Ragatz and Williams, now reinforced by Carrington, emphasize that in 1785 the British shipping interest decisively fought to limit the claims of the West Indians to trade with American carriers.[30] With major exceptions for 'emergencies', this prohibition remained in effect until the mid-1820s. The policy was particularly damaging to the planter interest in the mid-1780s and in 1805–8. The second structural pressure on the planters was the metropolitan policy of heavy fixed duties upon sugar. Duties on imports rose during each conflict and were never substantially reduced before abolition.

Carrington argues that these facts demonstrate the decline of the planter class and, therefore, of British West Indian slavery. This by no means follows. The maintenance of the Navigation Laws clearly underlined the dependence of the British shipping interest on the West Indies. Within its mercantilist perspective the West Indian shipping interest thereafter supported the West Indies against abolitionists. After slave trade abolition the West Indies in fact supplied one of the few outlets for the re-deployment of former slave ships until the end of the Continental blockade. Even more clearly, sugar duties were one of the fiscal mainstays of public revenue. No government considered risking a change during the course of, or immediately after, the French wars. Both the sugar revenues and the Navigation System force us to recognize the important differences for the empire between the short-run prosperity of the planter and the value of the sugar colonies. This, again, is why trade figures strike me as a better indicator of the significance at the imperial level than profitability or prices. The mercantilist perspective, as *Econocide* emphasizes, did allow abolitionists, regardless of growth or decline, to move separately against the slave trade when they could convince Parliament that no unmanageable short-run damage would accrue to the slave colonies in the circumstances of 1806–7.

Both the neo-mercantilist and *laissez-faire* arguments assume an imperial or world-market context. Another strategic defence of the decline theory focuses on intracolonial comparisons. As one would expect, this frame of reference is most frequently invoked by historians of the West Indies. In defending *Capitalism and Slavery* these historians maintain that *Econocide* does not sufficiently emphasize differential development within the islands.[31] They point out that some old colonies, at least, had passed their peak. On similar grounds Carrington in his lengthy critique of *Econocide* has systematically attempted to revive the Ragatzian perspective *in toto*. His own analysis gives to the decline of the old islands primacy of position. Carrington goes even further. He imputes to *Econocide* the

The Decline Thesis since Econocide   101

argument that 'the older islands (namely Barbados and the Leeward Islands) were not saturated as was generally believed but were developing with renewed strength'. Carrington considers that point critical to Drescher's study. In fact, *Econocide* explicitly argues exactly the opposite. Summarizing British Caribbean conditions in 1790, *Econocide* says: 'Taken as a whole, the slave colonies had exhausted neither their soil nor their potential. *Some, such as Barbados and the Leeward Islands, were considered to be at or past their optimum development. But this was only one segment of the islands*'[32] (italics added).

Econocide reiterates in its closing chapter for the period 1780–1833 as a whole, 'Metropolitan politicians would naturally think in imperial not regional terms. *Barbados had no special economic status as against Jamaica in 1788, and Jamaica had none vis-à-vis Trinidad in 1805 or Demarara in 1815*'. And, 'the dynamic of the colonial system was no more measured by the statistics of the seventeenth-century pioneers than were metropolitan trends by the statistics of Old Sarum'.[33] *Econocide* maintains that at *all* times from the end of the American war to Waterloo, and beyond, there were developing slave sectors. This was as visible to contemporaries as it should be to historians. Eric Williams' own favourite source for pre-1776, Sir Charles Whitworth, showed that as of 1790, Jamaica, Dominica and St Vincent had clearly expanded beyond their pre-war peaks. Other official sources showed that Jamaica, St Vincent and Trinidad were frontier *de jure* colonies as of 1802, to which one could add Demerara (*de facto*) in 1807 and Demerara, Mauritius and the Cape Colony (*de jure*) by 1815. Carrington's approach does indicate why many of the smaller islands were less apprehensive (but never to the point of advocacy) of abolition in 1807.

The method of reducing the decline theory of British slavery to the decline of some parts of British slavery does not, in fact, support Williams' turning point. Rather it undermines it and throws into question the very possibility of using such a theory in historical analysis. If, using Carrington's criteria, decline must be dated from the decline of the first slave area in an economic system, American slavery was declining almost before slavery crossed the Appalachians, when Pennsylvania legislated its gradual abolition. Using Carringtons's criteria, the decline of slavery in Delaware after 1800 would mean that

Southern slavery too was already in decline. In the West Indies Carrington's criteria dispose not only of *Econocide*'s nineteenth-century turning point, but of Williams' (1776) and Ragatz's (1763) as well. As Williams himself noted, 'as early as 1663, a mere twenty years after the rise of the sugar industry, Barbados was "decaying fast" and the complaints of soil exhaustion grew more numerous and more plaintive'.[34] This would, it is true, give economic decline a comfortable 150-year lead on abolition. It would, however, also mean that over 98 per cent of the slaves brought to America in British ships between 1620 and 1808 were boarded after the beginning of the decline of British slavery.[35] If, following Carrington, we use Deerr's 'old colony' sugar export figures rather than colonial complaints it still appears that Barbados reached its pre-abolition sugar peak in 1698, more than one hundred years before 1808. Nevis' pre-abolition peak was in 1710, Montserrat's in 1735.[36] Therefore, of the five little-old-islands possessed by Britain on the eve of the Seven Years' War, a majority were already long in decline. We would have to conclude that Ragatz was too late by a full generation and Williams by forty years in identifying the turning point. A reduction of British slavery to its insular parts reduces the very idea of rise and fall, whether of Drescher, Williams, Ragatz, or most other historians of Atlantic slavery, to chaos.

Carrington also uses the crop by crop performance of the British West Indies between 1775 and 1806 to test and to reaffirm the decline theory against *Econocide*. I again take fundamental issue with his method of disaggregation. *Econocide* showed that the sugar islands were both dynamic and flexible in the face of new opportunities. As new opportunities opened up for sugar, the British colonies became the largest colonial producing area in the world. Far from being exclusively wedded to monoculture, British slavery became *increasingly* polycultural in the decades between the Treaty of Versailles and abolition of the slave trade.

British dependency on slave grown imports clearly increased during the two decades prior to the abolition of the British slave trade. Table 4.3 shows that the primary slave products increased their relative contribution to total British imports. The fact that cotton and coffee gained on sugar does not alter the picture of the combined figures. Britain became more

Table 4.3 Slave-grown share of British imports, 1784–6 to 1814–6

Product	Current value (£000's) (1)	% predominantly grown by slaves (2)	% of total British imports (3)	% grown in slave importing areas (4)	% of total British imports in same (5)
		1784–6			
Sugar	2 614	100	11.5	100	11.5
Coffee	158	88	0.6	88	0.6
Cotton	1 817[a]	70	5.6	70	5.6
Total			17.7		17.7
All British imports	22 761				
		1804–6			
Sugar	6 879	97	12.0	97	12.0
Coffee	2 458	99	4.4	99	4.4
Cotton	5 628	89[a]	9.0	53[b]	5.4
Total			25.4		21.8
All British imports	55 558				
		1814–16			
Sugar	11 138	98	15.1	—	—
Coffee	2 784	79	3.1	—	—
Cotton	8 593	96	11.5	35	4.2
Total			29.7		4.2
All British imports	71 796				
		1824–6			
Sugar	6 722	93	9.4	—	—
Coffee	1 022	87	1.3	—	—
Cotton	7 452	86	9.7	18	2.0
Total			20.4		2.0
All British imports	66 389				

Notes: [a] Estimates of contributing areas from *Econocide*, pp. 84–5.
[b] US cotton production is excluded here from the slave importing zone, although abolition was not effected until 1808. Column (2) represents the actual percentage in 1804–6.
Source: Davis, *The Industrial Revolution and British Overseas Trade*, appendix on British imports.

dependent not only upon the slave zone but upon the slave importing areas as well. If slave based cotton production was entirely responsible for the increase in British exports between 1792 and 1806, half of that raw material was still dependent upon slave importing economies. Even (prematurely) excluding the United States from the slave importing roster (column (3)), 1804–6) does not alter the general picture (column (4)). If one also added rice and tobacco to the slave-produced share of British imports the dependency on slavery would rise still higher, to 23 per cent in 1784–6, 27 per cent in 1784–6, 27 per cent in 1804–6, and 32 per cent in 1814–6, according to Ralph Davis' figures.

Ralph Davis' post-*Econocide* figures on real trade values from 1794–6 to 1844–6 also show that while cotton and coffee accounted for only 28 per cent of the value of the 'big three' British slave staples in 1784–6 they accounted for more than 39 per cent in 1804–6.[37] On the eve of abolition slave production was tangibly diversifying as well as expanding. All of this remains hidden if each crop is treated in isolation. Not only did coffee emerge as the new 'second' crop to sugar after the American war, but sugar culture itself underwent a 'green revolution'. The introduction of Otaheite cane in the last decade of the eighteenth century increased yields per acre. The British colonies were pioneers in this transformation.[38]

Carrington offers a final structural argument in behalf of the Williams decline dating. This concerns the slave trade itself as an indicator. While most recent scholarship has tended to accept the Anstey–Drescher claim that the British slave trade peaked only after the American War, in the 1790s, David Richardson's findings seem to modify that claim.[39] His figures apparently indicate twin peaks, one just before the American War of Independence and a second only slightly higher, in the 1790s. By all counts the total American post-war volume exceeded any pre-war equivalent period. Most scholars also agree that the British trade was somewhat reduced by the Slave Carrying Act of 1799, further reduced by the abolition Act of 1806, and virtually annihilated by the Act of 1807. J. E. Inikori argues for a much higher 'hidden' trade than other scholars from 1800 to 1807.[40] *Econocide* was sceptical of the argument but emphasized that the impact of abolition would be magnified by Inikori's estimate.

Carrington disputes not the fact of expansion but its interpretation. He argues that the crucial point is not how *many* slaves were transported by British carriers but what percentage were re-exported from the old islands. 'One of the best indicators of West Indian prosperity during the eighteenth century', he claims, was the ability and readiness of the planters to purchase slaves. 'For most of the period up to 1775–6, the planters retained a majority of the slaves imported into the islands. After the American War, even if more slaves were imported into the islands than in the pre-1775 period, a larger number was also re-exported'.[41]

Jamaican data (the only island for which we have a full run of eighteenth century re-exports) show that most of the years in which a majority of slaves was re-exported come from the period *prior* to 1775–6.[42] This misreading of the data brings us to the larger issue of Carrington's use of re-exports as an indicator of decline.

Carrington argues that the percentage of re-exports should be used as an indicator of decline. Elsewhere I have argued that, based on Jamaica's data series, there was no direct correlation between the rate of planter profits and the rate of re-exports. I also showed that post-1800 re-export figures could be quite deceptive since a substantial number were recycled to *de jure* British colonies. An even larger number went to *de facto* British planters. Further evidence against any positive correlation between the percentage of retained slave imports and planter prosperity may be observed from Carrington's own Bellagio paper, 'The Economy of the British West Indies, 1775–1791: The Makings of the Williams/Drescher Controversy', Appendix V.[43] Ignoring for the moment the methodological difficulty in excluding slave import figures into the new frontier regions of Trinidad and Demerara, one can easily observe that the planters retained the highest percentages of slaves just when their profits were *lowest*. From 1788 to 1798 planters enjoyed an almost uninterrupted period of high profits. Yet the lowest retention rates are clustered precisely in that period (with the exception of 1798). Correspondingly the years 1800–1 and 1805 were years of low or falling prices, yet they seem to be characterized by high retention rates. There are enough anomalies, even from this pattern, to cast doubt on the relevance of profits to re-exports altogether, but it is at least quite clear

Table 4.4 Percentage of received slaves re-exported from Jamaica by five-year intervals, 1713–87

Period	% Re-exported	Period	% Re-exported
1713–1717	50.2	1758–1762	15.0
1718–1722	40.1	1763–1767	17.0
1723–1727	43.9	1768–1772	13.0
1728–1732	44.5	1773–1778	15.3
1733–1737	43.6	1778–1782	14.6
1738–1742	15.5	1783–1787	32.0
1743–1747	24.0	Years over 50% re-exports: 1709,	
1748–1752	22.1	1713, 1714, 1719, 1720, 1723, 1724,	
1753–1757	12.1	1730, 1731, 1733 (peak 69.9%), 1786	

Source: McCusker, 'The Rum Trade,' pp. 615–16.

that the hypothesis of low profits–high re-exports and vice versa is not borne out.

Finally, I wish to draw attention to the untenability of the whole Carrington premise on even longer-term grounds. In Table 4.4, I carry the percentage of Jamaican re-exports back to the Treaty of Utrecht. The reader can easily observe that using percentages of re-exports as an indicator of decline places the nadir of the most dynamic old British colony in the 'Asiento' years at the beginning of the *eighteenth* century. As given, Carrington's re-exports theory, like his 'little-old-colony' theory, leads us to a Herodian slaughter of the innocents. It would simply destroy the development paradigms of most historians including Williams. If we accept Carrington's premises, we have truly entered an age of paradigms lost.

Ebb and Flow

In terms of the larger issues one can spend less time with the post-*Econocide* views which draw on *Capitalism and Slavery* to explain the ups and downs of abolitionist fortunes. Like the spatial and product segmentations just discussed, these tend to look to very short-run developments to explain political decisions. Scholars reflecting on these questions do not necessarily take issue with the broader findings of *Econocide* or defend those of *Capitalism and Slavery*. For the post-American War decade Carrington upholds Williams' short-run arguments to the letter. He asserts, with Williams, that the slave system failed to recover its 1774–5 level of profitability during the years between the Treaty of Versailles (1783) and the St Domingue Revolution. I have again argued elsewhere that profits by and even before 1791 were well above their level of 1775.

Another post-war issue concerns the impact of the restrictions on American carriers to the British islands after 1783. Carrington maintains that shortages lasted until the St Domingue uprising. I again take the opposite position. In this encounter Carrington sticks with the Ragatzian position *tout court* – that St Domingue alone, and only momentarily, saved the tottering planters. Some historians slice the post-American War frame of reference even more finely. In an essay on Britain's policy towards St Domingue, David Geggus focuses on the state of the West Indies just prior to the abolitionist breakthrough in 1788–91.[44] He nods in *Econocide*'s direction by noting that production recovered pre-war levels by the mid-1780s. However, he faults the study for relying too heavily on the turbulent years after 1789 to make a case for the West Indies' recovery of its imperial position. If, however, Geggus had compared the '*non*-turbulent' pre-American war years (1771–4) with only the equally non-turbulent post-war and pre-French revolutionary years (1784–8), he would have found that the West Indies accounted for a higher percentage of British imports, exports, and total trade in the second period than the first. *Econocide* characterized the 1780s as a period of West Indian recovery. As with the whole metropolitan export trade, it was only in the 1790s that recovery gave way to new growth.

Many historians, including Geggus and Carrington, point to annual downturns in production, profits, trade shares and the slave trade during the period 1783–1807. There is no objection to using these for carefully delimited comparisons. But decline theorists could hardly insist that annual or even quinquennial downturns in an economic sector are sufficient to categorize it as a declining trend. Otherwise, almost every major British trade in the Empire, metropolitan and colonial alike, was declining at some point between 1783 and 1806. Even the superstar of the post-1783 period, British cottons, staggered badly in the 1790s. Exceptional critics like Minchinton, who apply such a rigorous criterion of cumulative trends to the British West Indian case, simply fail to note that by such a test no British trading zone in the world rose or fell continuously during every quinquennium of the century before Waterloo (see *Econocide*, Table 2). Cyclical and politically induced fluctuations were bound to be part of any economic activity.

Some objections to *Econocide* consisted in quoting 'high authorities' on short-term issues to explain general motives. In *every case* to date this comes down to the pleasant pastime of 'pick your pundit'.[45] Arguing for Williams' overproduction thesis one historian triumphantly cited a speech by the 'Leading Minister' in the Lords who in 1807 assured his House that abolition would save the planters from ruin. Hence concern about overproduction presumably predisposed the House to vote for abolition. The same historian neglects to observe that two weeks later the 'Leading Minister' of the other House assured *his* audience that abolition would lead to no decrease of production. That House then voted even more overwhelmingly for abolition. May we then conclude that the Commons was even more anxious about underproduction in 1807?

Aside from these possibilities, it is clear that the factors most important to Williams, a coalescence of antagonistic economic interests and a shift in political economy, simply have not been unearthed by further research as playing their allotted role in the decline and fall of slavery outlined by *Capitalism and Slavery*. This does not preclude incorporating negative short-term psychological effects of the American War on the West Indies on the slave interest. It does fundamentally challenge any account of abolition which incorporates either the decline of the West Indies or perceptions of the decline of the value of slavery to Britain during the generation after 1783. Just as Williams may have exaggerated the increasing importance of the West Indies to the imperial economy before 1775 so he appears, at the very least, to have exaggerated the diminution of its importance to Britain before emancipation. It is more likely that as in the case of American slavery two growing, if unequal, social systems faced each other, rather than a rising and a falling one.

PART THREE: ALTERNATIVES TO
WEST INDIAN DECLINE

Thus far we have dealt with arguments tending to defend elements of the Williams thesis as given within the parameters of *Capitalism and Slavery*. Some approaches actually narrow the framework of discussion. It is now important to consider some of the alternatives to the Williams economic decline thesis.

We can begin at the extremes. On the one hand, one might conclude, with Roger Anstey, that the sapping of the Ragatz–Williams decline theory means that the case for explaining abolition in 'terms of fundamental economic change is seriously if not totally undermined'.[46] On the other hand, from the Marxist side, Cecil Gutzmore, in his survey of the 'bourgeois' critiques of *Capitalism and Slavery*, similarly assumes that the effect of these critiques is to return the state of the question 'to the rather narrow Christian (even Methodist) humanitarianism of those who originally erected that tradition'.[47] The pendulum presumably swings back from the pristine economic determinism of *Capitalism and Slavery* to the pure moralism of the Coupland school.

Neither the expectations of Anstey nor the fears of Gutzmore have prevailed. The outcome to date is illustrated by many of those who accepted the main critique of the Williams thesis as valid, yet immediately seek alternative explanations somehow grounded in fundamental economic development. Pieter Emmer's was a typical response to *Econocide*: Drescher's new interpretation, he concluded, 'has overturned most of the factual implication of the Williams thesis. But still ... there remains something unassailable in this thesis concerning the connection between economics and abolition'.[48]

Econocide, some reviewers realized, did not at all dispute this. Philip Curtin noted that a staunch defender of a Marxian point of view could take a more roundabout approach, drawing a class struggle out of the religious ideology that pervaded British middle-class life in the eighteenth century. Alan Adamson, moving the argument toward the post-emancipation period, suggests that economic forces would be much more apparent in the struggle over the sugar duties. Richard Lopper also argues that a Marxist analysis can easily accommodate an abandonment of both the decline thesis and Williams' economic determinist reading of abolition.[49]

Embodied in many reactions, made as reservations or suggestions, are two fundamental propositions. The first of these might be called a historiographical gut feeling. The response goes something like this: 'It is surely no accident that abolition coincided with the industrial revolution.' The second fundamental proposition, however, seems to derive from a recognition, sometimes wholehearted, sometimes grudging, that the abolition of slavery cannot be explained by direct extrapolation from pure economic motives or mechanisms any more than from pure moral consciousness. Most of the alternative approaches thus far lean toward an attempt to find a new ideological base for abolitionism. The attack on the Coupland school of pure ideas by the Williams school of impure interests begins with a search for convincingly impure ideas. The principal target of scholarly concern has become the antislavery 'ideology' – some combination of economic and non-economic ideas which called forth the abolitionist crusade and permitted it to triumph. There has also been a renewed search for an ideological combination which will include both the abolitionist spokesmen and the political economists of industrializing Britain.

Perhaps the most apt conclusion to this survey of the decline thesis since *Econocide* would be to emphasize the enduring heritage of *Capitalism and Slavery*, the book which constituted the object of its critique. As long as British slavery and abolition were regarded as *sui generis*, primarily as moral categories, they were more likely to be treated commemoratively than analytically. *Capitalism and Slavery* was therefore a classical demonstration of the value of even deliberately simplistic history. It would be no gain whatever to the historiography of slavery if apparent gaps in the causal chain forged by Williams fragmented slavery scholarship into clusters of specialists with no common framework. Williams cast his story in a global economic setting and that setting must, if anything, be remapped and resynthesized.

Williams' last and most enduring message was that abolition could not have triumphed independently of economic developments linked to industrialization. This simple hypothesis has already proved to be more fruitful than those offered by historians in the whole century before him. *Capitalism and Slavery* changed the way in which we view abolition precisely because it riveted attention on the context rather than on heroes. Historians are unlikely again to suspend disbelief in the existence of 'three or four perfectly virtuous pages in the history of nations'.

NOTES

This essay was prepared during a fellowship at the Woodrow Wilson Center for Scholars. I wish to express my appreciation to the participants at the Bellagio conference on British Capitalism and British Slavery in 1984 for their extensive comments, and to Stanley Engerman in particular for his advice. Reviews of *Econocide* referred to in this essay are listed at the end of the notes.

1. Eric Williams, *Capitalism and Slavery* (1944, rept'd, 1966), hereafter *CS*.
2. *Ibid.*, p. 120.
3. *Ibid.*, p. 154.
4. 2nd Ser. xxi (1968) no. 2, 307–20. See also his 'A Re-interpretation of the Abolition of the British Slave Trade, 1806–07', *Economic History Review* 87(343) (1972), pp. 304–32.
5. *CS*, pp. 52–4, 225–6, tables; *Econocide*, pp. 16–25.
6. 'Economic Aspects of the Abolition Debate', in Christine Bolt and Seymour Drescher (eds.), *Anti-Slavery, Religion, and Reform: Essays in Memory of Roger Anstey* (Folkestone, England and Hamden, 1980), pp. 272–3.
7. Cf. Cecil Gutzmore, 'The Continuing Dispute over the Connections between the Capitalist Mode of Production and Chattel Slavery, presented at the Sesquecentennial of the Death of William Wilberforce and the Emancipation Act of 1833' (MSS) pp. 2–6.
8. '"Econocide" – Myth or Reality – The Question of West Indian Decline, 1783–1806' and the reply, 'Econocide, Capitalism and Slavery: A Commentary', in *Boletin de Estudios Latinoamericanos y del Caribe*, 36 (June 1984), pp. 13–67.
9. See n. 5.
10. *CS*, p. 225, n. 16.
11. See n. 5.
12. *Econocide*, p. 20, Figure 5.
13. Those reviews of *Econocide* which evidently accept the undermining of the Williams decline thesis are: W. J. Hausman, J. A. Casada, G. Heuman, L. J. Belliot, R. Anstey, D. Eltis, R. Lopper, J. Hogendorn, B. Hilton, J. Walvin, P. E. H. Hair, P. D. Curtin, R. Koch, I. R. Hancock, J. P. Greene, S. Daget, P. Emmer, J. A. Lesourd, Sv. E. Green-Pedersen. In the most novel portion of this essay on 'Williams and Drescher' in *Slavery and Abolition*, 4(3) (September 1983, 81–105), Walter Minchinton dismisses the utility of official British trade statistics for measuring trends in the relative significance of global trade zones, including the British West Indies. On grounds that these figures used static official prices, Minchinton insists that they do 'not enable us to assess properly the importance of the British West Indies for Great Britain' (*ibid.*, p. 87). He does not, however, address the fact that the other economic historians of the same period consider it quite feasible to measure relative trade shares on the basis of the official data (see, for example, François Crouzet's 'Toward an Export Economy', cited, below in Table 2). More important, he overlooks the fact that

Ralph Davis' *real* price data confirm the British West Indian trends at the end of the eighteenth century (see n. 37 below). Minchinton also overlooks the fact that the official figures were those used exclusively by contemporary MPs and publicists in arguments about the value of the British West Indies (see *Econocide*, p. 231, note). (Incidentally, Minchinton's summary dismissal of the official data works directly against his own conclusion that *Captialism and Slavery* remains a 'yardstick' for the study of abolition. If the official series cannot validate *Econocide*'s conclusions about the West Indies after 1775, how can the same data validate *Capitalism and Slavery*'s similar conclusions about the period before 1775?)

14. See, *inter alia*, Gutzmore, 'The Continuing Dispute', pp. 16–17; Review of A. Adamson.
15. Review of M. Craton. The most systematic and elegant elaboration to date of the implicit tension between abolition and the pattern of economic development yet written is David Eltis' 'Capitalism and Abolition: The Missed Opportunities of 1807–1865', typescript kindly circulated at Bellagio conference. It is a foretaste of Eltis' eagerly awaited two-volume synthesis on the nineteenth-century slave trade.
16. *CS*, p. 134.
17. *Ibid.*, p. 135.
18. J. R. Ward, 'The Profitability of Sugar Planting in the British West Indies, 1650–1834', *Economic History Review*, 2nd ser. 31 (1978); and his excellent unpublished sequel, 'The Profitability and Viability of British West Indian Plantation Slavery, 1807–1834'.
19. Review by M. Craton.
20. At the Bellagio conference of British Slavery and British Capitalism, Barbara Solow placed special emphasis on the significance of the eighteenth-century export trade in British economic development. See the general discussion in John J. McCusker and Russell R. Menard, *The Economy of British America, 1607–1789* (Chapel Hill and London, 1985), pp. 39–45.
21. See review essays by B. Solow and M. Turner; review by E. Goveia; Noel Deerr, *History of Sugar*, 2 vols (London, 1949–50), pp. 529–31.
22. *Econocide*, pp. 39–41.
23. See *Some Observations Showing the Dangers of Losing the Trade of the Slave Colonies, by a Planter* (1714), from the Huntington Library Collection, no. 146982.
24. *CS*, p. 122.
25. *Econocide*, pp. 46–51.
26. See Deerr, A History, p. 530, prices of sugar in London and Amsterdam, 1806. Just prior to the Commons debate of 1792, 5 January–5 March, British re-exports of sugar to Europe were running at about 300 per cent of the rate of average re-exports for 1787–90. (Calculated from *A Report from the Committee of Warehouses of the United East-India Company Relative to the Price of Sugar* (London, 1792), p. 23.) Below, I offer a table [Table 4.5], but only suggestively, comparing the ratios of British re-exports to 'British'/foreign sugar prices at points between 1765 and 1818. From the sources used, it is unclear whether different grades

Table 4.5 Re-exports of sugar compared to 'British'/foreign sugar ratios, 1765–1818 (selected periods)

Period	% of British imports re-exported (cwt) (1)	London prices/foreign prices × 100 (per British cwt) (2)
1761–5	23.8	124[a]
1771–5	4.5	144[b]
1781–5	10.0	136[c]
1791–5	24.5	—
1801–5	33.3	83[d]
1814–18	31.8(27.9)	88[e]

Note: Column (1): Parenthetical figure = British West Indian sugar only. Column (2): a = London compared to Amsterdam Muscovado; b = London compared to Nantes Muscovado; c = ditto, but Nantes prices for 1782–4 only; d = London/Amsterdam ratio, but Amsterdam prices 1801, 1804, 1806 only; e = London/Havana, ord. yellow.
Sources: Column (1): 1765–1805, *Econocide*, p. 80, 1814–1818, *PP*, 1847–8, LVIII; column (2): a and b London prices from R. Sheridan, *Sugar and Slavery: An Economic History of the British West Indies* (Baltimore, 1974), p. 497; Amsterdam prices, Deerr, *History*, p. 530; c Nantes prices from Deerr, *ibid.*, British prices from *ibid*. Mean of range given by Deerr; d same as c; e *PP*, 1847–8 (44), p. 3 of *Report*.

of sugar are being compared in the price series in different ports. In the re-export series it is also unclear how much 'foreign' sugar was being re-exported, especially in the war years: 1761–3; 1781–3; 1793–5; 1801; 1804–5. Five-year intervals are chosen both because Parliament preferred these multiyear averages, and because quantities of foreign sugar, listed as 'retained' for consumption in one year might have been imported in prior years. (See, for example, *PP* 1847–48, LVIII *Seasonal Paper* No. 400: '*Return of Quantities of Sugar*', etc. p. 3, n. lc.)

27. Temperley, 'Capitalism, Slavery and Ideology', *Past and Present* No. 75 (May, 1977), p. 101.
28. *Econocide*, p. 53.
29. P. J. Cain and A. G. Hopkins, 'The Political Economy of British Expansion Overseas, 1750–1914', *Economic History Review*, 2nd ser. 33(4) (November 1980), pp. 463–90. Referring to *Econocide*, Cain and Hopkins write: 'Contrary to a long-standing belief, the slave trade was not overthrown by powerful industrial interests cramped by colonial restrictions. Manufacturers were neither influential enough to overthrow the trade nor driven by economic logic to make the attempt' (p. 473, n.).
30. Carrington, 'Econocide–Myth'.

31. See reviews by Emmer, G. Heuman, and the essay by D. Geggus, 'The British Government and the Saint Domingue slave revolt, 1791–1793', *English Historical Review*, 96 (379) (April 1981), 287.
32. *Econocide*, p. 64.
33. *Ibid.*, pp. 165–6.
34. *CS*, p. 113.
35. P. Curtin, *The Slave Trade: A Census* (Madison, 1969), pp. 119, 216.
36. Deerr, *A History*, pp. 193–6.
37. R. Davis, *The Industrial Revolution and British Overseas Trade* (Leicester, 1979), pp. 89–125.
38. Deerr, *A History*, p. 21.
39. See for example P. E. Lovejoy, 'The Volume of the Atlantic Slave Trade: A Synthesis', *Journal of African History*, 23(4) (1982), pp. 473–501; James A. Rawley, *The Transatlantic Slave Trade: A History* (New York, 1981), p. 428; and D. Richardson, unpublished figures summarized in his Bellagio conference paper 'The Slave Trade, Sugar, and British Economic Growth 1748 to 1776'.
40. J. E. Inikori, 'Measuring the Atlantic Slave Trade: An Assessment of Curtin and Anstey', *Journal of African History*, 17 (1976), pp. 197–223; *Econocide*, pp. 211–3.
41. Carrington, 'Econocide–Myth', p. 42.
42. *Ibid.*, p. 43, Figure XXIII: Slave imports into and exports from the British West Indies, 1783–1805.
43. J. J. McCusker, 'The Rum Trade and the Balance of Payments of the Thirteen Continental Colonies, 1660–1776' (University of Pittsburgh, Ph. D. dissertation), 2 vols, 1970.
44. See n. 31 above.
45. Another historian cited yet another leading Minister who assured the Governor of Jamaica in 1808 that abolition had been a practical response to overproduction. Yet only nine months earlier the same MP had opposed abolition as impractical on grounds of planter demand for slaves. Is there any reason why one should prefer after-the-fact rationalizations to before-the-fact statements in determining motivation?
46. Anstey, *The Atlantic Slave Trade*, pp. 51–2.
47. Gutzmore, 'The Continuing Dispute', p. 26.
48. Emmer's review.
49. Reviews of Curtin, Adamson, and Lopper.

LIST OF REVIEWS OF *ECONOCIDE* COMPILED BY THE UNIVERSITY OF PITTSBURGH PRESS

William J. Hausman, in *Library Journal* (1 May 1977).
The Economist (7 January 1978).
James A. Casada, *Africana Journal*, 9(3) (1978).
Gad J. Heuman, *Journal of Imperial and Commonwealth History*, 7(1) (1978).
Leland J. Bellot, *The History Teacher* (February 1978).

Roger Anstey, *Times Literary Supplement* (19 May 1978).
J.-A. Lesourd, *Revue Historique*, 259 (January–June 1978).
Betty Fladeland, *American Historical Review* (June 1978).
Michael Craton, *Canadian Journal of History*, 13(2) (August 1978).
Betty Fladeland, *Modern Europe* (September 1978).
David Eltis, *The Business History Review*, 52(3) (Autumn 1978).
Elsa V. Goveia, *William and Mary Quarterly*, (October 1978).
Richard B. Sheridan, *The Journal of Economic History* (October 1978).
A. J. H. Latham, *Durham University Journal* (December 1978).
Richard Lopper, *Black Liberator*, 4(4) (December 1978).
Serge Daget, *Revue Française d'Histoire d'Outre-mer*, 65 (1978).
Jan Hogendorn, *International Journal of African Historical Studies*, 12(1) (1979).
Boyd Hilton, *English Historical Review* (January 1979).
Barbara L. Solow, *Journal of Economic Literature*, 17 (June 1979).
James Walvin, *The Historian* (August 1979).
Mary Turner, *Peasant Studies*, 8(4) (Fall 1979).
Alan H. Adamson, *Journal of Social History*, 13(1) (October 1979).
P. E. H. Hair, *International History Review* (October 1979).
D. A. G. Waddell, *History*, 212(1) (November 1979).
Philip D. Curtin, *Journal of Interdisciplinary History*, 9(3) (Winter 1979).
P. C. Emmer, *Belgisch Tijdschrift voor Filologie en Geschiedenis*, 67(3) (1979).
Rainer Koch, *Historische Zeitschrift*, B. 231 (1980).
I. R. Hancock, *Australian Journal of Politics and History*, 26(1) (1980).
Jack P. Greene, *Agricultural History*, 54(1) (January 1980).
Emma Lapansky, *Histoire Sociale – Social History* (May 1980).
Sv. E. Green-Pedersen, *Historisk Tidsskrift*.

Part II

Having analyzed the destruction of the British slave trade in terms of comparative political economy and mass mobilization, the essays in Part II compare British antislavery with a number of other national cases. Chapter 5 looks at Brazilian abolition from a multinational perspective, including those of the United States, Great Britain, and France. It continues to develop the comparison between 'Anglo-American' and 'Continental' models of antislavery. Chapter 6 looks at France's second emancipation (1848) in terms of its similarities to, and differences from, British emancipation. In both Brazil and France, ineffectual elite-centered antislavery required last-minute infusions of popular mobilization in order to carry their respective societies over the political threshold to slave emancipation.

Chapter 7, on Dutch antislavery, considers a neglected aspect of comparative antislavery. In the wake of the abandonment of the decline thesis, some historians undertook a search for new cases, and new capitalist models of abolition. (See, inter alia, *The Antislavery Debate: Capitalism and abolitionism as a problem in historical interpretation*, ed. Thomas Bender (1992) and my review essay on capitalism and abolition, in *History and Theory*, 32(3) (1993), pp. 311–29). The Dutch response to colonial slavery over the course of three centuries serves as an excellent testing ground for the link between capitalism and antislavery across a whole range of economic conditions, regions and 'stages' of political economy. Since Dutch antislavery remained a marginal 'Continental' variety from beginning to end historians can measure the potential of capitalism to stimulate abolitionism, and/or to facilitate political termination of slave labor. I conclude that, on close inspection, the 'Dutch test' turns out to be a killing field for any of the hypothesized casual linkages between capitalism and antislavery. The Dutch case was also discussed at a colloqium held at the University of Leiden in 1993. (See *Fifty Years Later: Antislavery, Capitalism and modernity in the Dutch orbit*, Gert Oostindie, ed. (Leiden, 1995, Pittsburgh, 1996.) The last essay in Part II, chapter 8, looks at European reactions to

John Brown's seizure of Harpèrs Ferry military arsenal in Virginia in 1859. It traces the varying reactions in Europe to the fate of John Brown as the United States moved towards civil war. Those reactions varied in intensity and valuation, according to histories of individual 'national' antislaveries, of attitudes towards revolutionary violence and of political formations in Europe.

5 Brazilian Abolition in Comparative Perspective (1988)*

On the eve of the age of abolition, even intellectuals who were morally opposed to slavery were far more impressed by its power and durability than by its weaknesses. Adam Smith reminded his students that only a small portion of the earth was being worked by free labor, and that it was unlikely that slavery would ever be totally abandoned. Across the channel, the Abbé Raynal could envision the end of New World slavery only through a fortuitous conjuncture of philosopher-kings in Europe or the appearance of a heroic Spartacus in the Americas. No historical trend toward general emancipation could be assumed.[1]

Little more than a century later, the passage of the 'Golden Law' through the Brazilian legislature – to the accompaniment of music, public demonstrations, and street festivities at every stage – was regarded as only a belated provincial rendezvous with progress. Until then, Brazilians had been humiliated by condescending references to their country as the last Christian nation that tolerated slavery, on a level with 'backward' African and Asiatic slaveholding societies.[2] Brazilian emancipation was hailed as opening a new stage in the 'civilizing' of Africa and Asia. Counting from the formation of the first abolitionist societies in the late 1780s, the Brazilian action almost precisely marked a 'century of progress'.

Perhaps because it occurred so late in a world dominated by a concept of libertarian progress, Brazilian abolition received relatively little attention from those who wrote general histories of slavery.[3] The demise of Brazilian slavery seemed to follow a path roughly prescribed by a dozen predecessors in the Americas and Europe. This impression may have been due in part to the fact that until recently there were

---

* *The Hispanic American Historical Review*, 68(3) (August 1968), pp. 429–60. © 1988 Duke University Press.

few extensive analyses of the Brazilian case,[4] a lack which was compounded by the 'North Atlantic' or even national orientation of most North American and European historians of slavery. Moreover, when Brazilian slavery has been treated in comparative perspective, the contrast is almost invariably with the US South.[5] In this study, I shall expand the range of cases to include a number of emancipations in areas which were subject to European polities during the nineteenth century.

Historians of abolition usually approach causal discussions along a range of analytical categories: demographic, economic, social, ideological, and political. The historiography of abolition in Brazil, as elsewhere, is usually embedded in implicit or explicit theories about the relative weight to be assigned to each of these facets of social development and to their long- or short-term significance in the outcome. This essay will address two major elements of Brazilian abolition in comparative perspective – the demographics and economics of late Brazilian slavery, and the peculiar characteristics of Brazilian abolitionism and its opposition. I should say at the outset that I am entirely dependent on the existing historiography for the details of Brazilian development.

DEMOGRAPHIC DEPENDENCY AND ECONOMIC VIABILITY

Slave Trade Abolition

As elsewhere in the New World, Brazilian slavery was stimulated by a shortage of labor relative to opportunities for rapid expansion in specialized commodity production. Like that of the Caribbean slave systems, the relative decline of the institution in Brazil was initially a consequence of external political pressures for the restriction of slave recruitment.[6] Exactly as in Cuba, Brazilian imports of African slaves had actually reached an all-time peak just before the enforcement of abolition in 1851.[7]

The impact of slave trade abolition on Brazil was similar to West Indian terminations in two other ways. Insofar as Brazil continued to expand its staple production, it increasingly had to rely on some combination of free and slave labor and a redistribution of its diminishing slave labor. The slave population inevitably declined, as a percentage both of the total labor force and of Brazilian capital. After 1851, that trend was inexorable and predictable.

Moreover, market pressures alone assured that, as in the British colonies and Cuba after ending slave importation from Africa, slave labor would be concentrated toward commodity production which could optimize the output from that form of labor. Certain economic sectors had to become less dependent on slavery. Without such inhibiting political restrictions on the flow of slave labor as occurred between islands of the British Caribbean in the decades after slave trade abolition in 1807,[8] there was a shift of Brazilian slaves from the city to the countryside in expanding frontier regions. This type of redistribution occurred even in the US South, where there was a positive and high rate of postabolition natural increase.[9]

In Brazil, local expansions of the slave labor force could come only from redistribution. Shortly after African migration ended, the north-eastern provinces which were losing slaves vainly attempted to follow the 'British' model by prohibiting the interprovincial slave trade. As the northeasterners noted, the interprovincial flow of slaves created growing differentials of dependency on, and commitment to, slavery.[10] But, by the time political fear became more important than economic interest to the importing south-central region (in the early 1880s), it was too late. By 1884, fewer than half the provinces of Brazil had populations of more than 10 percent slaves, and more than one-fourth of the provinces (mostly northern and northeastern) were even below 5 percent, the level at which many northern US states had opted for immediate emancipation.[11]

By the last quarter of the nineteenth century, the free population of the Northeast had grown sufficiently to facilitate the transition to free labor in that less dynamic region. Within southern Brazil itself, a new regional differentiation developed in the mid-1880s. As foreign immigration to São Paulo increased rapidly, the Paulista planters joined the ranks of the abolitionists, leaving the slaveowners of Rio de Janeiro and Minas Gerais in isolation.[12]

Two comparative demographic points can be emphasized. The regional divisions in Brazil developed over a much shorter period than in the southern United States, because of the different reproduction rates in the two slave societies. Also, free immigrants were few compared to those of the antebellum United States. As an alternative agricultural labor force they seem to have played a last-minute role, relieving the labor crisis of the Paulista planters, and helping to convert them to abolition in 1887–8. It would thus appear that highly organized foreign labor recruitment was more a response to the prospect of imminent abolition in the mid-1880s than a long-term causal variable.[13] For the generation after abolition of the slave trade, free mass immigration was an uncertain potential rather than an actuality.

Brazil's situation resembled the Caribbean model more than that of the United States in that abolition of the African slave trade condemned slavery to a speedy relative decline. The political significance of redistribution seems to have been dramatically borne out in only one generation. It reduced urban interest in the system and it stimulated higher slave prices and concentration of ownership. The frequently remarked Brazilian planters' acceptance of the 'inevitability' of slavery's decline (even when used as a political argument against the need for further abolitionist legislation) was based on a logical assessment of the data and an accurate reading of Caribbean history.[14]

A glance at the Cuban example reinforces both the general causal weight assigned to the ending of the slave trade and the political significance of regional differentiation resulting from its termination. The constriction of the African slave supply was a more drawn out and fluctuating process in Cuba than it was in Brazil. Cuban import flows were generally more volatile.[15] Cuban slave prices rose about as rapidly as Brazil's between the 1830s and 1860, but Cuban prices were always higher, and the total value of its staple exports grew faster. This indicates that market pressures for finding alternative sources of labor were felt more keenly in Cuba than in Brazil, and may explain Cuba's earlier recourse to non-African labor. In regional terms, Cuba's poorer eastern provinces were less able to afford either slave or Asiatic labor, and as in Brazil's Northeast, those Cuban provinces produced movements more willing to add elements of abolitionism to their political agenda in the 1860s and 1870s.[16]

Everywhere in the Euro–Americas, in bound labor systems, except the southern United States, recruitment from without played a crucial role. For centuries, expansion had been effected via the transoceanic slave trade, as in the case of Afro–Caribbean slavery; by binding the native population, as with Russian peasants; or by combining both methods, as in the Brazilian recruitment of both Indians and Africans. During the nineteenth century, Brazil followed the circum-Caribbean pattern which required transoceanic transfers of Africans for expansion.[17] Without such recruitment, all the systems (with the one exception noted) faced deteriorating active population ratios, as well as a variety of other difficulties. If, as David Eltis cogently argues, the 'natural limits' of slavery (in terms of changing technology, decreasing land–labor ratios, management techniques, lower profits from slave labor, or potential slave supply) were nowhere in sight at any point in the nineteenth century, many of the supposed contradictions and stresses observed within slave economies are primarily consequences of slave trade abolition, rather than contradictions between slavery and economic growth.[18]

Economic Growth

The degree of dependence of New World slave societies on external recruitment probably constitutes their most important socioeconomic characteristic from start to finish. As agricultural and extractive frontiers, they also tended to be more dependent for technological innovation and even for much of their cultural self-definition on the increasingly 'free' metropolises. Only rarely was one or another of these slave societies able to imagine itself as an autonomous economic and political actor,[19] and Brazil alone developed a domestically based slave trade with Africa well before the beginning of interventionist British abolitionist diplomacy. This stood Brazil's slaveowners in good stead during the semiclandestine stage of the slave trade after Waterloo. However, before restriction of the African labor supply, almost all slave economies were probably expanding faster in population and wealth than the metropolitan societies which dominated them politically. Even the roughest statistical approximations would have led one to conclude that Brazil in particular was more than matching

Portugal in total population growth, growth of the value of exports, and with regard to other similar indicators during the period before independence.

By most of the usual criteria of economic development, Brazilians were unlikely to have been impressed by the 'progress' of Portugal at the beginning of the nineteenth century. With a population of only 2 000 000 in 1700, between 300 000 and 500 000 Portuguese departed for Brazil over the course of the eighteenth century. On the eve of its own movement for independence, Brazilian agricultural growth contrasted markedly with relative Portuguese industrial and agricultural stagnation, and Brazilian reexports largely accounted for Portugal's trade surplus with England.[20]

In the second half of the nineteenth century, Brazilians, especially those who traveled abroad, increasingly measured themselves against a broader West, in which the long-term weaknesses of their society became more manifest with each passing decade. In this respect, the significant comparisons were not those of the marketplace such as crop output, productivity, profits, the net worth of slaveholders, or the aggregate wealth of the nation. What was important was Brazil's relative dearth of railroads, canals, towns, factories, schools, and books. The echoes of Alexis de Tocqueville's contrast between the bustle of free societies and the stagnation of slave societies in the United States resonated among the Brazilian elite.[21] Long before 1850, it was clear that Brazil's demographic dependency on Africa was the most critical ingredient in slavery's viability as an economic system.

Brazil also contributes to the labor 'flexibility' debate in slavery historiography. The argument has often been made that slaves were 'immobilized' labor compared with wage laborers.[22] Whether or not slaveowners in the South proved to be more market responsive than entrepreneurs using free labor in the North in the antebellum United States, Brazilian slavery seems to have been as flexible and fluid as that of the US South in the redistribution of labor in the generation after slave trade abolition. Comparing the interregional slave migrations within the US South and Brazil, Robert Slenes concludes that, in proportion to the populations of the respective exporting regions, 'the two migration currents were about the same size'.[23] In regional terms, it would appear that the 'exporting' Brazilian slave areas were divesting at a faster rate than those in the upper South of the United States during the generation before their respective emancipations.

As can be seen in the cases of the British West Indies, the United States, Cuba, and Brazil, all of the dynamic plantation economies produced a variety of crops so long as the traffic with Africa remained unimpeded. In the British Caribbean and the US South, that situation ended in 1808. Thereafter, the former moved toward a concentration on sugar and the latter toward cotton. In Cuba, the trend was toward expansion of all produce into the 1830s. With increasing constriction in the 1840s the slave labor force began to concentrate on sugar production and to increase its productivity. After full prohibition of the African labor supply and the beginning of gradual emancipation in 1870, the convergence of slavery and sugar became even more pronounced. In 1862, the major sugar zones of Cuba (Matanzas and Santa Clara) had 46 percent of Cuba's slave population; by 1877 they had 57 percent. A 'ruralization' of slavery, similar to that of the US cotton zone and the Brazilian coffee zone, occurred in Cuba.[24]

Of course, this demographic/economic flexibility came at the cost of regional political divergence. Contrary to convergence models of abolition, we confront the paradox that Brazilian economic and political variables operated against each other in some respects. Economic winners hastened their institution's political decline, while the economic losers for a time futilely attempted to retard slave labor flexibility by warning of political divergence.[25] Eventually Ceará, the most distressed province in preemancipation Brazil (where the only transferable capital left by 1880 was in slaves), became the pioneer province in emancipation. Moreover, the trend toward free labor in the Brazilian Northeast after 1850 was not associated with industrialization as in the US Northeast: industry did not come first to Ceará or to Amazonas as it did to Massachusetts. After 1850, urbanization proceeded more swiftly in the cities located adjacent to the principal slave holding and slave-importing provinces of the south–center than those in the slave-exporting Northeast. European immigration also flowed primarily to just those areas that were among the last to be converted to abolition in 1877–8. Many of the indicators of 'progress' rhetorically used to demonstrate the greater dynamism of the northern

United States in the analysis of antebellum slavery (industrialization, transportation, urbanization, immigration) seemed to favor the more dynamic slave regions of Brazil.[26]

The Brazilian case therefore suggests that the enterprises, urban areas, and provinces least involved in economic growth and modernization were the first to turn against slavery. This is consistent with Eltis's conclusion that the burgeoning of

Table 5.1 Distribution of foreigners, United States and Brazil, 1860 and 1872

United States 1860	% of all foreigners	% of total population	Brazil 1872	% of all foreigners	% of total population
Free states and western territories	86.5	17.5	Provinces with the lowest proportion of slaves[a]	13.2	1.2
Slave states	13.5	3.5	Provinces with the greatest proportion of slaves[b]	86.8	2.9

Notes: On the eve of secession in 1860, there were four million foreigners in the United States. Indeed, there were more foreigners in the southern slave states in 1860 than in all of Brazil at the time of the Rio Branco Law. However, insofar as attracting free European immigration was concerned, the northern United States already contained more than four times as many foreigners in 1860 as the South of 1860 and Brazil of 1872 combined. Whether measured by total migrations or in *per capita* terms, the flow of European free migration was clearly toward the free labor zone of North America.
[a] Includes 11 provinces at, or below, the median proportion of slaves.
[b] Includes 9 provinces and the Município Neutro (Rio de Janeiro) above the median.
Sources: *The Statistical History of the United States, From Colonial Times to the Present* (Stanford, 1965), pp. 11–12; *Population of the United States in 1860* (Washington, 1864), p. 300; *Recenseamento da População do Imperio do Brasil ... agosto de 1872*, Quadros geraes.

Table 5.2 Percentage of the labor force in selected urban areas

Area	Slaves	Foreigners	Slaves in province
Rio de Janeiro	21.1	34.7	45.2 (Rio de Janeiro)
Pôrto Alegre	23.4	13.9	18.7 (Rio Grande do sul)
São Paulo	15.0	9.9	21.6 (São Paulo)
Recife	16.7	10.1	14.3 (Pernambuco)
Brazil			11.9 (Provincial median)

Sources: For the percentage of the labor force in the four largest cities, Merrick and Graham, *Population and Economic Development*, p. 73; for the median provincial percentages, see Table 5.1 above.

nineteenth-century European and North American capitalism fueled the general expansion of slavery in terms of investment, consumer demand, and technological innovation.[27] However, there was no area of Brazil, before the mid-1800s, which could assume the role of a 'free labor' abolitionist zone, as in the Anglo–American (i.e. British and United States) case. Until late in the emancipation process, 'pressure from without' came predominantly from beyond the Brazilian polity.

POLITICAL ABOLITION

Comparative analysis of the politics of Brazilian emancipation might begin with any one of a number of salient criteria. One can distinguish between violence and nonviolence in the process;[28] between abolitions which came from 'above' (Russia, the Netherlands, etc.) and those which came from 'below' (Haiti);[29] between gradual and partial abolitions (Pennsylvania, Argentina, Venezuela) and simultaneous and total abolitions (France, Massachusetts); or between compensated emancipations (Britain, France, Denmark) and uncompensated emancipations (the United States, Brazil). Some of these taxonomies seem designed to engender terminological disputes. For example, if we include all legislative acts, from minor restrictions on further recruitment to complete and immediate freedom of contract for all labor, all abolitions, including even the Haitian revolutionary case, were gradual. Similarly, there is simply no case in the plantation Americas in which slaveholders prostrated themselves before economic forces and consensually agreed to initiate abolition.[30] From the historical point of view, all emancipations in the plantation Americas were initiated by exogenous pressures on the planter class.[31]

In formal terms, Brazilian slavery was gradually brought to an end by parliamentary legislation. Abolition occurred in three major political stages: the effective prohibition of the African slave trade in 1851; the passage of the 'free birth' (Rio Branco) law in 1871; and the passage of the 'Golden Law' of emancipation in 1888. The first stage virtually terminated transatlantic recruitment of slaves. The second deprived the slave system of its means of endogenous reproduction. The third registered the accelerating impact of the extraparliamentary demolition of chattel slavery.

Considering all three stages as part of a single historical development, how can one best view this process in comparative terms? In a study of British and French antislavery in the period between 1780 and the end of the US Civil War, I suggested a contrast between an Anglo–American and a continental European model of abolitionism.[32] The distinguishing characteristics of the Anglo–American variants were their relatively broad appeal and long duration. Citizens in Great Britain and the United States attempted to bring public pressure to bear on reluctant or hostile economic interests and hesitant agencies of the state. They used mass propaganda, petitions, newspapers, public meetings, lawsuits, and boycotts, presenting ever more radical antislavery action as a moral and political imperative. They achieved, at least occasionally, a reputation for fanaticism. Organizationally, this form of abolitionism tended to be decentralized in structure, and rooted in widely dispersed local communities. Anglo–Americans usually aimed at inclusiveness, welcoming participants who were otherwise excluded from the ordinary political process by reason of gender, religion, race, or class.

The 'continental' variants usually had different tendencies. Their leaders were reluctant or unable to seek mass recruitment. They concentrated on plans of abolition (submitted to, or commissioned by, the central government) containing elaborate provisions for postemancipation labor control and planter compensation. They often attempted to act as brokers between external pressure groups (including British abolitionists) and their own slaveowners. Public discussion was restricted to the capital or the chief commercial center. Continental abolitionists, in other words, preferred to work quietly from within and from above. They almost never were considered as fanatics, even by their adversaries. Continental variants also tended to be limited in duration. A small movement would typically form in response to an external (usually British) stimulus. It would last only until the abolition of its nation's own slave trade or slave system. Continental abolitionist societies remained satellites of their British counterpart, and failed to capture any mass following on their own soil.

French abolition was a partly anomalous case. During the Great French Revolution, the source of collective mobilization for emancipation was the slaves in the French Caribbean. Even so, during most of France's age of abolition (1788–1848), the movement was a continental variant – a discontinuous series of elite groupings, unable and usually unwilling to stimulate mass appeals. French slave emancipation occurred in two surges (1793–4 and 1848), with an intervening restoration of slavery under Napoleon wherever his military forces prevailed. Every major French abolitionist thrust (1794, 1815, 1831, and 1848) came in the wake of a revolution, with little abolitionist mobilization in the metropolis; France was a case of abolition without mass abolitionism.[33]

In the Spanish empire, abolition was generally contingent on the fate of colonial mobilizations for national independence. The process on the American continent extended over half a century until the 1860s. Some areas with relatively small slave systems enacted total emancipation in one legal step, in the immediate aftermath of political independence. Others, like Venezuela, Peru, and Argentina, began the process during the independence struggle but moved through slow stages with frequent retrenchments. Cuba, however, was Spain's most important New World slave colony, and its nineteenth-century path to abolition clearly reveals the significance of the absence of strong metropolitan antislavery mobilization. Cuba's dependency on Spain imposed few ideological or political constraints on its slave system for the first two-thirds of the century. On the contrary, Spain was the most extreme example of the 'continental' variant of abolitionism; not even a nominal movement existed before the US Civil War. Until southern secession, the United States also provided a formidable counterweight to British abolitionist diplomacy, and was undoubtedly decisive in permitting Africans to reach Cuba for more than a decade after the Brazilian slave trade crisis of 1850. Even after the northern victory in 1865 and the emergence of political abolitionism in Spain, much of the initiative for abolition within the Spanish empire came from foreign countries and the colonial periphery (Cuba and Puerto Rico).[34]

Brazil appears to have shared some characteristics of both major variants of abolitionism. Before the late 1860s, Brazil conformed pretty closely to the continental European model. During the final phase, in the 1880s, it came to more closely resemble the Anglo–American variant, and developed its own original characteristics of popular mobilization.

For almost 60 years, from the Anglo–Portuguese treaty of 1810 to the end of the US Civil War, Brazil conformed to the European pattern in the sense that exogenous forces played a far greater role than endogenous ones in the timing of moves toward abolition. Great Britain's role was preponderant in linking the achievement of independence with formal abolition treaties. Britain also intervened in Brazilian domestic slavery over *emancipado* issues, i.e. over the treatment of ostensibly free Africans who had been rescued from illegal slaving ships. Even more blatantly than in the European context, moreover, the British government 'colonized' abolitionism in Brazil through secret subsidies and covert agents.[35]

If slave trade abolition was the first and most important step in the destruction process, it is instructive to consider the Brazilian case in comparative political perspective. Throughout the tropical Americas, the abolition of the slave trade was opposed by expanding plantation areas before such legislation was passed, and was massively evaded afterward for as long as the enforcing polity was willing to connive at large-scale smuggling. A huge proportion of Brazil's slave labor force in the second third of the nineteenth century entered the country after the first prohibition in 1831.[36] Given the economic incentive for expansion, however, it is noteworthy that nowhere in the Americas did slaveowners attempt to resist slave trade abolition with military force. The US South was clearly the most acquiescent, with a majority of southern legislators willing to abolish imports at the first constitutional opportunity, in 1807. (Indeed, even those states that originally made constitutional postponement of the abolition question a prerequisite of entry into the union did not make perpetuation a sine qua non of union.) Even in secession, the Confederacy did not move to reopen the slave trade. Elsewhere (as in the British case) the majority of slaveowners engaged in protracted lobbying efforts against prohibition.[37] Yet a minority of planters readily acquiesced, and in no case did ending of the trade cause a major internal upheaval in slave societies.

The Brazilian case is especially interesting in political terms. Brazil – along with Cuba – was one of the last two slave societies in the Americas to effectively prohibit African recruitment. Despite other similarities to the US South, there had been relatively little endogenous political activity in Brazil against the illegal traffic during the generation before 1850, certainly nothing comparable in scale to British agitation in favor of abolition. The major push for Brazilian abolition of the trade thus came from outside the nation – in a virtual *casus belli*, in June of 1850. When the British navy mounted an attack on slave ships within Brazilian territorial waters, a number of remarkable results ensued. Unlike the localized impact of naval interventions on the coast of Africa, the entire slave trade to Brazil was brought to a precipitous end.[38] The only nominally independent slave society in the Americas acquiesced in the total elimination of what had been its major source of plantation labor recruitment for centuries. Since the Brazilian elite's commitment to slavery was a primary source of common loyalty,[39] such rapid enforcement and the inaction of the traders, slaveowners, and potential slaveowners are indeed striking, although not out of line with developments elsewhere.

From the perspective of established slaveowners, a general restriction on their long-run powers of expansion was an obvious setback, but its acceptance both spared them the short-term trade losses entailed in a British naval blockade and, as in the US South, offered the medium-term gains of a rise in slave prices flowing from abolition. The immediate losers were outsiders on the verge of becoming slaveholders. The acquiescing planters were mortgaging their political future.

A second important observation concerns the absence of attempts to use public opinion or mass demonstrations, either against the British violators by proslavers or against the Portuguese slavers by supporters of the British demands. The political decision was made behind closed doors, in secret session. Popular opinion might have been welcome after the Chamber had acted, but it was not incorporated into the decision-making process itself either for resistance or for acquiescence.[40]

Sectoral Divisions

Comparative analysis also seems to support those interpretations of Brazilian abolition which emphasize the significance of regional and sectoral differentiation without the need for recourse to sociopsychological divisions of the planter class along progressive-bourgeois and traditionalist–paternalist lines.[41] The demographic decline of slaves produced by termination of the slave trade, combined with the differential expansion of the slave-based economy, produced an accelerated emptying of certain economic sectors which had still been tied into slavery under the lower labor costs of the African slave trade. The same regional erosion occurred in the United States, but over a much longer period. Some of the southern calculations about the need for secession in 1860 were based on perceived trends of slavery's decline in the border states.[42]

The British West Indian case offers an interesting exception to regional erosion that supports the general model. Despite the slave price gap which opened up between the developed and the frontier colonies between British slave trade abolition in 1807 and emancipation in 1833, none of the British slave colonies broke ranks before 1833 in the manner of Amazonas and Ceará in Brazil. The ability of British slaveowners to transfer slaves to high-price areas was legally curtailed. Consequently, the process of regional divestment could not occur.[43] Redistribution of labor occurred only between crops or within separate island labor markets. One of the principal advantages of the use of slave labor over free workers was thus reversed in the British case during the interregnum between slave trade abolition and emancipation.[44]

As already mentioned, by the time the political consequences of the free market in slaves clearly outweighed the economic advantages to slaveowners in Brazil, it was far too late. The social consensus in favor of slavery at the time of independence had dissolved. The relationship between abolition and the increasing economic concentration of slavery seems as clear as in the case of geographical redistribution. It has been shown that for the US South there was 'a striking increase in the percentage of farm operations with no slaves', from less than 40 percent in 1850 to approximately 50 percent in 1860. Not only was the percentage of southerners in the total US population falling, but the percentage of southern families who owned slaves was also steadily dropping in the generation before 1860. The rising proportion of slaveless white families was probably more significant politically than any distinction between large and small slaveholders, because a southerner who owned just two slaves and *nothing else* was as rich as the average antebellum northerner. The need to maintain the loyalty of the nonslaveholding backbone of the electorate was the major task of the dominant party in the South.[45]

In addition to the effects of regional redistribution, rising Brazilian slave prices after 1850 must have prevented more and more Brazilians from entering into slaveowning altogether. Aspirations to ownership and a stake in the future of the system receded, as the free population increased more rapidly than the slave. I have found no figures on the percentage growth of slavelessness in Brazil after 1850, but the available analyses of slave redistribution, price trends, and slave/free population ratios after 1850 all point in the direction of a parallel to the antebellum South. The short-term benefits to existing owners of capital may conceivably have weakened their resolve to oppose abolition of the slave trade in 1850, but thereafter the same factors weakened the potential appeal of slavery to nonowners, eroding the consensual base of slavery.

The Politics of the Planters

The early historiographical focus on planters in Brazilian abolition appears to be quite reasonable, in view of their general dominance and cohesiveness in imperial Brazilian society. Since the abolitionist process was, from the slaveowners' perspective, first initiated from without, the Brazilian case can perhaps be most frutifully examined within the comparative context of responses to abolitionist threats.

There were certain similarities between the slaveowners' situations in Brazil and the US South on the eve of the external threats to their respective slaveries. Plantation profits were generally increasing in both economies during the first half of the nineteenth century, which should have encouraged counterabolitionist action. The same upward trend was true of long-term demand for their staples.[46]

But there were divergences between the two economies which made for very different outlooks in contemplating courses of action. The coffee planters of the Brazilian south–center would have been less buoyed by the nature of their market in 1850 or in 1871 than were their US counterparts. The latter might rationally have anticipated that secession would succeed without violence. Their major premise was that the South, 'safely entrenched behind her cotton bags ... can defy the civilized world – for the civilized world depends on the cotton of the South'. Their optimism was supported by northern disarray and by the fears voiced in England about a cotton famine.[47]

The situation of the Brazilian planters in 1850 was quite different. They were presented at the outset with a military *fait accompli* which offered only the choice between preparation for war and acquiescence in the ending of the slave trade. No one was under the illusion that a British blockade of Brazilian coffee or sugar exports would quickly bring a major component of the English economy to its knees. The British public and government could always be tougher toward coffee- and sugar-producing areas than toward cotton-producing ones. Only a political regime able to dismiss short-term economic considerations could seriously have considered challenging the British navy. There is no indication that Brazilian society was remotely organized for a scorched trade policy in the mid-nineteenth century, and the Brazilian government seems to have played a continental-style mediating role between Britain and Brazil's slaveowners.

After 1865, the timing of the initial movement toward gradual emancipation in Brazil also seems to have been dominated by external events, including emancipation in the United States and the Spanish Caribbean and the Paraguayan War. Early explorations of popular channels of abolitionism (extraparliamentary organization and newspaper appeals) were confined to a very small section of the elite until the national legislation was actually presented in the form of a 'free womb' emancipation bill in 1871.[48]

By 1871, the model of emancipation by birth, as Robert Conrad notes, had been among the tested formulas for emancipation for almost a century. It had most recently been employed in the Spanish colonies the year before.[49] One might, of course, emphasize the limitations of the Rio Branco Law in order to enhance the significance of the mass mobilization phase of the 1880s. It should be noted, however, that the law certainly cut down the projected duration of slavery from a multigenerational perspective to the lifespan of a slave. It definitively set the clock running on termination. Subsequent popular mobilization made a difference of perhaps 10 to 15 years in the duration of Brazilian slavery. Although abolitionists in the 1880s were quick to note that slaves born in 1870 could live for another 60 to 70 years,[50] the active slave population would have been so small and so aging a proportion of the labor force by 1900 that it is difficult to imagine further resistance to accelerated, and even compensated, immediate emancipation. Compensation based on the European model would have become far more palatable as the pool of prime, able-bodied slaves evaporated. In some other areas where gradual legislation was passed (e.g. New York State, 1799) the tendency was for acceleration of the emancipation clock as the slave labor pool shrank and aged.[51]

Brazil's was the only plantation society to peacefully enact free womb emancipation entirely from within. In 1870, Brazil was operating under far less serious direct external and internal threats than Cuba.[52] Why then did Brazil adopt a law which was so definitive about the outer time limit of its slave system, and one which did not offer a guarantee of compensation to planters against the eventuality of further accelerated emancipation?

Conrad's study indicates that during the gradual emancipation debate an area *within* Brazil – the Northeast – began to play the role of mediating the transition to a free labor system. However, the social dynamics of realignment within the Northeast are still insufficiently clear.[53] Were the northeastern deputies of still substantial slave areas responsive to slaveholders who already felt secure in their ability to make the transition to free labor over another generation? The willingness of slaveowners from Pernambuco or Bahia to support the law, when between 12 and 20 percent of their populations were still slaves, stands in stark contrast to Delaware's refusal to consider a compensated emancipation proposal by Abraham Lincoln in 1861, when that state had fewer than 2000 remaining slaves.

The opposition to the Rio Branco Law raises equally interesting questions. It was located primarily in the dynamic South and south–center (although São Paulo divided evenly).[54] Given the region's expanding need for interprovincial labor recruitment, why was the resistance not far greater when the Rio Branco bill was introduced? Faced with the historical record, the planters could hardly have been in doubt that abolitionists, like Oliver Twist, always came back for more. Where was the cry of 'no emancipation without compensation', which had unified British, French, Dutch, and Danish colonial planters before their respective emancipations, often postponing abolition for decades? The Rio Branco Law was obviously no more than a stop-gap measure for those Brazilians who wished to 'catch up' with their century.

The behavior of the Brazilian slaveholders can be contrasted most dramatically with that of the southern United States after Lincoln's election climaxed a decade of escalating sectional crisis. In Brazil, there was some sectional revitalization of federalism in response to the developing emancipationism of the late 1860s and a resurgence of republicanism in reaction to gradual emancipation demands in 1870–1. But there seems to have been no serious move in the Brazilian South to either overthrow the regime or withdraw from it. For the period 1865–71, the limits of political mobilization on both sides are again evident, but those on the part of Brazil's dynamic southern slaveowners are more intriguing because it was their future which was being most compromised.

The historian of North Atlantic abolitions is therefore struck by the absence of a united front of the major slaveholding provinces against the gradual termination of the institution.

Supporters of reform could argue their case before thousands in the theaters of Rio de Janeiro, a city whose hinterland was one of the three most 'hard core' slave provinces, with a delegation in the Chamber of Deputies that voted by a ratio of three to one against the law.[55] (The fact that the Município Neutro deputies also voted 3 to 0 against the law indicates that as late as 1870 neither economic modernization, nor urbanization, nor slave disinvestment had yet converted the enfranchised notables of Rio.[56]) The proslavery forces did not even attempt to match the preemptive censorship against abolitionism which was so characteristic of the antebellum US South. Could New Orleans have been, like Rio, the venue for the largest antislavery debates in the entire country during the Kansas–Nebraska controversy or the 1860 election?

The disunity of slaveowners at the national level circa 1870 and the weakness of civil threats at the regional level stand in contrast not only to the southern states of the United States in the late 1850s but even to Jamaica. In 1830–1, the first mass petition for immediate emancipation in Great Britain, combined with new ministerial restrictions on the planters' disciplinary powers, triggered the most vigorous proslavery countermobilization in Jamaican history. Public assemblies throughout the island threatened secession. As a result, the last round of imperial restrictions was virtually suspended. (On the other hand, planter mobilization also helped to stimulate the most widespread slave revolt in British Caribbean history a few months later.[57]) By contrast, Brazilian elite suspicion of popular mobilization, revealed in the crisis of 1850, may again have kept planter action to a low level of nonviolent opposition in 1870. A detailed consideration of the slaveowners' perceptions and actions in 1870–2 would make an important addition to the historiography of Brazilian abolition and of the demise of New World slavery.

Popular Abolitionism

In the final phase of emancipation (1880–8), Brazil became the only non-English-speaking country to develop a full-blown, Anglo–American-style variant of antislavery. Brazilian mass abolitionism was largely confined to the years just before the Golden Law of 1888.[58] As in the British case, Brazilian emancipation was enacted by the regular legislative process, and, as in the British case, the legislature lagged behind popular action. The early phase of the Brazilian popular movement drew on Anglo–American recipes for mobilization: newspaper publicity, mass rallies, autonomous abolitionist local organizations, and the underground railroad.[59] In the final phase, however, Brazilian abolitionism was distinctive and inventive. The first public rallies in Brazil were held in theaters and concert halls rather than in the town halls, courts, churches, and chapels which formed the centers of British and US abolitionist rallies. Anglo–American antislavery mobilized in the image of familiar political structures: through town meetings, formal petitions, and deputations to the legislature. Abolitionist meetings followed the rules and discourse of parliamentary procedures. At critical moments, Anglo–American electoral campaigns had to address slavery as a central national issue. Candidates were forced to take explicit positions on slavery-related questions before aroused, and ultimately decision-making, audiences.[60] Brazilian popular mobilization apparently flowed more easily from the familiar modes of public entertainment than political organization. The proportion of programs devoted to music and poetry at rallies would probably have surprised a veteran of the British antislavery lecture campaigns. Petitioning in particular seems to have played less of a role in Brazil than in Anglo–American abolitionism. Although petitioning was permissible in both imperial Brazil and monarchical France, in neither country was it central to the antislavery movement.[61]

Yet the inventiveness of Brazilian popular abolitionism extended far beyond the public concert and the victory carnival. Perhaps because of the inertia of its political system, Brazilian abolitionism's distinguishing characteristic was to be seen in decentralized direct action. Brazil created two new patterns of direct and nonviolent action which enabled much of the nation to dismantle its slave system without any special enabling legislation, province by province, municipality by municipality, and even city block by city block.

There are few more dramatic stories in the history of abolition than the collective liberations of Ceará, Goiás, and Paraná in the mid-1880s. For the first time in Brazilian history, 'free' labor zones, analogous to the European metropolis or the US North, were established in whole provinces, as well as in urban areas of all major regions in Brazil. Popular liberations were enacted entirely outside the formal political and bureaucratic channels of the central government. When local ordinances were involved, they were likely to be ratifying what had already taken place.[62] Never before in the history of Brazil had mass political agitation simultaneously extended over the whole territory of the nation or involved so many Brazilians. As with Anglo–American abolitionism, Brazilian mobilization afforded an entrée for large numbers of people who had not previously participated in the national political process. From accounts of participation in the victory celebrations, it would also appear that far more people identified with abolition in 1888 than with the establishment of the republic in 1889.[63]

A second Brazilian form of direct action was equally original in style, scale, and effectiveness. Once de facto zones of freedom were established in provincial and urban areas, the Brazilian 'underground railroad' came into its own. By any measure it was the largest such network in the history of New World slavery. The very term 'underground railroad' is something of a misnomer. It defers too much to its US predecessor. Fleeing slaves often used the Brazilian *overground* railway itself. More often than in the United States, flight was undertaken collectively, with whole plantations being simultaneously abandoned. Abolitionist initiatives were indeed so open and so numerous that the policing system simply broke down in entire provinces.[64] In contrast to most emancipations, Brazilian planters seem to have had to conduct their counter-attacks without access to either the full panoply of official coercion or the active cooperation of the free masses.[65] At critical moments in the spread of collective flight, the cities and the armed forces proved unreliable and indeed hostile to enforcers of the law.

Although a nonviolent termination of slavery by the refusal of slaves to continue working without wages had been unsuccessfully attempted at a late stage in the British emancipation process, the inability of Brazilian officials to mobilize the coercive forces of the state was decisive in the accelerating success of the Brazilian movement. Therefore, in the late nineteenth century, Brazil came as close to demonstrating a 'withering away of the estate', despite planter opposition, as any slave system in the Americas except Haiti's.

Violence was not absent from Brazilian abolition. However, given the size of its slave population and the scale of its movement, Brazilian emancipation lies at the nonviolent end of the spectrum. In recounting the bloodiest incidents, historians indicate implicitly that violence and brutality were regarded as exceptional, not normative. Bloodshed shocked the public, rather than polarizing it. The fact that one of the worst incidents of vigilante violence involved two US veterans of the Confederate Army, who taunted Brazilian slaveowners for their lack of manhood and honor, is certainly illustrative. In this instance the government of one of the major slave provinces of Brazil was forced, by public opinion, to indict the participants, although the charges were not pursued to a conclusion.[66]

When the slaves engaged in violence, they seem to have directed their attacks toward overseers, and only occasionally toward masters. The fact that many surrendered themselves to the authorities immediately after such incidents indicates a substantial level of trust, at least in the nonbrutality of the authorities. Virtually absent are accounts reminiscent of the horrors of St Domingue, with slaves burning their plantations and eventually extending the repertoire of vengeance to the women and children of their owners. (Also entirely absent are the scenes of calculated terrorism as carried out by planters and public authorities both before and after the St Domingue uprising, including all the refinements of torture.) Even the British West Indies had experienced the largest slave uprising in their history less than two years before emancipation. The Brazilian slaves, by contrast, appear to have concluded that neither bloody insurrections nor guerrilla warfare were necessary or productive.[67]

Most significant, in comparative terms, was a fourth class of participants in the abolition process, the free masses, who seem to have played their major role in Brazilian abolition less as laborers than as political actors. It is not elite attitudes toward the laboring masses but attitudes of the nonslave masses toward slavery and abolition that most need further articulation by historians.[68] Slavery as an institution was ultimately dependent on those who were neither masters nor slaves. Masters required more than just passive acquiescence to support their system of domination. During the eighteenth century, British West Indians began to lose control over the slaves they brought to England when the London populace failed to cooperate in returning runaways.[69] But the free population in Brazil did more than refuse to condone planter violence and to tolerate the formation of free towns at the edges of the cities. Nonslaveholders participated as emissaries to the countryside, encouraging large-scale flight. They made it impossible for slaveowners and their employees to deal with resistance by ordinary policing and patrol methods. The phenomenon of abolitionists fanning out into the countryside with relative impunity was novel in plantation slave societies: elsewhere, abolitionists and slaves were usually separated by thousands of miles of water or (as in the United States) by the solidarity of a very hostile free local population. How to account both for Brazilian permeability to abolitionism and for the failure of the slaveowners to sufficiently mobilize against the British ultimatum in 1850, gradual abolition in 1871, or popular abolition in the mid-1880s remains the most intriguing political question about Brazil in comparative perspective.

RACIAL IDEOLOGY AND ABOLITION

The ideological mobilization of Brazilian masters was in one respect more analogous to that found in the British, French, and Russian empires than to that of the United States. The pro-slavery 'positive good' argument of the US South, so highly articulated in both religious and racial terms, played a relatively minor role in Brazilian political discourse. As in the Caribbean and in Russia, Brazilian planters invoked arguments based more on economic necessity, social order, and the advantages of gradual change than on slavery as a superior form of economic, racial, and social organisation.[70] This occurred despite the fact that theories of innate racial superiority and social Darwinism were attaining ever-increasing respectability in Europe and the United States during the decades just before Brazilian emancipation.

In his comparative study of US and Russian slavery, Peter Kolchin concludes that the extent to which bondsmen were considered to be outsiders affected the nature and vigor of the defense of servitude. Slaves in the US South were regarded as alien in origin and nature. They belonged to a racial minority of 'outsiders', and most members of that minority were slaves. Hence, the equation of slaves as both black and alien could be more existentially sustained. In Russia, the peasants, perceived as 'natives', were the overwhelming majority of the population.[71] The formulation of a racially based mobilization of proslavery ideology was thus dependent on the degree of overlap between racial and juridical divisions. In this respect, Brazil conceived of itself as intrinsically multiracial long after whites in the United States were determined to think of theirs as a country of white people. There was no major movement in Brazil to reexport free blacks to Africa, although some abolitionists called for racial removal in the 1830s.[72] At the very time that a movement to deport free blacks was being launched in the United States, serious proposals were still being made in Brazil to replace the threatened supply of slaves by recruiting free Africans. In Brazil, the importation of Chinese workers also continued to be seriously debated when the United States was moving to prohibit their immigration. (The unresponsiveness to Chinese immigration projects seems to have come as much from the Chinese as from the Brazilian side.[73])

In terms of race, the crucial difference between Brazil and the US South as it affected the political process was not potential sources of labor recruitment but the relative proportions of slaves and free blacks. For the politics of abolition, the 'degrees of freedom' were more important than the degrees of constriction. At the time of independence, the Brazilian free colored population was already almost a third as great as the slave population. A communally based mobilization in defense of unfree labor would presumably have required (among other things) a free majority racially distinguished from the slave population. In the Brazilian situation, slaveholders could not, at any point during the crisis of their system, mobilize either a credible political–military defense against external pressure or a sectional defense against internal pressures. In this they resembled Caribbean slave societies rather than the US South. Caribbean planters did not have the option of mobilizing free masses in the colonial areas.

The Russian situation was analogous. There were no nonserf 'masses' to mobilize in defense of the existing social structure, only peasants who identified more closely with the serfs than with the lords.[74]

In Brazil and Cuba, a mass mobilization of all free people in defense of slavery would have required risking a social revolution, appealing to a racially mixed, disenfranchised rural population. The Iberian slave polities were distinctive in having developed a free sector which was racially more mixed and socially more hierarchical than that of the United States. Politically speaking, the 'free' masses of Brazil and Cuba were the functional equivalents of the free masses of continental Europe, useless or worse to the planters in a long-term struggle against external abolitionism.[75] On the other hand, the free colored urban masses of Brazil, equally uninvolved in the national political process, were also not generally accessible to the abolitionists. Emília Viotti da Costa and June Hahner note the failure of abolitionism to attract large numbers of former slaves and free colored workers. Brazilian abolitionists were aware of this problem as late as the very eve of emancipation.[76]

Comparative analysis therefore seems to highlight the significance of political organization and demography in accounting for Brazil's path toward abolition. The planters of the US South, accustomed for two generations to sharing decision making with the vast number of individuals owning few or no slaves, had forged a regional identity resting on economic and racial solidarity which Brazilian planters had never, and probably could never have, replicated in their hierarchical regime of 'notables'.[77] Lacking both the political and racial building blocks for a slaveowner *herrenvolk* democracy, the planters tacked cautiously within the narrow boundaries of their political system against the combined pressures of a shrinking demographic base, an expanding national economy, and a contemptuous free world. In 1830, Brazil was still one of many unenfranchised, illiterate, unindustrialized nations with a large, permanently bound labor force. Two generations later, it stood virtually alone. Regional divestment, urban-rural and crop redistributions, concentration of slave ownership, and above all Brazil's increasing divergence from the Western model of civil liberty weighed against the status quo.

As conflicts of interest and outlook grew wider the consensus of slaveholders eroded. As their numbers dwindled, demoralized slaveowners faced an increasingly popular abolitionism without the potential for a racially grounded antiabolitionism.[78]

It is important to note that not all Brazilian planters subscribed to the European model of civil progress implied in the antislavery ideology. Moreover, the high price of slaves until the final wave of abolitionist mobilization indicates that Brazilian slaveowners, like their counterparts in Cuba, conducted their slave enterprises within relatively short-term time horizons, even after the implementation of gradual emancipation legislation. But three final observations about Brazilian ideology and self-identification are worth making. First, as in much of Latin America, a Europeanized social future, including the demise of slave labor, remained the dominant forecast of Brazil's destiny. Second, some of those who most vigorously rejected the model of Europeanization in other respects (for example, Sílvio Romero's *História da literatura brasileira* in 1888), emphatically supported an egalitarian and fusionistic racial destiny for Brazil.[79] And third, the 'patriarchal' vision of Brazil did not fade away without many nostalgic literary evocations. However, no school arose in Brazil during the nineteenth century which successfully crystallized that diffuse counteregalitarian mentality into a cultural identification with the perpetuation of slavery. Brazilian planters remained closer to the ideological norm of the Americas than to that of the antebellum US South.

CONCLUSION

Brazilian abolition seems to offer some intriguing contrasts with abolition in other slave societies. There was no profound revolutionary crisis in Brazil before 1888 to stimulate the extension of abolitionist appeals to broader social sectors, and not until the Paraguayan War of the 1860s did Brazil experience military problems even slightly analogous to those which accelerated moves toward abolition in much of Spanish America. At the same time, a distinctive political characteristic of the process in Brazil was the inability of planters to rally the country around the principle of slavery, and to use exogenous threats as a catalyst for effective countermobilization. The midnineteenth century was a moment when nationalism was emerging throughout the West as a rallying point for intensive state-building. The US South linked its bid for national independence to its 'peculiar' institution. The southerners failed to achieve nationhood, but only after a massive military and political mobilization of resources. Brazil, however, never developed an interregional nationalism against the British in 1830–50, or a regional nationalism against gradual abolition in 1865–72 and immediate abolition in 1880–8. Brazilian slaveowners lacked the tradition of, or the means for, orderly popular mobilization, and they clearly hesitated to construct such mechanisms before 1850, when slavery was still a consensual institution. Even a planter-led popular mobilization entailed the risk of losing control over the political process at a time when abolitionist attacks were as yet cautious and sporadic. Much like the French *pays légal* of the 1830s and 1840s, Brazilian planters clung to a regime of notables.

Concentrating on the planters and the cities, students of Brazilian abolition have paid less attention to the rural free population. Only recently has there been a historiographical focus on small-scale cultivators which would allow historians to speculate why the free poor were never asked to defend their traditional community on a scale or intensity equal to what occurred in the southern United States. Did planters never even imagine appealing to the rural free masses in favor of slavery because of their distrust of their neighbors? Was the relationship between slaves and free people in the rural areas different in Brazil because of the cumulative effect of manumissions and the consequent existence of bonds which did not exist in the racially more polarized US South? Or did southern US planters play a role that had no parallel in Brazil – shielding nonslaveholders from low wages and the risks of the world market, and guaranteeing the free masses considerable comfort by contemporary world standards?[80] Although historians duly note tensions which existed between yeomen and slaveowners of the antebellum United States, the relative strength of the southern commitment to slavery remains a critical benchmark for comparisons with Brazil. The South had become politically democratic for the white male population in the half-century before the secession crisis, and the abolition of slavery was not on the southern political agenda because no substantial group of southern nonslaveholders elected men to state office who fundamentally challenged that institution. To secessionist leaders, nonslaveholders may still have posed political problems, but in the struggle that followed far more was asked of them and given by them than the planters of Brazil requested even of themselves.

Equally significant in Brazil was the dearth of nonelectoral alternatives through which to popularize antislavery. The Catholic church, like established churches everywhere, proved very reluctant to mount any challenge to the status quo in general, and to Brazilian slavery in particular. There was no counterpart in Brazil to the dissenting denominations of early nineteenth-century Anglo–American society that facilitated local and regional abolitionist organization. As the French case also showed, a highly centralized religious authority was not easily accessible to abolitionist penetration.

Newspapers and other means of mass communication were alternative sources of mobilization. Here one could note the limitations of Brazilian literacy and a weaker national communications network compared with Anglo–America. In general, Brazil lacked the national network of voluntary associations which so impressed de Tocqueville in the nineteenth-century United States. Brazilian abolitionists therefore had to improvise along different lines. The result was to add some startling pages to the history of slavery. In the last phase, it was an extraparliamentary abolitionism, forcing a reluctant legislature and a demoralized planter elite to verify a fait accompli.

In the end, two major characteristics force themselves on our attention. Brazil presents us with an example of a planter class which, though it successfully resisted termination of the slave trade for two generations, could not after that successfully mobilize against abolitionism, even with a constitution made to order for its domination of society. Secondly, Brazil offers us the case of an urban abolitionist movement which had to effect emancipation primarily through ingenious ad hoc agitation and temporary coalitions of diverse groups largely outside the political framework. Abolitionists could dismantle slavery but could not dictate any of the terms of social change beyond that. The Golden Law, like the first French emancipation decree in 1794, was a tersely worded death warrant for a collapsing structure. The very brevity of the law revealed the limits of Brazilian abolitionism – no compensation for the slaveholders, no welfare for the slaves, no planned transition to a new order. In this respect, it is noteworthy that the major monographs on Brazilian abolition discuss postabolition Brazil almost exclusively in terms of the fate of former masters and former slaves, and are virtually silent on the continuity and impact of antislavery. The abolitionist movement appears to have dissoved even more quickly than it had formed. There was no concerted movement to aid the freed slaves, and neither was Brazilian abolitionism an ideological and organizational exemplar for a multitude of other reform mobilizations as in Anglo–America, although it did have echoes in the *jacobinos'* agitation of the 1890s.[81] Brazil offered its slaveholders little leverage to resist external pressures for liberation, but it provided the abolitionists with little leverage to follow through after slave emancipation. Brazilian abolition seems to have lacked the means of political reproduction.

NOTES

Also published in R. Scott, S. Drescher *et al.*, *The Abolition of Slavery and the Aftermath of Emancipation in Brazil* (Durham, NC, 1988), pp. 23–54; and in P. Finkelman, ed., *Comparative Issues in Slavery*, 18 vols. (New York, 1989) XVIII, pp. 69–100; trans. Jaime Rodrigues 'A Abolicão Brasileira em Perspectiva Comparativa', *História Social*, 2 (1995), pp. 115–62.

I would like to thank George Reid Andrews, Stanley L. Engerman, Frederic C. Jaher, and Rebecca J. Scott for their helpful suggestions.

1. Adam Smith, *Lectures on Jurisprudence*, R. L. Meek, D. D. Raphael, and P. G. Stein, eds. (Oxford, 1978), p. 181; G. T. F. Raynal, *Histoire philosophique et politique des établissements et du commerce des européens dans les deux Indes*, 7 vols. (Geneva, 1780).
2. David Brion Davis, *Slavery and Human Progress* (New York, 1984), p. 298; Robert E. Conrad, *The Destruction of Brazilian Slavery, 1850–1888* (Berkeley, 1972), p. 71. It was, of course, European-oriented members of Brazil's elite who felt most strongly that their country was humiliated

by slavery and that it was a nation which played no role in building civilization or prosperity. See Joaquim Nabuco, *Abolitionism: The Brazilian Antislavery Struggle*, Conrad, trans. (Urbana, 1977), pp. 4, 108, 117–18. On the influence of European and US models on Brazilian concepts of progress and slavery, see Richard Graham, *Britain and the Onset of Modernization in Brazil, 1850–1914* (Cambridge, 1968), esp. chs. 6 and 10, and 'Causes for the Abolition of Negro Slavery in Brazil: An Interpretive Essay', *HAHR*, 46(2) (May 1966), pp. 123–37; and E. Bradford Burns, *The Poverty of Progress: Latin America in the nineteenth century* (Berkeley, 1980), ch. 2.

3. For good general syntheses which treat Brazilian abolition primarily as a mopping-up operation by modernizers, see C. Duncan Rice, *The Rise and Fall of Black Slavery* (London, 1975), pp. 370–81; and Edward Reynolds, *Stand the Storm: A history of the Atlantic slave trade* (London, New York, 1985), pp. 90–2. The historiography of Brazilian abolition is sometimes elaborated within a broader model of social progress in which the inherent inefficiencies or 'contradictions' of slave labor utilization converge with other causes of technological and economic retardation. For a good example of this 'convergence' thesis, see Emília Viotti da Costa, *The Brazilian Empire: Myths and histories* (Chicago, 1985), pp. 148–71 and *Da senzala à colônia* (São Paulo, 1966), ch. 5. The issue of the efficiency of slave labor is sometimes not distinguished from the issue of technological progress in general. See the perceptive discussion in Peter L. Eisenberg, *The Sugar Industry in Pernambuco: Modernization without change, 1840–1910* (Berkeley, 1974), ch. 3 and n. 18 below.

4. But recently, see da Costa, *The Brazilian Empire*, ch. 6; Robert Brent Toplin, *The Abolition of Slavery in Brazil* (New York, 1972); and Conrad, *The Destruction*. The pervasive structural foundations of Brazilian slavery are presented in greatest detail by Stuart B. Schwartz, *Sugar Plantations in the Formation of Brazilian Society: Bahia, 1550–1835* (Cambridge, 1985), esp. ch. 16 and Robert Wayne Slenes, 'The Demography and Economics of Brazilian Slavery: 1850–1888' (Ph.D. dissertation, Stanford University, 1975).

5. Carl Degler, *Neither Black nor White: Slavery and race relations in Brazil and the United States* (Madison, 1986); Frank Tannenbaum, *Slave and Citizen: The Negro in the Americas* (New York, 1947); Stanley Elkins, *Slavery, a Problem in American Institutional and Intellectual Life* (Chicago, 1959); Arnold Sio, 'Interpretations of Slavery: The Slave Status in the Americas', *Comparative Studies in Society and History*, 7(3) (April 1965), pp. 289–308; David Brion Davis, *The Problem of Slavery in Western Culture* (Ithaca, 1966), chs. 8 and 9. Even Rebecca J. Scott who analyzes Cuba, the other late emancipation in Latin America, makes only a passing reference to Brazil (*Slave Emancipation in Cuba: The transition to free labor 1860–1899* [Princeton, 1985], p. 284). However, Scott recognizes the comparative opportunities afforded by the Cuban and Brazilian cases in her comments on Eric Foner, *Nothing But Freedom: Emancipation and its legacy* (Baton Rouge, 1983), in 'Comparing Emancipations: A Review Essay', *Journal of Social History*, 20(3) (Spring 1987),

pp. 565–83, esp. pp. 574–5. See also Davis, *Slavery and Human Progress*, pp. 294–7. For US–Brazilian comparisons, see also Eugene D. Genovese, *The World the Slaveholders Made: Two essays in interpretation* (New York, 1969), part one.

6. Leslie Bethell, *The Abolition of the Brazilian Slave Trade: Britain, Brazil, and the slave trade question, 1807–1869* (Cambridge, 1970), p. 385; Conrad, *The Destruction*, pp. 65–9. On the US linkage between abolition of the trade and decline of slavery, see n. 14 and 25 below. For a summary of economic models used to explain the rise and continuation of the slave trade, see Robert W. Fogel, *Without Consent or Contract: The rise and fall of American slavery* [New York, 1989], ch. 1.

7. David Eltis, *Economic Growth and the Ending of the Transatlantic Slave Trade* (New York, 1987), App. A.

8. David Eltis, 'The Traffic in Slaves between the British West India Colonies, 1807–1833', *Economic History Review*, 25(1) (February 1972), pp. 55–64. For the urban decline in the British West Indies after 1807, see B. W. Higman, *Slave Populations of the British Caribbean, 1807–1834* (Baltimore, 1984), pp. 92–9; for the urban decline in Brazilian slavery, see Mary C. Karasch, *Slave Life in Rio de Janeiro, 1808–1850* (Princeton, 1987), p. 61, Table 3.1.

9. Compare the percentage reductions in numbers of slaves in Ceará, Pernambuco, Bahia, and Sergipe in Brazil's Northeast from 1864 to 1884 with those in the northern tier of US slave states – Maryland, Virginia, Kentucky, and Missouri – from 1840 to 1860. Also compare Conrad, *The Destruction*, App. 3 with Bureau of the Census, *Negro Population in the United States, 1790–1915* (New York, 1968), p. 57, Table 6. On the general shift of slave labor toward the south–center, see also da Costa, *Da senzala*, pp. 132–7. For the impact of slave trade constriction and concentration of ownership in Cuba, see Jordi Maluquer de Motes, 'Abolicionismo y resistencia a la abolición en la España del siglo XIX', *Anuario de Estudios Americanos*, 43 (1986), pp. 311–31, esp. pp. 323–4.

10. Conrad, *The Destruction*, pp. 65–9. According to Conrad, the nonimporting areas of the Northeast might have begun to consider the potential increase of prices for their slaves even before abolition of the trade in 1850–1. The antiabolitionist 'Barbacena Project' of 1848 was opposed by some representatives of the northern provinces. See Conrad, 'The Struggle for the Abolition of the Brazilian Slave Trade: 1808–1853' (Ph.D. dissertation, Columbia University, 1967), pp. 289–303. Some indication of the impact of slave trade abolition on the northeastern planters is the fact that, circa 1850, slaves normally outnumbered free laborers on Pernambuco sugar plantations by more than 3:1. But 'by 1872 free workers outnumbered slaves in all occupational categories, from 14:1 in unskilled labor and 5:1 in agricultural labor, to 3:1 in domestic labor'. See Eisenberg, *The Sugar Industry*, p. 180.

11. Conrad, *The Destruction*. Just ten years earlier, in 1874, 14 of the 21 provinces of Brazil had slave populations of more than 10 percent, and only 2 had levels of under 5 percent. In the declining regional

economy of the Northeast slavery became a relatively more urban phenomenon. See Thomas W. Merrick and Douglas H. Graham, *Population and Economic Development in Brazil, 1800 to the Present* (Baltimore, 1979), pp. 69–71.
12. Slenes, 'The Demography and Economics', chs. 6–8. See also Merrick and Graham, *Population*, pp. 82–3.
13. Toplin, *The Abolition of Slavery*, p. 162.
14. The relative demographic decline of US slavery was different from that of Brazil and the Caribbean area primarily in that it was drawn out over a longer period because of a high rate of natural reproduction. Without African imports to match free European migration in the half century before 1860, that decline became progressively more apparent. Peter Kolchin's recent comparison of US and Russian masters interestingly concludes that the US slaveowners were both more entrepreneurial and more paternalistic than their absentee and rentier-minded counterparts among the Russian nobility. The decisive division of slaveowner 'mentalities' therefore occurs between the capitalist–paternalist masters of the US South, on the one hand, and the capitalist–rentier lords of Russia, on the other. In Brazil, too, entrepreneurial and paternalistic characteristics are arguably combined. Kolchin, *Unfree Labor: American slavery and Russian serfdom* (Cambridge, MA, 1987), pp. 126–56, 357–61; Slenes, 'The Demography and Economics', ch. 11.
15. One can measure the comparative volatility of these two most important slave-importing areas of the Americas during the last generation of the transatlantic slave trade. During the period 1826–50, Brazil's average quinquennial importation of slaves was 192 500. The widest deviations from this mean were a low of 93 700 (or 49 percent of the average) in 1831–5, and a high of 257 500 (or 139 percent) in 1846–50. By contrast, Cuba's quinquennial average importation in the period 1836–60 was 53 500 slaves. The widest deviations from this mean were a low of 15 400 (or 29 percent) in 1846–50 and a high of 95 700 (or 179 percent) in 1836–40. Three of Cuba's five quinquennia fell outside the Brazilian extremes. The same general conclusion holds if the time span is doubled. During the 50 years between 1801 and 1850, Brazil's highest quinquennial average importation (1846–50) was 2.75 times greater than its lowest (1831–5). During the 50 years between 1811 and 1860, Cuba's highest quinquennial average (1816–20) was 8.3 times greater than its lowest (1846–50). My calculations are derived from figures in Eltis, *Economic Growth*, pp. 243–4, Tables A.1 and A.2.
16. Between 1862 and 1877, the slave populations of Cuba's eastern provinces declined by 77 percent, while in the great sugar provinces of the West the decline was only 31 percent. The differential impact of the Ten years War had much to do with this contrast. As in Brazil, however, where the staple prospered, slavery persisted. See Scott, *Slave Emancipation*, p. 87.
17. Eltis, *Economic Growth*, part two. As late as 1830, Brazilians turned toward interior recruitment of Indian labor when British pressure

seemed to threaten importations from Africa. See Conrad, 'The Struggle for the Abolition of the Brazilian Slave Trade', pp. 216–17.
18. Eltis, *Economic Growth*, p. 14. In the cases of the British West Indies, the US South, and Cuba the claims of a contradiction between slavery and technology, or slavery and productivity, are challenged by recent economic analysis. For Cuba, see Scott, *Slave Emancipation*, pp. 26–8; for the British West Indies, see R. Keith Aufhauser, 'Slavery and Technological Change', *The Journal of Economic History*, 34(1) (March 1974), pp. 34–50; for the United States, see Robert William Fogel and Stanley L. Engerman, *Time on the Cross: The economics of American Negro slavery*, 2 vols. (Boston, 1974), I, ch. 6 and Fogel, *Without Consent or Contract*, ch. 3. The discussion of Brazilian slavery within a historiographical framework of rise, prosperity, and decline is well illustrated in Stanley J. Stein's excellent *Vassouras: A Brazilian Coffee County, 1850–1900: The roles of planter and slave in a plantation society*, reprint ed. (Princeton, 1985), part 4. This approach was recently challenged by Slenes, 'Grandeza ou decadência? O mercado de escravos e a economia cafeeira da Província do Rio de Janeiro, 1850–1888', in *Brasil: História econômica e demográfica*, Iraci del Nero da Costa, ed. (São Paulo, 1986), pp. 103–55. Free labor, however constricted, was a second best alternative among the most entrepreneurial Paulistas. See Verena Stolcke and Michael M. Hall, 'The Introduction of Free Labour on São Paulo Coffee Plantations', *Journal of Peasant Studies*, 10(2) (January 1983), pp. 170–200. The Paulista planters of Rio Claro continued to buy slaves until the eve of abolition. See Warren Dean, *Rio Claro: A Brazilian plantation system, 1820–1920* (Stanford, 1976), p. 52.
19. Perhaps those who came closest to independence were the US southern elites in 1776 and 1860, and the Brazilian planters at the time of national independence. Only the 1860 southerners, however, explicitly claimed that their peculiar institution might operate indefinitely against the free labor trend in the Western world.
20. See the essays by Maria Luiza Marcílio and Dauril Alden, in *The Cambridge History of Latin America*, Bethell, ed. (Cambridge, 1984–), II, pp. 37–63 and 602–60, esp. pp. 602–12 and 649–53. The abolition of slavery in Portugal in 1773 had no visible impact on its economic growth. Even at the end of the age of Brazilian slavery, Portugal remained 'backward by any contemporary standard', and 'only the eye of faith could detect much in the way of economic development there'. Eric J. Hobsbawm, *The Age of Empire 1875–1914* (New York, 1987), p. 18.
21. See Alexis de Tocqueville, *Democracy in America*, 2 vols., J. P. Mayer, ed. (Garden City, NY, 1969), pp. 345–8. It should be noted that in *per capita* terms the railroad milage of the US South was almost equal to that of the North just before secession. See Fogel and Engerman, *Time on the Cross*, I, pp. 254–5. Graham argues that, compared with Brazil, the slave South of the United States was far from being economically underdeveloped. See 'Slavery and Economic Development: Brazil and the United States South in the Nineteenth Century',

Comparative Studies in Society and History, 23(4) (October 1981), pp. 620–55. On the development of railway building in the south–central provinces of Brazil, see C. F. van Delden Laerne, *Brazil and Java: Report on coffee-culture* (London and The Hague, 1885), ch. 8. In 1889, the provinces of Rio de Janeiro, São Paulo, and Minas Gerais had 65 percent of Brazil's total railroad milage. See Mircea Buescu, 'Regional Inequalities in Brazil During the Second Half of the Nineteenth Century', *Disparities in Economic Development Since the Industrial Revolution*, Paul Bairoch and Maurice Levy-Leboyer, eds. (London, 1981/1985), pp. 349–58. For an interpretation of Brazilian slave trade abolition tied closely to the political economy of transportation development, see Luiz-Felipe de Alencastro, 'Répercussions de la suppression de la traite des noirs au Brésil', delivered at the Colloque International sur la Traite des Noirs, Nantes, 1988.

22. See Genovese, *The Political Economy of Slavery: Studies in the economy and society of the slave south* (New York, 1965), p. 227.
23. Slenes, 'The Demography and Economics', pp. 145 ff. See also Anyda Marchant, *Viscount Maúa and the Empire of Brazil* (Berkeley, 1965), p. 269.
24. On Cuban slave concentration, consult Eltis, *Economic Growth*, pp. 190–3 and Scott, *Slave Emancipation in Cuba*, pp. 86–90.
25. Conrad, *The Destruction*, pp. 65–9. In the case of the United States, the movement of slaves toward the frontier initially strengthened the institution by providing for the entrance of new slave states to match the free labor settlement to the north. Later, the movement of slaves out of some border states aroused anxiety about a declining political commitment to slavery in those areas. I designate as convergence theories of abolition those which assume that all or most of the major economic variables (labor, credit, technology, productivity, profitability) combined with each other to induce the abolition process. For a recent elaboration of the general case against such a role for economic growth in slave zones of the nineteenth-century Americas, see Eltis, *Economic Growth*, passim.
26. See Temperley, 'Capitalism, Slavery, and Ideology', *Past and Present*, 75 (May 1977), pp. 94–118. See Davis, *Slavery and Human Progress*, p. 110, for the classic Emersonian comparison of freedom and slavery. It should be noted that even the antebellum South compared favorably with Europe on a number of indexes of 'progress.' See Fogel and Engerman, *Time on the Cross*, I, p. 256 and II, pp. 163–4.

Regional comparisons indicate that immigrant flows could hardly have played the same role in Brazil as they did in the United States after 1850. At the time that Brazil passed its gradual emancipation law, the overwhelming proportion of its foreigners resided in those provinces with the highest percentage of slaves—exactly the inverse of the situation in the United States on the eve of its Civil War (see Table 5.1).

Regarding urban areas, a relatively high level of slave labor (either within urban areas or in the adjacent province) does not appear to have been a major deterrent to those foreigners who located themselves in Brazil. Four major cities with substantial foreign populations had substantial slave populations. They were also located in provinces with above median slave populations (see Table 5.2).

27. Regarding manufacturing, slaves in Rio de Janeiro were beginning to be incorporated into nineteenth-century factory employment when the abolition of the slave trade and the coffee boom drained slaves from the cities to the plantation areas. See Eulália M. Lachmeyer Lobo, 'A história do Rio de Janeiro' (Rio de Janeiro, 1975), mimeograph, as summarized in Merrick and Graham, *Population*, p. 51; see also Karasch, 'From Porterage to Proprietorship: African occupations in Rio de Janeiro 1808–1850', in *Race and Slavery in the Western Hemisphere: Quantitative studies*, Engerman and Genovese, eds. (Princeton, 1975), pp. 369–93. This is consistent with Claudia Dale Goldin's conclusion that slaves in the US South were drawn out of urban areas by strong agricultural demand (*Urban Slavery in the American South, 1820–1860: A quantitative history* [Chicago, 1976], conclusion).
28. Genovese, *The World the Slaveholders Made*.
29. Kolchin, *Unfree Labor*, pp. 49–51.
30. Genovese, *The World the Slaveholders Made*, p. 14.
31. For the first wave of abolition see Davis, *The Problem of Slavery in the Age of Revolution, 1770–1823* (Ithaca, 1975), chs. 1 and 2. For Haiti, see C. L. R. James, *The Black Jacobins: Toussaint L'Ouverture and the San Domingo Revolution* (London, 1938). For the Spanish Caribbean, see, *inter alia*, Arthur F. Corwin, *Spain and the Abolition of Slavery in Cuba, 1817–1886* (Austin, 1967).
32. Seymour Drescher, 'Two Variants of Antislavery: Religious Organization and Social Mobilization in Britain and France, 1780–1870', in *Anti-Slavery, Religion, and Reform: Essays in memory of Roger Anstey*, Christine Bolt and Drescher, eds. (Folkestone and Hamden, 1980), pp. 43–63; see also Chapter 2 in this volume.
33. Drescher, *Capitalism and Antislavery: British mobilization in comparative perspective* (London and New York, 1987), ch. 3; Davis, *The Problem of Slavery in the Age of Revolution*, pp. 137–48.
34. On Spanish American abolition in general see Leslie B. Rout, *The African Experience in Spanish America, 1502 to the Present Day* (New York, 1976); Herbert S. Klein, *African Slavery in Latin America and the Caribbean* (New York, 1986), ch. 11. For Venezuela, see John V. Lombardi, *The Decline and Abolition of Negro Slavery in Venezuela, 1820–1854* (Westport, 1971). For Argentina, see George Reid Andrews, *The Afro-Argentines of Buenos Aires, 1800–1900* (Madison, 1980). For Cuba and Puerto Rico, see Corwin, *Spain*, esp. chs. 6–15 and David R. Murray, *Odious Commerce: Britain, Spain and the abolition of the Cuban slave trade* (Cambridge, 1980). Maluquer characterizes Spanish policy toward Cuban slavery and the slave trade before 1860 as a politics of silence and inaction. See 'Abolicionismo', Maluquer, pp. 312–22. A shadowy abolitionist society appears to have been formed in Madrid in 1835 (*ibid.*, pp. 315–16). As with its more public Parisian counterpart, the probable stimulus was the implementation of British slave emancipation in the West Indies in 1834. See Drescher,

Dilemmas of Democracy: Tocqueville and Modernization (Pittsburgh, 1968), pp. 155–66.
35. Bethell, *The Abolition of the Brazilian Slave Trade*, p. 313; Eltis, *Economic Growth*, pp. 114–19, 140–1, 214–16.
36. Eltis, *Economic Growth*, pp. 243–4. Table A.1.
37. See Drescher, *Econocide: British Slavery in the Era of Abolition* (Pittsburgh, 1977), p. 181.
38. Bethell, *The Abolition of the Brazilian Slave Trade*, pp. 380–3.
39. A. J. R. Russell-Wood, ed., 'Preconditions and Precipitants of the Independence Movement in Portuguese America', *From Colony to Nation: Essays on the Independence of Brazil* (Baltimore, 1975), p. 38.
40. Bethell, *The Abolition of the Brazilian Slave Trade*, pp. 335–41. Eisenberg, *The Sugar Industry*, p. 152, speaks of the British action as an 'unreturnable insult'. On the other hand, there was agitation in the late antebellum South to reopen the slave trade, in order to diffuse ownership and support for slavery.
41. See Toplin, *The Abolition of Slavery*, ch. 1; Genovese, *The World The Slaveholders Made*, pp. 75–93; Elizabeth Fox-Genovese and Eugene D. Genovese, in *Fruits of Merchant Capital: Slavery and bougeois property in the rise and expansion of capitalism* (New York, 1983), pp. 47–8, reiterate their emphasis on the basically seigneurial labor relationships of northeastern Brazil, but their conclusion (pp. 394–5) places all slaveholders within the same antimodern category. For a discussion of alternative models of planter behavior, see Slenes, 'The Demography and Economics', ch. 1.
42. Compare Slenes, 'The Demography and Economics,' ch. 11 and Gavin Wright, *The Political Economy of the Cotton South: Households, markets, and wealth in the nineteenth century* (New York, 1978), p. 37, and n. 9 above.
43. Peter F. Dixon, 'The Politics of Emancipation: The movement for the abolition of slavery in the British West Indies, 1807–1833' (D. Phil. thesis, Oxford University, 1971); Eltis, *Economic Growth*, pp. 8–9.
44. Higman, *Slave Populations of the British Caribbean 1807–1834* (Baltimore, 1984), pp. 67–9.
45. Wright, *The Political Economy of the Cotton South*, pp. 34–5. On southern fears of a class division between slaveholders and 'no-property men,' see Michael F. Holt, *The Political Crisis of the 1850s* (New York, 1978), pp. 225–6, 246–7. See also Paul D. Escott, *Many Excellent People: Power and privilege in North Carolina, 1850–1900* (Chapel Hill, 1985), ch. 2.
46. For the United States, see Fogel and Engerman, *Time on the Cross*, pp. 92–4; for Brazil, see Eltis, *Economic Growth*, p. 186. Slave prices in Pernambuco almost doubled during the 1850s, and reached an all-time peak in 1879 (Eisenberg, *The Sugar Industry*, p. 153). 'In coffee-producing Rio de Janeiro, moreover, nominal slave prices rose even higher, and reached a peak in the late 1870s at a level nearly four times that of the early 1850s. The coffee sector's greater prosperity allowed the coffee planters to outbid the sugar planters for slaves, and after 1850 Pernambuco began shipping slaves south' (*ibid.*, p. 156).

47. Wright, *The Political Economy of the Cotton South*, pp. 146–7.
48. Conrad, *The Destruction*, ch. 5
49. *Ibid.*, pp. 87–90; Corwin, *Spain*, ch. 13.
50. See Toplin, *The Abolition of Slavery*, ch. 2, pp. 92–6.
51. Arthur Zilversmit, *The First Emancipation: The abolition of slavery in the North* (Chicago, 1967), pp. 212–13.
52. See Corwin, *Spain*, pp. 144–71, 294–9; Scott, *Slave Emancipation*, chs. 2 and 3; and Murray, *Odious Commerce*, ch. 14.
53. Conrad, *The Destruction*, pp. 91–3. Even as late as 1884–5 in northeastern Brazil it was possible for small elite electorates of less than a thousand voters to nearly defeat Nabuco's candidacy for the Chamber of Deputies. Nabuco was defeated in his bid for reelection in Recife in 1886. See Carolina Nabuco, *The Life of Joaquim Nabuco* (Stanford, 1950), chs. 11 and 13.
54. Conrad, *The Destruction*, p. 301, Table 21.
55. *Ibid.*, p. 93.
56. *Ibid.*, p. 301, Table 21. As late as 1870, more than one fifth of Rio's population was still slave. Karasch, *Slave Life*, p. 61, Table 3.1.
57. See Dixon, 'The Politics of Emancipation', p. 203; Drescher, *Capitalism*, pp. 106–8; Mary Turner, *Slaves and Missionaries; The disintegration of Jamaican slave society, 1787–1834* (Urbana, 1982), p. 163.
58. Conrad, *The Destruction*, ch. 9; Toplin, *The Abolition of Slavery*, ch. 3.
59. Conrad, *The Destruction*, 193 ff.; Toplin, *The Abolition of Slavery*, pp. 86 ff.
60. Drescher, *Capitalism*, ch. 4.
61. *Ibid.* For recourse to the theaters see, *inter alia*, Carolina Nabuco, *The Life of Joaquim Nabuco*, p. 74. The Spanish abolitionist society, like that of Brazil, initially tended to favor artistic appeals rather than conventional political rallies (Maluquer, 'Abolicionismo', p. 324). Spanish and Cuban abolitionism also adopted petitioning as a tactic in the early 1880s. See Corwin, *Spain*, p. 309.
62. Conrad, *The Destruction*, ch. 11.
63. Toplin, The *Abolition of Slavery*, p. 256; June E. Hahner, *Poverty and Politics: The urban poor in Brazil, 1870–1920* (Albuquerque, 1986), p. 72.
64. Toplin, *The Abolition of Slavery*, ch. 8; Conrad, *The Destruction*, ch. 16.
65. Toplin, *The Abolition of Slavery*, p. 213. Planter organization against abolitionism in the northeastern provinces seems to have come very late, in reaction to the Ceará abolition of 1883–84, and the planters themselves were deeply divided over the question of gradualism vs. immediatism (Eisenberg, *The Sugar Industry*, pp. 166–70). The Cuban path to abolition followed the earlier Spanish American pattern. Until after the US Civil War the Spanish military presence and political repression made open proslavery and nonviolent antislavery mobilization impossible. See Robert L. Paquette, *Sugar is Made with Blood* (Middletown, Conn. 1988). The Ten Years War for national independence in 1868–78 opened the door to selective manumissions for military purposes and partial abolition in areas under rebel control. But if insurrection accelerated gradual abolition in the 1870s, the

settlement of the conflict inhibited popular agitation in favor of the final emancipation legislation of the 1880s.

66. Toplin, *The Abolition of Slavery*, pp. 212–13; Conrad, *The Destruction*, pp. 256–7. The most violent series of confrontations apparently occurred in the plantation areas of Campos in Rio de Janeiro, where fazendeiro-led gangs resorted to 'lynch law'. Even in Campos, however, the power of the slaveowners was openly challenged by abolitionist leaders and armed defenders. See Toplin, *The Abolition of Slavery*, pp. 220–2.

67. Compare James, *The Black Jacobins*, with the accounts in da Costa, Toplin, and Conrad. On the Jamaica uprising in 1831–2, see Michael Craton, *Testing the Chains: Resistance to slavery in the British West Indies* (Ithaca, 1982), ch. 22.

68. Relations between the elite and the free poor in the countryside are analyzed for one locality in Hebe Maria Mattos de Castro, *Ao sul da história* (São Paulo, 1987), but the link between those relationships and the national political process of abolition has not yet been systematically investigated.

69. Drescher, *Capitalism*, ch. 2.

70. Toplin, *The Abolition of Slavery*, p. 131; Conrad, *The Destruction*, p. 167. Spanish defenders of the status quo, like their Brazilian counterparts, stressed economic necessity or political constraints, not the intrinsic superiority of slavery. See Maluquer, 'Abolicionismo', p. 321. Compare with the Anglo–American positive good argument in Marcus Cunliffe, *Chattel Slavery and Wage Slavery: The Anglo–American context 1830–1960* (Athens, GA, 1979), ch. 1.

71. Kolchin, *Unfree Labor*, pp. 170–91.

72. Repatriationist ideologies based on racism were not absent in Brazil. Early abolitionists in particular argued for the removal of former slaves from Brazilian society. See Manuela Carneiro da Cunha, *Negros, estrangeiros: Os escravos libertos e sua volta à África* (São Paulo, 1985), pp. 84–6. Once again, it is the lower level of collective action for these ends in Brazil compared with the United States that is striking.

73. Conrad, *The Destruction*, pp. 33–6, 133.

74. Kolchin, *Unfree Labor*, pp. 177–83.

75. The role of the Spanish 'Volunteers' as defenders of the imperial connection and the traditional political economy during Cuba's Ten Years War may demonstrate how ethno–cultural interests could be linked to a defense of slavery. Communal or cultural loyalties could even cause slaves to reject outsiders with abolitionist agendas as they did in some British islands during the Anglo–French conflict of the 1790s. On the British Caribbean, see David Geggus, 'The Enigma of Jamaica in the 1790s: New light on the causes of slave rebellions', *William and Mary Quarterly*, 44(2) (April 1987), pp. 274–99, esp. p. 292 and Craton, *Testing the Chains*, pp. 180–210. In both cases, however, the planters were auxiliaries to imperial military forces.

76. Da Costa, *Da senzala*, p. 438. Hahner emphasizes that color–class divisions within Brazil's cities contributed to the fact that 'most dark-skinned Brazilians did not participate in the formal abolitionist

movement', and class divisions were evident within the movement as well (*Poverty and Politics*, pp. 67–68).

77. A majority of Brazil's population in the early nineteenth century was deemed 'marginal', both to the economy and to the polity. See Caio Prado, Jr., *The Colonial Background of Modern Brazil*, Suzette Macedo, trans. (Berkeley, 1967), pp. 328–32; and Michael C. McBeth, 'The Brazilian Recruit during the First Empire: Slave or Soldier?', in *Essays Concerning the Socioeconomic History of Brazil and Portuguese India*, Alden and Dean, eds. (Gainesville, 1977), pp. 71–86. There appears to have been considerable ideological, as well as social, continuity of attitudes toward the *desclassificados* in the colonial period. See, e.g., Laura de Mello C. Souza, *Desclassificados do ouro: A pobreza mineira no século XVIII* (Rio de Janeiro, 1982) and Andrews, 'Race and the State in Colonial Brazil', *Latin American Research Review*, 19(3) (1984), pp. 203–16. Compare this configuration of class relations with Fletcher M. Green, *Democracy in the Old South, and Other Essays* (Nashville, 1969), ch. 3; Steven Hahn, *The Roots of Southern Populism: Yeoman farmers and the transformation of the Georgia upcountry, 1850–1890* (New York, 1983), p. 99; Fox-Genovese and Genovese, *Fruits*, ch. 9; and John McCardell, *The Idea of a Southern Nation: Southern nationalists and Southern nationalism, 1830–1860* (New York, 1979), pp. 319–35.

78. On late divisions among the planters, see Toplin, *The Abolition of Slavery*, ch. 9 and Conrad, *The Destruction*, ch. 16.

79. Burns, *The Poverty of Progress*, pp. 62–3, 79.

80. Hahn, *The Roots of Southern Populism*, p. 88; Fox-Genovese and Genovese, *Fruits*, p. 250; Holt, *The Political Crisis of the 1850s*, ch. 8. For the relatively high wages of free laborers in the South, see Fogel, *Without Consent*, p. 155.

81. Brian Harrison, 'A Genealogy of Reform in Modern Britain', in Bolt and Drescher, *Anti-Slavery*, pp. 119–48 and *Peaceable Kingdom: Stability and change in modern Britain* (Oxford, 1982), ch. 8. In isolated instances, the Brazilian abolitionist mobilization did have an organizational and ideological spillover effect analogous to that of the English mass mobilizations a half century earlier. Rio typographers sought to transfer the abolitionist momentum into 'a new abolition for the *free slaves*', and their intensive participation in the abolitionist victory celebration played a role in stimulating a more militant labor organization. See Hahner, *Poverty and Politics*, pp. 86–7. Indeed, the rarity of successful social movements in Brazil may have contributed to the psychological impact of abolition among skilled workers (*ibid.*, 87).

6 British Way, French Way: Opinion Building and Revolution in the Second French Slave Emancipation (1991)*

After a generation of enormous scholarly fecundity, interest in the history of the Atlantic slave system shows no signs of subsiding. It now constitutes one of the liveliest fields of comparative and interdisciplinary history. A recent flurry of centennial activities marking the history of abolition will probably continue unabated into bicentennial commemorations in 1991 of the St Domingue slave uprising and the quincentenary in 1992 of Columbus's voyage.[1] This luxuriant centennialization is grounded in a distinctive set of historical benchmarks. Little more than two centuries ago, personal bondage was the prevailing form of labor in most of the world. Personal freedom, not slavery, was the peculiar institution. In 1772, Arthur Young estimated that only 33 million of the world's 775 million inhabitants could be called free. Adam Smith offered a similarly somber ratio to his students and prophesied that slavery was unlikely to disappear for ages, if ever.[2]

During the next century, a transformation occurred in the Atlantic slave labor system. It required profound changes in historical and moral frames of reference as well as in political and economic institutions. Once conceived primarily in terms of a Whiggish history of human progress, the transition entailed the development of complex and countervailing expansions of slavery and antislavery.[3]

From the limited defeat of slaveholders in England in 1772 through the passage of Brazil's 'Golden Law' of emancipation in 1888, every seaboard society in the Atlantic world was

---

*The American Historical Review, 96(3) (June 1991), pp. 709–34. © 1991 The American Historical Association.

affected by interdependent contractions and extensions of slavery. One Western polity after another eventually abolished its African slave trade. In the Danish and British dominions and the United States of America, the trade ended in the first decade of the nineteenth century. The Dutch, French, Brazilian, and Cuban slave trades closed in the second, fourth, sixth, and seventh decades of the century, respectively.[4] Chattel slavery itself began to be abolished in the non-plantation northern United States in the 1780s. French colonial slavery was temporarily (and in Haiti, permanently) abolished in the 1790s. On the Spanish–American mainland, the emancipation process, initiated during the wars of liberation, extended over half a century. British colonial emancipation came in the 1830s and Swedish, Danish, and French emancipation followed in the 1840s. Slavery was ended in the US South and the Dutch American colonies in the 1860s and in Cuba and Brazil in the 1880s.[5]

Although each of these processes has generated its own historiographical tradition, the most significant ones, quantitatively and qualitatively, deal with the American, British, and French cases.[6] In world-historical terms, British abolition is important both because of its predominant role in the ending of the Atlantic slave trade and because its slave emancipation became a stimulus and foil for other polities. Slaveholders, abolitionist societies, and political elites viewed British emancipation as the 'great experiment' in the transition from slave to free labor.[7]

The history of British imperial slavery reflects the perception of British abolition as a long-term structural process. Historians now routinely discuss variables of demography, economics, political economy, ideology, class relationships, popular organization, and slave resistance in an international context. The principal historiographical issues revolve around the significance of countervailing tensions and ecological constraints on actions and outcomes.[8]

In contrast, French historiography has been dominated by the most successful slave uprising in the Americas. For historians of slave resistance and of French slavery, the transformative power of revolutionary violence emerges as the pivotal moment in the history of Atlantic slavery. The first French emancipation decree in February 1794 was not only contingent on but was constrained by the forces of self-liberated West Indian slaves on the one hand and the impending British invasion on the other. The synergy of the French revolutionary ethos and the slave armies of St Domingue are often treated as the turning points in the history of slave resistance and emancipation.[9]

Compared to British abolition, the most distinctive characteristic of the first French emancipation was the disintegration of metropolitan power over the course of events. From 1789, the contested question of policy toward slavery and the slave trade was inextricably entangled in struggles for colonial self-rule and racial equality. Planters' hopes for political autonomy and economic liberalization were combined with deep fears of metropolitan abolitionism and colonial free colored demands for civil rights. For three years, the colonial interest succeeded in keeping the slave trade and slavery off the agenda of the Constituent and Legislative assemblies despite the enormous social and ideological transformatioin within France.

Metropolitan antislavery was at best the concern of a small minority, increasingly distracted by bitter struggles over the direction and survival of the French Revolution. Among the revolutionaries themselves, bitter internal divisions tended to fragment perspectives on colonial developments. The disintegration of the political order and the economic system in the islands became a source of mutual accusation. Only a few months before the emancipation decree of 16 Pluviôse, An II (February 4 1794), responsibility for the devastation of St Domingue was still one of the counts of treason leveled against Brissot de Warville and other antislavery Girondists.[10]

The fate of the first French slave system was determined more by the changing colonial and international situation than by metropolitan mobilization. The major juridical steps toward slave emancipation were decreed by Civil Commissioners in the colonies as emergency legislation. Although the ideological ground for 16 Pluviôse had been prepared by fiery public debates and pamphlet wars, emancipation in the colonies is best understood as a desperate response to wartime contingencies. In the wake of the revolution, this first emancipation remained, in the eyes of both metropolitan elites and later historical assessments, 'The Formula for Loss of Control'.[11]

Accounts of the second French slave emancipation, forty-six years after Napoleon's restoration of the institution, have remained heavily indebted to the revolutionary heritage. The abolition of 1848 superficially replicates the heroic and spasmodic French pattern of 1794. That the 1848 emancipation was punctuated by a slave uprising in Martinique, just before the arrival of the Parisian decree, reinforces the concept that the ending of the second French slavery derived from the same interaction of metropolitan and West Indian upheavals.

These twin secenarios of revolutionary transformation have reduced analytical incentives to investigate the historical context of the second French emancipation. There is a strong temptation to dismiss pre-1848 opinion building in a causal dissociation between July Monarchy procrastination, dominated by an inconclusive debate over the British model of emancipation, and the revolutionary efficacy of February 1848. As David Brion Davis has remarked, French emancipation 'came in a reassuringly French way, at the hands of the left, led by [Victor] Schoelcher, an atheist untainted by British evangelicalism, echoing the events of the Revolution of 1789, and in response to both domestic and colonial turmoil'.[12]

A somewhat different assessment of the second French emancipation has recently emerged. In a Marxist analysis, Robin Blackburn suggested a close analogy between French antislavery in the 1840s and British antislavery in the 1830s. During the late July Monarchy, the French mobilized against slavery in the same constellation of forces that impelled British parliamentary reform and slave emancipation. Louis Philippe's *juste milieu* echoed the context of late Hanoverian Britain. French antislavery on the eve of 1848 is conceived as the French analog to British antislavery, as part of a broad-based uprising against an oligarchic regime. Guizot is the French counterpart to William Pitt or George Canning, Louis Philippe to William IV. Paralleling the British agitation for metropolitan political reform, the abolition of slavery in 1848 was part of the resurgence of metropolitan agitation that led from the banquets of 1847 to the February Revolution. In the context of class polarization, the French antislavery campaign was 'only a descant to this chorus of agitation, but both had a momentum dangerous for the prevailing order'.[13]

Blackburn, however, relied more on ideological inference than empirical reference. He posited an increasingly interlocking combination of ideologies and social movements, with massive working-class unrest, the mobilization of the frustrated 'political classes', and mass abolitionist agitation fusing into a mutually reinforcing juggernaut in February 1848. The bourgeois revolutionary leadership, aware of its historical obligation and 'the pressure of a new type of class struggle', had 'to reassure the proletarian masses that its ideals were not to be degraded by the sordid interests of slaveholders'.[14]

An alternative picture of the relationship of prerevolutionary abolitionism to emancipation has been presented by Lawrence Jennings. In 1846–7, some French abolitionists decided to adopt modes of agitation that had proven successful in Britain for more than half a century. Without an efficient religious and organizational network, the hastily composed French campaign 'could not possibly succeed'. British-inspired efforts to persuade French departmental councils to call for an end to slavery had no 'measurable effect on either these bodies or the Paris government'. The 'apparent victory' of the British approach 'was a shallow one'. French emancipation did not flow organically from a popular agitation, concluded Jennings, but coincidentally from the actions of an elite vanguard that displaced the *pays legal* notables. The decision to eradicate slavery in 1848 was more analogous to the Convention's spasm of emancipationism in 1794 than to the long-agitated British emancipation of 1833.[15]

How are we to relate these two images of French abolitionism, the one popular, driven by class hostility, cumulative in impact, and analogous to its British exemplar in structure, with just a Gallic revolutionary touch, the other minuscule, discontinuous, and reenacted in the incidental mode of the Great French Revolution? All recent accounts concur that one of the prevailing characteristics of organized French antislavery was its elitism. For most of its history between 1788 and 1848, French abolitionism was distinguished by its narrow political, social, and geographical base. It fits into what might be called the Continental, as distinguished from the Anglo–American, variant of antislavery. The prevailing features of Anglo–American antislavery were its relatively massive appeal, decentralized organization, and extended duration. Citizens in the United States and Great Britain attempted to develop associational mechanisms for bringing popular pressure to bear on hostile economic interests and hesitant agencies of the state. They used mass propaganda, petitions, newspapers, public meetings, lawsuits, boycotts, and electoral campaigns to develop an antislavery constituency. They aimed at inclusiveness of membership, welcoming participants who were otherwise excluded from the ordinary political process by reason of gender, religion, race, or class.[16]

French abolitionism, like most of its Continental counterparts, usually had very different characteristics. Its leaders were reluctant to seek mass recruitment. They preferred to work quietly on elaborate projects of abolition with the sanction of the state, often acting as brokers between external pressure groups (including British abolitionists) and their own slaveholding interests. Usually concentrated in the capital or chief commercial center of the nation, Continentals preferred to work in established governmental channels.

French antislavery, however, operated under peculiar historical conditions that made it somewhat anomalous within the 'Continental' variety. In 1794, revolutionary France briefly incorporated slave liberation into a general program for revolutionary warfare. In 1802, Napoleon gave France the distinction of being the only Western nation to restore its overseas slave system. His restoration failed only in Haiti, where a brutal racial war resulted in the final expulsion of the French. Post-Napoleonic France was therefore heir to a complex history that linked French overseas initiatives to revolutionary violence, bloody restorations, military debacles, and colonial economic disaster. Postrevolutionary French abolitionism could not adopt the nationalist triumphalism so characteristic of its counterpart across the English Channel.

Even nonviolent mass agitation seemed threatening. Until the very eve of the February Revolution, abolitionists proposed plans of emancipation that were responsive to both slaveowner and conservative sensibilities. They made allowance for delays in implementation, for compensation funds, and for the continuity of plantation labor. Immediate and complete emancipation was not even considered as an abolitionist program until less than a year before the Revolution of 1848. The abolitionism that emerged during the Constitutional Monarchy (1815–48) was as cautious in its recruitment as in its programs. With a limited membership, the movement was dominated by parliamentary and bureaucratic notables. Membership fees were high. Neither workers nor women were invited to join. One active abolitionist, Cyrille C. A. Bissette, was apparently kept at arm's length because he was an *homme de couleur*.[17]

French abolitionism was also 'Continental' in being responsive primarily to exogenous (that is, British) initiatives. The impetus for the original 'Amis de Noirs' in 1788 had been the formation of the London Abolitionist Society the year before. The first emancipation decree of 1794 came largely in response to a combination of unmanageable slave uprisings and British military threats in the Caribbean. Napoleon restored slavery immediately after the peace treaty of Amiens (1802), which assured the uninterrupted flow of his troops to the colonies. Napoleon's own decree of slave-trade abolition during his 'Hundred Days' in 1815 was designed to forestall British hostilities. The revival of organized French abolitionism 1834 was again a direct response to the implementation of British slave emancipation. The rationale for considering emancipation plans during the following decade stemmed from strategic concerns with potential 'revolutionary' contagion from the British colonies and fears of British revolutionary warfare in the event of an Anglo–French conflict. Until the eve of the February Revolution, British policy was the principal exogenous stimulus to French action or inaction.[18]

***

The narrow confines of abolitionist mobilization for most of the July Monarchy set clear limits on the ideology and the pace of moves toward slave emancipation. On the one hand, a few eminent abolitionists made periodic motions in Parliament. The result was a sequence of decorous governmental investigations, piling up data and suggesting a range of legislative strategies. The abolitionists backed up their parliamentary activities with intermittent publications and articles in sympathetic Parisian neswpapers. There was no strong link between individual abolitionist deputies and their local constituents, who were never informed of their representatives' abolitionist initiatives in electoral campaigns. Abolitionist parliamentary activity remained confined to prominent members in Paris.[19]

On the other side of the emancipation question lay the colonial interest. It was headed by paid delegates, who sat as members of the two parliamentary chambers by virture of their metropolitan constituencies. The delegates of the four slave colonies (Bourbon, French Guiana, Guadeloupe, and Martinique) were in continuous contact with their respective colonial councils. They usually managed to present a united front on issues involving potential changes in the slave system. The colonials also had allies in the French provinces, especially among merchants in the Atlantic port cities. In this regard, the colonial interest was more national than that of the abolitionists. Through their delegate-legislators, the colonists possessed a lobby in the legislature and at the Ministry of the Navy and the Colonies.

The colonial interest also parried the propaganda thrusts of the abolitionist press. Given the restraints on political association, the press of the July Monarchy was the main channel of public opinion. The colonial delegates subsidized sympathetic editors through heavy subscriptions and direct grants to publicists. They compiled accounts of sums disbursed and assured their overseas paymasters that such subsidies ensured news and views favorable to the slaveholders' perspective. Occasional shifts of press support were carefully registered.[20]

The prominent French abolitionists wanted to avoid even the appearance of a radical or 'fanatical' movement. They considered themselves engaged in a rational dialogue with the colonists and other metropolitan notables. They were committed to plans that ensured social order and sugar production during the transition from slavery to free labor. The idea of orderly and rational social change was embodied in a middle-of-the-road newspaper's declaration that French slavery would not be brought to an end by a revolutionary *journée* at the Bastille or at the Hôtel del Ville. The emancipation plan suggested by the French abolitionist members of the governmental commission of 1840–2 allowed for a significant delay in implementation and constraints on the participation of slaves in the full system of metropolitan civil rights. French abolitionists anticipated the proletariazation of ex-slaves as the lasting solution to plantation labor problems.[21]

If abolitionists did not generally accept the colonial hypothesis that slave property was as absolute and natural as any other, they agreed that slavery was a form of legal property nurtured by the metropolis. Planters who had invested capital in the security of French law were entitled to some indemnification for losses suffered through the eradication of that form of property. The language of property and the principle of no emancipation without indemnification was shared throughout the elite. In Parliament, abolitionists were reminded that the financial situation of the French government did not allow for an addition of 150 to 250 million francs to the national debt in order to provide compensation for slaveowners. New fiscal embarrassments, of course, continually succeeded old ones: the burdens of building the railroad system, of fortifying Paris, of conquering Algeria, of economic recession.[22]

A decade after British emancipation, there was a feeling of satisfaction on the pro-slavery side. The colonial delegates presented a united front against any major change. The colonial councils believed that their strategy of blanket resistance had proven successful against a variety of abolitionist proposals. The government was determined to reject any legislation that would incur a heavy financial cost. Baron Mackau, the minister of the navy and the colonies, was disposed to defend the colonial status quo. Metropolitan capital was again flowing outward to the colonies.[23]

By the mid-1840s, the French abolitionists themselves regarded the British precedent as a very mixed argument in favor of abolition. On the one hand, British emancipation had been completed without violence and with a rise in the ex-slaves' standard of living. On the other hand, there had been a decrease in plantation labor and output, counteracted only by an expensive policy of metropolitan protection for colonial sugar. As fears of revolution and war subsided in France, the economic difficulties of the British colonies seemed increasingly important. Abolitionists were aware that the momentum of the previous decade was slipping away from them[24]

So apparent were the political constraints on abolitionist initiatives that André Jardin and A.-J. Tudesq used the politics of slave emancipation as the prime example of how the July Monarchy could be paralyzed by opposing pressure groups. A decade of French discussion produced only the 'preparatory' Mackau Laws of 1845. These laws provided for little more than the slaves' right to purchase their own freedom and for increased religious instruction. According to Jardin and Tudesq, a pro-slavery minority had thwarted both governmental and public opinion favorable to emancipation by purchasing a sympathetic press.[25]

Given the constraints of indemnification and potential labor problems, moreover, it is by no means clear that the government wished to move toward emancipation. The Guizot administration was insistent about the Gordian knot of public funding. Nor did any likely alternative administration promise a different policy. Adolphe Thiers, the principal leader of the opposition in the 1840s, was, if anything, more unsympathetic than Guizot to any imitation of the British experiment. In his view, the recently freed British colonies were a total failure, an example of the 'base and barbarous idleness offered by Negroes left to their own devices'.[26]

Regarding Jardin and Tudesq's observation about a pro-emancipation public, however, there is no evidence that opinion favored rapid legislative action. A decade after British emancipation, the French colonial delegates and the abolitionists agreed that the French public gave no indication that emancipation should be a political order of the day. Far more typical was the press's praise of the government's 'sage lenteur' in approaching a complex problem. Guizot seemed more concerned with the public's hostility toward British activity against suspected French slavers than with French attitudes toward colonial slaveholders.[27]

Finally, as a result of the expanding French conquest of Algeria, there was far more territory with slaves under French sovereignty by the mid-1840s than there had been at the time of the July Revolution in 1830. In the name of internal security, General Bugeaud, the French military commander in Algeria, refused to take action against indigenous slaveholders. He even protested against interfering with the Arab slave trade, which he viewed as a principal means of expanding trade with the African interior. The frustrated tone of the British abolitionist press, the embarrassed correspondence of the French abolitionist society, and the complacent correspondence of the colonial delegates with their employers all testify to a regression from the modest abolitionist momentum of the 1830s.[28]

***

The first attempt to imitate 'British' methods of agitation came from outside the world of the notables under the sponsorship of a working-class newspaper. A few months after Guizot's firm indication that the state of finances prohibited a decision on emancipation, the skilled artisans of Paris launched a drive for signatures. Petitions were initially gathered at printing shops. The Parisians were joined by workers of Lyons, who emphasized the sharper class consciousness of their signers by designating themselves 'proletarians'. Although they evoked the example of their sans-culottes predecessors in the Great Revolution, the petitioners carefully emphasized the reformist intention of their campaign. They claimed the right to use the legal mechanisms of constitutional government for the pacific solution of slavery – for 'the organization of labor for *all*', and for 'the emancipation of all'. The explicit model for such extraparliamentary mobilization was the 'genius' of British petitioning. The workers noted that French rights of association and collective demonstration, still severely impeded by law and administrative surveillance, now had to be developed. The petitioners even accepted as valid the notables' concern that slavery should not be followed 'by vices and idleness' or by 'pillage and murder – savage liberty'.[29]

Although it had the approval of individual members of the French Abolitionist Society, the petition was explicitly a workers' artifact. The signers included carpenters, cabinet-makers, mechanics, clock makers, tailors, sculptors, jewelers, rope makers, foundry workers, laundresses, dressmakers, milliners, house painters, stoneworkers, sawyers, artists, and engravers. Both the Parisian 'ouvriers' and the Lyons 'prolétaires' welcomed female signatories. By Anglo–American standards, the results of the canvass were quite modest. Fewer than 9000 signatures were presented to the Chamber of Deputies (7126 from Paris and 1704 from Lyons).[30]

To the colonial interest, the reception of the petitions was disturbing but not devastating. The petitions were the opportunity for antislavery speeches in the Chambers and for a renewed press discussion. But the petitioners, by virtue of their highly localized geographical and social origins, did not represent the limited electorate, the 'legal country', whose opinion counted most in the July Monarchy. As Thomas Jollivet, Martinique's delegate, summarized it, the Chamber of Deputies, in forwarding the petitions to Minister Mackau, had reaffirmed its general approval of the principle of emancipation but not its immediate implementation. Jollivet concluded that both the Chambers and the public were still better disposed toward the colonies than they had been before the furor over the right-of-search controversy in 1841–2.[31]

The only legislative sequel to the discussions of slavery in 1844 was the 'Mackau Laws' of 1845. Given Mackau's statement that no further 'preparatory' legislation was contemplated, the colonial agents assumed that these laws were the limit of concessions to abolitionist demands. The workers' petitions had not appreciably altered the prospects of French abolitionism, and a subsidized press could still be counted on to parry the abolitionist press. Early in 1846, the abolitionists were still referring to the 'regression' of the emancipation question.[32]

At this juncture, the British Anti-Slavery Society played a major and perhaps crucial role in suggesting, exhorting, and supporting another petition campaign in 1846–7. In 1844–5, British emancipationists increased their missions to France. They expanded their geographical contacts in the hope of stimulating support from provinces outside Paris. They succeeded in convincing a Montauban professor, Guillaume de Félice, to compose an abolitionist pamphlet calling for a British-style popular movement and to organize provincial committees. They underwrote the distribution of Félice's pamphlet and some of the expenses of Cyrille Bissette, the most active petition gatherer in Paris.[33]

Quantitatively, the results of the second campaign were hardly more impressive than the first. Just over 10 700 signatures were submitted to the two Chambers in the spring of 1847. Even at its relatively modest beginning, sixty years before, British popular abolitionism had outperformed the second French petition campaign. In 1788, the first abolitionist petition from Manchester alone, a city with fewer than 50 000 souls, produced the same number of the signatures as came from all of France sixty years later. By 1833, one man in five was signed up for immediate emancipation in Great Britain. Less than one in a thousand had yet done so in the French campaign of 1846–7. Organizationally, the French abolitionist movement still remained divided. The elite abolitionist society would not even print the petitions for the 1846 campaign. In these respects, the diagnosis of July Monarchy abolitionism, as characterized by Jardin, Tudesq, and Jennings, is confirmed.[34]

Despite the quantitative contrast with its robust British counterpart, however, the French movement was clearly operating in a new way. In conscious imitation of the British model, the French religious network began to make itself accessible to abolitionist action. French Protestants were already heavily overrepresented in the 1846–7 campaign and promised to remain a major conduit for a new campaign in 1848. Even more striking was the entrance of the Catholic clergy and popular press into the antislavery movement. As late as 1845, Catholic officialdom assumed a general attitude of strict neutrality on the question of emancipation. In France, both the theological curriculum and the training of colonial clergy encouraged consideration of slavery as secondary to pastoral duties. When urged by British abolitionists to use its influence in favor of emancipation in 1842, the archdiocese of Paris responded by reiterating the need for preparing slaves for freedom through religious instruction.[35] A dramatic change occurred during the 1846–7 campaign. Bissette took the emancipation petition to a large clerical retreat meeting in Paris. Hundreds of the Catholic clergy, including three bishops, signed up. A few months later, the archbishop of Paris seemed to remove impediments on further clerical participation. The liberal Abbé Dupanloup offered assurances that 20 000 clergy would sign an 1848 petition. The adherence of Louis Veuillot's *L'Univers* indicated that this figure was well within the power of Catholic mobilization. In the spring of 1847, his newspaper had managed to accumulate almost 90 000 pro-clerical adherents to a petition on educational legislation.[36]

By the fall of 1847, the third petition campaign was becoming more systematic than its predecessors, with the creation of a bureau of correspondence and the distribution of printed petition forms. Three petition-gathering agencies (Protestant, Catholic, and secular radical) were operating in addition to the elite abolitionist society. Frenchwomen were asked to sign their own petitions, following the precedent of their British counterparts a generation before. French abolitionism seemed poised to become a popular movement.

***

Did this nascent social movement have any appreciable effect in forwarding emancipation? Jennings argued no, citing the still obvious divisions in the movement, its lack of measurable impact in the provinces, and, above all, the government's refusal to take any major initiative between the presentation of the 1847 petitions and the overthrow of the regime the following year. David Brion Davis agreed that as late as 1847 there was no prospect of hastening slavery's demise. Blackburn, by contrast, emphasized the broad social aspirations, if not achievements, of the 1847 petition, the temporal coincidence between the banquets and the abolitionist campaign, and the fact that the February Revolution subsequently empowered radicals who identified themselves with emancipation in the colonies.[37]

The alleged linkage between metropolitan French and colonial reformism is far weaker than Blackburn assumed. If one were to try and measure the salience of abolitionism on the basis of the public banquet campaign of 1847, the evidence is actually nil. Of the many issues evoked by the banqueters, colonial slavery was conspicuous by its absence. Just one week before the revolution, the deeply abolitionist *Le Semeur* lamented:

> Hasn't the reader more than once observed that in the reformist banquets, where everything is discussed, our poor slaves haven't obtained the least space? The lot of the working classes in our country has elicited generous advocacy, and we are as happy about that as anyone. But the incomparably more abject condition of the blacks in our Antilles has been left in the shadows. Someone informed us that an honorable Deputy would speak in favor of the abolition of slavery at the Lille banquet, but we recall how this banquet was so torn apart by political disputes that the slaves lost the chance for the one mention that was to have been made of their miserable fate ... When it moves beyond the Chambers to address the masses, the opposition is an echo, and when it ignores the cause of the slaves, it is because France itself is but feebly stirred.[38]

Le Semeur concluded that, contrary to their British forerunners, the reformers were not being pushed by popular interest to make even symbolic obeisance to the issue of emancipation. Blackburn's linkage of abolitionism to the metropolitan political revival of 1847 therefore remains stranded at the weakest level of causal analysis–temporal coincidence. The question of emancipation was no more prominent on the reformist agenda of 1847 than it had been in the *cahiers de doléances* of 1789.

A comparison between the petitions of 1844 and 1847 also shows that Blackburn's faith in the linkage of rising working-class militancy to rising abolitionist agitation is not borne out by social analysis. The petition of 1844 had been around 90 per cent working class, its signers pointedly designating themselves as workers and proletarians. Although the majority of signers in 1847 were still residents of Paris and Lyons, the petitions had lost their working-class character. Those who headed up many of the petitions identified themselves as members of the elite: electors, mayors, magistrates, merchants, businessmen, clergy, lawyers, pharmacists, professors, and military officers.[39]

Yet there is abundant evidence that the campaign of 1846–7 did have a measurable impact in France and indicated a renewal of abolitionist momentum on an unprecedented scale. Every year, the general councils of French departments could issue *voeux*, or resolutions, on current political or social issues. The table shows that there had been small surges of departmental resolutions in favor of emancipation following British slave emancipation (1834) and again following the ending of British colonial apprenticeship (1838). Conciliar *voeux* then dropped off in the early 1840s. The first 'workers' petition of 1844 found no echo among the departmental notables. Then, in 1847, the number of abolition resolutions suddenly rose to twice the level of the previous peak years of 1838–9. Sixteen departments took action on slavery for the first time. Never had more than a quarter of the nation's departments simultaneously taken a stand in favor of slave emancipation (Table 6.1).[40]

The most immediate political effect of the petitions was registered beyond the metropolis. The government felt the need to anticipate the rising tide of abolition in some direction. During the previous parliamentary session, the two Chambers had received, and forwarded to the minister of war, petitions of notables requesting the abolition of slavery in Algeria. There

Table 6.1 Resolutions in favour of emancipation presented by Conseils-Généraux of French departments, 1835–47

Date	Number	Number from new departments
1835	5	5
1836	6	1
1837	5	3
1838	12	3
1839	11	1
1840	6	1
1841	7	1
1842	4	0
1843	4	0
1844	3	0
1845	3	0
1846	4	1
1847	24	16

Note: *Of the twenty-five councils that considered a motion on emancipation in 1847, one voted to table the motion, twelve supported immediate or very rapid emancipation, and twelve favoured emancipation while insisting on suitable compensation, precautions, or guarantees of labor. This is a revision of the earlier breakdown of *voeux* in Drescher, *Capitalism and Antislavery*, p. 226.
Source: ANSOM, Généralités 156 (1301), 'Voeux des Conseils-Généraux pour l'abolition', 1835–47.

the matter rested until April 24 1847, when the popular petition was presented to acclaim in the Chamber of Deputies.

The same day, the minister of war dispatched a note to Marshal Bugeaud, the conqueror and governor-general of Algeria, indicating the government's need to bring the slave trade and slavery to a speedy end in the colony. The minister's haste was visible in the letter itself. Almost one-third of the original text (including a portion in which the minister undiplomatically confessed that he disagreed with the judgment of the abolitionists) was struck out and replaced by less self-revelatory wording.[41]

Although he acknowledged the difficulties that such a transformation would create for the colonial administration, the minister concluded that 'the state of opinion' and British diplomatic successes in obtaining abolitionist promulgations in Tunis, Cairo, and Constantinople made it prudent for France to take preemptive action. Over the vitriolic opposition of the stunned and outraged governor-general, the minister dispatched the draft of an ordinance of emancipation on June 2. It was worded to prohibit immediately slave trading and slaveholding by Europeans and Algerian Jews and, in deference to Bugeaud's objections, to postpone abolition among the Muslim population to no later than 1852.[42]

The most important indicator of the petition's impact, however, can be observed in the reaction of the colonial delegates and colonists. In the months leading up to the presentation of the petitions, the delegates viewed the campaign with increasing anxiety. The convergence of press support for emancipation seemed particularly ominous when reinforced by a petition of 800 French priests meeting in Paris. Even before the petitions reached the Chambers, Delegate Jollivet sent word that 'public opinion is turning against us'. All the Parisian 'organs of liberalism', from *Le Constitutionnel* to *La Réforme*, were 'preaching emancipation'. The press 'anticipates our defeat and the Tribune [the Chambers] will complete it'.[43]

The discussion of the petition in the Chamber of Deputies on April 24 and 26 1847, was a disaster for the colonists. The cautious resistance of Minister Mackau was swept aside. Jollivet was driven from the rostrum in derision. Traditional defenders of the colonists on both the nationalist Left and the legitimist Right remained silent. Catholic leaders spoke in favor of the petition, and even the conservative Center, wrote Jollivet, 'abandoned us'. Martinique's humiliated delegate warned that abolition had just advanced by a decade. Within weeks, Mackau, abandoned by Guizot, resigned.[44]

If Jollivet's accounts of the situation decomposed into jeremiads after his personal humiliation, the assessment of Guadeloupe's delegate was even more somber. E. de Jabrun had been away from Paris during the debates and was not personally devastated by the parliamentary *journées*. However, he witnessed the 'movement of ideas' stirred up in the provinces by the Chamber's emotional discussion and later reflected in the department resolutions: 'All France would have applauded some kind of emancipation, had the Chamber been voting on it.'[45]

What struck the delegate most forcefully was that the indemnity question no longer offered unassailable security against serious legislation. A fundamental component of the 'British' model of emancipation might itself be compromised if the government sought to ingratiate itself further with parliamentary abolitionists. Long-dismissed alternatives, such as the freeing of slave children at birth, or of slaves illegally imported after the abolition of the French slave trade, were again being mooted. Such piecemeal abolition would mean emancipation 'at the cheapest possible price' for the legislators. The planters were facing the combined risk of reduced indemnification and decimated labor gangs.[46]

The colonists, hitherto united in opposition to emancipation, broke ranks. Some delegates urged a continuation of the old tactics and simply demanded more funds in order to counteract the abolitionist gains in the press. Others regarded the old strategy as bankrupt. Bourbon's council failed to supply increased press funds. French Guiana was too poor to furnish further resources for a major counteroffensive in the metropolis. And Guadeloupe, responding to its delegate's advice, passed over into the ranks of those favoring total and simultaneous emancipation.

Guadeloupe's delegates and some colonial residents in Paris decided that the petitions were literally the handwriting on the wall. The next wave might inundate the whole system. Guadeloupe's delegates therefore proposed a series of bold preventive measures. They first contacted the old eminent abolitionists, Broglie and Tocqueville, who had quietly withdrawn from abolitionist activity. The delegates also advised Guadeloupe's council to do an about-face and to outflank all partial plans by a demand for total emancipation, the regulation of labor, and an indemnity.[47]

The distance traveled by some French slaveowners in 1847 was most startling at the ideological level. Until the mid-1840s, the French colonial interest aligned itself unambiguously with the sanctity of property. Colonists grounded their claims to indemnification on the absolute and natural right of property, as well as on French positive law. A regime that so clearly relied on degrees of property to distinguish a 'legal country' of electables and voters from the vast mass of less privileged citizens was sensitive to such proprietary claims. The Guizot government's main reason for not proceeding to emancipation was the necessity for fair compensation, a precondition unchallenged by any potential heads of governments during the July Monarchy. Plantation slaveholders had envisioned transitions solely within the ambit of capitalism.

For more than a decade before 1847, however, French socialists had been suggesting that abolitionism was a false path to slave emancipation. Abolitionists looked no further than integrating colonial labor into the European capitalist model, producing emancipation-cum-proletarianization. Socialists with colonial links began to devise schemes to bypass *laissez-faire* abolitionism by an 'organization of labor'. This would give the colonial worker 'social protection' and guarantee a labor supply to the employers in communities or corporations styled after Charles Fourier.[48]

The colonial planters and their delegates in Paris were aware of the socialist critique of abolition. Not one delegate or colonial council, however, so much as suggested a collectivist alternative to agents of government or to any of the various parliamentary commissions on French emancipation before the abolitionists turned to mass petitioning. Nevertheless, in the summer of 1847, many slaveholders in Paris and in Guadeloupe began to espouse the Fourierist language of labor. A majority of the Colonial Council of Guadeloupe adopted a plan of 'association' to supersede slavery. The plan would avert the threat of piecemeal metropolitan emancipation by 'full and indemnified' emancipation. Association would also presumably avoid the progressive disorganization of plantation labor by maintaining the plantation and sugar production as the foundation of the colonial economy. Finally, association might obviate certain difficulties encountered in Britain's colonies, where after emancipation the wages system had increased cash-flow problems and reduced plantation labor.[49]

The Guadeloupe plan did offer some resemblance to the Fourierist organization of labor. It was a sharecropping system, providing for a tripartite division of proceeds from production: one-third to labor, one-third to capital, and one-third to 'talent'. It contained detailed rules for collective discipline, as well as welfare provisions for childhood, old age, and illness. But the plan stipulated that the shares for both managerial 'talent' and for capital would accrue to the planters, who would retain authority over the new 'organizations of labor'. It also stipulated an initial five-year period during which the ex-slaves could not leave their new associations.[50]

The appeal of the Guadeloupe planters to metropolitan opinion was one of the most remarkable in the history of slavery. Nowhere else in the Americas did planters come so close to adopting the rhetoric of socialism in contemplating the transition to free labor, complete with a five-year labor plan. Where but in Paris on the eve of 1848 could slave planters have even imagined that such 'advanced' rhetoric might gain them more sympathy than hostility?

Yet, during the final months of the July Monarchy, the impact of both the Guadeloupe plan and the abolitionist agitation seemed equally meager in terms of new legislation. Mackau's successor, the duc de Montebello, gave private assurances that the government was not preparing a major move toward emancipation. Indeed, he indicated a firm resolve not to be swept up in public opinion. When the Guadeloupe plan, accepting the principle of immediate emancipation, was presented as an address to the king, it was coolly received. The plan was declared too 'advanced', and those colonial delegates who had rejected Guadeloupe's great leap forward felt vindicated in having stood on their traditional proprietary defense. At the opening of the Chambers session in 1848, the king's speech made no reference at all to colonial slavery.[51]

Martinique's council decided to cling to the slave system as long as the metropolis would allow it. Although slave discipline had deteriorated in response to metropolitan agitation, sugar exports from both Guadeloupe and Martinique in 1847 were up sharply over the previous year. Some of that increase might be attributed to the generally better harvest conditions of 1847, but, even so, the increase in the two French islands was clearly greater than it was in British Dominica, which lay between them. Moreover, in 1847, the British West Indies began to show the devastating effects of the dismantling of British imperial sugar protection. Bankruptcies were rampant, and the Jamaican and Barbadian banking systems were collapsing.

Regarding Algeria, the minister of war was still assuring Guizot, in February 1848, that the emancipation ordinance drafted nine months before was receiving his closest attention. At the same time, he reminded his colleague, who had to respond to pressure from the British ambassador, that the situation was a delicate one. The Muslim population seemed to regard possession of slaves as a right. 'The interests of domination enjoin us not to brusquely change a state of things which we implicitly promised to respect upon the capitulation of Algiers.' Against the customs of the Muslim majority across the Mediterranean, Bugeaud's earlier dismissal of abolitionism in France retained residual weight. Where, Bugeaud had demanded to know, were the voices of millions of peasants and workers in France aligned with those of the liberal 'théoriciens'?[52]

Yet the question of emancipation was no longer what it had been as late as 1844, when a small number of eminent abolitionists, colonists, and ministers engaged in a leisurely discourse with no real need to act. All of the protagonists were now keenly aware of the rising potential of pressure from without. If 10 000 petitioners could hasten the departure of a minister and increase the plausibility of 'partial' emancipations, what might successive petitions of 100 000 or more not achieve? By the fall of 1847, the French abolitionists had settled into the perspective of British social movements. The government was henceforth to be assailed, year in and year out, by a rising tide of petition signers and propaganda. The political costs of defending the status quo increased. As one colonial delegate asked, how long would the government be willing to sacrifice its comfort for the sake of the colonists?[53]

Thus the abolitionists prepared to launch the 'third wave' with enthusiasm. By the beginning of the 1848 session, they already claimed 30 000 signatures. The petitions that began to arrive in January of 1848 were from small provincial villages that had never before participated in abolition activity. For the first time, abolitionists were able to make use of the clerical networks that had been so useful to their British counterparts in the gathering of signatures. France was about to create a national movement at the village level, led by mayors, magistrates, priests, and pastors.[54]

***

The February Revolution of 1848 overtook the tactics of abolitionists, colonists, and ministers alike. The Provisional Government, although dominated by a majority who had favored abolition before 1848, initially drew back from an immediate emancipation. On February 28, the first dispatch from Paris of the colonial delegates rejoiced that the Republic would, in the words of its own proclamation, organize 'liberty in *accord with the sacred principle of acquired rights* and the interests of labor'. Martinique's other delegate, Charles Dupin, was surprised and delighted to find himself in such harmony with François Arago, the new minister of the colonies. Dupin felt that he could move in perfect accord with the minister 'until the elected national assembly will have legislated the terms of colonial liberty'. The government was proceeding 'under conservative principles'.[55]

The situation changed dramatically on March 3. Victor Schoelcher returned from a voyage to Senegal. By 1848, Schoelcher had become France's most knowledgeable and indefatigable expert on slavery. He was the first and only French abolitionist to have visited the British, French, and Spanish Caribbean islands, Haiti, Egypt, and West Africa; he singlehandedly put abolition on the agenda of scientific congresses in France. Schoelcher was at the center of the petition campaign of 1847–8 and produced a long, model petition, with advice on how to turn the operation into a full-blown British-style campaign. His affiliation with the political group associated with the newspaper *La Réforme* allowed him to conduct a continuous assault on the slave interest.[56]

Schoelcher's timely return to France was fortuitous. His advent to power was not, however, because the *Réforme* group had just entrenched itself in the new government. In a dramatic personal intervention, Schoelcher convinced Arago and the Provisional Government to prepare an emancipation decree in the shortest possible time. He was immediately chosen to preside over the emancipation committee. Within eight weeks, the emancipation decree was approved by the Provisional Government and published the day before the meeting of the National Assembly.[57]

Public opinion, as measured through the press, was not concerned with either emancipation or the colonies in February and early March of 1848. Nor does any account of the revolutionary crowds in Paris mention their having demanded colonial slave emancipation. The revolutionaries at the Hôtel de Ville demanded immediate working-class representation in the government, a Republic, the right to work, and the red flag. Colonial slave emancipation was about as distant from the Parisian crowds in February of 1848 as it had been from the banquets a few months earlier. The Provisional Government therefore had a relatively free hand in formulating its pronouncements on colonial slavery, both in its cautious proclamation of February 28 and in its dramatic decision for immediate emancipation on March 4.[58]

Popular pressures for emancipation were as little evident among the colonial slaves as they were in metropolitan France. Prior to Schoelcher's return to Paris, the government received no news of colonial crowds like the ones in Paris that prompted the establishment of the national workshops. Indeed, before the revolution, there was no large-scale slave agitation, certainly nothing remotely like the 'Baptist War' in Jamaica, less than two years before British emancipation. The first major French slave uprising of the decade came only in May 1848, in anticipation of the imminent Parisian emancipation decree.[59]

The initial cautious proclamation of February 28 therefore indicates the lack of a sense of emergency. Except for the organization of a *Club des Amis des Noirs* in Paris, the formation of Schoelcher's emancipation committee seems to have mobilized more notables in favor of postponement than of emancipation. A dozen provincial chambers of commerce petitioned the minister of the navy and the colonies for a delay. They and some colonial delegates requested that the decision be left to the forthcoming National Assembly.[60]

Schoelcher, however, as head of the emancipation committee, saw to it that the decree was edited, approved, and published before the convocation of the National Constituent Assembly. He feared awaiting consideration by the elected representatives. When questioned in July about his preemption of the nation's prerogative, he replied that if the emancipation committee had waited on the approval of the National Assembly, 'slavery would still be in place in the territory of the French Republic'. A National Assembly willing to risk a Parisian insurrection by closing down the costly national workshops would have hesitated to enact immediate slave emancipation-cum-indemnity. It might also have responded quite as ruthlessly to the slave insurrection in Martinique as it did to the working-class challenge in Paris.[61]

Public opinion did not propel Schoelcher toward immediate abolition. Nor did his prominence as the architect of slave emancipation assure him of electoral popularity in revolutionary Paris. When he ran for the Constituent Assembly in April 1848, he received only 6000 Parisian votes, as against 260 000 for Lamartine and 105 000 for Lamennais, the least successful elected candidate. He ran far behind even such unsuccessful radical reformers as Raspail, Léroux, Considérant, and Cabet. Schoelcher was to play his major parliamentary role in the Second Republic as the representative of colonial ex-slaves.[62]

Nevertheless, Schoelcher had greater freedom of action in Paris during the spring of 1848 than any abolitionist in the history of slavery. The metropolitan conservatives were momentarily immobilized. The French planters, already dejected by the campaign of 1847, could not look abroad for succor as had their predecessors in 1793–4. The Paris crowds made no colonial demands. The possible reaction of the slaves was a matter of speculation, but Schoelcher could reasonably claim to be forestalling just such a situation of bloody confrontation as that which faced the Convention in February 1794. Knowing that a decision on slavery was likely to precipitate a decision on compensation, Schoelcher initiated an emancipation process that turned out to be more like the nonviolent British transition of 1834 than the hecatombs of 1791–1804.

***

Was the decree of 1848 therefore as 'totally extraneous' to July Monarchy abolitionism as the decree of 1794 was to the *Amis des Noirs* of 1789? The emancipation of 1848 was more deeply embedded in metropolitan political culture than was its predecessor. The Second Republic did not require four years to decide in favor of immediate emancipation. The gathering of over 10 000 names and the hearty reception of the petitions in 1847 publicly ratified the commitment of a significant segment of the monarchy's political elite to immediate emancipation.

Such prominent reformers were identified with colonial transformation in a manner beyond even the radical imagination of 1830 in the July Revolution.

There is another important sense in which the search for British analogs in French abolitionism is heuristically fruitful. When the February Revolution overthrew the monarchy, it also interrupted the development of a cross-class and ecumenical movement that had already put the previous regime under tangible pressure to enter into a transition to freedom, either along the lines of the British experiment of 1834–8, or Denmark's (British-inspired) legislation of 1847. By 1847, the French abolitionist movement was far more popular than its counterparts in Sweden, Denmark, or the Netherlands. The imminence of metropolitan emancipation was therefore more predictable in 1847 than it had been in 1793.[63]

Even without the 1848 Revolution, French slavery would have soon come to an end. Suppose a France that had somehow avoided the twin traumas of February 1848 and the Bonapartist coup of December 1851. Assume the continued growth of the abolitionist movement and of slave unruliness in raising the political and police costs of the status quo. Take account of the slowly shrinking slave population, the declining economic value of the French slave colonies, and the consequently ever-diminishing fiscal costs of indemnification.[64] Given this combination of actual and most probable trends, it is difficult to imagine any scenario in which French slavery could have survived the metropolitan economic boom of the 1850s. Finally, shame and pride also counted for something among a political elite imbued with the mid-century conception that their nation was falling behind in the great procession of human progress. Even the relatively minuscule mobilization of 1847 had caused Guizot to speculate privately that in 1848 he would introduce some legislation to 'restore France to her moral level among the civilized nations'.[65]

It is difficult to conceive of nonrevolutionary conditions in which French slavery would have outlasted the sixth decade of the nineteenth century. Somewhere between the ten-year transition to emancipation suggested by the Broglie Commission's abolitionist majority in 1843 and the twenty years favored by the commission's pro-colonial minority, French slavery would probably have been terminated by the regular legislative process. Although the actual date of the second emancipation was fortuitous, and the implementation more rapid than in normal circumstances, French abolition was not an accident.⁶⁶

Some of the benefits of France's mode of emancipation in 1848 seem clear. The slaves were spared another decade of existence as chattels and wageless laborers. For the first time in history, representatives of a black majority took their regularly elected places in a parliamentary democracy. But France's revolutionary acceleration came at a price. The newly freed blacks were exposed to the rapid retrenchment of their rights as citizens and workers as France again stumbled toward Bonapartist domination. A decade after 1848, French ships were again sailing from Africa with involuntary *engagés*, bought, 'liberated', and dispatched to the colonies to work off the purchase price of their freedom. The only abolitionist movement on hand to oppose this traffic was located in Britain, where Victor Schoelcher fumed in exile. The 'reassuringly French way' of revolutionary emancipation had also shattered the fragile coalition of liberals, radicals, church people, and workers that was forming on the eve of the February Revolution. Whatever the 'deceptions' of the British model, French emancipation provided its own generous portion of shattered illusions for metropolitans and colonials alike.⁶⁷

NOTES

I should like to thank Stanley L. Engerman and Daniel P. Resnick for their helpful comments.

1. Beginning with the sesquicentennial commemoration of British slave emancipation at the University of Hull in 1983, a number of anniversaries have left collective volumes in their wakes. Of the four-volume series *Legacies of West Indian Slavery* (London, 1985), see especially *Out of Slavery*, Jack Hayward, ed.; and *Abolition and Its Aftermath*, David Richardson, ed.; also *Anuario de estudios americanos*, 43 (1986); *Estudios sobre la abolición de la esclavitud*, Francisco de Solano, ed. (Madrid, 1986); *British Capitalism and Caribbean Slavery: The legacy of Eric Williams*, Barbara L. Solow and Stanley L. Engerman, eds. (Cambridge, 1987); *Hispanic American Historical Review*, 68(3) (1988), anniversary issue on Brazilian emancipation, also published as Rebecca J. Scott, *et al.*, *The Abolition of Slavery and the Aftermath of Emancipation in Brazil*

(Durham, NC, 1988); *The Meaning of Freedom: Economics, politics and culture after slavery*, Frank McGlynn and Seymour Drescher, eds. [Pittsburgh, 1992]; *The Atlantic Slave Trade: Who gained and who lost?* J. E. Inikori and S. L. Engerman, eds. [Durham, NC and London, 1992]; and a number of forthcoming publications from Brazilian Centennial Conferences in 1988.

2. Arthur Young, *Political Essays Concerning the Present State of the British Empire* (London, 1772), pp. 20–1; Adam Smith, *Lectures on Jurisprudence*, R. L. Meek, *et al.*, eds. (Oxford, 1978), pp. 181, 186–7.

3. See, among others, Seymour Drescher, *Econocide: British Slavery in the Era of Abolition* (Pittsburgh, 1977); David Brion Davis, *Slavery and Human Progress* (New York, 1984); and David Brion Davis, *The Problem of Slavery in Western Culture*, rev. edn. (New York, 1988); esp. pp. 153–64; David Eltis, *Economic Growth and the Ending of the Transatlantic Slave Trade* (New York, 1987); Robin Blackburn, *The Overthrow of Colonial Slavery 1776–1848* (London, 1988); Robert W. Fogel, *Without Consent or Contract: The rise and fall of American Negro slavery*, 4 vols. (New York, 1989–92), 1.

4. Eltis, *Economic Growth*, pp. 243–9, Tables A.1–A.7 (imports of slaves into the Americas).

5. On the general chronology, see C. Duncan Rice, *The Rise and Fall of Black Slavery* (London, 1975). For the period 1770–1823, see David Brion Davis, 'A Calendar of Events...', *The Problem of Slavery in the Age of Revolution 1770–1823* (Ithaca, 1975), pp. 23–6. On Latin American chronology, see Herbert S. Klein, *African Slavery in Latin America and the Caribbean* (New York, 1986), ch. 11.

6. See Joseph C. Miller, *Slavery: A worldwide bibliography 1900–1982* (White Plains, NY, 1985), and his updates in *Slavery and Abolition: A Journal of Comparative Studies*. This essay will deal with the British and French cases that have been historiographically designated as the exemplars or models for the abolitions of other polities.

7. See William A. Green, *British Slave Emancipation: The sugar colonies and the great experiment, 1830–1865* (Oxford, 1976).

8. See, among others, Eric Williams, *Capitalism and Slavery* (Chapel Hill, NC 1944); Roger T. Anstey, *The Atlantic Slave Trade and British Abolition, 1760–1810* (London, 1975), part 3; Howard Temperley, 'Capitalism, Slavery and Ideology', *Past and Present*, 75 (1997), pp. 44–118; Drescher, *Econocide*; Thomas L. Haskell, 'Capitalism and the Origins of the Humanitarian Sensibility: Some analytical considerations', *American Historical Review*, 90 (April and June 1985), pp. 339–61 and 547–66; David Brion Davis, John Ashworth, and Thomas L. Haskell, *American Historical Review Forum* on abolitionism, capitalism, and ideological hegemony, *American Historical Review*, 92 (October 1987), pp. 797–878; Eltis, *Economic Growth*; James Walvin, *England, Slaves and Freedom, 1776–1838* (London, 1986), part 2; Seymour Drescher, *Capitalism and Antislavery: British Mobilization in Comparative Perspective* (New York, 1987), ch. 5; *Slavery and British Society 1776–1846*, James Walvin, ed. (London, 1982); Solow and Engerman, eds., *British Capitalism and Caribbean Slavery*, part 3.

9. On the centrality of the Haitian revolution as a turning point in slave history, see C. L. R. James, *The Black Jacobins: Toussaint L'Ouverture and the San Domingo revolution* (1938; rpt. edn., New York, 1963); Eugene D. Genovese, *From Rebellion to Revolution: Afro-American Slave Revolts in the making of the New World* (New York, 1979), ch. 3; Elizabeth Fox-Genovese and E. D. Genovese, 'Epilogue', *Fruits of Merchant Capital: Slavery and bourgeois property in the rise and expansion of capitalism* (Oxford, 1983), pp. 404–13. For a similar emphasis, see Blackburn, *The Overthrow*, p. 30, 259–60. However, compare David Geggus, 'The French and Haitian Revolutions and Resistance to Slavery in the Americas', *Revue française d'histoire d'outre-mer*, 76 (1989), pp. 107–24. On the role of the Haitian Revolution in furthering or delaying the abolitionist process in Britain, see David Geggus, 'British Opinion and the Emergence of Haiti 1791–1805', in Walvin, ed., *Slavery and British Society*, pp. 123–49; and David Geggus, 'Haiti and the Abolitionists: Opinion, Propaganda and International Politics in Britain and France, 1804–1838', in Richardson, ed., *Abolition and Its Aftermath*, pp. 113–40. On the impact of British slave resistance in the abolition process, see Michael Craton, *Testing the Chains: Slave rebellions in the British West Indies, 1629–1832* (Ithaca, 1982). On the distinction between violence and nonviolence in the comparative history of slave emancipation, see, among others, Frank Tannenbaum, *Slave and Citizen: The Negro in the Americas* (New York, 1947), p. 105 and following; Eugene D. Genovese, *The World the Slave-holders Made: Two essays in interpretation* (1969; rpt. edn., Middletown, Mass., 1988), part 1; Seymour Drescher, 'Two Variants of Antislavery: Religious Organization and Social Mobilization in Britain and France, 1780–1870', in *Anti-Slavery, Religion and Reform: Essays in memory of Roger Anstey*, Christine Bolt and Seymour Drescher, eds. (Folkestone and Hamden, 1980), pp. 43–63, see Chapter 2; Davis, *Slavery and Human Progress*, parts 2 and 3; Peter Kolchin, *Unfree Labor: American Slavery and Russian serfdom* (Cambridge, Mass., 1987), epilogue; Seymour Drescher, 'Brazilian Abolition in Comparative Perspective', *Hispanic American Historical Review*, 68 (1988), pp. 429–60; see also Chapter 5 in this volume.

10. See David Geggus, 'Racial Equality, Slavery, and Colonial Secession during the Constituent Assembly', *American Historical Review*, 94 (December 1989), pp. 1290–1308; Yves Bénot, *La Revolution française et la fin des colonies* (Paris, 1988), ch. 7; Jean Tarrade, 'Les Colonies et les principes de 1789: Les Assemblées révolutionnaires face au problème de l'esclavage', *Revue française d'histoire d'outre-mer*, 76 (1989), pp. 9–34; and Blackburn, *The Overthrow*, ch. 6.

11. Davis, *The Problem of Slavery in the Age of Revolution*, pp. 137–48; also Geggus, 'Racial Equality', pp. 1304–5.

12. Davis, *Slavery and Human Progress*, p. 284. For Davis, this is one of the principal ways in which British emancipation functioned as 'A Deceptive Model' (p. 224). On the dissociation between prerevolutionary abolitionism and emancipation, compare the successive volumes of the Cambridge History of Modern France: André Jardin and A.-J. Tudesq, *Restoration and Reaction, 1815–1848*, Elbourg Forster, trans. (Cambridge, 1983),

p. 135; and Maurice Agulhon, *The Republican Experiment, 1849–1852*, Janet Lloyd, trans. (Cambridge, 1983), pp. 27, 111. For a similar comparison of monarchical paralysis with republican revolutionary breakthrough, see Philippe Vigier's two 'Que sais-je?' volumes: *La Monarchie de juillet* (Paris, 1962, 1982), pp. 109–10, and *La Seconde République* (Paris, 1967), p. 24. See also A.-J. Tudesq, *Les Grands Notables en France (1840–1849): Etude historique d'une psychologie sociale*, 2 vols. (Paris, 1964), 2, pp. 843–52, 1050. On slave resistance treated separately, see Edouard de Lépine, 'Sur l'abolition de l'esclavage', in *Questions sur l'histoire antillaise* (Fort-de-France, 1978), pp. 25–166; and Léo Elisabeth, *L'Abolition de l'esclavage à la Martinique* (Martinique, 1983), esp. pp. 33–80.

13. Blackburn, *The Overthrow*, pp. 493–500. Few histories of the Revolution of 1848 devote more than the most cursory reference to the abolition of colonial slavery. See, for example, Georges Duveau, *1848: The making of a revolution*, Anne Carter, trans. (New York, 1967), p. 77. Where historians of France offer any causal statement, emancipation is the logical or 'normal' consequence of universal male suffrage and the general humanitarianism of the Republicans of 1848. A minor ancillary theme may be a clash of economic interests – colonial cane versus metropolitan indigenous sugar-beet producers. See Agulhon, *The Republican Experiment*, p. 27, 111; William B. Cohen, *The French Encounter with Africans: White response to blacks 1530–1880* (Bloomington, Ind., 1980), pp. 192–3; Jean Dautry, *1848 et la IIe République* (Paris, 1957), pp. 101–2. In Gaston Martin's *L'Abolition de l'esclavage* (Paris, 1948), the prerevolutionary petition campaigns serve to illustrate Victor Schoelcher's prowess in converting the masses to his 'Humanitarian Gospel' (pp. 41–2, 49–50).

14. Blackburn, *The Overthrow*, pp. 494, 505–6. Blackburn's scenario for 1848 is strikingly parallel to his account of the first metropolitan emancipation. The decree of 1794 arose in the context of 'a subterranean current of rude popular egalitarianism', anti-absolutist, anti-nobilist, anti-capitalist, and proto-socialist. In both his narratives, the emancipatory moment becomes a revolutionary tableau, with all lines of action converging harmoniously on a central point (pp. 223–25, 261).

15. Lawrence Jennings, *French Reaction to British Slave Emancipation* (Baton Rouge, La., 1988), ch. 7, esp. pp. 185, 190, 193–4.

16. Drescher, *Capitalism and Antislavery*, ch. 3. Dale W. Tomich, in *Slavery in the Circuit of Sugar: Martinique and the world economy, 1830–1848* (Baltimore, Md., 1990), pp. 284–6, challenged the growing body of scholarly opinion that affirms a disjuncture between economic and political factors in the abolition process in the Americas, including Blackburn's treatment of French slave emancipation in 1848. Tomich charged that such scholarship isolates political and economic variables, emptying them of their historical context. His study, however, takes no account of French responses to the economic consequences of British slave emancipation, as discussed by Jennings. On the political side, Tomich's assertion that French slavery 'was the object of mounting governmental and popular pressure throughout the period

from 1830 to 1848' (p. 58) also overlooks a decade of historiography on the feebleness of such pressure during most of the July Monarchy. For further discussion of the historical debate over the role of capitalism in abolition, see David Brion Davis, 'The Perils of Doing History by Ahistorical Abstraction: A reply to Thomas L. Haskell's AHR *Forum* reply', in Thomas Bender, ed., *The Antislavery Debate* (Berkeley, 1992), n. 13: 'Even scholars as far separated ideologically as Robin Blackburn and Robert William Fogel agree that the triumphs of abolitionism in Britain and the United States must be explained in political, not economic terms.' If Davis sees a flaw in the explanations of Blackburn and Fogel, it derives from their relative insensitivity to 'the central importance of religious motivation' *(ibid.)*. MS. kindly furnished by the author. In the French case, however, Davis himself does not consider religious motivation to have been of central importance in either of the slave emancipations. See Davis, *Slavery and Human Progress*, p. 284.

17. Drescher, 'Two Variants of Anti-Slavery', pp. 43–63; Seymour Drescher, *Dilemmas of Democracy: Tocqueville and Modernization* (Pittsburgh, 1968), p. 163. On Bissette's persecution in Martinique, which became a metropolitan *cause célèbre*, see Shelby McCloy, *The Negro in the French West Indies* (Lexington, Ky., 1966), pp. 135–6. Bissette was listed as a corresponding member of the British Anti-Slavery Society (see *British and Foreign Anti-Slavery Reporter* [June 1, 1847] p. 91).
18. See Daniel P. Resnick, '*The Société des Amis des Noirs* and the Abolition of Slavery', *French Historical Studies*, 7 (1972), pp. 558–69; Serge Daget, 'A Model of the French Abolitionist Movement ', in Bolt and Drescher, eds., *Anti-Slavery*, pp. 64–79; Ruth F. Necheles, *The Abbé Grégoire 1788–1831: The Odyssey of an Egalitarian* (Westport, 1971), chs. 10, 11; and Jennings, *French Reaction*, p. 201.
19. See Tudesq, *Les Grands Notables*, pp. 839–40; Drescher, *Capitalism and Antislavery*, pp. 56–7, 203n; and Jennings, *French Reaction*, ch. 4.
20. See Tudesq, *Les Grands Notables*, pp. 838–43; Lawrence Jennings, 'La Presse havraise et l'esclavage', *Revue historique*, 272 (1984), pp. 45–71. For details on press subsidies and sympathies, see Bibliothèque Nationale, Nouvelles Acquisitions, Fr. (hereafter, BN, Nouv. Acq.) 3631, Collection Schoelcher, Martinique, compte de M. Jollivet ... (1842–8).
21. See *Le Constitutionnnel*, June 30 1841, on the deprecation of revolutionary symbolism. The culminating example of social planning by notables for emancipation was the official report of the Duc de Broglie, *Commission instituée, par décision royale du 26 mai 1840, pour l'examen des questions relatives à l'esclavage et à la constitution publique des colonies: Procès-verbaux* (Paris, 1840–2); and *Rapport* (Paris, March 1843) (hereafter, Broglie Commission *Rapport*). See also Alexis de Tocqueville's parliamentary 'Rapport sur l'abolition' (1839) and 'Sur l'émancipation des esclaves' (1843), both published in the Gaillimard edition of his *Oeuvres*, Tome III, *Ecrits et discours politiques*, 3 vols. (Paris, 1962–90), 1, pp. 41–111; and translated in *Tocqueville and Beaumont on Social Reform*, Seymour Drescher, ed. (New York, 1968), part 3, pp. 98–173.
22. Broglie Commission *Rapport*, pp. 263–70; and Tudesq, *Les Grands Notables*, p. 847.

23. BN, Nouv. Acq. 3631, Collection Schoelcher, report of Jollivet, Delegate for Martinique, March 13 1843; May 13 and 28 1843.
24. Green, *British Slave Emancipation*, ch. 8. French abolitionist perspectives are detailed in Jennings, *French Reaction*, pp. 103, 119, 178–80. For colonialist perspectives, see BN, Nouv. Acq. 3631, the reports of Baron Dupin and Jollivet, January 1845 to August 1846.
25. Jardin and Tudesq, *Restoration and Reaction*, p. 135.
26. Louis-Adolphe Thiers, *Histoire du Consulat et de l'Empire*, 21 vols. (Paris, 1845), 4: 176. In his history, Thiers was only repeating what he had said as president of the council of ministers in 1840.
27. A. Cochut, 'De la Société coloniale: Abolition de l'esclavage', *Revue des deux mondes*, 3 (1843), pp. 177–228, 185–6. See Archives des Affaires Etrangères, Les Etats-Unis (Paris), 98 (1842), for Guizot's reference to A. F. de Bacourt (March 4), on the 'exaggerated manifestations of public opinion' (Guizot deleted this phrase in the communication). In 1842, the one abolitionist attempt to hold an Anglo–French public meeting in Paris was prohibited by the government on the grounds that it would incite disorder. French planters used the absence of abolitionist public opinion in France as a strong argument against governmental action. See France, Ministère de la Marine et des Colonies, *Questions relatives à l'abolition de l'esclavage ...* (Paris, 1840), Conseil Colonial de la Guadeloupe, session de 1840, 46.
28. On abolitionist morale in the early 1840s, see Jennings, *French Reaction*, pp. 170–80. Colonial expectations about the prospects of French slavery might also be measured in terms of price differentials between children and adults over time. A sharp relative drop in the former would have indicated a rising fear of proximate emancipation. However, calculations from Guadeloupe slave prices between 1825 and 1845 indicate that prices for children between ages one and thirteen declined 36 percent, only very slightly more than prices for slaves between fourteen and forty years old (33 percent). This does not mean that political events, especially British emancipation, had no impact on slave prices. In Guadeloupe, during the five years before British emancipation (1830–4), prices offered for seafaring slaves rose 4 percent over the previous period (1825–9), making them the only occupational group in 1830–4 whose prices did not decline. However, in the following five years (1835–9), immediately after British emancipation, this trend was reversed. Prices for seafaring slaves (with easy access to free islands) declined 37 percent, more rapidly than for those of any other group. The sources for these calculations are: France, Ministère de la Marine et des Colonies, *Questions relatives à l'abolition de l'esclavage* (Paris, 1843), part 3, *Délibérations et avis du Conseil spécial de la Guadeloupe*, 'Tableau récapitulatif des prix des ventes d' esclaves ... de 1825 à 1839'; 'Résumé des transmissions de Noirs effectués à la Guadeloupe depuis 1825 jusqu'à 1839'; and Archives Nationales (AN), K3, Comité des Colonies (Juillet–Octobre 1848), Tableau A (Revised), 'Relève des ventes d'esclaves par catégories d'âge et par années.'
29. See *L'Union, Bulletin des ouvriers, rédigé et publié par eux-mêmes* (February 1844), 2, pp. 1–2. For similar remarks in the Parisian working-class

press, see *L'Atelier* (May 1843), pp. 66–7; (May 1844), p. 119. In the Chamber of Deputies on June 28 1843, over the protests of abolitionists, Guizot estimated the cost of slave emancipation at from 220 to 250 million francs; see Drescher, *Tocqueville and Beaumont on Social Reform*, p. 172 and n.
30. Drescher, *Capitalism and Antislavery*, pp.132–3. See also AN, Petitions to the Chamber of Deputies, C2425 (1844), 233.
31. BN, Nouv. Acq. 3631, Collection Schoelcher, account of Delegate Jollivet, May 13 1844.
32. *Ibid.*, account of Martinique Delegate Baron Dupin, April 12 1845, and Jollivet's letter of September 28 1845. For analogous assessments by the abolitionists, see Jennings, *French Reaction*, p. 188.
33. See Guillaume de Félice, *Emancipation immédiate et complète des esclaves: Appel aux abolitionistes* [sic] (Paris, 1846). See Jennings, *French Reaction*, pp. 181–9, for an excellent discussion of the British role in the 1846 campaign.
34. Seymour Drescher, 'Public Opinion and the Destruction of British Slavery', in *Slavery and British Society*, James Walvin, ed. (London, 1982), pp. 22–48. Unfortunately, no historian has been able to locate the papers of the French petition campaigns. The network must be inferred from the Anglo–French correspondence in the Rhodes House Anti-Slavery Papers (Oxford), from notices of activities in British and French periodicals, and from the local elites who inscribed their names at the head of the lists of subscribers. Given the constraints of French association laws, potential signers could not be convened at publicly advertised meetings as they were in Great Britain or the United States. Abolitionist mobilization by mail and personal contact was again used by the French Protestant clergy in support of the North during the American Civil War.
35. Drescher, 'Two Variants', pp. 51–52. For comparative analyses of Anglo–French missionary movements in relation to abolitionism, see also Bernard Salvaing, 'Missionnaires catholiques françaises et protestants britanniques face à l'Afrique: Le Cas de la Côte du Benin et du Pays Yoruba (1841–1891)', *Revue française d'histoire d'outre-mer*, 71 (1948), pp. 31–57; and Paule Brasseur, 'Libermann et l'abolition de l'esclavage', *ibid.*, 73 (1986), 335–46. On the comparative impact of abolitionsm on racism, see Seymour Drescher, 'The Ending of the Slave Trade and the Evolution of European Scientific Racism', *Social Science History*, 14 (1990), pp. 415–50.
36. Drescher, 'Two Variants', pp. 51–2, 61n.
37. Jennings, *French Reaction*, pp. 191, 194; Davis, *Slavery and Human Progress*, p. 283; Blackburn, *The Overthrow*, pp. 494–5. Daget and Drescher concluded that, although the size and number of the French petitions is not evidence of a British-style popularity in French abolitionism, they do indicate the beginning of popular interest and an expression of solidarity by many workers of Paris and Lyons with the colonial slaves. See Daget, 'A Model', pp. 74–5; Drescher, *Capitalism and Antislavery*, pp. 132–3.
38. *Le Semeur*, February 16 1848.

39. On slavery in the *cahiers* of 1789, see Beatrice F. Hyslop, *French Nationalism in 1789 according to the General Cahiers* (New York, 1934), p. 142; and Drescher, *Capitalism, and Antislavery*, pp. 53–5. On the petitions of 1847, see Archives Nationales, Section Outre-Mer (hereafter, ANSOM), Aix-en-Provence, Généralités 197 (1489), 47 cahiers.

40 Evidence for an 'economic' sugar interest behind the departmental *voeux* on slavery is weak. Only one of the five major sugar-beet departments on the eve of 1848 was among those that continually voted for emancipation resolutions. Only one other 'beet' department voted for such *voeux* more than once. On sugar-beet distribution, see E. Boizard and H. Tardieu, *Histoire de la législation des sucres, 1664–1891* (Paris, 1891).

41. AN, F80 1699 (Algeria), 'Minute' from the Minister of War, 'Direction des affaires de l'Algérie, Bureau de l'administration générale et des affairs arabes, Projet de l'abolition de l'esclavage en Algérie', Paris, April 24 1847 to (Marshal Bugeaud) the Duc d'Isly. Significantly, just a month before this dispatch, an internally written 'Note pour le Ministre' (*ibid.*) emphasized the religious, political, and topographical obstacles to ending even the slave trade in Algeria.

42. See BN, Nouv, Acq. 3631, Bugeaud's reply (May 2 1847), and the Minister's second dispatch (June 2, 1847), enclosing a 'Projet d'Ordonnance pour l'abolition de l'esclavage en Algérie'. Further evidence of the campaign's impact may lie within the metropolitan strongholds of the colonial interest. Bordeaux's press had been overwhelmingly hostile to antislavery initiatives during the 1840s. In April and May of 1847, however, the normally antiabolitionist *Guienne* 'unexpectedly opened its columns to a series of seven long articles containing passages highly critical of slavery'. See L. C. Jennings, 'Slavery and the Bordeaux Press', in *French History*, 3 (1989), pp. 273–92.

43. BN, Nouv. Acq. 3631, May 14 1847
44. BN, Nouv. Acq. 3631, May 14 1847.
45. BN, Nouv. Acq. 3631, E. de Jabrun, Delegate of Guadeloupe, letter to Martinique, September 12 1847.
46. BN, Nouv. Acq. 3631, Jabrun to General J.-J. Ambert, President of the Colonial Council of Guadeloupe, June 15 1847.
47. BN, Nouv. Acq. 3631, Jabrun to Martinique, September 12 1847. In contemplating the future of their labor force, Guadeloupe's planters had no incentive to invoke their own revolutionary past rather than the British model. The output of their major staple crops had declined by two-thirds or more during the revolutionary decade. See Christian Schnakenbourg, *Histoire de l'industrie sucrière en Guadeloupe aux XIXe et XXe siècles*: Tome I, *La Crise du système esclavagiste 1835–1847* (Paris, 1980), pp. 122, 138.
48. As late as their participation in the proceedings of the Broglie Commission, not a single colonial council deviated from the proprietary defense, insisting on the indivisibility of property and denouncing 'anti-social' doctrines. See ANSOM, Généralités 171 (1379), Report of the Committee of Guadeloupe's Council, charged with the examination

of the Broglie *Rapport* (July 1843), p. 106; 'Saint-Simonianism had its day ... Abolitionism still pursues its course, more adroitly embedding itself among the powerful ... All is mere vanity in the new socialist ideas, whether spread on one side of the ocean or the other.' The willingness of Guadeloupe planters to consider sharecropping does not seem to be related to its decade of 'free labor' in the revolutionary era. Concerning the organization of labor, Guadeloupe's council in 1840 declared slavery to be 'in reality only the organization of the proletariat'. Its own early experiment was conflated with Haiti's as proving the universal inferiority of free labor in the Caribbean. See France, Ministère de la Marine et des Colonies, *Questions relatives à l'abolition de l'esclavage: Avis des Conseils coloniaux* (Paris, 1840), pp. 55–7; and ANSOM, Généralitiés 161 (1323), Observations of the Conseil des Délégues on Tocquevillie's 'Report on Abolition', December 20 1839. French Guiana had a similarly negative attitude toward its episode of revolutionary emancipation. See *Avis des Conseils coloniaux*, Conseil Colonial de la Guyane Française (1840–41), p. 114.

49. On the entry of socialist ideas into plans for colonial development and emancipation, see Jack Hayward, 'From Utopian Socialism, via Abolitionism to the Colonisation of French Guiana: Jules Lechevalier's West Indian Fiascos, 1838–44', in Serve Daget, ed., *Colloque internationale sur la traite des noirs, Nantes, 1985*, 3 vols. (Nantes, 1988), 1. My source is the unpublished version of 1985. The socialist critique of liberal abolition was evoked by each step in British emancipation. See Charles Fourier, 'Aveuglement du liberalisme', *La Phalange*, 2(28) (July 12 1833), pp. 331–2; and 'Abolition de l'esclavage', 2(46) (November 15 1839), p. 785.

50. ANSOM, Généralités 173 (1388), Guadeloupe's Projects of Emancipation, sent to the King, November 17 1847. On the Fourierists' exhortations to the colonists in 1847, see the *Démocratie pacifique*, February 21 1847. Its model for the organization of labor was a form of sharecropping based on an experiment in British Mauritius (*ibid.*, February 28).

51. BN, Nouv. Acq. 3631, Dejean de la Batie to Martinique, August 10, 1847; Dupin to Martinique, February 9 1848. Early in 1848, a document sent to the minister of the navy noted that 'phalansteries' had been tried, without success, in France, England, Germany, and Africa. See ANSOM, Généralités 173 (1388), Paris, February 11 1848. Apparently, not all of the colonists of Guadeloupe were happy about their delegate's initiative in the new organization of labor. The governor of Guadeloupe, M. J. F. Layrle, wrote to the minister of the navy on December 24 and 25 1847, that the project of association was both languishing and suspect: 'the colonists ... have organized association as they would wish to organize servitude. Their project, such as it is, would be nothing but the continuation of slavery with an indemnity for the masters'. Montebello, the new colonial minister, dismissed 'association' as a dream. BN, Nouv. Acq. 3631, report of Jollivet, September 12 1847. For abolitionist suspicion of the planters' conversion to association, see *Le Semeur*, February 9 1848; and ANSOM,

Généralités 162 (1324), Commission de l'Abolition de l'Esclavage, *Procès-verbaux*, 2d session, March 4, and *Annexes*, May 7.
52. The annual production figures are taken from Noel Deerr, *The History of Sugar*, 2 vols. (London, 1949–50), 1, pp. 235–42. For the plight of the British West Indies on the eve of the Revolution of 1848, see Green, *British Slave Emancipation*, pp. 233–44; and ANSOM, Généralités 173 (1388), Address of' Martinique's Council to the King, January 8 1848. On governmental reluctance to implement emancipation in Algeria, see above, nn. 40 and 41; and *ibid.*, the 'Minute' to Foreign Minister Guizot, marked 'Confidential,' February 4 1848. On Bugeaud's attitude, see his reply of May 2 1847, and n. 28 above.
53. BN, Nouv. Acq. 3631, letter of Jabrun to General Ambert, June 15 1847; and ANSOM, Généralités 173 (1388), letter of Reiset and Jabrun, June 29 1847. See also Montebello's warning to Jollivet, just ten days before the February Revolution, that present legislation no longer sufficed for 'the needs of the future'. Jollivet's own registered assessment was that 'all is finished', unless a full-scale press campaign could counter press hostility and the new petitions of the abolitionists; *ibid.*, reports of Jollivet, January 30 and February 14 1848. In the Chamber of Peers, the liberal Catholic comte Arthur de Beugnot was preparing to launch the abolitionist drive of 1848.
54. Symptomatic of the changing status of French abolitionism was the fact that when a new abolitionist movement was launched in Germany, in January 1848, it sent a birth notice to the secretary of the French Abolitionist Society. For the briefest of moments, Continental abolitionists no longer corresponded exclusively with and through London. See the copy of the *Aufruf zur bildung eines Deutschen Nationalvereins für Abschaffung der Sklaverei*, in the Château de Presles (papers of the Carnot family). The copy is addressed to Dutrône, the secretary of the French Abolitionist Society.
55. BN, Nouv. Acq. 3631, dispatch of Dupin, February 28 1848. The delegates of Guadeloupe and Bourbon suggested that the Republic adopt the association plan as the basis of emancipation. See George Boussenot, *L'Affaire legitimus et la race noire* (Paris, 1912), p. 25. On the temporization of the Provisional Government's first colonial dispatch, see also 'Note sur certaines episodes de la Révolution de 1848 à la Martinique', by J. B. C. J. Colson, in Jacques Adélaide-Merlande, ed., *Documents d'histoire antillaise et guyanaise 1814–1914* (n.p., 1979), pp. 155–6.
56. Among Victor Schoelcher's many writings, see especially *Colonies étrangères et Haiti, résultats de l'émancipation anglais* (Paris, 1842–3); *Des colonies françaises: Abolition immédiate de l'esclavage* (Paris, 1842); *Histoire de l'esclavage pendant les deux dernières années* (Paris, 1847); *De la Pétition des ouvriers pour l'abolition immédiate de l'esclavage* (Paris, 1844), *Société française pour l'abolition de l'esclavage* (n.p., 1847). On Schoelcher's intervention at learned society meetings, see *Congrès scientifique de France 12ᵉ session tenue à Nîmes* (Nîmes, 1845), pp. 312–13, 467–93.
57. Janine Alexandre-Debray, *Victor Schoelcher, ou la mystique d'un athée* (Paris, 1980), pp. 124–8. See also Louis Blanc, *1848: Historical Revelations* (1858; rpt. edn., New York, 1971), pp. 267–9.

58. Blackburn, *The Overthrow*, p. 496. I have uncovered virtually no evidence of proletarian expectations regarding colonial labor in the spring of 1848, as posited by Blackburn (*The Overthrow*, p. 506). As far as one can gather from the official proceedings, the Schoelcher commission was not subjected to mass abolitionist interventions. Neither the language nor the rituals of metropolitan labor were concerned with overseas slavery. Indeed, as Paris approached its peak of class polarization in June, Schoelcher was the target of a charge often aimed at British abolitionists, of narrowly focusing on slave liberation rather than the universal emancipation of labor (Etienne Cabet, in *Le Populaire*, June 4 1848). For examples of the profoundly Franco and Eurocentric vision of 1848, see *Le Banquet social: Journal du XIIe arrondissement*, April 25 1848; and *Le Christ républicain*, June 18–21 1848

59. Slave discipline deteriorated in the Antilles after news arrived of the Chamber of Deputies' response to the abolitionist petition in April 1847. But public disorders remained 'extremely rare' (*La Réforme*, July 26 1847) The first news of the colonial reaction to the February Revolution did not reach France until the end of April 1848. Before the decree was promulgated by the government, the colonies still appeared to be 'tranquil', though in a state of expectant and 'profound emotion'. See *L'Assemblée nationale*, April 27 1848; and *La Réforme*, April 26, 28, May 8, and June 15 1848. On the discussion of Jamaica's 'Baptist War' of 1831, see Drescher, *Capitalism and Antislavery*, pp. 106–9, and 232 nn. 53–58. Metropolitan abolitionists viewed the emancipation process as complete by the beginning of May 1848. In a published letter 'To my Overseas brothers, the Black Slaves and Mulattoes', D. Poléma, a 'Negresse de la Martinique', urged her compatriots to return to work 'after the battle' in imitation of 'those to whom we owe our liberty'; *La Réforme*, May 2 1848.

60. See Drescher, *Capitalism and Antislavery*, p. 203, n. 21. On the radical *Club des Amis des Noirs*, see AN, C942, Enquête sur les evenements de mai et juin 1848, Tome III, Pièces diverses, 4th dossier. The flurry of mercantile protests against immediate emancipation found little echo either in the press or in the electoral campaign for the National Assembly. The conservatives focused their propaganda on the national workshops, Louis Blanc, communism, socialism, and the surtax on land. Their defense of the 'sacred interests' of religion, family, and property did not include a defense of property rights in persons. See Tudesq, *Les Grands Notables*, 2, pp. 1050–1, 1063. For the counter-petitions, see ANSOM, Généralités 153 (1275). On the colonial lobby, see E. Tersen, 'La Commission d'abolition de l'esclavage (4 mars–21 juillet 1848)', in *Actes du Congrès historique du centenaire de la Révolution de 1848* (Paris, 1948), pp. 295–301. *La Réforme* was the most abolitionist of the Parisian dailies toward the end of the monarchy, devoting almost one column a week to slavery just before the revolution. After February, its colonial coverage almost vanished. Colonial correspondence, which arrived too late to influence the Schoelcher commission's deliberations, seemed to favor a rapid and definitive end to

the postrevolutionary interregnum. See *La Réforme*, April 26, 28, May 8, June 15, and June 30 1848. On the final flurry of lobbying before the publication of the decree, see *ibid.*, April 30–May 3 1848.

61. AN, K2, Compensation Commission, Procès-verbaux, 9ᵉ Séance, July 12 1848. Members of the *Club des Amis des Noirs* were also fearful that the National Assembly might revoke the emancipation decree. (AN, C942, Enquête, dossier 4, procès-verbaux, meeting of May 20). The details of the Martinique slave uprising were reported to the National Assembly on June 22, the very eve of the climactic working-class uprising in Paris. The account occasioned an emotional reaction in the Assembly, including a denunciation of the Provisional Government for its precipitate promise of freedom. The French government had quelled similar resistance in 1831, stimulated by the July Revolution. See Léo Elisabeth, 'La Domination française, de la paix d'Amiens à 1870', in Pierre Pluchon, ed., *Histoire des Antilles et de la Guyane* (Toulouse, 1982), p. 395.

62. Alexandre-Debray, *Victor Schoelcher*, p. 140. Schoelcher fared no better during the supplementary Parisian elections to the National Assembly in June 1848. He was not supported by the electoral coalition of workers' corporations, national workshops, radical clubs and newspapers. See *L'Aimable faubourien; L'Apôtre du peuple; Les Bêtises de la semaine; Le Conspiration des poudres; L'Epoque; L'Organisation du travail; Le Populaire; Le Représentant du peuple; Le Travail; Le Travailleur par Mère Duchene; La Vraie République* (issues of June 3–6 1848).

63. See Svend E. Green-Pedersen, 'From Danish Abolition to Danish Emancipation: Some Considerations about the British versus the French Influence', unpublished Ms. kindly furnished by the author. In discussing French emancipation, Aimé Césaire reversed Karl Marx's scathing comparison of 1848 with 1789. For Césaire, the 'farce-mais grandiose' is the theatrical emancipation of 16 Pluviôse An II: 'Slavery is abolished in ten minutes of embraces, fainting and tears'. It is the emancipation of April 1848 that is 'sérieux.' Aimé Césaire, 'Victor Schoelcher et l'abolition de l'esclavage', in Victor Schoelcher, *Esclavage et Colonisation*, E. Tersen, ed. (Paris, 1948), pp. 25–6. On the evanescence of 16 Pluviôse, see also Robert Stein, 'The Revolution of 1789 and the Abolition of Slavery', *Canadian Journal of History*, 17 (December 1982), pp. 447–68.

64. On long-term economic trends in the slave colonies, see Schnakenbourg, *Histoire*; and Tomich, *Slavery in the Circuit of Sugar*. Note that at the highest compensation rate suggested for masters by the Broglie Commission, the cost of indemnification to each person in France would have been one-seventh what it cost his or her British counterpart in 1833. See Drescher, 'Public Opinion', p. 45.

65. Alexandre-Debray, *Victor Schoelcher*, p. 114. Guizot's remark was made to the comte de Montalembert on August 12 1847. In 1846–7, the arsenal of shame expanded enormously for French abolitionists. Sweden legislated emancipation for its small slave colony of St Bartholomew. Denmark enacted a program of gradual emancipation. The bey of Tunis decreed the end of slavery within his

jurisdiction. In Algiers itself, the Jewish congregation decided to prohibit slavery. The press did not fail to flaunt this flurry of antislavery among Protestants, Muslims, and Jews. Unaware of the government's draft ordinance for Algeria, *Le Semeur* asked whether France was content to have only Catholic powers unrepresented in the abolitionist ranks and to let non-Europeans outperform France in fostering progress; *Le Semeur*, November 26 1846, May 20 and October 13 1847; *L'Atelier*, 7 (April 1847), p. 487. For the impact of British abolitionism on Swedish emancipation, see Ernst Ekman, 'Sweden, the Slave Trade and Slavery, 1784-1847', *Revue française d'histoire d'outre-mer*, 62 (1975), pp. 221-31.

66. French colonial postemancipation also deserves a larger niche in comparative studies. Eric Foner's stimulating *Nothing But Freedom: Emancipation and Its Legacy* (Baton Rouge, La., 1983), p. 3, assumes that the United States was 'the only society where the freed slaves, within a few years of emancipation, enjoyed full political rights and a real measure of political power'. Steven Hahn's wide-ranging comparative study of postemancipation societies also omits the French example of 1848; see 'Class and State in Postemancipation Societies: Southern Planters in Comparative Perspective', *American Historical Review*, 95 (February 1990), pp. 75-98. By the time of US emancipation, the French colonial freedmen had gone through a full cycle of political empowerment and political impotence.

67. The steady erosion of abolitionism after 1848 is documented in Lawrence Jennings's account of official tolerance for French slaveowners in foreign countries after colonial emancipation; see 'L'Abolition de l'esclavage par la IIe République et ses effets en Louisiane 1848-1858', in *Revue française d'histoire d'outre-mer*, 56 (1969), pp. 375-97. It was not only that Bonapartist imperial policy repeated itself in the Second Empire. Most ex-abolitionists in France seem to have greeted the erosion of freedmen's rights with the same 'Gallic shrug of the shoulders' offered by most Jacobins when rights for colonial free blacks were revoked by the National Assembly in the fall of 1791. See Michael L. Kennedy, *The Jacobin Clubs in the French Revolution: The First Years* (Princeton, 1982), p. 209. On the significance of potential resistance by the freed population in preventing abrogation of certain articles of the emancipation decree after 1848, see ANSOM, Généralités 119 (1059), Decree of April 27 1848, Modifications, 1848-1860; Pierre Lascade, *Esclavage et immigration: La Question de la main-d'oeuvre aux Antilles* (Paris, 1907), pp. 55-78.

7 The Long Goodbye: Dutch Capitalism and Antislavery in Comparative Perspective (1994)*

'Is there any other point to which you would wish to draw my attention?'
'To the curious incident of the dog in the night-time.'
'The dog did nothing in the night-time.'
'That was the curious incident,' remarked Sherlock Holmes.
(Arthur Conan Doyle, 'The Adventure of Silver Blaze,' *The Memoirs of Sherlock Holmes* [New York, 1893]).

'If the world were to come to an end, I would go to Holland, where everything happens fifty years later.' Pieter Emmer opens his discussion of Dutch abolition with this apocryphal aphorism (ascribed to Heinrich Heine). Of all the northern European imperial powers, the Dutch were the last to legislate colonial slave emancipation, thirty years after their British counterparts across the North Sea.[1] They perfunctorily abolished slavery in 1863, after their Swedish, Danish, and French neighbors. Historians of slavery seem to have repeated the procrastination. They have been equally slow to view the Dutch case as a valuable opportunity for comparative analysis.

The relationship between capitalism and antislavery has primarily been debated by historians of Anglo–American slavery. For almost a centruy and a half after abolitionism assaulted the slave systems of the Atlantic economy, the historiography of Anglo–American antislavery was solidly embedded in what has come to be called the Progressive or Whig

---

The American Historical Review, 99(1) (February 1994), pp. 44–69. © 1994 The American Historical Association.

interpretation of history. Historians assumed that the ending of chattel slavery reflected the modern development of civilized behavior, led by the English-speaking world. Slavery constituted a moral and material fetter, which antislavery shattered in one area after another. The process moved from the most progressive areas toward the most backward, from the Somerset decision of 1772 in England to Brazil's 'Golden Law' of emancipation in 1888, and then on to the termination of coerced labor in Africa and Asia.

Perhaps the most controversial aspect of the historiography of abolition since World War II has been the new prominence accorded to economically based motives, forces, and conflicts in accounting for the transition from slavery to freedom. In this linkage of economic development to slavery, Eric Williams' *Capitalism and Slavery* was but a forerunner.[2] For more than a generation, the historical debate over abolition in Anglo–America has been centered on a bedrock economic question: Was abolition facilitated by the decline of slave economies or the rise of capitalist industrial systems, and how did economic and non-economic considerations figure in this process?

It is now clear that, in at least one important sense, slavery was no peculiar institution. The slave trade was an 'uncommon market', to use Henry Gemery and Jan Hogendorn's terms, only in that its commodities and capital were human beings, not because buyers, or sellers, or users of slaves and their products behaved differently from those in other markets. Since economically grounded models plausibly account for the establishment and growth of slave systems, many historians were tempted to explain the destruction process by similar economically generated forces. Williams explained abolition in terms of an economically induced decline of British slavery and rise of industrialism in the wake of the American Revolution. Historians of slavery in the United States, the British empire, and elsewhere also explained abolition by recourse to a variety of internal economic contradictions and uncontrollable world market forces.[3]

A generation of research on the various slave economies in the Americas has increasingly shown, however, that slavery was economically viable throughout the age of emancipation, even while it was being hobbled and destroyed in one entity after another. Political processes unraveled economically viable systems of production, often at the peak of their significance to the world market. Slave labor productivity was, in short, not economically regressive or inferior, a fact that challenged abolitionist conceptions of progress and abolition.[4]

If no inherent weakness in slave labor led to the rise and triumph of antislavery, how else might an economic causal relationship be established? A number of historians emphasized the declining value of the colonies to the imperial metropolis. Some have hypothesized that capitalist elites and intellectuals were so impressed by the economic performance of their own dynamic free labor societies that they simply dismissed equally compelling evidence of dynamism in slave labor economies and assumed that a transformation to free labor could only accelerate growth and prosperity everywhere.[5] Others have reformulated the connection in terms of a transformation within metropolitan class relationships during the early industrial revolution. Capitalist industrialization required a new free labor discipline, a discipline widely resisted by working people still rooted in an older moral economy. The pioneers of Anglo–American antislavery legitimized the new discipline by denouncing antithetical labor systems, especially the institution of chattel slavery.[6] In this perspective, abolition validated both ruling class and capitalist hegemony during a period of severe social and military threats – the period of the French Revolution and Napoleon. Abolitionism acted as a screening device, which simultaneously underwrote the old British aristocratic political order and the new industrial order.[7]

All of these accounts stress what has been called the 'free labor ideology'. Spokesmen for antislavery targeted slavery or coerced labor as inferior in efficiency, motivation, or ease of discipline to wage labor. Metropolitan abolitionism promised the universal superiority of free labor. Thus the antislavery movement, like Adam Smith's transformation of political economy, 'reflected the needs and values of the emerging capitalist order'.[8]

The free labor ideology, however, is not the only economically based link that has been forged between capitalism and antislavery. In another conceptualization of the connection, capitalism stimulated antislavery not through its relationship to free labor superiority or to class interests but through the impact of market activity on values and perceptions, yielding a new 'cognitive style in Europe'.[9] Humanitarianism in general and British abolitionism in particular arose from the interplay of market-fostered values, not through the dialectic of class conflict.[10]

But, while historians' focus on the relationship between capitalism and antislavery inside the English-speaking world intensified, the potential value of other national experiences has become increasingly apparent. Similar or divergent outcomes could clarify the nature of the interaction between 'one of the most palpable realities of Western economic history [slavery] and one of the slipperiest abstractions of the Western intellectual heritage [capitalism]'.[11] The history of the Netherlands is of particular comparative value for a number of reasons. If the pattern of Dutch economic and political development was not precisely that of Britain and France, the Dutch did anticipate and share with Britain a relative economic precocity and economic expansion overseas during the first three quarters of the seventeenth century. After a further century of relative prosperity but slackened growth, the Dutch standard of living in the 1770s still remained among the highest in Europe. Socially and politically, Dutch society was dominated by a bourgeois oligarchy that had broken decisively with the aristocratic landholding ethos of neighboring societies. Throughout the seventeenth and eighteenth centuries, the Netherlands was a republic dominated by a narrow political class and characterized by a high degree of provincial autonomy.

By contrast, more in the manner of France than Britain, the Netherlands entered three decades of acute economic distress, overseas disasters, and political upheaval between the 1780s and the fall of Napoleon. A discernably new period began with the creation of a kingdom of the Netherlands in 1814 and with the partial restoration of the Dutch overseas empire. The Netherlands now diverged in its economic, political, and imperial history from Britain and France. For more than half a century, it lagged behind its near neighbors in economic growth, political democratization, revolutionary challenges, and imperial expansion. It is this 'third' Dutch period, coinciding with the final dismantling of the British, French, and Dutch overseas slave systems, that has been the primary focus of what little comparative use of the Netherlands does appear in the literature of antislavery.

Yet a historiography focused solely on the nineteenth-century Netherlands risks the loss of extraordinarily fruitful comparisons that can be drawn from outside the conventional temporal frame of reference. Presumably, given a market model, a 'strong antislavery movement should have emerged in Holland, which was certainly involved in mercantile capitalism, in long-distance commerce, in world markets, and in complex banking and credit. Surely, the Dutch learned to attend to the remote consequences of their actions, and there must have been as many potential humanitarians per capita in the Dutch population as in Britain or the United States. Yet, despite repeated prodding from British abolitionists, the Dutch remained stolidly indifferent to the whole abolitionist campaign'.[12] Even as abolitionism was reaching its peak of intensity in Anglo–America, only the faintest echo could be heard in the Netherlands.[13]

The point is critical because the market was more significant in the fifteenth-century Mediterranean economy ('the birth place of modern plantation slavery') than it was in many areas of nineteenth-century rural and abolitionist America. And, in the Dutch case, the *early* modern Netherlands fully met the market criteria for a capitalist, non-abolitionist, counter example. For the century of its primacy in world trade, Holland exemplified a 'market-oriented society, whose members continued to see slavery as nothing worse than a necessary evil'.[14] Seventeenth-century Holland, with the largest overseas trade *per capita* of any nation in the world, was the envy of much larger monarchical states. It had a substantial stake in the Atlantic slave system. It possessed a highly diversified economy, tied to the needs of its commercial hegemony and nourished by the most complex banking and market institutions of its time. Its wage levels and standard of living were the highest in Europe for well over a century.[15]

Moreover, in terms of humanitarian sensibility, Holland was internationally noted for its institutions of charity. It experienced no shortage of moral and ideological attacks on the improper accumulation and use of wealth – what Simon Schama has called 'the embarrassment of riches'. The Netherlands' religious spokesmen offered an unbroken criticism of the potential immoralities of commerce. Even more pointedly, the Dutch began their seventeenth-century transatlantic slaving venture with occasional moral doubts about the propriety of trading in human beings and with legal inhibitions on slave owning at home. Masters understood that when they brought slaves to the Netherlands they implicitly manumitted them. Yet, for two centuries, Holland nurtured few antislavery arguments and no abolitionist movement whatever.[16]

***

One might usefully distinguish three periods of the Dutch case: generations of expanding capitalism in the seventeenth century, the turbulent decades around the time of the French Revolution, and the nineteenth century. More telling than the virtual absence of abolitionism in the stagnant post-Napoleonic Dutch economy, even with its diminishing dependence on slavery, is the fact that Dutch abolitionism failed to emerge either in the seventeenth century, when the Netherlands was at or near its peak of economic dynamism, or in the early eighteenth century, when the slave system was an important and growing branch of Dutch trade. Between the end of the Thirty Years' War (1648) and the end of the War of the Spanish Succession (1713), the Afro-Caribbean trade was one of the Netherlands' three principal 'rich trades'. For six more decades, a growing Dutch slave trade and an expanding plantation system no more stimulated the emergence of abolitionism during the eighteenth century than it had during the seventeenth.[17]

If abolitionism was a market-linked phenomenon, one could dismiss the Dutch case only by employing a 'Goldilocks model' of capitalism and antislavery. Before the American Revolution, Dutch slavery was 'too big' to be attacked in the Netherlands. After Napoleon, it was 'too small' to be noticed. (We will have more to say about the revolutionary and Napoleonic interregnum.) Apparently, only in Anglo–America was the salience of slavery 'just right' for capitalist-inspired antislavery in the age of abolition.

If the Dutch case undermines the'market model' of abolitionism, it also challenges the industrial 'free labor ideology' model, whose supporters should 'find it puzzling that the Dutch bourgeoisie passed up the opportunity to legitimize wage labor, accumulate moral capital, and bolster its own self-esteem by attacking slavery'.[18] This puzzle has led some historians to make a sharp distinction between mercantilist and industrial capitalism as the stimulating economic context for antislavery. The linkage is more precisely located in the new social world created when merchant capitalism was being transformed by industrialization:'The Netherlands, for all of its precocity in merchant capitalism fell well behind even Belgium in industrialization. It was the difference in the timing of industrialization that most sharply distinguished the British from the Dutch economy.' Is a vital clue to be discovered in the fact that Holland's 'anemic antislavery voices coincided with the country's delayed industrialization'? Significant industrialization came late to the Netherlands, long after industrial capitalist surges in Britain, France, Belgium, and the United States.[19]

Industrial capitalism remains the most plausible general context in which to link economic growth with abolition. If antislavery 'reflected the needs and values of an emerging capitalist order' in Bntain,[20] the Dutch case might also be used to test the early *industrial* capitalist model of antislavery. However, the distinction between an early industrializing Britain in the eighteenth century and a late industrializing Netherlands in the nineteenth century is not the only relevant comparison. The Netherlands' first period of rapid industrial growth anticipated rather than followed Great Britain's. In the mid-seventeenth century, at the time when the Dutch West India Company was integrating Afro–Caribbean slavery into Holland's economic empire, the town of Leiden was having its greatest impact on the European textile industry.[21] Around 1650, Dutch industry attained a margin of superiority in the production of fabrics that was maintained until the eighteenth century. At the peak of Dutch economic growth, in the generation after 1650, the cloth industry made a vastly greater contribution to Holland's overseas commerce than during any previous phase of its economy.[22] Dutch machinery was a technological pacesetter in the competitive international textile trade. Leiden and other interior inland towns were actually the source of much of the start-up capital for the Dutch West India Company. In general, Dutch industries, geared to export, expanded and grew even more competitive during the last third of the seventeenth century.[23]

This rising tide of Dutch industrialization has important consequences for any hypothesis that links abolitionism to rising industrial capitalism. In seventeenth-century Europe, the Dutch Republic was not only the leading center of commercial capitalism, it was also the first European country to have a large urban proletariat and 'the first in which the urban proletariat formed a large proportion of the total work-force'. Even excluding those who worked at sea, well over 100 000 people were employed in the main urban industries. The 'proletariat' in the broadest sense was larger still.[24]

The Dutch Republic remained the world's economic leader for most of the seventeenth century. In 1700, its *per capita* income was half again as high as Great Britain's. Only 40 percent of the Dutch labor force was agricultural, compared with 60 percent in Britain. The Netherlands' international trade was as large as Britain's, with a population only one-fifth as large. Its costs were comparatively low because of its efficient canal system. Its capitalist manufacturing sector was as important a source of Dutch profits then as at present. In 1700, the Dutch economy had a higher proportion of its labor force in industry than the British economy did 120 years later. Even with the fastest-growing economy in Europe, eighteenth-century Britain did not surpass Holland's seventeenth-century performance in income per head.

The Netherlands anticipated Europe's age of industrialization in a number of other ways. By the mid-seventeenth century, the Dutch rural economy had acquired characteristics often identified by economic historians as prerequisites for general economic growth. One-third of the residents of the Netherlands were urbanized, a percentage not reached by Great Britain a century later. England alone, while far more populous than the Dutch Republic, did not have a greater urban population, even in absolute numbers, before the eighteenth century. The enormous outflow of men into the overseas trades and the high mortality of seamen in the Dutch East and West Indies stimulated a heavy rural and foreign influx. In relation to other highly mobile areas of preindustrial Europe, Dutch cities were extraordinary magnets. More than a quarter of all persons marrying in seventeenth and early eighteenth-century Amsterdam had been born outside the Dutch Republic.[25]

Dutch urban industrial growth also exhibited a number of other characteristics that were later repeated in the British case. Women and girls, who made up about 30 percent of Leiden's labor force, worked harder and for lower wages than the average male laborer. In the more crowded industrial towns, 'night piecework was necessary to make up a living wage for a household'.[26] Such centers would seem to have provided an urban context analogous to those areas of late eighteenth and early nineteenth-century Britain that became centers of abolitionism. The Dutch case is relevant to the social stress model of capitalist abolition. Many Dutch social problems, including alcoholism, urban crime, unemployment, and resistance to falling wages, appeared likewise a century later in other nascent capitalist societies. Dutch ideologues also offered similar rationalizations and solace for Dutch social problems.

Other supposed preconditions for the emergence of abolitionism in early nineteenth-century Britain prevailed in the late seventeenth-century Netherlands. A plethora of Dutch publications delineated the mutual obligations between rich and poor within an idealized framework of natural harmony. The Dutch Revolt of the sixteenth century had already generated an ideology that affirmed the inseparability of freedom of conscience, political liberty, and personal freedom: freedom of body, goods, and mind. Influential writers like Johan van Beverwijck, Jakob Cats, Hugo Grotius, and other inventors of the national tradition expounded Dutch culture in terms of a patriotic liberation covenant. These writers abundantly exploited 'the Exodus metaphor (from southern fleshpots to northern freedom)'. In that trope, the Dutch people were 'the old/new Batavians, guardians of the *waare vrijheid* [true liberty]. They were the reborn Hebrews, children of the Covenant. Where had they come from? From slavery and idolatry, through ordeal, to freedom and godliness'. When the Dutch launched the most expansive slave trade of the early seventeenth century in Asia, Africa, and the Americas, they had only recently achieved political independence and developed a tradition of individual freedom and God-fearing righteousness. Although slave trading and slavery had been sanctioned by the Dutch East India Company as early as the 1620s, doubts about the morality of the trade existed at the very start of the Dutch

West India Company and lingered on after the company increased its involvement in African slavery in the 1630s. Thus the working conditions and the ideological arsenal accessible to the seventeenth-century Dutch seem congruent enough with those of late eighteenth-century Britain that the complete absence of any abolitionist movement or hegemonic displacement process whatsoever may offer a significant counterfactual condition for testing scenarios linking early capitalist industrialization to antislavery.[27]

***

Why was the reservoir of distaste for slavery in the Dutch metropolis not tapped by Dutch capitalism? Why was there no utilization of abolition of the slave trade between 1672 and 1713 as an ideological device for a beleaguered and war-weary populace? Why did a critical mass of Dutch libertarian symbolism, industrialization, economic crisis, proletarianization, and military threat not anticipate some major parallel to abolitionism? Abolition could have served the beleaguered Dutch as well against the enslaving 'Pharaoh', Louis XIV of France, as it served the British against Napoleon after his victories at Jena and Auerstädt. Indeed, this 'patriotic' dimension (so important to some recent accounts of the hegemonic function of British slave trade abolition) could have been of service during the entire half-century of Dutch eminence in the slave trade.[28] The desperate Dutch needed every source of patriotic solidarity they could muster at many moments between the 1640s and the early 1700s.

Remarkably, even after the British had apparently demonstrated abolition's hegemonic potential, Dutch slave trade abolition in 1814 was not used to create any domestic ideological advantage for the restored House of Orange. The only recorded reaction to Dutch abolition was an internal memo to the king by an unknown author displeased with the royal decree. The government's subsequent moves toward slave emancipation came in hesitant responses to the British, French, Swedish, and Danish emancipations between 1833 and 1848, in the form of cautious administrative and parliamentary proposals.[29]

Since the relatively more rapid industrialization of Belgium has also been alluded to in relation to the Dutch case, it may be heuristically useful to speculate about the fate of abolition in the Netherlands had Belgium remained part of a united kingdom after 1830. One might begin by noting that the Habsburg Netherlands became one of the last European entrants into the Atlantic slave system. The merchants of Ostend eagerly seized the opportunity afforded to them as neutrals in the American war of independence to gain a foothold in the slave trade. Belgian capital flowed into the French slave system.[30]

In its brief political union with the Dutch provinces after 1814, the southern Netherlands had an opportunity to display its attitude toward the abolitionist process. Four years after the royal prohibition of the slave trade, legislation was requested from the States-General to establish penal sanctions against merchants who might be tempted to continue the trade. After a brief debate, the vote was taken. Every one of the small minority of five who voted against the legislation was a representative from the southern provinces. While it would be hazardous to tie their votes exclusively to their economic orientation, it is significant that they all opposed the motion on capitalist grounds. They were disturbed by the fact that convicted violators would be deprived for life of their *patente*, or license to trade. The opponents of the law regarded this penalty as an attack on the industrious segment ('l'homme industrieux') of the nation.[31]

It is clear that Belgians did not stimulate any antislavery movement until 1830. It might be argued that Belgium's industrial 'take-off' did not occur until after independence. The incipient dynamism of the south was less evident until then. In 1830, the north was 40 percent urban, the south still only 25 percent, and population was increasing more rapidly in the north. The steady expansion of the Belgian metallurgical and textile industries was most apparent after the postrevolutionary turmoil.[32]

It seems unlikely that even continued unity would have produced an acceleration of slave emancipation in the generation after 1830. As late as the 1880s, Belgians showed scant interest in their monarch's acquisition of a vast area of the slave-ridden Congo basin for his imperial new 'Free State' in Africa. When Cardinal Lavigerie visited Brussels in 1888, on behalf of an international Catholic movement against the

African slave trade, his sermon berated the Belgian nation 'for not supporting her king's great humanitarian work in Africa'. The idea for an international congress in Brussels to end the slave trade originated in Britain. The Congress met in Brussels because of British fears that an invitation to London would be viewed as still one more hegemonic gambit.[33] As late as 1903, the initial public reaction in Belgium to charges from Britain that the 'Free State' had developed a vast and violent new system of coerced labor offers little encouragement for any inference that the industrializing southern Netherlands would have generated more action against slavery in either hemisphere than its northern neighbors manifested.[34]

The profile of Dutch antislavery, whether during the Netherlands' economic primacy around 1650, or at the peak of its African slave-trading traffic around 1760, or in its economically retarded phase after 1800, remained closer to its Danish, French, Swedish, and Spanish counterparts than to that of the Anglo–Americans. Nowhere on the European continent was abolitionism a durable mass movement, and nowhere was the enactment of antislavery legislation used to legitimize the claims of either traditional political elites or new industrial ones.

***

Incorporating the Netherlands into a comparative perspective is fruitful in testing another general theoretical framework that links capitalism to antislavery. In a recent history of the ending of colonial slavery, Robin Blackburn attempted to relate the rise and triumph of abolitionism to the dynamics of emerging European bourgeois society. Blackburn rejects the hypothesis that capitalist development directly triggered antislavery, since slavery neither collapsed economically in the Americas nor was destroyed by rival metropolitan economic interests. Rather, 'slave systems were overthrown in stormy class struggles in both colonies and metropolis'. In this sense, the capitalist order created new class struggles and political crises that implicated and destroyed slavery.[35]

Blackburn's principal nominees for what he terms increased 'dynamic density' in bourgeois society are Britain (at various moments between 1788 and 1838) and France (during the

French Revolution and again in the 1840s). In Blackburn's account, the Franco–Caribbean explosion of 1789–1804 was the turning point in the history of the antislavery movement, emerging from an unparalleled metropolitan political crisis and the most successful slave uprising in history.

France in the early 1790s admirably fulfills Blackburn's optimal conditions for the acceleration and triumph of antislavery. The alleged turning point of Caribbean slave revolution in St Domingue coincided with the climax of the radical French Revoltition in Paris, in which all remaining feudal rights and non-capitalist forms of property were being swept away in an environment hostile to both inequality and great commercial interests. The Jacobins gave slave emancipation their own hegemonic twist, sacrificing a distant and precarious colonial interest to consolidate popular opinion at home. (The British, with 'proto-revolutionary' situations in the 1790s and 1830s, are classified along with France as a zone of bourgeois capitalist expansion, class conflict, and abolitionism.)[36]

What of the Netherlands' place in this more populist model of capitalist antislavery? Blackburn's *The Overthrow of Colonial Slavery, 1776–1848* categorizes the Netherlands alongside Spain and Denmark in the column of non-starters – societies that failed to develop antislavery movements and that experienced a retarded development of their industrial bourgeois capitalist order. Blackburn offers no comment on Holland's precocious seventeenth-century industrialization or on its lead over France in urban, industrial, commercial, and bourgeois development throughout the seventeenth and eighteenth centunes. Many historians have, of course, questioned even France's proximity to an industrial capitalist order in 1789.

Blackburn's most salient criterion, however, is the catalyst of political rupture and class conflict, occurring in circumstances in which the voice of the slave holders was marginalized. Here, the Netherlands probably fits his prescription for bourgeois democratic abolition far better than Britain and, in some respects, for far longer than revolutionary France as well. Blackburn emphasizes the impact of the American Revolution on the rise of British abolitionism. Yet how much greater was the impact of that conflict on the Netherlands as a result of the fourth Anglo–Dutch war (1780–1784)? The entire Dutch slaving fleet was captured by the British, a loss from which the Dutch only partially recovered. The war was a disaster for Holland's entire merchant marine and for its free port colonies.[37] The conflict had scarcely ended when the Netherlands experienced its deepest political crisis in a century.

Recent historians of the eighteenth-century Dutch Republic have discovered a number of other relevant parallels between the contemporary Dutch and British cases. In the republic, as in Britain, there was an upsurge in popular mobilization. 'In the 1780s ... there was petitioning in the republic on a scale never seen belore', signature-gathering by the thousands, and a link of Enlightenment participatory politics and aggressive nationalism. 'Just as in Britain during the latter decades of the century, the link also existed in the Dutch Republic between political radicalism and what we may describe as an industrial vision.' Josiah Wedgwood, the Staffordshire industrialist who furnished the British with the image of the African in chains that symbolized the abolitionist movement, also stippled the Patriots and Orangists with images of their heroes. Wedgwood, the exemplar of the industrial abolitionist in Britain, was himself the model for Patriot revolutionaries across the North Sea. There was a conjuncture between the Dutch 'industrial vision' of the late eighteenth century and attraction to the Patriot cause.[38] The Orangist–Patriot civil conflict and the abortive revolution that ensued were settled in 1787 only by the intervention of foreign troops.

All this conflict was but the harbinger of a generation of national upheavals to come. The next three decades brought one disaster after another: war, invasion, revolution, occupation, naval blockade, levies of tribute, mass conscriptions into foreign armies, and outright annexation into Napoleon's empire. Finally, the revolutions of 1830 entailed yet another crisis and one more national humiliation. The seceding Belgian provinces had been compensation for Dutch acquiescence in British demands for the abolition of the Dutch African slave trade in 1814 and for the surrender of important overseas colonies to the British. Between 1780 and 1830, the Netherlands therefore experienced as much military defeat, economic distress, and political turmoil as any colonial metropole except France.[39]

As for the marginalization of the colonial planter class, so important to Blackburn's model, before the French Revolution the Dutch slave Caribbean had already afforded more evidence of decline than any other European plantation system. Between 1770 and 1789, the Dutch colonial share of North Atlantic sugar imports shrank more rapidly than any other sector of the plantation Americas. The relative decline of the Dutch colonies continued into the early nineteenth century.[40] Even in peacetime, the disastrous collapse of Surinam's speculative boom in the early 1770s meant that its exports could no longer pay the interest on the colony's loans, let alone repay the principal. The West Indies' negative trade balance accounted for much of the reduction in the Dutch slave trade at the end of the eighteenth century.[41]

After 1795, the parallel occupations of the Netherlands by the French and of the Dutch colonies by the British served to isolate the colonial planters from the metropolis. The long separation probably helps explain the relative indifference in the Netherlands to the abolition of the slave trade that accompanied the restoration of 1814. 'The country's largest slave-worked colony mattered little to Dutch industry and trade.' There was no collective protest against abolition even by the sugar refiners of Amsterdam. Their imports came from a far wider range of plantations than the Dutch West Indies.[42]

Finally, the threat of collective slave resistance, which plays a large role in Blackburn's model, was at least as prominent in the Dutch case as anywhere else. In 1763, a slave uprising in Berbice nearly engulfed the whole colony of more than 4000 slaves. It was probably the largest, the longest, and most successful slave revolt in the Caribbean before the St Domingue uprising of 1791. The Dutch took a year and a half to suppress the Berbice revolt, and many plantations were not rebuilt.[43]

The Netherlands therefore meets all of Blackburn's criteria for abolition: political conflict, economic decline, and slave unrest. It even meets one of Eric Williams' major prerequisites for the abolitionist take-off in Britain – relative imperial insignificance. There was no need to search for an imagined 'swing' of interest to the east in the Netherlands after the 1770s, because for more than a century the Dutch had regarded the East Indies as their prime overseas enterprise.

If relative colonial economic decline could be said to have eased the path to abolition anywhere in Europe, Dutch antislavery should have been 'overdetermined' during the last generation of the eighteenth century.[44]

***

The complete absence of the Batavian Republic from Blackburn's account of the 'bourgeois democratic' revolutions is a noticeable gap in his history of antislavery. The reason is clear. The prerevolutionary period in the Netherlands produced only the faintest echoes of hostility toward slavery in the form of Latin treatises, anonymous poems, and occasional polemics. These were 'isolated expressions hardly noticed by the general public'.[45] In 1791, almost three years after the first abolition debates in the British Parliament and two years into the French Revolution, the Dutch States-General formally announced (in a regulation designed to stimulate the Dutch slave trade) that 'as long as no one had thought of a method to provide the colonies with the necessary hands to do the labor the "Negro trade" cannot be separated from the growth and prosperity of these colonies, as well as the commerce which results from them'.[46]

The climactic Dutch political crisis occurred in 1794–5. The Batavian Republic was the first and the most important of the 'sister' republics sponsored by the French revolutionaries. It was a model for other French satellites and the first regime (including that of France) to adopt 'Liberty, Equality, Fraternity' as its official motto. The Dutch Revolution was an extension of the Patriot movement of the 1780s, supported by a broad middle stratum of classes, from journeymen to members of the social elite. Dutch 'Jacobins' were eager to abolish privileges and to establish a 'revolutionary government'.[47]

In January 1795, the French seized Amsterdam and the Batavian Republic was declared. The question of colonial slave emancipation, however, was raised only once. In the republic's constituent National Assembly, a motion for slave emancipation and the abolition of the Dutch slave trade received an unenthusiastic reception. The French experience was, if anything, invoked as a warning. Any 'action might very well lead to a violent insurrection as bad as anything in St. Domingue and was bound to bring ruin to many virtuous and patriotic burghers'.[48] The issue was buried.

The French made no effort to pressure their republican allies to adopt a slave emancipation policy for their colonies. On the contrary. Traditionally, the Caribbean island of St Martin was jointly shared by the two metropolitan powers. St Martin's French slaves had not been freed by the French emancipation decree of 1794 because of the prior Dutch occupation of the French sector. In 1795, the French took charge of both halves of the island. They promptly planted a tree of liberty on the Dutch side, but the slaves remained slaves. French revolutionary policy turned out to have been more strategic and less universalistic than many historians have supposed.[49]

When a large-scale slave revolt broke out in the Dutch Caribbean in August 1795, the Batavian National Assembly was not impelled toward any abolitionist initiative whatsoever. At the peak of the Curaçao uprising, the rebels probably numbered 2000, more than a third of the slaves on the island. The French made no move to aid the rebels from their own Caribbean strongholds.[50] As far as both the Dutch and the French governments of 1795–1800 were concerned, the Batavian Republic's Declaration of Rights stopped at the North Sea. When the French later attempted to seize Curaçao, they proclaimed the status quo regarding slavery. When Napoleon restored slavery in the French colonies in 1802, he was merely realigning the French colonial order with that of his Dutch satellite. The last Dutch regime officially to sanction the revival of the African slave trade, following the peace of Amiens in 1802, was the Dutch Republic. In 1814, it was the Netherlands' monarch who abolished the slave trade, under pressure from the ambassador of His Britannic Majesty.[51]

As far as the Dutch Caribbean is concerned, Batavia's sterile revolution casts a long ironic shadow on the 'meaning' of French revolutionary emancipation. Even when one adds to an already bourgeois society like the Netherlands all of the active ingredients in the bourgeois revolutionary model – successive revolutionary crises, overwhelming military threats, a long-term decline in the economic value of colonial slavery, a past and present threat of massive slave resistance, class struggles, and a patriotic republican ideology – the Dutch still come up short of an abolitionist movement, let alone any memorable page in Blackburn's narrative of abolitionism.

In ironic and precise verification of Heinrich Heine's dictum, the Dutch, after being nudged into slave abolition, waited for literally half a century before implementing slave emancipation. Even then, the dynamic and profitable sector of the Dutch imperial economy, which, in effect, covered the compensation costs of Caribbean emancipation, was the coerced labor system of the Dutch East Indies. Other than in helping to fund slave emancipation, the Dutch East Indies provided little stimulus for moving toward an imperial free labor policy. The dismantling of colonial slavery in the West began during the heyday of the coercive 'Cultivation System' in Java. In the east, the decisive shift toward wage labor came only in the 1870s and 1880s. True to their tradition, the Dutch became the last Europeans to sign the Brussels Act of 1890 for the repression of the African slave trade. 'The Dutch played out their resistance to the bitter end, signing the treaty only at the last possible moment.' As usual, they held out for commercial reasons, in protest against the advantages given by the treaty to Leopold II, king of the Belgians and ruler of the Congo Free State.[52]

From beginning to end, the role of Dutch metropolitan capitalism in the abolition of slavery was nil. The present consensus is that nineteenth-century Dutch industrialization did not get under way until Europe's 'second' industrial revolution, well after the ending of Dutch colonial slavery. This casts doubt on the applicability of an industrial or capitalist-industrial model, in any of its dynamic periods, to Dutch abolition.

***

Historians relying on the experience of Britain, France, or the United States have traced a clear evidentiary path from 'capitalism' in accounting for the origins, the evolttion, and the triumph of antislavery. Yet the Netherlands was actually more typical than anomalous in having no major abolitionist movement and more 'Continental' in moving toward emancipation without great domestic pressure. Capitalism, whether mercantile, industrial, or bourgeois, has thus far offered very little purchase for explaining the timing of Dutch abolition.[53]

The cases of Hispanic American and Brazilian slave emancipation inspire as little confidence in the association of capitalist development and abolition as does the Dutch. A number of historians have noted that, although the belated emancipation of Cuban and Brazilian slaves is often attributed to the comparative retardation of capitalist development in Spain and Brazil, the most dynamic economic and technological sectors in Cuba, Spain, and Brazil failed to back the abolitionist cause. Rebecca Scott showed that the most successful sugar planters of Cuba clung most tenaciously to the slave system. In Spain, the Catalan business lobby, the most market-oriented sector of the Spanish economy, defended both slavery and its own privileged trade with the country's slave colonies. Brazil was, of course, long independent of its Portuguese metropolis, whose economic development was, to say the least, unimpressive. Within Brazil itself, urbanization, improved transportation, and foreign immigration were most evident in the expanding slave areas. Regarding manufacturing, Rio de Janeiro was beginning to incorporate slaves into factories when the mid-century abolition of the African slave trade and the coffee boom combined to drain slaves from the cities. Nowhere was abolition particularly associated with economic growth within the Iberian cultural zone on either side of the Atlantic. Capitalists came on board only when the slave systems were in advanced stages of political destruction from international pressures, nationalist uprisings, or slave resistance.[54]

One other historiographical trend merits comment. Once one begins to explore the intriguing ground of Dutch retardation in detail, scholarship tends to displace some originally economically grounded arguments with those that explicitly rely on demographics, politics, culture, and religion. Whatever the resemblance and parallels between the Dutch and the English in their metropolitan economic, political, and religious development in the seventeenth and early eighteenth centuries, the Dutch overseas imperial system was far closer to those of the Continent than that of Anglo–America in one crucial respect. Unlike the English, the Dutch never successfully established a colonial zone dominated by its own ethnic group or replicated the metropolitan political institutions and civil status for the majority of its laborers. In the century before the age of abolition, only the North American British settler empire maintained a preponderance of free over slave labor and developed a 'European' religious,cultural, and political infrastructure beyond the Atlantic.

For the Dutch, as for other Continental Europeans, the majority of the labor force in their zones of settlement remained racially and juridically distinct from the metropolis.[55] By the beginning of the eighteenth century, all of their possessions were slave or bound-labor societies. A major reason that the Dutch encouraged foreign settlers and tolerated religious diversity in their overseas colonies was the enormous difficulty they had in luring native Netherlanders to their settlements.[56]

By contrast, the seventeenth-century British colonial venture in North America was decidedly aided by the fact that England's net rate of migration reached its peak in the four decades between 1630 and 1670 and was supplemented thereafter by other European immigrant flows. Even in absolute numbers, English migration attained magnitudes not matched again until after the Napoleonic wars. At the beginning of this great English surge, in the early 1630s, the Dutch West India Company's directors in Amsterdam were lamenting that anyone in Holland 'with the slightest desire to work will find it easy to make a living here, and thus will think twice before going far from home on an uncertain venture'. For its part, the Dutch East India Company did not encourage large-scale European immigration to South Africa, the one area that might have replicated the Anglo–American experience of European settlement in a temperate zone.[57]

One must not attribute the emergence of abolitionism to a uniquely English ethno–religious sensibility any more than to economic precociousness. It was the Dutch-speaking immigrants of Germantown Pennsylvania who produced the first collective petition in the Americas calling for the prohibition of slavery in the new Quaker settlement. And it was the weighty English Friends who tabled that and other antislavery initiatives for two generations thereafter.[58] The Cape Colony in Africa, which still had almost as many free burghers as slaves in the early eighteenth century, occasionally produced a colonist who wistfully regretted that the introduction of slaves had not been prevented from the outset. In 1717, the directors of the Dutch East India Company asked the Cape colonists whether slaves should continue to be imported into the colony or whether European labor immigration should be encouraged instead. One respondent offered arguments that were later to be more vigorously and collectively asserted in the British empire: that free labor was more productive than slave, that security would be increased by more free Europeans, and that indentured immigrants would ultimately increase the numbers of small proprietors and expand prosperity. By 1717, however, even that Dutch colony was demographically already a slave society. Most settlers responded to the question in cost-benefit terms: that it was cheaper to purchase and use slaves, that European immigrants would impoverish the colony because they would regard manual labor in the colony as degrading and would rather remain impoverished than work as slaves.[59] Well before the second quarter of that century, most descendants of Europeans in the Dutch imperial world envisioned their societies as irrevocably different from Europe's.[60]

Only in the British Continental Colonies, after a century of social experimentation and development, was a completely free labor and predominantly white community imagined as a viable long-term probability. The band of self-governing English colonies with black slave populations numbering less than half the total inhabitants produced the first intermittent attempts to reduce slave imports and then to eliminate slavery altogether. Everywhere north of the Carolinas, religious, racial, demographic, and political arguments in favor of restricting or eliminating the further inflow of African slaves increased after the 1750s. All these arguments rested on the notion that in one part of the New World it was possible to replicate and even to accelerate the trajectory of civil freedom as it had evolved in northwestern Europe.

The white inhabitants of the Continental British colonies regarded themselves as participants in, and extenders of, British liberty, and they were so regarded by their counterparts in the metropolis. When, on the eve of the American Revolution, Arthur Young calculated the world's free population, the subjects of His Britannic Majesty were the only people in the overseas world included in his zone of freedom.[61]

Freedom was not merely a passive geographical construction. If envisioning abolition required a century of gestation even in the Anglo–American zone, as late as the 1780s nothing in Dutch (or Danish or Portuguese or Spanish) transatlantic discourse matched the decades of transatlantic discussion of slavery in the British imperium. Well before the middle of the eighteenth century, one British colonizing society unsuccessfully attempted to establish a non-slave community in Georgia. The American Revolution of 1776 accelerated political actions against the transatlantic slave trade. During the next generation, the northern states of the United States became the first American legislatures to constitutionally undermine slavery or to initiate gradual emancipation. A number of southern states moved to expand white suffrage, perpetuate slavery, and shut down the avenues to emancipation. None of these debates and initiatives had any parallel among the settlements of the Dutch colonial empire.[62]

Evangelicals, lured across the Atlantic by burgeoning European communities in America, had to wrestle with a range of choices about the implications of slavery that was completely absent from the bifurcated world of the Dutch empire, with its free-labor metropolis and its bound-labor colonies. By the 1780s, the 'Quaker International', and its transatlantic consensus against slavery, was reinforced by a thickening network of antislavery religious dissent in Britain and North America.[63] Antislavery was one of the ideological movements that survived and counteracted the political rupture of Anglo–America after the War of Independence. Not until the St Domingue revolution of 1791 was there to be comparable transatlantic pressure for abolition. Antislavery in France had little connection with overseas white settlers, and Continental abolitionism remained a fragile social formation even in revolutionary France.[64]

In prerevolutionary Europe itself, an increasing number of slaves brought from the Americas created an unresolved problem of property in persons. In Britain, the courts found it difficult, and ultimately unfeasible, to reconcile the libertarian thrust of the legal tradition with the requirements of colonial slave law. The influx of freed blacks in the wake of the American Revolution also stimulated the founding of Sierra Leone, the first colonial 'free soil' experiment in Africa. In the case of France, the rapid growth of a free-colored population in St Domingue and the presence of an affluent branch of that community in Paris in 1789 contributed to the early intrusion of racial questions into the debates of the French revolutionary assemblies. The flow of black slaves and free blacks into the Netherlands was demographically and socially far less significant and presented far less of a socio–judicial problem than in England or France. When there was a legal clarification of the status of slaves in the Dutch metropolis, four years after the Somerset case in England, it was a 'Continental' response, more akin to the reaction to the eighteenth-century black presence in France than to the Somerset decision. The States-General decreed that Dutch slave holders could encapsulate their colonial property in the free metropolis. Black slaves brought from the colonies were thereby treated like overseas commodities. They could be legally 'warehoused' for reexportation within a limited period.[65]

The impact of slave resistance on the abolitionist process is also difficult to assess. In the French case, the St Domingue slave uprising of 1791 clearly played a large, indeed, the critical, role in the French emancipation decree of 1794. The effects of slave resistance in other colonial sectors and in the process as a whole is more uncertain. For more than a century, the Dutch confronted the largest maroon community *per capita* in the Americas. Their Guiana colonies were 'a theater of perpetual war' by the mid-eighteenth century. Yet, until well into the following century, all the turmoil, uncertainty, and costs of repression generated no abolition movement or state-sponsored programs for terminating slavery. Dutch emancipation was enacted after a very long period of relative quiescence in the slave colonies.[66]

***

The events of the American and French revolutions produced no Dutch reorientation on overseas slavery. The Dutch and British cases serve to emphasize the different paths taken by two of the most economically developed, religiously diverse, and politically constitutional societies of Europe in the seventeenth and eighteenth centuries. The Dutch, it turns out, offered an ordinary rather than an exceptional goodbye to slavery. In the insulation of their metropolitan political culture from overseas social arrangements, the Dutch remained within the bifurcated world of early modern Europe until far into the nineteenth century.[67] In the imperial preponderance of their tropical and slave colonies, in their persistence as a trading empire in tropical staples, in their dearth of transoceanic religious networks, the Dutch diverged far more in politico–religious than in economic terms from the Anglo–Americans.

The Dutch case may clarify another aspect of the problematic relationship between economic development and antislavery. Whatever the economic implications of any specific case, proponents of this relationship still maintain that the ideological challenge to slavery 'itself reflects fundamental long-term economic forces'.[68] In other words, over the long term, antislavery is still widely conceptualized as a 'superstructure', reflecting an economic 'base'. The Dutch case presents us with the following relevant conundrum: a society identified as a pioneer of modern capitalism from the early seventeenth century, one unencumbered by serfdom for centuries more before that, yet one that failed to generate a major antislavery movement by the standards of the age. Indeed, legally coerced labor continued to exist until the twentieth century, when it was finally eliminated by the Dutch state.

Half a century's investigations of the relationship between capitalism and antislavery have increasingly uncovered the contradictory consequences of antislavery for British capitalism without a clear determination of whether abolitionism diminished or complicated the birth pains of early industrialization.[69] By contrast, the case of the Netherlands makes clear that Dutch capitalism, whether mercantile or industrial, whether in oligarchical or revolutionary phases, created no significant antislavery movement. Nor did antislavery at any point significantly legitimize Dutch capitalist industrialization. In terms of mutual cause and effect, the more closely one investigates the relationship the more trivial the outcome appears.

Nevertheless, the hope of encompassing the century of slave emancipation within the ambit of economic development continues to fascinate historians of slavery. They are inexorably drawn to the institution's termination by collectivities professing the social norms of individual liberty, civil equality, free enterprise, and free labor. Few seem prepared to settle for only the weakest and blandest construction of the linkage – that the wealth generated within the North Atlantic economies allowed for the acceptance of alternative forms of labor if slave holding, however competitive, became morally embarrassing or politically inconvenient. If inconvenience alone were at issue, Europe could have managed to do without chattel slavery well before the age of abolition.

The Dutch dog that didn't bark now joins a larger pack of non-events that challenge a number of stronger formulations of the relationship between economic development and antislavery. It is not as easy as it once appeared to formulate an empirically satisfactory account of the antislavery consequences of European world-capitalism, whether mercantile, industrial, or bourgeois.

Taken in comparative perspective, the Dutch case enables us to make or to reinforce a number of observations about the antislavery process. First, the seventeenth, eighteenth, and early nineteenth centuries do not mark incommensurable 'stages' in Western capitalism and modern slavery. There were zones of both commercial and industrial capitalism in all three centuries. The various segments of Atlantic slavery were likewise not universally rising or declining during the same period. Less well recognized, antislavery sentiments were not limited to any of these centuries. Indeed, the Dutch were remarkably precocious in having developed a politically effective sentiment against metropolitan slavery centuries before the traditional age of abolition.[70]

It is the context in which that sentiment was nurtured into an overwhelming and irreversible political process that is at issue. Here, too, the Dutch case is relevant. Neither a dynamic seventeenth-century metropolitan economy nor a distressed late eighteenth-century economy on both sides of the Atlantic stimulated Dutch antislavery. Therein lies the chief significance of the Netherlands for the capitalism and antislavery debate. For a period of Dutch involvement extending over almost two and a half centuries, we can audit the economic dimension of the relationship with overseas slavery in the relative absence of strong political and cultural pressures against the system. As with other major cases thus far investigated, the economic context offers the weakest positive support for and the strongest counter-abolitionist argument against the antislavery process. In light of the eagerness with which scholars have fruitfully juxtaposed cases of slavery drawn from two hemispheres and three millennia, comparing antislavery among neighbors with close cultural, political, and economic ties over three centuries hardly appears a daunting or fanciful project. Our appetites and our critical sense should be as whetted for comparative antislavery as for comparative slavery.

Comparative regional and national analysis suggests that the breakthroughs to collective abolitionism and the triumphs of antislavery are not to be sought primarily in the impact of the usual economic markers of the capitalist industrial revolution – the shift from agriculture, the rise of the large-scale factory, or the new forms of managerial discipline. Antislavery seems to have been more dependent on the invention of new forms of collective behavior and on communal expansions of the rights of individuals, of social roles, of public membership, which accompanied the rise of Britain and its settler societies to prominence and world primacy. As the discussion broadens, the rise of antislavery has to be imagined less as a correlate of expanding new class domination than as one of the new modes of social mobilization. More expansive conceptions of liberty influenced Vermont farmers, Yorkshire women, or Caribbean slaves at least as much as they did entrepreneurial and abolitionist elites in the economic capitals of Anglo-America.[71]

In its British and North American variants, antislavery did intersect with rapid industrial development in ways that are still much debated. The major retrospective stimulus to clarifying that intersection, however, is that once antislavery was consensually embedded in British, and later American, opinion and law, those nations made it increasingly difficult for other societies to avoid placing abolition on their own political agendas. A century after the launching of the British abolitionist movement, the link between capitalism and slavery was finally broken in the New World and well on the way to dissolution in the Old.

NOTES

For their critical judgment and helpful comments, I owe thanks to Robin Blackburn, Natalie Z. Davis, David Eltis, Pieter C. Emmer, Stanley L.

Engerman, William W. Freehling, P. W. Klein, Gert Oostindie, and Robert L. Paquette; to the Seminar on Caribbean Societies at the University of London's Institute of Commonwealth Studies; to the Workshop on Migration and Missionary Activities at the international conference on the interaction between the Low Countries and the Americas, 1492–1992 (Leiden and Amsterdam, June 1992); to the participants at the Conference on the Lesser Antilles in the Age of European Expansion at Hamilton College (Clinton, New York, October 1992); and to the participants in the conference on Dutch Capitalism and Antislavery at the Royal Institute of Linguistics and Anthropology KITLV (Leiden, October 1993). Many suggestions that could not be incorporated into this article appeared in other versions, published in *The Lesser Antilles in the Age of European Expansion*, Robert L. Paquette and Stanley L. Engerman, eds (Gainesville FL, 1996), pp. 345–367; and G. Oostindie, ed. *Fifty years Later: Antislavery, Capitalism and modernity in the Dutch Orbit* (Leiden, 1995; Pittsburgh, 1996) pp. 25–66.

1. P. C. Emmer, 'Anti-Slavery and the Dutch: Abolition without Reform', in Christine Bolt and Seymour Drescher, eds., *Anti-Slavery, Religion, and Reform: Essays in memory of Roger Anstey* (Folkstone 1980), pp. 80–98; and Gert Oostindie, 'The Enlightenment, Christianity, and the Suriname Slave', esp. p. 14, unpublished MS, kindly provided by the author.

2. In addition to Eric Williams, *Capitalism and Slavery* (Chapel Hill, NC 1944), chs. 6–10, see Eric Williams, *From Columbus to Castro: The History of the Caribbean, 1492–1969* (New York, 1970), ch. 17. For reviews of the historiographical trends, see S. Drescher, 'Trends in der Historiographie des Abolitionismus', *Geschichte und Gesellschaft* (special issue on *Sklaverei in der modernen Geschichte*), 16 (1990), pp. 187–211; Stanley L. Engerman, 'Slavery and Emancipation in Comparative Perspective: A look at some recent debates', *Journal of Economic History*, 46 (1986), pp. 317–39.

3. On free labor as the peculiar institution, see M. I. Finley, 'A Peculiar Institution?', *Times Literary Supplement*, 3877 (July 2 1976), p. 819; and Seymour Drescher, *Capitalism and Antislavery: British mobilization in comparative perspective* (New York, 1986), pp. x, 17–18. On the economics of the slave trade, see Henry A. Gemery and Jan S. Hogendorn, eds., *The Uncommon Market: Essays in the Economic History of the Atlantic Slave Trade* (New York, 1979). Although Williams' initial work focused specifically on the destruction of the British slave system by British capitalists, he later extended his thesis to claim that the hostility of metropolitan capitalism in general was a major factor in the abolition of the other northern imperial slave systems, including the Dutch; Williams, *From Columbus to Castro*, pp. 280–90. The economic argument for the abolition of slavery took two basic forms. The first was that slavery became increasingly unprofitable. The second was that, whether or not it remained profitable, it became decreasingly important economically in the various political systems to which it was attached. In addition to the references in note 2, see, among others, S. Drescher, 'Le declin du système esclavagiste britannique et l'abolition de la traite', *Annales: E.S.C.*, 31 (1976), pp. 414–35; *Econocide: British Slavery in the Era of Abolition*

(Pittsburgh, 1977); Howard Temperley, 'Capitalism, Slavery and Ideology', *Past and Present*, 75 (1977), pp. 94–118; David Eltis, *Economic Growth and the Ending of the Transatlantic Slave Trade* (New York, 1987), ch. 1; Barbara L. Solow and Stanley L. Engerman, eds., *British Capitalism and Caribbean Slavery: The legacy of Eric Williams* (New York, 1987); Robert W. Fogel, et al., *Without Consent or Contract: The rise and fall of American slavery*, 4 vols. (New York, 1989–92), 1: ch. 3; David Brion Davis, *The Problem of Slavery in Western Culture* (1966; rev. edn., New York, 1988), p. 153 ff; and David Eltis, 'Europeans and the Rise and Fall of African Slavery in the Americas: An interpretation', *American Historical Review*, 98 (December 1993), pp. 1399–1423.

4. See Drescher, *Econocide*, ch. 10; Eltis, *Economic Growth*, ch. 1; Robert W. Fogel and Stanley L. Engerman, *Time on the Cross: The economics of American Negro slavery*, 2 vols. (1974; rpt. edn., New York, 1989); Fogel, *Without Consent*, ch. 10; Davis, *The Problem of Slavery*, 153 ff. David Brion Davis, 'The Significance of Excluding Slavery from the Old Northwest in 1787', *Indiana Magazine of History*, 84 (March 1988), pp. 75–89; Gavin Wright, 'What Was Slavery', *Social Concept*, 6 (1991), pp. 29–51.

5. Temperley, 'Capitalism', pp. 117–18; Eltis, *Economic Growth*, pp. 17–28, 102–06. There is a general assumption that 'it is no historical accident that the rise of the "bourgeois state", with its belief in 'possessive individualism' should have led to an attack on various systems of forced labor, such as slavery and serfdom'; Stanley L. Engerman, 'Coerced and Free Labor: Property Rights and the Development of the Labor Force', *Explorations in Economic History*, 29 (1992), pp. 1–29, quote on p. 3. Engerman, however, notes the tension between moral and economic arguments in the attack.

6. David Brion Davis, *The Problem of Slavery in the Age of Revolution, 1770–1823* (Itchaca, 1975), chs. 5, 8, and 9, esp. pp. 453–68 (henceforth, *Slavery in Revolution*). See also Thomas C. Holt, 'Explaining Abolition', a review essay in *Journal of Social History*, 24 (1990), pp. 371–78; and Holt, *The Problem of Freedom: Race, labor, and politics in Jamaica and Britain, 1832–1938* (Baltimore, Md., 1992), ch. 1

7. Holt, 'Explaining Abolition', p. 373. Davis also noted that antislavery could appeal to 'various aspiring groups, including skilled workers'. He restricts his emphasis on the hegemonic antislavery of industrial capitalists and political elites to the early industrial period in Britain. See 'The Perils of Doing History by Ahistorical Abstraction: A reply to Thomas L. Haskell's *AHR Forum* Reply', in Thomas Bender, ed., *The Antislavery Debate: Capitalism and abolitionism as a problem in historical interpretation* (Berkeley, Calif., 1992), pp. 290–309.

8. See Davis, *Slavery in Revolution*, p. 350; and John Ashworth, 'Capitalism, Class, and Antislavery', in Bender, *The Antislavery Debate*, 263–89.

9. See Thomas L. Haskell, 'Capitalism and the Origins of the Humanitarian Sensibility', in Bender, *The Antislavery Debate*, pp. 107–60; and the subsequent discussion by Davis, Ashworth, and Haskell, *ibid.*, p. 161 ff. Haskell's two-part essay was first published in the *American Hisorical Review*, 90 (April–June 1985), pp. 399–61; 547–66. See also

S. Drescher, 'Review Essay: Thomas Bender ed. *The Antislavery Debate, Capitalism and Abolitionism as a problem in Historical Interpretation*', *History and Theory*, 32 (1993), pp. 311–29.

10. For further explorations of the relationship between British capitalism and slavery, see Solow and Engerman, *British Capitalism and Caribbean Slavery*, esp. parts 2, 3, and 4; Eltis, *Economic Growth*, ch. 2; and Robin Blackburn, *The Overthrow of Colonial Slavery, 1776–1848* (London, 1988).

11. Gavin Wright, 'Capitalism and Slavery on the Islands: A lesson from the mainland,' in Solow and Engerman, eds., *British Capitalism and Caribbean Slavery*, pp. 283–302. For other international comparisons, see, among others, Bolt and Drescher, *Anti-Slavery, Religion, and Reform*, part 1; David Brion Davis, *Slavery and Human Progress* (New York, 1984), parts 2 and 3; Drescher, *Capitalism and Antislavery*, ch. 3; S. Drescher, 'Brazilian Abolition in Comparative Perspective', *Hispanic American Historical Review*, 68 (August 1988), pp. 429–60; Fogel, *Without Consent*, part 1; Thomas Holt, 'An Empire over the Mind: Emancipation, race and ideology in the British West Indies and the American South', in J. Morgan Kousser and James M. McPherson, eds., *Region, Race, and Reconstruction: Essays in Honor of C. Vann Woodward* (New York, 1982)

12. David Brion Davis, 'Reflections on Abolitionism and Ideological Hegemony', in Bender, *The Antislavery Debate*, pp. 161–79.

13. Ironically, the 'decline' of Dutch slavery correlates much more closely with the rise of *British* abolitionism. See below, n. 41, and compare Johannes Menne Postma, *The Dutch in the Atlantic Slave Trade, 1600–1815* (Cambridge, 1990), pp. 215, 275, 284–303, with Drescher, *Econocide*, ch. 3.

14. See Thomas L. Haskell, 'Convention and Hegemonic Interest in the Debate over Antislavery', in Bender, *The Antislavery Debate*, pp. 200–59, esp. pp. 233–4; and Davis, 'The Perils of Doing History', p. 294. Haskell's argument, connecting the economic insignificance of slavery with the propensity to abolish it, recalls the opposite formulation by Adam Smith. In *An Inquiry into the Nature and Causes of the Wealth of Nations* (1776), Smith commented wryly: 'The late resolution of the Quakers in Pennsylvania to set at liberty all their negro slaves, may satisfy us that their number cannot be very great. Had they made any considerable part of their property, such a resolution could never have been agreed' (New York, 1937 edn.), 366. Smith, and a sizable number of later historians, including economic historians, considered the economic insignificance of slavery to be the relevant factor in ensuring an early and rapid Quaker abolition. Haskell links slavery's economic insignificance to a *delay* in Dutch abolition. Neither Smith's nor Haskell's arguments work easily for both the Pennsylvania Quakers and the Dutch.

15. See Karel Davids and Leo Noordegraaf, eds., *The Dutch Economy in the Golden Age* (Amsterdam, 1993); and n. 25 below.

16. See Simon Schama, *The Embarrassment of Riches: An interpretation of Dutch culture in the Golden Age* (New York, 1987), ch. 5; Davis,

'The Perils of Doing History', p. 295. On implicit metropolitan manumission, see Robert Ross, 'The Last Years of the Slave Trade to the Cape Colony', *Slavery and Abolition*, 9 (1988), pp. 209–19, citing J. A. van der Chijs, ed., *Nederlandisch–Indisch Plakaatboek: 1602–1811*, 17 vols. (Batavia and the Hague, 1885–1900), 4, p. 57; and Robert Ross, *Cape of Torments: Slavery and resistance in South Africa* (London, 1983), pp. 73–4. According to some historians, slaves were legally free on arrival in the Netherlands, See James C. Armstrong and Nigel A. Worden, 'The Slave, 1652–1834', in *The Shaping of South African Society, 1652–1840*, Richard Elphick and Herman Giliomee, eds. (Middletown, Conn., 1988), pp. 109–83, 116; and Richard Elphick and Robert Shell, 'Intergroup Relations: Khoikoi, settlers, slaves and free Blacks, 1653–1795', in *ibid.*, pp. 210–11. Other historians assert that the Dutch legal system never reached an unambiguous position on the question. All agree that slavery's status within the metropolis was problematical. See Gert Oostindie, 'Prelude to the Exodus: Surinamers in the Netherlands, 1667–1960s', in *Resistance and Rebellion in suriname: Old and New*, Gary Brana-Shute, ed. (Williamsburg, Va., 1990), pp. 231–58, esp. 232–3.

17. See Jonathan I. Israel, *Dutch Primacy in World Trade, 1585–1740* (Oxford, 1989), chs. 6–7, esp. p. 296. The Dutch seaborne empire, the first fully global empire of trade, was also 'the first to combine trade hegemony with great power status on land as well as sea, a pattern again subsequently repeated in the case of eighteenth-century Britain'; Jonathan I. Israel, *Empires and Entrepots: The Dutch, the Spanish Monarchy, and the Jews, 1585–1713* (London, 1990), p. x. On slave trade figures, see Postma, *The Dutch in the Atlantic Slave Trade*, esp. pp. 250–1, 280–303, 308–61. Up to the 1770s, the Dutch slave system remained a significant component of the imperial economy; pp. 280–3.

18. Haskell, 'Convention', p. 233, replying to Davis. In a modified form, Eltis adopted Haskell's approach ('Europeans and the Rise and Fall of African Slavery', pp. 1416–17, 1420–1).

19. Davis, 'The Perils of Doing History' 296, 308–9; Oostindie, 'The Enlightenment', p. 5. For one Dutch historian, it was self-evident that the ending of Dutch slavery 'was caused by the industrial revolution'; Cornelis C. Goslinga, *The Dutch in the Caribbean and in Surinam 1791/5–1942* (Assen, 1990), p. 265. On the limits of Dutch economic development, see Frederick Krantz and Paul M. Hohenberg, eds., *Failed Transitions to Modern Industrial Society: Renaissance Italy and seventeenth century Holland* (Montreal, 1975).

20. Davis, *Slavery in Revolution*, p. 350; David Brion Davis, 'Capitalism, Abolitionism and Hegemony', in Solow and Engerman, *British Capitalism*, pp. 209–27, esp. p. 221; and the studies of Temperley, Eltis, and Ashworth cited above.

21. Israel, *Dutch Primacy*, p. 260.
22. Israel, *Dutch Primacy*, p. 260.
23. Israel, *Dutch Primacy*, p. 348.
24. Israel, *Dutch Primacy*, p. 355. For the view of seafarers as a 'proletarian' work-force under conditions of early modern capitalism, see Marcus

Rediker, *Between the Devil and the Deep Blue Sea: Merchant seamen, pirates, and the Anglo–American maritime World, 1700–1750* (Cambridge, 1987), chs. 2–4. On seamen as among the vanguard of British working-class antislavery sympathizers, see Eltis, 'Europeans and the Rise and Fall of African Slavery', p. 1421. In the early eighteenth century, the Dutch economy employed 50 000 sailors in the merchant marine, the ocean fisheries, the Atlantic, and the East Indies. Some recent studies highlight the long-term tensions in class relations between workers and capitalists in a variety of Dutch industries between 1650 and 1800. See, for example, two papers presented at the AHA annual meeting on December 28 1992: Joyce M. Mastboom, 'Guild or Union? A Case Study of Rural Dutch Weavers, 1682–1750'; and Karel A. Davids, 'Artisans, Urban Governments, and Industrial Decline in Holland, 1670–1800'.

25. See Angus Maddison, *Phases of Capitalist Development* (Oxford, 1982), pp. 29–35; Jan de Vries, *European Urbanization 1500–1800* (Cambridge, Mass., 1984), pp. 39, 210–12, 361 n. 15. In 1675, the population of the Netherlands was more than 45 percent urban, its peak before the abolition of Dutch slavery. See Jan de Vries, 'Problems in the Measurement, Description, and Analysis of Historical Urbanization', in *Urbanization in History: A process of dynamic interactions*, A. D. van der Woude, et al., eds. (Oxford, 1990), pp. 43–60, 47, Table 3.2. See also Jan de Vries, 'An Inquiry into the Behavior of Wages in the Dutch Republic and the Southern Netherlands from 1580 to 1800', in *Dutch Capitalism and World Capitalism*, Maurice Aymard, ed. (Cambridge, 1982), pp. 37–61, 44; and Jan de Vries, *The Dutch Rural Economy in the Golden Age, 1500–1700* (New Haven, Conn., 1974), ch. 7

26. Schama, *The Embarrassment of Riches*, p. 168. A. T. Van Deursen, *Plain Lives in a Golden Age: Popular culture, religion and society in seventeenth-century Holland*, Maarten Ultee, trans. (cambridge, 1991), pp. 8–9, 17–20.

27. Martin van Gelderen, *The Political Thought of the Dutch Revolt, 1555–1590* (Cambridge, 1992), pp. 119, 142, 161, 257–8; Schama, *The Embarrassment of Riches*, pp. 45, 68, and ch. 2, sec. 2, 'Scripture'. It should be emphasized that *waare vrijheid* was a political concept with no particular meaning in regard to labor relations. (My thanks to Professor P. W. Klein for this clarification.) See also Ernest van den Boogaart and Pieter C. Emmer, 'The Dutch Participation in the Atlantic Slave Trade, 1596–1650', in Gemery and Hogendorn, *The Uncommon Market*, pp. 353–75; Postma, *The Dutch in the Atlantic Slave Trade*, pp. 10–14; J. Fox, 'For Good and Sufficient Reasons: An examination of early Dutch East India Company Ordinances on slaves and slavery', in Anthony Reid, ed., *Slavery, Bondage and Dependency in Southeast Asia* (New York, 1983), pp. 246–62. The 'patriotic' dimension of antislavery is of some importance in Davis' account of British slave trade abolition. Davis, *Slavery in Revolution*, pp. 449–50. See also David Turely, *The Culture of English Antislavery, 1780–1860* (London, 1991), pp. 178–81.

28. Schama, *The Embarrassment of Riches*, pp. 53, 220, 27–77.

29. See Pieter C. Emmer, 'Abolition of the Slave Trade and the Mixed Courts', in *The Abolition of the Atlantic Slave Trade*, Davis Eltis and James Walvin, eds. (Madison, 1981), pp. 177–90; and Goslinga, *The Dutch in the Caribbean*, ch. 7. After the passage of British abolition, Holland was taunted by English poets for having failed, in an excess of capitalist greed, to extend its own liberties abroad. The result was Dutch degeneration – moral, economic, and political. See James Montgomery, 'The West Indies', and Elizabeth Benger, 'A Poem Occasioned by the Abolition of the Slave Trade in 1806' [*sic*], in *Poems on the Abolition of the Slave Trade* (London, 1809), pp. 18, 130. Gert Oostindie suggests that slave trade abolition might have been resented as a humiliating condition imposed by Britain. Therefore, slave trade abolition could not easily have been used to hegemonic advantage after 1814. In any event, the day of slave emancipation in the Netherlands passed with as little public agitation or celebration in 1863 as had slave trade abolition forty-nine years before. See J. M. Van Winter, 'Public Opinion in the Netherlands on the Abolition of Slavery', in *Dutch Authors on West Indian History: A historiographical selection*, M. A. P. Meilink-Roelofsz, ed. (The Hague, 1982), pp. 100–28.
30. Drescher, *Capitalism and Antislavery*, pp. 170–1.
31. *Verslag des Handelinger van de Tweede Kamer der Staaten-Generaal, Gerdurende de Zitting van 1818–1819, Gehouden te Brussel* ('s Gravenhage, 1861), 9th Sitting, November 12 1818, pp. 16–24. (My thanks to Pieter Emmer for calling this debate to my attention.)
32. See Joel Mokyr, *Industrialization in the Low Countries, 1795–1850* (New Haven, Conn., 1976), ch. 2; E. H. Kossmann, *The Low Countries, 1780–1940* (Oxford, 1978), pp. 129–35, 210–16.
33. Suzanne Miers, *Britain and the Ending of the Slave Trade* (New york, 1975), pp. 205–7. On the role of Anglophobia in the abolition process, see n. 68 below.
34. See William Roger Louis and Jean Stengers, eds., *E. D. Morel's History of The Congo Reform Movement* (Oxford, 1968), p. 149 ff.
35. Blackburn, *The Overthrow*, 520. Thomas Holt uses a similar frame of reference. His crucial connection between capitalism and antislavery is located in 'the emerging bourgeois social relations of the seventeenth and eighteenth centuries'. A bourgeois movement and ideology, rooted in the Enlightenment, then assaulted slavery in a dual revolution: 'The political upheavals inspired by the French revolution set the destruction of slavery in motion; the ideology thrown up by Britain's free labor economy provided the model for what should replace slavery.' Holt, *The Problem of Freedom: Race, Labor and Politics in Jamaica and Britain, 1832–1938* (Baltimore, 1992), pp. xxii, 3–9, 21–26.
36. Blackburn, *The Overthrow*, chs. 5, 6, pp. 519–20.
37. Blackburn, *The Overthrow*, pp. 133–4, 158n.; Postma, *The Dutch in the Atlantic Slave Trade*, pp. 165, 284–5. The annual average of transported slaves fell to less than one-fifth of the 1770–9 level in the period 1780–1803. Postma, *The Dutch in the Atlantic Slave Trade*, p. 295.

38. On Dutch revolutionary mobilization and industrial progressivism, see Nicolaas C. F. van Sas, 'The Patriot Revolution: New perspectives', and Margaret C. Jacob, 'Radicalism in the Dutch Enlightenment', in *The Dutch Republic in the Eighteenth Century: Decline, enlightenment, and revolution*, Margaret C. Jacob and Wijnand W. Mijnhardt, eds. (Ithaca, 1992), pp. 91–119 and 224–40. On the significance of Wedgwood as an abolitionist industrialist, see Davis, *Slavery in Revolution*, pp. 460–1.
39. See Simon Schama, *Patriots and Liberators: Revolution in the Netherlands, 1780–1813* (New York, 1977), *passim*.
40. Drescher, *Econocide*, pp. 48, 77. The Danish, with the only other relatively declining system between 1770 and 1789, had a share-loss less than half as great as the Dutch. The Dutch colonies' share of the Caribbean slave population fell from 9.6 percent in 1750 to 4.6 percent in 1830. Only the French, with the loss of Haiti, had a greater relative loss during the same period. On population trends, see Stanley L. Engerman and B. W. Higman, 'The Demographic Structure of the Caribbean Slave Societies in the Eighteenth and Nineteenth Centuries', in *General History of the Caribbean* III, *The slave societies of the Caribbean*, Franklin W. Kinght ed. (UNESCO, 1997), pp. 45–104, esp. pp. 48–57, table 2.1. (My thanks to Stanley Engerman for making this chapter available before publicaion.)
41. P. C. Emmer, 'The Dutch and the Making of the Second Atlantic System', in *Slavery and the Rise of the Atlantic System*, Barbara L. Solow, ed. (Cambridge, Mass., 1991), pp. 75–96, esp. p. 93. On the Dutch East India Company, see S. Abeyaserkere, 'Slaves in Batavia: Insights from a slave register', in Reid, *Slavery, Bondage and Dependency in Southeast Asia*, pp. 286–311. Much of the literature of the period after the early 1770s reflects an increasingly pessimistic mood about Dutch plantation slavery, continuing until slave emancipation in 1863. See Gert Oostindie, 'The Economics of Suriname Slavery', in *Economic and Social History of the Netherlands* 5 (1993) pp. 1–24, esp. 3 and n. 7. (My thanks to Professor Oostindie for making this article available before publication.)
42. Postma, *The Dutch in the Atlantic Slave Trade*, p. 78.
43. Goslinga, *The Dutch in the Caribbean*, ch. 15; Postma, *The Dutch in the Atlantic Slave Trade*, pp. 215–17.
44. On the supposed British swing to the east after 1780, see Drescher, *Econocide*, pp. 54 and 235n.
45. Postma, *The Dutch in the Atlantic Slave Trade*, pp. 292–3. See also G. J. Schutte, *De Nederlandse Patriotten en de Kolonien: Een onderzoek naar hun denkbulden en optreden 1770–1800* (Groningen, 1974), pp. 220–3.
46. Postma, *The Dutch in the Atlantic Slave Trade*, p. 286 (November 1789).
47. R. R. Palmer, *The Age of the Democratic Revolution: A political history of Europe and America, 1760–1800*, 2 vols. (Princeton, 1959), 2, p. 180 and following. The first Dutch constitution was composed under the direct influence of the French ambassador to the Hague. See D. R. C. Verhagen, *L'influence de la Révolution Française sur la première constitution Hollandaise du 23 avril 1798* (Utrecht, 1949). Its section on

Dutch Capitalism and Antislavery 229

colonies (VII) included nothing about the juridical status of the inhabitants.
48. Schama, *Patriots and Liberators*, pp. 260–1. A proposed plan for gradual abolition by a French colonial official and a Dutch planter in Demerara was included in the Dutch translation of John Gabriel Stedman's *Narrative of a Five Years Expedition against the Revolted Negroes of Surinam in 1799–1800 (Reize naar Surinamen)*, cited in Oostindie, 'The Enlightenment', 4–5, note. It was not taken up by the government. A recent study on the political mobilization of women in the Netherlands in the 1780s and 1790s does not indicate any antislavery dimension in their activities. See Wayne P. te Brake, Rudolf M. Dekker and Lottee C. van de Pol, 'Women and Political Culture in the Dutch Revolutions', in *Women and Politics in the Age of the Democratic Revolution*, Harriet B. Applewhite and Darline G. Levy, eds. (Ann Arbor, Mich., 1990), pp. 109–46.
49. Goslinga, *The Dutch in the Caribbean*, p. 146.
50. Goslinga, *The Dutch in the Caribbean*, ch. 1.
51. Postma, *The Dutch in the Atlantic Slave Trade*, p. 290. When the Cape Colony was briefly restored to Dutch sovereignty in 1802, the Batavian Republic considered the possibility that slavery was unnecessary there, but conlonial administrators generally agreed with Governor Janssens that the abolition of slavery 'would overturn all property' and immiserate the colony. No action was taken. See Elphick and Giliomee, *The Shaping of South African Society*, pp. 163, 337.
52. Emmer, 'Anti-Slavery and the Dutch', p. 83; Mokyr, *Industrialization in the Low Countries*, p. 83. Slave emancipation occurred in July 1863 without fanfare or celebration in the metropolis. See J. M. van Winter, 'Public Opinion in the Netherlands on the Abolition of Slavery', in Meilink-Roelofsz, *Dutch Authors on West Indian History*, pp. 100–28. On the East Indies' labor system, see Nico Dros, 'Javanese Labour Relations in a Changing Rural Economy, 1830–1870', *Economic and Social History in the Netherlands*, 3 (1991), pp. 133–53; Peter Boomgaard, *Children of the Colonial State: Population growth and economic development in Java, 1795–1880* (Amsterdam, 1989), p. 39. On Dutch resistance to the Brussels treaty, see Miers, *Britain and the Ending*, pp. 287–92. 'The Dutch Foreign Minister, 'an honourable man', winced when the British Ambassador smugly informed him that Britain, 'unlike others' regarded trading interests as a secondary matter'; Miers, p. 281.
53. See, among others, S. Drescher, 'Two Variants of Anti-Slavery: Religious organization and social mobilization in Britain and France, 1780–1870', in Bolt and Drescher, *Anti-Slavery, Religion, and Reform*, pp. 43–63; see also Chapter 2 in this volume; Drescher, *Capitalism and Antislavery*, ch. 3; and Davis, 'The Perils of Doing History', p. 296. Only Brazilian and, to a lesser extent, French abolitionism on the eve of their respective slave emancipations might qualify as approaching the status of broad social movements. See Drescher, 'Brazilian Abolition', pp. 450–4; and Seymour Drescher, 'British Way, French Way: Opinion Building and Revolution in the Second French Slave

Emancipation,' *American Historical Review*, 96 (June 1991), pp. 709–34; see also Chapter 6 in this volume.

54. On Spanish and Brazilian abolition, see Arthur Corwin, *Spain and the Abolition of Slavery in Cuba* (Austin, Tex., 1967); Rebecca J. Scott, *Slave Emancipation in Cuba; The transition to free labor, 1860–1899* (Princeton, 1985); Robert E. Conrad, *The Destruction of Brazilian Slavery, 1850–1888* (Berkeley, Calif., 1972); Rebecca J. Scott, Seymour Drescher et al., *The Abolition of Slavery and the Aftermath of Emancipation in Brazil* (Durham, N.C., 1988); Robin Blackburn, 'Abolitionism and Emancipation in comparative Perspective' (unpublished Ms., kindly furnished by the author). In the mid-nineteenth century, the industrial interests of Catalonia (the 'Manchester of Spain') were closely linked to the preservation of the Cuban connection, including their trade privileges and the continuity of plantation staple production. See Raymond Carr, *Spain 1808–1975*, 2d edn. (Oxford, 1982), pp. 199–201, 307–9, 323; C. A. M. Hennessy, *The Federal Republic in Spain* (Oxford, 1962). pp. 64–8; Earl Ray Beck, *A Time of Triumph and of Sorrow: Spanish politics during the reign of Alfonso XII, 1874–1885* (London 1979), pp. 114–20; and especially Robert Whitney, 'The Political Economy of Abolition: The Hispano-Cuban elite and Cuban slavery', *Slavery and Abolition*, 13 (August 1992), pp. 20–36. The list of opponents of the first abolition bill (for Puerto Rico) 'reads like a "Who's Who" of Spain's most prominent capitalists and political figures'; Whitney, p. 29. Peru, another late emancipating nation (1855), is equally illustrative of the weak link between antislavery and rapid industrialization or the emergence of a 'national entrepreneurial bourgeoisie'. See Peter Blanchard, *Slavery and Abolition in Early Republican Peru* (Wilmington, Del., 1992), pp. 135–7, 189–207. Venezuela, which remained an agricultural export economy throughout the century before final emancipation in 1854, was equally notable for an absence of abolitionism. It entirely lacked 'the panoply of a crusade', popular abolitionism, or antislavery campaigns. See John V. Lombardi, 'The Abolition of Slavery in Venezuela: A nonevent', in *Slavery and Race Relations in Latin America*, Robert Brent Toplin, ed. (Westport, 1974), pp. 228–52. Fogel and Engerman showed that even by northern European standards, the US slave South ranked high among the world's industrial and financial economies in 1860. See *Time on the Cross*, pp. 254–7; and Larry Schweikart, *Banking in the American South from the Age of Jackson to Reconstruction* (Baton Rouge, La., 1987), pp. 254–66.

55. Before the beginning of the eighteenth century, the ratio of black slaves to Europeans in Surinam, the major Dutch colony in the Americas, was already more than 4 to 1. In South Africa, slaves outnumbered free white burghers by the second decade of the eighteenth century. By the 1730s, the demographic ratio of slaves to freemen in certain areas of the colony was similar to that of contemporary South Carolina. For Guiana estimates, see John J. McCusker, 'The Rum Trade and the Balance of Payments of the Thirteen Continental Colonies, 1660–1775', 2 vols. (Ph.D. dissertation, University of Pittsburgh, 1970),

1, p. 601. On the Cape Colony, see Nigel Worden, *Slavery in Dutch South Africa* (Cambridge, 1985), pp. 10–12.

56. Even the New Netherlands colony in America remained weak, vulnerable, and ethnically diverse before the British conquest because of the scattered pattern of settlement. It also lacked cultural and political support networks and leaders interested in reproducing Dutch culture. See A. G. Roeber, 'The Origin of Whatever Is Not English among Us', in *Strangers within the Realm: Cultural margins of the first British Empire*, Bernard Bailyn and Philip D. Morgan, eds. (Chapel Hill, N.C., 1991), pp. 220–83. The Dutch seaborne empire relied heavily on foreigners and recently naturalized citizens, Sephardic Jews, Huguenots, Germans, etc. for its seventeenth-century colonial ventures in Brazil, the Caribbean, the Guianas, and the Cape Colony. Until the late eithteenth century, Surinam was governed by a quasi-public Societeit van Suriname, not directly by the Dutch state. This was an additonal buffer against perceptions of metropolitan responsibility. There was no impetus toward abolition or emancipation from the colonies themselves. In religious terms, Moravian missionaries were active in the Dutch Caribbean colonies from the 1730s onward. For well over a century, however, they ensured their acceptability among the planters by emphasizing (like their evangelical counterparts in the British Caribbean until the 1820s) their 'neutrality' on the issue of slavery. Compare Oostindie, 'The Enlightenment', pp. 8–13, with Drescher, *Capitalism and Antislavery*, pp. 117–23. The Dutch did not manage to establish a transatlantic communications network like that of the Anglo–Americans by the mid-eighteenth century. See Susan O'Brien, 'A Transatlantic Community of Saints: The great awakening and the first evangelical network, 1735–1755', *American Historical Review*, 91 (October 1986), pp. 811–32; and Eltis, 'Europeans and the Rise and Fall of African Slavery', pp. 1421–2.

57. On English migration flows, see E. A. Wrigley and R. S. Schofield, *The Population History of England, 1541–1871: A reconstruction* (Cambridge, Mass., 1981), pp. 219–20. In 1700, blacks represented 36 percent of the population of British America and 12.5 percent of the Continental Colonies. On the eve of the American Revolution, the respective percentages were 32.5 and 25 percent. On the Dutch West India Company's difficulties, see J. G. Van Dillen, 'The West India Company, Calvinism and Politics', in Meilink-Roelofsz, *Dutch Authors on West Indian History*, pp. 149–86, esp. p. 175.

58. See Roger Bruns, ed., *Am I Not a Man and a Brother: The antislavery crusade of revolutionary America, 1688–1788* (New York, 1977), pp. 3–4; Stephanie Grauman Wolf, *Urban Village: Population, community, and family structure in Germantown Pennsylvania, 1683–1800* (Princeton, 1976), p. 129; Jean R. Soderlund, *Quakers and Slavery: A divided spirit* (Princeton, 1985); and Gary Nash and Jean Soderlund, *Freedom by Degrees: emancipation in Pennsylvania and its aftermath* (New York, 1991), on the tortuous road to abolition in Pennsylvania. In abandoning the notion of a wide gap between English and Dutch economic development to account for British antislavery, one may be tempted to posit

alternative Anglo-Dutch 'gaps' in communications networks and national 'sensitivity' to the overseas world. Eltis concludes that because of their superiority in transatlantic migration, the English 'must have dwarfed' the Dutch in the intensity of transoceanic communications and in popular awareness of the world beyond Europe. (See Eltis, 'Europeans and the Rise and Fall of African Slavery', pp. 1421–2.) However, 'the greatest migration into the English Atlantic between 1675 and 1740 was neither English speaking nor European nor voluntary'. Improving English Atlantic communication intensified slavery. Ian K. Steele, *The English Atlantic 1675–1740: An exploration of communication and community* (New York, 1986), p. 252.

59. See Worden, *Slavery*, pp. 16–17; and *The Reports of Chavonnes and His Council*, in *The Van Riebeeck Society Publications*, 1 (Cape Town, 1918), pp. 85–112. The distribution of slaves was as important in the colony as their relative importance as laborers. By 1750, almost half the free male population had at least one slave. See Elphick and Giliomee, *The Shaping of South African Society*, pp. 135, 541.

60. On the role of projected futures in the emergence of autonomous communities in the Americas. see Benedict Anderson. *Imagined Communities: Reflections on the origins and spread of nationalism* (London, 1983). Comparing Vermont's Dutch and Yankee communities, Randolph A. Roth notes the far greater propensity of the latter to engage in reform movements, including antislavery, during the six decades after 1790. He emphasizes the long-term impact of the distinctive character of prerevolutionary town life and politics in the Anglo-American world, compared with the more parochial and less voluntaristic Dutch. Roth, *The Democratic Dilemma: Religions, reform, and the social order in the Connecticut River Valley of Vermont, 1791–1850* (Cambridge, 1987), 302–4. Roth notes the historiographic perspective that concludes that the Dutch entered politics primarily to advance or protect economic interests, not to reform society, a pattern typical of ethnic groups of the Middle Colonies; pp. 385–6, n. 6.

61. [Arthur Young] *Political Essays Concerning the Present State of the British Empire* (London, 1772), pp. 20–1. On the Continental Colonies as an imagined community without slaves, see Arthur Lee, *An Essay in Vindication of the Continental Colonies of America from a Censure of Mr. Adam Smith, in His 'Theory of Moral Sentiments* [1759]', *with Some Reflections on Slavery in General* (London, 1764).

62. On the American Revolution and antislavery, see Arthur Zilversmit, *The First Emancipation: The Abolition of slavery in the North* (Chicago, 1967); and Ira Berlin and Ronald Hoffman, eds., *Slavery and Freedom in the Age of the American Revolution* (Charlottesville, Va., 1983).

63 See Davis, *Slavery in Revolution*, chs. 4 and 5. On Georgia as an imagined community free of slavery, see J. E. Crowley, *This Sheba, Self: The conceptualization of economic life in Eighteenth-Century America* (Baltimore, Md., 1974), pp. 30–34; Betty Wood, 'James Edward Oglethorpe Race, and slavery', in Phinizy Spalding and Harvey H. Jackson, eds., *Oglethorpe in Perspective: Georgia's founder after two hundred years* (Tuscaloosa, Ala., 1989), pp. 66–79; *The Most Delightful*

Dutch Capitalism and Antislavery 233

Country of the Universe: Promotional literature of the colony of Georgia, 1717–1734, Trevor R. Reese, intro. (Savannah, Ga., 1972), p. 183. The flow of slaves from the Dutch colonies to the Netherlands was miniscule compared with the British case. Compare Oostindie, 'The Enlightenment', 5n.; and Drescher, *Capitalism and Antislavery*, ch. 3.

64. See Yves Benot, *La Révolution française et la fin des colonies* (Paris, 1987); and Jean Tarrade, 'Les colonies et les principes de 1789: Les Assemblées révolutionnaires face au problème de l'esclavage', *Revue française d'histoire d'Outre-mer*, 76 (1989), pp. 9–34.

65. On the number of Surinam slaves in the eighteenth-century Netherlands, see Gert Oostindie and Emy Maduro, eds., *In Het Land van de Overheerser: II Antillianen en Surinamers in Nederland, 1634/1667–1954* (Dordrecht, 1986), p. 7. For the text of the Dutch declaration of 1776, see 'Placaat van de Staaten Generaal ... 23 Mey 1776', in *ibid.*, pp. 15–16. (This text was brought to my attention by Professor Oostindie.) Also see Cornelis C. Goslinga, *The Dutch in the Caribbean and in the Guianas, 1680–1791* (Assen, 1985), p. 553. On the tensions produced by mobile blacks in Britain and France, see Drescher, *Capitalism and Antislavery*, ch. 2; John Garrigus, 'Blue and Brown: Contraband Indigo and the Rise of a Free Colored Planter Class in French Saint-Dominque'; and Sue Peabody, 'Race, Slavery and French Law: The legal context of the "Police des Noirs"' (MSS. kindly provided by the authors). For the French Revolution, see David Geggus, 'Racial Equality, Slavery, and Colonial Secession during the Constituent Assembly', *American Historical Review*, 94 (December 1989), pp. 1290–1308.

66. Slave resistance models of abolition have also proliferated during the past generation. They emphasize the role and agency of slave resistance in achieving emancipation or in accelerating metropolitan antislavery action. This model has been most successfully applied to the case of the first French slave emancipation, and there have been attempts to extend it throughout the slave Americas. See, for example, Eugene D. Genovese, *From Rebellion to Revolution: Afro-American slave revolts in the making of the modern world* (Baton Rouge, La., 1979); Michael Craton, *Testing the Chains: Resistance to slavery in the British West Indies* (Ithaca, 1982); James Walvin, ed., *Slavery and British Society, 1776–1846* (London, 1982), chs. 5, 6; David Richardson, ed., *Abolition and Its Aftermath* (London, 1985), part B; and Blackburn, *The Overthrow*, chs. 5, 6, and 9. Here, too, the Dutch case logically qualifies as the preeminent candidate for a slave resistance model of abolition before 1790. Postma calculated that there may have been up to 300 revolts on Dutch slavers in the course of the transatlantic slave trade (Postma, *The Dutch in the Atlantic Slave Trade*, p. 167). Surinam was 'a theater of perpetual war'; see John Gabriel Stedman, *Narrative of a Five Years Expedition against the Revolted Negroes of Surinam, in Guiana, on the Wild Coast of South America, from the Year 1772 to 1777 ...*, Richard Price and Sally Price, eds. (Baltimore, Md., 1988), 'Introduction', p. xiv. The maroon population of the Dutch colonies was by far the largest in the Caribbean area throughout the period of slavery. See

also Richard Price, *The Guiana Maroons: A historical and biographical Introduction* (Baltimore, 1976). Although Surinam's preemancipation period was not preceded by a major slave uprising, the metropolitan debates were punctuated by discussions of covert resistance and open unrest at the moments of British and French emancipation. See Michael Craton, 'The Transition from Slavery to Free Wage Labour in the Caribbean, 1780–1890: A survey with particular reference to recent scholarship', *Slavery and Abolition*, 13 (August 1992), pp. 37–67, esp. p. 46.

67. See Drescher, *Capitalism and Antislavery*, ch. 1.
68. In considering the longer-term relationship between capitalism and servile labor, one can note both the persistence of slavery in the commercialized societies of Mediterranean Europe and the disappearance of chattel slavery in an economically expanding northern Europe from the mid-tenth to the mid-fourteenth century. The Dutch appropriately present the most paradoxical evidence, illustrated by the early decline of personal bondage in the Low Countries and the late ending of slavery and other forms of bound labor overseas. On the significance of time horizons in the capitalism and antislavery debate, see Stanley L. Engerman, 'Chicken Little, Anna Karenina, and the Economics of Slavery: Two reflections on historical analysis, with examples drawn mostly from the study of slavery', *Social Science History*, 17 (1993), pp. 161–71. Davis vigorously argues against the long-term causal significance of the capitalist market as a stimulus to antislavery: 'The Perils of Doing History', pp. 291–2.
69. Ashworth, 'Capitalism, Class, and Antislavery', pp. 286–7.
70. See Postma, *The Dutch in the Atlantic Slave Trade*, p. 11; Drescher, *Capitalism and Antislavery*, p. 15; Davis, *Slavery in Revolution*, p. 214n.
71. Compare Drescher, 'Two Variants', pp. 43–63; Drescher, *Capitalism and Antislavery*, chs. 4, 6, 7; Seymour Drescher, 'Whose Abolition? Popular Pressure and the Ending of the British Slave Trade' (*Past and Present*, August 1994); Edward Magdol, *The Antislavery Rank and File: A social profile of the abolitionists' constituency* (New York, 1986), pp. 57–8, 137–40; John Ashworth, 'Capitalism and Humanitarianism', pp. 189–98, and 'Capitalism, Class, and Antislavery', pp. 274–81, Davis, 'The Perils of Doing History', pp. 291–3, all in Bender, *Antislavery Debate*. A full discussion of Anglo–American capitalism and antislavery must also articulate differences between antislaveries as well as between capitalisms. There were anti-slave trade, anti-black, humanitarian, egalitarian, religious, and secular variants, sometimes operating separately and sometimes in tandem or tension.

8 Servile Insurrection and John Brown's Body in Europe (1993)*

The most famous and graphic European image to appear in the wake of the raid on Harpers Ferry, Virginia, in October 1859 was an engraving entitled *John Brown*. Against a dark landscape and a dull cloudy sky, a small human figure hangs from a gallows. The body's features are almost completely obscured in shadow. From the heavens alone come shafts of light breaking through the dreary obscurity. They touch the gallows and the figure. Beneath the illustration are the words: 'Pro Christo – Sicut Christus, John Brown, – Charleston. Designed by Victor Hugo'.[1]

The engraving was the frontispiece to the most widely publicized commentary on John Brown to reach the United States from across the Atlantic. Hugo's 'Letter on John Brown', written in early December 1859 and directed to the editor of a London newspaper, was reprinted in newspapers and pamphlets on both sides of the Atlantic. It was viewed by American abolitionists as a document that would 'be read by millions with thrilling emotions'. In it France's most famous contemporary writer proclaimed in exclamatory prose that the whole civilized world (that is, England, France, and Germany) was witnessing with horror a travesty of justice – 'not in Turkey, but in America!' 'The champion of Christ ... slaughtered by the American Republic', 'the assassination of Emancipation by Liberty', 'something more terrible than Cain slaying Abel ... Washington slaying Spartacus!' Hugo wrote the letter as an impassioned public plea to save Brown from execution. The engraving was appended to later publications of the letter to portray Brown as a crucified Christian martyr and slave emancipator, with the gibbet as his cross.[2]

Journal of American History, 80(2) (September 1993), pp. 499–524.

Hugo's letter became the most prized gem among the overseas commentaries on John Brown published by William Lloyd Garrison in the *Liberator* during the winter of 1859–1860. The American Anti-Slavery Society gave prominence to 'opinions from over Sea', including Hugo's, in its annual report of May 1860, entitled *The Anti-Slavery History of the John Brown Year*. The report prayerfully observed that the judgments of a foreign country 'in some sort, foreshadow those of future times'. To a bitterly divided United States, Hugo's letter was touted as typical of the meaning given John Brown's death by all civilized world opinion.[3]

Historians of the Civil War era in the United States have approached the John Brown affair almost exclusively as a domestic conflict with domestic impacts. Any venturing beyond North America has been limited to identifying a few European celebrities who took note of Brown in their writings or private correspondence. Yet a wider range of overseas observers were sufficiently stirred to link Brown's fate to major themes of nineteenth-century Western culture: civilization and barbarism, Europeans and non-Europeans, slavery and human progress, and, above all, the role of violence in the pursuit of, and resistance to, social change.

THE STRUCTURE OF COMMUNICATION

If the aftershocks of the attack on Harpers Ferry reverberated across the Atlantic, the fate of John Brown was not of equal interest throughout Europe. Nor did the turmoil in America stimulate the impassioned intervention of Europe's intellectuals. Probably American abolitionists seized so eagerly upon Hugo's letter because he was the only eminent European intellectual to proclaim, with maximum publicity, his unreserved support of Brown's act. From American reprints of European reactions it is the comparative silence, rather than the outspokenness, of Europe's intellectuals that is striking. Hugo was the only European celebrity whose words were directly quoted in the *Liberator* or the annual report of the American Anti Slavery Society. For the most part, Brown intruded upon European consciousness only in the anonymity of press reports and editorials. The European response to the

Harpers Ferry affair and its aftermath was almost exclusively journalistic.

There was also a clear geographical pattern to transatlantic attention. Interest in the various phases of the affair was far more evident in the newspapers of Britain than in those of the Continent, and far more intense in northern England and southern Scotland than in other areas of Britain. On the Continent published discussion of John Brown seems to have been most extensive in France, but still far less abundant than the British commentary. In most of the Continent's newspapers, Brown's fate did not elicit more than one editorial comment. Even the affair's most dramatic moment, the execution, usually figured only as a brief news item.[4]

Newspapers in maritime nations with well-developed Atlantic trading networks often had private correspondents reporting on events in America. There was a clear diminution of interest and coverage from Atlantic maritime countries to the interior regions of Europe.[5] The communications network, however, was not the principal factor influencing European reaction to the John Brown crisis in America. Garrison's *Liberator* was typical in emphasizing the European response as an overwhelmingly British phenomenon. By the 1850s Anglo–American trade, immigration, tourism, cultural exchange, and political interaction were all far better developed than any other links between Europe and the United States. In addition to the steady flow of people from the British Isles to the United States, forty thousand American tourists a year visited England, and the lion's share of American overseas exports went to Great Britain.[6] As regards interest in John Brown, the most significant network was the political and cultural link between the American and British antislavery movements. By 1859 this Anglo–American network had been in place for more than a generation. Ideas, money, convention delegates, petitions, addresses, abolitionist lecturers, and runaway slaves crisscrossed the Atlantic. There was a pattern of continuous communication, punctuated by periodic mass mobilizations. Since the British abolitionists had long since succeeded in dismantling the legal apparatus supporting British colonial slavery (from 1833 to 1838), the persistence of slavery in the United States, where it was both vigorously expanding and dominated by an English-speaking planter class, was of prime concern to British abolitionists.[7]

While the Anglo–American antislavery connection was a generation old, its British component was in serious decline by the late 1850s. British abolitionism was fragmented, highly localized, reduced in numbers and local chapters, and dependent on the residual loyalty of affluent individual families for day-to-day operations. Nevertheless, antislavery retained a broader and more powerful constituency in Britain than anywhere in contemporary Europe. Moreover, just as interest in Brown was greater in Britain than on the Continent, so it was greater in the traditional heartland of British abolitionism – industrial northern England and southern Scotland. Antislavery embers still glowed in the old 'petition' towns – where masses had readily mobilized to petition against slavery in the preceding decades – such as Halifax, Bolton, Leeds, Sheffield, Newcastle upon Tyne, Glasgow and Edinburgh. Only there were public meetings called to hear lectures about John Brown and American slavery in the winter of 1859–60.[8]

THE STRUCTURE OF INTERPRETATION

If the intensity of interest in John Brown depended on an established network of information and political interaction, European judgments on the John Brown affair were shaped even more by the mentality of the mid-nineteenth century, which exalted Europe's civilizing mission. Brown's story unfolded within a larger conceptual world that identified the meaning and significance of his actions and those of his fellow citizens. Europe and its extensions formed a core world of standards and behaviors connoted by the term 'civilization'. Revolutionaries used the binary formula of civilization/barbarism or civilization/savagery as readily as did conservatives. In a later hagiographical book about John Brown, a French revolutionary exile expressed special disgust for American 'Red Indian' slaveholders, implying a level of human degradation for their slaves even worse than for those of civilized white masters. Hugo's reference to the whole 'civilized world' in his letter on Brown casually located that world in western Europe and the United States. Barbarity or savagery was generally characteristic of those non-European areas, cultures, peoples, or behaviors that contradicted the patterns or aspirations of the civilized core. The people of the United States (or at least its cultivated classes) were generally accorded full membership in the 'civilized world' and often placed at its forefront by European observers. Hence the invective with which Hugo treated the 'corruption' of one of the world's leading civilized sectors.[9]

In this conceptual world, civilization was not only a condition but also a process, comprising both an internal transformation of the North Atlantic core and the latter's gradual incorporation of the uncivilized periphery. One might emphasize material, intellectual, or moral aspects of that transformation, but even traditionalists within Europe acknowledged a dynamic alteration of the non-European world. The United States was recognized as a prime agent of this transformation. Even those who rejected some aspects of such 'progress' understood that the rest of the world was becoming increasingly synchronized with the European core. Most of the media that took note of John Brown generally qualified the United States as a progressive member of the 'civilized world'.

Those Europeans describing world trends around 1860 tended to regard the civilizing process as dependent on the expansion of European settlement overseas. In the various overlapping taxonomies used to subdivide Europeans, the United States was usually included with Great Britain and the white-settler colonies in its empire. Britons and Americans were united by ties of language, culture, religion, law, and economy; by a shared heritage of representative institutions; and by relative immunity to both midcentury Continental revolutions and royal authoritarianism. There was an increasing tendency to conflate these similarities as shared characteristics of the 'Anglo–Saxon race'. The rhetorical emphasis on Anglo–Saxonism as an indelible and distinctive biological inheritance was far commoner by the end of the 1850s than it had been even a generation before.[10]

By the mid-nineteenth century, the older linkage of the Anglo–Saxon myth with individual liberty and political freedom within England had undergone a profound change. The myth was now casually associated with the idea that the people of the entire planet were being molded to the qualities of a superior Anglo–Saxon physical stock. Human moral, political, and economic progress was dependent on, and evidenced by, the geographical expansion and dominance of that dynamic race, the one most capable of transforming the less endowed. Newspapers encountered little criticism in Britain when they spoke with pride of Anglo–Saxon energy in peopling the world, or even when they described, with philosophical resignation, expansion of the United States southward toward Central America as the great leavening agent of the Americas.[11]

Since attachment to liberty was a putative characteristic of Anglo–Saxons, antislavery could be incorporated into the racial mythos and the emancipation of slaves in the British Empire used as evidence of Anglo–Saxon superiority. Midcentury British journalists never tired of citing Britain's leading role against the African slave trade and colonial slavery. Even radical American abolitionists (including Theodore Parker, one of John Brown's early supporters) could combine Anglo-Saxonism with vigorous opposition to the extension of slavery.[12]

If Europeans generally included the United States within the ambit of civilization, the existence and especially the expansion of the slave system posed a conundrum for the conceptualizers of progress. By 1859 the ending of personal bondage was becoming a key indicator of the civilizing process. In the century before the Harpers Ferry raid, the absence or removal of personal bondage had become a distinguishing feature of Europe's high state of civilization. Serfdom had been abolished in central Europe. The Russian government was drawing up plans to end serfdom in its last European stronghold. Slavery had beaten an uneven retreat in large parts of the Americas. Only the United States seemed to be moving against the thrust of history. Its slave system was still expanding – economically, demographically, and politically. Far from bending to the prevailing doctrine of progress, southern slaveholders were increasingly vocal about preserving and extending their dynamic institution.[13]

Nevertheless, until the late 1850s, the weight of planetary evidence for emancipation allowed Europeans to explain away American slaveholders' victories as a distressing exception and to search the horizon for countervailing signs. If the end of

American slavery was 'but a question of time', Europe was relieved of responsibility for encouraging immediate, and risking violent, emancipation. The ideology of civilization, peaceful progress, and racial superiority jostled uncomfortably alongside portents of disruptive and violent threats to that ideology. In mid-November 1859, in the same issue that reported the news of 'Old Brown's' trial, the *London Times* editorialized on its principal anxiety about America, the possibility of a war over the San Juan Islands on the disputed border between the United States and British Columbia. It drew a fearful picture of the potential reversal of Anglo–Saxon progress:

> Europe and Asia would look on with surprise and exultation, watching paroxysms of frenzy among that terrible Anglo–Saxon race which had seemed to monopolize the ALMIGHTY'S permission to go forth and people the earth; wondering to see that vast family whose expansion they had envied, whose industrial energy they had found it vain to emulate, and whose free thoughts, wafted over the world, were ever sowing themselves in uncongenial soils, now engaged in the mad enterprise of destroying their common property and shedding their own blood.

Still the race's ability to resolve its problems without recourse to violence would triumph once again. Whatever the unsavory qualities of Britons' 'American cousins', 'the respectable portion of the great American people ... has sentiments as civilized as those of the same classes in Europe'. It was into this frame of reference that the reported events of John Brown's raid were placed in Europe.[14]

THE SALIENCE OF THE JOHN BROWN AFFAIR

The news of the seizure of Harpers Ferry reached Europe at the end of October. Discussion of Brown's fate peaked toward the end of December, after the arrival of news of his execution and its aftermath. There was a final surge of discussion early in January, following the publication of President James Buchanan's state of the union address. Thereafter, except in British antislavery circles, discussion of Brown almost ceased. European concern was limited, even at the peak of interest. Most Cotinental and many British newspapers carried only brief notices of the trial and execution.

Initially, many European observers dismissed the political significance of the raid on Harpers Ferry altogether by describing it as a riot. The correspondent of the *Independance Belge*, published in Brussels, observed that in size Brown's attempt qualified as no more than a minor European *émeute*. The most eloquent evidence that the John Brown affair had limited salience in Europe was its omission from year's end editorial retrospectives. Reviewing the year 1859 and sometimes the whole decade, editors failed to perceive any major implications for the future in the incident. Harpers Ferry did not even make the list of significant events in *The Annual Register of World Events* for 1859.[15]

The proceedings in northern Virginia and their aftermath throughout the United States were overshadowed by the unfolding events in the Italian peninsula. Europe's attention was focused on the reverberations of the victory of the French emperor, Louis Napoleon, over the Habsburg monarchy in Lombardy, the continuing process of Italian unification, the fate of the papal territories in central Italy, the shifting balance of power in western Europe, and the possibilities of an Anglo–French conflict. If any revolutionary possessed true celebrity status in Europe, it was Giuseppe Garibaldi. In the winter of 1859–60, his past and potential role in Italian unification was a source of endless speculation. Even in the British radical and abolitionist press, it was 'general Garibaldi', not 'captain Brown', whose moves and words were monitored to gauge the danger of future violence. Brown made none of the annual lists of the illustrious deceased with which many newspapers closed their books on the past year's events.[16]

THE CORE TENSION: SERVILE INSURRECTION AND HUMAN FORTITUDE

If the news emanating from the distant hills of Virginia could hardly compete with the intrigue and anticipation generated by political and diplomatic maneuvers on both sides of the Alps, John Brown made Europeans aware, in more personalized terms than ever before, of the depth of the crisis looming across the Atlantic. The traditional image of a prosperous, philistine, invincible United States was transformed. The first news of Harpers Ferry conjured up one of the most shocking terms of nineteenth-century political rhetoric. Newspapers reiterated the same sketchy details in almost identical words. Somewhere between five hundred and seven hundred slaves had risen in 'servile' or 'Negro' insurrection somewhere in Virginia and seized an arsenal, with some destruction of life and of lines of communication.[17]

Servile insurrection resonated with historically loaded meanings from two sources. The first was ancient Roman history. From classical antiquity Europe derived stories of desperate slave revolts followed by ruthless suppressions in which no quarter was given and no bounds set on vengeance. In its earliest editorial accounts of the Harpers Ferry uprising the *London Times* referred, with Victorian propriety, to history's averting its face from the unspeakable cruelties of this aspect of the ancient world.[18]

The second source of Europe's image of servile insurrection was a more recent event. The St Domingue uprising of 1791 and the Haitian war of independence of 1803 against the first Napoleon furnished the ultimate image of servile insurrection – a war of scorched earth, mutual mutilation and extermination. The combatants did not respect the civilized taboos regarding innocence, age, sex, or helplessness. Imprinted on European memory was the image of the brutal climax to that insurrection, the massacre of whites by Jean Jacques Dessalines, the leader of the Haitian army of independence, after his moment of victory.[19]

By the mid-nineteenth century, there were two sharply bifurcated images of black slaves in particular and Africans in general. One presented blacks as fundamentally passive, either docile and gentle by nature or dulled into permanent submissiveness by the dehumanizing experience of slavery. The basis for the other image was rage – blacks as creatures of suppression and brutalization, who, when offered the opportunity, retaliated with blind vengeance. Both images could be ascribed to people in a state of primitiveness, savagery, or barbarism. This was a condition indigenous to sub-Saharan Africa and intensified in the plantation societies of the New World.

The transition from slavery to freedom could well be accomplished without unfettered violence, as the slave emancipations of the 1830s and 1840s in British, French, and Scandinavian colonies in the Caribbean demonstrated. But a sudden collapse of authority could also lead to bloody chaos.[20]

Most initial news reports on Harpers Ferry used 'servile' or 'Negro' insurrection in their headlines. Almost all also used adjectives like 'horrible' or 'fearful' to describe the envisioned consequences of unleashing the 'hell hounds' of such an uprising. Sketchy news allowed editorialists to invoke the supposed natural rebelliousness of black slaves. Throughout the later infusions of information, the label *servile insurrection*, with its connotations of pillage, mutilation, torture, rape, and brutality, clung to the affair. After about a week, the failure of the slaves to rise and the relatively easy capture of the raiders became clear. Newspapers that pursued the story now began to offer, again in bare outline, the second major image of the affair – the mad or audacious leader of the raid who had survived the ordeal and was being indicted for murder and treason. All reports included a number of points. To his followers, the leader of the aborted uprising was a truly patriarchal figure ('Old Brown') and a warrior ('Captain Brown'). Brown's New England heritage, his participation in the Kansas guerrilla wars, his stoic resignation to his fate, the impressive courage with which he bore physical wounds, and, above all, his calm and defiant appeal to an authority higher than his Virginia judges gradually fleshed out the central character of the story.[21]

Literally by his presence, Brown shifted the focus away from the imagined bodies of helpless innocents sacrificed to savage insurrection. Even reporters who claimed that they were abolitionists peppered their early accounts with disapproving nouns like 'madman' or 'fanatic'. Those were later accompanied by less negative historical symbols: Oliver Cromwell, Puritan, Ironside, Spartacus. 'Old Brown' was a man weathered but not bent by bitter struggles that had cost him two sons. Almost all reports remarked on the haste of the proceedings, which brought Brown into court bedridden with his wounds. To the initial descriptions of the leader as insane or fanatic were joined terms of understanding and even justification. The Kansas battle-ground had produced a wild old man, 'maddened' by fate, or even the 'injured soul' of a hero. Other descriptors harked back to the distant past – the 'enthusiasm' of Puritanism, the 'lofty' fanaticism of the Reformation – or to the noble tragedy of an Othello 'who loved his fellow man not wisely but too well'.[22]

Brown's composure amid overwhelming hostility and power helped to displace, or at least to dilute, the all-pervasive obsession with servile insurrection. The waters of the Potomac at Harpers Ferry were metaphorically mixed with the waters of the Nile. In his apologia Brown spoke of having wished merely to liberate and to draw off the slaves, rather than to stir up an uncontrollable servile or racial conflict. Few European newspaper reporters discussed the evidence that might have clashed with the image of a flight to freedom. Brown's invocation of divine law received the broadest coverage, making him both victim and judge of an all-too-inhumane institution.

Precisely because a black servile insurrection had utterly failed to occur, attention shifted to the free white prisoner. Hugo's exclamatory dichotomies captured the decisive shift. Brown 'sounded to these men, these oppressed brothers the rallying cry of Freedom. The slaves, enervated by servitude, made no response to the appeal. Slavery afflicts the soul with Weakness!' Brown's own strength of soul was correspondingly magnified.[23] There was an exceptionally broad consensus that for a man of violence Brown was an extraordinary individual. The dramatic appeal of his courtroom behavior induced the *Monde Illustré* of Paris to feature the affair in its issue of December 1859.[24]

The execution was the most heavily reported moment of the affair. The reports all emphasized Brown's 'firmness' and 'courage'. Some accounts described his final interview with his wife as unemotional; others emphasized its congruence with the stoic character he had manifested during the trial. Brown had chosen the quintessentially nineteenth-century male role at Harpers Ferry. The one insertion of the feminine Mary Brown into the drama conformed, in exquisite detail, to the proprieities of the nineteenth century and to its vision of antiquity. Mrs Brown was, at least in the more sympathetic European accounts, 'courageous without insensibility, tender without weakness, and her bearing in the last interview was worthy of a Roman wife'. The more attention reports allotted to the details of Brown's personal behavior, the more the real captive superseded the hypothetical servile war. Of all the European reports, the *Liberator* chose for its first reprint the comments of the *London Morning Star* under the headline 'THERE WAS NO "BUNKUM" IN BROWN'. The *Star* emphasized the general admiration for the raw courage of 'OSSOWATOMIE BROWN', his 'true grit', with 'no fine sand'. Finally, every report on the execution noted the unwavering body standing with the rope around its neck for several minutes. On the threshold of eternity, 'he neither blenched nor wearied'.[25]

Closely linked to the language used to describe the execution was the meaning assigned to Brown's death. Just as the initial reports of the raid had employed the language of unfiltered violence, so the language of martyrdom was immediately embedded in sympathetic reflections on the execution. Very few editorials offered Brown to their readers as an unqualified martyr, but most referred to the use of that term by many Americans.[26]

SERVILE INSURRECTION AND THE SOUTH

If the images of mass insurrection and of Brown's indomitable individual fortitude dominated portrayals of the Harpers Ferry affair, images of fear and terror quickly became affixed to John Brown's captors and indeed to the whole South. Since most of the correspondents and the American newspaper sources of European papers were situated in the North, few accounts interpreted the events from a southern perspective.

A central judgment of the South emerged from the very first news of Harpers Ferry; it was elaborated through the later stages of the affair. The South became a region, a society, under the grip of a single overwhelming emotion – panic. Southern panic and its consequences informed almost every European report on the affair. An initial acceptance of Virginia's mobilization as necessary against a massive and unfathomable threat gave way to widespread disparagement of the South's over-reaction. This sense of emotional disproportion made itself felt in most aspects of reporting. One correspondent bewailed the difficulty of explaining the massive mobilization of whites in Virginia and throughout the South in response to what his readers would have properly regarded as no more than a routine disturbance if it had occurred in Europe. Even sympathetic newspapers allowed unmistakable notes of pity or contempt into their comments on the 'sad picture of panic' among the southerners. The contrast between that panic and the South's self-proclaimed chivalric virtues invited occasional sneers about southern manliness, by reference to its fear in feminine terms. Most significant, it was not simply those who most identified or sympathized with the abolitionists who condemned the South's panic. Some of the most conservative European newspapers were contemptuous of the hasty trial and execution. The rush to indictment, judgment, and execution increased the European journalistic unease. There was a very general conclusion that the South, by its over-reaction, had helped transform a senseless adventure into an act of heroism and a political crisis.[27]

The more conservative European newspapers acknowledged the existence of grievances that justified some action by the South. They pointedly balanced accounts of southern fear with references to provocative northern 'fanaticism'. Even such reports, however, emphasized that fanaticism was only one tendency within the North. The more virulent manifestations of southern behavior were taken to illustrate the tendency and tenor of the region. Because of the differences between social conditions in Europe and the southern United States, many southern acts appeared both excessive and irrational. Especially incomprehensible were the campaigns to intimidate people of color and white outsiders. Even observers who sympathized with the decision to execute Brown found the widespread 'colorophobia' reported in various states incomprehensible in light of the failure of the uprising. Motions introduced in southern state legislatures to expel or enslave resident free blacks seemed signs of a society gone out of control. The legislative agitation was rendered even more 'outrageous' by news of southern threats and mob violence against northern tradesmen and European workers suspected of being sources of disaffection. There was a steady progression of discomfort, from comments on the 'barbarous' haste in trying 'Old Brown' to reports about incidents of extralegal popular behavior from Virginia to Texas.[28]

European newspapers began to use the rhetoric of insurrection and revolution against the planters. They affixed to the South terms drawn from the French Revolution – the Great Fear and the Reign of Terror. The South's cultivated self-image as a traditional society, paternally ruled by its rural gentry, was now shattered by journalistic analogies to the angry peasant crowds of provincial France in 1789 or to the revolutionary terrorists of Paris in 1794. For Europeans, the story that began in late October 1859 with the evocation of a savage servile insurrection became one recounting lawless coercion in the South in winter 1860.[29]

If the John Brown affair undermined sympathy for the slaveholder-dominated South among conservatives, it diminished sympathy with a slaveholder-dominated America among both radicals and conservatives. Hugo was not alone in identifying the action of Virginia as that of the United States. Especially on the Continent, the United States as a whole was held responsible for the execution of Brown and his followers. For traditionalists and monarchists, Virginia's behavior was but the latest illustration of a fundamental affinity between republics and slavery extending back to the pagan Mediterranean world.

In Paris, one commentary on Harpers Ferry quickly escalated into a debate between traditionalists and secularists on the papacy, whose temporal claims in Italy were in peril. How could one expect real progress toward the termination of slavery, declared the Catholic and monarchist *L'Union*, until the world was converted to the one true apostolic faith? The secular Parisian press immediately countered with the observation that nineteen hundred years of traditional Catholicism had not ended slavery. The papacy still made no effort to excommunicate or otherwise discipline slaveholders in the vast territories in the Americas served by its clergy and within societies swearing allegiance to Rome. In this discussion, reflections on the fate of John Brown immediately shifted into a debate about the merits or evils of various European regimes.[30]

For some continental Europeans, the outcome of the Harpers Ferry affair proved that the United States had betrayed its revolutionary heritage. It was sinking even below the level of a Russia now clearly committed to the emancipation of serfs.

Europe's submerged nations and classes had little to hope for from such an America. If Brown was recognized as a revolutionary comrade, his society was denied its place at the forefront of progress. Such revolutionary exiles as Karl Marx paid little attention to the personal fate of Brown but wondered instead whether the raid, like the coming Russian emancipation, might not signal the spread of great social upheavals beyond the boundaries of revolutionary Europe in 1848.[31]

In Britain, there was a less one-dimensional understanding of the United States. The differentiation between South and North and even of regions within these two geographical areas was axiomatic. The discussion of the meaning of the John Brown affair revolved around the significance accorded to three major concepts: slavery, violence, and race. Arguing from the South's mood after Harpers Ferry or (less frequently) from the potential for slave rebellion, Britons reached a general consensus on the long-term social fragility of the South. The political power of the South in the federal system and the economic power produced by the southern domination of world cotton production were short-term advantages that would yield, in the long run, to the general pattern of European development. There remained only two long-term solutions to the problem crystallized by John Brown – emancipation by violence and blood or a gradual elimination of the slave labor system. The pathway to gradual emancipation was unclear, but the successive European emancipations had shown that, one way or another, America was destined to end slavery. The capture and execution of Brown might be interpreted as a short-term setback for emancipation, but not as an alteration of the course of history.[32]

THE THUNDERER: SERVILE INSURRECTION v. ANGLO-SAXONISM

If the long-term course of world history remained clear, Brown's raid did not convince all European commentators that he had furthered the cause of emancipation. Yet even periodicals that denounced the raid did not show a lasting sympathy with Brown's captors. The *Times* of London offers the outstanding European example of how an articulated intention to offer a balanced, detached interpretation, including even an attempt at a sympathetic view of the southern reaction, was undermined by the flow of events and the escalating passions over John Brown. In the mid-nineteenth century the *Times*, nicknamed *The Thunderer*, was widely regarded as the most authoritative single organ of British public opinion. The *Times* regarded slave emancipation as one of the glories of British history, irrefutable evidence of human progress. Britain's legal and peaceful implementation of emancipation, which recognized both human and property rights, was the very model for social change in the civilized world. The *Times* confidently foresaw a nonviolent transformation of the peculiar institution in the United States.[33]

Refusing to regard slavery as the exclusive, or even the central, issue of the Brown affair, the *Times* placed it in the context of the economics of cotton, of the political prospects for American self-government and federalism, and of the racial relationship between Anglo–Saxons and Africans. Weighing these factors, the *Times* denounced the northern fanatics who endangered Anglo–Saxon destiny, economically, politically, and racially. If the Virginians had hanged a 'poor old man', he remained simply a malefactor, not a martyr. Personal courage could not exonerate a movement that threatened to wipe out the gains of two hundred years of Anglo–Saxon economic and moral progress in North America or to reduce the southern states, of the 'purest English blood', to 'the level of Haiti or Costa Rica'. The *Times* returned again and again to the ultimate talisman of servile insurrection and Haitian-style scenes of murdered planters and ravished white women. In this spirit, the *Times* welcomed anti-Brown manifestations in the North, even quoting (without denunciation) a proslavery rally in New York that promulgated both racist and biblical arguments for slavery. This, concluded the *Times*, was evidence of the trend of public opinion in the United States produced by John Brown's raid.[34]

The stance taken by the *Times* provoked rejoinders from other British publications. For abolitionists the most useful responses were those in periodicals not previously implicated in abolitionist initiatives. The *Economist*, a free-trade periodical that usually steered clear of abolitionist causes, was sufficiently alarmed to intervene directly against the *Times*. Karl Marx and Friedrich Engels were so impressed with the *Economist's* editorial that they dispatched it to the United States for reprinting in the pro-Republican *New York Tribune*. In its rebuttal the *Economist* pointedly contrasted the alarmist view of the raid promulgated by the *Times* and the paper's passivity toward proslavery arguments. When the *Times* treated southern planters as innocent sufferers rather than the 'headstrong, domineering, insolent, cruel, offensive, irritating and bullying party', after half a century of fruitless nonviolent abolitionist preaching, the *Times* betrayed the English antislavery tradition. The sin of civil strife was now almost wholly on the heads of the slave states. The *Economist* was not surprised by the 'insolent doctrines' of Anglo–Saxon race superiority that were often 'half-echoed' by the most popular organ of English opinion. The true surprise had been the equivocation of the *Times* on slavery itself. The *Economist* refused to allow such thoughts to 'go forth to the world with that *imprimatur* of English public opinion on them which their mere insertion in *The Times* gives'.[35]

The *London Daily News*, a major mass-circulation competitor of the *Times* whose comments were reprinted in the United States, was far readier than the *Economist* to sympathize with Brown's motives. Nevertheless, his calamitous mistakes were regretted 'by the true friends of the negro throughout the North'. That his success would have been 'the commencement of anarchy' was the 'prevalent opinion and feeling of the North'. But Brown, the North, the *News*, and most Englishmen would all agree that 'no power in human society could make it wrong to strike down a slaveholder'. So why should the North make itself the accomplice in the perpetuation of slavery? Above all, why should *Englishmen* declare 'that *our* credit or interest' lay in the maintenance of a hateful domination? 'Our religion, laws, and manners forbid and annihilate Slavery'. Even British racial ideology was sent into the field in favor of emancipation: 'The Anglo–Saxon race, of all races of mankind, can assert its superiority without invading the rights of other races less favored in their development'.

Seeing no likelihood of either further insurrection or the dissolution of the Union as the result of Harpers Ferry, the *News* saw no reason whatever to sanction the *Times*' casual equivocation on slavery.[36]

For a few weeks the *Times* continued to blame New England and abolitionist agitation for growing northern acceptance of proslavery arguments and for turning the upper South against gradual emancipation. But, as it chronicled the spate of initiatives against free blacks in the South, it quickly and positively distanced itself from proslavery arguments. It emphatically deplored new marks of 'political reprobation' toward the African race, 'which may well make the philanthropist despair'. The *Times* ridiculed the American embassy's denial, on grounds of race, of a travel visa to Sarah Remond, an American black abolitionist traveling in Britain. It quoted with disdain President James Buchanan's state of the union address, which reaffirmed that property in persons could be carried into any United States territory. It described, in tones of civilized outrage, atrocities committed 'against coloured seamen' on an American vessel on the high seas and indicted in a British court. It contemptuously dismissed the statement by Henry Wise, the governor of Virginia, equating British aid to runaway Negroes with the invasion of Harpers Ferry. For such southern vitriol, the Thunderer reserved the deepest of its ethnic slurs. Wise's 'climax of Southern extravagance', the *Times* editorialized, 'reminds one more of Irish "patriotic" oratory than of anything coming from a reasonable part of the world'[37]

With this racio–cultural demotion of Virginia's chief executive, the rhetoric of Anglo–Saxon unity had vanished. Even the *Times*' usually careful distinctions between and within North and South were dismissed in a cascade of disgust. If Britain could not yet afford to turn its back on American cotton, its leading newspaper would waste no sympathy on the fanatics of either section. 'Neither England nor our American colonies have anything to envy in the social state of the Slave-holding Republic'. Whether insurrectionary or not, the clouded future of the United States decoupled it from a British empire destined for brighter horizons. In its rapid editorial spin away from the South, the *Times* showed the antebellum limits to British conservative sympathy.[38]

THE BRITISH ABOLITIONIST RESPONSE

Insurrection, not race, was the nightmare haunting John Brown's sympathizers as the news of his trial, execution and sanctification successively made its way across the Atlantic. Wendell Phillips might tell the abolitionist faithful in Massachusetts that 'the lesson of the hour is insurrection', but this was the lesson neither of the hour nor of the affair for most British abolitionists.[39]

Harpers Ferry intruded on British discourse at a peak of British self-confidence in nonrevolutionary change. Charles Dickens had just published *A Tale of Two Cities*, emphasizing the retrospective world of difference between Paris and London during the great French Revolution. Signs of stress in Britain were not to be found 'in diplomacy, war, or Parliament'. Loftily surveying the world at the close of 1859, the British press reflected with complacency and pride on Britain's immunity to revolution during the previous half century of European upheaval. Of all the world's major powers, Britain was the only one that did not either look uneasily backward on recent revolutionary violence and post-revolutionary bureaucratic despotism or gaze vertiginously forward into the abyss of civil conflict or social transformation.

The attempted insurrection at Harpers Ferry, even without any added overtones of slave or racial violence, posed difficulties for a society that so assiduously cultivated a non-revolutionary ideology. For a decade Britons had heard a torrent of rhetoric on the Anglo–Saxon knack for compromise. When the *Times* wished to reverse the positive spin on Brown's religious convictions, it called attention to his draft constitution, which sanctioned the seizure of property, and linked his religious pedigree to the anabaptists, Puritans, Fifth Monarchy men, and French republicans in the era of the July Monarchy.[40]

If the revolutionary element in Brown's raid was a challenge to British public ideology at the end of the 1850s, it was a particular embarrassment to those Britons who took the most active interest in John Brown. The central historical tenet of the British abolitionist movement was that it had succeeded (in true English fashion) by the peaceful conquest of public opinion. Whatever the factional differences within British and American antislavery during the three decades before Harpers Ferry, there had been general agreement on nonviolence as the only moral and practicable way to slave emancipation.[41]

The initial impulse of abolitionists in Britain was to distance their movement from the dreaded image of violent insurrection. The *Anti-Slavery Reporter,* organ of the British and Foreign Anti Slavery Society, was circumspect in its first references to Harpers Ferry. It noted that Brown would have many sympathizers, especially among 'those [that is, not us] who justify employment of arms'. Even among 'those who took the opposite position', that is, representatives of the British and Foreign Anti Slavery Society, there were 'few who would not heartily commiserate with him, while they [that is, we] disapprove of his rash attempt'. The *Reporter* pointedly echoed the Quaker *Friends Review* for its final comment: 'the principal actors must have been labouring under a species of insanity, or the blindest fanaticism'. Considering the means 'inconsistent with Christianity and totally indefensible on religious grounds', they profoundly deplored the raid.[42]

Abolitionists in Britain did not all remain as defensive and anxious to bury the event as the *Anti-Slavery Reporter.* As John Brown's performance altered his image, Harriet Martineau resoundingly denied the least possibility of insanity, leaving it to better-informed Americans whether his 'scheme' was wild or hopeless. But Martineau quickly shifted the focus from the actual or revolutionary potential of Brown to his more Christian virtues. He was no mere European (above all no *Irish*) revolutionary. He had none of 'the passion, frenzy and selfish vanity' of the political agitators on Martineau's side of the Atlantic. At the end, only the figure of the solitary upright victim-hero on the gallows remains in Martineau's letter. The uncomfortable havoc of revolutionary violence disappears as completely as in the impenetrable horizon of Hugo's engraving.[43]

Brown's reputation within British antislavery can best be observed in a series of explanatory lectures offered on his career during the winter of 1859–60. One of the two principal speakers was Frederick Douglass, a veteran spokesman for American black abolitionism. Douglass reached Liverpool late in November 1859. When Douglass left the United States, he was probably deeply uncertain as to what connection he wanted to admit to Brown's action, or what to say about it. The day the raid was announced in Philadelphia, Douglass had given a routine lecture there without mentioning the raid, 'as if he did not want to acknowledge the fact that Brown had committed himself, and as if Douglass himself were innocent of any knowledge of it'.[44]

Arriving in England after a hurried flight via Canada, he began his lecture tour with the same distancing strategy. Douglass's first published remarks about Brown and the raid were designed to dispose of that implicit question humorously. Alluding to his initial visit to England as a runaway slave, he quipped, 'I've always been more distinguished for running than for fighting'. Now he was a runaway again, returning 'to the home of all oppressed nations'. In coming to England he had simply stuck to his original plans and repeated his previous flight. But neither Douglass' personal relationship with Brown nor his supposed manliness in staying or running was important in British abolitionist circles. He was continually greeted and sent off to cheers and enthusiasm during the tour. His principal problem with a British abolitionist audience was to address their concern about Brown's own appeal to arms.[45]

As news of Brown's impressive posture in captivity increased the possibilities of throwing a more sympathetic light on the entire affair, Douglass began a strategy of breaking down the dichotomy between Christianity and violence and of making the courageous 'tiger' show his teeth in the most benign manner. Douglass introduced his later discussions by acknowledging that even the most sympathetic British audiences might find it difficult to condone Brown's project. Resurrecting one of Brown's earlier schemes, he pictured him, not as a revolutionary launching a new constitution, but as a Moses. Brown had intended simply to unleash a great exodus of the enslaved up the 'corridor' of the Appalachian Mountains to freedom, leading the freed masses to the promised (and gloriously British) land (Canada/Canaan). Brown had not intended to shed blood; like Moses, he had intervened between the death-dealing master and the slave. Harpers Ferry was transferred to the banks of the Nile. With a bit of good fortune, Brown might have been another George Washington. With ill fortune, he became an apostle and martyr. Step by step, the audience witnessed a rhetorical metamorphosis. From a seemingly wild and hopeless venture, whose success would have produced immeasurable bloodshed, Brown's raid reemerged in British meeting halls as a bloodless representative of British-style patriotism and biblical salvation.[46]

In four months of well-attended meetings, Douglass' translation of Brown was always received with cheers and resolutions of thanks. He was quickly joined on the John Brown circuit by Britain's own premier veteran antislavery lecturer, George Thompson. As the American and the Englishman separately toured a dozen towns in northern England and southern Scotland, Thompson's message on Brown (although, as a Garrisonian, Thompson differed with Douglass on the nature of the American polity) dovetailed with that of Douglass. Yet Thompson's lectures were equally revealing. Following the enrollment of Brown among the glorious (and safely)* dead, he 'supplemented his discourse with a few observations on the offense for which Brown suffered'. He condemned 'the instrumentality which [Brown] employed for the accomplishment of a humane, good and Christian object'. Thompson concluded that Brown had better served the cause by failing and dying than he ever could have by succeeding. In other words, the promulgation of truth, the renovation of public opinion, and legal change (the tripartite tradition of abolitionism) should continue. Harpers Ferry had usefully jolted the public mind, but the raid offered an event, a leader, and a model of action that no one should follow.[47]

Sarah Remond, sharing the platform with Douglass at Wakefield in January 1860, praised Brown's motives but placed herself 'decidedly against such attempts as the one he had undertaken, the power of moral suasion being of itself sufficient to effect the object they had in view'. Douglass had the same message for his audiences, once he shifted from the glorious sacrifice of 1859 to what was to be done in 1860. Peaceful agitation remained the proper policy not only for British supporters of American emancipation but for American abolitionists as well. The message delivered to, and echoed by, British abolitionists seems clear: Granted Brown's beatification, and the abolitionists' splendid attempt to snatch martyrdom from madness, one such victory was more than enough.[48]

One can also measure the behavioral limits of British abolitionist sympathy with John Brown in comparative terms. Before Brown died there was no collective mobilization in Britain either before, or in response to, Hugo's desperate appeal. Yet British abolitionists had mounted just such a mass appeal fifteen years before to stay the execution of another John Brown, under sentence of death for aiding the flight of a fugitive slave. In 1844 a South Carolina judge sentenced one John L. Brown, a native of Maine, 'to hang by the neck until your body be dead'. The sentence reached Great Britain in March 1844. It ignited widespread media discussion. Public meetings in Liverpool, Edinburgh, Glasgow, and Dublin passed resolutions warning that if Brown were executed, the ghost of the murdered man 'would shame American travellers whenever they set foot on the shores of England'.[49]

However, the most imposing British activity for John L. Brown was the nationwide circulation of a collective clerical address directed to the governor of South Carolina. It originated in Lancashire, the English county in which mass abolitionist petitioning had begun in 1787. The clerical memorial quickly obtained thirteen hundred signatures of ministers and other notables. It was dispatched, along with accounts of the proceedings in Glasgow, Edinburgh, and Liverpool, to the United States via the American ambassador in London. The cause of John L. Brown was even raised in Parliament, skirting the proprieties of noninterference in foreign legal proceedings. For the *Liberator*, in 1844, no single event in the United States since the beginning of antislavery agitation had ever 'so powerfully affected the public mind in Great Britain'. The commutation of John L. Brown's sentence was attributed to a surge of public sentiment that overawed even the South.[50]

The British mobilization of 1844 had not been forgotten fifteen years later. Responding to the publication of Hugo's appeal in the *London Daily News*, a correspondent reminded its readers that John L. Brown's sentence had kicked up an antislavery storm in Britain and that his life had been saved. British religious and benevolent feeling was 'surely as strong and vigorous as it was in 1844'. Victor Hugo had led the way. The newspapers and churches of Britain could follow. But the appeal was not taken up by the press, nor by the churches, nor by the abolitionist societies of northern

England and southern Scotland. Indeed, none of these bodies had needed Hugo's letter to remind them of past mobilizations. Nor was the correspondent wrong in assuming that significant religious, benevolent, and even antislavery sentiment remained alive in Britain. Four years after Harpers Ferry, there was another considerable mobilization in favor of the North. British antislavery still had a usable past. One may therefore surmise that the difference between 'young' John Brown in 1844 and 'old' John Brown in 1859 lay less in the state of British feelings about antislavery than in differences between the two cases. Frederick Douglass might urge that old Brown had come to liberate, not to annihilate or to confiscate, but even the warmest crowds drew a thin red line between the bloodless crime of 1844 and the seizure of an arsenal and hostages amid deadly gunfire.[51]

Another mobilization closer in time to Harpers Ferry than the John L. Brown affair shows how the abolitionist core could expand to impressive proportions around the right symbol. The greatest mobilization of British antislavery in the 1850s centered on a group of completely invented heroes, the characters of *Uncle Tom's Cabin*. Harriet Beecher Stowe had more readers and certainly received more nationwide adulation and public acclaim in Britain than in America. Her visit to Britain in 1852 resembled a triumphal progress. Antislavery factions managed to mute their differences. A popular antislavery 'Address' from the 'Women of England to their Sisters, the Women of the United States of America' accumulated a half million signatures. An *Uncle Tom Penny Offering* campaign netted the author twenty thousand dollars (in lieu of forgone royalties) before her departure. Historians of British abolition treat Stowe's visit as *the* abolitionist event of the decade.[52]

By contrast, the Douglass–Thompson lectures, the outstanding public event of the John Brown affair, constituted a regional, not a national, phenomenon. Brown received neither the benefit of a collective appeal for his life nor a mass outpouring of condolence afterward. There was apparently no John Brown's penny (nor even farthing) subscription launched in his memory or collected for his widow. The abolitionists' response mirrored the general British attitude toward the John Brown affair. No part of the political spectrum welcomed or sanctioned an escalation of violence as the best or most likely way of erasing America's peculiar institution. In this respect a common political culture seems to have overridden the fault lines in British society.

ECLIPSE AND REVIVAL

The British and Foreign Anti Slavery Society, in its annual report of July 1860, characterized Brown's raid, trial, and execution as 'matters of history'. It was now more interested in the ongoing process of southern 'proscription'. The pro-abolitionist *Edinburgh Review*, in October 1860, described the Harpers Ferry insurrection as an 'aggression of so utterly unjustifiable and absurd a character (notwithstanding the lofty qualities of John Brown who led it)' that it might have given a triumph to Virginia and to the federal government, had they acted with restraint. Instead a 'Reign of Terror' had unfolded in the South, marking the period since Harpers Ferry as 'revolutionary'. Some northerners, if less directly violent than southerners, fed the fires of revolution. Long 'trains of pilgrims were seeking the graves of John Brown and his sons'. Escapes of Brown's accomplices from federal agents proliferated. Public meetings quickened 'the blood of old men, in memory of revolutionary days'.[53]

For three years after his execution, John Brown's attempt was no more than an item on the checklist of events leading up to southern secession. The relationship of the North to slavery remained deeply ambiguous until the middle of the Civil War. It was the Emancipation Proclamation that brought John Brown modestly back into European public discourse. The London Emancipation Committee had been founded in 1859 to sustain a Garrisonian organization in the metropolis. It did not hold a public meeting until three years after the Harpers Ferry affair. In 1863, changing its name to the London Emancipation Society, it finally was able to attract a large membership and to receive intellectual and political support from John Stuart Mill, John Bright and Richard Cobden.[54]

On December 2 1863, the society organized its first public meeting in commemoration of John Brown's execution. After three years of bloody conflict and the prospect of settling the emancipation issue by the sword, the abolitionist speeches at the crowded Whittington Club were stocked like an arsenal. With French troops ensconced in Mexico, the chairman felt free to draw on the parallels of December 2 in 1851 (when liberty was 'garroted' in France) and in 1859, when a liberator's death heralded the emancipation of a race. Brown was no longer a solitary victim on the scaffold-cross but the might-have-been Garibaldi of America, whose song of resurrection became the American 'Marseillaise'. Warrior analogies abounded. Cromwell, Washington, Garibaldi, Giuseppe Mazzini and Louis Kossuth were all John Browns. In language that might have come from Otto von Bismarck, the new Iron Chancellor of Prussia, the speakers proclaimed that the issue would now be settled, not by soft voices, but by the cannon's iron lips, the saber's tongue and the artillery's thunder. Brown was marched briskly through an honor roll of national liberation warriors in whose company no Englishman at the Whittington Club could feel ill at ease. General Dessalines was absent. In December 1863, the soul of John Brown led a Union army, not a slave revolution.[55]

Brown underwent an even more militant metamorphosis on the Continent during the closing stages of the American Civil War. In 1859 some of Europe's revolutionaries had viewed Brown's execution as simply one more grim benchmark in the post-1848 reaction. The execution at Charles Town marked the United States as belonging to the same implacable system as Europe's bourgeois and feudal regimes. The Emancipation Proclamation allowed revolutionaries to incorporate the conflict into a broader world-liberation scenario. In 1864, from revolutionary exile in Belgium, Pierre Vesnier published Europe's longest work on Brown, *Le martyr de la liberté des nègres; ou, John Brown, le Christ des noirs*. Vesnier, a French journalist, had fled first to Geneva and then to Brussels after Louis Napoleon's coup of December 2 1851. A member of the International, he was elected to the General Council of the Paris Commune in 1871 and was regarded as an ultrarevolutionary even by other members. Vesnier dedicated his book to all the suffering and degraded of the earth – to the immense mass of black, brown and yellow servitude that covered Africa, Asia, and much of America and to the proletarians of Europe, still slaving in the galleys of barbarous civilization. The book was structured according to the 'passion' of John Brown – in thirteen stations, or days, of suffering, from his capture at Harpers Ferry to his execution/crucifixion.[56] Brown's life was the eternal story of good versus evil, attuned to a continental European timetable. He was born in the energized generation of the great revolution, along with a list of heroes somewhat different from that offered in London's Whittington Club. Etienne Cabet, Auguste Blanqui, Louis de Saint-Just, Vincent Ogé, the marquis de Lafayette, and Robert Blum joined Kossuth and Garibaldi. Brown's inquisitors also joined the Duke of Alba, the 'Catholic Pharisees' of Belgium, Pontius Pilate, the Austrian field marshal Joseph Radetzky, and all despots from the pharaohs to the Bourbons.

Vesnier embraced, with exaltation, the primordial taboo of 'servile insurrection'. The St Domingue revolution, the last resort of Brown's detractors in 1859, was recounted by Vesnier with zest. Revolutionary massacre linked the Haitian past to the American present. If the blacks of the United States South made 'their night of August 24' (date of the Parisian massacres of 1792), 'their Sicilian Vespers', their 'Saint Bartholomew of the whites, they would fulfill a great obligation, because slavery, that crime of crimes ... justifies everything, authorizes everything' committed by its victims. Vesnier's formula was the 'frightful and yet only possible and desirable solution to the terrible struggle which desolates the United States'. 'The Negro race will exterminate the white race, it being necessary that one die so that the other may live'.[57]

Vesnier invoked both racism and race to justify a massacre of southerners. Prejudice decreed that the two races could not live together. Whites were not suited to cultivating in the tropics without blacks. In case the reader had missed the iron necessity of his solution, Vesnier left no adjectival hiding place:

> The only desirable, just, useful, opportune, indispensable, solution is that the black race remain alone, in free possession of the soil, which it alone can cultivate ... That, terrible as it is, is the only solution that a sincere friend of humanity and justice can maintain.[58]

Ideas coursed swiftly through four hundred pages of revolutionary martyrology and policy recipes. Brown himself, according to Vesnier, had been innocent of a genocidal solution, having only the bloodless exodus model in mind. Vesnier was less forbearing. Since Brown had been executed on false charges, Vesnier decreed that each minute of Brown's thirty-odd-minute agony on the gallows would have to be repaid with 100 000 lives. He did not mention that his sentence required the death of one-tenth of the entire United States population, including all races of both North and South in 1860. After hundreds of pages on revolutions through the millennia (in which Jesus of Nazareth and all his apostles were condemned as sanctioners of slavery), Vesnier returned to Brown in a 'Coda', with a song entitled 'The Soul of John Brown and the Marseillaise of the Blacks'. Brown was thus fully incorporated into European revolutionary tradition.[59]

Seven years after writing his book, Vesnier found himself in the maelstrom of the Paris Commune. As the editor in chief of its official journal, he denounced all moderates. Later, reviewing his own revolutionary moment for posterity, Vesnier dispensed with the language of extermination. The Commune never struck down an unarmed enemy, he wrote, and John Brown and servile insurrections in the Americas found no place in Vesnier's history.[60]

During the American Civil War, most European supporters of the abolitionist cause were far less enthusiastic than Vesnier for servile insurrection. They were pleased that, for the most part, slaves ran away to the Union armies rather than recreating St Domingue in the South. Four years after Brown's execution, the *London Daily News* contentedly noted that the much-conjured servile massacres had not come to pass, proving that 'it is not the negroes' way to rise in violent insurrection, unless driven to despair by the absence of any prospect of redemption by other means'.[61]

The public apotheosis of John Brown as the martyr–liberator of the American slaves lasted only a short time. The commemoration of 1863 in London was not repeated. For most Europeans, a new figure, not associated with slave uprisings, displaced Brown as emancipation's martyr in April 1865. In Paris thousands flocked to the United States embassy on hearing of President Abraham Lincoln's assassination. Politicians signed collective addresses to 'Lincoln the glorious martyr of duty'. In other European cities, newspapers and magazines devoted front pages to his life and death, and working-class rallies presented their condolences to the American people.[62]

The distance between the reactions to the deaths of Lincoln and Brown may best be gauged in similar commemorative tributes. Immediately after Lincoln's assassination, a provincial French newspaper, supported by the Parisian press, launched a campaign to pay for a gold medal intended for Lincoln's widow. The names of forty thousand subscribers were eventually published. Some organizers of the Lincoln medal made explicit the analogy between the deaths of Brown and Lincoln. But only in 1870 did they organize to commission a similar gold medal for Brown's widow, and only in 1874 was the medal dispatched to the United States.[63]

Although John Brown did not figure in Vesnier's history of the Paris Commune, the memory of that uprising cast its own shadow over Brown. One had to beware of French republicans, even when bearing gifts. When the picture of the medal and the French committee's letter was appended to a book on John Brown in the 1880s, Frank Preston Stearns, its editor, felt compelled to argue that although some committee members were implicated in the Commune, only one was culpable. The French referred to themselves as 'French republicans'. Stearns referred to them as 'French philanthropists'. Name by name, the editor exonerated the signatories. Victor Hugo, then at the peak of his popularity, presented no problem. Etienne Arago had been mayor of Paris during the siege of 1870, but he was 'not a communist'. Victor Schoelcher, the emancipator of slaves in the French colonies in 1848, was a respectable senator of the Third Republic. Other signatories were designated as republicans, 'moderate' or 'advanced'. Louis Blanc, although a 'visionary' socialist and a 'prejudiced writer', had not been part of the Commune. Only one, Melvil Bloncourt, condemned to death in 1874, was designated as 'unworthy of the rest'. The real trouble was that in America anarchists, socialists, women's rights eccentrics, and teetotalers attached themselves to Brown's memory 'like barnacles to a whale'.[64]

After the entire gold medal committee had passed through the nitric acid test of social and political respectability, only one committee member, 'whose character was now better known', had failed the test. Stearns asked, 'Is there not commonly a Judas among every twelve men?' Just as an American abolitionist had metaphorically transformed Spartacus into Moses before the tolerant eyes of British abolitionists, so now the guardian of Brown's memory transmuted French republicans into apostles. Ritually cleansed of its insurrectionary taint, John Brown's gold piece uncomfortably occupied the commemorative niche never filled by John Brown's penny. So Stearns made John Brown's memory safe for French republicans. By then, for all but a few European scholars, abolitionists, and revolutionaries, the old twin images of insurrection at Harpers Ferry and the indomitable old man at Charles Town were already distant and fading memories.[65]

NOTES

I would like to acknowledge the advice and comments of Richard Blackett, David Brion Davis, Stanley Engerman, William W. Freehling, Laurence Glasco, Van Beck Hall, and the staff and anonymous referees of the *Journal of American History*, and, especially, Susan Armeny. A more extensive version of this article is published in, *His Soul Goes Marching On*, Paul Finkelman, ed. (Charlotteville, Va, 1995), pp. 253–95.

1. Victor Hugo, *John Brown* (Paris, 1861), frontispiece. The Latin inscription can be translated, 'For Christ – Like Christ'.
2. Victor Hugo to editor, *London News*, December 9 1859; republished in *Letters on American Slavery* (Boston, 1860), pp. 3–6. See also Louis Ruchames (ed.), *A John Brown Reader* (London, 1959), pp. 268–70. When he wrote the letter, on December 2 1859, Hugo believed that the execution had been postponed until mid-December.
3. American Anti Slavery Society, *The Anti-Slavery History of the John Brown Year: Being the Twenty-Seventh Annual Report of the American Anti-Slavery Society* (1861; New York, 1969), pp. 157–66. On American reactions to Hugo's letter, see Monique Lebreton-Savigny, *Victor Hugo et les américains (1828–1885)* (Paris, 1971), pp. 221–64. Hugo's letter did not encounter universal acclaim. It was *'un bellisimo escrito'* for the *Madrid Credito*, December 28 1859. It was an *'eloquente-lettera'* for the *Giornali di Roma*, December 19 1859. But it was 'an address which burlesque's enthusiasm and dignity' for the *Belfast Daily Mercury*, December 28 1859.

Hugo was not involved in the French abolitionist movement before the second French slave emancipation in 1848. On that emancipation, see Seymour Drescher, 'British Way, French Way: Opinion building and revolution in the second French slave emancipation', *American Historical Review*, 96 (June 1991), pp. 709–34; see also Chapter 6 in this volume.

4. Fears of imitation may have encouraged some editors to restrict coverage to a single sentence on the subject. See *Lisbon Illustraçao Luso-Brasiliera*, December 31 1859. For mainland Europe, my newspaper selection was based on the collections in the British Library (in Hendon), the Library of Congress, and the New York Public Library. These included one or more papers in Amsterdam, Berlin, Brussels, Copenhagen, Leipzig, Lisbon, Madrid, Milan, Naples, Paris, Rome, Stockholm and Vienna. Except in Paris, editorial attention was very sparse in all of these cities, the most cosmopolitan in their countries and the most likely to show interest in distant news. I infer that my sample probably did not underestimate the attention to John Brown in most other European areas. For Britain I examined daily or weekly coverage in dozens of newspapers, from Aberdeen to Exeter, covering the general spectrum of British politics. I gave special attention to the traditional heartland of antislavery over the previous three generations – the cities of northern England and southern Scotland. For the origins of regional differentiation, see Seymour Drescher, *Capitalism and Antislavery: British mobilization in comparative perspective* (New York, 1987), pp. 71–88. The indexes of the *London Times* and the *Paris Temps* for 1861–5 were used as indicators of the frequency of coverage in the mass press after early 1860.

5. English sources in general and the *London Times* in particular disproportionately formed the basis for the selection and description of events in European newspapers farther from the transatlantic flow of information. The *Neue Amsterdamsche Courant*, for example, listed all United States items under 'Engelsche Post'. See also *Copenhagen Dagbladet*, December 22 1859; and *Naples Giornale del Regno delle Due Sicilie*, November 29 1859, January 20 1860. On the *London Times* and the United States, see Martin Crawford, *The Anglo-American Crisis of the Mid-Nineteenth Century*: The *Times and America, 1850–1862* (Athens, Ga., 1987).

6. Jim Potter, 'Atlantic Economy, 1815–1860: The USA and the Industrial Revolution in Britain', in *Studies in the Industrial Revolution*, ed. L. S. Pressnell (London, 1960), pp. 244, 248–57.

7. See, for example, Betty Fladeland, *Men and Brothers: Anglo-American antislavery cooperation* (Urbana, 1972), esp. chs. 15; Howard Temperley, *British Antislavery, 1833–1870* (London, 1972), chs. 10–12; Christine Bolt, *The Anti-Slavery Movement and Reconstruction: A study in Anglo-American cooperation, 1833–77* (London, 1969), pp. 1–25; C. Duncan Rice, *The Scots Abolitionists, 1833–1861* (Baton Rouge, 1981), pp. 151–88; R. J. M. Blackett, *Building an Antislavery Wall: Black Americans in the Atlantic abolitionist movement, 1830–1860* (Baton Rouge, 1983); C. Peter Ripley, ed., *The Black Abolitionist Papers* (5 vols., Chapel Hill, 1985–92), I; Clare Taylor, ed., *British and American Abolitionists: An episode in transatlantic understanding* (Edinburgh, 1974); and David Turley, *The Culture of English Antislavery, 1780–1860* (London, 1991).

8. On the decline of abolitionism in the 1850s, see Temperley, *British Antislavery*, pp. 221–47; and Rice, *The Scots Abolitionists*, pp. 151–4. On the minor continental European abolitionist movements, see Seymour Drescher, 'British Way, French Way', esp. pp. 711, n. 9, pp. 733, nn. 63, 65. From announcements and direct reports, I have determined that between December 1859 and April 1860, abolitionist lecturers spoke on Brown in Bradford, Halifax, Sheffield, Ulverston, Leeds, Wakefield, Bolton, Edinburgh, Glasgow, Preston, Leigh, Dundee, Perth and Dublin.
9. On *progress*, see David Brion Davis, *Slavery and Human Progress* (New York, 1984), esp. pp. 107–68, 231–58. On *civilization*, see *London Morning Post*, January 1 1860; Pierre Vesnier, *Le martyr de la liberté des nègres; ou, John Brown, le Christ des noirs* (Berlin, 1864), pp. 383; and Hugo: 'that like France, like England, like Germany, she [America] is one of the great agents of civilization; that she sometimes even leaves Europe in the rear by the sublime audacity of some of her progressive movements'. *London News*, December 9 1859.
10. See Reginald Horsman, *Race and Manifest Destiny: The origins of American racial Anglo–Saxonism* (Cambridge, Mass., 1981): Douglas A. Lorimer, *Colour, Class, and the Victorians: English attitudes to the Negro in the mid-nineteenth century* (Leicester, 1978); Christine Bolt, *Victorian Attitudes to Race* (London, 1971); Leon Poliakov, *The Aryan Myth: A history of racist and nationalist ideas in Europe*, trans. Edmund Howard (New York, 1974); and George W. Stocking, Jr., *Victorian Anthropology* (New York, 1987).
11. *London Times*, November 17 1859; *Brussels Independence Belge*, January 5 1860; Horsman, *Race and Manifest Destiny*, pp. 272–97. For abolitionist recognition of racial expansion as a mark of greatness pride, see *Liberator*, May 7 1844. For the analogous vision of Britain as the 'mother of empires' and its children as the seeds of 'free communities in all parts of the globe', expressed in a letter to a prolabor paper, see 'Northumbrian' to editor, *London Reynold's Newspaper*, November 20 1859. For the argument that American blacks did not challenge British racism lest they alienate potential supporters, see Blackett, *Building an Antislavery Wall*, p. 160. But black abolitionists shared the general propensity to invoke racial typologies, even if they differed from those of Anglo–Saxonists. See the remarks of Rev. Sella Martin, in *The Martyrdom of John Brown. The proceedings of a public meeting held in London on the 2nd of December 1863 to commemorate the fourth anniversary of John Brown's death* (London, 1864), p. 22. On Anglo–Saxonism in mid-Victorian Britain, see Billie Melman, 'Claiming the Nation's Past: The invention of an Anglo–Saxon tradition', *Journal of Contemporary History*, 26 (September 1991), pp. 575–95.
12. On Theodore Parker's acceptance of racial doctrines, see Horsman, *Race and Manifest Destiny*, pp. 178–80.
13. On the breakdown of servile systems in Europe, see Jerome Blum, *The End of the Old Order in Rural Europe* (Princeton, 1978). On the United States South, see Davis, *Slavery and Human Progress*, pp. 233–44; Robert

William Fogel and Stanley L. Engerman, *Time on the Cross: The economics of American negro slavery* (2 vols., Boston, 1974), I, pp. 103–5; Robert William Fogel, *Without Consent or Contract: The rise and fall of American Slavery* (New York, 1989), pp. 81–113; and Drew Gilpin Faust, ed., *The Ideology of Slavery: Proslavery thought in the antebellum South, 1830–1860* (Baton Rouge, 1981), pp. 274–99. On southern slavery's recognized potential for expansion, see the citation of the *Economist's* forecast in *Belfast Daily Mercury*, December 27 1859.

14. Crawford, *The Anglo–American Crisis of the Mid-Nineteenth Century*, p. 57; *London Times*, April 22 1857, November 17 1859. The last editorial was reprinted by the *Manchester Guardian*, November 18 1859. See also *Carlisle Journal*, January 6 1860; and *Bradford Observer*, January 12 1860.

15. See, for example, *Brussels Independence Belge*, November 16 1859; *Liverpool Daily Post*, November 7, 1859; and *London Illustrated News*, December 31 1859. *The Annual Register of World Events: A review of the year 1859* (London, 1860).

16. See, for example, *Edinburgh Caledonian Mercury*, November 18 1859; *London Daily News*, December 18 1859; and *Glasgow Times and Western Counties Chronicle*, November 2, 9, 16, 23, 30, December 1, 14, 21 1859. The radical *London Leader* displayed the same priority. Exceptionally, however, the *Leader's* 'National Outlook for 1860' noted that, in the 'great Anglo–Saxon republic the year will be ever-memorable for the first, we fear not the last, outbreak of a servile insurrection'. *London Leader*, January 7 1860, p. 3. In central and southern Europe, newspaper accounts were sporadic, and editorial attention extremely terse.

17. See, for example, *Paris Constitutionnel*, October 29 1859; *Liverpool Daily Post*, October 28 1859; *Manchester Daily Examiner*, October 28 1859; *Leeds Mercury*, October 29 1859; *Edinburgh North Briton*, October 29 1859; *Brussels Nord*, November 2 1859; and *Giornale di Roma*, November 15 1859.

18. *London Times*, November 5 1859.

19. So closely associated was 'Negro insurrection' with the St. Domingue revolution, that the first account in *Madrid Credito* began: 'In Harper's Ferry (Haity) an insurrection of 800 Negroes has taken place'. *Madrid Credito*, November 6 1859. See also *London Times*, December 23 1859; and *London Morning Herald*, January 1 1860.

20. See Lorimer, *Colour, Class, and the Victorians*, ch. 4. For a contemporary editorial, see *London Times*, November 3 1859.

21. See *Fife Saturday Press*, November 12 1859; *Manchester Daily Examiner*, December 20 1859; *Edinburgh Caledonian Mercury*, November 14 1859; *Paris Siècle*, December 21 1859; *Glasgow Sentinel*, December 24 1859; *Paris Constitutionnel*, December 19 1859; *Berlin Neue Preussische Zeitung*, December 20 1859; *Paris Journal des Debats*, December 18, 24 1859; *Edinburgh North Briton*, November 19 1859; *London Morning Chronicle*, December 17 1859; *Aberdeen Journal*, December 21 1859; *Paris Monde Illustré*, December 17 1859; *Leeds Mercury*, January 14 1860. *Paris Union*, November 16 1859; *Glasgow Advertiser*, December 24 1859; *Birmingham Journal*, December 17, 1859; *Wiener [Vienna] Zeitung*, November 18 1859.

22. *Edinburgh Caledonian Mercury*, December 20 1859.

23. *Fife Saturday Press*, November 12 1859; *Edinburgh Caledonian Mercury*, December 16 1859; *Leeds Mercury*, December 22 1859; *London News*, December 9 1859.
24. See Lebreton-Savigny, *Victor Hugo et les américains*, p. 240; *Paris Monde Illustré*, December 17 1859. The *London Illustrated News*, by contrast, offered no artistic dramatizations of the trial or execution.
25. *London Morning Star*, reprinted in the *Liberator*, January 20 1860. See also *Bristol Times*, December 24 1859; *Leipzig Deutsche Allgemeine Zeitung*, December 20 1859; and *Belfast Daily Mercury*, December 19 1859. An occasional editorial dilated on the treatment of Brown's corpse as a symptom of southern anxiety. So fearful of his returning to life were his executioners, 'that a brave and noble captain prescribed a dose of arsenic, and others suggested decapitation'. *Belfast Banner of Ulster*, December 29 1859.
26. *Liverpool Daily Post*, December 14, 16 1859, January 9 1860; *Firth Saturday Press*, December 24 1859; *Manchester Daily Examiner*, December 20 1859; *Edinburgh Caledonian Mercury*, December 20 1859; *Paris Union*, December 21 1859; *Brussels Independance Belge*, December 17 1859; *London Morning Herald*, December 20 1859; *Paris Journal des Debats*, December 24 1859; *Bristol Western Daily Press*, December 17 1859; *Brussels Nord*, December 23 1859; *Edinburgh North Briton*, December 31 1859; *Glasgow Times*, December 21 1859; *London Illustrated News*, December 24 1859. For a good example of editorial symmetry between heroic classical/Christian martyr on one side and fire-and-blood vengeance on the other, see 'A Martyr or a Criminal?', *Aberdeen Journal*, December 21 1859.
27. Every account in the European press referred to the first news of Harpers Ferry as a 'servile' or a 'Negro' insurrection. See *Leeds Intelligencer*, October 29 1859; *Leeds and West Riding Express*, October 29, 1859; *London Leader*, October 30 1859; *Edinburgh North Briton*, October 29, 1859; *Paris Union*, November 2–3 1859; *Paris Constitutionnel*, October 29 1859; *Brussels Nord*, November 6 1859; *Liverpool Daily Post*, October 28 1859; *Glasgow Advertiser*, October 29 1859; *Fife Saturday Press*, October 29 1859; *Manchester Daily Examiner and Times*, November 1 1859; *Manchester Guardian*, October 29, November 1 1859; *Edinburgh Caledonian Mercury*, October 29 1859; *London Times*, December 6 1859; *Edinburgh Caledonian Mercury*, December 16, 20 1859; *Brussels Independance Belge*, December 8 1859; *Leipzig Deutsche Allegemeine Zeitung*, December 20 1859; *Glasgow Times*, December 2 1859; *London Reynold's Newspaper*, November 6 1859; *Copenhagen Faedrelandet*, November 1 1859; *Naples Giornale del Regno delle Due Sicilie*, November 12 1859; and *Dublin Evening Mail*, December 23 1859. A French newspaper scorned 'the barbarity with which the people of Virginia have condemned a political prisoner, after having deprived him of the privilege of a free defense'. *Paris Univers*, November 25 1859. American abolitionists singled out the judgment for quotation because it came from an ultraconservative and pro-papal organ. American Anti Slavery Society. *The Anti-Slavery History of the John Brown Year*, p. 161. A few conservative newspapers found the southern reaction understandable in view of some abolitionists' defense of violence.

28. For ascriptions of fanaticism to both sides, see *Birmingham Daily Post*, January 4 1860; and *Giornali di Roma*, January 12 1860. For reports of southern behavior as bizarre and incomprehensible, even to generally conservative newspapers, see *Birmingham Daily Post*, January 9, 18 1860; and *Manchester Guardian*, December 27, 1859, January 5, 14 1860. The *Manchester Guardian* referred to southern behavior as 'that of men who totter and reel and rave at the prospect of calamities which they see to be inevitable'. See *ibid.*, January 30 1860. See also the *Glasgow Advertiser*, December 24 1859; *Warwick and Warwickshire Advertiser*, January 14 1860; and *Glasgow Sentinel*, December 10 1859.
29. See, for example, *Manchester Guardian*, December 27 1859, January 5, 9, 14, 26, February 6 1860; *London Leader*, December 24 1859, January 7, 28 1860; *London Morning Post*, January 2, 11, 24 1860; *Manchester Daily Examiner*, January 24 1860; *Leeds Mercury*, January 1860; *London Morning Herald*, January 3 1860. One newspaper wrote that 'Hispanic American commonwealths would be constitutional utopias' by comparison with the situation developing in the slave states. *Birmingham Daily Post*, January 2 1860.
30. See *Paris Union*, December 10 1859; *Paris Siècle*, December 17 1859, January 13 1860.
31. On Hugo's indifference to disunion, see Hubert Juin, *Victor Hugo* (3 vols., Paris, 1980–6), II, p. 438. See also *Paris Siècle*, January 13, 1860. Like Hugo, Alexander Herzen was more impressed by the execution of Brown as a betrayal of the American democratic dream. See Hans Rogger, 'Russia and the Civil War', in *Heard round the World: The impact abroad of the Civil War*, ed. Harold Hyman (New York, 1969), pp. 196–9. For the most sympathetic recognition of the 'feelings of the Southerners' exasperated by antislavery agitation, see *Dublin Nation*, November 26, December 3 1859. On the strains between Anglo–American abolitionists and Irish nationalists, see Gilbert Osofsky, 'Abolitionists, Irish Immigrants, and the Dilemmas of Romantic Nationalism'. *American Historical Review*, 80 (October 1975), pp. 889–912.
32. *Manchester Guardian*, January 14, February 6 1860; *Edinburgh Caledonian Mercury*, December 20 1859; *Paris Union*, December 21 1859; *Glasgow Sentinel*, January 4, 1860; *Leeds Mercury*, January 10, 1860; *Leeds and West Riding Express*, January 14 1860. Some conservative newspapers were less definitive about the outcome, but none asserted that slavery would ultimately emerge victorious. See *Paris Constitutionnel*, January 20 1860; *Leeds Intelligencer*, January 14, 28 1860; E. Forcade, 'Chronique de la quinzaine, 31 decembre 1859', *Revue des Deux Mondes*, 25 (January 1860), 232; *Paris Siècle*, January 13 1860.
33. On the commitment of the *London Times* to progressive gradual abolition, see Crawford, *The Anglo–American Crisis of the Mid-Nineteenth Century*, pp. 56–61. On the *Times'* policy of deflating projects emanating from 'Exeter Hall', the favorite location for mass meetings of London abolitionists, see Howard Temperley, *White Dreams, Black Africa: The British antislavery expedition to the River Niger, 1841–1842* (London, 1991), pp. 60–3. *London Times*, January 6, 14, 19 1860.

34. See editorials, *London Times*, December 19, 23, 28 1859. Its evaluation of the affair was quoted by other papers, including Ernest Jones's *Cabinet Newspaper*, December 24 1859. It indicates the standing of the *Times* that even Jones, an ex-Chartist imprisoned for sedition in 1848, could follow its line.
35. See *Karl Marx, Friedrich Engels Gesamtausgabe* (20 vols., Berlin 1972–), XVIII, part 1, pp. 623–7: 'English Feeling on the American Slavery Question', printed in the *New York Daily Tribune*, January 19 1860, and dated London, December 31, 1859.
36. *London Daily News*, reprinted in *New York Times*, January 18 1860; and analyzed at length in *Leipzig Deutsche Allgemeine Zeitung*, January 7, 1860; For vigorous reaction against the *London Times*, position, see also *Liverpool Mercury*, January 7 1860; *Sheffield Independent*, January 21 1860; *Bradford Observer*, January 12 1860; and *London Morning Star*, January 9 1860.
37. *London Times*, January 3, 11, 14, 17, 19 1860. The *London Times* was correct in concluding that Henry Wise's words, including his request for a retaliatory invasion of Canada, might please Irish nationalists. See *Dublin Irishman*, January 14 1860.
38. *London Times*, January 30 1860. For similar congratulations to Britain on its freedom from extremes, from the revolutionary madness of France, the deadening despotism of Austria, the mob legislation and 'revolver logic' of the United States, see *Birmingham Post*, January 9 1860.
39. *Liberator*, November 7 1859.
40. *London Times*, November 21 1859.
41. On nonviolence among British abolitionists, see Temperley, *British Antislavery*, pp. 170–2, 176–83, 252–4. See also Fladeland, *Men and Brothers*, pp. 376–81; and Rice, *The Scots Abolitionists*, p. 188.
42. Excerpt from the *London Examiner*, in *Liberator*, December 9 1859; *Anti-Slavery Reporter*, December 1 1859, pp. 272.
43. Harriet Martineau to the *National Anti-Slavery Standard*, in *New York Times*, January 5 1860.
44. William S. McFeely, *Frederick Douglass*, (New York, 1991), pp. 193–200, esp. p. 197.
45. *Ibid.*, p. 197. See also *Halifax Courier*, December 3 1859; and John W. Blassingame *et al.*, eds., *The Frederick Douglass Papers* (3 vols., New Haven, 1979–), II, pp. 141–2.
46. On Frederick Douglass' speeches at Leeds and Newcastle-on-Tyne, see *Anti-Slavery Reporter*, January 1 1860; and *ibid.*, and May 1 1860.
47. *Bolton Guardian*, March 24 1860; McFeely, *Frederick Douglass*, p. 204; *Anti-Slavery Reporter*, January 1 1860.
48. The proabolitonist *Leeds Mercury* was explicit: 'Nothing could be more disastrous to all classes, nothing could be more wicked after the example of Brown's failure, than another attempt of the same kind'. *Leeds Mercury*, January 10 1860.
49. *Liberator*, April 26 1844; Fladeland, *Men and Brothers*, pp. 295–6. According to Fladeland, the slave was reputed to be his mistress.
50. *Liberator*, March 1, April 26, May 7 1844. The parliamentary and public intervention demonstrated how quickly the British could mobilize on the slimmest bits of information. Because the news of John L. Brown's

sentencing first came through New Orleans, both Lord Brougham and Lord Denman spoke in Parliament on behalf of a sentencing in the state of *Louisiana*. See UK, *Hansard Parliamentary Debates* 3d. ser., vol. 73 (1844), cols. 491–2, 1156–60.
51. *London Daily News*, December 10 1859.
52. See Fladeland, *Men and Brothers*, pp. 350–8; Temperley, *British Antislavery*, pp. 224–8; Rice, *The Scots Abolitionists*, pp. 173–88; and Glasgow Emancipation Society, *Uncle Tom Penny Offering* (n.p., n.d.).
53. *Anti-Slavery Reporter*, July 2 1860, 158; Harriet Martineau, 'The US under the Presidentship of Mr. Buchanan', *Edinburgh Review*, 112 (October 1860), pp. 292–3.
54. Temperley, *British Antislavery*, pp. 254–5; Bolt, *The Anti-Slavery Movement and Reconstruction*, p. 31.
55. See *Martyrdom of John Brown*, pp. 3–15. For other works inspired by Brown, see Jacques Fernand, *John Brown et ses amis* (Paris, 1861); Alphonse Pagès, 'John Brown', in *Chroniques Judiciaires* (Paris, 1866); and H. Emile Chevalier and Florien Pharaon, *Un drame esclavagiste* (Paris, n.d.). Before late 1862, John Brown's action at Harpers Ferry was at least as useful to the pro-Southern as to the pro-Northern press in Britain. See, for example, Joseph Barker, 'Slavery and the Civil War; or, John Brown and the Harper's Ferry Insurrection', *Barker's Review*, September 6 1862, pp. 1–7. (Richard Blackett kindly brought this item to my attention.) On reactions to Brown among prominent European revolutionaries, see Herbert Aptheker, *Abolitionism: A revolutionary movement* (Boston, 1989), pp. 137–8; and Jerry Zedlicke, 'The Image of America in Poland, 1776–1945', *Reviews in American History*, 14 (December 1986), 669–86, esp. pp. 673–74.
56. Vesnier, *Le martyr de la liberté des nègres*, dedication. See William Serman, *La Commune de Paris (1871)* (Paris, 1986), pp. 311, 536.
57. *Ibid.*, pp. 217–28.
58. *Ibid.*, p. 219.
59. *Ibid.*, pp. 292–4, 348–54, 378.
60. Pierre Vesnier, *Comment a Peri la Commune* (Paris, 1892), p. x. With the fall of the Commune Vesnier fled to London, where he joined the Society of Refugees. He was soon expelled from it as a police spy.
61. *London Daily News*, December 3 1863. Although the *New York Herald Tribune* described British working-class demonstrations for suffrage in 1866 under the heading, 'John Brown's soul Is Marching On', the demonstrators preferred to use the nonviolence of New England democracy as their American example. See *New York Herald Tribune*, December 5 1866; *London Times*, September 26, October 9 1866.
62. For the massive and sympathetic response to the assassination of Lincoln, see, for example, Donaldson Jordan and Edwin J. Pratt, *Europe and the American Civil War* (Boston, 1931), pp. 261–4; Hyman, ed., *Heard round the World*, pp. 161–2; E. D. Adams, *Great Britain and the American Civil War* (2 vols., New York, 1925), pp. 257–64; Albert A. Waldman, *Lincoln and the Russians* (Cleveland, 1952), pp. 261–2, 269–76. At least two liberal newspapers in Paris linked the deaths of Brown and Lincoln as joint victims of the battle against slavery. See *Paris Siècle and Paris*

Presse, April 28 1865, reprinted in *New York Times*, May 16 1865. Brown's death was also recalled at the Wakefield sympathy meeting in England following Lincoln's assassination. See Richard Blackett, 'Contested Ground: British working class reactions to the Assassination of President Lincoln', January 1992 (in Seymour Drescher's possession). This essay was kindly furnished by the author.

63. Serge Gavronsky, *The French Liberal Opposition and the American Civil War* (New York, 1968), pp. 241–2.
64. Hermann von Holst, *John Brown*, ed. Frank Preston Stearns, trans. P. Marcou (1883; Boston, 1888), appendix, pp. 189–94. The French committee sent the gold medal to Brown's widow on October 21 1874. See Juin, *Victor Hugo*, III, p. 198.
65. European interest in John Brown did not lapse altogether. For later Soviet historiographic concern, see Rogger, 'Russia and the Civil War', p. 199, n. 3. I have not pursued another resonance of John Brown's body in Europe, its durability as an enormously popular song. The tune was still part of the children's group singing repertoire in the twentieth century, albeit in many humorous variations (courtesy of the memory of Walter Laqueur). That, however, is surely another story.

Part III

Having considered the interactions of economically, religiously and politically motivated groups in Part II the essays in Part III focus upon other lively themes in the historiography of slavery and antislavery. Tracing the pattern of scientific racism in France and Britain in the era of slave trade abolition, the presence or absence of mass abolitionism affected the development of racial science in Europe. Chapter 10 addresses issues raised by the temptation to compare the slave trade to the more recent phenomenon of the Holocaust, and Chapter 11 assesses the place of Jewish merchants in the slave trade. Together they illustrate the potential and the limits of slavery and the slave trade as subjects of comparative analysis.

Chapters 12 and 13 combine two review essays on *Capitalism and Slavery* written ten years apart (1987 and 1997). They assess Eric Williams' two famous theses and the current state of scholarly opinion after subsequent decades of empirical research and theoretical analysis. Chapter 14 addresses another hypothesis that preceeded and followed *Capitalism and Slavery*. With the decline of direct economic 'interest' explanations for the ending of slavery, some historians have sought to explain its demise in terms of economically inspired ideas – a hegemonic 'free labor ideology'. Its unchallenged power arguably buried slavery despite the latter's increasingly acknowledged economic rationality and viability. This ideological explanation, presented as a triumphant example of bourgeois 'false consciousness', is here empirically tested in the same manner as the economic decline thesis of slavery before it. In New World slave societies the clash of economic reality with the ideology of free labor usually exacerbated post-emancipation differences between exmasters and exslaves and decisively contributed to the aura of disappointment that pervades the historiography of post-emancipation plantation societies throughout the Americas: 'With few exceptions, the conditions of the ex-slaves converged more towards the relatively impoverished levels of the Afro–Asian tropics than those of the old North Atlantic world or of the New Pacific Rim.' (See the Introduction to *The Meaning of Freedom: Economics*

Politics and Culture after Slavery, Frank McGlynn and Seymour Drescher, eds. (1992).

One import of these studies is that those who value freedom must not deceive themselves into believing that liberations give societies everything that they wish for: 'liberty is liberty, not equality or fairness or justice or culture, or human happiness or a quiet conscience' (Isaiah Berlin). The good things that freedom brings are often seen only as time passes and, even then, it is easy to mistake the cause that brought them about.

9 The Ending of the Slave Trade and the Evolution of European Scientific Racism (1990)*

How might a discussion of the ending of the Atlantic slave trade in relation to the development of European racism illuminate the question of who gained and who lost? The question can be approached at three levels. The first concerns the degree to which the racial attitudes of Europeans were affected by the process of termination. The second would be how the people of Europe and of Afro–America were affected by the termination itself. The third and broadest aspect would be the long-term effects of that complex process. It seems to me that the answers become more speculative as the scope of potential impact broadens, as the discussion moves from a concern with attitudes and ideology to social conditions, as the geographical scope broadens, and as the temporal dimension to be considered expands to encompass the twentieth century. The first level, the relation of the processes of abolition to racism, is the primary focus of this paper; a few brief remarks on the second and third issues are reserved for the conclusion.

We must begin by distinguishing between process and outcome. There was a long ending as well as an end to the slave trade. The process extended unevenly over almost a century, and well beyond a century if one includes all overseas and trans-Saharan slaving. Sometimes the ending and the end were virtually simultaneous. The Dutch, for example, lost their trade *de facto* during the French Revolution and the Napoleonic Wars and then renounced it *de jure*, under British pressure at the end of that conflict. For the British, the abolition process was drawn out over a century, broadening in clear public

---

Social Science History, 14(3) (Fall 1990), pp. 415–50. © 1990 The Social Science History Association.

stages from a campaign against slaving by British nationals in 1788 into a policy commitment against chattel slavery throughout the world. One could theoretically formulate a complex accounting system for various groups throughout the world who gained or lost from that policy, including nonpecuniary benefits such as status, power, popularity, and organizational experience in almost endless variations.

In opening his recent discussion of Eric Williams' *Capitalism and Slavery* (1944), Gavin Wright (1987, p. 283) notes that Williams chose to relate 'one of the most palpable realities of Western economic history to one of the slipperiest abstractions of the Western intellectual heritage'. Some of the same difficulties arise in relating the ending of the slave trade to European racism. The abolition process extended over the same century which witnessed the emergence of European scientific racism. Scholars of the latter, just like scholars of abolitionism, locate both in the Enlightenment and in the religious revivals of the eighteenth century (Mosse, 1978; Poliakov, 1974; Davis, 1966). There is also general agreement that the third quarter of the nineteenth century, which saw the definitive end of the Atlantic slave trade (Eltis, 1987), also witnessed the full flowering of scientific racism and its broad diffusion into the popular culture of the West (Lorimer, 1978; Biddiss, 1970; Bolt, 1971).

Both historians of slavery and those of racism have also naturally had a good deal to say about the correlation of one ideology with the other, both in America and in Europe. Although before the rise of political abolitionism[1] those seeking to invoke racial theories sometimes proclaimed antislavery sentiments or lamented the use of their writings in defense of slavery, and slave owners sometimes sneered at racial dehumanization by scientists, there was an increasing crossover in arguments between the two ideologies during the second third of the nineteenth century.

The relationship between abolitionism and racism was, at the very least, more complex than that between racism and the defense of slavery, although many historians have attempted to emphasize the degree of overlap. In the Americas, where large black and white populations lived in close proximity to one another, hostility to the slave trade and slavery was frequently combined with strong hostility to the presence or expansion of the black population. At points in the antislavery debates in the United States, Cuba and Brazil, aspects of antislavery were linked by some agitators to a program for making their nations safer for Euroamericans. Indeed, there has been a good deal of debate over the degree to which negrophobia played a role in intensifying the debate over the future of slavery in the mid-nineteenth-century United States. The combination of abolitionism and hostility to blacks, however, occurred much more rarely in Europe.

Where the black and white components of the Atlantic empires were largely separated by vast distances, the question of the future status of blacks could be regarded as principally, if not exclusively, a problem of overseas territories. In 1770, on the eve of the age of abolition, black people probably amounted to less than 0.2 per cent of the British metropolitan population and 0.02 per cent of the French. On the American mainland, the black share of the population ranged from 2 per cent in Massachusetts to 60 per cent in South Carolina. And in the French and British sugar islands, the black share of the population was about 90 per cent (a little less in Barbados). In West Africa, the preponderance of the black population was higher still. It was only in the more 'mixed' belt of the Americas that antislavery and antislave appeals could overlap.

If nothing else, the temporal conjuncture between racism and abolitionism in Europe should alert us to deep tensions and paradoxes more counterintuitive than those between slavery and racism. Whatever its premises or overtones of cultural imperialism, abolitionism in societies where the slaves and free people were widely separated by oceans, where slavery was 'beyond the line', rhetorically assumed a fundamental equality as its core motto. 'Am I not a man and a brother?' (and, later, 'Am I not a woman and a sister?') was its 'inclusive' idiom. Racial thought saw as its goal the division of human beings into group types, usually hierarchically related and often polarized into pairs of opposing characteristics. Its practitioners sought to delineate biocultural boundaries, coinciding with innate and heritable mental and moral differences.

Attempts to deal with abolitionism and racism as equally central historical themes reveal some of the difficulties in relating them. The most recent study of race relations and slavery in Britain by a historian who has done much research on both subjects emphasizes the pervasive long-term hostility by whites toward blacks over the past three centuries. This general current was temporarily interrupted by a massive countercampaign against the slave trade and slavery at the end of the eighteenth and the beginning of the nineteenth centuries. Thereafter there was a wholesale reversion to the more disdainful racial attitudes, intensified by the surge of imperialism in the final third of the nineteenth century (Walvin, 1986). Since antislavery was a parenthesis between two eras of racism, the basis of the more benign attitude of the abolitionist era remains somewhat obscure.

I would like to take a slightly different tack in relating the attack on the slave trade to the evolution of racism. The most thorough historians of European responses to blacks during the critical century before 1860 have concentrated upon single countries, chronicling intellectual trends over time (Lorimer, 1978; Curtin, 1964; Cohen, 1980). I would like to look more comparatively at the political environment for racism in the two greatest European imperial powers of the century after 1760, asking whether one can account for divergences in prevailing attitudes toward, or discourse about, blacks in terms of the political context within each society.[2]

One must first lay out the similarities. Historians have been struck by the durability and continuity of images of African cultural inferiority before and after the century of slave trade abolition (Curtin, 1964, p. 479; Cohen, 1980, pp. 291–2). French and British reactions were not only analogous in this respect but part of a general Western attitude towards much of the non-Western world. It must be remembered that both before aud after the century of the ending of the Atlantic slave trade, Europeans regarded large numbers of people on all continents and of all colors with disdain. To wander through the travel books and geographies of the eighteenth century is a voyage through shades of contempt: the 'unnatural' Circassians bartered their own of every age and sex; the Georgians sold their children or kidnapped others for the markets of lslam, killing those for whom no market was available; East Asians were linked to wife sacrifice and infanticide; Brazilian Indians were identified with cannibalism, as were the natives of New Zealand (*The Beauties of Nature*, 1763–64, 10, p. 140; II, pp. 132–7; 13, p. 78; *Atlas Geographus*, 1711–17, 5, p. 271; Carver, 1779, p. 663; Boulle, 1986). Thus, if West Africans were categorized as degraded by the selling of their 'own', they were neither exclusively condemned for any social or cultural practice nor linked to exclusively negative characteristics. Italians and Russians were as likely to be identified with some 'unnatural' (i.e. alien) behavior as the Chinese. The age of abolitionism heightened the intensity and frequency of positive and negative African and black imaging, but those images neither were born nor died with that historical epoch.

Perhaps the most significant point is that such stereotyping was broadly diffused over the peoples of the earth and that there seems to have been little difference of image between the French and British writings of the preabolitionist period. Initial and enduring images of Africans were drawn from a shared international literature deriving from European and Arabic sources as well as from French and British travelers. In addition, both Britain and France established major slave-owning colonies in the Americas and slave-trading enclaves on the African coast (Davis, 1984, pp. 51–82; Curtin, 1975; Fryer, 1984).

Both Britain and France were also confronted by social problems stemming from the importation of slaves from Africa and the Caribbean into Europe. This resulted in black resident populations in the thousands by the second half of the eighteenth century. Both metropolises also faced demands for the termination of their slave trades and slave systems during the last quarter of the eighteenth and the first half of the nineteenth centuries. Finally, race became a major explanation of human variation, behavior, and history only in the period when the Atlantic slave trade was being driven from its last areas of demand in the Latin Americas. Biological and anthropological paradigms were therefore deeply influenced by white and black relationships in slavery, war, revolution, and abolition.

The rise of scientific racism induced not a radical shift in the characteristics ascribed to Africans or to blacks in general but a reworking of those characteristics in different frames of reference. Abolitionists as well as defenders of slavery and the slave trade concurred in many aspects of the image of blacks. Indeed, the most militant abolitionists insisted on a broad range of evils created by the slave trade and the slave environment in Africa, although they often balanced such negative images with an insistence on the greater civility and higher culture of areas not affected by the trade. The issues of typicality or exceptionality, of durability or reversibility, were to play an important role in the debates over the nature of racial relationships. It should be noted that the abolitionist perspective was not confined to whites. Haitian writers also accepted 'the idea that civilization was most fully developed in Europe'. This was due to 'historical and cultural factors, rather than to any racial inferiority of Africans' (Nicholls, 1988).

The great difference between abolitionists and anti- (or perhaps non-) abolitionists lay in the emphasis placed upon the potential for rapid change, whatever the supposed deficiencies in African or Afro–American societies in the New World. For agitational purposes the early abolitionists tended to emphasize the distance between slavery and freedom and the dramatic potential metamorphosis entailed in abolition itself. Indeed, it was precisely because the abolitionists linked negative characteristics so causally and so completely to the African slave trade and to colonial slavery that they could assure their contemporaries of a more rapid civilizing of blacks than of any other 'backward' people on the globe. For a brief period, at the end of the eighteenth century, more hopes were raised for the transformation of Africa than for any other part of the globe by the elimination of institutions believed to be completely subject to European political legislation. This general frame of reference also made a difference in European assessments of postabolition race relations. Britain and France differed not in the range of racial attitudes but in frequencies, intensity, and timing. It is in this sense that the political context of the abolition of the slave trade seems to have made a critical difference in the intellectual milieu of evolving racial thought and racism.

I have suggested elsewhere that one can empirically distinguish between modes of British and of French abolition (Drescher, 1980, 1987, ch. 3). For more than half a century the distinguishing characteristic of the British movement was its breadth and continuity. British citizens brought public pressure to bear on reluctant or hostile economic interests and hesitant politicians decade after decade. Time and again between the 1780s and 1840s they inundated their country with propaganda, newspaper advertisements, lectures, mass meetings, petitions, lawsuits, and boycotts, presenting ever more radical abolition agendas as moral and political imperatives. Organizationally, British abolition tended to be decentralized in structure and rooted in widely dispersed local communities. The movement was increasingly inclusive, welcoming adherents who were otherwise remote from the political process by reason of gender, religion, race, or class. Equally important for our present purpose, abolitionism constituted a continuous social presence, refracting, as we shall see, other forms of cultural production.

French abolition presented a different picture during the six decades between the establishment of the abolitionist *Société des Amis des Noirs* in 1788 and the second French slave emancipation in 1848. During the Great French Revolution, the first slave emancipation, decreed in 1794, was primarily the result of exogenous pressures, a massive slave uprising in St Domingue combined with the prospect of British colonial conquest throughout the Caribbean. During almost two-thirds of France's age of abolition (1788–1848), there was simply no identifiable abolitionist movement whatever. What existed during the remaining third was a discontinuous series of small elite groups in the French capital unable, and usually unwilling, to encourage mass appeals. French abolitionists concentrated on formulating plans of abolition, often in their roles as members of the French legislature, including systems of postemancipation labor control and planter compensation. Briefly put, French abolitionism never captured a visible mass following. French slave trade abolition, unlike British abolition, occurred in four uneven surges (1794, 1815, 1831, 1861) with restorations in 1802, 1814, and, depending on definition, 1858–61. British slave trade abolition occurred in a series of increasingly constrictive measures in 1788, 1799, 1806, and 1807, with ever widening moves towards international suppression between 1814 and 1867.

By the second decade of the nineteenth century, the divergent patterns were set. With the passage of British slave trade abolition, William Wilberforce had become a national hero who symbolized liberty because of his parliamentary leadership in the crusade. His closest counterpart across the Channel, the Abbé Grégoire (one of the few abolitionist who had survived the vagaries of the revolutionary purges, and who lived in internal exile after 1814), was identified as an incendiary of the St Domingue revolution. Grégoire's very presence inhibited the formation of another French abolitionist organization for almost a generation (Drescher, 1980, p. 59; 1987, p. 200, n. 12; Jennings, 1988).

France's first and hasty abolition had struck Grégoire and his friends in the *Amis des Noirs* as a 'disastrous measure' (Cohen, 1980, p. 153 and n.). Antislavery had not had time to become a settled popular issue in revolutionary France (Drescher 1987, p. 200, n. 12; Daget, 1980, pp. 67–8). In 1794 the police reported mixed reactions in the streets of Paris. Some people responded favorably, but women in the marketplace were heard to say, 'My God, they are giving us black sisters, we shall never be able to live with people like that' (Cohen , 1980, p. 113). Thus, neither organizationally nor socially did abolitionism have the chance to become rooted in France before emancipation as it did in Britain.

Were racial concepts affected by these different political contexts? It is agreed that the first major attack on slavery in England produced a surge in racially justified defenses of the institution. The steady percolation of black slaves into both Britain and France as a result of the slave trade and slavery created legal and social issues about the status of slaves in societies without colonial slave law. A series of attacks on the rights of owners in England culminated in the famous Somerset case of 1772 (Davis, 1975, ch. 10; Drescher, 1987, ch. 2; Oldham, 1988). West Indian racists sought to exploit the image of African cultural inferiority by using it to argue for permanent inferiority and irreversible degeneration (Barker, 1978, ch. 3; pp. 77–8).

Soon after the Somerset decision, the Jamaican planter Edward Long (1774) published the most extensive racially grounded argument in defense of slavery written before the age of abolition. *The History of Jamaica*, published in three volumes, contained a vitriolic linkage of Negroes to the animal world. Long assigned blacks to an intermediate species between Europeans and 'Orangoutangs'. He metaphorically associated blacks with beasts by writing of their 'bestial and fetid smell' and categorically affirmed that their children, like animals, matured more rapidly than those of whites; that even their lice were black; and that they were 'brutish' people (*ibid.*, 2, pp. 353–71). Long was widely read and accepted as an empirical authority by naturalists and anthropologists for generations.

To what extent did Long's sharp distancing of blacks from whites reflect English as well as planter attitudes? David Brion Davis (1966, p. 461) warns that we must not presume that Long 'was totally unrepresentative of his time'. But that statement allows a good deal of leeway between small and substantial agreement with Long's assessment. Peter Fryer (1984, p. 161) extends Davis' vague caution into the positive statement that Long's 'opinions were shared by many and that racism had more than a foothold in England'.

Both these statements are too vague for comparative analysis of racism's impact on policy toward slavery in Britain and France. It is important to recall that Long's writings were published in the wake of the most sustained discussion on slavery which had hitherto occurred in England, a discussion which took place in the courts and newspapers as well as in pamphlets and books.

In France the same concern about the presence of blacks induced the French government in 1764 to prohibit their entry into the metropolis. This was modified in 1777 by a decree confining colonial slaves accompanying their masters to special depots to await deportation when their masters returned to the colonies. An equally important explicit racial motive in the decree's preamble stated: 'The Negroes are multiplying every day in France. They marry Europeans, the houses of prostitution are infected by them, the colors mix, the blood is changing.'

On the other hand, legal restraints were never placed upon black entry into or residence in Britain, despite the fact that the black population there, as a percentage of the general population, was probably more than 10 times greater than in contemporary France (Cohen, 1980, p. 112). Moreover, at the same time that English law was becoming more explicit about the lack of restrictions on incoming blacks, the French government was increasing the level of restraint. This may not mean, as Cohen speculates, that there was less hostility to blacks in Britain than in France. The words of the French decree indicate that part of the problem was precisely the tolerance of many black people by the French as socially acceptable marriage partners. The decree's statement that 'they marry Europeans' is an indicator of integration rather than of hostility, and the government appeared to be seeking to stem a popular tendency.

Intermarriage in England was similarly denounced by anti-black writers. The difference between the increasing legal restrictions in France and their absence in Britain probably lay in the countries' different political contexts. The French monarchy was more accessible to highly organized domestic elites, had to consult fewer interests, and allowed for less expression of public opinion in law making (Drescher, 1987, pp. 173-4; Boulle, 1986, p. 224). In parliamentary Britain, with its less developed institutions for state policing, the masters utterly failed to win support for legislation affirming their property rights. It seems clear that the political context in which the planters operated had more to do with the different legal response to black people in the metropolis than did a presumed difference in relative racial hostility.

These battles of the 1760s and 1770s were merely preliminary skirmishes. The late 1780s saw the formation of abolitionist organizations in both Britain and France, the former explicitly aiming to achieve the complete and immediate abolition of the slave trade. However, the two movements diverged from the outset. Abolitionism became one of the, if not the, most popular movements of the next 50 years in Britain. Abolitionists sent more petitions to Parliament in 1788 and again in 1792 than the adherents of any other movement in the history of Parliament to that date, or indeed for two decades to come. Meanwhile the short-lived French Amis des Noirs remained confined within their elite membership, unable effectively to counter the proslave mobilization at the beginning of the French Revolution (Drescher, 1987, p. 200; Quinney, 1967). They had to look to Britain and the Caribbean to stimulate attention in the French National Assembly.

The difference between the two movements was also reflected in the influence of racial arguments on the debates about legislation for the colonies. When British defenders of the slave trade first became alarmed by the campaign against the trade in 1788, they quickly tested the efficacy of racial arguments in defense of their cause. The most sustained argument for black racial inferiority appeared, significantly, as a series of letters in the same year to the London *Morning Chronicle* over the pseudonym Civis. Anthony Barker (1978) plausibly argues that Civis's trial balloon actually demonstrated a long-established balance of public opinion in favor of the Negro's human integrity. Civis introduced his own theory of racial hierarchy by announcing that he was entering the argument 'on that side of the question, which has scarce found a single defender'. By the end of the exchange of letters in the *Morning Chronicle*, the opponents of Civis outnumbered his defenders eight to one (*ibid.*, p. 160; Drescher, 1987, p. 180).

Perhaps even more telling in the British discourse was the relative use of racial arguments drawn from Long's *History of Jamaica*. Very few proslave trade spokesmen used his racial slurs in their propaganda, and none at all did so in Parliament. On the contrary, it was the abolitionists who quoted Long to illustrate the depth of prejudice among the slave interest (Wilberforce, 1807, pp. 54–61). By the end of the campaign to outlaw the British slave trade in 1807, Wilberforce casually referred to the idea 'that the Negroes were an inferior race of beings' in the *past* tense, although he acknowledged the persistence of assertions of mental and moral inferiority. He felt free to quote Long at length, with the assurance that his readers would react 'with astonishment, as well as with disgust' (*ibid.*, p. 57). Neither in the press nor in Parliament was there an indication of preoccupation with theories of racial inferiority, much less an acceptance of them. Abolitionists repeatedly employed the notion of inferiority as an accusation, often vigorously denied, against the slave traders. The opening round of slave trade debates therefore set a pattern which was to last through the debates on British emancipation in the 1830s. The merchants and planters restricted their defense of slavery largely to reasons of law, politics, and, above all, economic expediency (Curtin, 1964, p. 240). Lack of training rather than innate inferiority was the element of black behavior most salient to their argument.

The British abolitionist initiative also led to an upsurge of writings more favorable to the image of Africa, emphasizing the potential for rapid social and cultural change in that continent. Abolitionist literature tended to emphasize African society as desperately requiring change but hitherto imprisoned in the violence of the slave trade. The antislave trade campaign thus coincided with a flurry of blueprints for the founding of free settlements in Africa and to the establishment of a 'province of freedom' in Sierra Leone. This colonization effort and the one on Bulama Island marked the high point of expectations for Africa in the decade between the end of the war with the United States in 1783 and the beginning of the war with the France in 1793. It also coicided with a peak of 'noble savage' literature as applied to Africans, and to writings which emphasized the existence of higher civilizations in the interior, beyond the devastation wrought by the slave trade. The abolitionist initiatives thus led to an upsurge of writings with favorable prognoses for Afro–America, whose regeneration would begin with the ending of the Atlantic slave trade (*ibid.*, 48–55).

While disappointment with the progress of Sierra Leone was accompanied by a clear diminution of British expectations about the rate of possible change in Africa, that disillusionment was insignificant compared with the impact of the St Domingue revolution and Napoleon's disastrous failure to subdue the Haitians. In France, the abolitionists found themselves in a much weaker position, and the immediate intrusion of the question of the status of the free colored population in the French islands resulted in the diffusion of caricatures in the brochures distributed by the proslave white lobbyists in the National Assembly (Debbasch, 1967, p. 157).[3]

In 1807 it was still possible in Britain to conceive of the formal abolition of the slave trade as part of a progressive providential plan and to hail that event with a poem about Africa, in the noble savage tradition. James Montgomery's (1828, 1, pp. 63–4) poem 'The West Indies' could even envision the emergence of a military hero, an African Jenghis Khan, who would unify his continent by conquest. In contemporary France no such evocations were possible. African conquerors rather suggested Dessalines' defeat of Napoleon's army in Haiti. So, while Wilberforce could dismiss hostile racial arguments while being hailed as Britain's symbol of liberation, across the Channel the Abbé Grégoire (1808) was now an isolated voice, reduced to publicizing black literary achievements against a rising tide of antiblack hostility in France.

The French transformation could be observed within the work of a single author. In 1802, just as Napoleon was restoring slavery in the French colonies, Sylvain Golbéry published his *Fragmens d'un voyage en Afrique*, containing his observations in Africa during the late 1780s. Many of the original notes indicated a moment when positive images of Africa were in fashion. Other passages, depicting blacks as savages and slavery as a worthy institution, were 'probably added just before publication, in the atmosphere of Negrophobia caused by the St Domingue uprisings' (Cohen, 1980, p. 69).[4]

Golbéry's book was published only one year before the Englishman Thomas Winterbottom's *Account of the Native Africans in the Neighborhood of Sierra Leone*. While Golbéry ascribed to Africans a natural racial inclination to 'sloth', Winterbottom denied all direct influence of race. Golbéry ironically portrayed Africans as happy in their lazy and unconscious ignorance. Winterbottom, an abolitionist doctor in Sierra Leone in the 1790s, found Africa to be plagued by poverty, ignorance, polygyny and slavery. The dominant frame of reference in both countries had shifted away from expectations of dramatic change, but the revolutions in the French colonies had depressed sympathy for black victims of the slave trade to a far greater extent in France than in Britain. Soon after the renewal of hostilities with France, British cartoons symbolized the imprisonment and death of Toussaint L'Ouverture under Napoleon as one of the crimes of the French despot, despite the fact that L'Ouverture had defeated the British forces in St Domingue only a few years before.

An analogous trend can be observed in scientific writings as well as in trade accounts and caricatures. As the biologists and anthropologists of the early nineteenth century attempted to disentangle factors of environment and heredity and to relate their findings to the biblical worldview, both British and French scientists generally accepted the premise of African cultural deficiency, a premise they shared with abolitionists and missionaries. They also assumed that blacks belonged to a distinct group, whether characterized as a 'race' (subspecies) or a 'species'. Scientific differences arose concerning the degree to which racial inheritance inhibited the progress of 'civilization'. This question was frequently related to the 'place' of the black in nature and the role of slavery and the slave trade in future relations between Europeans and Africans. As the prestige of scientists increased, developments in their disciplines therefore impinged upon the abolition debates. To the extent that inherited characteristics determined black behavior, the dramatic power of abolition was implicitly diminished.

One of the principal questions facing the scientists was the duration of the racial divisions formulated during the previous century. One position, monogenesis, which derived from biblical texts, was the hypothesis that all humans were descended from a single set of parents. The alternative theory, polygenesis, was at odds with the scriptural account. Polygenesis maximized the biological and permanent distance between races by hypothesizing separate creations for each of them. During the eighteenth century both hypotheses had supporters, although monogenesis was the accepted position of the majority in both countries.

The combined impact of the rise of British abolitionism and the French Revolution seems to have marked a fork in the road for the scientists of Britain and France. The theory of polygenesis was clearly declining in Britain during the early nineteenth century, and English physical anthropologists 'were more moderate in their anti-negro strictures' (Curtin, 1964, p. 229). They were less inclined to emphasize the clarity of racial boundaries. Their writings were generally more favorable to Africans than they had been before the 1780s or would become after the 1830s (*ibid.*, p. 235).

The dominant figure in British anthropology during this period was James Cowles Prichard, who abandoned the eighteenth century's linkage of racial classification with a traditionally conceived 'great chain of being'. Prichard, closely associated with the humanitarian movement, emphasized the perfectability of all human beings and insisted upon the overlapping characteristics of human groups. The usual 'characters ascribed to the negro' were, for Prichard (1826, 1, p. 233), 'distributed to different nations in all manner of ways, and combined in each instance with more or fewer characters belonging to the European or Asiatic'.

Meanwhile, the center of the polygenist school of anthropology of racial hierarchy moved to France, where it was represented by Bory de Saint-Vincent and Geoffroy Saint-Hilaire, aided by the virulently negative descriptions of Jean-Joseph Virey (Poliakov, 1974, pp. 181–2, 220). The mental inferiority of blacks became a central thesis of those who insisted upon race as the principal determinant in human behavior and history. The change in French scientific as well as in travel literature may be observed in the writings of Georges de Cuvier, the dominant authority in French comparative anatomy. In 1790 the young Cuvier was among the critics of authors who proclaimed the inherent inferiority of blacks and who likened them to apes. A generation later, although still monogenist, his own *Animal Kingdom* spoke of the similarity of Negro features to those of apes. 'The hordes which compose this race', he concluded, 'have always been savages' (Cuvier, 1817, p. 94). The English editors of even this French monogenist found it necessary to challenge Cuvier's remarks on African capabilities and to insist upon the importance of education and moral causes in human behavior (Curtin, 1964, pp. 235–6).

Philip Curtin attributes British resistance to polygenism largely to the rising current of Evangelicalism and the conservative reaction to the French Revolution. Those variables, if viewed comparatively, strike me as not fully adequate to explain the divergence. It is clear that Evangelicalism was rising in the United States as well as in Britain during the whole first half of the nineteenth century. Yet this did not prevent Virey's polygenetic and anti-African arguments of 1800 and Long's 'facts' from being translated by J. H. Guenebault (1837) of South Carolina in the 1830s, following the first northern mass abolitionist mobilization against southern slavery. Nor did it prevent the rapid emergence of a vigorous polygenist 'American school' of anthropology in the following decade (Stanton, 1960). Evangelicalism clearly had severe limitations as a brake upon the cultural formation of scientific racial ideology.

Although Curtin may be correct in seeing the evangelical ideology as a restraint upon polygenism, environmentalism was in retreat in the United States as early as the second decade of the nineteenth century. Faith in the plasticity of humanity diminished. Curtin himself aptly notes that Britain exported antislavery crusaders to America in the 1830s and received in return the American scientific racism of the 1850s. Finally, in comparative perspectives, attributing the decline of British polygenism to the French Revolution raises the question of why the French scientists did not react even more strongly against what was certainly a more traumatic event for them than for their counterparts across the Channel.

A third historical factor might be at least as significant: the presence or absence of an abolitionist political 'mentality' during the early decades of the nineteenth century. The impact of the difference can be illustrated, if not demonstrated, in a number of ways. As early as 1795, when the evangelical movement was certainly less powerful in Britain than it was to become in the nineteenth century, Charles White challenged the monogenist position with a series of lectures entitled *An Account of the Regulur Gradations in Man*.[5] White, a Manchester doctor, gave his lectures in the heartland of early popular abolitionism. It is noteworthy that he felt free to challenge monogenesis but not slavery. He declared himself in favor not just of ending the British slave trade (the political target of abolitionists in 1790s) but of abolishing slavery itself throughout the world. White has often been cited as evidence that polygenists could be abolitionists, but it might be truer to say that White concealed himself from an exposed theological position behind the mantle of a very popular ideology. Since White was not a prominent member of Manchester abolitionism, even his abolitionism should be treated with caution (Barker, 1978, pp. 167–73). Examples of French polygenist antislavery writers would make much more convincing evidence for the polygenist-abolitionist link.

William Lawrence (1819), writing two decades later and attacked on suspicion of unbelief, likewise claimed that his views of white mental and moral preeminence were no barrier to humanitarianism (Curtin, 1964, pp. 232, 239–40). Like White, he included a vigorous attack on slavery and the slave trade in his scientific lectures. The result is that we have examples of British scientists who were accused of heterodoxy being stridently antislavery but none, whether polygenist or monogenist being proslavery. Lawrence even softened his stereotype of the 'African Character' with a balancing list of African virtues, so that their 'moral inferiority' would not seem as deep as their 'mental'.

Against those who infer that the division between polygenists and monogenists was neutral as regards their propensity to be for or against slavery, Curtin logically concludes that radical polygenesis offered far more rhetorical comfort to proslavery advocates. Even if abolitionists conceded the inferiority of African culture, the early diminution of biologically racist arguments in Britain between 1790 and 1840 probably owed much to the ideological pervasiveness of abolitionism. Historians of British race thinking may also have underestimated British abolitionism's cultural impact when they wrote that humanitarians did not claim full equality for all races but only the admission of common ancestry and the right to freedom out of Christian 'charity'. There was far more 'rights of man' rhetoric in abolitionist demands and propaganda than is usually recognized (Walvin, 1982; Drescher, 1982).[6] But this is a matter for further investigation.

Even within the monogenetic scientific tradition one recalls that the derogatory remarks by the monogenist Cuvier on the capabilities of blacks were not printed in England without editorial challenge. In France, neither leading polygenists nor monogenists apparently felt the need to dissociate themselves publicly from proslavery. Just one year after Napoleon's restoration of slavery in the colonies, Henri de Saint-Simon wrote that the French had erred in emancipating an inferior race: 'The revolutionaries applied the principles of equality to the Negroes: had they consulted the physiologists, they would have learned that the Negro, in accordance with his formation, is not susceptible under equal conditions of education, of being raised to the same level of intelligence as [the] European' (Poliakov, 1971, p. 221). The interest in racial science remained strong in the Saint-Simonian tradition. In the 1830s Victor Courtet de l'Isle (1837) identified race as the foundation of political science and the primary cause of human history. At the very moment that colonial slavery was being brought to an end in the British colonies Courtet de l'Isle justified placing blacks at the bottom of the human scale by referring to their enslavement and to the African slave trade as their most distinguishing characteristic: 'They have enslaved no foreign race; they have only enslaved each other' (cited in Poliakov, 1974, p. 228).

In Britain, the strongest resistance to the extreme formulations of racial hierarchy came not just from evangelicals, and certainly not from those most frightened by the French Revolution, but from humanitarians associated with ongoing activities for improving the lot of black slaves. Curtin has uncovered the most telling example of the British pro-African argument in the Reverend Richard Watson's (1834–7, 2, p. 94) 'Religious Instruction of Slaves in the West India Colonies Advocated and Defended', a sermon of 1824. Watson's classic argument, reprinted and paraphrased for decades, linked the planters and the racial scientists as twin spokesmen for racial inequality (Curtin, 1964, pp. 242, 285). Humanitarian writers may have entrapped themselves in a theory of inferiority by their own rhetorical distaste for African slavery, customs and culture, but their commitment to antislavery apparently made some difference in their rhetoric about race. For two full generations, this difference was crucial for the history of slavery and, as we shall speculate, perhaps more than of slavery alone.

Thus far we have investigated the impact of abolitionism on a series of individual thinkers. But it would be useful if we could go beyond the classic terrain of intellectual history to the institutional mentality of the human sciences in Britain and France during the ending of the slave trade. At the beginning of the Victorian era new fields of social inquiry, both humanitarian and scientific, were becoming formalized into separate disciplines and organizations. In Britain, the first anthropological societies came out of a fusion of James Cowles Prichard's biological orientation and the political concerns of humanitarians. A committee formed in 1837 to channel ethnological data to Thomas Fowell Buxton's Parliamentary Committee on the Aborigines became a new humanitarian Organization, the Aborigines Protection Society. It functioned partly as a political group and partly as an ethnological society, with Buxton as the nominal chairman and Thomas Hodgkin, a Quaker humanitarian, as its driving force.

Hodgkin wrote to William F. Edwards, an English scientist resident in Paris, and suggested the formation of an analogous French organization. Edwards agreed, but his orientation and that of his interested French colleagues were scientific, not humanitarian. Thus the Parisian Société Ethnologique, formed in 1841, reversed the British priority, making investigation primary and protection secondary. A formal ethnological society was not established in England until 1843, and Hodgkin continued to be its guiding spirit, hosting its meetings at his house. Across the Channel, Edwards had been inspired by the French racial theories of the historians Amédée and

Augustin Thierry to develop a racial map of Europe, based upon facial features, head shape, and bodily measurements. Traveling through Europe from France to Hungary, Edwards (1829) designated the boundary lines of transition between one European 'race' and another. Consequently, the charter purpose of the Parisian society, to discover 'the principal elements that distinguish human races', was a reflection of its founder's priorities (*Mémoires*, 1841–7, 1, p. 64). Both societies drew up racial/ethnic questionnaires; Hodgkin drew upon Edwards' initial version, but Hodgkin's questionnaire was more concerned with political institutions and Edwards' with material culture and physical measurements.

The difference between the British and French societies did not, of course, reflect only the founders' priorities. The participants in the French society included the Saint-Simonians Courtet de l'Isle and Gustave d'Eichthal, the naturalist Geoffroy Saint-Hilaire, the historian Jules Michelet, the physical anthropologists Armand de Quatrefages and D. M. Morton (of Philadelphia), and, significantly, spokesmen for the French colonial planters (*ibid*., 1, pp. 3–14).

Ironically, the French society, which had initially distanced itself from directly humanitarian concerns, was the one which became most heavily involved in the question of slavery. Both societies had been formed shortly after the abolition of British colonial apprenticeship (1838) and before the second French emancipation (1848). Seeking to take advantage of the renewed discussion of French slavery in the Chamber of Deputies in 1847, the Société Ethnologique decided to intervene with a parallel scientific discussion. This would demonstrate the national utility of ethnology, 'which along with all of the other sciences, must not concern itself solely with gathering facts, but also with establishing doctrines' (*ibid*., 2, p. 64). The question which the members thought most relevant was, 'What are the distinctive natures of the white race and of the black race and the conditions of association of these two races?' (*ibid*.). It will be noted that the question was posed in such a way as to maximize racial distinctions explicitly and therefore implicitly to maximize the potential role of those who studied such differences. More important, for the first time in European history the views of ethnologists were to be aired in an open exchange, with the possibility of immediate confrontation.

The meetings on the question extended over several months. The principal speakers included not only leading French anthropologists and ethnologists but representatives of the French slave colonies and Victor Schoelcher, who had recently emerged as France's leading abolitionist writer. As a member of the revolutionary provisional government in 1848, Schoelcher was to preside over the emancipation of French colonial slaves.

The opening speaker was Gustave d'Eichthal, secretary of the society. He made three points which were accepted by the overwhelming majority of those who followed him: (1) that the two groups under discussion divided all of mankind between them in one way or another; (2) that the white race was preeminently the race of intellectual superiority, scientific creativity and progress; and (3) that the two races were related to each other by differences in social characteristics, psychological constitution, and economic function. D'Eichthal's own analogy was to the relation between the two genders, with whites represented by the male, active, intellectual principle of humanity and blacks by the female, passive, sensual principle. Whatever their future relationship, these essential and opposite characteristics would presumably have to constitute the basis of association between them (*ibid.*, pp. 64–72).

The past racial relationship of whites and blacks was defined in dyads of domination/subordination and of superiority/inferiority, although the terms of future domination remained unspecified. For those who raised questions about difficulties of racial definition, there were learned references to various anatomical measurements, from skull shapes and cranial cavities to calves. Overlapping characteristics could be explained in terms of the relative mixture between white and black, as elements of a conceptual pyramid running down from fair northern Europeans to south-central Africans.

Significantly, it was not physical measurements which were regarded as the key characteristics, but social relationships of power and, above all, of slavery. When challenged or queried about anomalies in physical measurements, those who were committed to rigorous hierarchical boundaries would ask, rhetorically, which races had given the world slaves and which had produced masters (*ibid.*, 65–74, 85–92, 186–91). Thus the geographical areas furnishing slaves and fueling the slave trade were offered as *prima facie* evidence both of group definition and of the empirical relationship between the two major races. The circularity of the argument with regard to the political question which science was supposed to illuminate was not recognized. From beginning to end the bond between the two races was bondage, one group consistently ruling over another. Just one century before, David Hume (1875, 252n.) had offered an analogous 'bottom line' empirical assertion of a uniform and constant difference of civilization between whites and other 'complexions'. For the overwhelming majority of the French participants, on the very eve of the second French emancipation, this was still the core distinction in the white/black dichotomy: civilization and domination at one end of humanity, slavery and savagery at the other.

Most speakers seemed indifferent, if not actually hostile, to the process of abolition which had recently been consummated across the Channel. Armand de Quatrefages alluded to the fact that the British planters were attempting to reconstitute new forms of coerced labor, demonstrating the constancy of the traditional relationship between whites and blacks in tropical regions. He echoed the bitter jibes made against 'perfidious Albion' in the French Chambers during the early 1840s over an Anglo–French treaty for a mutual right of search. Quatrefages derisively asserted that English ships were hypocritically still being used in the transatlantic slave trade (*Mémoires*, 1841–7, 2, pp. 74–5). This elicited a lively rejoinder from an abolitionist at the society's next meeting. The presiding officer then decided that in light of such a serious charge the minutes should dissociate the society from the opinions of its individual speakers (*ibid.*, p. 82).

Another minor fracas arose when one colonial delegate cited a French colonial document which stated that native American Indians were more difficult to civilize than blacks. Two participants quickly rose to defend the mental capacity of the Indians, and a third speaker reiterated the point at the following meeting (*ibid.*, pp. 93–5). Within the discussion's dichotomous terms of reference, Indians and Asiatics, significantly, were placed closer to whites than to blacks by those major speakers who dealt with the entire racial spectrum. In order to underline the chasm between whites and blacks, Amerasians were placed in the autocivilizing category (*ibid.*, pp. 64, 185). By all except one major abolitionist participant, blacks were at best allowed compensatory 'moral' or emotional capacities in place of their designated lack of 'talent' for science, fine art, or monumental architecture. Only certain artistic forms were offered as indicators of such talent.

Given a frame of reference so deeply informed by the master–slave relationship, what were the suggested optimal forms of association for whites and blacks, and how could such associations lead to social change in the direction of 'civilization'? Most speakers assumed that the purest characteristics of blacks could be found only on their continent of origin, and even there, only among those Africans least affected by contact with white Arabs to the north and east and by white Europeans to the west, south, and east. This mode of reasoning thus discounted the abundant evidence of economic, political, religious and artistic development cited by Victor Schoelcher in his vigorous defense of Africans before the society (*ibid.*, pp. 151–74).

Implicitly taking issue with the abolitionist model, the ethnologists found the 'basic' African characteristics to be low technology, little trade, few cities, enslavabilily, undeveloped cultures, and physical features farthest removed from Europeans. Moreover, these characteristics were documented as the areas of least change in the direction of 'civilization'. This conformed to an important proslavery argument, that African economic and cultural development had been greatest in those areas of most intense contact with Europeans in the slaving ports of West Africa. The most inferior Africans were the groups generally enslaved by other Africans.

Slavery, not freedom, was thus the primary mechanism of social change at the bottom of the human scale. The French colonial representative at the meetings implied that the slave trade had been the principal mechanism for 'improving' the blacks, since improvement for Africans originating in the areas of enslavement occurred only in the slave colonies. Creoles improved both morally and physically in the colonies; the children of Africans lost the 'muzzle-like' faces of their parents (*ibid.*, pp. 85–6, 91–2). The biological orientation of the majority of participants logically led to a discussion of 'improvement' by crossbreeding between whites and blacks. There were assertions about the intellectual improvement wrought by such crossbreeding. The colonial delegate, auxious to maximize the positive effects of creolization by racial mixture, declared that mulattoes were virtually identical with whites in intelligence. A metropolitan speaker countered that they must be just average between blacks and whites. A third participant issued the usual scholarly call for more 'experimentation' and observation to settle the question; this motion was accepted by the society (*ibid.*, pp. 93–4, 98).

There was almost no discussion of the implicit premise that, if improvement could occur only in the islands and under conditions of biological crossbreeding, the *ending* of the slave trade was endangering the civilizing process. Nor was any concern expressed about the pattern of extramarital and exploitive behavior implicit in crossbreeding, which had angered abolitionists across the Channel for generations. The Reverend Watson's bitter characterization of planters and racial scientists as conspirators against human equality carried little weight across the Channel. The tone of the discussion was as cool as if one had been discussing the selective breeding of domestic animals. The generally biological metaphors dovetailed well with the first speaker's characterization of the two races as 'genders'.

There was general accord on the superiority of creoles, although one physical anthropologist wondered whether the change observed in colonial-born children would be permanent (*ibid.*, pp. 87, 95). Such a concern obviously reflected the central premise of biological determinism which formed the starting point for most anthropometric assertions. Another speaker, obviously with his eye on the impending emancipation of French slaves, wondered if one could breed for a new form of social organization. None of the speakers, of course, anticipated the proximity of French emancipation just a few months later. No African or black Caribbean participants were invited. Blacks were 'represented' at the sessions only as objects, through the various African skulls in the society's collection. The one living black brought into the society was a resident of Paris who posed as a model for local artists. He was brought in for visual observation, and no counterpart white model was placed 'on stage'. The audience presumably needed none.

Only one major dissident voice challenged the cosy consensus of the discussion, its complacent assumptions of clear-cut racial boundaries and immense mental differences, or its offhand use of biological metaphors and analogies. Victor Schoelcher conducted a vigorous but almost solitary counter-attack against the empirical premises of the discussants. He began with a ringing affirmation of the absolute equality of all races. To demonstrate that relationships of civilization changed over time, he contrasted the antiquity of Egyptian civilization with the 'barbarism' of the Gauls and Germans in antiquity. He cited passage after passage of contemporary travel accounts of Africa to illustrate the existence of fine material cultures, high skills, large towns, legal order, political authority, elite literacy, secure property, market economies and humane relationships. He conceded that Africa lagged in modern scientific and industrial achievements but insisted that large sectors of the European, and indeed the French, peasantry were at about the same level of social development as their African counterparts.

Above all, Schoelcher emphasized two facets of Afro–American history not considered by the other discussants. The first was that the slave trade itself was responsible for much of the social disorganization and psychological degradation considered by other speakers as inherently African. The second was that the body of evidence which other participants had used in framing their characterizations was limited. Here Schoelcher cited not only examples of African educators, judges and politicians but accounts of free blacks fulfilling management functions in the newly emancipated British colonies. On evidential grounds Schoelcher was most upset by the society's willingness to accept without question statements about blacks made by a commission of Martinique planters in response to a legislative initiative undertaken by an abolitionist.

For the most part, Schoelcher's approach was heavily empirical. He drew from British and French explorers and from the Abbé Grégoire's catalogue of creative blacks. He patriotically tried to sever the association of abolition with Great Britain by recalling that the first French emancipation had preceded decisive English action. Finally, he insisted that the approach of most speakers offered implicit comfort to the defenders of slavery and even to those who emphasized the beneficent effects of an Atlantic slave trade already condemned by French law (*ibid.*, 151–74).

Schoelcher's two interventions in the debate were therefore an elaboration on his major premise of the absolute equality of the black and white races. One other member of the society very briefly intervened to plead for discarding the criteria of physical anthropology and ethnology in the name of 'spiritual capacities'. But that spiritual appeal served only to close the ethnological ranks in the name of scientific objectivity (*ibid*., 96–8). Those few participants who felt it necessary to respond to Schoelcher's accusation of abetting the slave owners insisted that they were interested only in the scientific value of the discussion. The possible implications of facts could hardly be allowed to interfere with the advancement of scientific knowledge (*ibid*., pp. 173, 191).

Such was the position taken by Victor Courtet de l'Isle. Courtet de l'Isle had already worked out a systematically racial philosophy of history a decade before the Société Ethnologique's discussion of 1847, and before the soon-to-be more famous essays of Robert Knox (1850) in Britain and of Arthur de Gobineau (1853–5) in France.[7] Courtet de l'Isle simply brushed aside Schoelcher's cascade of illustrative facts with one methodological sweep of the hand. The abolitionist had gathered bits and pieces of evidence from all over Africa but had made allowance neither for the exogenous influence of more advanced non-African cultures nor for racial differences within Africa. Thus the original dichotomous notion of a single sub-Saharan African race was now redefined by Courtet de l'Isle to allow for infinite graduations. 'True' or 'pure' African cultural potential was to be found only in the continent's least developed area (*Mémoires*, 1841–7, 2, pp. 190–6).

Thus, all of Schoelcher's massive counterevidence could be attributed to the presence of Europeans or Arabs, or to the fact that the more gifted Africans were not 'true Negroes' but belonged to people with different physical characteristics (indicated by the possession of hair or of anatomical features closer to the European 'norm' than in other parts of Africa). All of Schoelcher's evidence could be discounted, concluded Courtet de l'Isle, in the face of a clear, single, worldwide, and color-coded correlation. In the final analysis, he maintained, racial categorizations had an irreducibly aesthetic component. Everywhere in the world, the beautiful, the powerful, and the creative coincided. The closer faces came to resembling the

Greek statues of Apollo, the fairer the skin, the bluer the eyes, the greater was their possessor's domination of other racial groups and the greater was the distance between them (*ibid.*, pp. 184, 187).

Courtet de l'Isle first offered the society a quick world tour through the Americas, the Pacific islands, India, and Europe. Everywhere lighter was brighter, darker was duller; blacker was outcast, savage, or enslaved. Africa merely mirrored the globe. If such 'facts' pointed to a constant of superiority/ inferiority *à la* Hume this was not a defense of abuses of power but a bowing to the power of 'sad truths', but truths nevertheless (*ibid.*, p. 192).

Thus ended, without resolution, the most extensive discussion of race ever conducted by a scientific body up to that time, in meetings which ran over a period of months during the spring and summer of 1847. A number of its facets are worth summarizing. Most of the discussants adhered to an ideal of rigorous empiricism. In this, they resembled most defenders of the slave trade until the end of the Napoleonic Wars and most supporters of slavery before 1848. The existing racial 'map' of the world indicated to them that the relationship between darker- and lighter-skinned peoples, where they overlapped, was one of fair-skinned dominance.

This dominance, significantly, was qualified more as a product of intellectual power and inherent qualities than as a condition imposed by force. The discussants refused to recognize the implications of all examples which did not fit the pattern. Nor did they care to note the trend in Western polities toward the ending of the slave trade and chattel slavery. The ethnological debate of 1847 ended with no resolution to the question it had posed for itself, with no detailed agenda for further research, and without having influenced the political process in the least. By the following summer, French slavery and the Société Ethnologique had both disappeared, fatalities of the Revolution of 1848.

As the Atlantic slave trade lurched to an end during the two decades after 1848, the trends of Anglo–French racial thought again seemed to converge. The British 'age of humanitarianism' was drawing to a close and with it the era of Prichard's supremacy in anthropology (Curtin, 1964, ch. 15; Stocking, 1987, ch. 7). British antislavery, which had been able to mobilize hundreds of thousands in the five decades before 1840, fragmented and ebbed (Temperley, 1972). When Courtet de l'Isle published his race-centered analysis of humanity in the 1830s, he had no counterpart in Britain. But within two years of his uncompromising defense of racial science before the Société Ethnologique, Thomas Carlyle (1849) signaled the resurgence of virulent antiblack racism in England with the publication of his 'Occasional Discourse on the Nigger Question'. By the time Gobineau began to unveil his *Essai sur l'inégalité des races humaines* in 1853, Robert Knox (1850) had already published a book-length work on 'the races of man' in Britain (developed out of lectures in 1846). Knox (*ibid.*, p. v) declared, 'Race is everything: literature, science, art – in a word civilization depends on it'. If Knox's ideas about race struggle were still those of a minority, and the British ethnological society still supported potential equality of development, humanitarian abolitionism had clearly ceased to exercise its quasi-omnipotence of the previous generation.

A decade later, when the Atlantic trade was drawing to a definitive close, there were already enough Britons who disliked the philanthropic links of the Ethnological Society to break away and form the Anthropological Society of London, under the leadership of a physician, James Hunt. Hunt's papers on the nature and status of the Negro equaled in disdain any assertions of inferiority produced on the other side of the Channel. Hunt by no means went unchallenged; his anti-Negro lecture at the British Association was greeted by 'hisses and catcalls' (Lorimer, 1978, p. 138). Hunt consequently believed himself to be breaking new scientific ground against a hostile pro-Negro cultural consensus in England:

> It is not a little remarkable that the subject [the 'station' of the Negro in the genus *Homo*] is one which has never been discussed before a scientific audience in this Metropolis. In France, in America and in Germany, the physical and mental characters of the Negro have been frequently discussed, and England alone has neglected to pay that attention to the question which its importance demands (Hunt, 1865).

The Prichardian humanitarian school was his target, as was a supposedly still widespread British opinion of 'the equality of the Negro and European' (which Hunt attributed to 'little real knowledge' on the part of Europeans; *ibid.*, pp. 3, 4, 31). Hunt's own theses would probably have satisfied the most rigorous racist of the earlier Parisian meeting, including its slaveholder representatives.[8]

In a faint echo of White and Lawrence before him, Hunt did draw the line against being identified as an outright advocate of the 'slave trade' (his quotes). However, a qualification immediately followed. Hunt insisted that the Negro was, after all, much better off as a slave in the Confederate States of America or in the British West Indies before emancipation than as a part of Africa's 'savage state' or as a resident, 'emancipated (from work?)', of the contemporary West India Islands. Even Hunt's slave trade disclaimer was almost facetious. He advocated that the transporting of those Africans enslaved for crimes be reintroduced (*ibid.*, pp. 54–6). Indeed, a Confederate agent resident in England who served on the anthropological society's council was sufficiently pleased with its views to donate funds to it through his secret service accounts. He gave special prominence to Hunt's views, which included designation of the Negro as a distinct species, assertion of the proximity of the Negro to the apes, and affirmation of the intellectual inferiority of the black race and its civilizability only under European domination (Lorimer, 1978, pp. 138–9). By 1863 the Anthropological Society of London was clearly on the same wavelength as its new French counterpart, the Société d'Anthropologie de Paris, dominated by Hunt's friend, Paul Broca. The Anglo–French patterns of scientific racial thought were far less distinctive by 1860 than they had been during the first four decades of the century.

CONCLUSION

What light can the ending of the slave trade throw upon the concept of winners and losers in relation to the evolution of European racism? If racial attitudes were altered temporarily by the ending of the trade, we must still deal with the contention that the entire abolitionist process altered the path of racism very little. For those who see late-nineteenth-century racism largely as the continuation and intensification of earlier xenophobia and arrogance, toward blacks in particular, abolition was hardly more than a dramatic, quite anomalous interlude in a pattern of general hostility (Walvin, 1986, ch. 4, p. 91). On the other hand, for those who see mid-Victorian racism as a novel response to nineteenth-century industrialization and class formation, and one common to all of late-nineteenth-century Europe, the political intensity of the abolitionist process in Britain is equally superfluous (Lorimer, 1978, esp. p. 208). In the latter case, abolition was both too early and too peripheral in orientation to have had an impact on what is conceived to have been a pan-European phenomenon of the last half of the century. In other words, if British and European racism both wound up in roughly the same cultural place by the 1860s, the end of the slave trade, ideologically speaking, was no more than part of the prehistory of late-nineteenth-century scientific and popular racism.

But did European societies end up in quite the same place? First, it must be noted that British policy continued to be more activist against the slave trade and slavery than any of its European counterparts, even during the generation after 1850, the decades usually identified as the period of a more thorough Western shift toward a racialist vision of the world. A much-depleted British antislavery lobby remained in continuous existence and occasionally exercised real influence upon the course of events (Miers, 1975). Thus the new configuration of racist culture was too weak to remove the antislavery component from British policy. That policy continued to subject British diplomacy and colonial rule to greater tensions and outcomes than would probably have emerged without any antislavery pressure. However much the conservative bias of British antislavery may have increased, it continued to provide reasons 'for doing something about African savagery', while 'racism provided a reason for not doing too much' (Cooper, 1980, p. 32).

The extent to which humanitarian ideology inflected the general trends in European policy toward African slavery can still be best worked out comparatively, rather than in the framework of analysis of a single polity. The postabolition turn toward indentured Asian labor has been designated by one historian as 'a new system of slavery' but by another as 'the great escape' (Tinker, 1974; Emmer, 1985). In some ways the new system was clearly uncharacteristic of the previous forced labor transfers from Africa. Once again the abolitionist tradition appears to have exercised a limiting and cost-increasing role in which the old characteristics of the slave trade acted as a negative reference even at the height of late-nineteenth-century European racism.

Another question as to winners and losers concerns the impact of the age of humanitarianism (or the abolitionist interlude, depending on the historian) on the lives of the peoples of Africa. One historian recently concluded that in several important respects the damage to Africa was less severe than has been contended (Eltis, 1987, chs. 5, 13). Others may claim that the ending of the slave trade did little to improve the lives of Africans. The analytical point of departure here might have to be counterfactual rather than simply comparative. What would have happened to Africa if the British, like the French under Napoleon and during the early Bourbon restoration, had allowed the slave trade to continue? What if, under the impact of rising racism, governments had used racism as a reason for 'not doing too much' and had allowed the unrestricted flow of slaves to Latin America and perhaps elsewhere during the whole of the nineteenth century? David Eltis (*ibid.*, p. 64), while denying that the initial impact of British abolition on Africa was significant, concludes that without abolition in the first half of the nineteenth century, the increased demand for slaves under the impact of European economic growth might well have had a major and sustained impact, producing levels of slave exports in excess of the 1780s' peak. 'Indeed, it is possible that few regions in Africa would have escaped population decline in the face of industrialization in the West' (*ibid.*, p. 71). And Eltis takes no stock of the nondemographic consequences or of the whole catalogue of pain and suffering elaborated by the abolitionists.

Thus the question of timing becomes quite important. The earlier (and longer) Britain diverged from the relative Continental passivity toward the slave trade during the early decades of the nineteenth century, the more antislavery ideology provided reasons and pressure for 'doing more' against the existing Atlantic slave system, the more these reasons and pressure exceeded those that racism provided for 'not doing too much', and the more profound the long-term consequences were for Africa and probably for the Americas as well. David Brion

Davis (1983) has imagined a more conservative world as the outcome of a failed American Revolution. One might equally imagine a South African-style outcome for large parts of the British Empire in the absence of the abolitionist movement and its successes. One can easily imagine an analogous outcome in Brazil. The more dependent nineteenth-century capitalism became on slavery, the more difficult, delayed, and perhaps violent the ultimate outcome would have been.

Finally, the long-term impact of the 'ending' on European racism must also be considered. Lorimer's (1978, pp. 208–10) study of British racism concludes that, despite differences in the intensity of racial antipathy in late-nineteenth-century Europe, British and Continental racism shared important features: they emerged in the same time period (the 1850s and 1860s), were popularized in the 1870s and 1880s, and persisted, with much-diminished scientific respectability, to the present. Yet in terms of world history the differences of abolitionist intensity may actually have been more important than the racist similarities. Let us allow our imaginations to thrust forward one last time, from the beginning of the last third of the nineteenth century, where we halted our story, to the end of the first third of the twentieth century. In the summer of 1933 the British marked the centennial of their colonial slave emancipation with an international celebration. Despite the self-congratulatory rationalizations for postabolition British imperialism in Africa, the event was primarily hailed as a milestone in the movement of humanity towards common liberty and equality.

However, the same newspapers which reported the flags of 50 nations unfurling together at Wilberforce's birthplace carried vivid accounts of the new Nazi regime driving Jews into the streets to perform forced labor at degrading tasks (Drescher, 1985). Given this juxtaposition of events on the pages of British newspapers, one might have expected contemporary editors or historians to note the contrast that the combined centenaries of Wilberforce's death and slave emancipation made with the emerging outlines of the 'thousand-year Reich' across the North Sea. After all, in 1807, the triumph of abolition in Britain had been contrasted with the deeds of the warlord of France across the Channel. No one seems to have made the comparison in 1933. Moreover, only a few isolated black voices from the colonies noted that 1933 marked almost 100 years of British metropolitan retreat before the forces of white settler racism abroad and Anglo–Saxon supremacist ideology at home. Perhaps it was too much to ask of a weary and beleaguered empire that it share the memory of its moral zenith with the story of subsequent compromises and accommodations of white supremacy in Africa, the West Indies, Asia, and the South Pacific.

The commemorations of abolition did not, therefore, signal the revival of a new national consciousness against the lengthening shadow of an even more virulent racism to the east. The ultimately antiracist component of the war waged against Hitler was an unanticipated and belated consequence of its horrors and not a primary cause for which the struggle was undertaken by any of the Allies.

Yet the contrast between abolitionism and Nazism was latent, if not evoked, in the centennial of 1933. The British national rituals of black liberation and civic incorporation did contrast sharply with the Nazi rituals of exclusion, racial purification, and dehumanization. The following decade was to show that the logic of racism could ultimately mean the difference between life and death on a new and unimagined scale. At least until the postwar wave of non-European migrations to Europe, the ending of the slave trade, one of the most successful human rights movements in history, may have cast a longer shadow than we recognize.

NOTES

The author would like to thank Stanley L. Engerman, Henry Gemery, George L. Mosse and Lionel Rothkrug for their helpful comments. This essay is a part of a larger project on public opinion and the abolition of slavery in comparative perspective.

This chapter was also published in J. E. Inikori and S. L. Engerman, eds., *The Atlantic Slave Trade: Effects on economies, societies and peoples in Africa, the Americas, and Europe* (Durham, NC 1992), pp. 361–96.

1. Especially before the rise of abolitionism, West Indians might refuse to align themselves with the emergent scientific racial anatomists of the eighteenth century. The writer of *Observations from a Gentleman*

in *Town to His Friend in the Country Relative to the Sugar Colonies* (1781, pp. 23–4) took issue with a French philosopher 'whose scrutinous observations into the interiors of a negro, have pronounced him to be not of the human species'. The 'observer' rejected the philosopher's findings on the grounds of the Negro's capacity for speech, rationality, and reproduction. On Arthur de Gobineau's discomfort on being linked to proslavery, see Biddiss, 1970, pp. 145–7.

2. For analogous attempts to study ideology comparatively, see Kennedy and Nicholls (1981). For an Anglo–French comparison using religious mobilization as a variable, see Drescher (1980).

3. On colonial racial arguments, see, for example, the *Observations sur les hommes de couleur des colonies* (1790), by César de l'Escale de Vérone, quoted in Poliakov (1974, p. 360, n. 7). Yet early in the assembly debates most prominent representatives of the slave interest attempted to align themselves with Enlightenment empiricism, arguing for the continuance of the civil restrictions on free blacks and people of color on the grounds of economic necessity and the security of the social order. Like Long's scientific racism, an analogous argument, published in 1790 in St Domingue, was publicized in France by antislavery writers such as Grégoire, Brissot and Milscnet (see Bénot, 1989, pp. 83–5). The turmoil of revolutionary and military change was so swift and erratic in both France and the French islands that there was little leisure for the formulation of grand theories of racial inequality. The result was that the prerevolutionary environmental optimism about potential change, which was analogous to British optimism between 1785 and 1795, vanished much more thoroughly from France by the beginning of the nineteenth century with Napoleon's restoration of slavery to the islands and segregationist legislation in the metropolis (see Cohen, 1980, pp. 118–20; Debbasch, 1967, pp. 234–51). There was a direct relationship between the rate and intensity of revolutionary change and the intensification of racial ideology. On the intensification in France, see Boulle (1986, pp. 227–9).

4. On the literary shift, see Hoffman (1973, pp. 131–6).

5. Published in London in 1799. Robin Blackburn (1988, pp.154–7), who sees in White part of a racist reaction to the French and St Domingue revolutions, fails to explain why White took a radical antislavery position while elaborating his doctrines of racial inferiority. Blackburn (*ibid.*, p. 156) does not distinguish between postrevolutionary attitudes toward race in Britain, France, or the United States.

6. Where the acquiescene in slavery remained an element of the national ideology, as in the United States (Jordan, 1968, pp. 530–8) well into the 1840s, even the hegemony of Christian doctrine, whether in its ritualistic or evangelical variants, did not slow the rapid decline of environmentalism regarding questions of race or of theories of black inferiority.

7. It should be noted that full-blown defenses of slavery which rejected the principle of civic equality could run into more difficulty than books defending racial inequality (see Ride, 1843, pp. 57–8).

8. The image of the Negro as a case of arrested human development was being eleaborated in the Société d'Anthropologie de Paris at the same time. See Pruner-Bey (1861, esp. p. 336), comparing blacks to children and likening them to 'the most patient, and often the most useful animal'. Such was the normal level of discourse in the anthropological societies of London and Paris at the time of the American Civil War.

REFERENCES

Atlas Geographus (1711–17) 5 vols. (London: John Nutt).
Barker, Anthony J. (1978) *The African Link: British attitudes to the Negro in the era of the Atlantic slave trade, 1550–1807* (London: Frank Cass).
The Beauties of Nature and Art Displayed (1763–4) 13 vols. (London: G. Robinson).
Bénot, Yves (1989) *La révolution française et la fin des colonies* (Paris: Editions La Découverte).
Biddiss, Michael D. (1970) *Father of Racist Ideology: The social and political thought of Count Gobineau* (New York: Weybright & Talley).
Blackburn, Robin (1988) *The Overthrow of Colonial Slavery, 1776–1848* (London: Verso).
Bolt, Christine (1971) *Victorian Attitudes to Race* (London: Routledge & Kegan Paul).
Boulle, Pierre H. (1986) 'In Defense of Slavery: Eighteenth-century opposition to abolition and the origins of a racist ideology in France', in Frederick Krantz (ed.), *History from Below: Studies in popular protest and popular ideology in Honor of George Rude* (Montreal: Concordia University), pp. 221–41.
Carlyle, Thomas (1849) 'Occasional Discourse on the Nigger Question', *Fraser's Magazine*, 40, pp. 670–9.
Carver, Jonathan (1779) *The New Universal Traveller* (London: G. Robinson).
Cohen, William B. (1980) *The French Encounter with Africans: White response to blacks, 1530–1880* (Bloomington: Indiana University Press).
Cooper, Frederick (1980) *From Slaves to Squatters: Plantation labor and agriculture in Zanzibar and Coastal Kenya, 1800–1925* (New Haven: Yale University Press).
Courtet de l'Isle, Victor (1837) *La science politique fondée sur la science de l'homme* (Paris: A. Bertrand).
Curtin, Phillip D. (1964) *The Image of Africa: British ideas and action, 1780–1850* (Madison: University of Wisconsin Press).
Curtin, Phillip D. (1975) *Economic Change in Pre-Colonial Africa: Senegambia in the era of the slave trade*, 2 vols. (Madison: University of Wisconsin Press).
Cuvier, Georges de (1817) *Le règne animal: Distribué d'après son organisation* (Paris: Deterville).
Daget, Serge (1980) 'A Model of the French Abolitionist Movement and its Variations', in C. Bolt and S. Drescher (eds.), *Anti-Slavery, Religion, and Reform* (Folkestone: William Dawson), pp. 64–9.

Davis, David Brion (1966) *The Problem of Slavery in Western Culture* (Ithaca: Cornell University Press).
Davis, David Brion (1975) *The Problem of Slavery in the Age of Revolution, 1770–1823* (Ithaca: Cornell University Press).
Davis, David Brion (1983) 'American Slavery and the American Revolution', in Ira Berlin and Ronald Hoffman (eds.), *Slavery and Freedom in the Age of the American Revolution* (Charlottesville: University Press of Virginia), pp. 262–80.
Davis, David Brion (1984) *Slavery and Human Progress* (New York: Oxford University Press).
Debbasch, Yvan (1967) *Couleur et liberté: Le jeu du critère éthnique dans un ordre juridique esclavagiste* (Paris: Dalloz).
Drescher, Seymour (1980) 'Two Variants of Anti-Slavery: Religious organization and social mobilization in Britain and France, 1780–1870', in Christine Bolt and Seymour Drescher (eds.), *Anti-Slavery, Religion, and Reform: Essays in memory of Roger Anstey* (Folkestone and Hamden: William Dawson), pp. 43–63; see also Chapter 2 in this volume.
Drescher, Seymour (1982) 'Public Opinion and the Destruction of British Slavery', in J. Walvin (ed.), *Slavery and British Society, 1776–1848* (London: Macmillan), pp. 22–48.
Drescher, Seymour (1985) 'The Historical Context of British Abolition', in David Richardson (ed.), *Abolition and Its Aftermath: The historical context, 1790–1916* (London: Frank Cass), pp. 3–24.
Drescher, Seymour (1987) *Capitalism and Antislavery: British mobilization in comparative perspective* (New York: Oxford University Press).
Edwards, William F. (1829) *Des caractères physiologiques des races humaines* (Paris: Compère Jeune).
Eltis, David (1987) *Economic Growth and the Ending of the Transatlantic Slave Trade* (New York: Oxford University Press).
Emmer, Pieter C. (1985) 'The Great Escape: The migration of female indentured servants from British India to Surinam', in David Richardson (ed.), *Abolition and Its Aftermath: The historical context, 1790–1916* (London: Frank Cass), pp. 245–66.
Fryer, Peter (1984) *Staying Power: Black people in Britain since 1504* (Atlantic Highlands: Humanities).
Gobineau, Arthur de (1853–5) *Essai sur l'inégalité de races humaines*, 4 vols. (Pairs: Firmin-Didot).
Golbéry, Sylvain-Meinrad-Xavier de (1802) *Fragmens d'un voyage en Afrique fait pendant les années 1785–1787* (Paris: Treuttel et Würtz).
Grégoire, Abbé (1808) *De la littérature des nègres, ou recherches sur leurs facultés intellectuels, leurs qualités morales et leur littérature* (Paris: Maradon).
Guenebault, J. H. (1837) *The Natural History of the Negro Race* (Charleston: D. J. Dowling).
Hoffman, Léon-François (1973) *Le nègre romantique: Personnage littéraire et obsession collective* (Paris: Payot).
Hume, David (1875) *Essays, Moral, Political, and Literary* (London: Longmans).
Hunt, James (1865) 'On the Negro's place in nature', Memoirs Read Before the Anthropological Society of London, 1, pp. 1–60.

Jennings, Lawrence C. (1988) *French Reaction to British Slave Emancipation* (Baton Rouge: Louisiana State University Press).

Jordan, Winthrop (1968) *White over Black: American attitudes toward the negro, 1550–1812* (Chapel Hill: University of North Carolina Press).

Kennedy, Paul, and Anthony Nicholls (1981) *Nationalist and Racialist Movements in Britain and Germany before 1914* (London: Macmillan).

Knox, Robert (1850) *The Races of Men: A fragment* (London: H. Renshaw).

Lawrence, William (1819) *Lectures on Physiology, Zoology, and the Natural History of Man* (London: J. Callow).

Long, Edward (1774) *The History of Jamaica*, 3 vols. (London: T. Lowndes).

Lorimer, Douglas A. (1978) *Colour, Class, and the Victorians: English attitudes to the negro in the mid-nineteenth century* (New York: Holmes & Meir).

Mémoires de la Société Ethnologique de Paris (1841–7), 2 vols. (Paris: Dondet-Duprey).

Miers, Suzanne (1975) *Britain and the Ending of the Slave Trade* (New York: Africana Publishing).

Montgomery, James (1828) *Poetical Works*, 4 vols. (London: Longman, Rees, Orme, etc.).

Mosse, George L. (1978) *Toward the Final Solution: A history of European racism* (New York: Howard Fertig).

Nicholls, David (1988) 'Haiti: Race, Slavery, and Independence (1804–1825)', in Léonie J. Archer (ed.) *Slavery and Other Forms of Unfree Labour* (London: Routledge), pp. 225–38.

Observations from a Gentleman in Town to His Friend in the Country Relative to the Sugar Colonies (1781) (London: R. Ayre).

Oldham, James (1988) 'New light on Mansfield and Slavery'. *Journal of British Studies*, 27, pp. 45–68.

Poliakov, Leon (1971) *Le mythe aryen* (Paris: Calmann-Lévy).

Poliakov, Leon (1974) *The Aryan Myth: A history of racist and nationalist ideas in europe*, trans. Edmund Howard (New York: Basic Books).

Prichard, James C. (1826) *Researches into the Physical History of Man*, 2nd edn., 2 vols. (London: John & Arthur Arch).

Pruner-Bey, Franz (1861) 'Mémoire sur les Nègres' (lecture of 21 February), *Bulletins de la Société d'Anthropologie de Paris*, 2, pp. 293–336.

Quinney, Valerie (1967) 'The Committee on Colonies of the French Constituent Assembly, 1789–91', Ph.D. disseratation, University of Wisconsin – Madison.

Ride, Alphonse (1843) *Esclavage et liberté* (Paris: H.-L. Delloye).

Stanton, William (1960) *The Leopard's Spots: Scientific attitudes toward race in America, 1815–1859* (Chicago: University of Chicago Press).

Stocking, George W. (1987) *Victorian Anthropology* (New York: Free Press).

Temperley, Howard (1972) *British Antislavery, 1833–1870* (London: Longmans).

Tinker, Hugh (1974) *A New System of Slavery: The export of Indian labour overseas, 1830–1920* (London: Oxford University Press).

Walvin, James (1982) 'The Propaganda of Anti-Slavery', in J. Walvin (ed.), *Slavery and British Society, 1776–1847* (London: Macmillan), pp. 49–68.

Walvin, James (1986) *England, Slaves, and Freedom, 1776–1838* (London: Macmillan).

Watson, Richard (1834–7) *Works*, 12 vols. (London: John Mason).
Wilberforce, William (1807) *A Letter on the Abolition of the Slave Trade* (London: Luke Hansard & Sons).
Williams, Eric (1944) *Capitalism and Slavery* (Chapel Hill: University of North Carolina Press).
Winterbottom, Thomas (1803) *An Account of the Native Africans in the Neighborhood of Sierra Leone*.
Wright, Gavin (1987) 'Capitalism and Slavery on the Islands: A lesson from the mainland', in Barbara L. Solow and Stanley L. Engerman (eds.), *British Capitalism and Caribbean Slavery: The legacy of Eric Williams* (Cambridge: Cambridge University Press), pp. 283–302.

10 The Atlantic Slave Trade and the Holocaust: A Comparative Analysis (1996)*

THE COMPARATIVE IMPULSE

The vastness of some historical events and processes attracts scholars into postulates marked by singularity. Like the Holocaust, modern slavery intuitively appeals to the historical imagination as a candidate for uniqueness: 'There was nothing quite like black slavery, in scale, importance or consequence', writes one of slavery's recent chroniclers.[1] Beyond slavery's challenge to scholarly understanding, recently, considerable popular pressure has generated a demand that greater attention be paid to the story of slaves and their descendants in the world at large. The enormous increase in scholarly discussion and in the public visibility of the Holocaust in the United States has contributed to corresponding reflections on the place of slavery in American and world history. In April 1995, a *New York Times* front-page story on the commemoration of slavery reported that 'some scholars compare this widespread reflection to that of Jews who have vigilantly preserved memories of the Holocaust'.[2] Because both phenomena are so intimately tied to stories of mass degradation, dispersion and death, they elicit not only scholarly analysis but tempt philosophers, theologians, and politicians into competitions over comparative victimization.

In an early comparison, a historian of American slavery attempted to analogize the psychology of Nazi concentration camp inmates with the trauma of enslavement in order to explain what was considered to be the cultural annihilation

---

* Chapter 4 in Alan S. Rosenbaum (ed.), *Is the Holocaust Unique? Perspectives on comparative genocide* (Boulder: Westview, 1996). © 1996 Westview Press, Inc., a Division of HarperCollins Publishers, Inc.

and long-term infantilization of blacks in America. Subsequent research and discussion of this putative analogy indicated that the original comparison had been premised on deficient knowledge about both systems. Since the 1970s, the research on both subjects has, if anything, widened the distance between the Holocaust and New World slavery. A generation of slavery scholarship has increasingly demonstrated the ability of slaves not only to sustain themselves but to create systems of culture, family, community, enterprise and consumption from the sixteenth to the nineteenth centuries.[3]

Histories of slavery in the Americas now routinely devote much of their pages to such themes as the development of religion, family life, women and children, leisure and the arts, independent economic activities, consumption patterns and individual and collective forms of resistance. The whole scholarly enterprise now focuses on a system that endured and expanded for almost four centuries and produced an enormous variety of human interaction. Slaves created patterns of human relationships as complex as any to be found outside the distinctive economy of the Atlantic system. African Americans were part of a durable system in which the enslaved played key roles as actors in 'an ever-widening social and economic space'.[4]

By contrast, historians of the Holocaust must analyze human behavior, thought, and Institutional development within a time-frame of years, not centuries. Analytical questions about intergenerational patterns of production and reproduction, modes of family- and community-building, and the evolution of economic activity over many generations are irrelevant. There were, of course, rapidly changing patterns of work, culture and even artistic expression, but they unfolded in terms of months and years, not decades, generations and centuries. Except for isolated individual fugitives hidden by gentiles and pockets of Jewish armed partisans, the Holocaust is a tale of rapidly *narrowing* economic and social space, physical concentration, immiseration and annihilation.[5] A recognition of the divergence of the two 'institutions' was quickly grasped in the wake of the initial comparison. It remains the starting point in any contrast of slavery in the Americas with the Holocaust in Europe.

If there is one aspect of African slavery that might be fruitfully linked to an analysis of the Holocaust, it is probably the process of initial enslavement. Coerced transfers of sub-Saharan Africans fed slave systems of the Mediterranean, Atlantic, and Indian Ocean basins for ten centuries. The largest component of this forced migration after 1500 was the transatlantic slave trade. During three and a half centuries, from the early 1500s to the 1860s, up to 12 million Africans were loaded and transported in dreadful conditions to the tropical and subtropical zones of the Americas. In the process, probably twice as many were seized in the African interior.

One historian has estimated that in the peak century and a half of the intercontinental forced migration from Africa (1700–1850), 'twenty-one million persons were captured in Africa, seven million of whom were brought into domestic slavery [within Africa itself]'. The human cost of sustaining the combined slave systems to the west, north, and east of sub-Saharan Africa between 1500 and 1900 was an estimated 'four million people who lost their lives as a direct result of enslavement', plus others who died prematurely.[6] Of the nearly 12 million in the Atlantic slave trade, around 15 percent, or up to 2 million more, died on the Atlantic voyage – the dreaded 'Middle Passage' – and the first year of 'seasoning'. In the Americas, the death rates dropped gradually to levels approximating those projected in Africa.[7] Averages offer only an inkling of the intensity of suffering in particular regions, communities, barracoons and slave ships or in the diverse situations to which slaves were delivered in the Americas. In terms of conditions of life as well as of death, the long journey from the African interior was the peak period of pain, discomfort, psychological dislocation and degradation in the Atlantic system. Within the parameters of the slave trade, comparisons with the Holocaust may, therefore, be more meaningful, even if the differences remain overwhelming.

MARKET VERSUS NONMARKET FORCES

A fundamental comparison may begin with the terms given by those who organized the two systems. The Holocaust was envisioned as a 'final solution' to a problem: Jews were beings whose very existence was a threat and whose physical disappearance was regarded as one of the highest priorities of the Nazi leadership. The success of the enterprise required rapid institutional innovation aud was measured in a time frame calculated in months and years. The Atlantic slave trade developed incrementally with millennia of institutional precedents. The initial age of European transoceanic expansion from the fifteenth to the seventeenth centuries slowly added a new dimension to the expansion of African slavery. Europeans discovered by stages that they could best tap the mineral and agricultural potential of the Atlantic basin with massive rearrangements of labor. The rapid depletion of New World populations led to experiments in various forms of imported, coerced labor from both Europe and Africa. In large parts of the New World, as in Africa, slaves proved to be an economically optimal form of labor for slaveholders. The context of the development of the slave trade was, therefore, both long-term and incremental. For hundreds of years, the Americas presented enormous tracts of sparsely populated land and subsoil minerals suitable for profitable production and overseas export. During the same period, Europeans developed capital and communications networks capable of directing the transportation of American production to all parts of the Atlantic world. Simultaneously, Africans expanded and intensified their internal networks of enslavement, and Europeans tapped into those networks of enslavement for long-distance, coerced migration.[8]

Historians of slavery intensely dispute the slave trade's long-term effects on each region of the Atlantic system – whether and how much slavery stimulated or constrained development in Europe, the Americas and Africa.[9] There is, however, a generally shared consensus about two points. First, there was no single collectivity, whether defined in political, geographical, religious, or racial terms, that dominated the entire trade complex at any point. Indeed, it is the fragmentation of power that assured the system was sustained as a competitive system. Second, whatever groups entered into and departed from this vast complex of human and material transfers, the central mechanism driving its general expansion for well over three centuries was the economic gain accruing to those who remained in it. Economic considerations and the attempt to bend economic outcomes to advantage by additions of political constraints define the terms in which participants entered or exited from the trade.[10]

Almost every scholarly work on the slave trade also acknowledges or infers the primacy of economics or political economy as the nexus of the flow of forced labor within the system.[11] Only the captives, transferred from owner to owner in a network of exchanges that often extended for months from the interior of Africa to the interior of the Americas, had no bargaining power in the stream of transfers. What drove the movement of human beings along the network was the value-added potential at the end of the process and the ability of individuals and states to tap into that delivery system. If the slave trade was what some historians have termed an 'uncommon market', *uncommon* is clearly the modifier; *market* is the noun. What ensured that the trade continued was the dream of wealth flowing back into the system as returns on previous investments in human beings. And though the slave trade epitomized the reduction of human beings to the category of things, it was also the slaveholder's conception of the enslaved as potentially *valuable* things that sustained the system of exchange. From the perspective of all those involved in the traffic, the longer that all able-bodied slaves remained alive, the greater was their potential to add to the wealth, status, and power of the traders and slaveholders. The slaves' status as property and as productive instrument, analogous to 'laboring cattle', ensured that their disablement or death registered as costs to their owners.[12]

The Holocaust of 1941–5 developed in a different context and was driven by different motivations. It was confined to a single continent. It reached its greatest intensity in European areas and against populations that had been least directly involved in the Atlantic slave trade. Unlike the latter, it was dominated by one hegemonic political entity: the Nazi regime. It functioned most effectively, according to its own directors, where the Nazis had unimpeded institutional authority to implement their plans. Where Nazi political power was less direct and more limited, the system worked less effectively or thoroughly.[13] Rather than attempting to convert underpopulated or underexploited areas into optimal producers of wealth, the perpetrators conceived of the areas under their influence as already overrun with undesirable populations afflicted with human pollutants. Even before the decision for the Final Solution, the Nazis assigned a very high political priority to methods of quarantine and expulsion of Jews into zones far beyond Europe. Africans, Europeans and Americans in the Atlantic slave trade measured their success in terms of the numbers of captives landed and sold alive. In the Nazi system, every Jew destroyed was a gain in 'racial' security and a once-for-all economic gain in confiscated goods.[14]

The slave trade was an open-ended process. Its voluntary participants (the traders) wished to perpetuate it. As a forced migration, it devastated areas of Africa and changed the balance of population groups within the Americas. Regarding the impact on the population of Africa, a major historical debate revolves around the question of whether the population of western or west–central Africa would have been substantially larger in 1700 or 1850 in the absence of the transatlantic branch of the slave trade. However, it never so depleted western and west–central Africa as to threaten the Atlantic system.[15] By contrast, the Holocaust was directed against specific groups within Europe and had very specific effects on those groups. Millions of Jewish deaths were so concentrated in time and place that the impact of overall and short-term depletion of the target population was dramatic and definitive.

As a 'way of death', the slave trade was kept in being by the maintenance of a continuous flow of living human bodies who were a means to the production of labor. The Holocaust was kept in motion by the production of dead human bodies. The two systems, therefore, reveal dramatically different tempos of mortality. Joseph Miller, a historian of the Angolan slave trade, has drawn a profile of 'Annualized Mortality Rates Among Slaves from Capture Through Seasoning'. He depicts a typical trade cycle extending over four years (fourteen months in transit and almost three years of seasoning in the New World).[16] For African slaves, the highest rate of loss would have occurred in the first fourteen weeks of captivity: on the journey through Africa, within the coastal holding quarters (the barracoons), and during the Atlantic Middle Passage. Ironically, one of Miller's four-year cycles is as long as the whole period of the Holocaust.

The mortality profile of the Holocaust victims is dissimilar from that of Angolan slaves. In some areas, whole communities were massacred on the spot. In the wake of the invasion of Russia in 1941, the *Einsatzgruppen*, of special killing squads, and their auxiliaries rounded up and slaughtered tens of thousands of Jews in open areas near their homes.[17] For one stage of the slave trade, Miller notes that annualizing the death rate in the slave barracoons 'would produce a preposterous annual rate' of 1440 per 1000 per year. Raul Hilberg also notes the futility of offering annualized infant mortality rates of over 1000 per 1000 in the ghetto experience. At Auschwitz between July 1942 and March 1943, even among those Jews and non-Jews not immediately killed on arrival, the 'annualized' death-rate was more than 2400 per 1000. It would be even more absurd to speak of the series of mass slaughters during the early months of the Nazi sweep through the various regions of the Soviet Union in terms of 'annual' mortality.[18] What is clear is that in this opening phase of the Final Solution in the East, the primacy of on-the-spot maximum annihilation was manifest in the documentary reports making their way back up through the Nazi chain of command.

For the millions of Jews who resided elsewhere in Nazi-dominated Europe, the Holocaust proceeded rapidly, from late 1941 to early 1945, through stages of identification, concentration, and deportation.[19] Short of death for victims of the Atlantic slave trade, one peak of collective suffering came early in the process of enslavement: the trauma of uprooting, family disintegration, and physical restraint (shackling). A fresh set of afflictions accompanied the march to the sea, including attrition from epidemic disease, hunger, and thirst. In this African side of the process, large numbers of slaves were siphoned off into local populations. Others, however, were added to the enslaved caravans along the line of travel as criminal and 'tribute' slaves. Captives were sometimes used as beasts of burden, carrying other commodities down to the coast, thereby offsetting some of the costs of transportation for their captors. At the coast there would be some respite from shortages of food and water experienced en route. However, the slave would have exchanged the conditions of forced marches in shackles for the dangers and discomfort of sedentary imprisonment. Concentrations of people from different disease environments increased the appalling toll of disease. The 'slave pens' in Benguela, Angola, 'were about 17 meters square with walls three meters or more in height'. With 'two square meters per individual', the barracoons contained 150 to 200 slaves, often enclosed together with pigs and goats.[20]

Few aspects of the trade expressed the valuelessness of dead slaves more clearly than the slave merchants' habit of dumping bodies of the dead in a heap in a small cemetery or depositing them in shallow graves in great numbers as food for scavenging birds and animals. On the western shore of the Atlantic in Rio de Janeiro, slave traders heaped up their decomposing losses in a mountain of earth awaiting weekly burials. On those occasions when slaves died too quickly for burial, the decomposing corpses were partially burned, giving off a terrible odor.[21]

TRANSIT

For those captives not retained in Africa who survived the barracoons, the most distinctive part of the Atlantic slave trade was the transoceanic journey. The Middle Passage was a voyage lasting from weeks to months in an environment that none of the enslaved had ever experienced in their lives. In the Holocaust, there is no precise counterpart to the Middle Passage. For European Jews, a completed *seaborne* voyage actually represented redemption. During the Nazi period, one transatlantic voyage of Jews illustrates the contrasting contexts of the two systems. In the famous case of the aborted journey of the *Saint Louis* to Cuba and the United States in 1939, the passengers' forced return to the Old World meant captivity and destruction.

For enslaved Africans, the boarding process often signaled their transfer to the authority of Europeans. The state, the church, and the owners might affix their own seals of ownership upon each boarding victim through the repeated application of hot irons to their bodies. Europeans branded slaves as marks of ownership exactly as they branded their cattle or horses or as goods clearing customs. In addition to the marks of capitalist ownership, some states might add their separate brand of royal arms, denoting vassalage to the crown. Representatives of the Church could add a cross branding to the royal arms as a mark of baptism. Under certain jurisdictions, the branding process might continue in the Americas where slaveowners affixed their own signs and renamed their new human properties or designated them as runaways.[22]

For deported Jews, the passage to the death camps in boxcars was also like nothing they had ever experienced before. Lack of food, water, heat, or sufficient air circulation created a human environment rife with futile disputes – by 'curses, kicks and blows ... a human mass extended across the floor, confused and continuous, sluggish and aching, rising here and there in sudden convulsions and immediately collapsing again in exhaustion'. The journey of two or three days ended when the crash of opening doors and barked orders forced the passengers out onto platforms.[23] The closest analogue to the branding of Africans was the tattooing of inmates at Auschwitz after selection. They were not renamed but numbered, signifying their transition to the condition of anonymous state property. Only by showing one's 'baptism' (number) could an inmate get his or her daily ration of soup.[24]

For Africans, the ordeal of oceanic transit could last from weeks to months. Many of the Africans were sick, and all must have been terrified boarding an object that they had never seen, heaving upon a medium they had never experienced. The passengers were arranged in tightly packed horizontal rows lying shoulder-to-shoulder along the length of the ship and were even curled around the mast. The males were linked together in irons, making it difficult for them to 'turn or move, to attempt to rise or lie down', without injuring each other. The collisions and curses that accompanied the crowding were further intensified by fights at feeding times and during attempts to relieve themselves. Overflowing lavatory buckets and the effluvium of digestive tract diseases added to the discomfort of stifling air. From the beginning of the voyage, the holds were covered with blood and mucus and were so hot that the surgeons could visit the slaves only for short periods at a time. To the many incubating intestinal diseases that the slaves had brought on board with them were added the nausea of seasickness.[25] Accounts of the pervasive sensory impact of excrement on the slave ships correspond to Holocaust reports of the wall of feces three feet high in one ghetto lavatory and a concentration camp latrine at Auschwitz where a system with a capacity for 150 was used each morning by 7000 people.

The Atlantic Slave Trade and the Holocaust

With many inmates stricken with diarrhea and dysentery and with no more than ten minutes allowed for bodily functions, people were knee-deep in excrement.[26]

Cruelty and arbitrary abuse added to the toll of hunger, thirst and disease in both systems, but most slaves who died of hunger and thirst did so as the consequence of unanticipated long voyages. The railroads to Auschwitz moved relatively close to a schedule, the precision of which was the pride of the German railway bureaucracy. Trains rolled when they had been cleared for through passage to their destination. What one historian calls the 'floating tombs' of the African trade had their literal equivalents during the Holocaust. Trucks in transit to death camps sometimes served as gas chambers.[27]

Crews of African ships were at much greater risk than were the Nazi guards and their auxiliaries. Slave crews faced considerable danger from tropical disease, hunger and thirst. They had no recourse to reinforcements in the event of a slave uprising when slaves were released from their hold below deck for daily exercise. Above all, ship's captains in the slave trade had a stake in the survival of their human cargo. Every sale at the end of the voyage meant revenue for the state and profits for the traders. Every dead body meant some loss on invested capital.

Nothing better illustrates the legal difference between the two systems than one of the most bizarre slave trade cases ever heard in an English Court – the *Zong* case, argued in Britain in 1783. The slave ship *Zong* had sailed from Africa to the Caribbean in 1781 loaded with 470 slaves bound for Jamaica. After twelve weeks under sail, it had already lost over sixty Africans and seventeen crew members. In order to preserve the rapidly dwindling water reserves, save the remaining 'cargo', and allow the investors to claim a loss under their insurance policy, the captain threw 131 of the sickest slaves to their deaths. (Unlike losses due to capture or insurrection, losses of slaves due to death by suicide or sickness were routinely uninsurable.) Designated victims were selected in daily batches by the *Zong*'s crew. They were pushed overboard in sight of the remaining slaves. Consequently, ten more slaves, witnessing the selections, threw themselves overboard.

The underwriters refused to pay for those cast into the sea. A civil suit was brought by the investors. The case was argued in the court of Lord Chief Justice Mansfield, famous for having declared in 1772 that colonial slave law did not apply within England. Counsel for the slavers logically brushed aside the whole question of murder, on the ground that in terms of the suit the *Zong* slaves were goods and property. The only question before the court was whether some property had been rationally jettisoned at sea in order to preserve the rest. Mansfield agreed: 'Though it shocks one very much ... the case of the slaves was the same as if horses or cattle had been thrown overboard.'[28]

Nothing like the *Zong* case came before a German court over the disposal of captive Jews – nor could it in Nazi 'actions' or shipments. No one who engaged in either the authorized killing of or who *refused* to kill Jews was the object of legal action. There was no property over which such a case could have arisen – no acknowledgment of the monetary value of persons, no contract for the sale of persons, no description of the sex and age of the deceased at the point of loading, no lawful insurance upon the human cargo, and no inquest into reasons for the deaths of any or all of a transported group. The passengers' fares were payable to the railway system whether or not they arrived alive (one-way for Jews, round-trip for their guards). The fares were paid for by funds previously confiscated from the victims themselves. No suits were filed for uncompleted journeys due to death en route. There was literally no 'interest' in the survival of the passengers en route.

Both captive Africans and Jews were designated as 'pieces', but Africans were more highly differentiated goods because an African's status was derived from the exchange value of an adult male for a piece of imported textile. A set of categories designated slaves who were less than full 'pieces', in order to indicate their lower exchange value, ranged according to age, health and strength. The 'use-value' of the ideal African piece was clear. By contrast, all Jews who were not deemed of 'full' immediate labor value were immediately sent to the furnace. Their only use-value was that of certain 'pieces' of their bodies.[29]

DIVERGENCE

At journey's end, the fate of the captives diverged. In the transatlantic slave trade, landfall marked the end of the seaborne horrors. Slaves very often arrived disabled, covered with sores, and suffering from fevers, but the sight of land and the removal of shackles excited a transient feeling of joy. The captives were offered fresh food. They were bathed, 'bodies cleansed and oiled', and given gifts of tobacco and pipes. In some ports, a priest might come aboard to reassure the terrified passengers that they had not been transported in order to be eaten on disembarkation. The next stage of the process involved further psychological humiliation. Captives had to endure long and repeated physical inspections by prospective buyers. Slaves were offered for sale almost naked to prevent deception. The healthiest and strongest went first. The remaining ('refuse') slaves were sometimes taken on to other ports or sent onshore to taverns and public auctions. Further separations from relatives or shipboard companions at this point added to the trauma of sale. If slaves survived this series of traumas, they might enter a period of relative recovery ('seasoning'), along with the imposition of a new name, instruction in a new language, and coercion in a new work discipline.[30]

For Jews in transit, the moment of arrival marked not a lessening but the most dangerous, single moment of their collective suffering. As they arrived, they were unloaded onto a vast platform. Compared to the purchase of African slaves, the rail-side inspection of Jews was extraordinarily casual. SS men or other agents of the state moved quickly through the silent crowd interrogating only a few: 'How old? Healthy or ill?' Mothers who did not wish to be separated from children were told to remain with their children. The SS decided, often in a fraction of a second, between life and death. In a few minutes from the opening of a railway car, the overwhelming majority were on their way to the gas chamber. A mentality of superfluity enveloped the whole process. Only in this context can one fully appreciate Primo Levi's opening phrase in *Survival at Auschwitz*: 'It was my good fortune to be deported to Auschwitz only in 1944, that is, after the German Government had decided, owing to the growing scarcity of labor, to lengthen the average life span of the prisoners destined for elimination.'[31]

The slave trade was always predicated on the value of the captives as potential laborers. Well before the decision for the 'Final Solution' to the 'Jewish question' by mass murder in 1941, the Nazi regime had also realized the potential utility of coerced Jewish labor following the captives' pauperization. In Germany, a series of decrees between 1938 and 1941 mobilized all able-bodied Jewish labor within the Reich and occupied Poland, sustained at a standard of remuneration and nutrition far below that of the non-Jewish populations around them. On the eve of the invasion of Russia, more than 100 000 had been conscripted in Germany alone.[32] In the occupied Polish territories between 1939 and 1941, a running debate ensued between attritionists (favoring accelerated starvation) and utilitarians (favoring temporary use of Jewish labor for producing at least the equivalent of their temporary upkeep). The debate revolved around local policy options while awaiting decisions from above about the disposition of the Jewish population. Some ghettos briefly succeeded in achieving the status of short-term economic (not long-term demographic) viability. By the end of 1941, a portion of ghettoized adult able-bodied Jews was contributing to the Nazi economy and war production at minimal survival levels. Had the Nazis decided in favor of exploitation rather than liquidation of the Warsaw ghetto in the summer of 1942 and had the harsh living conditions and the high death rate remained at levels of the first half of that year (i.e. over 1000 per cent of the prewar monthly rate), 'it would have taken eight years for all of Warsaw's Jews to die out'.[33]

The German invasion of Russia was accompanied not only by a moving frontier of massacre to its east but by the creation of death camps. The decision for mass annihilation in the already conquered territories was taken at a moment when the Nazis looked forward to total victory in the East. In such a context, the Slavic populations under Nazi control were also perceived to be superfluous – one more obstacle to the movement of an Aryanized frontier to the east. Enormous numbers of Russian prisoners of war were allowed to starve to death during this early period of the Holocaust. The Nazis, therefore, anticipated no major economic impediments to their twin ideal of general racial reorganization and accelerated Jewish annihilation. By stressing the parasitic concept in relation to both economic and racial development, the Nazis could also formulate the annihilation of Jews in terms of accelerated economic modernization. In addition to its public health dimension, the Final Solution would eliminate petty bourgeois impediments to the growth of large-scale industrial organization. This 'imagined economy' of some Nazi bureaucrats drew on both capitalist and Communist visions of the industrial future.[34]

The division of 'visions of labor' between slave traders and Nazi officials illustrates another divergence between the Holocaust and the transatlantic slave trade. Jews were of demographically negative value to the Nazi New Order. To the sponsors of the slave trade, Africans were indispensable, or at least optimal, to economic and imperial development. The failure of slaves to achieve a positive reproduction rate in the tropical Americas (thereby requiring continuous infusions of Africans for sustained economic growth) was perceived as a shortcoming, not a virtue, of the Atlantic system.

LABOR

In policy terms, these divergences between the two systems are even more marked for the period of the Holocaust after the stalling of the German blitzkrieg against the Soviet Union. By the end of 1941, the conflict had settled into an extended struggle. German economic mobilization for war was intensified. As more Germans were required for military service, massive inputs of new labor were needed to fuel the German war machine. At that critical moment, the Nazis finalized the Final Solution into a rational bureaucratic annihilation. German industrialists began scrambling for alternative sources of labor, including the remnants of the Russian prisoners of war. The moment that killing operations against the Jews accelerated, the economic pressure increased. Thus, by 1944 there were more than 7.5 million coerced laborers in the heart of Europe, compared with less than 6 million African slaves in the Americas in 1860 after more than three centuries of the Atlantic slave trade.[35]

However, the rising number of Germany's slave laborers failed to boost productivity. The disciplinary habits and indifference to human suffering, developed during the era of superfluity, hindered the introduction of rationalized allocation or management of labor and precluded the development of incentives among prisoners. 'Until the very end the Nazis pursued the policy of maximum results with minimum investments.'

The system was most effective not in raising productivity but 'in squaring the economic postulates of German industrial circles with the plans to exterminate the Jews and certain categories of slaves, which had been outlined in the first years of the war by Nazi leaders and put into practice by the SS'.[36] Primo Levi's opening phrase about his own 'good fortune' in arriving at Auschwitz in May 1944 was, therefore, also an obituary on the fate of his fellow Jews. When Levi was arrested, the overwhelming majority of Jews in Nazi-controlled Europe had already been murdered.

The labor shortage caused a small slowdown in the killing process. For three years, individual Jews engaged in desperate attempts to ensure themselves against deportation to the death camps by retaining their status as slaves. Even small children grasped the significance of labor qualification as a final, frail barrier between death and brief survival. 'How deeply this labor-sustained psychology had penetrated into the Jewish community is illustrated by a small incident observed by a Pole. In 1943 when an SS officer (Sturmbannführer Reinecke) seized a three-year-old Jewish girl in order to deport her to a killing center, she pleaded for her life by showing him her hands and explaining that she could work. In vain.'[37]

The comparative figures on enslavement and annihilation between 1941 and 1945 show that the ideology of Jewish elimination took precedence over the ideology of production in Nazi policy. Time and again Jews were deported before requested replacements arrived. At the highest political levels, economic reasoning was treated with condescension or contempt. Even when grudging concessions were made to urgent requests for the temporary retention of Jewish slave labor, it was understood that 'corresponding to the wish of the *Führer* the Jews are to disappear one day'.[38] Hitler personally overruled a request by the bureaucrat responsible for labor supply to postpone the removal of Jews from German soil in vital armaments factories. Josef Goebbels rejoiced that the arguments of 'economic experts and industrialists, to the effect that they cannot do without so-called Jewish precision work, do not impress him [Hitler]'.[39]

In Nazi Europe, it was usually capitalists and bureaucrats in direct control of Jews who tried to rationalize labor mobilization on the road to elimination. This underlines the difference between the two historical processes that we emphasized at the outset. In the Atlantic system, political rulers – both African and European – tapped into and tried to manipulate a competitive market that they could never hope to fully master. They failed in their attempts to control the flow of slaves to or at the coast or to monopolize the seaborne transit of slaves. If they succeeded temporarily, the effect was either to stifle the slave trade to their own zones of power, to draw new competitors into the trade, or to stimulate the formation of new networks of trade and production.[40] In the Holocaust, the power relationship between state and capitalists was reversed. It was the political leadership that literally controlled the switches governing the flow of captive populations into war industry or death factories.

Europeans in both systems converged in acquiring adult males as slaves. This group was heavily overrepresented among those boarded on the African coast. It also was overrepresented among those selected for survival at Auschwitz and elsewhere. (One must note, however, that adult males were the *first* group targeted for mass killing by the Nazi *Einsatzgruppen* in the East during the summer of 'superfluity' in 1941.)[41] The Nazis, however, chose their labor force from a full demographic range of human beings. Mothers, children, and the aged were transported in the same shipments as young males and were usually designated for death on arrival. In the slave trade, African captors and traders substantially altered the sex and age distribution of captives offered for sale to European traders. Among Africans, captive women and children had considerable value.[42] Women and children in the slave trade who died from hunger, nutritional deficiencies, thirst, exposure and disease perished for reasons beyond the determination of their captors. Under the Nazis, Jewish children who died in large numbers for these same reasons perished because of Nazi decisions to withhold food and medicine available to the surrounding population.

If one turns from victims to perpetrators, one professional group appears to have played a significant role in both processes. Doctors in the British slave trade were rewarded for saving lives en route to the Americas. A recent economic historian specializing in the medical history of the slave trade has concluded that doctors, for all of their limitations, succeeded in reducing mortality on the slave ships. Moreover, in the end, the greatest contribution to Africans by some 'Guinea surgeons' in the Atlantic system was their testimony about conditions aboard slave ships. Physicians enjoyed quite a different role in the Holocaust. In Auschwitz, conclude two historians, doctors presided over the killing of most of the 1 million victims of that camp. They chose between labor and death, decided when the gassed victims were dead, rationalized the selection and cremation process, and lent the prestige of their profession to the whole operation, converting mass murder into a medical procedure. Nazi doctors rationalized the public health ideology of annihilation. They spent more time and care in examining some of the dead than most of the living. They conducted ferocious experiments on the bodies of the living. Jews who never saw a Nazi doctor during the years of the Holocaust stood a far better chance of survival than those who did.[43]

RACISM

Justification for the two systems also overlapped. 'Race' was used as a rationale for sustaining both processes. 'No other slave system', writes one recent historian of British slavery, 'was so regulated and determined by the question of race'.[44] Historians of slavery might make an equally strong claim about the rationale for collecting vast numbers of coerced laborers at work sites throughout Nazi-dominated Europe. Jews, Gypsies and Slavs were not only ranked in racial 'value' but their bodies were at the disposal of the state for experiments, as well as for labor brigades and brothels.

Ironically, race may have played a limited role as a justifying concept in the launching and early expansion of the Atlantic slave trade. This finding has generated a long and inclusive debate on the role of antiblack racism as a cause or consequence of the enslavement of Africans.[45] Slavery was hardly synonymous with Africans nor were Africans with slaves when the Portuguese first began to purchase Africans in the mid-fifteenth century. Africans did not regard themselves as a unitary 'race', and Europeans continued to enslave people from other portions of the world well into the age of exploration. From their earliest transoceanic voyages down to the eighteenth century, various European groups continued to enslave people in the Mediterranean, Africa, the sub-Sahara, America and Asia. At the beginning of the Atlantic slave trade, only peoples of European descent were considered nonenslavable in the full sense of becoming inheritable reproductive property. Many non-European groups were only gradually exempted from enslavement by Europeans. By 1750, sub-Saharan Africans and their descendants constituted the overwhelming majority of slaves in the Americas and the exclusive source of slaves for the transatlantic trade. As the African slave trade persisted, the racial link embedded itself ever more deeply in the ideological fabric of European consciousness, especially in the Americas. In the process of dehumanization, European holders of African slaves intrinsically linked them to domestic animals or pets. Inventories consistently listed the value of slaves first and that of livestock second. Unlike Jewish captives, however, Africans 'were not generally likened to predators, or to vermin', or to invisible carriers of disease.[46]

At no time, moreover, was the linkage between Africans and slaves fully congruent. European states and slave traders were fully aware that their slave-trading partners in Africa (princes, warriors and merchants) possessed some of the same distinctive physical features as the enslaved. Treaties were signed and contracts were made by Europeans with Africans. Europeans paid tribute and customs to Africans. Military, economic, and marital alliances were formed with Africans. Africans were educated in European schools. Legal and administrative precautions were taken against wrongful seizures or enslavements of Africans. General characterizations of Africans as being more uncivilized or barbarous than Europeans, therefore, did not preclude an enormous range of political, economic, family, and cultural exchanges with Africans as equals in those relationships.[47]

Whatever the constraints against enslaving non-Africans, the identification of slavery with Africans in the Americas was a residual result of centuries of experimentation with various African and non-African groups, not the outcome of an imagined racial selection before the beginning of the Atlantic slave trade. Considerations of race came to define the outer limits of enslavability, not the designated status of Africans as slaves. The color-coded racial hierarchy was designed by

Europeans to stabilize an asymmetrical distribution of transatlantic power over the long term. Given the indispensability of the slaves, renegotiations of master–slave relationships began almost from the moment slaves arrived in the New World. If racism undergirded the African slave trade, it was an effect rather than a cause of that system.[48]

Ironically, the closest analogue in European culture to a 'racially' defined fear of contamination during the early period of the transatlantic slave trade was the Iberian obsession with 'purity of blood'. For two centuries after 1500, Spanish and Portuguese authorities conducted ongoing hunts for 'Judaizing' descendants of Jews converted to Christianity. Such *conversos* or 'New Christians' were indefinitely branded by their ancestral link to the Jewish tradition. In the Iberian settler societies, racial legislation was primarily concerned with the regulation of nonslave groups, including New Christians, Indians, and free people of 'mixed' race. For slaves, legal codes inherited from *pre-Atlantic* Roman law constituted the primary juridical nexus for grounding master–slave, free–slave, and slave–slave relationships.[49]

Racism fulfilled a different systemic function during the Holocaust. The difference was not that Jews were defined primarily by the religious affiliation of their grandparents rather than by ancestral geographic origin or by color. For the Nazis, a racial revolution was needed to unravel past legal and social integration. Racial legislation also prescribed a new system of individual classification in order to unravel the results of religious intermarriage. The regime intended that one precisely designated group would, one way or another, disappear. Nazi racial policy was, in this sense, committed to *a* final solution – a policy of 'disappearance' – long before the particular physical implementation that began in 1941.[50] Thus, if European statesmen and merchants measured success in the slave trade in terms of ships and colonies increasingly filled with aliens, success for National Socialists was measured in terms of body counts and empty horizons. Rudolf Höss, the commandant of Auschwitz, not only arranged to return to his killing center in 1944 so that he could personally oversee the destruction of Hungarian Jewry but claimed credit for annihilating 2.5 million, rather than the 1.25 million, people actually murdered there.[51]

The slave trade and the Holocaust are characterized by another striking difference. For the first three centuries of the transatlantic slave trade, only isolated voices – no government – attempted to prohibit slaving by its own citizens. There was no need for concealment and no international declaration against the Atlantic slave trade until more than three centuries into the duration of the system. Every European state with ports on the Atlantic participated in the trade at one time or another. Participants in the Atlantic system operated within the comforting context of doing or seeing ordinary and customary things, even at times when they expressed personal revulsion or reservation about some particularly brutal action within that system.

The Holocaust differed from the slave trade in that it was not described by its perpetrators as conforming to some ancient and universal practice. The Nazis were cognizant that they were radical innovators and directors of an operation that they themselves had begun and that they alone were capable of seeing through to completion. Their commitment was crucial to the process. Indeed, they knew that they had bet their lives on a project that would be considered a war crime were they to be defeated.

CONCLUSION

This brief overview emphasizes the difficulty of comparing two events so disparate in space, time, intention, duration, and outcome. Yet the urge to find analogues to one's suffering is unquenchably human. What could be more encouraging than to see the recent surge of historical interest in the Holocaust as a model for calling attention to other human catastrophes? The African slave trade had, in its turn, served Jews as a means of making sense of catastrophic oppression, for apprehending the disorienting cruelty of the world. It was reflexive for Anne Frank to draw upon Europe's dark chapter in Africa in order to come to terms with her own terrifying present: 'Every night people are being picked up without warning and that is awful particularly for old and sick people, they treat them just like slaves in the olden days. The poor old people are taken outside at night and then they have to walk ... in a whole procession with children and everything ... They are sent to Ferdinand Bolstraat and from there back again and that's how they plague these poor people. Also they throw water over them if they scream.' Beyond the evocation of comprehensible and distant past horrors lay only fragments of other incomprehensible and distant present horrors: 'If it is as bad as this in Holland whatever will it be like in the distant and barbarous regions they are sent to? We assume most of them are murdered. The English radio speaks of their being gassed perhaps the quickest way to die.'[52]

Anne Frank's successive entries should serve as a caution to scholars. In comparing historical catastrophes, there is a temptation to argue as though one could arrive at a hierarchy of suffering or cruelty or radical evil such that only one such process reaches the apogee of uniqueness. Systems of human action are like Tolstoy's happy and unhappy marriages, all alike in some ways but each different in its own.

NOTES

I wish to thank Stanley L. Engerman, George Mosse, and Alexander Orbach for their helpful comments.

1. James Walvin, *Black Ivory: A history of British slavery* (Washington, DC.: Howard University Press, 1994), p. ix. For a parallel and much more ambitious claim for the Holocaust, see Steven T. Katz, *The Holocaust in Historical Context*, 3 vols. (New York: Oxford University Press), 1, p. 1.
2. *New York Times*, April 2 1995, p. 1.
3. See Stanley Elkins, *Slavery: A problem in American institutional and intellectual life* (Chicago: University of Chicago Press, 1959), pp. 104–15; Earle E. Thorpe, 'Chattel Slavery and Concentration Camps', *Negro History Bulletin* (May 1962), pp. 171–6; republished in *The Debate over Slavery: Stanley Elkins and his critics*, ed. Ann J. Lane (Urbana: University of Illinois Press, 1971), pp. 23–42; Sidney W. Mintz, 'Slavery and Emergent Capitalisms', in *Slavery in the New World*, ed. Laura Foner and Eugene D. Genovese (Englewood Cliffs, NJ: Prentice-Hall, 1969), pp. 27–37; Laurence Mordekhai Thomas, *Vessels of Evil: American slavery and the Holocaust* (Philadelphia: Temple University Press, 1993), esp. pp. 117–47. See the introduction to Martin A. Klein, *Breaking the Chains: Slavery, bondage, and emancipation in modern Africa and Asia* (Madison: University of Wisconsin Press, 1993), pp. 11–12. In a reappraisal, Elkins did not seem inclined

to defend the heuristic value of the analogy in comparison with other institutions such as asylums and prisons. See Elkins, 'Slavery and Ideology', in Lane, *Debate over Slavery*, pp. 325–78; John Thornton, *Africa and the Africans in the Making of the Atlantic World, 1400–1680* (Cambridge: Cambridge University Press), pp. 152–82, 206–53.
4. See, most recently, the essays in Larry E. Hudson Jr., ed., *Working Toward Freedom: Slave society and domestic economy in the American South* (Rochester, NY: University of Rochester Press, 1994), p. viii; and Stanley L. Engerman, 'Concluding Reflections', in *ibid.*, pp. 233–41. See also the essays in *The Slaves' Economy: Independent production by slaves in the Americas*, a special issue of *Slavery and Abolition*, 12(1) (May 1991); and Robert W. Fogel, *Without Consent or Contract: The rise and fall of American slavery* (New York: Norton, 1989), pp. 154–98.
5. See Raul Hilberg, *The Destruction of the European Jews*, rev. and definitive ed., 3 vols. (New York: Holmes & Meier, 1985).
6. See Paul E. Lovejoy, 'The Impact of the Atlantic Slave Trade on Africa: A review of the literature', *Journal of African History*, 30 (1989), pp. 365–94, esp. p. 387.
7. Patrick Manning, 'The Slave Trade: The formal demography of a global system', in *The Atlantic Slave Trade: Effects on economies, societies and peoples in Africa, the Americas, and Europe*, ed. J. I. Inikori and S. L. Engerman (Durham, NC: Duke University Press, 1992), pp. 117–41, esp. pp. 119–20; Philip D. Curtin, *The Atlantic Slave Trade: A census* (Madison: University of Wisconsin Press, 1969); David Eltis, *Economic Growth and the Ending of the Transatlantic Slave Trade* (New York: Oxford University Press, 1987); *idem.*, 'Free and Coerced Transatlantic Migrations: Some comparisons', *American Historical Review*, 88(2) (1983), pp. 251–80; J. D. Fage, 'African Societies and the Atlantic Slave Trade', *Past and Present*, 125 (1989), pp. 97–115; David Eltis, David Richardson and Stephen Behrendt, 'The Structure of the Atlantic Slave Trade, 1597–1867' (unpublished typescript).
8. See, *inter alia*, Thornton, *Africa and the Africans*; Inikori and Engerman, *The Atlantic Slave Trade*; Herbert Klein, *The Middle Passage: Comparative studies in the Atlantic slave trade* (Princeton: Princeton University Press, 1978); David Brion Davis, *Slavery and Human Progress* (New York: Oxford University Press, 1984); Orlando Patterson, *Slavery and Social Death* (Cambridge: Harvard University Press, 1982).
9. See Paul Lovejoy, *Transformations in Slavery: A history of slavery in Africa* (Cambridge: Cambridge University Press, 1983); *idem.*, 'The Impact of the Atlantic Slave Trade'; and Patrick Manning, 'The Impact of Slave Trade Exports on the Population of the Western Coast of Africa, 1700–1850', in *De la Traite à l'esclavage*, ed. Serge Daget (Nantes, France: Société française d'histoire d'outre-mer, 1988), pp. 111–34. Compare, with David Eltis, *Economic Growth*, pp. 64–71; John Thornton, 'The Slave Trade in Eighteenth Century Angola: Effects on demographic structures', *Canadian Journal of African Studies*, 14(3) (1980), pp. 417–27; and Martin A. Klein, 'The Impact of the Atlantic Slave Trade on the Societies of the Western Sudan', in Inikori and Engerman, eds., *Atlantic Slave Trade*, pp. 25–47.

10. William A. Darity, 'A General Equilibrium Model of the Eighteenth Century Atlantic Slave Trade: A least-likely test for the Caribbean school', *Research in Economic History*, 7 (1982), pp. 287–326; Hilary McD. Beckles, 'The Economic Origins of Black Slavery in the British West Indies, 1640–1680: A tentative analysis of the Barbados model', *Journal of Caribbean History*, 16 (1982), pp. 35–56; Raymond L. Cohn and Richard A. Jensen, 'The Determinants of Slave Mortality Rates on the Middle Passage', *Explorations in Economic History*, 10(2) (1982), pp. 173–6; David W. Galenson, 'The Atlantic Slave Trade and the Barbados Market, 1673–1723', *Journal of Economic History*, 42(3) (1982), pp. 491–511; Herbert S. Klein, 'Novas Interpretaoes do trafico de Escravos do Atlantico', *Revista de Historia*, 120 (1989), pp. 3–25.
11. See, *inter alia*, Inikori and Engerman, *Atlantic Slave Trade*; Barbara L. Solow and Stanley L. Engerman, eds., *British Capitalism and Caribbean Slavery* (Cambridge: Cambridge University Press, 1987); Barbara L. Solow, ed., *Slavery and the Rise of the Atlantic System* (New York: Cambridge University Press, 1991); David W. Galenson, *Traders, Planters, and Slaves: Market behavior in early English America* (New York: Cambridge University Press, 1986); Janet J. Ewald, 'Slavery in Africa and the Slave Trades from Africa', *American Historical Review*, 97 (1992), pp. 465–85; Julian Gwyn, 'The Economics of the Transatlantic Slave Trade: A review', *Social History*, 25 (1992), pp. 151–62. On the contrasting meaning of humans as 'things' in the Atlantic system and in the Nazi system, see Claudia Koonz, 'Genocide and Eugenics: The language of power', in *Lessons and Legacies: The meaning of the Holocaust in a changing world*, ed. Peter Hayes (Evanston, Ill.: Northwestern University Press, 1991), pp. 155–77; David Brion Davis, *The Problem of Slavery in Western Culture* (Ithaca: Cornell University Press, 1966), ch. 2, pp. 31–5; and Sidney Mintz, ed., *Esclave = facteur de production: l'economie politique de l'esclavage* (Paris: Dunod, 1981).
12. See Henry A. Gemery and Jan S. Hogendorn, eds., *The Uncommon Market: Essays in the economic history of the Atlantic slave trade* (New York: Academic Press, 1979), on the 'Western' transoceanic trade; and *The Economics of the Indian Ocean Slave Trade in the Nineteenth Century* (Special Issue), *Slavery and Abolition*, 9 (December 1988).
13. See, above all, Hilberg, *The Destruction*, 2, pp. 543–860.
14. See Claudia Koonz, 'Genocide and Eugenics', pp. 162 ff; Robert Jay Lifton and Amy Hackett, 'Nazi Doctors', in *Anatomy of the Auschwitz Death Camps*, ed. Michael Berenbaum (Bloomington: Indiana University Press, 1994), pp. 301–16.
15. See David Eltis, 'Free and Coerced Transatlantic Migrations: Some comparisons', *American Historical Review*, 88(2) (1983), pp. 251–80; Stanley L. Engerman and Kenneth L. Sokoloff, 'Factor Endowments, Institutions and Differential Paths of Growth Among New World Economies: A view from economic historians of the United States', in *Why Did Latin America Fall Behind?*, ed. Stephen Haber (Stanford: Stanford University Press, 1966). On depopulation in Africa, compare Manning, 'The Slave Trade', in Inikori and Engerman, *The Atlantic Slave Trade*, pp. 117–41, and Eltis, *Economic Growth*, pp. 64–71.

16. See Joseph C. Miller, *Way of Death: Merchant capitalism and the Angolan slave trade, 1730–1830* (Madison: University of Wisconsin Press, 1988), p. 439, figure 11.1. Miller's data base is quite small and lower estimates have been suggested by other authors. For example, Miller estimates an average loss of 35 percent from the point of capture to arrival at the coast, with a further loss of 10–15 percent in the port towns, yielding a total depletion in Africa of 45 percent (*ibid.*, p. 440). Patrick Manning estimates an interior loss of about 15 percent ('The Slave Trade', p. 121); as does John Thornton, 'The Demographic Effect of the Slave Trade on Western Africa 1500–1850', in *African Historical Demography*, II, *Proceedings of a Seminar* (Edinburgh: University of Edinburgh, 1977), pp. 693–720. Manning notes that population loss in Africa, though relatively less serious than the depopulations of the Americas and Oceania, was caused in large part by human agency. This characteristic would bring the slave trade closer to the Holocaust in terms of agency than other population catastrophes; Manning, *Slavery and African Life: Occidental, oriental, and African slave trades* (Cambridge: Cambridge University Press, 1990), p. 87.
17. See Yitzhak Arad, 'The Holocaust of Soviet Jewry in the Occupied Territories of the Soviet Union', *Yad Vashem Studies*, 21 (1991), pp. 1–47.
18. Compare Miller, *Way of Death*, p. 401, n. 89, with Raul Hilberg, 'Opening Remarks: The Discovery of the Holocaust', in Hayes, *Lessons and Legacies*, pp. 11–19, esp. pp. 15–16; Yisrael Gutman, 'Auschwitz – An overview', in *Anatomy of the Auschwitz Death Camp*, ed. Yisrael Gutman and Michael Berenbaum (Bloomington: Indiana University Press, 1994), pp. 5–33. It is important to note that the Auschwitz mortality figure applies only to the 400 000 (of 1.5 million) who were given inmate status, registered, numbered and left alive for some time. The majority of arrivals were killed immediately. See Franciszek Piper, 'The System of Prisoner Exploitation', in Gutman and Berenbaum, *Anatomy of the Auschwitz Death Camp*, pp. 34–49; and 'The Number of Victims', *ibid.*, pp. 61–76.
19. Hilberg, *The Destruction*, 1.
20. Miller, *Way of Death*, pp. 379–401; Philip Curtin, *Economic Change in Precolonial Africa: Sengambia in the era of the slave trade* (Madison: University of Wisconsin Press, 1975), pp. 168–73, 277–8.
21. Miller, *Way of Death*, pp. 391–2.
22. Miller, *Way of Death*, pp. 404–6; Walvin, *Black Ivory*, pp. 250–1, 284–92; see also Herbert S. Klein, *The Middle Passage: Comparative studies in the Atlantic slave trade* (Princeton: Princeton University Press, 1978).
23. Levi, *Survival in Auschwitz*, pp. 17–20.
24. *Ibid.*, pp. 27–8.
25. See Thornton, *Africa*, pp. 153–62. For eyewitness accounts by a slave and a surgeon, see Olaudah Equiano, *The Interesting Narrative of the Life of Olaudah Equiano*, 2 vols. (London, 1789) 1, pp. 78–80; Alexander Falconbridge, *An Account of the Slave Trade on the Coast of Africa* (London: J. Phillips, 1788), p. 25.
26. Robert-Jan Van Pelt, 'A Site in Search of a Mission', in Gutman and Berenbaum, *Anatomy of the Auschwitz Death Camp*, pp. 93–154, esp. pp. 130–2. See also Terrence Des Pres, *The Survivor: An anatomy of life*

in the death camps (New York: Oxford University Press, 1976), p. 60, describing the 'excremental assault' on the inmates. See also Hilberg, *Destruction*, 2, p. 490.
27. Arad, 'The Holocaust of Soviet Jewry', p. 14.
28. Walvin, *Black Ivory*, pp. 16–20.
29. That captive Jews were more readily imagined to be criminals than slaves may also be inferred from the case of the Ukrainian who consented to find refuge for two Jewish children whose father feared an imminent Nazi 'action' in his ghetto. When the children were discovered, Bazyli Antoniak was accused of complicity in harboring 'criminals', not stolen goods. He was convicted and sentenced to death, despite the fact that the children, aged six and seven, were too young to be charged as criminals. Ingo Müller, *Hitler's Justice: The courts of the Third Reich*, trans. Deborah Lucas Schneider (Cambridge: Harvard University Press, 1991), p. 164. Jews under Nazi control were, however, of value to Jewish groups outside the range of Nazi power. For details of the futile negotiations on the ransoming of Jews, see Yehuda Bauer, *Jews for Sale? Nazi–Jewish negotiations, 1933–1945* (New Haven: Yale University Press, 1994). On the value of corpses, see Andrzej Strzelecki, 'The Plunder of the Victims and Their Corpses', in Gutman and Berenbaum, *Anatomy of the Auschwitz Death Camp*, pp. 246–66. Under the auspices of Breslau University, a doctoral dissertation was published in 1940, 'On the Possibilities of Recycling Gold from the Mouths of the Dead'; Miller, *Way of Death* pp. 66–9; Levi, *Survival*, p. 16.
30. Thornton, *Africa*, pp. 162–82; Walvin, *Black Ivory*, pp. 59–66; Miller, *Way of Death*, pp. 445ff.
31. Levi, *Survival*, pp. 9–21. See also Paul Hoedeman, *Hitler or Hippocrates* (Sussex England: Book Guild, 1991), pp. 187–93; Franciszek Piper, 'Gas Chambers and Crematoria', in Gutman and Berenbaum, *Anatomy of the Auschwitz Death Camp*, pp. 157–82.
32. Konrad Kwiet, 'Forced Labour of German Jews in Nazi Germany', in *Leo Baeck Institute: Year Book*, 36 (London: Secker & Warburg, 1991), pp. 389–410, esp. p. 393.
33. Isaiah Trunk, 'Epidemics and Mortality in the Warsaw Ghetto, 1939–1942', in *The Nazi Holocaust: Historical articles on the destruction of European Jews*, ed. Michael R. Marrus, 9 vols. (Westport, Conn.: Meckler, 1989), 6; 1, p. 43; Christopher R. Browning, *The Path to Genocide: Essays on launching the final solution* (Cambridge: Cambridge University Press, 1992), pp. 34–51, 130–41. For an alternative and detailed account of the Warsaw ghetto, see Charles G. Roland, *Courage Under Siege: Starvation, disease, and death in the Warsaw Ghetto* (New York: Oxford University Press, 1992).
34. Browning, *The Path*, pp. 59–61; 111–22.
35. *Ibid*., pp. 73–4; Ulrich Herbert, 'Labour and Extermination: Economic interest and the primacy of *Weltanschauung* in National Socialism', *Past and Present*, 138 (1993), pp. 144–95; Peter Hayes, 'Profits and Persecution: Corporate involvement in the Holocaust', in *Perspectives on the Holocaust: Essays in honor of Raul Hilberg*, ed. James S. Pacy and Alan P. Wertheimer (Boulder: Westview Press, 1995), pp. 51–73.

36. Franciszek Piper, 'The System of Economic Exploitation', p. 47. For an extended discussion of the role of utilitarian and nonutilitarian rationalizations of the Holocaust, see the essays by Susanne Heime and Götz Aly, Dan Diner, David Bankier and Ulrich Herbert, in *Yad Vashem Studies*, 24, ed. Aharon Weiss (Jerusalem: Yad Vashem, 1994), pp. 45–145. However configured, the Holocaust frame of reference assumed a 'surplus' of people. The slave trade frame of reference assumed a deficit of laborers.
37. Hilberg, *Destruction*, 2, p. 529.
38. Himmler, quoted in Kwiet, 'Forced Labour', p. 403 (October 1942).
39. From J. Goebbels, *Tagebuck*, 2 March and 30 September 1943, quoted in Kwiet, 'Forced Labour', pp. 403–4.
40. Thornton, *Africa*, pp. 53–71.
41. Arad, 'The Holocaust of Soviet Jewry', p. 23.
42. Miller, *Way of Death*, pp. 159–63. On attitudes toward women and children in the African slave trade and in Auschwitz, compare Claire C. Robertson and Martin A. Klein, eds., *Women and Slavery in Africa* (Madison: University of Wisconsin Press, 1983), esp. the introduction, 'Women's Importance in African Slave Systems', pp. 3–25; Irena Strzelecka, 'Women', in Gutman and Berenbaum, *Anatomy of the Auschwitz Death Camp*, pp. 393–411; and Helena Kubica, 'Children', *ibid.*, pp. 412–27.
43. See Richard B. Sheridan, 'The Guinea Surgeons on the Middle Passage: The provision of medical services in the British slave trade', *International Journal of African Historical Studies*, 14 (1981), pp. 601–25; *idem.*, *Doctors and Slaves: A medical and demographic history of slavery in the British West Indies, 1680–1834* (Cambridge: Cambridge University Press, 1985), pp. 108–26; Robert Jay Lifton and Amy Hackett, 'Nazi Doctors', p. 303. On the role of Nazi medicine in the process of mass murder, see also Robert Jay Lifton, *The Nazi Doctors: Medical killing and the psychology of genocide* (New York: Basic Books, 1986); Götz Aly, Peter Chroust and Christian Pross, *Cleansing the Fatherland: Nazi medicine and racial hygiene* (Baltimore: Johns Hopkins University Press, 1994); Hoedeman, *Hitler or Hippocrates*.
44. Walvin, *Black Ivory*, p. ix; Anna Pawelczynska, *Values and Violence in Auschwitz: A sociological analysis* (Berkeley: University of California Press, 1979), pp. 54–5.
45. See, *inter alia*, William A. Green, 'Race and Slavery: Considerations on the Williams thesis', in Solow and Engerman, eds., *British Capitalism*, pp. 25–50; Thornton, *Africa*, pp. 137–8; 143–51.
46. Winthrop D. Jordan, *White Over Black: American attitudes toward the Negro, 1550–1812* (Chapel Hill: University of North Carolina Press, 1968); David Eltis, 'Europeans and the Rise and Fall of African Slavery in the Americas: An interpretation', *American Historical Review*, 98 (1993), pp. 1399–1423; Philip D. Morgan, 'Slaves and Livestock in Eighteenth-Century Jamaica: Vineyard pen, 1750–1751', *William and Mary Quarterly*, 52 (1995), pp. 47–76.
47. See, *inter alia*, Philip D. Curtin, *The Image of Africa: British ideas and action, 1780–1850* (Madison: University of Wisconsin Press, 1964); William B. Cohen, *The French Encounter with Africans: White response to blacks, 1530–1880* (Bloomington: Indiana University Press, 1980).

48. Magnus Mörner, *Race Mixture in the History of Latin America* (Boston: Little Brown, 1967).
49. Albert A. Sicroff, *Les Statutes de pureté de sangre en Espagne, au XVI, et XVII siècles* (Paris, 1955).
50. Koonz, 'Genocide and Eugenics'; George L. Mosse, *Toward the Final Solution: A history of European racism* (New York: Harper & Row, 1978), pp. 215–31.
51. Franciszek Piper, 'The Number of Victims', in Gutman and Berenbaum *Anatomy of the Auschwitz Death Camp*, pp. 61–76, esp. p. 614.
52. *The Diary of Anne Frank: The critical edition* (New York: Doubleday, 1987), pp. 265, 273, 316: entries of October 6, 9, and November 19, 1942.

11 The Role of Jews in the Transatlantic Slave Trade (1993)*

I

Hostility to Jews has a long history in the West. They have been used to signify the antithetical, unassimilable, threatening, other, the malevolent outsider responsible as a people for killing the God/Saviour, for undermining the belief in one true faith and for exercising enormous and mysterious power over rulers, peoples and economic activity.

A peculiar internal coherence is often ascribed to them, whether in religious, cultural or racial terms, depending upon the dominant conceptual metaphors of the time. As vast uncontrolled historical processes or world-shaking events unfolded, Jews were assigned a principal role as instigators or disseminators of the process, especially by those who condemned or feared the phenomenon in question. Over the past two centuries, Jews have been designated as the architects of the French and Russian Revolutions, as initiators of the two world wars, as the generators of democracy, of capitalism and of communism. Responsibility for world-wide epidemics and for the disintegration of the Soviet Union has been added to this long and open-ended series of manipulations of the course of history.

Developers of these conspiracy or dominance theories usually cite in support of their arguments a small number of highly-prominent individuals or brief moments of collective Jewish success contemporary with the time period or location of the event. They correspondingly ignore or trivialize the

---

Immigrants and Minorities, 12(2) (July 1993), pp. 113–25. An extended version of the chapter will appear as 'Jews and New Christians in the Atlantic Slave Trade', in *Jews and the Expansion of Europe to the West 1450–1825*, ed. Paolo Bernadini (forthcoming from Berghahn Books, 1999).

counter-evidence of Jewish helplessness, impoverishment persecution, expulsion and mass murder which are prominent elements of the record for so much of the last millennium of Western and world history.

Attaching principal responsibility to Jews for the initiation and organization of the African slave trade therefore fits into a clear historical tradition. Until recently a dominant role in the African slave trade had not been among the primary responsibilities assigned to the Jews. In July 1991, however, the Chairman of the Black Studies department of the City College of the City University of New York identified Jews as foremost among the principal financiers, planners, organizers and sustainers of the Atlantic slave trade and the transatlantic slave system.[2] It is no accident that this perspective bypasses the general historical patterns of Jewish history as well as the specific way in which two major diasporas, Jewish and African, partially coincided during the first two and a half centuries after the European encounter with sub-Saharan Africa and the settlement of the Americas.

The story of the black African diaspora has been the focus of major reinvestigations during the past generation. The general outlines of the story are now clearer and more widely disseminated in the curricula of American secondary and higher education and research publications than ever before.[3] For half a century before the voyages of Columbus, thousands of Africans were forcibly transported northward across the Atlantic to serve as coerced labour in Europe and, for more than three centuries after Columbus, at least four out of every five transatlantic migrants were black Africans rather than white Europeans. Ironically, only in that part of the Americas which became the United States did the European migration stream (often also coming in various forms of coerced labour) outnumber African slaves. In terms of pre-1850 migration patterns, the transatlantic movement was far more African than European.[4]

Less familiar is the diaspora which was occurring among the Jews of Europe after 1450. The Holocaust of the twentieth century was not the first near-elimination of Jewry from Western and Central Europe. That situation first occurred in the later fifteenth century, almost simultaneously with the beginning of the transoceanic African slave diaspora. After a century of increasing persecution of the Spanish Jews, their general expulsion or forced conversion was implemented in 1492, only a few months before the launching of Columbus's first expedition. The mass expulsion from Spain was followed by the coerced mass baptism of the 70 000 or so Jews (mostly Spanish refugees) who resided in Portugal in 1497. These events paralleled the expulsion of Jews from most of Northern and Southern Italy between 1491 and 1510, and from most of the Swiss and German lands between 1490 and 1520.

The final denouement of these successive expulsions came between 1520 and 1550. This last phase was the result of princely and ecclesiastical authorities as much as of popular mobilization. Except for areas directly under the authority of the Holy Roman Emperors (the Habsburgs) the collapse of Jewish life in both Catholic and Protestant Europe was virtually complete by 1570. Open allegiance to Judaism was entirely extinguished in Spain, Portugal, Italy south of Rome, the Netherlands, England, France, the Germanies and northern Italy. In isolated areas where Jews were not physically expelled, the Jewish role in Western and Central Europe had become altogether marginal. The age of European exploration was therefore also initially the age of 'the most fundamental restructuring of Jewish life in Europe' between the Roman destruction of the Jewish nation and the later German annihilation of the twentieth century.[5]

By 1570 the major centres of Jewish life had shifted definitively eastward to the Ottoman dominions in the Balkans and the Levant and to Poland–Lithuania in north-eastern Europe. In 1492 Polish Jewry amounted to only around 30 000 less than the Jewish population of Italy and one-fifth of Spanish Jewry. By the end of the sixteenth century, Polish Jewry had increased by up to five times or only slightly less than Spanish Jewry on the eve of expulsion. The overwhelming mass of European Jewry in the four centuries of the Atlantic slave trade therefore lived outside of the area of Europe which was most directly involved in the Atlantic economy. The role of the Jews in the Atlantic slave trade becomes clearer in the light of the framework of these two diaspora movements at the dawn of the early modern era – one moving north and west from Africa, the other moving north and east within Europe and the Levant.

That there was a Jewish involvement with the slave trade is not a new discovery. The nature of the involvement, however, requires further elaboration. A small fragment of the Jewish diaspora fled northward in Europe and westward into the Americas, there becoming entwined with the African slave trade. So often and so long barred by Western European societies from securing high political positions, large landholdings, high military rank, the right to participate in established crafts, professions, commercial and educational institutions, and even denied full rights to residence in most of the West, a small minority of European Jewry succeeded in re-entering the areas of Western domination. Since they remained at the social margin of society, they could prosper only by moving into high risk and new areas of economic development. In the expanding Western European economy after the Columbian voyages, this meant getting footholds within the new markets at the fringes of Europe, primarily in its overseas enclaves. One of these new 'products' was human beings. It was here that Jews, or descendants of Jews, appeared on the roster of Europe's slave trade.

II

With this as background, we may address the specific issue of Jewish involvement in the African slave trade. Were Jews, as claimed, the principal mediators of slavery's transference from the medieval Mediterranean world to the islands of the Atlantic and to the Americas in the wake of European expansion? Regarding the initiation of the various European slave trades, the answer is unequivocal. In none of the major transatlantic slaving zones within or outside of Europe was the slave traffic initiated by Jews, individually or collectively. Even in the earlier medieval systems of Spain and of Central and Eastern Europe, Jewish slaving was an extension of non-Jewish conquest and raiding armies.[6] The slave trades within Europe were initiated by non-Jews, Christians, pagans or Muslims. On the eve of the Muslim conquest of Spain, for example, the last Visigothic Christian king was hunting down and flogging Jews at the same time as he was pursuing fugitive slaves. Only when the Moorish conquest had settled down into cross-border raiding between Christians and Moslems did Jews play a significant mercantile role in the Iberian slave trade. At that point, the position of Jews as intermediaries on both sides of the political/religious border offered advantages to both sides in slaving activities.

By the late medieval period, however, when the prototype of the slave plantation system began its diffusion from the Eastern to the Western Christian Mediterranean, Jews played no role in the process. In the period of the Latin–Byzantine supremacy, Jews were forbidden from acquiring non-Jewish slaves. They are absent from the list of the areas's slave traders. The mercantile city-states of Italy dominated and sponsored the transfer of sugar plantation and slave systems across the Mediterranean and into the Atlantic islands.[7]

A similar observation may be made concerning the origins of the Atlantic slave trade itself. The Portuguese who opened up the Euro–African Atlantic slave trade in the mid-fifteenth century were Christians, funded and dispatched under the exclusive authority of a Portuguese prince seeking to outflank Moslem-controlled trade routes. Once Europeans reached the Americas, the Spaniards who undertook wholesale enslavements of native populations were Catholic Conquistadors. Far more rigorously than in Latin Byzantium, Jews were officially barred by the Iberian monarchs of both Portugal and Spain from settling in their overseas transatlantic empires.

All of the great trading companies which dominated the Atlantic slave trade in the seventeenth century – those of Portugal, Brazil, Holland, France and England – began as exclusive monopolies, organized and headed by Christian rulers. In the foundation of all of these major Atlantic slave trade systems, the role of Jews was at best a subordinate one. Only in the ephemeral schemes and ventures of some Baltic rulers, such as those of the Great Elector of Brandenburg (the Brandenburg Africa Company of 1682), and of Duke James of Courland, did wealthy Jews of Amsterdam and Hamburg play an entrepreneurial role. In these instances, too, however, the slaving ventures were state-sponsored and state-dominated enterprises. The ultimate decision-makers were always the political rulers, who more often than not were religiously intolerant sovereigns as well.[8]

III

If Jews did not found any of the major European transatlantic slave trades, what role did they play in organizing or financing them once established? Two of the largest slaving powers, England and France, were responsible for shipping at least 40 per cent of the total number of African slaves to the New World.[9] In these two cases, Jewish participation was so insignificant that historians of the slave trade no more than occasionally cite a few Jewish individuals or families in French or English seaports who engaged in slaving activities. These were rare instances among the hundreds of Catholic and Protestant investors who dominated all of the trades of England and France, including the African. Were one to include in such an accounting additional thousands of Europeans and Africans who commanded or manned the slave ships, or the Afro–Europeans and Africans who participated in the trade on the African supply side, the relative significance of the Jewish role in these enterprises would diminish even further.

This leaves us with the Spanish, Portuguese and Dutch slave trades as the remaining potential sources of a major Jewish role in the transatlantic slave trade. Spain relied upon the fleets, mercantile networks and capital of other European powers to monopoly contracts or *asientos*. Before the third decade of the seventeenth century, that is, for more than a century and a quarter after the mass expulsions of the 1490s, the Spanish *asiento* was entirely in the hands of the Genoese and Flemish capitalists. During the first century after 1492 when memories of or affiliations with Jewish traditions might have been most intense, Spanish *New Christians*, whether 'grandees' or otherwise, simply had no opportunity to take the lead in organizing, financing or otherwise directing the Atlantic slave trade to Spanish America. The Portuguese in the late sixteenth and early seventeenth centuries, succeeded by the Dutch in the mid-seventeenth century, were the principal early carriers to the Spanish possessions. The French and the British moved in as major competitors for the Spanish slaving *asientos* at the end of the seventeenth century.

The Portuguese slave trade creates a knotty problem for any historian who undertakes to apportion shares of participation in the slave trade by confessional affiliation. Descendants of

The Role of Jews in the Transatlantic Slave Trade 345

Jews did play a significant role in the sixteenth and early seventeenth century transatlantic slave trades as they did in all of the European and transoceanic trades of Portugal's seaborne empire from Asia to Angola, and from Mexico to Cartagena. Until the mid-seventeenth century their linkages with overseas Jews helped to sustain their mercantile position in Portugal. However, the Portuguese case amply demonstrates the difficulty of apportioning the slave trade by religious categories, especially as applied to Iberians.

Portugal's Jews, as indicated above, were forcibly Christianized through mass baptism in 1497. The resultant population was designated as a separate legal category of *Conversos* or *New Christians*, just as the previously-converted Spanish Jews had been. After one generation, the term *New Christians* therefore became an oxymoron, a hereditary legal category designating a suspect and underprivileged social class. For centuries after 1497 *'New' Christians* lived under the same kinds of legal, occupational and social restrictions previously applied by European rulers against openly-professing Jews.[10] As early as the late sixteenth century, when Portuguese *New Christians* were allowed to re-enter Spain, a large number were sincere Catholics, neither adhering to Jewish traditions nor desiring to maintain cultural ties with the Iberian Jewish diaspora outside the Iberian peninsula. The most definitive evidence of prominent Jewish connections in the Portuguese *New Christian* slave trade lies in the activities of Duarte Dias Henriques, who farmed the Crown monopoly for exporting slaves from Angola in 1607–14. He also helped to maintain Jewish institutions in Palestine.[11]

Of course, if one accepts the Inquisition's legal definition, all descendants of those converted at the end of the fifteenth century may be classified as secret or 'occult' Jews, or *Marranos*. In Iberian legal terms *New Christians* lacked the 'purity of blood' of Old Christians'. In this perspective descendants of Jews took any opportunity to escape the Inquisition's jurisdiction to subvert the faith and to revenge themselves for the humiliation of coerced ancestral conversion. From the Inquisition's perspective any *New Christians* involved in the slave system would be classified as potential 'Jews'.[12]

Modern scholars, overwhelmingly rejecting this racist and biologizing definition, treat the problem of Iberian Jewish identity as a historical process, with each generation of *New Christians* probably having fewer members who regarded themselves as Jews, or having any desire to revert or convert to Judaism. Even at the outset, at the end of the fifteenth century, the majority of converted Portuguese Jews did not consist of *forced* converts. It was the Inquisition which, within the jurisdiction of the Spanish and Portuguese empires, froze the identity of the descendants of *New Christians* and prevented their complete assimilation into the 'old' Catholic fold.[13]

Finally, the bulk of the Luso–Brazilian (Portuguese) slave trade occurred in the eighteenth and nineteenth centuries, eight to twelve generations after the initial mass conversion. Scholars have not assigned a 'Jewish' role of any kind to that period of the slave trade which accounts for five-sixths of the Africans landed in Brazil. When the Portuguese monarchy later removed all disabling impositions from the *New Christians* and invited the return of descendants of Jews who had fled Portugal centuries before, there was no large-scale reversion or conversion to Jewish practice among the old *New Christians* of Portugal nor any other collective manifestation of crypto-Jewish identity.

It therefore becomes crucial whether one uses cultural or racial criteria in considering the role of Jews in organizing and financing the forced transfer of African slaves to the Portuguese Americas. By 1650, there is overwhelming evidence that the Jewish diaspora outside Iberia and the *New Christians* who remained within the peninsula had also taken divergent paths regarding the slave trade. During the Dutch–Portuguese struggle for Brazil in the 1640s, it was Portuguese *New Christians* who financed the successful Portuguese expedition to recapture Brazil from the Dutch, who tolerated open Jewish practice in that colony. The ritual public burning in Lisbon of one of the captured Brazilian Jews marked a definitive cultural and commercial alienation between the main Jewish refugee community in Holland and the *New Christians* in Portugal.[14]

Hardest to disentangle is the Jewish role in the Portuguese African slave trade of the sixteenth century. As indicated above. Jews had no part in the founding or the initial financing of Portugal's slave trade. It was only after the mass conversion of 1497 that *New Christians* could have entered the slave trade.

Here too, attempts to identify even second-generation *New Christians* as 'Jews' leads in to a conceptual morass. How should one categorize the children of forcibly-baptized Jews who were deported to the island of São Tome in the Atlantic soon after the forced conversion of the parents? Since many deportees were allotted African slaves as wives, how does one proceed to disentangle the hereditary identity of subsequent generations of Afro–Europeans in the manner of the Inquisition?

It was the persecution, not the religious affinities of the *New Christians* driven or fleeing to the peripheral zones of Africa and America, which helped to determine their role in the expansion of the transatlantic slave trade. One of the frontier trades to which *New Christians* had easy access was the slave trade. They could quickly move into this 'new' trade and then out into other branches of economic activity once they had established themselves. There is ample evidence that the sixteenth-century *New Christians* were linked with diaspora Judaism. These early Iberian *New Christians* played a subordinate role as intermediaries in the transatlantic slave trade.[15]

IV

The Dutch slave trade is one instance about which we can be certain of unambiguous Jewish participation in the Afro–Caribbean slave trade. Unlike the Portuguese or Spanish *Conversos*, the Jews of Holland possessed a recognized corporate religious status. Even in Holland, of course, Jews were restricted from entering certain occupations and were excluded from political office. In the Dutch American colonies, Jews were likewise prohibited from engaging in the direct purchase of slaves on the African coast. But in the colonies they could settle as Jews and acquire and sell slaves once imported from Africa.

In the Netherlands itself, they could invest freely in the Dutch West India Company, which had the monopoly of Dutch African purchases until well into the eighteenth century. Since the mid-seventeenth century was the period in which the Dutch controlled a substantial portion of the Atlantic slave trade, the Jewish role in the Atlantic trade could, therefore, have been both substantial and important for a generation after 1640, via the Dutch trade. It turns out, however, that Jews played a limited and subordinate role, both managerially and financially, among the major Dutch slavers. They did not serve on the *Heren X*, the directorate of the Dutch West India Company. Their investment share amounted to only 0.5 per cent (or one two-hundredths) of the company's capital.[16]

Elsewhere in Northern Europe, the last third of the seventeenth century marked the high point of Jewish involvement in the scramble for the Afro–Caribbean trades. Whether as occasional agents for negotiating Spanish *asiento* contracts or as go-betweens for the founding of new West Indian trading companies, a handful of wealthy Jews negotiated with European rulers and merchants who were anxious to get into the expanding Afro–Caribbean economic systems of the late seventeenth century. But this flurry of Jewish entrepreneurial activity in Northern Europe signified almost nothing for Africa. Jews were most important in organizing the most insignificant slave trades. All of the Baltic states together accounted for less than 0.7 per cent of Africans transported to the New World.

The *indirect* significance of Jews in the Atlantic system was more important than was their role in organizing the forced migration of Africans to the Americas. They were active in the transportation and processing of certain tropical commodities–sugar, diamonds and tropical wood. In the generation after 1640 Jews were also among the transmitters of tropical plantation technology and know-how throughout the Caribbean. As artisans, as managerial experts on plantations and as mercantile pioneers, they helped to expand the production and transportation networks of new tropical products which their co-religionists often then processed in Europe. Here, and not in the slave trade, the forced diaspora of the Jews did contribute, at least briefly, to the mid-seventeenth century expansion of sugar and slavery. Fleeing from Brazil with the defeat of the Dutch, they scattered through the Caribbean, becoming plantation owners and merchants in the Dutch, English and French colonies.

Jewish participation in the slave system was greatest under Dutch sovereignty. On the island of Curaçao, Jews became re-export agents of the Dutch West India Company, selling slaves, manufactures and commodities to the Spanish mainland,

The Role of Jews in the Transatlantic Slave Trade 349

and to the British and French colonies. Jews also became a significant mainland settler group among the white colonists of Dutch Guiana in the second half of the seventeenth century. At one point the Dutch colonies contained the largest Jewish community in the Americas. They had their own self-governing community, 'Joden Savanne' (Jewish Savanah), in Surinam. In this medium-sized colony, they became a substantial segment of the propertied classes, including the possession of slave plantations. They were extractors of coerced labour and the owners of human bodies for three full centuries before Dutch slave emancipation (1863).[17]

V

What then was the overall role of the Jews in organizing and financing the transatlantic slave trade? The four most substantial trades – the British and French trades of the late seventeenth and eighteenth centuries and the Brazilian and Cuban slave trades of the eighteenth and nineteenth centuries – accounted for almost 90 per cent of the forced African migration to the Americas. In those four great trades, the Jewish role ranged from marginal to virtually nil.

Only by conflating *New Christians* with Jews can the latter be said to have been major participants in the sixteenth- and seventeenth-century Iberian slave trades. Jews played their largest role in the Dutch slave trade, but even here, they lacked the organizational and financial significance of their more powerful Christian neighbours. Finally, in the minor Danish and the miniscule Brandenburg, Swedish and Courland slave trades, Jews did play significant entrepreneurial or organizational roles. But even were we absurdly to assign *all* Africans transported under the flags of Denmark, Sweden, Brandenburg, etc. to a 'Jewish' account, all of these 'Baltic' trades combined did not account for as much as 0.7 per cent of Europe's transatlantic slave trade.

In any global analysis of the transatlantic slave trade, including Islamic and other Old World participants, Jews could not qualify as major players compared to other social groups, whether categorized by religion, race, class or ethnicity. Moreover, the futility of assigning responsibility for the Atlantic slave trade by religious or cultural groups should already be apparent. The transatlantic slave trade entailed a vast number of interlocking economic ventures and divided along political lines. It engaged the interest of warriors, sailors, merchants and artisans, people of both sexes and all races from Scandinavia to Southern Africa. Ironically, the only major state in Europe whose people or rulers evinced no interest whatever in getting into the Afro–Caribbean system during the four centuries after Columbus' voyages was the kingdom of Poland, proportionally the most 'Jewish' area of Europe until its final partition in the 1790s. This irony is of recent vintage because, for five centuries, no one imagined European Jewry to be dominant in the transatlantic slave trade.

The scholarship of modern slavery confirms the conventional assessment. Historians of the slave trade have devoted little attention to Jews as a distinct social group in the long and terrible story of its operation as revealed by the texts and indexes of scholarly histories of the slave trade. They rate attention only in detailed monographs of the individual European slave trades, works which focus on mid-seventeenth century Brazil, and on the seventeenth-century Caribbean.

To find extended attention devoted to Jews in the Atlantic slave trade, one therefore has to go to the scholarship of modern Jewry, rather than of slavery. That is precisely why proponents of a Judeo-centric slave trade ironically depend upon historians and biographers of Jews for their information. The paradox is easily explained. The Atlantic slave system was more important to certain segments of early modern Jewry than early modern Jewry was to the Atlantic slave system.

In evaluating the role of Jews in New World slavery, no serious scholar would mitigate the basic fact that Jews bought, used, sold, and otherwise coerced human beings in whom they held rights as chattels. One does not, however, have to grossly exaggerate the significance of a religious group which neither initiated the transatlantic slave trade, nor controlled any of its major components in Europe, Africa, or the Americas. This was the function of groups and rulers belonging to other faiths – Christian, Muslim and pagan. They dominated the world which generated both the African and the Jewish diasporas after 1450.

The Role of Jews in the Transatlantic Slave Trade

In terms of the relationship between these two groups, the most important underlying fact remains that they constituted two contemporary cohorts of people driven from their habitations at about the same moment in world history. In the Old World, the two diasporas rarely overlapped. In the Americas, it was a tragic irony that Jews, like other oppressed groups in Europe, could conceive of the New World as a land of promise while sustaining and enriching themselves through the enslavement of others. Prosperity and liberty for Jews, as for other Western migrants, entailed participation in systems of coercion, degradation, and indifference to the fate of non-Europeans. In the tropical Americas, liberation for Jews was eased by the enslavement of Africans. Only centuries after millions of Africans had contributed so tragically to the establishment of freer Jewish diasporas in the New World, did they achieve their own liberation from enslavement.[18]

NOTES

1. See Norman Cohn, *Warrant for Genocide: The Myth of the Jewish world-conspiracy and the Protocols of the Elders of Zion* (London, 1967) and Henry Gates, Jr., 'Black Demagogues and Psuedo-Scholars', *The New York Times*, 20 July 1992, p. 11.
2. See text of a speech by Leonard Jeffries, 20 July 1991, at the Empire State Black Arts and Cultural Festival in Albany, New York, reprinted in *New York Newsday*, Monday, 18 August 1991, pp. 3, 25–9:

    So I said, 'Where do you want us to start? What period of history? You want us to start in the Spanish–Portuguese period of the starting of the slave trade in the 1400s and 1500s? Do you want us to move it from Seville and Lisbon on to Amsterdam and Hamburg, where the new Jewish community continued the slave trade for the Dutch, the Germans, and the English? Or do you want us to move it to Brazil and the Caribbean and Curaçao, which became a new Amsterdam, the new center of the slave trade in the western world centered around the Jewish immigrants that moved into Curaçao? Or do you want us to move it to New York and Rhode Island? Where do you want us to start?'
      When do you want us to start? Do you want to go to Amsterdam? Then get a book by Jonathan Israel on 'European Jewry in the Age of Mercantilism, 1550–1750'.
      And there's a picture of the Amsterdam synagogue, which was the center of slave trading for the Dutch. Amsterdam became a leading port in this period of time for slaving. And it was around this synagogue that the slaving system was established ...

We'll have the ten major books relating to the Jewish community (the wealthy Jewish community) and enslavement.

In Spain, there were the grandees, managing the money of the Spanish throne. In Germany in the 16- and 1700s there were the court Jews, managing the political and economic apparatus of Europe, the Hapsburg Empire, the German states, etcetera. We have the names. We know who they were, what they were, what they controlled. We know when they set up the Dutch East Indian (sic) Co., Dutch West Indian (sic) Co., the Portuguese Company, the Brazilian Company. We know who and what documents. We know that even when they converted to Christianity, they maintained links with their Jewish community brothers who had not converted; and that's why they had a network around the world.

They became the lifetime of the fallen Roman Empire in the 15- and 1600s, and they began to institutionalize a trade link with the Middle East.

3. See, *inter alia*, Phillip Curtin, *The Atlantic Slave Trade: A census* (Madison, 1969); David Eltis, *Economic Growth and the Ending of the Transatlantic Slave Trade* (New York, 1987); Robert William Fogel, *Without Consent or Contract: The rise and fall of American slavery* (New York, 1989).
4. David Eltis, 'Free and Coerced Transatlantic Migration: Some Comparisons', *American Historical Review*, 88 (1983), pp. 251–80.
5. Jonathan I. Israel, *European Jewry in the Age of Mercantilism, 1550–1750* (Oxford: Oxford University Press, 1985). Long before the Iberian rulers, the kings of England and France had expelled the Jews of their realms.
6. See Charles Verlinden, *L'esclavage dans l'Europe medievale*, 2 vols. (Brugge and Ghent, 1955–77) and Pierre Bonnassie (trans. Jean Birrell), *From Slavery to Feudalism in South-Western Europe* (Cambridge: Cambridge University Press, 1991), pp. 96–9.
7. It is important to emphasize that there was no general inhibition against slave-holding or slave-dealing in any of the major religious communities of the early medieval period. Jews apparently participated in the slave trades of Southwestern and East Central Europe as fully as circumstances permitted. Nor did Jews merely designate slavery as a necessary evil in a mundane present. The large-scale enslavement of gentiles was often part of their messianic future, as well. In terms of Europe's historical slave trades, however, the role of the Jews waxed and waned in the ninth and tenth centuries CE, almost half a millennium before the burgeoning of the transatlantic slave trade. See Verlinden, *L'esclavage dans l'Europe Medievale*, 1, pp. 216–19, 245, 672, 707–16. Note that Verlinden's second volume covering the late medieval Italian Mediterranean colonies, the Latin Levant and the Byzantine Empire, contains no index reference to Jews as 'merchants of slaves'. See also Charles Verlinden (trans. Yvonne Freccero), *The Beginnings of Modern Colonization: Eleven essays with an introduction* (Ithaca, NY, 1970), Parts II and III; Steven B. Bowman, *The Jews of Byzantium 1204–1453* (Alabama, 1985), pp. 118–9.

The Role of Jews in the Transatlantic Slave Trade   353

8. Israel, *European Jewry*, p. 139.
9. Based upon Curtin, *The Atlantic Slave Trade*, p. 88. Revisions of estimates since Curtin do not substantially alter his percentages. See Paul E. Lovejoy, 'Volume of the Atlantic Slave Trade: A synthesis'. *Journal of African History*, 23 (1982), pp. 473–501.
10. Israel, *European Jewry*, pp. 24–5, 58–9, and Salo Baron, *A Social and Religious History of Jews*, XIII, pp. 141–55, 264, 275–7. On the complexity of the 'New Christian' identity over three centuries see Anita Novinsky, 'Sephardim in Brazil: The New Christians', in R. D. Barnett and W. M. Schwab (eds.), *The Sephardi Heritage*, 2 vols. (Grendon, Northants, 1989), II, pp. 431–44.
11. Israel, *European Jewry*, pp. 58. 11; C. R. Boxer, *The Portuguese Seaborne Empire, 1415–1825* (Newark, NJ, 1965), pp. 266–7, 331, and Daniel M. Sweschinski, 'Conflict and Opportunity in Europe's Other Sea', *American Jewish History* (December 1982), pp. 218–38. On the complexity of the cultural identity of the early settlers of São Tome, see David Birmingham, *Trade and Conflict in Angola* (Oxford: Oxford University Press, 1966), p. 25: Jews and criminals were sent to the island. Each settler was given a slave wife from the Kongo, and their offspring became planters. See also Pierre Chaunu, *Seville et l'Atlantique 1504–1650*, 8 vols. (Paris, 1959), VII, pp. 60–85, 277–86; Frederic Mauru, *Portugal et l'Atlantique* (Paris, 1960), p. 162 and Edgar R. Samuel, 'The Trade of the "New Christians" of Portugal in the Seventeenth Century', in Barnett and Schwab, *The Sephardi Heritage*, II, pp. 100–14.
12. See Leon Poliakov, *Histoire de l'antisemitisme*, 3 vols. (Paris, 1961), II, *De Mahomet aux Marranes*, ch.10, 11. See also Jeffries' speech, p. 27.
13. There is a long and complex debate about the religious and cultural status of the *Conversos* and their descendants in Iberia even before the establishment of the Spanish Inquisition. B. Netanyahu shows that the Jewish leadership outside Iberia assumed the erosion of Jewish identity to be the norm and concludes that as early as the early sixteenth century, the majority of converted Portuguese Jewry did not consist of *forced* converts. Exceptions to this normative position were made to first-generation Portuguese converts, but not to those who were children of converts and certainly not to descendants for generations. *The marranos of Spain From the Late XIVth to the Early XVIth Century According to Contemporary Hebrew Sources*, 2nd edn. (New York, 1973), pp. 211–15. It was the inquisition which froze the identity of the New Christians in assuming the propensity to crypto-Judaism.
14. Israel, 'Dutch Sephardi Jewry, Millenarian Politics, and the struggle for Brazil (1640–1654)', in David S. Katz and Jonathan I. Israel (eds.), *Skeptics, Millenarians and Jews* (Leiden and New York, 1990), pp. 76–97. On Brazilian Jewry, see Arnold Wiznitzer, *Jews in Colonial Brazil* (New York, 1960).
15. See Edgar R. Samuel, 'The Trade of the "New Christians" of Portugal in the Seventeenth Century', in Barnett and Schwab, *The Shepardi Heritage*, II, pp. 100–14. In the first century of the transatlantic slave trade, 'the distribution and marketing of sugar were in the hands of the Italians, who also predominated as slave traders', and the same capitalists who

financed the latter trade reaped the main profits from it. See Kenneth Maxwell, '¡Adios Columbus!, *New York Review of Books*, 28 January 1983, pp. 38–45; and Ruth Pike, *Enterprise and Adventure: The Genoese in Seville and the Opening of the New World* (Ithaca, NY, 1966).

16. Private correspondence with Professor Pieter C. Emmer, of the Institute for the History of European Expansion, 8 October, 1991. See also Johannes Menne Postma, *The Dutch in the Atlantic Slave Trade* (Cambridge: Cambridge University Press, 1990), for the most recent estimate of the Dutch slave trade. In the British West Indies, 'Jewish activity in the slave trade was neither as great as rumored nor as negligible as claimed', Stephen Alexander Fortune, *Merchants and Jews: The struggle for British West Indian commerce, 1650–1750* (Gainesville, FL, 1984), pp. 162–3.

17. See, *inter alia*, the volume by Cornelius Ch. Goslinga, *The Dutch in the Caribbean and in Surinam 1791–1942* (Assen and Maastricht, 1990) and Isaac S. and Suzanne A. Emmanuel, *History of the Jews of the Netherlands Antilles*, 2 vols. (Cincinnati, 1970), pp. 41–8, 78–80, 226.

18. See, above all, David Brion Davis, *Slavery and Human Progress* (New York, 1984), Part I, ch. 6, 'Jews and the Children of Strangers', for an excellent overview of Jews and New World slavery by a historian of slavery.

12 Eric Williams: British Capitalism and British Slavery (1987)*

THE MAKING OF *CAPITALISM AND SLAVERY*

Just over forty years ago the University of North Carolina Press published *Capitalism and Slavery*.[1] Its author was a young Trinidadian, Eric E. Williams, then teaching at Howard University in Washington, DC. If one criterion of a classic is its ability to reorient our most basic way of viewing an object or a concept, Eric Williams' study supremely passes that test.

For more than a century following British slave emancipation in 1833–8 the historical context of British slavery and its demise remained virtually unaltered. The Centenary of the Emancipation Act in 1933 was unabashedly celebrated by Britain as an imperial triumph in behalf of humanity. The London *Times* appropriately headlined its account of the principal festivities as 'The Centenary of Wilberforce', the Liberator who had died dramatically only days before the Emancipation Bill cleared its last hurdle in Parliament. Hull, the hometown of Wilberforce, was the logical center of commemoration. A great civic procession, led by the Lord Mayor and a host of dignitaries and descendants of Wilberforce, filed past his home, his grammar school, and his statue. The proceedings were solemnly consecrated by the Archbishop of York, to the accompaniment of choral hymns and spirituals. At the appropriate moment in the proceedings the flags of fifty nations unfurled before twenty thousand participants.[2]

For the celebrants at Hull, and for its scholarly interpreters, there seemed little ambiguity about either the historical concept of the original event or its long-range significance. Professors G. M. Trevelyan in the *Times* and Reginald Coupland at Hull agreed that the abolition was an act of the British

---

History and Theory: Studies in the Philosophy of History, 26(2) (1987), pp. 180–96. © 1987 Wesleyan University.

nation which had lifted mankind to a higher moral plane and nurtured the religious and secular optimism of the Victorian Age. These historians riveted the national memory on that gallant band of evangelical 'Saints' whose leader's remains had been honored with a funeral at Westminster Abbey. The beneficiaries of emancipation were also appropriately evoked – at the horizon of the event. The historians pointed first to the grateful slaves who had solemnly assembled on the hills on August 1 1834 to greet the rising sun of freedom from the East, and to the natives of Africa, still unaware, in 1833, that half a century later British domination would bring the disappearance of slavery in their own 'heart of darkness'. Such was the imperial historical vision of 1933.[3]

With the exception of the African postscript, the British historians of the 1930s had made no change whatever in the ideological context of Thomas Clarkson's first history of abolition. A corrupted nation was roused by a band of prophets who gave humanity a decisive victory over avarice, materialism, and brutal exploitation. Here, if anywhere in the mainstream of the Anglo–American historiographical tradition, was a watershed in the Whig interpretation of history. Clarkson had actually provided a watershed map of pre-abolitionist history. It began with scattered rivulets of isolated thinkers in the sixteenth century broadening into a vast transcontinental sea of abolitionism at the end of the eighteenth.[4] In the 1930s the story of slavery remained a progressive political narrative fleshed out with religious inspiration. Historians never wearied of recalling W. E. H. Lecky's famous dictum that the crusade against slavery was probably 'among the three or four perfectly virtuous pages comprised in the history of nations'.[5] The story was dramatic, the motives clear, and the ending happy. In 1833 Britain had been made safe for reform, the West Indies for freedom, and Africa for penetration.

Now consider the situation half a century after that Centennial. On August 1 1984, Prime Minister Forbes Burnham of Guyana told a rally of 5000 in Georgetown that Britain had freed the slaves not for humanitarian reasons but because slavery had become unprofitable, risky and expensive. Similar sentiments were voiced by the Minister of Sports Culture and Youth Affairs at an international conference on slavery held in Trinidad two days earlier.[6] Perhaps the most dramatic evidence of the shift was registered in Hull. In 1983 the Sesquicentennial of Emancipation was concluded by an international conference on social change in the West Indies after slavery. There were no sessions devoted to British antislavery, nor to its statesmen, nor to its Saints, nor to its historians. There was no paper on Hull's own Wilberforce. One was reminded of William Cobbett's little list of things that would not be missed when he was forced to flee England in 1816. At least where he was going, he noted, there would be no Wilberforces: 'No Wilberforces! Think of *that*! No Wilberforces!'[7]

What happened in the intervening fifty years between the two commemorations is in no small measure because of *Capitalism and Slavery*. When an international conference on British Capitalism and Caribbean slavery was convened at Bellagio, Italy on the 150th anniversary of British slave emancipation, it was appropriately focused on Eric Williams, and his major scholarly legacy.[8]

Among other things, *Capitalism and Slavery* marked Williams' personal declaration of independence from imperial tradition. He was born in the capital of Trinidad in 1911, the firstborn and pride of a post-office official. He grew up under a government not responsible to its population, in an economy not owned by its natives, and among inhabitants who were considered 'hewers of wood and drawers of water' for their foreign overloads.[9]

Because of his exceptional talents as a student, young Eric ascended rapidly through a very narrow Trinidadian educational channel which culminated in a scholarship to Oxford. To be groomed for such a rare and coveted opportunity was to be made continuously aware of the distance between one's formal training and one's colonial environment. Eric was given a thoroughly English education. As he later observed in his autobiography, 'this was only another way of saying that it was un-West Indian. My training was divorced from anything remotely suggestive of Trinidad and the West Indies'.[10] Not until years after he left Trinidad was West Indian history included In the island's secondary school curriculum.

At Oxford he at first continued his upward trajectory, gaining a 'first' in history and his doctorate in 1938. Yet he also experienced one supreme moment of disappointment, when he failed to win a prize Fellowship at All Souls College.

Whether, as Williams himself noted, he had not qualified because of his ranking in the examinations, or because color or colonialism had some part in the rejection, he retrospectively concluded that no 'native', however acculturated, could then fit into All Souls, or any other Oxford senior common room.

A number of Williams' most salient traits as an historian are evident from his account of these years. He already found Oxford's emphasis on political narrative far less interesting than glimpses of human development gleaned from the great creations of art and literature: "The suffering unleashed by the Industrial Revolution found poetic expression in Shelley's 'Song to the Men of England'" and 'to see Versailles was to see *Le Roi Soleil*; it was also to feel the deluge which came after him'.[11] Second, despite Williams's later immersion in political life, he retained a staunchly long-term perspective on the human condition. He saw humanity as having passed through a series of discrete stages. Each of its great cultural manifestations was symbolic of the age or stage in which it appeared. Hamlet's dilemma, for example, summed up the transition from feudalism to individualism. Williams shared this historical frame of reference with both his Whiggish and Marxian contemporaries.[12]

At Oxford he was also drawn to an aspect of British colonial history which was of enormous significance to his own people, West Indian slavery and its abolition. For Williams the traditional idealistic interpretation was doubly unsatisfactory. Historiographically, it minimized the role of slavery and of the Caribbean colonies in British economic history, especially the industrial revolution. It likewise minimized the role of British economic history in the abolition of plantation slavery and the slave trade. Politically, it allowed imperial historians to justify their twentieth-century empire in the afterglow of a nineteenth-century crusade. The British, wrote Coupland, the historian laureate of the centenary, would 'do justice to Africa because they are heirs and guardians of a great tradition'. To question this 'great tradition' of antislavery was to undermine the moral legitimation of British imperial overlordship.[13]

Surprisingly, in view of his scathing remarks on Coupland's scholarship in *Capitalism and Slavery* and in his autobiographical reminiscence, Williams' 1938 thesis was couched as a very modest addition, rather than as a challenge, to the prevailing English interpretation. 'The Economic Aspect of the Abolition of the West Indian Slave Trade and Slavery' was more limited in scope than was the later book. It dealt only with the abolitionist period, 1780–1833. More strikingly, it lacked those broad and incisive statements about the overriding importance of economic forces and motives which are the *leitmotif* of *Capitalism and Slavery*. Perhaps this was owing to the fact that Coupland was one of his thesis examiners. In any event, the dissertation explicitly cautioned against reading a preponderance of economic motives into the story of abolition. Williams supported the prevailing idealistic interpretation in accounting for the actions of the abolitionist leaders and of the British public. 'In the humanitarian and religious excitement', he wrote, 'there was nothing in any way savoring of economic considerations. The people were moved by the conviction that slavery was a disgusting and immoral system and had to go'. According to Howard Temperley, there was virtually no hint of economic determinism in the 1938 thesis.[14]

Perhaps it was not his Oxford days but his subsequent period at Howard University and in the West Indies which stimulated him to break irrevocably with both the idealistic frame of reference and the narrative framework of the Clarkson–Coupland tradition and to follow the suggestive interpretation of his fellow Trinidadian C. L. R. James in the *Black Jacobins*, which also appeared in 1938. A comparison between Williams' thesis and his 1944 version might make a fascinating point of departure for a scholarly study on the sources of *Capitalism and Slavery*.

In any event, there is little doubt that the examiners would scarcely have recognized the book. Its first half was entirely new, tracing the rise and development of the British Atlantic slave system from the early seventeenth century through the American Revolutionary War, where the dissertation had begun.[15] The second half also included a new chapter on the role of slaves and slavery, which had also not been in the dissertation. If the second half did not entail much new research, its format was transformed. It was not only a highly condensed version of the original thesis, but the narrative had given way to a structural reorganization. The period 1783–1833 was now treated as a single unit of time and divided into topical chapters: 'The Development of British Capitalism', 'The New Industrial Order', and so on. Within the age of abolition, the diachronic historian became a synchronic social scientist.

The author's attraction to the imagery of creative literature was also given freer stylistic rein in 1944. Historical figures were ushered onto the scene like characters from a novel: 'Wilberforce with his effeminate face appears small in stature' '[he] was familiar with all that went on in the hold of a slave ship but ignored what went on at the bottom of the mineshaft.' Regions, too, were metaphorically personified. The sugar islands were alternatively a Rip Van Winkle drugged by mercantilism, a Humpty Dumpty falling irretrievably, or an Oliver Twist always asking for more. Williams clearly had more fun writing the book in Washington than he had writing the thesis in Oxford, and he considerably lightened the reader's burden by coining sentences as dramatic as his characters: 'Slavery was not born of racism; rather, racism was the consequence of slavery.'[16]

Despite its focus on Britain and its Caribbean colonies, *Capitalism and Slavery* was initially more widely noticed in America than in Britain, where the *Times Literary Supplement* alone gave it a formal review. Almost all commentators recognized the study as a lively addition to the historiography of slavery and the empire. The enthusiasm of reviewers ranged from Elizabeth Donnan's guarded compliments in the *American Historical Review* to Henry Steele Commager's hosanna to *Capitalism and Slavery* in the *New York Herald Tribune*, as the most lucid, penetrating and original work in its field.[17]

Most reviews began with a brief assenting summary of Williams' account of the contribution of slavery to early British capitalism, what Donnan called a 'familiar story well told'. Only William Gee, in the *American Sociological Review* objected to Williams' effusive account of the contribution of coerced black labor to capitalism. Like other early commentators, Gee seemed as much disturbed by the tone as by the substance of the argument, and on moral rather than on statistical or logical grounds. It pained Gee that an 'eternally wrong' institution such as slavery, which had left such poverty and degradation in its wake, should be raised to the rank of indispensable contributor to modern capitalism.

Others focused on the more novel and contentious part of the book, where the abolition process was presented as illustrative of raw economic determinism. Commager wholeheartedly endorsed Williams' assessment of the British abolitionists as the 'unconscious mouthpiece' of the 'new industrial interest'. Denis Brogan, in the *TLS*, also accepted Williams' argument for the predominance of capitalist interests over moral indignation, although some (unidentified) parts of Williams' brief struck Brogan as being based on bold guesses rather than on demonstrated causal links.

Initially most reservations about *Capitalism and Slavery* stemmed from its unrelenting debunking of noneconomic factors and motives. Some commentators were puzzled by Williams' dismissal of the abolitionists as not only causally superfluous but as hypocritical. Donnan wondered why humanitarians should be treated as hypocrites just because economic interests happened to coincide with their moral perceptions. G. R. Mellor soon echoed this line of criticism, including Donnan's implicit acceptance of moral and economic conjuncture, in his *British Imperial Trusteeship, 1783–1850*.[18]

For Frank Tannenbaum in the *Political Science Quarterly*, however, *Capitalism and Slavery*'s unrelenting economic determinism posed a much broader threat to the study of slavery in the Americas. He feared that Williams's acerbic and often cynical reductionism would divert scholarship from the whole range of racial, psychological, ideological and moral variables which were significant in the history of New World slave societies and their very different paths to abolition. Although Williams had prefaced his monograph by pointedly emphasizing that it was not a study of the institution of slavery, Tannenbaum, like Donnan and Mellor, was more disturbed by what was left out of the study or implied by it than what was included. He took issue with Williams' assessment of the significance of race in the establishment of Caribbean slavery, but he offered no challenge to Williams' major theses, that slavery had risen to amazing importance under the aegis of a benign British mercantilism until the American Revolution, and had thereafter fallen even more dramatically under the hostile attacks of *laissez-faire* capitalists.[19]

The most widespread note of dissent therefore involved a defense of the humanitarian motives of the abolitionists, based on a rejection or devaluation of economic determinism as an adequate interpretative frame of reference. No initial reviewer seems to have questioned the empirical grounding of Williams' alignment of economic forces or his timing of the rise and fall of British slavery. In the absence of either sustained affirmation or systematic critique, Williams' theses percolated rather than flowed into historiographical discourse for reasons which would make an interesting study in its own right.[20]

There was, however, a measurable impact. One has only to compare Coupland's account of the abolition of the slave trade in the *Cambridge History of the British Empire* in 1940 with J. D. Hargreaves's discussion of the subject in *The New Cambridge Modern History* in 1965. In Coupland's account all economic forces were aligned against abolition and only noneconomic forces took a part with it. Twenty-five years later, referring specifically to Williams, Hargreaves was content merely to affirm that 'national virtue' had combined with and perhaps accelerated the underlying economic decline of the Afro–Caribbean complex. The idealism of Coupland was clearly in retreat from its historiographical monopoly. The obvious difference between the two versions lay less in the substantive assignment of causal weight to economic and noneconomic factors than in Hargreaves' assumption that contemporary economic trends, which clearly favored abolition, now had to be given more explicit recognition.[21]

It should be emphasized that the mere inclusion of economic forces and motives in the history of British abolition was no novelty in 1944. Abolitionist historiography had always incorporated the economic motives of the slave interests in discussing the legislative process, especially in the battle over the slave trade. For Frank Klingberg in the 1920s, as for Roger Anstey fifty years later, a peculiar economic conjuncture had played a role in the passage of British foreign slave trade abolition in 1806. This conjuncture was embedded in a context. 'Without abolitionist leadership, however, there would have been failure.'[22] The humanitarians were the structural constant, and economic interests and motives were variables. Williams' innovation was to offer a history of abolition in which the structural and conjunctural roles of capitalism and humanitarianism were reversed.

The immediate response to *Capitalism and Slavery* among black and radical scholars was less muted. In the *Journal of Negro History* Carter G. Woodson drew attention to Williams' intense factuality and hailed the work as 'the beginning of the scientific study of slavery' in international perspective. He rightly anticipated its strong appeal to those who were aligning themselves against British imperialism.[23] Marxists might have been more concerned than Woodson and the *TLS* reviewer that Williams' argument lacked an explicit Marxian formulation despite its unrelenting economic determinism. Nevertheless, *Capitalism and Slavery*'s factual phalanx, its focus on the Caribbean, and its economistic debunking quickly made it a bible among colonial students in Britain. By the 1950s Williams' theses were already 'orthodox' at the University College of the West Indies. They became integral elements of the 'Caribbean School' of social scientists and historians. They had an honored place in political discourse and touristic literature as well.[24]

With the publication of *Capitalism and Slavery*, Williams' own intellectual perspective on the subject was set. His later major historical works, *British Historians and the West Indies* (1964) and *From Columbus to Castro: The History of the Caribbean 1492–1969* (1970), elaborated his criticisms of British historiography and extended the major theses of *Capitalism and Slavery* to Caribbean history as a whole.[25]

THE ARGUMENT

Capitalism and Slavery is a study of the relationship between British economic development on the one hand and the British Afro–Caribbean slave system on the other. Williams leaves no doubt about the fundamental causal flow in that relationship. Down through the third quarter of the eighteenth century, capitalism and the capitalists uniformly supported their overseas creation and were supported by it. Following slavery's continuous decline in the wake of the American Revolution, the capitalists regrouped to destroy first the British slave trade and then British colonial slavery.[26] Moreover, these two phases of slavery, its rise and its fall, corresponded to two major phases of British political economy – mercantilism before 1776 and *laissez-faire* after.²⁷ Finally, postemancipation developments in British capitalism accounted for the diminution of sympathy for the freed blacks during the generation after the end of Negro Apprenticeship in 1838.

These were Williams' central and most revolutionary hypotheses. The historiographical mainstream had always considered each 'stage' of the rise and fall of slavery to be dominated by different sets of forces and motives. It was universally acknowledged that slavery had been sustained by those seeking to maximize individual, class, and national wealth. But slavery, it was also believed, had been opposed and overthrown by precisely those who had been most detached from profit-maximizing interests: humanists, philosophers, and religious evangelicals. In the traditional account, abolition had marked a shift of political power from the interested to the disinterested. The two were deemed as different in their origins, motives, and prevailing ideologies as the second British empire was from the first.²⁸

Capitalism and Slavery, with its insistence on the priority of economic motives at every significant juncture, broke most decisively with the tradition which emphasized the primacy of the humanitarian tradition in the destruction of slavery. To disregard the humanitarian tradition completely, wrote Williams, 'would be to commit a grave historical error and to ignore one of the greatest propaganda movements of all time'.²⁹ But even the focus and intensity of this propaganda movement was dictated, he emphasized, by the contemporary balance of British investments in the East Indies and trade with the Americas. *Capitalism and Slavery* calibrated the economic basis of shifting abolitionist policy at the end of the eighteenth century as carefully as it calibrated the shift of British shipping interests from indentured British islanders to enslaved Africans in the mid-seventeenth century.³⁰

Armed with his paradigm, Williams came to some dramatic conclusions about the relationship of capitalism to both the rise and fall of slavery. In the first half of the book he argued that the West Indies became the hub of the British empire. The Afro–American economy was shifted to the center of world history. Slavery had provided nothing less than the export demand and trade network for the British industrial revolution.³¹ He statistically demonstrated the 'amazing value' of the British Caribbean slave colonies by showing their rising share of total British overseas trade during the first three-quarters of the eighteenth century. Even more boldly, Williams declared that British colonial slave production, fueled by the lucrative slave trade, 'provided one of the main streams of that accumulation of capital in England which financed the Industrial Revolution'. The same conclusions about the slave trade and industrialization were reiterated twenty-five years later in *From Columbus to Castro*.[32]

This first argument of *Capitalism and Slavery* ultimately triggered a flurry of investigations. To date, the overwhelming majority of recent scholars have challenged Williams' hypothesis on the centrality of the African slave trade to British industrialization. Insofar as one reads Williams strictly, the critics on statistical grounds seem to have had the better of the argument. These scholars have concluded that the slave trade was not inordinately profitable to imperial investors, and that its profits simply could not have been large enough to be considered the or even *a* 'major contributing factor' in British capital formation. A few individuals in Lancashire might have funneled slave trade profits into the new manufacturing sectors, but they were no more than incidental in financing British economic growth. Second, the overall 'profitability' of the slave system to Britain has been hotly disputed by economic historians, using neoclassical models of analysis. Some even conclude that the slave colonies were a net capital loss to the metropolis. Finally, as Hilary Beckles observes, in terms of general impact most historians of British industrialization from Eric Hobsbawm to Phyllis Deane have given no more than a passing glance to the slave trade hypothesis of *Capitalism and Slavery*.[33]

A less controversial if less novel hypothesis of the first half of *Capitalism and Slavery* deals with motivations of the actors and the government rather than with the effects of slavery. Regarding motives, almost all historians before and after Williams have agreed that economic calculations were overriding in stimulating the creation and maintenance of the British Atlantic slave system. If anything, slavery scholarship after *Capitalism and Slavery* has added new strength to the role of economic variables and models. Beginning with the famous essay on the profitability of slavery by Conrad and Meyer in

1958, scholars developed ever more refined models to explain the economic mechanisms behind transitions and fluctuations of bound labor up and down the Americas. Gemery and Hogendorn's recent designation of the slave trade as an 'uncommon market' is meant only to refer to the fact that the traded commodities were human beings, not that the buyers, sellers, or owners of slaves behaved differently from those in other markets or capitalist enterprises. As economic men, their actions as well as their profits were far more 'normal' than postabolitionist generations cared to admit. Williams evidently was also accurate in stressing that coerced labor in the Caribbean had often been too narrowly identified with black slavery, which allowed too much weight to racial variables in what was basically an economic phenomenon.[34]

The most revolutionary section of *Capitalism and Slavery* was its second half, dealing with the 'fall' of British slavery. We have seen that the published version of Williams' treatment of the abolition process was revolutionary even with regard to his own Oxford thesis. In 1944 Williams explained the destruction of slavery by the very economic groups, forces, and motives which had been developed by the system and finally turned against it. Here, Williams launched a two-pronged argument, linking the demolition of slavery to changes in the British imperial economy, and applicable to world capitalism as a whole.

The first prong stressed changes in the economic relationship between the British metropolis and the slave colonies after American independence. Until then, all vested interests on the metropolitan side had united in support of colonial slavery. After 1783, a 'momentous year', each of those interests successively came out against monopoly and the West Indian slave system. This was because henceforth the colonies simply failed to sustain their assigned role as producers and customers. On the colonial side the fatal year was 1776, the year of Adam Smith's *Wealth of Nations* and Thomas Jefferson's *Declaration of Independence*: 'Far from accentuating the value of the sugar islands, American independence marked the beginning of their uninterrupted decline …' Moreover, even in terms of planter profits, 'the West Indian economic system was also so unprofitable that for this reason alone its destruction was inevitable'.[35]

The second prong of Williams' 'decline thesis' related to a rapid 'shift' in British political economy. American independence undermined Britain's 'mercantilist' policy and the economic rationale that had sustained it. Since the slave colonies were imperial monopolies, the attack on monopoly became an attack on slavery and vice versa. Planters and mercantilists had ganged together and were hanged together. The demise of slavery went hand in hand with the rise of *laissez-faire*. Industrial capitalism which had been nurtured through the umbilical cord of colonial slavery therefore cut the constriction on its further growth.

At a less global and structural level *Capitalism and Slavery* offered a detailed recipe of economic motives and conjunctures for all major successes or setbacks in the abolition process. The American War, the apogee and revolution of slave St Domingue, and the imperial 'swing to the East' all had clearly allotted roles in the story. But the clinching argument culminated in the ultimate power of the marketplace: 'Overproduction in 1807 demanded abolition; overproduction in 1833 demanded emancipation.'[36] Each and every tightening of the abolitionist noose could be traced, without any recourse to shilly-shallying idealism, to the interplay of economic forces and motives. The 'brilliant band' which led one of the 'greatest propaganda movements of all time' added sound and fury but, in the end, signified nothing in explaining the timing or direction of British policy.[37] The closing chapters, on the 'Saints' and on the slaves, are codas to a symphony of economic determinism.

Although some objections on details or putative abolitionist motivation were periodically raised, Williams' structural argument and its account of the major economic conjunctures corresponding to the dismantling of the slave trade and of slavery became deeply ingrained in British historiography. By 1964 the author of a foreword to a second edition of Coupland's history of antislavery would assert only that Coupland and Williams were both right because each was writing about different things.[38] Both the 'decline' of the West Indies and the 'rise' of *laissez-faire* after 1776 were readily incorporated into the Anglo–American mainstream because each of these concepts was already accepted as a separate element of colonial history. Coupland and the Imperial School had made the

American Revolutionary War the dividing line between the first 'mercantilist' and the second *'laissez-faire'* British empire. Williams' West Indian decline thesis relied on *The Fall of the Planter Class in the British West Indies*, a detailed account by Lowell Ragatz, to whom Williams dedicated his own study. Ragatz also placed his dividing line between the 'rising' and 'falling' planter class just prior to the American Revolution. Williams gave these two sequences of British historiography an ingenious twist.[39] The combined weight of periodization and trajectory seemed to have provided *Capitalism and Slavery* with a hard core of simple 'facts'.

From the mid-1970s, however, a new generation of scholars began to undermine the major structural and empirical bases for the argument in the second half of *Capitalism and Slavery*. The late Roger Anstey's study of the Atlantic slave trade took issue with Williams' analysis of parliamentary motives. In *Econocide* I offered a reinterpretation of the economic relationship between Britain and its slave colonies. Even using Williams' own empirical measure of value, the timing of West Indian decline was erroneous. The West Indies' significance to imperial trade continued long after 1776. Other scholars challenged the Ragatz–Williams assertion of a dramatic decline in sugar plantation profitability in the period following American independence. The economic decline of the West Indies therefore followed rather than preceded the political measures which curtailed British slavery's capacity for expansion and competitiveness.[40]

The second or ideological prong of Williams' account, the Coupland–Williams dating of the swing to the 'new' political economy of *laissez-faire*, was also vigorously disputed. Anomalies abounded when one actually tested Williams' putative correlation between antislavery and antimonopoly. For almost a century, while Britons paid more for their colonial sugar than they would have in the international market, slavery remained secure. Between 1790 and 1833, precisely during the period when slavery came under attack, British sugar prices approached or were actually below foreign market prices. The biggest price gap between British and foreign sugars therefore occurred only *before* and *after* the attack on the slave system. Paradoxically, *emancipation* made the Caribbean colonies prime targets during the antimonopoly crusade of the

1840s. So none of the major premises in the Williams paradigm were performing their assigned roles during the abolitionist era.[41]

In a sense, the critiques of the second half of *Capitalism and Slavery* mirror those addressed to the first part. Just as Williams inflated the rising slave trade's direct weight in the industrial revolution, so he accelerated the fall of the West Indies in accounting for the demise of slavery. Neither in terms of profits, productivity, or political economy did the West Indies account for the timing and pace of abolition. As for the metropolis, 'contrary to a long-standing belief, the slave trade was not overthrown by powerful industrial interests cramped by colonial restrictions. Manufacturers were neither influential enough to overthrow the trade nor driven by economic logic to make the attempt'.[42]

THE LEGACY

What then is the significance of *Capitalism and Slavery* in the perspective of more than forty years? One alternative always at hand is to treat *Capitalism and Slavery*, either inspirationally or patronizingly, as an exercise in history-as-rhetoric rather than history-as-scholarship. 'Written in white-hot rage', wrote one scholar, 'a capacity for which helps to explain its author's subsequent career in politics and statesmanship, *Capitalism and Slavery* is a classic of English political literature and a remarkable achievement in the genre of the polemic'.[43] Attention is thereby directed towards Williams' stature as a pioneer of 'Third World' scholarship. *Capitalism and Slavery* was, after all, along with C. L. R. James's *Black Jacobins*, one of the historiographical manifestoes of anti-imperialist scholarship on the eve of decolonization. This strategy takes advantage of Williams' remarkable blend of colorful prose and cynical economic determinism which inspired a whole generation of West Indian social scientists and historians. It does show us why the book is more than a classic of scholarship.

At the same time it leaves open the strong suspicion that *Capitalism and Slavery* is something *less* than a classic of historical scholarship. There is perhaps a subtle implication in such praise that a 'Third-World' book need not or should not be judged by first-rate standards. This frame of reference undervalues the impact of *Capitalism and Slavery* in one world where Williams felt most proud to have it stand – the republic of letters.

Therefore one cannot overlook the fact that Williams' ideological commitments and rhetorical devices complicated and weakened his historical interpretation of British abolition in ways that have been effectively analyzed by Howard Temperley.[44] To understand the wider impact of *Capitalism and Slavery*, however, one must look beyond those hypotheses and conclusions which have turned out to be untenable or dubious at best, and consider the new directions Williams charted for scholarly investigation. His insistent focus on the role of extra-European coercive labor and trade systems helped to inspire broader 'dependency' and world-economy theories of economic development. If the Williams hypothesis about rising slavery and early British industrialization is quite vulnerable to statistical analyses, quantitative methods alone cannot address other potentially important questions about the strategic role of the eighteenth-century colonial trades in providing jobs for otherwise underemployed British workers. Overseas markets provided incentives towards cost-reducing technologies, and colonial trades stimulated certain institutional changes in capital mobilization. There were no lengthier or more complex chains of credit than those evolved in the Euro–Afro–Caribbean triangular exchanges. Jacob Price cautiously suggests that the colonial sector 'may well have been the hothouse of the British economy, where progressive institutional innovations were forced decades or generations ahead of the times they 'normally' appeared elsewhere in the economy'.[45] Thus slavery's contribution to capital accumulation may have been much less dramatic than Williams claimed but may have played a role nevertheless.

Capitalism and Slavery was even more directly responsible for pioneering the systematic investigation of the relation of slavery's fall to British industrialization. Even among those who accept the most far-reaching critiques of Williams' analysis remain attracted to the hypothesis that it is surely no accident that abolition occured during a period of accelerated British economic development.[46] However, instead of emphasizing the interplay of capitalist high rollers in the manner of

Capitalism and Slavery, some historians have been sifting through the sociocultural development of Britain in search of a new ideological base for antislavery. They now look for some *combination* of humanitarian ideology and political economy to explain the rise and triumph of abolitionism. Howard Temperley has extrapolated the victory of abolition from metropolitan capitalism's triumphant free labor ideology. David Brion Davis, viewing the same period, finds the source of abolitionism even more in the stresses than in the successes of industrial capitalism. During the 'Age of Revolution' abolitionism presumably acted as a hegemonic 'displacement' from metropolitan problems at home towards problems overseas. Thomas Haskell has attempted to locate the origins of antislavery in the expanding market relationships of the eighteenth century.[47]

A second post-Williams school has concentrated on socioeconomic developments among the West Indian slaves themselves, especially in their evolving forms of resistance, although this approach seems to owe more to the inspiration of C. L. R. James than of Williams.[48] A third approach to abolition continues Williams' focus on the politicoeconomic evolution of the industrializing metropolis. This approach, however, is less concerned with Williams' captains of industry than with the most neglected sector in *Capitalism and Slavery*, the metropolitan masses.[49] They made the British abolition process distinctive from the ebbing of slavery in the ancient Mediterranean, in Medieval Europe or in early modern Russia.

The achievement of *Capitalism and Slavery* is that Williams made it impossible for historians ever to return to the posture of splendid moral isolation which characterized the story of British slave emancipation for more than a century. Williams' foremost aim was to insist as never before on the *banality* of the history of slavery. Even Roger Anstey, the most outstanding laborer in the traditional vineyard, distilled a scenario for the abolition of the slave trade which involved a specific economic conjuncture to explain the passage of at least one portion of the legislation. Anstey's own detailed work on the slave trade reiterated that abolitionists could sometimes be as *ökonomistisch* and *realpolitisch* as their enemies.[50]

As long as British abolition was regarded as *sui generis*, and part of the history of morals rather than a social institution and part of an evolving society, it was more likely to be treated commemoratively than analytically. *Capitalism and Slavery* is therefore a classical demonstration of the value of even deliberately simplistic history. It would be no gain whatever to the historiography of slavery if the apparent weakness of the economic links forged by Williams himself left slavery scholarship fragmented into clusters of specialists with no common framework. Williams cast his story in a global economic setting and that context must be retained and reworked.

Williams' most enduring message was that abolition could not have triumphed independently of economic developments linked to industrialization. This simple hypothesis has already proven to be more fruitful than those offered by historians in the century before him. Historians can never again suspend disbelief in the existence of three or four perfectly virtuous pages in the history of nations. They may indeed fall into the opposite trap and confuse the banality of most human actors, whether for evil or for good, with their collective human achievements.

NOTES

1. Eric E. Williams, *Capitalism and Slavery* (Chapel Hill, NC, 1944).
2. See *The Times*, 29 July 1933, esp. pp. 13–14.
3. See *ibid.*, also 24, 25 July; 2, 4, 5, 9 August 1933; also S. Drescher, 'The Historical Context of British Abolition', in *Abolition and Its Aftermath: The Historical Context, 1790–1916*, ed. David Richardson (London, 1985), pp. 3–24.
4. Thomas Clarkson, *The History of the Rise, Progress, and Accomplishment of the Abolition of the Atlantic Slave-Trade by the British Parliament* [1808], 2 vols. (London, 1968), fold-out-attached to p. 258.
5. W. E. H. Lecky, *A History of European Morals* [1869], 6th edn. (London, 1884), I, p. 153; also cited in Roger Anstey, 'The Historical Debate on the Abolition of the British Slave Trade', in *Liverpool, the African Slave Trade and Abolition*, ed. R. Anstey and P. E. H. Hair, *Historic Society of Lancashire and Cheshire Occasional Series*, 2 (1976), pp. 157–66.
6. Howard Temperley, 'Eric Williams and Abolition: The Birth of a New Orthodoxy', in *British Capitalism and Caribbean Slavery*: *The legacy of Eric Williams*, ed. B. L. Solow and S. L. Engerman (Cambridge, 1987), pp. 229–57.

7. R. Coupland, *Wilberforce: A Narrative* [1923] (New York, 1968), p. 422. On the 1983 conference, see the three volumes in the *Legacies of West Indian Slavery* series, papers given during the 'William Wilberforce 150th anniversary celebrations at the University of Hull, July, 1983'; *Abolition and its Aftermath: The Historical Context 1790–1916*, ed. David Richardson; *Dual Legacies in the Contemporary Caribbean; Continuing aspects of British and French dominion*, ed. Paul Sutton; *The Caribbean in Europe: Aspects of the West Indian experience in Britain, France and the Netherlands*, ed. Colin Brock (all, London, 1985). A fourth volume, *Out of slavery: Abolition and After*, ed. Jack Hayward, containing a series of lectures given at Hull during the winter and spring of 1983, includes three lectures dealing with Wilberforce, but the relative displacement of Wilberforce and the Saints by the West Indians at the climax of the commemoration is dramatically clear.
8. Solow and Engerman, eds., *British Capitalism*.
9. Eric Williams, *Inward Hunger: The education of a Prime Minister* (Chicago, 1969), p. 11.
10. *Ibid.*, p. 35.
11. *Ibid.*, pp. 42–3.
12. *Ibid.*, ch. 4
13. *Ibid.*, pp. 49–50.
14. This paragraph is based on the research and analysis of Howard Temperley, who compares the 1938 thesis with the 1944 book in his essay 'Eric Williams and Abolition'.
15. *Idem.* Some of the concepts which were to appear in the first part of *Capitalism and Slavery* must have been formulated very soon after Williams wrote his thesis. See Williams, 'The Golden Age of the Slave System in Britain', awarded a prize by the Association for the Study of Negro Life and History, in New Orleans (October 1939), and published in the *Journal of Negro History*, 25 (1940), pp. 60–106. Williams' devaluation of the humanitarian factor in the abolition process began at least as early as 1942. See Williams, 'The British West Indian Slave Trade after its Abolition in 1807', *Journal of Negro History*, 27 (1942), pp. 175–91.
16. *Capitalism and Slavery*, p. 7, and *passim*.
17. See reviews by: Wilson Gee, *American Sociological Review*, 10 (1945), pp. 566–7; Elizabeth Donnan, *American Historical Review*, 50 (1945), pp. 782–3; H. S. Commager, *Weekly Book Review, New York Herald Tribune Books* (4 February 1945), p. 5; as well as *in Book Week*, *The Nation*, and *Commonweal* (February 1945), *Booklist* (June 1945), and by Denis Brogan, *Times Literary Supplement* (26 May 1945), p. 250.
18. G. R. Mellor, *British Imperial Trusteeship, 1783–1850* (London, 1951), pp. 118–20.
19. See Frank Tannenbaum, 'A Note on the Economic Interpretation of History', *Political Science Quarterly*, 61 (June, 1946), pp. 247–53; and his 'The Destiny of the Negro in the Western Hemisphere' *ibid.*, pp. 1–41. Tannenbaum also chided Williams for extending his scorn for humanitarian sentimentality to the point of impugning the scholarship of his former teachers. For Williams' response see *British Historians and the West Indies* [1964], pp. 224–32. See also reviews in *Commonweal* and the *Nation*, and Eugene D. Genovese, 'Materialism and Idealism in the History

of Negro Slavery in the Americas', *Journal of Social History*, 1 (1968), pp. 371–94.

20. S. Drescher, 'The Decline Thesis of British Slavery since *Econocide*', in *Slavery and Abolition*, 6 (May 1986), pp. 3–24, esp. 4; see also Chapter 4 in this volume. After reading this essay Stanley Engerman wondered whether the impact of *Capitalism and Slavery* would have been as great had Williams published his study in 1904 instead of 1944. Without analyzing all the probable components of a reasonable guess, we actually have a bit of evidence of the response (or absence thereof) to a detailed 1905 economic interpretation of the abolition of the British slave trade: Frank Hochstetter's *Die wirtschaftlichen und politischen Motive für die Abschaffung des britischen Sklavenhandels im Jahre 1806–7* (Leipzig, 1905). *Die wirtschaftlichen ... Motive* was dismissed by Coupland as a work of the 'perfidious Albion' school of German historiography. Frank Klingberg was willing to accord a contingent role to economic conjuncture, and even praised Hochstetter's study, in a footnote, as 'the best treatment of the economic motives for abolition'. See *The Anti-Slavery Movement in England* (New Haven, 1926), p. 130 n. Hochstetter's study made so little general impresson on Anglo–American historiography that Williams did not mention it in the bibliography of *Capitalism and Slavery*. For a brief reference to parallels between Hochstetter and Williams, see Roger Anstey, 'The Historical Debate on the Abolition of the British Slave Trade', pp. 159–160. Anstey acknowledged Hochstetter's interpretation in *The Atlantic Slave Trade and British Abolition, 1767–1810* (London, 1975), p. xxi.

When the traditional school had something to say about the economics of the colonial slave system it usually followed its abolitionist predecessors in describing British slavery as risky, inefficient, and debt-ridden. It was a 'lottery', constantly threatening its participants with bankruptcy. See W. L. Mathieson, *British Slavery and Its Abolition, 1823–1838* (London, 1926), p. 11. The trouble with this 'perennial ruin' theme was that it was perennial. As a result, its precise causal role in the rise of slavery and the triumph of abolitionism could not be identified. This had not mattered very much to historians uninterested in the role of economic forces and motives. They readily admitted that there might have been economic reasons for abolition. Such an 'appeal to expediency, however, was or *should have been* superfluous and irrelevant'. See Mathieson, *England in Transition 1789–1832* (London, 1920), p. 7 (my emphasis). The question struck them as so inherently a moral one that the 'appropriate' grounds of motivation could be read back into the narrative without the least professional discomfort.

Black scholarship was insufficiently institutionalized in 1904 to offer a perch for a book like *Capitalism and Slavery*. An outstanding scholar like W. E. B. DuBois might have saved Williams from Hochstetter's virtual oblivion, but it is dubious whether *Capitalism and Slavery* could have entered Anglo–American historiography as a dominant paradigm before the World Wars and the Great Depression had shattered the ideology of European moral progress. Fifty years before Williams, DuBois's own history of American slave trade suppression recognized the existence of strong economic motives but did not overtly challenge the Anglo–American tradition in the way Williams' did. The abolition of slavery was, after all, the peer less example of that ideology. See also David Brion Davis, *Slavery and Human Progress* (New York, 1984), especially part three, ch. 3.

21. Compare R. Coupland, 'The Abolition of the Slave Trade', in *The Cambridge History of the British Empire*, II, *The Growth of the New Empire, 1783–1870*, ed. J. H. Rose, et al. (Cambridge, 1940, 1961, 1968), pp. 188–216 with J. D. Hargreaves, 'Relations with Africa', in *The New Cambridge Modern History*, VIII, *The American and French Revolutions, 1763–1793*, ed. A. Goodwin (Cambridge, 1965), pp. 236–51. In his chronological sequel to Coupland's chapter on abolition in the Cambridge *British Empire*, W. L. Mathieson's chapter, 'The Emancipation of the Slaves, 1807–1838' (pp. 309–36), made emancipation a question of the economic interests vs. the abolitionist passions. The same was true of Paul Knaplund's brief observations on the subject in his chapter on 'Colonial Problems and Colonial Policy, 1815–37', in the same volume (p. 291). The limits of Williams' impact on the *New Cambridge Modern History*, however, can be seen in H. G. Schenk's chapter, 'Revolutionary Influences and Conservatism in Literature and Thought' in vol. IX, *War and Peace in An Age of Upheaval, 1793–1830*, ed. C. W. Crawley, pp. 91–117. Schenk's account of abolitionism was entirely within the Clarksonian–Coupland tradition.

22. Klingberg, *The Anti-Slavery Movement in England*, pp. 129–30.

23. Carter G. Woodson, review in the *Journal of Negro History*, 30 (1945), pp. 93–5. For a similar emphasis on the triumphant 'factuality' of *Capitalism and Slavery*, see Johnson U. J. Asiegbu, *Slavery and the Politics of Liberation, 1787–1861: A study of liberated African emigration and British anti-slavery policy* (New York, 1969), p. 157.

24. See H. McD. Beckles, 'Down But Not Out: Eric Williams' 'Capitalism and Slavery' after Nearly 40 Years of Criticism', *Bulletin of Eastern Caribbean Affairs* (May–June 1982); Temperley, 'Eric Williams'; Elsa V. Goveia, 'New Shibboleths for Old', *Social and Economic Studies*, 10 (1964), p. 53; Williams, *Inward Hunger*, pp. 93–4; C. Duncan Rice, 'Humanity Sold for Sugar: The British abolitionist response to free trade in slave-grown sugar', *Historical Journal*, 13 (1970), p. 403. By the mid-1970s, two major bibliographical surveys regarded *Capitalism and Slavery* as the point of departure for modern historical scholarship on the British Caribbean. See W. K. Marshall, 'Review of Historical Writing on the Commonwealth Caribbean since 1940', *Social and Economic Studies*, 24 (1975), pp. 271–307; W. A. Green, 'Caribbean Historiography, 1600–1900', *Journal of Interdisciplinary History*, 7 (1977), pp. 509–30. For tourists, Air Jamaica makes Williams' point succinctly: 'When the sugar industry began to decline, slavery was finally abolished.' 'Jamaica A to Z', in *Skywritings* (February 1986), p. 42. David Brion Davis kindly pointed out this citation to me. For a survey of earlier criticism see the comments by Roger Anstey, John

Hargreaves and Duncan Rice in 'The Trans-Atlantic Slave Trade from West Africa', ed. Christopher Frye, mimeographed proceedings of a seminar held in the Centre of African Studies, University of Edinburgh, 4 and 5 June 1965. For subsequent criticisms see S. Drescher, *Econocide: British Slavery in the Era of Abolition* (Pittsburgh, 1977), pp. 1–5, 226–7 and n. 33.
25. *British Historians and the West Indies; From Columbus to Castro: The History of the Caribbean, 1492–1969* (New York, 1970).
26. *Capitalism and Slavery*, p. 120.
27. *Ibid.*, ch. 7; *From Columbus to Castro*, pp. 280–5.
28. See above, n. 21–22, as well as Anstey, 'Historical Debate', pp. 157–9.
29. *Capitalism and Slavery*, p. 178.
30. *Ibid.*, chs. 1, 7–9.
31. *Ibid.*, chs. 2–5. See also *Inward Hunger*, p. 94.
32. *Capitalism and Slavery*, pp. 52–5, and statistical tables, pp. 225–6; *From Columbus to Castro*, p. 148.
33. Stanley L. Engerman, 'The Slave Trade and British Capital Formation in the Eighteenth Century: A comment on the Williams thesis', *Business History Review*, 46 (1972), quotation on p. 441. See also Roger T. Anstey, '*Capitalism and Slavery*: A critique', *Economic History Review*, 2nd ser., 21 (1968), pp. 307–20; Anstey, *The Atlantic Slave Trade*, ch. 2. Robert Paul Thomas and Richard Nelson Bean, 'The Fishers of Men: The profits of the slave trade', *Journal of Economic History*, 34 (1974), pp. 885–914; S. Drescher, 'Le "declin" du système esclavagiste britannique et l'abolition de la traite', trans. C. Carlier, *Annales: Economies, Sociétés, Civilisations*, 31 (1976), pp. 414–35; David Richardson, 'Profitability in the Bristol–Liverpool Slave Trade', *Revue Française d'Histoire d'Outre-Mer*, 62 (1975), pp. 301–8; and Pierre H. Boulle, 'Marchandises de traite et développement industriel dans la France et l'Angleterre du XVIIIème siècle', *ibid.*, pp. 309–30. For recent nuanced defenses of Williams, see William A. Darity, Jr., 'A General Equilibrium Model of the Eighteenth-Century Atlantic Slave Trade: A least-likely test for the Caribbean school', *Research in Economic History*, 7 (1982), pp. 287–326. Barbara L. Solow, 'Caribbean Slavery and British Growth: The Eric Williams hypothesis', *Journal of Development Economics*, 17 (1985), pp. 99–115; and various essays in *British Capitalism*. For summary accounts of British economic history's reaction to Williams' industrialization hypothesis, see John J. McCusker and Russell R. Menard, *The Economy of British America, 1607–1789* (Chapel Hill, 1985), pp. 40–3, and Beckles, 'Down But Not Out'.
34. See, among others, D. W. Galenson's survey of the literature in *White Servitude in Colonial America* (New York, 1981), pp. 141–68; R. W. Fogel, *Without Consent or Contract: The rise and fall of American slavery* (New York, 1989), ch. VI: 'Population and Politics', (kindly sent by the author in typescript). On the timing of the switch to African slave labor, see R. N. Bean and R. P. Thomas, 'The Fishers of Men: The profits of the slave trade', *Journal of Economic History*, 34 (1974), pp. 885–914; H. A. Gemery and J. S. Hogendorn, 'The Atlantic Slave Trade: A tentative economic model', *Journal of African History*, 15

(1974), p. 225; R. C. Batie, 'Why Sugar? Economic cycles and the changing of staples in the English and French Antilles, 1624–54', *Journal of Caribbean History*, 10 (1976), pp. 8–9; H. McD. Beckles, 'The Economic Origins of Black Slavery in the British West Indies, 1640–1680: A tentative analysis of the Barbados model', *Journal of Caribbean History*, 16 (1982), pp. 36–56; and *The Uncommon Market: Essays in economic history of the Atlantic slave trade*, ed. H. A. Gemery and J. S. Hogendorn (New York, 1979).

35. *Capitalism and Slavery*, passim, esp. pp. 39, 120, 135, 154; S. Drescher, *Econocide*, ch. I.
36. *Capitalism and Slavery*, p. 37.
37. *Ibid.*, p. 178.
38. R. Coupland, *The British Anti-Slavery Movement*, with new introduction by J. D. Fage (London, 1964), pp. xix–xxi.
39. See the *Cambridge History of the British Empire*, II, p. v; *Capitalism and Slavery*, pp. 124–45.
40. See Anstey, *The Atlantic Slave Trade*, pt. I; Drescher, *Econocide*, passim.
41. Drescher, 'Decline Thesis', pp. 10–11, 22n., 26; Temperley, 'Eric Williams', pp. 18–20, 34 n. 27, 28.
42. P. J. Cain and A. G. Hopkins, 'The Political Economy of British Expansion Overseas, 1750–1914', *Economic History Review*, 2nd. ser., 33 (1980), pp. 463–90, 473 n. See also *Econocide*, ch. 10; S. Engerman, 'Slavery and Emancipation in Comparative Perspective: A look at some recent debates', *Journal of Economic History*, 46 (1986), pp. 317–39, esp. pp. 330–3; D. Eltis, *Economic Growth and the Ending of the Transatlantic Slave Trade* (New York, 1987).
43. P. E. H. Hair, review of *Econocide*, in *International History Review*, 1 (1979), pp. 567–9. Alan Bullock uses an analogous argument in his introduction to Williams' *British Historians*.
44. Temperley, 'Eric Williams', pp. 12–28.
45. Jacob Price, 'Colonial Trade and British Economic Development, 1660–1775', *Lex et Scientia* 14 (1978), pp. 101–26. See also E. Wallerstein, *The Modern World-System: Capitalist agriculture and the origins of the European world-economy in the sixteenth century* (New York, 1974); Wallerstein, *The Modern-World System*, II: *Mercantilism and the consolidation of the European world-economy 1600–1750* (New York, 1980): A. G. Frank, *World Accumulation, 1492–1789* (London, 1978); Frank, *Dependent Accumulation and Underdevelopment* (London, 1978); and S. Amin, *Accumulation on a World Scale: A critique of the theory of underdevelopment*, trans. Brian Pearce (New York, 1974). For an incisive critique of this hypothesis see Patrick O'Brien, 'European Economic Development: The contribution of the periphery', *Economic History Review*, 2nd. ser., 35 (1982), pp. 1–18, as well as the discussion by Wallerstein and O'Brien in *ibid.*, 36 (1983), pp. 580–5.
46. Pieter C. Emmer, review of *Econocide*, in *Belgisch Tijdschrift voor Filologie en Geschiedenis*, 57 (1979).
47. Howard Temperley, 'Capitalism, Slavery and Ideology', *Past and Present*, 75 (1997), pp. 94–118, and 'Anti-Slavery as Form of Cultural Imperialism', In *Anti-Slavery, Religion and Reform: Essays in memory of*

Roger Anstey, ed. Christine Bolt and Seymour Drescher (Folkestone and Hamden, 1980), pp. 335–50; David Brion Davis, *The Problem of Slavery in the Age of Revolution, 1770–1823* (Ithaca, 1975), and *Slavery and Human Progress* (New York, 1984). Davis more clearly delimits his 'hegemony' thesis in 'Capitalism, Abolitionism, and Hegemony', *British Capitalism*. See also Thomas Haskell, 'Capitalism and the Origins of the Humanitarian Sensibility', *American Historical Review*, 90 (April 1985), pp. 339–61, and *ibid.*, 90 (June 1985) pp. 547–66, and n. 6, above.

48. See Michael Craton, *Testing the Chains: Slave rebellions in the British West Indies* (Ithaca, 1982); Hilary Beckles, *Black Rebellion in Barbados: The struggle against slavery, 1627–1838* (Bridgetown, 1984); David Barry Gaspar, *Bondsmen and Rebels: A case study of master slave relations in Antigua* (Baltimore, 1985).

49. See James Walvin, 'The Public Campaign in England against Slavery', in *The Abolition of the Atlantic Slave Trade*, ed. David Eltis and James Walvin (Madison, 1981); S. Drecher, 'Public Opinion and the Destruction of British Colonial Slavery', in *Slavery and British Society*, ed. J. Walvin (London, 1982), pp. 22–48; Drescher, *Capitalism and Anti-Slavery: British mobilization in comparative perspective* (London and New York, 1987).

50. Anstey, *The Atlantic Slave Trade*, ch. 15.

13 *Capitalism and Slavery* after Fifty Years (1997)*

Ten years ago I began an assessment of *Capitalism and Slavery* with my understanding of a classic: 'If one criterion of a classic is its ability to reorient our most basic way of viewing an object or a concept, Eric Williams' study supremely passes that test'.[1] The passage of a fifth decade has provided abundant evidence of the pivotal status of *Capitalism and Slavery*. The original publisher reprinted the book in 1994 with a new Introduction by Colin A. Palmer.[2] Hilary Beckles, Selwyn Carrington, William Darity and Thomas Holt, among others, have assessed Eric Williams' impact upon, and inspiration for, West Indian scholars. Most recently, Walter Minchinton has demonstrated the sustained discussion of the Williams–Drescher debate among historians of Caribbean slavery. During the past decade Barbara Solow edited the results of two international conferences inspired by Williams' scholarship. And, on the eve of the fiftieth anniversary of *Capitalism and Slavery*, Joseph Inikori delivered his Elsa Goveia Memorial Lecture on 'Slavery and the Rise of Capitalism'.[3]

Perhaps the best point of departure is the collective volume that emerged from the fortieth anniversary conference on *Capitalism and Slavery*, held at Bellagio, Italy, and was published in 1987. The editors, Barbara L. Solow and Stanley L. Engerman, divided the non-biographical contributions into three parts, corresponding to three major hypotheses on the relationship between economic development and slavery in the British empire. We may appropriately test the first hypothesis most briefly. Williams only briefly broached the subject and his assessment has not been of major historiographical interest in the subsequent literature. Williams took the position that economic factors rather than racism occupied pride of place in the switch to African labour in the plantation Americas, that slavery 'was not born of racism' but rather slavery led to

---

* *Slavery and Abolition*, 18(3) (December 1997), pp. 212–27. © 1997 Frank Cass & Co. Ltd.

racism. Although some recent interpretations make racial preferences and inhibitions central to the choice of African labour, Williams' order of priorities, if not his either – or approach, is supported by a survey of hundreds of articles. They show virtual unanimity on the primacy of economics in accounting for the turn toward slave labour. Non-economic factors, such as race or religion, entered into the development of New World slavery only as a limiting parameter. Such factors affected the historical sequence by which entire human groups (Christians, Jews, Muslim North Africans, Native Americans) were excluded from liability to enslavement in the Atlantic system.

Since Williams published his book, the main change in the historiographical context of origins is an increase in the number and variety of actors brought into the process. That broader context complicates the role of any exclusively 'African' racial component of the slave trade. From the fifteenth to the eighteenth centuries, slavery, even the English colonial varieties, was hardly synonymous with Africans. Nor were Africans synonymous with slaves. In the African sector of the Atlantic system Europeans were forced to regard Africans (and Afro–Europeans) as autonomous and even locally dominant participants in the slave trade. They were often dominant militarily and were certainly dominant in terms of their massive presence and limited vulnerability to local diseases. Even in the Americas, Africans did not arrive only as captives and deracinated slaves.

While not rejecting the significance of economic factors, the new context of the slave trade reaches beyond the ports of embarkation into the interior of Africa. It thus breaks with the bipolar world of white rulers and black subalterns that Williams inherited from the imperialist world vision of the early twentieth century.[4] If such globalization necessarily lay beyond the horizon of Williams' generation of historians, *Capitalism and Slavery* remains consistent with current historiography in emphasizing the economic nexus of the origins of the modern New World slave system.

A second and more central hypothesis of *Capitalism and Slavery* was Williams' dramatic revaluation of the role of the slave trade and slavery in the rise of British capitalism and especially in the British industrial revolution. Williams' assertion of extraordinary profits for the slave trade was one of his first empirical affirmations to come under attack. The slave trade's primacy in funding British growth now has few defenders, even among those who argue for high profits.[5]

A more interesting question concerns the role of the British slave system as a whole in British metropolitan economic growth. There has been a double shift of historiographical emphasis in regard to the link between slavery and the rise of capitalism. The first relates to the rapid development of comparative analysis, well illustrated in Barbara Solow's second edited volume, *Slavery and the Rise of the Atlantic System* (1991). One of its important and conclusive findings seems to be that the further one proceeds outside the British orbit, the greater is the evidence against a generic linkage between New World slavery and the rise of European industrial capitalism.

Perhaps the most spectacular negative example is Portugal, which sponsored slaving, slavery and coerced labour systems for well over four centuries in areas as diverse as Asia, Europe, the Atlantic islands, Africa and Brazil. Whatever Portuguese slavery may have contributed to British industrial expansion, it did little for the Portuguese themselves. At the end of its long legal toleration of chattel slavery, Portugal, as Eric Hobsbawm noted, 'was small, feeble, backward by any contemporary standard ... and only the eye of faith could detect much in the way of economic development'.[6] Pieter Emmer, a Dutch historian of European expansion, has recently concluded that Dutch investment in overseas slavery may well have considerably retarded industrial development in the Netherlands.[7]

Such a devaluation of the generative role of slavery only impacts on the Williams' thesis insofar as one extends the model to the Northern European colonies, as he did in *From Columbus to Castro* (1970). Ironically, the greatest contribution of the slave trade to industrialization within a Continental European economy may have occurred only after, and because of, the abolition of the British slave trade in 1807. A recent study of Spanish economic development concludes that the slave trade to Cuba, accelerated by the cessation of British Caribbean imports, became crucial for the formation of industrial capital in Spain. The Spanish industrialists were to be among the last in a long line of economic interests hostile to closing down the Atlantic slave system. For Continental Europe as a whole, the slave empires would seem to justify

Patrick O'Brien's judgement about the impact of the overseas world on metropolitan economic development – 'the periphery was peripheral'.[8]

Nevertheless, one of those unforeseen shifts of historiographical focus points to a new and significant shift in the evaluation of slavery's role in capitalist development, one that encompasses the Atlantic world rather than Europe alone. In Barbara Solow's second collection, O'Brien and Engerman conclude that slavery accelerated the 'Americanization' of British imperial trade in the eighteenth century: 'the development of an Atlantic economy is impossible to imagine without slavery and the slave trade.' In drawing attention to the centrality of slavery in the British imperial economy of the eighteenth century, Williams was surely a harbinger of what recently seems to have been ratified as a paradigmatic shift. The concept of 'Atlanticization' differs from the argument in *Capitalism and Slavery*. Even as regards the British case, O'Brien and Engerman appear carefully to avoid saying that it is impossible to imagine European *industrialization* without slavery and the slave trade. They do not argue that slavery played a major role even in British industrialization. Engerman further elaborates his reservations in an article on the Atlantic economy in relation to those of Britain, America, Africa and elsewhere. He remains exceedingly sceptical about the specific timing and mechanisms of Williams's account of slavery's contribution to British industrialization. The 'necessary magnitudes' strike him as too small to bear the causal weight Williams assigned to them, 'considering Britain's lack of uniqueness in regard to its slave systems and its uniqueness in regard to industrial development'.

Moreover, one must bear in mind another challenge to the traditional concept of British economic development. Economic historians have radically challenged the very notion of a British industrial 'revolution' in the period that was crucial to Williams' thesis. Complaints by some historians of slavery that *Capitalism and Slavery* has been neglected or even suppressed by economic historians of British industrialization, overlook this tendency to view metropolitan growth as more drawn out than it has been portrayed in the conventional account. One historian of slavery has gone even further in this direction than the most radical of 'gradualists' in British economic history.

Joseph Inikori has recently suggested that Great Britain, far from emerging as the leading 'capitalist' nation of the period 1780–1830, did not become either capitalist *or* industrial until well after the British had already completely abolished their slave system. For most historians of slavery, however, capitalism is still considered to have been characteristic of at least some Northern European societies (such as England and the Netherlands) as early as the seventeenth century.[9]

Although Williams did not specifically frame his account of early modern slavery in terms of the whole Atlantic economy, his story of eighteenth-century slavery is consistent with some recent efforts to analyse the impact of Atlanticization on British economic growth and policy. In place of Williams' own emphasis on the overall profits of the slave trade and the British-protected tropical slave economy, for example, historians have turned their attention to the role of overseas slavery in stimulating British capitalist networks and institutional developments, in providing a major growth sector for British overseas exports, and in constituting a market for British goods in periods of major political and military threat – brought to a climax by Napoleon's Continental Blockade.

The broadening consensus on slavery's decisive role in the creation of the Atlantic economic system has therefore continued to stimulate the more unresolved debate over slavery's precise contribution to British industrialization. In the most recent summary of that debate, Robin Blackburn reaffirms the conclusion that Britain's surge ahead of its Continental rivals during the half century or so before Waterloo occurred when, and because, the economic contribution of the British slave sector to British growth was at its peak. Correspondingly, the ending of the slave trade decelerated the 'resource increment' of that sector to metropolitan growth. To that extent, Williams' strategy of linking slavery to shifting patterns of British overseas capitalism remains fruitful.[10]

However, this new and more rigorous assertion of slavery's effects on the rise of British capitalism has effectively undermined the central chronology of *Capitalism and Slavery*'s second major economic thesis. Williams asserted that, following the American Revolution, the economic decline of British Caribbean stimulated the destruction of British slavery by British industrial capitalists. Williams' thesis rested upon a dramatic reversal of the power between two major class actors: 'old' planters and 'new' capitalists. Williams' account therefore depended crucially upon the timing of British slavery's economic decline and the triumph of industrial free trade capitalism. This has produced a profound disjunction in the historiography of *Capitalism and Slavery*. Many of those who have recently argued in favour of a strong positive contribution of 'rising slavery' to British economic development (*inter alia* O'Brien, Engerman, Solow, Crouzet, Inikori, Cuenca-Esteban and Blackburn) have explicitly or implicitly undermined Williams' 'decline thesis'. For all of these historians there was simply no late eighteenth-century reversal of the economic role of the slave Americas. They have all demonstrated the continuity of slavery's contribution to British trade at least into the early nineteenth century. As Robin Blackburn succinctly concludes, 'the slave systems of the late-eighteenth and early nineteenth century New World had far outstripped those of the earlier mercantilist epoch. Although New World slavery now confronted mortal antagonists, it had yet to reach its apogee'. The implications of their collective economic finding is unavoidable: if the slave colonies made a significant contribution to British economic growth in the generations before 1783 they were as or more significant in the generation after 1783, the 'take-off' period in the conventional Industrial Revolution.[11] Although still vigorously disputed by one historian, the New World foundations of the decline thesis in Williams' own terms has thus been undermined.[12]

This reversal of Williams' decline thesis has even become retroactive. In 1988, a generation after the publication of his Pulitzer Prize-winning *Problem of Slavery in Western Culture*, David Brion Davis wrote that an intellectual revolution had taken place in the historiography of British slavery.[13] Davis' original affirmation of Williams' decline thesis was dropped from the republished version of the *Problem of Slavery* in 1988. This change is especially significant for some historians who had relied on the original formulation as authoritative support for that thesis.[14]

Another important component of the Williams' decline thesis has undergone a similar major challenge, the metropolitan side of his original equation. Williams' principal metropolitan actor in slavery's destruction was a grand coalition of British industrialists, East India investors and free traders, coalescing in the wake of the American and Industrial Revolutions. It is now widely noted that Britain's 'swing' towards both free trade and India did not seriously begin until more than four decades after peace with America, and a generation after abolitionists had their initial victories in parliament. Moreover, the pioneering industrial bourgeoisie was divided over abolitionist policies from the outset. The cotton interest of Manchester, the site of Britain's first mass abolitionist mobilization, was less united against the slave trade than almost every other occupational group in that city.[15] Economic interests, even when they had specific conflicts with those invested in slavery, usually had no desire whatever to undermine the foundations of what they considered as a legal form of property and trade.

The industrial bourgeoisie as a collectivity is, therefore, no longer allotted more than a peripheral and often a negative role in the crucial turn against the British slave trade. Cain and Hopkins' recent major overview of British imperialism emphasizes the continued policy preponderance of the gentlemanly capitalism of landowner mercantile interests in the formulation of early nineteenth-century imperial policy and the insignificance of an industrialist interest in abolition in particular: 'the important point is that it [abolition] was not promoted by a rising industrial bourgeoisie seeking to reach the goals of liberty and free trade set for it by a later generations of Whig historians',[16] among whom one may, in this regard, number Eric Williams.

In the absence of a capitalist economic bloc, some historians have invoked the emergence of an ideology rather than an interest. They posit a 'mentality' of bourgeois industrial hostility to slavery in the late eighteenth century.[17] The substitution of an intangible capitalist spirit or ideology for tangible capitalist interests, has actually tended to drive *Capitalism and Slavery* to the historiographic periphery. The outstanding recent example of this approach is *The Antislavery Debate: Capitalism and abolitionism as a problem in historical interpretation*, edited by Thomas Bender. In well over three hundred pages of citation-filled arguments, four historians each offer Williams credit for opening the discussion and promptly dismiss his arguments as outmoded or unsustainable. It seems clear that historians who consider the actual economic trends of

Caribbean slavery as virtually irrelevant to the rise of British antislavery are disposed to view the explanation of slavery's fall in *Capitalism and Slavery* as obsolete.[18]

On the other hand, for decades some historians of slave systems outside the British Caribbean have hypothesized that Williams' account of slavery's fall might be more applicable to slave systems other than the British. While the United States seems to be the region where such a correlation is most plauible, Williams himself suggested its general relevance for the Caribbean.[19] However, the classic decline theory has also been challenged by historians of other major slave systems in the Americas.[20]

In this way economic trends and the economic viability of slavery throughout the Americas has become a topic of intense and increasing interest. In one case after another, historians have demonstrated that the economics of slavery were more of an obstacle than an incentive to abolitionist initiatives. For the United States, Cuba and Brazil historians agree on a general hypothesis of economic viability. Even after slavery was slowly drained of its full potential by the abolition of the Atlantic slave trade the option of emancipation in the Caribbean was resisted for economic reasons.[21] Outside the Anglophone orbit, the coincidence of European capitalist industrialization and the endings of New World slavery during the nineteenth century remain elusive. Rather than demonstrating a pattern of abolition followed elsewhere, British anti-slavery may actually have constituted an exceptional metropolitan case, posing as a rule. Only as a political and military threat did British bring abolitionist pressure to bear on coerced labour throughout the globe, a pressure often counteracted by its own capitalists.[22]

If economic historians have slowly created a new framework for relating capitalism to slavery, social historians and social scientists have developed a corresponding challenge to Williams' assumptions about the transition to free labour. For Williams, as for most of his contemporaries, the story of abolition was primarily a history of elites. The major actors were 'class' actors: slavers, planters, merchants, bankers, industrialists and politicians. The novelty of *Capitalism and Slavery* lay above all in the dominant causal role it accorded to what have come to be called 'hegemonic' interests. In *Capitalism and Slavery*, slave resistance finally undermined the system, but only a generation after the metropolitan capitalists had turned against it. Slave resistance became historiographically significant only after a new generation of scholarship on culture, resistance and gender had transformed the social history of slavery. Thereafter, Williams' own bipolar model of slaves and capitalists was replaced by a complex mosaic of slaves as autonomous individual agents and social actors. Significantly, two Marxist-oriented historians who have stressed the key role of slaves in the ending of slavery turn to C. L. R. James's *Black Jacobins* for inspiration. Eugene Genovese and Robin Blackburn both view the Haitian (not the American or Industrial) Revolution as the turning point in the history of slavery. Thus, Blackburn's *Overthrow of Colonial Slavery* (1988) judged Williams' capitalist-driven model to be 'mechanical and unsatisfactory', while Genovese's *From Rebellion to Revolution* simply relegated *Capitalism and Slavery* to the 'other works' section of his bibliographical essay.[23]

Correspondingly, historians who initially followed Williams on the relation of slavery to the rise of British capitalism gave less attention to the experience of slaves or to their adjustments to freedom after emancipation. A partial shift of historiographical attention away from the imperial economic nexus has resulted in more consideration being given to colonial and creole perspectives: to the output of slave provision grounds, to marronage, to internal markets, and to changes in standards and styles of living. Nevertheless, as Barry Higman observes, the plantation system played so large a role in imperial policy and Caribbean labour relations, that the field of debate emphasized by *Capitalism and Slavery* remains important.[24]

Finally, the abolitionists. In its designation of the abolitionists as but one more elite (a 'brilliant band'), *Capitalism and Slavery* remained entirely conventional. Williams not only confirmed abolitionism as a top-down operation but sharply devalued its causal role. Even more belatedly than in the case of the slaves, the metropolitan masses have begun to find their place in the historiographies of both British slavery and of British metropolitan development.[25] As recently as ten years ago, abolitionists had not been integrated into the history of the modern social movement. The abolitionist rank-and-file were decontextualized by 'Whig' historiography into altruistic but passive respondents to an elite-led crusade. This perspective obtained whether those elites were portrayed, by the 'imperial school', as altruistic agents of moral progress, or, by the anti-colonial school, as agents of capitalist industrialization.

Recently, and for the first time, the political power of popular anti-slavery is therefore being analysed as an independent variable, rather than subsumed as a chorus responding to elite propaganda. Even those who continue to focus on the role of elites in the implementation of British emancipation now sharply distinguish between popular and elite roles in the process.[26] Most importantly, it is now widely recognized that popular abolitionism was a principal transformer of the changing attitude toward slavery from the 1780s.

The abolitionist breakthrough has, for the first time, become the object of separate analysis in historical monographs. The recognition of this popular dimension of anti-slavery is also changing scholarly views of the general relationship between religious and economic change in Britain. The most recent historian of popular Methodism concludes that 'the abolition of slavery in the British colonies was neither an economic necessity whose time had come nor a disinterested political gesture from an established political elite, but was, to a considerable extent, a victory for new religious and political forces unleashed both by evangelical enthusiasm and by the structural changes in British society in the period of the Industrial Revolution'.[27]

Historians are recognizing the implications of fifty years' futile prospecting for a grand coalition of economically-based anti-slavery elites and their ideologies. Scholars now routinely investigate the cumulative impact of changing patterns of demography, migration, organization, culture and communication; of political agitation, shared beliefs and social interaction on both sides of, and across, the Atlantic.[28]

CONCLUSION

Is there an emergent perspective on *Capitalism and Slavery* after half a century? The debates of the past decade seem to have vindicated Williams' insistence upon, if not his precise formulations of, the significance of slavery in the formation of the modern world economy. The narrow grounds of his own arguments have been discarded or deepened in ways that neither his earliest enthusiasts nor detractors could have anticipated. Historians who once treated the overseas tropics as conceptually and empirically marginal to the long march of European development have grown used to treating the world beyond the line as a significant variable in their causal networks. This is as true for the new Marxist as for the New Economic History. Even those who systematically discount the paramountcy of New World 'primitive accumulation' in the economic transformation of the industrial world regard the concept as within the pale of causal plausibility.[29]

On the other hand, there is widespread recognition that, however suggestive it remains, *Capitalism and Slavery* is also a work of its time. David Brion Davis appropriately identified Williams' approach as a variant of the 'economistic' school, dating back to the Enlightenment. He endorsed a materialist philosophy of history, and a view of history as a progression of stages of society. Less consciously Williams also shared, with his more 'idealist' historiographical predecessors, a sense of British global expansion as a world-historical master narrative. The Industrial and the American revolutions were the twin turning points in that narrative. Those turning points were denoted by a series of transformations: in economic organization, from agriculture to industry; in political economy, from mercantilism to free trade; and, above all, in social relations, from slave to free labour. These metamorphoses were the conceptual building blocks of *Capitalism and Slavery*.

Each one of these pivotal benchmarks has been reassessed over the past half century. The very idea of history as a series of discrete stages of interlocking economic, social, political and ideological orders has been eroded. We are now more acutely aware that New World slavery was, economically, superbly equipped to cross the great divide between the 'first' and 'second' British empires, between mercantilism and *laissez-faire*, between commercial and industrial capitalism, between the windmill and the steam engine, between the horsecart and the railroad. Capitalism was supremely agnostic and pluralistic in its ability to coexist, and to thrive, with a whole range of labour systems right through the abolitionist century after

1780: with slavery; with indentured servitude; with sharecropping; with penal labour; with seasonal contract labour and with day labour; with penally constrained or unconstrained free labour. In the longer run, we can see more clearly than Williams' generation that the 'rise of free labour' during the conventional age of industrialization was, in some respects, a myth.[30]

The historical imagination is therefore now less constrained by the premise of a linear sequence of labour systems passed down to the twentieth century. We have become aware that we need not posit a normative labour system for each era and then have to consign 'anomalies' to geographical marginality or historical anachronicity. On the contrary, we are faced with the more difficult problem of making sense of the coexistence of various forms of sanctioned labour in the heart of nineteenth-century Britain. We must now also integrate into our analysis of Atlantic slavery subsequent examples of coerced labour and other forms of domination, sometimes more intentionally murderous and brutal in the twentieth century than in eighteenth-century Afro–America.[31]

Capitalism and Slavery pioneered in urging the integration of a multi-geographical economic perspective into the history of modern slavery. That perspective is only likely to accelerate as scholars analyse its Caribbean, metropolitan, imperial, or world-historical context. Humanists and social scientists will certainly continue to add layers of rhetorical complexity to the historians' task by uncovering new prisms of culture and class, of kinship, gender, age, colour and religion.[32] Historians will increasingly look to remote times and places for answers to questions about their own chosen time and region.

Ten years ago, I concluded that Williams' most enduring achievement lay in having made it impossible for British historians ever to return to the posture of splendid moral isolation which had characterized their story of slave emancipation for more than a century. However, that was not the end of the story. In reaction to the moral imperialism of the previous century, many of Williams' first generation of readers were content to draw from *Capitalism and Slavery* only a message of anti-colonial cynicism. As Denis Brogan concluded in his introduction to the first British edition, the book's principal lesson was that 'where your treasure is, there will your heart be also'.[33]

A second generation was not content with this simple inversion of Whiggish moralism. It was drawn back to the story's paradoxes, anomalies and ironies. Williams had compelled serious scholarship to study and to explain the whole history of British slavery, not just part of it, in terms of ordinary social reality and ordinary people. The most recent Marxist historian of capitalism and slavery in the United States concludes that even if the destruction of West Indian slavery was an act of 'econocide', rather than one that promoted the interests of a capitalist class, Williams can take some of the credit for placing capitalism on the modern historiographical agenda of slavery. One can make an even stronger retrospective claim. Williams can also claim the honours of a pioneer in definitively placing capitalism on the agenda of anti-slavery.[34]

Whatever the varying judgements upon Williams' methods and conclusions, this 'secularization' of British slavery is the irreversible legacy of *Capitalism and Slavery*. Secularization, not necessarily in the sense Williams intended – the displacement of prophets by profits – but in treating the rise and fall of slavery as a continuous historical process, capable of explanation at all stages within the same terms of causal analysis.

As with every attempt to make sense of human experience *Capitalism and Slavery* will in some respects seem increasingly dated. Indeed, any effort to turn *Capitalism and Slavery* into a sacred text, and to measure orthodoxies, apostasies and heresies by it, remains a risk for the future. Eric Williams was, after all, the founding father of a nation, and the intellectual voice of a region as well as a historian. The literary and the mass media may well enshrine his most striking formulations long after they no longer command the assent of professional historians, who spend their analytic lives uncovering new data and revising theories. In this regard, the appeal of *Capitalism and Slavery* may be enhanced by what one historian has called 'history as-rhetoric' rather than 'history-as-scholarship'. Those inclined to proffer *Capitalism and Slavery* as worthy of scholarly inspiration would do well to remind their readers that Williams' book became a classic because it challenged the heirs of a complacent historiography to take note of neglected dimensions of the story. Fifty years later Williams' message of the need to *challenge* is as worth repeating as his challenging message.[35]

NOTES

This article was first presented to a conference on 'Capitalism and Slavery, Fifty Years Later: Eric Williams and the Post-Colonial Caribbean', held on the St Augustine Campus of the University of the West Indies, Trinidad, 24–28 September 1996. In addition to the comments offered by the other participants, I wish to thank Stanley Engerman and James Walvin for their helpful comments.

1. Seymour Drescher, 'Eric Williams, *British Capitalism and British Slavery*', *History and Theory*, 26(2) (1987), pp. 180–96; see also Chapter 12 in this volume.
2. The University of North Carolina Press, 1944; 1994.
3. See Hilary M. Beckles, 'Capitalism and Slavery: The debate over Eric Williams', *Social and Economic Studies* (Jamaica), 33(4) (1984), pp. 171–89; William Darity, Jr., 'A General Equilibrium Model of the Eighteenth-Century Atlantic Slave Trade: A least-likely Test for the Caribbean School', *Research in Economic History*, 7 (1982), pp. 287–326; Thomas C. Holt, 'Explaining Abolition', *Journal of Social History*, 24(2) (1990), pp. 371–8; Selwyn H. H. Carrington, 'The State of the Debate on the Role of Capitalism in the Ending of the Slave System', *Journal of Caribbean History*, 22(1–2) (1988), pp. 20–41; Barabara L. Solow and Stanely L. Engerman (eds.), *British Capitalism and Caribbean Slavery: The legacy of Eric Williams* (Cambridge: Cambridge University Press, 1987); Barbara L. Solow (ed.), *Slavery and the Rise of the Atlantic System* (Cambridge: Cambridge University Press, 1991); Joseph E. Inikori, 'Slavery and the Rise of Capitalism', 1993 Elsa Goveia Memorial Lecture, Mona, University of the West Indies, 1993; Walter Minchinton, 'Abolition and Emancipation: Williams, Drescher and the Continuing Debate', in Roderick A. McDonald (ed.), *West Indian Accounts: Essays on the history of the British Caribbean and the atlantic economy* (University of the West Indies: The Press, 1996), pp. 253–73.
4. See *inter alia*, John Thornton, *Africa and the Africans in the Making of the Atlantic World, 1400–1680* (Cambridge: Cambridge University Press, 1992); Ira Berlin, 'From Creole to African: Atlantic creoles and the origins of African–Americans in mainland North America', *William and Mary Quarterly*, 53(2) (1996), p. 251.
5. See, most recently, David Hancock, *Citizens of the World: London merchants and the integration of the British atlantic community, 1735–1785* (Cambridge: Cambridge University Press, 1995), appendix IV, pp. 419–24.
6. E. J. Hobsbawm, *The Age of Empire, 1875–1914* (New York: Pantheon, 1987), p. 18.
7. P. C. Emmer, 'Capitalism Mistaken? The economic decline of Surinam and the plantation loans, 1773–1850: A rehabilitation', *Itinerario*, 20(1) (1996), pp. 11–18.
8. On Spain and Cuba, see Luis Alonso Alverey, 'Comercio exterior y formacion de capital financiero: el trafico de negros hispano–Cubano, 1821–1868', *Anuario de Estudios Americanos*, 51 (1994), pp. 75–92;

Robert Whitney, 'The Political Economy of Abolition: The Hispano–Cuban elite and Cuban slavery, 1868–1873', *Slavery and Abolition*, 13(1) (1992), pp. 20–36. On the general role of the periphery, see P. K. O'Brien, 'Economic Development: The contribution of the periphery', *Economic History Review*, 35 (1985), pp. 1–18; and *idem*, 'The Impact of the Revolutionary and Napoleonic Wars, 1793–1815 on the Long-Run Growth of the British Economy', *Economic History Review*, 12 (1989).

9. See P. K. O'Brien and S. L. Engerman, 'Exports and the Growth of the British Economy from the Glorious Revolution to the Peace of Amiens', in Solow, ed., *Slavery*, pp. 177–209; S. L. Engerman, 'The Atlantic Economy of the Eighteenth Century: Some speculations on economic development in Britain, America, Africa and elsewhere', *Journal of European Economic History*, 24(1) (Spring 1995), pp. 145–75; esp. pp. 168–9; and Kenneth Morgan, 'Atlantic Trade and British Economic Growth in the Eighteenth Century', in Peter Mathias and John A. Davis (eds.), *Nature of Industrialization, vol. IV, International Trade and British Economic Growth from the Eighteenth Century to the Present* (London: Blackwell, 1997). See also François Crouzet, 'Toward an Export Economy: British Exports during the Industrial Revolution', *Explorations in Economic History*, 17 (1980), pp. 48–93; see also n. 8 above. The revival of a positive assessment of Williams' hypothesis of slavery's major contribution to capitalist development has been linked to a general revaluation of the 'commercial revolution's' impact upon industrialization. See Joseph Inikori, 'Eric Williams and the Changing Explanations of the Industrial Revolution', presented to the 1996 Trinidad conference on *Capitalism and Slavery*.

10. Robin Blackburn, *The Making of New World Slavery* (London: Verso, 1997), pp. 544. See, *inter alia*, Jacob M. Price, 'Credit in the Slave Trade and Plantation Economies', in Solow, ed., *Slavery*, pp. 293–339; the essays of Solow, Inikori and David Richardson in Solow and Engerman, *British Capitalism*; Seymour Drescher, *Econocide: British Slavery in the era of abolition* (Pittsburg: University of Pittsburg Press, 1977), chs. 5–6, pp. 65–112; and most recently, Javier Cuenca-Esteban, 'Britain's Terms of Trade and the Americas, 1772–1831: Back to demand as a dynamic factor in British industrialization?', delivered at the Eleventh International Economic History Congress, Milan, 12 September 1994. I thank P. C. Emmer for bringing this paper to may attention. Emmer's commentary at the same session was extremely sceptical of attempts to demonstrate a link between intercontinental oceanic trade and markets on the one hand, and innovative change in metropolitan manufacturing on the other.

11. Robin Blackburn, *The Making of New World Slavery*, p. 544. The most recent estimate, that of Cuenca-Esteban, locates 'the turning point' in the very year that Britain abolished the slave trade. Until then, 'Britain's *net barter terms of trade* appear to have improved sharply' (p. 13, emphasis in the original). Only one of the historians at the fortieth anniversary conference on British Capitalism and Caribbean Slavery followed Williams in seeing the West Indian slave system ca 1775–1815

'as an obstacle to British growth' (Solow and Engerman, Introduction, *British Capitalism*, p. 15). The twelve years since that conference have witnessed a steady strengthening of the case against the Ragatz and Williams' versions of the decline thesis. See, *inter alia*, S. Drescher, 'The Decline Thesis of British Slavery since *Econocide*', *Slavery and Abolition*, 7(1) (1986), pp. 3–24, table 1; see also Chapter 4 in this volume. Robin Blackburn concludes: 'Dating the decline of the British West Indies from as early as 1783 is a myth which has been demolished', *The Making of New World Slavery*, p. 550, n. 58.

12. See S. H. H. Carrington and S. Drescher, 'Debate: Econocide and West Indian decline, 1783–1806', *Boletin de Estudios Latinoamericanos y del Caribe*, 36 (1984), pp. 13–67; S. Drescher, 'The Decline Thesis'. See also Carrington, *The British West Indies During the American Revolution* (Dordrecht, Holland and Providence, USA: Foris Publications, 1988); Carrington, 'The State of the Debate on the Role of Capitalism in the Ending of the Slave System', *Journal of Caribbean History*, 22(1 and 2) (1988), pp. 20–41. See also Michael Craton, 'The Transition from Slavery to Free Wage Labour in the Caribbean, 1790–1890', *Slavery and Abolition*, 13(2) (1992), pp. 37–67, esp. 51–2. For a balanced recent assessment, see B. W. Higman, 'Economic and Social Development of the British West Indies, From settlement to ca. 1850', in Stanley L. Engerman and Robert E. Gallman (eds.), *The Cambridge Economic History of the United States*, Vol. I, *The Colonial Era* (New York: Cambridge University Press, 1996), pp. 297–336.

13. David Brion Davis, 'The Benefit of Slavery', *New York Review of Books*, 31 March 1988.

14. Idem, *The Problem of Slavery in Western Culture* (New York: Oxford University Press, 1988), pp. 153–65. Those invoking Davis' authority seem to overlook this change. See Holt, 'Explaining Abolition', p. 377; re-quoted in Minchinton, 'Abolition and Emancipation', p. 265.

15. S. Drescher, 'Whose Abolition? Popular Pressure and the Ending of the British Slave Trade', *Past and Present*, 143 (1994), pp. 136–66.

16. P. J. Cain and A. G. Hopkins, *British Imperialism: Innovation and Expansion, 1688–1914* (London: Longmans, 1993), p. 84n. On the relative economic significance of West Indian vs. industrial wealth in Britain before emancipation, see W. D. Rubinstein, *Elites and the Wealthy in Modern British History* (Brighton: Harvester, 1987).

17. See, above all, Thomas C. Holt, *The Problem of Freedom*: *Race, labour, and politics in Jamaica and Britain, 1832–1938*. Holt's inspiration is David Brion Davis' *The Problem of Slavery in the Age of Revolution, 1770–1823* (Ithaca: Cornell University Press, 1975). Holt notes, however, that Davis had already distanced himself from his original position during the 1980s. See Holt, 'Of Human Progress and Intellectual Apostasy', *Reviews in American History*, 15 (March 1987), pp. 50–8.

18. See Thomas Bender (ed.), *The Antislavery Debate*: *Capitalism and abolitionism as a problem in historical interpretation* (Berkeley: University of California Press, 1992), pp. 1–2, 69–70, 119, 161, 180–1. On the simultaneous disappearance of Africa, the West Indies and *Capitalism and*

Slavery from the *Antislavery Debate*, see also David Ryden, 'Planters, Slaves and Decline', a paper presented at the 1996 Trinidad conference. For other recent works that build on the reassesment of the relationship between economics and culture during the past decade, see David Turley, *The Culture of English Antislavery, 1790–1860* (London: Routledge, 1991); and Judith Jennings, *The Business of Abolishing the British Slave Trade, 1783–1807* (London and Portland: Frank Cass, 1997). See also Martin A. Klein's concise summary of the state of the discussion, 'Slavery, the International Labour Market and the Emancipation of Slaves in the Nineteenth Century', in Paul E. Lovejoy and Nicholas Rogers (eds.), *Unfree Labour in the Development of the Atlantic World* (London and Portland: Frank Cass, 1994), pp. 197–220.

19. *From Columbus to Castro: The History of the Caribbean, 1492–1969* (New York: Harper & Row, 1970), ch. 17.
20. On the Spanish Caribbean see M. Moreno Fraginals, Frank Moya Pons and Stanley L. Engerman (eds.), *Between Slavery and Free Labour: The Spanish-speaking Caribbean in the nineteenth century* (Baltimore and London, 1985), on the French Caribbean see Dale W. Tomich, in *Slavery in the Circuit of Sugar: Martinique and the world economy, 1830–1848* (Baltimore: Johns Hopkins University Press, 1990); Josette Fallope, *Esclaves et Citoyens: les Noirs à la Guadaloupe au XIXe siècle dans le processus de résistance et d'intégration, 1802–1910* (Basse Terre: Société d'Histoire de la Guadeloupe, 1992). On Africa see, *inter alia*, Patrick Manning, *Slavery and African Life: Occidental, oriental, and African slave trades* (Cambridge: Cambridge University Press, 1990). On Portugal, see João Pedro Marques. 'Uma Revisão Critica Das Teorias. Sobre a abolicão do Trafico de Escravos Português', *Penelope* (1994), pp. 95–118.
21. See, *inter alia*, on the United States, R. W. Fogel and S. L. Engerman, *Time on the Cross: The economics of American negro slavery* (Boston: Little, Brown, 1974); R. W. Fogel *et al.*, *Without Consent or Contract* 4 vols. (New York: Norton, 1989–92); for Cuba, Rebecca Scott, *Slave Emancipation in Cuba: The transition to free labor, 1860–1899* (Princeton: Princeton University Press, 1985); Laird Bergad, Fe Iglesias Garcia and Maria del Carmen Barcia, *The Cuban Slave Market, 1790–1880* (Cambridge: Cambridge University Press, 1995); for Brazil, R. W. Slenes, 'The Demography and Economics of Brazilian Slavery: 1850–1888' (Ph.D. dissertation, Stanford University, 1975), and S. Drescher, 'Brazilian Abolition in Comparative Perspective', *Hispanic American Historical Review*, 68(3) (1988), pp. 429–60; see also Chapter 5 in this volume; for the nineteenth century Atlantic as a whole David Eltis, *Economic Growth and the Ending of the Transatlantic Slave Trade* (New York: Oxford University Press, 1987); for the French colonies, Pieter Emmer, 'Capitalism after Slavery? The French slave trade and slavery in the Atlantic 1500–1900', *Slavery and Abolition*, 14(3) (1993), pp. 234–47; for the Dutch Caribbean, Gert Oostindie, *Fifty Years Later: Antislavery, capitalism and modernity in the Dutch orbit* (Leiden: KITLV 1995 and Pittsburgh: University of Pittsburgh Press, 1996), pp. 89–178, essays by Edwin Horlinga, Alex van Stipriaan and Gert Oostindie; for the British Caribbean, S. Drescher, *Econocide: British slavery in the age of*

abolition (Pittsburgh: University of Pittsburgh Press, 1977); and John R. Ward, *British West Indian Slavery: The process of amelioration* (Oxford: Clarendon Press, 1988).

22. See S. Drescher, 'The Long Goodbye', in Oostindie (ed.), *Fifty Years Later*, esp. pp. 44–53; see also Chapter 7 in this volume; and S. L. Engerman, 'Emancipation in Comparative Perspective: A long and wide view', in *ibid.*, esp. pp. 227–33, and David Eltis, *Economic Growth*, *passim*. The spreading scepticism about both the decline thesis and the applicability of industrial of *laissez-faire* explanations of abolition are summarized in Julian Gwyn, 'The Economics of the Atlantic Slave Trade: A review', *Social History* [Canada], 25(49) (1992), pp. 151–62, and David Murray, 'Capitalism and Slavery in Cuba', *Slavery and Abolition*, 17(3) (December 1996), pp. 223–37. On scepticism about the correlation between political economy and anti-slavery in British Parliamentary voting behaviour, see Tom L. Franzmann, 'Antislavery and Political Economy in the Early Victorian House of Commons: A research note on 'capitalist Hegemony', *Journal of Social History*, 27 (1994), pp. 579–93.

23. On the erosion of a sharp demarcation line between slave and free labour, see *inter alia*, Mary Turner (ed.), *From Chattel Slaves to Wage Slaves: The Dynamics of Labour Bargaining in the Americas* (Kingston: Ian Randle, 1995), esp. pp. 1–10; and Michael Twaddle (ed.), *The Wages of Slavery: From chattel slavery to wage labour in Africa, the Caribbean and England* (London and Portland: Frank Cass, 1993). Robin Blackburn, *The Overthrow of Colonial Slavery, 1776–1848*, (London: Verso, 1988), p. 26; Eugene D. Genovese, *From Rebellion to Revolution: Afro-American slave revolts in the making of the modern world* (Baton Rouge, Louisiana State University Press, 1978), p. 159. Historians increasingly see a convergence of modes of labour regulation in slavery and industrializing free wage labour economies. Whether planters borrowed the time-discipline of the factory or vice-versa is another question. See Mark M. Smith, 'Old South Time in Comparative Perspective', *American Historical Review*, 101 (1996), pp. 1432–69.

24. Higman, 'Economic and Social Development of the British West Indies', pp. 329–31.

25. The image of the abolitionists as elite agents of divine power was classically presented by Reginald Coupland, in *The Empire in These Days* (London, 1935), p. 264; quoted in *Capitalism and Slavery*, p. 178. For the subsequent change in perspective see Holt, *The Problem of Freedom*, pp. 27–33.

26. See S. Drescher, *Capitalism and Antislavery: British mobilization in comparative perspective* (London: Macmillan, 1986; New York, Oxford University Press, 1987); J. R. Oldfield, *Popular Politics and British Anti-Slavery: The mobilization of public opinion against the slave trade, 1787–1807*; Leo D'Anjou, *Social Movements and Cultural Change: The first abolition campaign revisited* (New York: Aldine de Gruyton, 1996); S. Drescher, 'Public Opinion and the Destruction of British Colonial Slavery', in James Walvin (ed.), *Slavery and British Society, 1776–1846* (London: Macmillan, 1982), pp. 22–48; see also Chapter 3 in this volume; S. Drescher, 'Whose Abolition? Popular Pressure and the Ending of

the Slave Trade', *Past and Present*, 143 (1994), pp. 136–66, and Christopher L. Brown, 'Foundations of British Abolitionism, Beginnings to 1789' (Ph.D. dissertation, Oxford University, 1994).
27. David Hempton, *The Religion of the People: Methodism and popular religion c. 1750–1900* (London: Routledge, 1996), p. 165. For various emphases on popular anti-slavery see: Robin Blackburn, *The Overthrow of Colonial Slavery*; David Turley, *The Culture of English Anttislavery, 1780–1860* (London: Routledge, 1991); Betty Fladeland, *Abolitionists and Working-Class Problems in the Age of Industrialization* (Baton Rouge: University of Louisiana Press, 1984); S. Drescher, 'Cart Whip and Billy Roller: Antislavery and reform symbolism in industralizing Britain', *Journal of Social History*, 15 (1981), pp. 3–24; and Linda Colley, *Britons: Forging the nation, 1707–1837* (New Haven: Yale University Press, 1992).
28. On the metropolian side, see Sidney Tarrow, *Power in Movement: Social movements, collective action and politics* (Cambridge: Cambridge University Press, 1994); Charles Tilly, *Popular Contention in Great Britain, 1758–1834* (Cambridge, MA and London: Harvard University Press, 1995); John Markoff, *Waves of Democracy: Social Movements and Political changes* (Thousand Oaks, CA: Pine Forge Press, 1996); and Leo D'Anjou, *Social Movements and Cultural Change*. On the interaction between the British working classes and Caribbean slaves see, *inter alia*, Emilia Viotti da Costa, *Crowns of Glory, Tears of Blood: The Demerara slave rebellion of 1823* (New York: Oxford University Press, 1994), esp. pp. 283 ff.
29. However, for the most vigorous reassertion of the view that European industrialization was not dependent upon Afro–American Atlantic slave production, see David Eltis, 'Slavery and Freedom in the Modern World', in Stanley L. Engerman (ed.), *The Terms of Labor: Slavery, serfdom and free labor* (Stanford: Stanford University Press, 1999), ch. 1, and Paul Bairoch, *Economics and World History: Myths and paradoxes* (Chicago: University of Chicago Press, 1993). pp. 59–98.
30. See Robert Steinfeld, *The Invention of Free Labor: The employment relation in English and American law and culture, 1350–1870* (Chapel Hill: University of North Carolina Press, 1991); and his 'The Myth of the Rise of Free Labor: A critique of historical stage theory'.
31. See Drescher, 'Epilogue', in *Fifty Years Later*, pp. 254–9
32. On gender see: Hilary Beckles, *Natural Rebels: A social history of enslaved black women in Barbados* (New Brunswick, NJ: Rutgers University Press, 1989); Verene Shepherd, Bridget Brereton and Barbara Bailey (eds.), *Engendering History: Caribbean women in historical perspective* (New York: St Martin's Press, 1995); Moira Ferguson, *Subject to Others: British women writers and colonial slavery, 1670–1834* (London and New York: Routledge, 1992); Clare Midgley, 'Slave Sugar Boycott, Female Activism and the Domestic Base of British Anti-Slavery Culture', *Slavery and Abolition*, 17(3) (December 1996), pp. 137–62.
33. Introduction to the 1964 edition. On Williams' portrait of abolitionism as a cynically disguised humanitarian triumph, see David Brion Davis, 'Capitalism, Abolitionism, and Hegemony', in Solow and Engerman, *British Capitalism*, p. 209. Williams' image continues to reverberate.

See, for example, Markman Ellis, *The Politics of Sensibility: Race, Gender, and Commerce in the Sentimental Novel* (Cambridge: Cambridge University Press, 1996), pp. 50–1. On the explicitly anti-colonialist and didactic intent of *Capitalism and Slavery*, see Williams, *British Historians and the West Indies* (London, 1966), p. 12. For further discussion see Howard Temperley, 'Eric Williams and Abolition: The birth of a new orthodoxy', in Solow and Engerman, eds., *British Capitalism*, pp. 229–57.

34. See John Ashworth, *Slavery, Capitalism and Politics in the Antebellum Republic*, Vol. 1: *Commerce and Compromise, 1820–1850* (Cambridge: Cambridge University Press, 1995), p. 147. For Williams' predecessors see Drescher, 'Eric Williams'.

35. For a good pedagogical example of Readings for discussion see Hilary Beckles and Verene Shepherd (eds.), *Caribbean Slave Society and Economy: A student reader* (Kingston, Jamaica: I. Randle Publishers, 1991).

14 Free Labor vs Slave Labor: The British and Caribbean Cases (1999)*

'Free labor' made its first significant appearance as a legal and cultural construct in the Anglo–American world of the eighteenth century. In one sense labor became free wherever employers lost the legal right to invoke criminal penalties for premature departure or non-performance. The defining characteristic of free laborers was the degree to which their violations of voluntary labor agreements were not punishable by imprisonment or physical coercion. 'Free labor', however, was also used in another sense. In certain contexts the term applied to all labor performed by 'freemen', i.e. anyone who was not legally and permanently bound to labor for others. In this second sense the fundamental distinction was between freemen on one hand, and villeins, serfs and slaves on the other. In Great Britain a freeman might well be penally liable for breaches of contract late into the nineteenth century.[1]

This second distinction, between the labor of freemen and of slaves, underlay one of the great social transformations of the eighteenth and nineteenth centuries. The relative merits of each form of labor became crucial to a small number of articulate groups: abolitionist elites; the slave interest; pro- and anti-abolitionist pamphleteers; Members of Parliament; and political economists. Their arguments, however limited in scope, potentially affected the lives and well-being of millions who were generally indifferent to the particulars of the comparison. In turn, the political and economic outcome of the broader struggle over the fate of slavery affected the agendas and rhetorical strategies of the debaters. The origin, development and results of the long debate is the subject of this chapter.

---

*Chapter 2 in Stanley L. Engerman (ed.), *The Terms of Labor* (Stanford: Stanford University Press, 1999).

BEFORE ABOLITIONISM

On the eve of the American Revolutionary War the British dominions encompassed the largest slave system in the Americas. Of the two and a half million human chattels in the New World more than one-third were the property of the subjects of George III. Less than a century later the final segment of that original Anglo–American slave system was brought to an end in the American Civil War. In the interim the British themselves had abolished the portion of the slave system under their own control and assumed the diplomatic, naval and popular world leadership in ending the transatlantic slave trade.[2] The Anglo–American Atlantic system was terminated despite the fact that the slave population of the Americas more than doubled in the century before Lincoln's Emancipation Proclamation, and that more Africans were landed in the Americas during that same period than during the previous three centuries of the Atlantic slave trade. Liberation depended upon a complex political process in which hundred of thousands of individuals, agitating for abolition on both sides of the Atlantic, were pitted against hundreds of thousands of defenders of the system. Between the 1760s and the 1860s slavery was established, expanded, or resurrected in some areas while it was being curtailed, gradually abolished, or violently destroyed in others.

The dismantling process was accompanied by a major cultural struggle to devalue the slave trade, slavery, and the products derived from it. At the end of the Seven Years' War the overwhelming majority of articulate individuals in Britain counted Caribbean slaves as among the most valuable work force *per capita* in the world. By the time of British slave emancipation in 1833 the overwhelming majority of Britons condemned slave labor as incompatible with their religion, their civilization, their traditions and their honor. Some also undertook to demonstrate, in what the British called their 'great experiment', that their newly freed ex-slaves were also more productive than their still enslaved counterparts in other regions.[3] The entire slaveholding world was to see that emancipation was compatible both with the maintenance of the political order and with continuity of production, profitability and prosperity for both planters and workers. The great experiment would confirm the providential order governing the world – that 'right never comes wrong'.[4]

In many ways, this robust linkage between freedom and labor was unprecedented. For most of human history the expression 'free labor' was an oxymoron. Freedom and labor were conceptually assigned to separate spheres of human existence. In the ancient classical view a human activity so intimately linked to the provision of life-sustaining needs was inherently servile. It was the natural activity of those, like slaves and animals, who were the means of freeing citizens for participation in virtuous activity and thought. Correspondingly the 'free man' was one who 'neither lived under the constraint of, nor was employed for the benefit of, another'.[5] Even when labor was not confined to slaves or foreigners, it was considered best to restrict citizenship to non-mechanics or to regard mechanics as incomplete members of the community.

The inherent servility of labor perpetuated itself long after slavery had ceased to be characteristic of or even legally acceptable in early modern Europe. However, the attributes of civil freedom and citizenship could be expanded to include all of the natives of a society without severing the connection between labor and servility in the perspective of the elite. By the late sixteenth century the absence of slavery on the soil of a commonwealth might be extolled as characteristic of one's nation, while labor's inferiority and the fitness of laborers 'onlie to be ruled', was simultaneously affirmed. Jean Bodin, notably hostile to slavery, proud of its disappearance from France, and concerned to have the most servile subjects acknowledged as members of the community, still wanted those engaged in mechanical operations or hired for wages excluded from the exercise of government. Even when the distinction between voluntary and involuntary, or time-bound and indefinite, labor obligations began to become significant in legal and popular culture, labor itself remained understood as service – an alienation or limitation of one's property in ones own working capacity for the duration of a contract.[6]

While this division between autonomous personal status outside the work situation and service within it emerged in Northwestern Europe, a rigorously constraining form of slavery was simultaneously expanding overseas. By the eighteenth century it was impossible to imagine the Atlantic system without slavery and the slave trade.[7] New World coerced labor and European indentured servitude, widely institutionalized before the massive importation of Africans, were the original means of producing overseas commercial exports. By 1700 African slavery was the labor system of choice in the tropical Caribbean basin. Africa, Europe, and the Americas contributed varying elements of labor, capital, technology and commodities into a highly coordinated system of exchange and production. Inhabitants of all four Atlantic continents, as well as of Asia, dynamically expanded their involvement in the Atlantic economy. The century of antislavery initiatives against European-sponsored slave systems after 1780 were undertaken in the teeth of powerful economic incentives offered to its participants.[8]

In Africa and the Americas all societies from Canada to the Rio de la Plata and from Spain to the Cape Colony legalized chattel slavery. Even European states without slaveholding colonies in the Americas attempted to participate in the slave trade. In Northwestern European societies, however, chattel slavery was, from the beginning, anomalous to their internal legal and social orders.[9] Contrasting extremes of freedom and slavery in the Atlantic system were to be found in Northwestern Europe and their sugar island colonies in the West Indies. By 1700 the same Northwestern European societies that were so reluctant to enslave their own members took coerced African labor in the plantation Americas for granted.

Arguments varied but the combination of abundant, fertile and unhealthy land rewarded a division of labor that maximized African and slave labor. Slavery was rationalized, even racially, as essential to tropical labor.[10] Whether residually, as in Montesquieu's formulation, or empirically as in the surveys of Arthur Young and the French *Encyclopédie*, the tropics was considered the zone *par excellence* of unfree labor. Thus, even when labor itself was imagined as integral to an individual's autonomy and rights, the notion was initially considered irrelevant to the extra-European environment. The extensive early modern European literature on freedom bore little relevance to behavior and institutions in the transatlantic system or to the non-European inhabitants of the continents 'beyond the line'.[11]

Economic rather than political-rights' discussions reshaped Europe's vision of freedom's potential impact upon labor relations. Everywhere until the mid-eighteenth century (and in some areas well into the nineteenth) slavery was reckoned merely a different, not an inferior or incompatible, form of organizing labor in the enormously varied environments of the European world system. In economically-oriented thought, the motivations of laborers were now linked to the maximization of wealth. Laborers could be creative as well as 'mechanical' factors of production. Thus James Steuart, in the 1760s, distinguished between *industry* and *labor*. Labor remained relegated to servile unfreedom. Industry invoked voluntary, self-motivated work. Under slavery, the master could dictate the very motions of the worker; under liberty 'every head is at work, and every hand is improving in dexterity'. Did this mean that 'industry' was superior to 'labor?' On the contrary, what mattered was of the nature of the work. If some were slaves to others, free laborers were slaves to their wants. The free worker was assigned a mind but not an economic edge: where hands were needed slaves were preferable, where heads were appropriate the advantage lay with liberty. Large-scale manufacturing as well as agriculture could take advantage of the 'simplicity of slavery'. The most obvious example of slave labor's superiority was drawn from the West Indies: 'Could the sugar islands be cultivated to any advantage, by hired labor?'

For Steuart, what really limited resort to the potential benefits of using slavery everywhere was not the superior *industry* of free men, but the political 'spirit of the times'. The nature of labour maintenance in the islands, as well as the nature of slave production, reinforced the Caribbean slaveholders' advantage. The ability to purchase slave labor from Africa gave the planters a still wider range of choices and, 'were not the expenses of rearing children supposed to be great, would slaves ever be imported? Certainly not'. While Africa remained what James Steuart called the 'warren' of New World labor, the planter could shift some of the costs of reproduction and child mortality from Caribbean plantations across the Atlantic. In Europe massive recourse to slavery was not a political or moral option. Elsewhere, it was maintained for *non*-Europeans without wounding the metropolitan 'spirit of the times'. Therefore, New World bondage had been 'very *luckily*, if not *politically*' established to promote the economic well-being of the metropolis. Slavery was deployed in simple and laborious agricultural operations where hands, not heads, were wanted. Indeed, since slavery discouraged invention and industry, were any colony to rival the industry of the mother-country, one needed only to allow the unrestricted introduction of slaves, whose 'natural effect' would undercut competitive economic development.[12] Where both forms were permitted the nature of production and reproduction determined the choice between slavish and industrial labor.

For James Steuart the geographic separation between liberty and slavery remained clear and unproblematic. By the last third of the eighteenth century, however, the two zones began to impinge upon each other. An increasing stream of black slaves from the periphery to Europe generated continuous friction over the metropolitan status of colonists' claims to their property in persons. European legal systems faced a choice. Some, like those of England and Scotland in the 1770s, nullified slave law within their jurisdictions. Others, like those of France and the Netherlands, were brought around to temporarily allowing properly registered slaves to be warehoused in Europe for re-export abroad within a given time period.[13]

Equally significant was the development of colonies of predominantly European settlers in British North America, facilitating the New World extension of Europe's commercial and free labor societies. This development generated discussions of the effects of free and slave labor along the borderlands between predominantly free and servile labor forces. In the two decades before the American Revolution Virginia planters attempted to restrict the slave trade to their colony. They aimed to preserve the colony's racial balance. Some also wanted to capture more of the European movement of arts and skills from their rapidly improving neighbors to the North.[14] From his own perspective slightly to the North, Benjamin Franklin identified the psychological and demographic depletion wrought by slavery in the British Caribbean:

> The Negroes brought into the English Sugar Islands have greatly diminished the Whites there; the Poor are by this means deprived of Employment, while a few Families acquire vast Estates, ... The Slaves being worked too hard, and ill fed ...

the Deaths among them are more than the Births; so that a continual Supply is needed from Africa. The Northern Colonies having few Slaves increase in Whites. Slaves also pejorate the Families that use them; the white Children become proud, disgusted with Labour, and being educated in Idleness, are rendered unfit to get a Living by Industry.[15]

Franklin agreed with James Steuart about the difference between industry and slavery but drew a different colonial lesson for North Americans from the wealthy sugar islands.

Metropolitans were also using slavery as a way of distinguishing themselves from both their European predecessors and their non-European contemporaries. European 'moderns' embraced the notion that their societies were dedicated to expanding their collective wealth through trade and industry, and to legitimizing the material aspirations of ordinary people. As in Franklin's moral economy, idleness was linked to apathy, to enfeeblement and to sterility. Industry promoted productivity and reproductivity. Both the classical and Caribbean worlds, distinguished by dependence upon slavery, had been marked by demographic, technological and intellectual stagnation.[16]

The most distinguished metropolitan exponent of this new world view was Adam Smith. *An Inquiry into the Nature and Causes of the Wealth of Nations*, published in 1776, supplied a distinctive economic argument to the British abolitionist movement when it emerged a decade later. For Smith, wealth and liberty ('opulence and freedom') were the two greatest blessings one could possess. The modern world was a world of commerce, creating a network of interdependence and resting upon the joint voluntary labor of a great multitude of workmen.[17] The opening theme of the *Wealth of Nations* was labor. In its productivity, its division and its maintenance lay the chief source of societal improvement. The optimum source of labor itself was the free action of the laborer. Ample rewards for free labor increased the activity, the diligence and the expeditiousness of the very population whose satisfaction and freedom, as both workers and consumers, was the true aim of an 'opulent and free' society.

In such a world slavery was not only morally objectionable but economically defective. Freedom for laborers was as beneficial for the masters as for the workers. Smith encapsulated the argument:

> The experience of all ages and nations, I believe, demonstrates that the work done by slaves, though it appears to cost only their maintenance, is in the end, the dearest of any. A person who can acquire no property, can have no other interest but to eat as much and to labour as little as possible. Whatever work he does beyond what is sufficient to purchase his own maintenance can be squeezed out of him by violence only, and not by any interest of his own.'

The costs of the 'wear and tear' – of labor and its reproduction – were at the expense of employers of both freemen and slaves. But the former cost the master less since the self-maintenance of the poor was generally more frugal and efficient than the management of masters.[18] Smith's formulation became a general article of abolitionist faith, ordaining the ultimate triumph of voluntary labor.

No subsequent formulation proved to be so straightforward or so compelling to antislavery advocates during the next three generations of political struggle against the Atlantic slave trade and Caribbean slavery. The whole world of historical experience was scoured to bear further witness that slave labor was 'in the end the dearest of any'. Smith's own demonstration was historical. The *Wealth of Nations* envisioned a succession of dominant modes of production in Western Europe, corresponding to a series of economic stages from hunting and gathering, through ancient slavery, to modern voluntary wage labor. In this schema, of course, the New World presented a major problem.

If the Western European sequence argued in favor of the superiority of wage labor, the reverse seemed to have been the case across the ocean, above all in the West Indies, where slavery had superseded indentured servitude. Before writing the *Wealth of Nations*, Smith himself had noted that bound labor was the prevailing form on the planet. Moreover, he anticipated that slavery was unlikely to disappear from the world for ages to come, if ever.[19] He offered two reasons for this contrast between free labor optimality and bound labour ubiquity. The first was a general non-economic human trait, love of dominating. This motive, of course, was not particularly helpful in explaining why the same Western Europeans used one form of labor in Europe and another in the West Indies. The second reason was both economic and relevant to the paradox. It related to Smith's view of the generality of West Indian planters as agricultural profit-seekers, not feudal lords or rentier gentry.[20] The planters' choice of labor in the Caribbean was based more on profit than on pride or prejudice. Sugar was so valuable a product in Europe that the planter could afford the service of slaves. Indeed, the crop's profitability, with slavery, was greater than any other in the Atlantic world. In a book replete with policy assessments, the *Wealth of Nations* did not suggest that planters in the West Indies could increase their profits still further by emancipating their labor force.

If one read the *Wealth of Nations* less selectively than abolitionists were inclined to do, one could discover other serious qualifications to free labor superiority. But two relevant omissions from the *Wealth of Nations* were as great a boon to future abolitionists as its formulation of free labor superiority. In discussions of slavery in the Americas Smith spoke of only two types of laborers – freemen and slaves. Aside from apprentices and miners in Britain itself, Smith seemed uninterested, to the point of total silence, in the existence and history of convict or indentured labor in America – especially the seventeenth-century displacement of British indentured servants by slaves in the sugar islands.[21] The process would receive short shrift in the debates over the British slave system before emancipation. During the age of abolition European freemen and Caribbean slaves would be juxtaposed in a stark dichotomy.

Smith's second omission was even more significant. It concerned his major hypothesis about the relative costs of 'wear and tear' – the reproduction of 'the race of journeymen and servants'.[22] When he turned to the New World for evidence of slave labor's dearness, Smith seemed interested in the urban clusters of North America, not the plantations of the West Indies, where the reproduction costs of the 'race' of servants was supported by the warren of Africa. Left to themselves, the choice of all New World sugar planters of all nations had been to replace all other forms of labor by African chattel slaves.[23]

FROM ABOLITIONISM TO
BRITISH EMANCIPATION (1787–1833)

For abolitionists who cited Smith the antithesis between the slave colonies and Britain was clearer than anywhere else in the world. James Ramsay, the first major polemicist against Caribbean slavery in the 1780s, casually invoked the principle of free labor superiority against the existing system. Humanity could anticipate emancipation without qualms because 'he who can procure a freeman to work for him, will never employ a slave'. By a reckoning that was to be commonplace during the age of abolition, a free laborer doubled the output of a slave. Moreover, when the freeman died, his place was supplied by 'natural' generation, not at 'enormous expense' from the slave market. Thomas Clarkson, the abolitionist movement's first national canvasser, boasted that sugar was already being raised by free men in Cochin China at one-seventh the cost of the British Caribbean product.[24]

Faith in the superior efficacy of free labor (or labor as free as it was in eighteenth-century Britain) did not depend on a reading of Adam Smith. The 'fruitlessness of compulsive labour' was proved 'every day in every workhouse in the kingdom. There is in proof too, the felons in the hulks, who produce not a fourth part of the ballast which is raised by the adjoining barges, where men are working on their own account'. The problem was always whether this experience could be transferred overseas. For generations to come such calculations elicited the rejoinder that the amount of labor extracted from the exploited and insecure freeman must therefore be far greater than what was being extracted from slaves. In this respect, West Indian slaves must be better off than free English manufacturers and peasants. Ramsay's reply anticipated the general abolitionist response. Whether or not a European peasant reaped more of the necessities of life from his labor than a Caribbean slave, the free laborer's reward came from the 'charms of liberty itself'. Freedom softened his toil while it doubled his exertions. After work it secured him his own time, his family, his immunity from arbitrary cruelty. The putative attraction of lower costs of reproduction and security became articles of abolitionist faith.[25]

Another argument offered in opposition to major alterations of the British slave system was the universally acknowledged observation that freed slaves in the West Indies never remained in the cane fields. During the very early phase of the antislavery attack, when the slave trade was being targeted, abolitionists suggested hiring free blacks as domestics and returning slave domestics to the field as substitutes for forgone Africans.[26] Over the longer run, however, the abolitionists deployed the modernists' attack on slave labor's inherent servility and brutishness. West Indian free blacks did not work in the fields, and frequently remained idle, because planters demeaned labor. Slavery degraded labor, not the reverse. In a slave-tainted environment, what free persons would 'subject themselves to the driver's lash, who are not absolutely forced to submit to such a degradation?' The West Indian system's peculiar defect was 'its utter forgetfulness of *mind*' and motive in reducing humans to 'the vilest of brute species'.[27] If slavery polluted labor, every step towards freedom would restore the innate pride, intelligence and energy of labor.

From their first mass campaign against the African slave trade in 1788 to their agitation against colonial 'apprenticeship' fifty years later, abolitionists committed themselves to creating one world of labor relations. As William Wilberforce emphasized on the eve of the abolition of the British slave trade in 1807: '*the principles of justice are immutable in their nature and universal in their application; the duty at once, and the interest, of nations, no less than of individuals.*'[28] The supreme object and obligation of abolitionism was to dissolve 'the line'.

However, the abolitionist elite was far from comfortable about using the generic assertion of free labor superiority to guide policy making beyond the line. For decades, while theoretically armed with the good news of free labor superiority, most Parliamentary abolitionists opposed the immediate application of this immutable principle. Until well after the Napoleonic wars, and despite their creed of the unity of religion, justice and policy, abolitionists virtually ignored what historians have termed the 'free labor ideology' in its *economic* sense.[29] The principle of slave labor inefficiency was usually tucked modestly into the back pages of antislavery polemics.[30]

The abolitionist elite were even more circumspect in their direct appeals for popular action than in their tracts.

Their major *Abstract of Evidence* on the slave trade in 1791 simply avoided the free labor argument. The popular petitions reiterated this reticence. Fewer than one in twenty of the great mass petitions in 1792 referred to the inferiority of slave labor.[31] One rationale for this rhetorical reticence seemed to derive from the policy priorities of the abolitionist leaders between 1787 and their first major victory twenty years later. The abolitionists' first target was the African slave trade. In the West Indies slaves represented upwards of fifty to one hundred million pounds of sunken British capital. Direct attacks on the Caribbean system would also evoke plausible challenges against the unconstitutionality of Parliamentary emancipation. The planters could claim compensation for the confiscation of their legally sanctioned property. Finally, attacking slavery itself raised the spectre of overseas slave rebellion in response to public agitation for their emancipation.[32]

Nevertheless, in arguing that an inevitable improvement would result from giving the 'blessings of freedom' to the West Indian slaves, abolitionists continually exposed themselves to the charge of hypocrisy in postponing emancipation. In response, abolitionist leaders declared that 'insanity alone could dictate' immediate emancipation.[33] In 1807 they demonstrated this conviction. As the Slave Trade Abolition Bill reached its final stage in Parliament, a young MP made a motion envisioning the emancipation of all infants henceforth born in the colonies. Wilberforce immediately opposed this motion as unsafe and ruinous.[34]

The abolitionist rationale for delay was straightforward: too high a proportion of Caribbean slaves were African 'savages', debased by both superstition and enslavement. Slaves as a group required a long transition to absorb proper work habits, religion and civilization. Free labor would be superior only when, through gradual 'amelioration', the slow-growing plant of 'true liberty' overcame the slave's indolence and licentiousness. In his first writings on the subject, Henry Brougham, later a parliamentary pillar of antislavery, could not even imagine testing the principle of free labor among uncivilized Africans, the 'common enemy of civilized society'.[35] What the *Wealth of Nations* seemed to affirm as a universal effect of free agency in labor was deemed disastrous as an immediate policy in the West Indian situation of 1807. The singular situation therefore left the free labor ideology intact, because free labor superiority could be tested only by 'truly' free men.

Historians have tended to accept this formulation of abolitionist belief in free labor superiority as modified by the peculiar situation imposed upon the victims of the slave trade. The British elite as a whole has been widely characterized as adhering to the principle of free labor superiority until emancipation and beyond.[36] Was it just a peculiarity of the peculiar institution that rendered Caribbean slave laborers unfit to compete as free laborers, or did abolitionists themselves harbor deeper doubts about the ability of even never-enslaved free labor to compete with the contemporary slave system?

The most knowledgeable of the Saints in Parliament openly rejected the hypothesis of free labor superiority in the sugar islands. The abolitionists, of course, knew from the beginning that the least controversial way to end both the slave trade and the slave system of production was to supply free labor sugar at 'a *cheaper rate*'.[37] In the early 1790s they looked hopefully from one potential 'free labor' competitor to another, to the British East India Company, to North American maple sugar extractors, to the new African colony of Sierra Leone.[38] By the time abolitionists finally succeeded in prohibiting the British slave trade, in 1806–7, all of the original potential free labor alternatives had foundered. New World Slaves supplied more than 95 per cent of the North Atlantic's sugar.[39]

The strategy of postponing political agitation for emancipation to a distant future before the 1820s also muted the 'consumerist' aspects of the free labor argument. In focusing upon the acquisitive potential of self-motivated free laborers, the 'modernist' political economists had emphasized the 'positive' incentives for increasing consumption as well as production. Indeed, the mass consumption of slave grown products – tobacco, sugar, coffee and cotton – presumably induced British laborers to work more assiduously for erstwhile luxuries and amenities. Voluntary labor not only increased the sufficient supply of worldly goods but the range and value of metropolitan demand.[40]

Yet, as applied to the West Indies, neither abolitionist arguments nor their policies tended to have a consumptionist orientation. In focusing upon the slave trade abolitionists initially emphasized the vast potential of Africa, not the Caribbean. Eliminating the internecine warfare inspired by slaving would rapidly transform 'one-third of the inhabitable globe' into a vast emporium for British commerce. In the Caribbean, on the other hand, abolitionists could only offer a gradual increase in colonial purchases of British exports, contingent upon the slow improvement of the still-enslaved bulk of the population.[41] Moreover, another aspect of abolitionist behavior tended to depress, rather than to expand, the British consumption of West Indian produce. Beginning in 1791, an abolitionist consumers' mobilization launched a mass boycott against slave-grown sugar. The boycott's effect upon West Indian sugar producers was negligible, but it sometimes raised the cost of sugar to those consumers who purchased only ('free') East Indian sugar offered for sale in Britain.[42]

When slave trade abolition finally loomed in 1806, Joseph Barham, one of its few West Indian Parliamentary sympathizers, suggested that the time was ripe to venture beyond slave trade abolition and to economically challenge slavery itself. Barham suggested using Britain's recently acquired and undeveloped colony of Trinidad as an ideal laboratory for demonstrating the superiority of free labor. Barham wanted the British government to sponsor the migration of free Chinese laborers, famed for their good labor discipline. Wilberforce was initially inclined to support a project so favorably framed in favor of free labor. But the main author and strategist of the recent Foreign Abolition Bill of 1806 warned Wilberforce against supporting Barham's project. As the best informed abolitionist on the West Indies, James Stephen foresaw nothing but disaster in such an experiment.

Stephen had already registered his anonymous opinion that slave labor had a decisive advantage over both free and other forms of involuntary labor in the sugar islands. He argued primarily from his knowledge of the results of slave emancipation in the French colonies of St Domingue and in Guadeloupe during the previous decade. Stephen convinced Wilberforce that the experiment's failure would discredit all who sponsored it, including abolitionists. In print he again anonymously denounced the Trinidad free labor project as preposterous. The case of Trinidad throws crucial light on early abolitionist assumptions. In 1802, when Trinidad's development as a slave colony with an unimpeded African slave trade still seemed likely, Stephen urged the exclusive importation of 'free negroes'. Even then, Stephen assumed that slave labor was the most profitable form of labor. Free (and even indentured) labor had to be permanently protected against slave labor. From the beginning, Stephen could not assent to a competitive situation.[43]

A few years later, as a Member of Parliament, Stephen himself successfully opposed a petition for a similar free labor experiment, invoking the failure of the earlier Trinidad experiment as additional proof, that 'while slavery existed in the West Indies it was impossible that free labor could succeed in competition with it'.[44] When Stephen pronounced this conclusion, not a single abolitionist rose in Parliament to oppose or even soften this categorical dismissal of free labor superiority. Nor did any Parliamentary abolitionist of the next generation ever suggest another pilot experiment.

Following peace with France in 1814 and the revival of the French Atlantic slave trade, Stephen added a detailed codicil to his evaluation of relative labor competitiveness. British slavery, now dependent exclusively upon natural reproduction, would henceforth, Stephen predicted, be undercut by the foreign 'buying' systems. Painful as he found it to confess this to a Prime Minister who had always opposed slave trade abolition, Stephen even parted company with his abolitionist colleagues' principle that 'breeding' was cheaper than 'buying'. The British slave interest was unable to benefit politically from this private confession by their most knowledgeable and effective opponent.[45]

The abolitionist leadership launched a second major offensive against the British overseas slave system in 1823. They directly attacked British Caribbean slavery itself and requested Parliament to sponsor gradual legal emancipation. In attacking slavery abolitionists felt impelled to resurrect their long-muted free labor ideology. Adam Smith was resuscitated and a search was undertaken to cull further support from economists. In view of the burgeoning authority of political economy the results were meager. Few British political economists had bothered to reiterate, much less to elaborate, Smith's brief passages on slave and free labor. In the half century between the *Wealth of Nations* and the first campaign for gradual abolition there were probably fewer passages published comparing slavery and free labor by any major British political economist than had already appeared in the body of Smith's own work.

One of Smith's most renowned successors was, in fact, a source of anxiety and embarrassment to British abolitionists. France's J.-B. Say, in his famous *Treatise on Political Economy* (1803/rev. 1814), offered calculations which explicitly contradicted the *Wealth of Nations* on the productivity of colonial slavery. Say not only argued, like Smith, that West Indian slave labor was profitable and productive, but that slave labor, in cost-benefit terms, was *at least* as efficient as that of free labor in France.[46] These calculations were so disturbing to his English translator, that he took sharp issue with Say in a series of footnotes to the *Treatise*. Another British abolitionist felt it necessary to extract a letter from Say acknowledging at least that slavery was incompatible with modern economic development. Say's distinction was not unlike James Steuart's contrast between 'industry' and slavery.[47]

Given a golden opportunity to demonstrate the utility of their science in favor of a massively popular public policy, the political economists demurred. In Parliament, in 1828, the economist R. J. Wilmot Horton was as explicit as James Stephen had been seventeen years before: 'free labor would not be found as effectual as the labor of slaves in the production of sugar.' At the very peak of mass antislavery petitioning and Parliamentary debates on immediate emancipation in 1833, Montifort Longfield gave an inaugural lecture in the Chair of Political Economy at Trinity College, Dublin. He solemnly announced that the question was too complicated and too agitated 'to be fit for a Professor's chair'. Longfield would say only that 'when it is said that free labor is cheaper than that of slaves, or the contrary, the proposition must be considered false if taken universally'.[48] The Chair was the legacy of Adam Smith but the voice was the voice of James Steuart.

In the absence of academic mobilization, abolitionists reworked Adam Smith on their own, emphasizing his 'wear and tear' argument. Abolitionists reinforced Smith by comparing British Caribbean population statistics with Malthusian population principles. Malthus posited the general propensity of human populations to procreate to the limit of available natural resources. The British Caribbean after 1807 offered the anomaly of a generally declining slave population.[49] The abolitionists had no compunctions about comparing the West Indian slave population decrease to the high natural growth rate of slaves in the United States' South. West Indian defenders of their system countered by emphasizing the delayed effects of the slave trade abolition in accounting for declining slave populations. Their arguments were often statistically more sophisticated than those of the abolitionists, but they always carried the rhetorical burden of having to explain away the clear and simple fact of sugar island slave decline within an Anglo–American world of otherwise rapidly expanding populations.

In appealing to their countrymen for political steps toward emancipation, abolitionists now more insistently invoked the positive motives to labor as portrayed by the optimistic economics of the eighteenth century. Industry in a labor force implied a willing effort on the part of the worker. A worker, like all others, sought to 'better his condition'. He became bonded to an ever receding threshold of amenities. Freed slaves would be doing more than exchanging hunger for the lash. They would be making the same 'voluntary sacrifices of time and ease ... which influence other classes of mankind'. Abolitionists presented case after case of free men, from Java to Mexico, who were productively employed in the cultivation of tropical goods. These cases validated the hypothesis that the urge toward self-improvement offered more than sufficient security for the maintenance and even enhancement of West Indian sugar production after emancipation.[50]

No element of antislavery propaganda infuriated the West India interest as much as these sweeping assurances of improved labor performance after the ending of slavery. As far as the planters were concerned, abolitionists were propounding a general argument in defiance of transatlantic realities. The axiom of universal free labor superiority was extrapolated from a purely local experience. England was the country in Europe where the desires for greater varieties of products yielded 'the greatest improvement of which human nature is susceptible'. However, insisted the defenders of Caribbean slavery, political economists were well aware of how few laborers yet possessed the incentives requisite to this 'positive' motivation for labor. West Indians insisted that, even in the very heartland of industrial England, free men still alternated between working only against hunger when destitute and only for limited comforts and maximum leisure when well paid.[51]

In this perspective, accumulating leisure was a better way of 'bettering one's condition' than was maximizing one's income. Verification of this limited-aspirations hypothesis was found in the 'short week' favored by many free industrial workers in Britain, and in the aversion of plantation labor by all free blacks in the Caribbean. As a substitute for subsistence satisfaction, want creation remained more of an imagined future than a global reality. West Indians challenged

> the whole world to produce a single satisfactory precedent, where a similar ratio exists between population, capital and space, of slaves, in any numbers, who have been made free, executing the necessary duties of tropical sugar labour for wages [or any equivalent income] consistent with the maintenance of the ... necessary and average profits of plantations.

They denied even *'the probability of such a result'*.[52] Planters' demands for compensation stemmed from that argument.

In seeking verification for their arguments the condition of Haiti was of great interest to those who debated the merits of slavery and the merits of gradual abolition between the end of the Napoleonic Wars and the final mobilizations for immediate emancipation after 1830. For abolitionists, Haiti's reproductive performance was its principal asset. Although the numbers were hotly contested, Haiti's official figure, indicating a virtual doubling of the population from the outbreak of the slave revolution in 1791 to the 1820s, stood in sharp contrast to the declining slave population of Britain's sugar colonies. Haiti appeared to conform to Malthus' principle of high natural increase in regions of low population density.

On the other hand, Haiti's economic performance was a boon to West Indian propagandists who wished to demonstrate the inefficiency of free labor in the Caribbean. There was no disputing the fact that slave St Domingue's position as the world's premier producer of tropical exports had long since vanished. Haiti had been virtually eliminated as a producer for the

North Atlantic sugar market. The case of Haiti was still more complicated by debates over the place of its population on the spectrum between free and coerced labor. If slavery had disappeared, Haiti's rural code allowed for deep infringements on personal liberties in the name of labor continuity. Was it the level of coercion that caused Haiti's low productivity and competitive failure, or had coercion preserved whatever was left of Haiti's productive and competitive capacity? When the British Colonial Secretary introduced the motion for immediate emancipation in 1833, he simply claimed that the St Domingue case was inconclusive and irrelevant. Many abolitionists and anti-abolitionists agreed with him.[53]

Neither the arguments of Smith and Malthus, nor the relative performances of Haiti and the sugar colonies convinced the British government to accelerate slave emancipation. Two major abolitionist mass mobilizations and the post-Reform Act election of 1832, reinforced by the greatest slave uprising in the history of British colonization, forced emancipation on to the political agenda of the first Reform Parliament in 1833. No contemporary suggested that the efficiency of free labor was a significant motive in attracting any of the 1.3 million men and women who gathered at British public meetings to sign petitions for immediate emancipation.

Those responsible for the colonies had to be more concerned about the anticipated motivations and performance of slaves on the verge of freedom. At the Colonial Office, James Stephen's son James feared the effects of the choices that would become available to the majority of laborers in the British Caribbean. Drawing upon the experience of Britain's other developing overseas colonies, he and others concluded that as long as labor had the option of access to cheap land the cost of labor would remain high, probably too high for the full maintenance of the plantation system. Henry Taylor, the head of the Colonial Office's West India division, was dismissively skeptical about the doctrine that slave labor was dear in the Caribbean. Taylor, Stephen and Viscount Henry Howick, a convinced supporter of both emancipation and of *laissez-faire* in political economy, mulled over various combinations of legal constraints on prospective freedmen. Without exception all were designed to maximize the continuity of plantation labor.

Empirically, Colonial Office social planners and the slave interest were not far apart. In Parliamentary hearings before emancipation, West Indian planters overwhelmingly testified that freed slaves never returned to the cane fields. Slaveholders inferred that freed slaves probably would not work at the prices offered to the owners of rented slave gangs during slavery. There was clearly a market for *non*-gang labor, which could be roughly reckoned at the prices of those slaves who were allowed to hire themselves out in various other occupations. As for the field slaves themselves, there is no evidence that they had any interest whatever in their potential cost-effectiveness as free laborers for planters. No Parliamentary committee requested their testimony. Some leaders of the Jamaica slave uprising of 1831 seemed to have envisioned freedom in terms of working for wages. Others imagined remaining growers of sugar. Neither of these imagined futures (nor the destruction of crops and infrastructure occurring in so many uprisings) bespeaks a profit-and-production-oriented activity within the plantation complex.

Some historians assume the general dominance of a universalized 'free labor ideology' in Britain in 1833. However, the distinction between constraints upon labor in high and low density conditions was clearly assumed by all advocates of emancipation in the Colonial Office and in the Cabinet. They muted their public emphasis on the significance of the distinction for two reasons. Slaveholders were offering analogous arguments and would use them to argue for a delay in emancipation. Even after the House of Commons supported the government's general motion for immediate emancipation, such arguments could be used to maximize the coercive components in the detailed system of freed labor regulation. Abolitionists feared that West Indian planters would use any institutional opening to recreate an approximation of the old constraints. In Parliament, most abolitionists spoke in favor of reducing non-market constraints on ex-slaves to the absolute minimum that the majority would accept.

Outside Parliament, abolitionist propaganda stuck to the idea of an exclusive choice between *Wages or the Whip* (1833), backed by the Smithian generic pronouncement on slave labor inferiority. There was no middle ground left between slave labor and free labor.[54] Emancipation, insisted the abolitionists, would now vindicate the superiority of free labor, even for the capitalists. But what, as the slave interest protested, if it did not? We have only fleeting glimpses about how the abolitionist rank and file – those who attended abolitionist rallies and signed petitions – reacted to the pessimistic prognosis. Responding to West Indian predictions of falling production, Britain's most popular antislavery lecturer resolved the issue of post-emancipation production in a cascade of contempt. So what if Haitian exports were already down by two-thirds, and so what if the West Indian consumption of British exports were also to decrease? Would Ireland be worse off if she too exported less, keeping her produce 'for home consumption?' The only reported response was '*Loud Cheers*'. Even Haiti and Ireland, contemporary bywords for economic failure, could not deter cheering antislavery gatherings.[55]

FROM BRITISH EMANCIPATION TO AMERICAN EMANCIPATION

Between them, the great mass campaigns of 1831–3 and the Jamaica slave uprising of 1831 convinced Parliament and the Government that there was no longer any middle ground between slavery and immediate legal emancipation. Members of the Government and of Parliament, however, were not so sanguine about the potential outcome as were abolitionist crowds. The administration was deeply worried about the continuity of labor under a regime of wages. The Colonial Secretary, introducing the Emancipation Bill of 1833, called it a 'mighty experiment'. The notion stuck, and for a generation thereafter emancipation was referred to as 'the great experiment'. Radicals like Daniel O'Connell were prepared to express total confidence in the success of an immediate transition to wage labor, without either transitional limitations or monetary compensation. The abolitionist leadership, which had emphasized the need for special transitional measures in the Caribbean for forty years, also reversed itself. Responding to demands and priorities from out-of-doors, they moved successive amendments to minimize the delay in arriving at complete freedom of contract.

However, for the majority of the political nation – the Government, the colonial bureaucracy, the overwhelming majority in Parliament, the West Indian commercial interests – continuity of sugar production was of vital importance. The final Act reflected their deep uncertainty that free labor plantations would sustain, much less increase, their previous level of production and thereby undercut slave labor competitors.[56] The Emancipation Act provided for a huge compensation package of £20 million. Masters were allotted up to six years of mostly unfree labor ('apprenticeship') from their ex-slaves. Above all, protective duties were continued in favor of British colonial sugar. In one sense, the maintenance of protection was a remarkable commentary upon antislavery propaganda. For a decade, abolitionists had taunted the West India interest for clinging to protective duties in favor of their own slave-grown sugar. This showed that 'monopoly' alone shielded 'a forced cultivation' from competition with free (i.e. East Indian) sugar. If West Indian slave labor in the colonies was more productive than free labor, how did it happen 'that in the case of the West Indies all the recognized principles of political economy should be thus strangely reversed?' What could better demonstrate that free labor competition would eliminate slavery? Yet at their moment of triumph, the abolitionists fell strangely silent about the possibility of realigning the West Indies with 'all the recognized principles of political economy' and about convincing slave Cuba and slave Brazil of the inefficiency of slave-based 'forced cultivation'. Freely opposing the government on both the length of apprenticeship and on the terms of compensation, abolitionists silently consented to the continuity of protection.[57]

British legislators thus anticipated, although they underestimated, the 'wear and tear' on the labor supply and discipline that would result from the transition. A 'cushion' of West Indian surplus sugar for British domestic consumption had characterized British colonial production since the beginning of the nineteenth century. During the apprenticeship period (1834–8) the quantity of sugar exported from the British West Indies to the United Kingdom fell by 10 per cent, while the London sugar price rose 40 per cent.[58] Another wave of popular pressure forced the early termination of apprenticeship in 1838. West Indian production fell again. It now met less than two-thirds of British consumption.

The government erratically responded to pressures and counter-pressures from West Indian proprietors, freedmen, consumers, abolitionists and an increasingly powerful free trade movement. For the first time since 1807 British governments cautiously began to open the ex-slave colonies to transoceanic migrant workers: to voluntary and unencumbered labor from the Americas and Europe; and to indentured contract labor from Africa and Asia. The flow of free labor from the Americas and Europe proved to be both insufficient in numbers and ineffective in performance. The flow of indentured labor from Africa and Asia was also initially hampered by the still-powerful abolitionist lobby, which denounced indentured labor as a new system of slavery.[59] The Government also attempted to encourage the expansion of free labor sugar plantations in Africa and Asia. Its major African venture – the Niger expedition of 1840–1 – was a complete disaster. Further east, the effort was more successful, but mostly in areas where one or another form of coerced labor system was introduced – indentured Indian labor in British Mauritius and the 'Cultivation System' in Dutch Java.[60]

In terms of commercial pressures, the shortfall in Caribbean production combined with high metropolitan consumer prices to put both British colonial sugar producers and abolitionists on a collision course with the rising British free trade movement. A potential conflict had existed from the beginning of the abolitionist movement, when Dean Tucker had cautioned Ramsay that the Atlantic slave system would never really be undermined until sugar could be produced more cheaply by free men than by slaves. Tucker was totally wrong in one respect. During the fifty years after his warning British antislavery moved from victory to victory while sugar produced by non-slaves made little headway against slave produced sugar. Before emancipation all metropolitan attempts, like those of the abolitionist merchant James Cropper, to form an economic coalition of East Indians, British industrialists, free traders and abolitionists against the plantation slave system monopoly fell far short of abolitionist hopes or expectations.[61] The economic reason was clear. Almost as soon as political abolitionism got underway, British colonial sugar had almost ceased to be effectively raised above world market levels by the old British mercantilist legislation. From the 1790s until slave emancipation

> it was the world price which largely determined the remuneration which West Indian producers received ... Had Foreign

sugar been admitted at the same rate of duty it would not have affected the consumers by more than a few percentage points.[62]

If emancipation brought a sharp reduction in the exports of sugar and coffee to the metropolis from the British Caribbean, the first results seemed far more satisfactory from the perspective of the ex-slaves. Exports of sugar from the West Indies to Great Britain fell by nearly 30 per cent in the decade after the end of apprenticeship, but retained imports of clothing from Britain to the West Indies rose by more than 50 per cent between the years immediately before emancipation (1832–4) and the years following the abolition of apprenticeship (1839–44). Even more impressive was the sharp rise in West Indian wheat consumption. Wheat flour had never been more than an occasional luxury for most slaves, handed out to gangs assigned to hard labor, or as part of special Christmas rations. Given that basic tropical foods grew in abundance, imported flour and flour products were obvious post-emancipation indulgences. Imports of wheat flour to the British West Indies more than doubled from just before emancipation to just after apprenticeship.[63]

As emancipation loomed, West Indian planters had attempted to make the most of the earlier abolitionist concession that slaves did not yet have enough of civilized laborers' 'artificial wants'. In this sense the slaveowners' fears proved to be completely unfounded. Ex-slaves used their new wages and independent earnings to purchase riding horses, gigs and conspicuously fine clothes. One of the major missionary champions of emancipation in the colonies happily testified to members of parliament that freedmen in the islands 'were decidedly better off than English workmen'. A British Guiana magistrate asserted that 'the peasantry, as a body ... can boldly challenge comparison with the happiest and best paid laborers of the most fertile districts in England'. The consumerist aspects of freedom, which had remained marginal to the abolitionist case before emancipation now featured centrally in abolitionist discourse. References to the 30–40 per cent decrease in British West Indies sugar could be countered by noting the sharp rise in the ex-slaves' standard of living and the stimulus this gave to British manufacturers. Wages were high, new villages were founded and educational opportunities for ex-slaves expanded. At the end of apprenticeship even West Indian vagrancy and contract laws had to be made more lenient than they were in England. This legislation was rolled back in the 1840s, but only to the extent that it was made identical with British metropolitan labor statutes.[64]

The cost of these results, however, elicited a rising crescendo of hostile propaganda from consumer and free trade advocates in Britain. Emancipation dragged the question of free trade into the center of the debate over colonial sugar. The termination of colonial apprenticeship coincided with the reemergence of free trade as an urgent public issue. Two protected interests were quickly fused in political discourse: West Indian sugar and English corn. The limits of the free labor ideology in abolitionist circles was again demonstrated at the Second World Anti-Slavery Convention in 1843. A free trade group attempted to alter the slave-grown sugar exclusion plank of the first Convention in 1840. They argued for revision on the basis of free labor superiority, which the previous Convention had also unanimously upheld. Refusing to accept free labor superiority as grounds for approving a change of policy, the chairman convinced the meeting to move the previous question.

The campaign for ending protection of free labor sugar came to a climax in 1846. Abolition of the domestic British Corn Laws was swiftly followed by the progressive reduction of protective duties favoring British colonial sugar. The debate leading up to this change had disoriented the abolitionist rank and file, sharply reducing their leadership's former ability to mobilize the larger public. Some abolitionists believed that the demise of plantation sugar would result in the expansion of smallholding and the 'peasant option', or at least a combination of wages and subsistence farming satisfactory to the ex-slaves. Others feared that stagnant sugar production would be followed by a declining standard of living among free labor within the colonies and a negative assessment of the great experiment by other slaveholding societies. The latter tended to realign themselves with British West Indian planters in favor of continued protection. Free trade sympathizers countered that heavily protected sugar was already useless as evidence of free labor's superiority. The split fragmented the unified abolitionist movement in the mid-1840s.[65]

Within Parliament, even Members who most strongly regarded the well-being of the ex-slaves as the 'great experiment's' principal criterion of success could not ignore the governments' general criteria of political and economic success. A dwindling number of die-hard abolitionists were reduced to fighting rear-guard actions in favor of differential duties on sugar grown by 'free labor'. As the victory of world free trade over protected imperial free labor became imminent, its most ideologically interesting effect in Parliament was the unanticipated revival of James Stephen's overt argument against free labor superiority. In 1833, no one could have imagined that William Wilberforce's own son would announce in Parliament, just thirteen years after emancipation, that West Indian free labor could not compete with slaves. Samuel Wilberforce was as unequivocal in his pronouncement as the elder Stephen had been thirty-five years earlier: slave labor in the Caribbean was 'absolutely cheaper' than free labor in raising sugar.[66]

British sugar production stabilized and slowly revived after the crisis of trade liberalization. However, the revival came at the price of a shift in the terms of labor – the expansion of the market in East Asian indentured servants. What abolitionists in Parliament and in the Colonial Office had once denounced as a 'new system of slavery' was institutionalized as voluntary indentured migration to the British colonies. During the 1850s the magnitude of this new source of labor surpassed the transatlantic flow of African slaves, now reduced by aggressive British diplomatic and naval action. In contrast to the first four decades of the nineteenth century the British colonies recaptured the major share of labor flowing to the plantation Americas. While densely populated Barbados could expand production without recourse to the new bondsmen, the recovery of sugar in sparsely populated Trinidad and Guyana depended heavily upon them. Jamaica, with lower fertility and less recourse to migrant labor than Trinidad, and a far lower population density than Barbados, stagnated.[67]

Planters beyond the line were uniformly unimpressed with the great experiment. Even in relatively undynamic slave colonies, whose imperial governments were vaguely committed to eventual emancipation, slaveholders preferred the coercive discipline of their slave plantations to the results they observed in the British free labor colonies. Where planters could still acquire fresh slaves for use on fresh land, they bought; where they were asked to participate in planning for emancipation, they balked. In Britain the debate over the merits of free and slave labor now shifted from sugar to cotton. As the United States' sectional crisis deepened, the British metropolitan cotton interest vainly requested government encouragement for further experiments in free labor for producing a product, almost 90 per cent of which remained dependent upon slave labor. Former free trade industrialists of Manchester found themselves in the embarrassing position of pleading for political help in developing alternatives to American agriculture. During the American Civil War they were concerned about enhancing the level of production in the cotton-growing systems of India, Egypt, Algeria or Brazil, asking few questions about their levels of labor coercion.

THE IMPACT OF THE DEBATE IN BRITAIN

What were some of the long-term implications of the discussion of free vs slave labor, carried out in the British press, lecture halls and Parliament for nearly a century? The first was slavery's novelty as a major public issue after two millennia. Before 1750, the question of slavery's comparative cost and efficiency was not a matter of public debate anywhere in the world. In the New World tropics, it was generally assumed that *some* form of bound labor was necessary to establish and expand commercially viable agriculture, especially in those activities requiring the organization of labor on a large scale. Before the rise of political abolitionism, no economist, including Adam Smith, maintained that slavery was less valuable or more expensive than free labor in the Caribbean sugar islands. When political abolitionists raised the possibility of substituting free for slave labor, they assumed a process requiring considerable time. Most of the early leaders of post-emancipation St Domingue likewise imagined that they could not dispense with coerced labor.

Abolitionist propaganda abstractly valorized free labor. Yet the superiority of free labor, endlessly restated, never became the centerpiece of the abolitionist argument – or even one of its high rhetorical priorities. The coincidence between coerced labor and New World sugar production, right down to British emancipation, was simply too close to overcome the doubts of planters and governments. Abolitionist leaders were themselves divided over the ability of free labor to sustain sugar cultivation competitively in the West Indies. Therefore British abolitionists tended to argue piecemeal and not always consistently from one measure to the next. Until slave trade abolition in 1807, they argued that 'breeding' would prove to be more profitable than 'buying'. Between abolition and emancipation in 1833 they argued that wages were more effective than whips. The main point was always to limit the slave-holders' options: prohibiting transatlantic imports and constricting inter-colonial imports (1788–1834); constraining planters' abuse of laborers (1823–8); limiting apprenticeship and legal coercion (1834–8); maximizing the constraints on importing indentured labor (after 1838). During the 1830s and early 1840s abolitionists, at the height of their political influence, continued to narrow planter options, to denounce vagrancy laws and other modes of employer discipline and to counteract planter political domination. Some fought to maintain the briefly rising standard of living of the freedmen and to protect their bargaining position as workers against both metropolitan free traders and employers of indentured labor.[68] Over the long term, however, they could not persist in securing more protection for Caribbean free laborers than those available to metropolitans.

Insofar as abolitionists intensified the scrutiny of the conditions of slave labor in the sugar islands, they also stimulated scrutiny of free labor conditions at home. In the pre-abolitionist era the status of metropolitan laborers as 'freemen' seems to have been an unexamined assumption. Aside from specifically designated exceptions under law (Scottish miners, convicts and apprentices) all laborers in Britain and all Europeans in the Americas fell under the rubric of freemen. For Adam Smith 'the principal attributes of villanage and slavery being thus taken away from them they now, at least, became really free in our present sense of the word Freedom'.[69] In the *Wealth of Nations*, waged workmen were invariably designated as freemen and always as the opposite of slaves, or serfs.

Ironically, the abolitionists' politicization of the free–slave dichotomy stimulated a political culture that consistently engendered negative images of metropolitan free labor. In other words, contrary to a hypothesis that antislavery rendered the ills of metropolitan labor less visible, abolitionism forced some members of an otherwise united elite, out of sheer self-defense, to expose the social costs of British free labor. If abolitionist petitions were often disproportionately supported by urban workers, antiabolitionists generated polemical critiques of metropolitan conditions. They did their best to publicize every sore of the British poor, those employed and those unemployed, those imprisoned in parish poverty and those displaced by clearances. As soon as abolitionists won their first major legislative victories, metropolitan radicals quickly adopted the iconography and imagery of abolitionism to compare the sympathy offered to African slaves with the unheeded complaints of 'slaves at home'.

With the abolitionist shift of focus to gradual emancipation in the 1820s, both West Indians and spokesmen for British labor compared the conditions of labor and workers' standards of living on both sides of the Atlantic. Abolitionists themselves emphasized the peculiar elements of slave treatment in the sugar islands, setting slave labor apart from metropolitan labour (the whip, sexual domination). They avoided emphasizing hours of labour or material conditions of living, where differences were less obviously, if at all, in favor of metropolitan laborers.

Most significantly, each mass abolitionist mobilization escalated metaphors of enslavement in Britain by West Indians and among political radicals: in agitation against child factory labor, in protests against the hardening of the Poor Law, in arguing against the exploitation of women, and in organizing against the exclusion of the poor from the suffrage. Militant reformers found it advantageous to denounce waged labor as a variant of bondage – 'wage slavery'. Occasionally the analogy was embarrassing enough to stimulate abolitionists into publicly aligning themselves with a particular metropolitan reform (e.g. child labor protection). Antislavery's popularity in the decades immediately before and after emancipation (ca 1820–40) were peak years for negative comparisons of British with Caribbean labor. The slavery metaphor was also effectively incorporated into the campaign against penal transportation in the 1830s and 1840s: 'After 1834, to denounce any British institution as a form of slavery was to damn it.' This propensity was reinforced during the late 1830s and early 1840s by the temporary coincidence of rising living standards among the ex-slaves and the onset of the hungry forties in Britain. The stage had been set for inflammatory racial polemics like that of Thomas Carlyle, comparing affluent idle blacks in the islands with impoverished and overworked British laborers at home.[70]

Invoking slavery and freedom as the two mutually exclusive forms of labor therefore had important cultural repercussions. Before the rise of abolitionism, slavery performed a variety of ideological functions. It served to differentiate freeborn Britons (who 'never will be slaves') from an external world dominated by arbitrary power and abject servility. It also served to dramatize internal 'assaults' upon metropolitan freedom. Recasting the binary opposition of freedom and slavery in terms of specific relations of production in Britain and the West Indies paradoxically increased slavery's potential ideological functions. The contrast was used both to reinforce the distinctiveness of British liberty and to illustrate its decline or subversion. Moreover, the same groups often responded to both themes. At one moment large numbers of Britons (including workers) were mobilized to sign petitions condemning overseas enslavement as unworthy of their freeborn heritage. At another moment large numbers of people from the same groups were mobilized to condemn the decline of their own freedom or living conditions. The more detailed the criticism and the more popular the attack on colonial slavery, the more salient became the repertoire of antislavery rhetoric for deployment at home.[71]

Nevertheless, it is equally significant that the debate over colonial slavery did not lead to a concerted ideological attack against the elaborate provisions in English law to prevent servants, especially in agriculture, from leaving their masters before the terms of their service had expired. Even the slave interest's long litany of metropolitan ills failed to highlight the penal sanctions available to employers against laborers in Britain. The tactical reason for their omission seems clear. Had slave-holders concentrated on those sanctions, abolitionists would have pounced upon the differences between those sanctions and the array of uncontracted powers used by planters against their chattels. Abolitionists would have challenged West Indian planters to contract their power to match metropolitan legal standards. On the other hand, abolitionists seeking to stress the chasm between overseas slaves and domestic freemen rarely wanted to call attention to the very ancient fact that some British workers were still answerable with their bodies for breaching their labor agreements.

On only one occasion did abolitionists call attention to the penal constraints upon free metropolitan workers. In 1827, West Indian propagandists made much of the coercive provisions in Haiti's new Rural Code. Abolitionists quickly responded by referring to the sanctions listed in Blackstone's *Commentaries* against vagabondage and breaches of contract in England. Presumably, some forms of labor coercion were neither incompatible with civic freedom nor confined to the Caribbean. Nevertheless, abolitionists were obviously uncomfortable about discussing coerced labor at home. They self-protectively added 'We are not bound, neither are we disposed, to bestow any laudatory epithets either on [these laws of England] or on the corresponding clauses of the Haytian Code', or on their 'humanity'.[72]

Historians of slavery have hypothesized that British antislavery suppressed public awareness of evils closer to home may have been in looking for evidence in the wrong sector of the economy – in the emerging labor conditions of the Industrial Revolution.[73] Those 'new' metropolian ills were persistently targeted by West Indians and urban radicals alike. The increasing number of English women and children pushed into mines, mills, factories and workhouses did not go unnoticed. Nor did the large numbers of men, women and children pushed from their homes and fields in Scotland. If the debate over slavery omitted any aspect of metropolitan labor relations, it concerned the mechanisms for enforcing labor contracts of free-born English agricultural laborers.[74] The most 'traditional' of labor coercions was the least directly targeted abuse in the long debate over slavery.

For fifty years, the abolitionist leadership also successfully constrained the geographic terms of imperial labor relations. There was relatively little discussion of slavery in the British

East Indies before the Emancipation Act. The magnitude of slavery, and other forms of coerced labor, in India and Ceylon was not seriously considered until the termination of 'Apprenticeship' in 1838. Only then was India prominently placed on the British abolitionist agenda, and on that of the first World Anti-Slavery Convention held in London in 1840. The number of slaves in India was quickly recognized to be far greater than those who had already been liberated by the Act of 1833. Equally significant was the abolitionist recognition of Eastern diversity. Bondage in India seemed to lack the sharp 'capitalistic' features of slavery in the New World. This belated recognition of the variations and complexities of 'free' laborers in India was to become a defining characteristic of the post-emancipation generations.[75]

A century of debate over the relative merits of free vs slave labor had been initiated by a mass movement to eradicate the differences between conditions of labor in Britain and in her slave colonies. The superiority of free labor, 'demonstrated' universally by political economy and exemplified in the history of Western Europe, was projected 'beyond the line' in order to extend the benefits of freedom throughout the British empire and the entire world. After three generations of intense debate the discussion began to break out of the dualistic frame of reference in which both the abolitionists and their opponents, had conducted it.

As the political stakes were reduced, Herman Merivale offered a comprehensive retrospective of the process as part of a series of *Lectures on Colonization and the Colonies*. Delivered at Oxford in the immediate aftermath of colonial apprenticeship (1839–41), the *Lectures* were reprinted, with additional comments, on the eve of the American Civil War. Oxford's Professor of Political Economy and Undersecretary for the Colonies was now prepared to consider slavery as eminently fit for a Professor's chair, but the discussion acknowledged the impact of the abolitionist crusade. Merivale expressed his anxiety about presenting a 'mere economical consideration' on matters 'so deeply interesting to every social and moral feeling of our nature'.

Merivale also registered the impact of another historical process on the discussion of slavery. Surging British migration to the temperate zones of the planet encouraged a further globalization of the discussion of overseas labor. He sought to integrate Caribbean labor into the general phenomena of free labor scarcity in low density settler societies. In this frame of reference, Australian convict labor, not Caribbean slave labor, was the 'dearest labor of all'.[76] Merivale boldly brought Smith's unheralded reservations about the optimality of free labor to the foreground. He accepted the axiom of the dearness of slave labor with an italicized caveat: *'wherever abundance of free labour can be procured'*. 'Beyond the line' was back in action. In Merivale's reading, New World slavery reemerged as an eminently rational response to conditions in the Americas and the tropical Atlantic system. Within this frame of reference both Smith and Say could be recruited to support the unequivocal conclusion that it was more profitable to cultivate the virgin soil of the Americas by the 'dear labor' of slaves than to cultivate the depleted soil of Europe by the 'cheap labor' of freemen.[77]

Nor was slavery an anachronistic residue from an earlier stage of history. It was an integral part of the capitalist present. Not only could slave labor produce more agricultural value in Cuba than could free labor in France or in Germany, but it could continue to do so for the foreseeable future. Merivale made his economic prognosis unequivocal: 'no economical cause can be assigned on which we may rely for the extinction of slavery.' Abolitionists who hoped for a gradual redefinition of capitalist interests were delusional, at least until the forests of the Americas had been cleared and long tilled from the Atlantic to the Pacific. The gap in Smith's explicit analysis of the special nature of the Atlantic slave system allowed Merivale to imagine a hypothetically unending stream of slaves across the Atlantic economy unless checked by countervailing political power.

In this perspective, the abolition of the British slave trade in 1807 was 'the real death-blow' to British West Indian prosperity. The good news, at least for fellow economists, was that the coming of free trade in sugar had not caused, and might even have averted (through economic shock therapy), the complete downfall of the British West Indian sugar interest. The upshot of Merivale's analysis was that large-scale production of exportable tropical staples would probably continue to be organized by compulsory labor, whatever the results of the 'experiments then in progress'.

The Caribbean labor force would also continue to be non-European, partly the result of the high mortality rate of Europeans in the tropics. What had been conventional wisdom in the mid-eighteenth century was a global statistical conclusion a century later. Empirically, mounting evidence showed that the 'wear and tear' of Europeans was greater in the West Indies than in the temperate areas of the Americas or the South Pacific to which they were overwhelmingly choosing to migrate. In 1860, as in 1760, non-European compulsory labor was still the labor of choice for rational capitalists who chose to cultivate the vast undeveloped parts of the tropics. The robustness of Merivale's prediction was amply demonstrated during the century after British slave emancipation. The 20 millions who left India alone, mostly as indentured servants, between the 1830s and the 1910s amounted to twice the number of Africans forcibly landed in the Americas during the four centuries of the Atlantic slave trade.[78]

The phenomenon of indentured servitude, ignored by Adam Smith, forced itself back into the economists' field of vision. Merivale did not even bother to disguise the fact that the new stream of indentured servants flowing into the West Indies was not 'free' labor, even if it was not the old slavery. For Merivale, indentured servitude rather evoked the analogue of military recruitment, both in the benefits (reliability) and the drawbacks (inefficiency) brought by such recruits to the plantations. In the canefields, all of the potential dexterity, ingenuity, frugality, and efficiency of free laborers was not a sufficient substitute for the continuous presence, reliability and pliability of indentured servants, answerable with their bodies for breaches of contract.

Unlike their mid-eighteenth century predecessors, political economists of the mid-nineteenth century had no need to invoke extra-economic motivations, such as the urge to domineer, in order to explain the establishment and maintenance of slavery. The choice of slavery overseas could be entirely accounted for in terms of the peculiar – but widespread – combination of soil fertility, population densities and tropical commodities. J. E. Cairnes would offer the same combination of economically active ingredients to explain the character, career and aims of *The Slave Power* (1862) in the United States of America at the time of Southern secession. Neither Merivale nor Cairnes took issue with Smith's emphasis on the superior efficiency of free labor *qua* labor. They did take firm issue with the universality of that superiority. From the perspective of both capitalists in the tropics and economists in Britain, free labor simply had not been, nor was it now, 'superior' to slavery. Absent abolitionism, slavery was simply a way of organizing scarce or reluctant labor, a condition which recurred throughout human history rather than only at its beginning.[79]

Despite all these concessions to the rationality and profitability of slavery in their own and perhaps future generations, mid-nineteenth-century British political economists had more access to evidence in favor of the superiority of freedom than their eighteenth-century predecessors had possessed. Comparisons confined to British metropolitan and colonial labor systems had produced not-always-reassuring conclusions about the relative condition of European peasants and proletarians. However, the rapid development of nineteenth-century overseas zones of free labor also constituted a broadening evidentiary base in favor of freedom. Merivale's invocation of Alexis de Tocqueville's contrast between dynamic Ohio and sluggish Kentucky was only one striking example.[80] By 1860, industrial New England and the Mid-Atlantic states, agricultural Australia and North America, implied that freedom in general rather than free wage labor in particular promised a long run superiority of the free society tortoise over the slave society hare. Political Economy could not predict the distant moment when compulsory labor would succumb, but it forecast the ever more rapid expansion of prosperous free labor in the frontier of the temperate zone.

CONCLUSION

What, then, of the 'great experiment' in the British West Indies? The results were mixed, and especially disappointing to those who had held out the brightest hopes for simultaneous increases in commercial productivity and in the ex-slaves' standard of living. One great target audience of the experiment, the planters and governments of other slave societies, seemed particularly unimpressed. Although British Caribbean laborers in 1860 still seemed remarkably orderly in comparison with their

European counterparts, very few ex-slave colonies had demonstrated an ability to expand or even sustain production without the further aid of compulsory labor. Exemplary successes, like Barbados, were not frontier societies like the United States, Cuba and Brazil. Compared to the 'triumphant progress' of free labor communities in North America or in the Southern Pacific; or to the 'scarcely less brilliant, though sinister and insecure prosperity of Cuba and Louisiana', the British Caribbean colonies in 1860, seemed 'stationary at best, subsisting but not accumulating'.[81] They matched neither their American free labor brethren in their standard of living, nor their Cuban slave labor brethren in productivity. They were already assuming the status of less-developed-societies that would be theirs over the following century.[82]

For British consumers, the results were of diminishing significance. A decreasing proportion of their sugar came from the British West Indies. By 1860, the literature comparing comparisons between free labor in Britain and the British Caribbean was also diminishing in quantity and intensity. In general, the British Caribbean was a place 'where no marked improvement strikes the eye, even where there are no signs of absolute decay'.[83] 'Race' subtly gained credence as an explanatory device. Merivale vigorously defended black workers against 'the common' representation of them as destitute of the ordinary capacity of workers. In densely populated Barbados they were 'as regular in their daily labour as the operatives of the old communities of Europe'. Even there, however, their numbers made the planters less anxious to innovate. No ex-slave colony received an evaluation as clearly progressive.[84]

The imaginary line between free and slave labor that ran between Northwestern Europe and most of the world when the *Wealth of Nations* appeared had shifted a century later. Political action had ended or provided for the gradual ending of slavery throughout the zones of expanding European settlement. However, penally coerced labor continued to be the dominant form of labor in the production of commercial crops in the tropics. With the repositioning of the line between free and unfree labor, race loomed larger than ever as a dividing line in determining the migratory flow of labor.

The great debate over the relative merits of free and slave labor ended with the return of the excluded middle. In this sense the battle between advocates of slave and free labor in the Atlantic system was a dramatic interlude between periods of more nuanced assessments of the performance of labor under various regimes of constraint and choice. During the age of British abolitionism, political economists were probably more wary of offering deflationary assessments of free labor superiority than either before or after. Even at the height of abolitionist influence, however, there never seems to have been a moment when faith in the free labor ideology was consensual in Britain – not even among the abolitionist leadership.[85] It was still less so among other European, African and American elites.

In cultural terms, the true measure of the abolitionist achievement lay less in a national conversion to free labour superiority, than in the psychological 'wear and tear' of their moral and political agitation against the doubters. The overwhelming asymmetry of mass opinion that slavery had to come to an end may have caused a very brief suspension of disbelief in the high risk of commercial disaster. Colonial slavery did not, however, come under massive and sustained attack in Britain because it was incompatible with capitalism. Still less was it brought to an end because it was a defective form of capitalist labor. Antislavery mobilized against those general characteristics of colonial slavery that most distinguished it from contemporary legal and social relations in Western Europe. Viewed from Britain New World slavery rested upon an extraordinary, and extraordinarily brutal, exercise of power. It was institutionally, if not always empirically, indifferent to the dignity, the bodies and the relationships of the enslaved. Masters could claim nearly absolute property rights in the persons they bought or inherited. Such claims extended well beyond the demand for 'ordinary labor service', as the most dependent laborer understood that service in England. Masters routinely escaped public punishment for acts that would have cost them their liberty or their lives in the metropolis. In this sense, the supreme achievement of the abolitionists was to have shifted the terms of debate over the terms of colonial labor by eliminating chattel property from the range of options available to employers. In a process drawn out over three generations the attack upon slavery also set in motion a series of changes that altered the terms of labor in other parts of the globe as well.[86]

NOTES

I am grateful to the participants in the Terms of Labor project and the Working Class group of the Pittsburgh Center for Social History for their incisive and helpful suggestions. I would also like to offer particular thanks to Stanley Engerman, Van Beck Hall and Michael Jimenez for careful readings of earlier drafts of this chapter.

1. See Robert J. Steinfeld, *The Invention of Free Labor: The employment relation in English and American law and culture, 1350–1870* (Chapel Hill and London, 1991); and Steinfeld, 'The Myth of the Rise of Free Labor: A critique of historical stage theory' (MS, forthcoming). The controlling distinction was that a 'Free-man' had the proprietary right to sell future limited actions ('Service') for a limited duration. See John Locke, *Two Treatises of Government*, Peter Laslett, ed. (Cambridge, 1970), II, sec. 85. Locke's 'laws of nature' explicitly precluded anyone from purchasing rights in persons as opposed to rights in actions. It remains doubtful whether Locke extended this law to the Caribbean (See *ibid.*, I, sec. 130).
2. For overviews, see Robin Blackburn, *The Overthrow of Colonial Slavery, 1776–1848* (London, 1988); David Eltis, *Economic Growth and the Ending of the Transatlantic Slave Trade* (New York, 1987); Robert William Fogel, *Without Consent or Contract: The Rise and Fall of American Slavery* (New York, 1989), pt. two.
3. See William A. Green, *British Slave Emancipation: The sugar colonies and the great experiment, 1830–1865* (Oxford: Oxford University Press, 1976), ch. 7.
4. Charles Buxton, *Slavery and Freedom in the West Indies* (London, 1860), title page. Buxton's summary had already been published as 'The West Indies as They Were and Are', *Edinburgh Review* 109 (1859), pp. 216–36.
5. M. I. Finley, *Ancient Slavery and Modern Ideology* (New York, 1980), p. 90. Aristotle, *The Politics of Aristotle*, trans. Ernest Barker (Oxford, 1948), bk I; Christopher J. Berry, *The Idea of Luxury: A conceptual and historical investigation* (Cambridge, 1994), pp. 46–58.
6. Sir Thomas Smith, *De Republica Anglorum* (1583 rept. Cambridge, 1906), p. 46; Jean Bodin, *The Six Books of A Commonwealth*, ed. K. D. McRae (Cambridge, 1996), pp. 135–37.
7. P. K. O'Brien and S. L. Engerman, 'Exports and the Growth of the British Economy from the Glorious Revolution to the Peace of Amiens', in *Slavery and the Rise of the Atlantic System*, Barbara Solow, ed. (New York, 1991), p. 207.
8. See, *inter alia*, S. Drescher, *Capitalism and Antislavery: British mobilization in comparative perspective* (New York, 1987), pp. 1–12; Drescher, 'The Long Goodbye: Dutch Capitalism and Antislavery in Comparative Perspective', in Gert Oostindie, ed., *Fifty Years Later: Antislavery, capitalism and modernity in the Dutch orbit*, (Leiden and Pittsburgh, 1995 and 1996), pp. 25–66; see also Chapter 7 in this volume; David Eltis, *Economic Growth*, ch. 1.

9. Drescher, *Capitalism and Antislavery*, pp. 12–24.
10. Anthony J. Barker, *The African Link: British attitudes to the negro in the era of the slave trade, 1550–1807* (London, 1978), pp. 98–9. See also, David Eltis, 'Europeans and the Rise and Fall of African Slavery in the Americas: An interpretation', *American Historical Review*, 98 (1993): pp. 1399–1423; John Thornton, *Africa and the Africans in the Making of the Atlantic World, 1400–1680* (Cambridge, 1992).
11. Drescher, *Capitalism*, pp. 22–4. *Idem.*, 'Capitalism and Abolition: values and forces in Britain, 1783–1814', in Roger Anstey and P. E. H. Hair, eds., *Liverpool, The African Slave Trade, and Abolition* (Bristol, 1976), pp. 167–95.
12. Sir James Steuart, *An Inquiry into the Principles of Political Economy*, 2 vols. (London, 1767), I, p. 227.
13. Drescher, *Capitalism*, ch. 2; *idem.*, 'The Long Goodbye', pp. 49–50; David Brion Davis, *The Problem of Slavery in the Age of Revolution, 1770–1823* (Ithaca, 1975), ch. 10; Sue Peabody, *'There are No Slaves in France': The political culture of race and slavery in the ancien régime* (New York, 1996).
14. Bruce A. Ragsdale, *A Planters Republic: The search for economic independence in revolutionary America* (Madison, 1996).
15. Benjamin Franklin, 'Observations Concerning the Increase of Mankind', in L. W. Labaree, ed., *The Papers of Benjamin Franklin*, vol. 4 (New Haven, 1961), pp. 229–30.
16. Berry, *The idea of Luxury*, pp. 142–73, on Hume and Smith.
17. Adam Smith, *Lectures on Jurisprudence*, eds. R. Meek, D. Raphael and P. Stein (Indianapolis, 1982), p. 185; Smith, *Wealth of Nations*, eds. R. H. Campbell, A. S. Skinner and W. B. Todd (Indianapolis, 1981), pp. 22–3.
18. Smith, *Wealth of Nations*, pp. 387–8, 98. Abolitionists later frequently alluded to the high overhead costs of managing slaves. In an overall evaluation of plantation costs in 1833, however, one of the Colonial Office policy architects dismissed the 'managerial-costs' argument with a single sentence: 'What capitalist in any country carries on a manufacture with fewer hired superintendents for every hundred of laborers than the sugar planter?' [Henry Taylor] 'Colonial Office, January 1833. Memo: for the Cabinet', C0884/1, 58. [Hereafter, Taylor 'Memorandum'.]
19. Smith, *Lectures*, pp. 186–7.
20. Smith, *Wealth of Nations*, p. 70.
21. *Adam Smith's An Inquiry into the Nature and Causes of the Wealth of Nations: A concordance*, Fred R. Glahe, ed. (Lanham, MD, 1993). Early abolitionists mentioned the presence of indentured laborers to refute the idea of the impossibility of using European field labor in the Caribbean. They were less anxious to discuss its subsequent yielding to slave labor.
22. Smith, *Wealth of Nations*, p. 98.
23. *Ibid.*, p. 99. Defenders of the slave trade confidently appealed to the authority of Hume and Smith in defense of their system. See S. Drescher, 'Capitalism and Abolition', in Anstey and Hair, *Liverpool*, p. 195, n. 49, and chap. 1 in this volume.

24. James Ramsay, *Objections to the Abolition of the Slave Trade, with Answers* (London, 1788), p. 8; Thomas Clarkson, *Essay on the Impolicy of the African Slave Trade* (London, 1788); Clarkson, *The History of the Rise, Progress and Accomplishment of the Abolition of the African Slave Trade by the British Parliament*, 2 vols. (London, 1808), I, p. 86.
25. See *Morning Chronicle*, 15 September 1785, *ibid.*, 3 October 1785; *London Chronicle*, 29 September, 4 October 1785; Ramsay, *Objections*, pp. 8–9.
26. *Ibid.*, p. 104
27. William Wilberforce, *A Letter on the Abolition of the Slave Trade* (London, 1807), pp. 144, 210 (author's emphasis).
28. *Ibid.*, p. 104.
29. See, *inter alia*, Stanley L. Engerman and David Eltis, 'Economic Aspects of the Abolition Debate,' in Christine Bolt and Seymour Drescher, eds. *Anti-Slavery, Religion and Reform: Essays in memory of Roger Anstey* (Folkestone and Hamden, 1980), pp. 284–5; Jonathan A. Glickstein, *Concepts of Free Labor in Antebellum America* (New Haven, 1991); David Brion Davis, *The Problem of Slavery in the Age of Revolution, 1770–1823*, pp. 346–54; Howard Temperley, 'Capitalism, Slavery and Ideology', *Past and Present*, 75 (1977), pp. 94–118; *idem.*, 'Anti-Slavery as a Form of Cultural Imperialism', in Bolt and Drescher, *Anti-Slavery, Religion and Reform*, pp. 335–50; David Eltis, *Economic Growth*, pp. 20–4.
30. See, e.g., Wilberforce, *Letter*, p. 254.
31. Seymour Drescher, 'People and Parliament: The rhetoric of the British slave trade', *Journal of Interdisciplinary History*, 20 (1990), pp. 561–80.
32. Roger Anstey, *The Atlantic Slave Trade and British Abolition, 1760–1810* (Atlantic Highlands, NJ, 1975), p. 256. For the various valuations of capital invested in the British West Indies, see Seymour Drescher, *Econocide: British slavery in the era of abolition* (Pittsburgh, PA 1977), pp. 22–3.
33. Wilberforce, *Letter*, p. 257.
34. *Hansard's Parliamentary Debates*, 1st ser. vol. 9, 1807, March 17, cols 142–6.
35. H. Brougham, *An Inquiry into the Colonial Policy of the European Powers*, 2 vols. (Edinburgh, 1803), II, pp. 60–140 and 310–14; and Wilberforce, *Letter*, p. 259.
36. See, *inter alia*, Eltis, *Economic Growth*, p. 22; David Brion Davis, *Slavery and Human Progress* (New York, 1984), pp. 189–91.
37. Dean Tucker, *Reflections on … Great Britain and Ireland* (London, 1785), quoted in F. O. Shyllon, *James Ramsay: The unknown abolitionist*, p. 77.
38. Drescher, *Econocide* pp. 114–19.
39. *Ibid.*, pp. 76–83.
40. See David Eltis, *Economic Growth*, p. 20; and Sidney W. Mintz, *Sweetness and Power: The place of sugar in modern history* (New York: 1985), pp. 61–73.
41. See, e.g., Wilberforce, *Letter*, pp. 262–4.
42. Drescher, *Capitalism and Antislavery*, pp. 78–9, Clare Midgley, 'Slave Sugar Boycotts, Female Activism and the Domestic Base of British Anti-Slavery Culture', *Slavery and Abolition*, 17 (1996), pp. 137–62.

43. *Capitalism and Antislavery*, p. 243; Stephen, *Crisis of the Sugar Colonies*, (London, 1802), pp. 185–9. Stephen's estimates of St Domingue's production under Toussaint L'Ouverture are still regarded as reliable. See Mats Lundahl, 'Toussaint L'Ouverture and the War Economy of Saint-Domingue, 1796–1802', *Slavery and Abolition*, 6(2) (1985), pp. 122–38.
44. *Parliamentary Debates* vol. 19 (April 4 1811), col. 710.
45. Drescher, *Econocide*, pp. 156–9.
46. J.-B. Say, *Traité d'economie politique*, 2 vols. (Paris, 1814), I, p. 283. For a similar conclusion about sugar and slavery from an English economist's perspective, see J. R. McCulloch's *The Principles of Political Economy*, 4th edn. (London, 1849), pt. III, ch. II, sec. 2, pp. 437–9. McCulloch was one of Britain's most popular political economists between the opening of the campaign for gradual emancipation in 1823 and the ending of colonial apprenticeship in 1838. See also S. Drescher, 'Cart Whip and Billy Roller: Antislavery and reform symbolism in industrializing Britain', *Journal of Social History*, 15 (1981), pp. 3–24, esp. pp. 5–6. Characteristically, Jeremy Bentham subscribed precisely to Smith's comparison of free and slave labor, but never doubted the abolition of slavery's unprofitability to the slave-owners. Despite decades of friendly relations with Wilberforce, Bentham offered no public support whatever to the campaign for gradual abolition in the 1820s. See Lea Campos Baralevi, *Bentham and the Oppressed* (New York, 1984), pp. 154–6.
47. Hodgson, *A Letter to M. Jean Baptiste Say on the Comparative Expense of Free and Slave Labor*, 2nd. edn. (London, 1823), p. 60.
48. See Montifort Longfield, *Lectures on Political Economy* (Dublin, 1834), p. 71 (*Parliamentary Debates*, 2nd ser., 1828, vol. 18, cols. 1026–1027), and Wilmot-Horton, *First Letter to the Freeholders of the County of York, on Negro Slavery: being an inquiry into the claims of the West Indians for equitable compensation* (London, 1830), p. 7.
49. B. W. Higman, 'Slavery and the Development of Demographic Theory in the Age of the Industrial Revolution', in James Walvin, ed., *Slavery and British Society* (London, 1982), pp. 164–94.
50. See, *inter alia*, *The Petition and Memorial of the Planters of Demerara and Berbice on the subject of Manumission, Examined* (London, 1827), pp. 21–48.
51. Sir J. R. Wilmot Horton, *Speech in the House of Commons, 6 March 1828, with notes and appendix* (London, 1828), Appendix B, p. 73; Alexander MacDonnell, *Considerations on Negro Slavery* (London, 1824), pp. 62–8. While some historians assume that the 'consumer revolution' was well underway by the eighteenth century, others date its spread to the working classes after 1850. See E. Hobsbawm, *Industry and Empire* (Harmondsworth, 1968), p. 74.
52. MacDonnell, *Considerations*, pp. 63, 69; Wilmot Horton, *Speech*, p. 73; Gilbert Mathison, *A Critical View of the West India Question ... In a letter addressed to the Right Hon. Robert Wilmot Horton* (London, 1827), pp. 77–8.
53. See David Geggus, 'Haiti and the Abolitionists: Opinion, propaganda and international politics in Britain and France, 1804–1838', in

Abolition and its Aftermath: The historical context, 1790–1916, David Richardson, ed. (London, 1985), pp. 113–40; David Eltis, 'Abolitionist Perceptions of Society after Slavery', in *Slavery and British Society 1776–1846*, James Walvin, ed. (London, 1982), pp. 195–213.

54. Drescher, *Capitalism and Antislavery*, chs. 5–6. See also Harriet Martineau, *Tale of Demerara, Illustrations of Political Economy* (London, 1832); Josiah Conder, *Wages or the Whip* (London, 1833): discussed by Patricia Hollis, 'Anti-Slavery and British Working-Class Radicalism', in Bolt and Drescher, *Anti-Slavery*, pp. 294–315. See also Davis, *Slavery and Human Progress*, pp. 189, 214–22; and Thomas C. Holt, *The Problem of Freedom: Race, labor, and politics in Jamaica and Britain, 1832–1938* (Baltimore, 1992), pp. 48–53. On slave motivations, see Michael Craton, *Testing the Chains: Resistance to slavery in the British West Indies* (Ithaca and London, 1982), pp. 300–4. Before British emancipation the French Revolutionary colonial experience also indicated a high probability of partial or total withdrawal from plantation agriculture unless limited by coercive restraints.

55. George Thompson, *Speech on Colonial Slavery ... at ... Manchester*, 13 August 1832, quoted in Drescher, *Capitalism*, pp. 266, n. 1. For Henry Taylor, at the Colonial Office, the strength of popular demands was such that immediate emancipation without any compensation seemed to be a real possibility by the beginning of 1833. The West Indians' only hope lay with those classes and politicians who valued property, legality and political economy. See Taylor, 'Memorandum', pp. 62–3.

56. On the Bill's development and passage, see Holt, *Problem of Freedom*, pp. 42–50; and Green, *British Slave Emancipation*, ch. 4. Thomas Fowell Buxton specifically invoked the automatic and immediate efficacy of wages among free men as insuring adequate labor. See *Parliamentary Debates*, 3rd ser. vol. 10 (June 10 1833), col. 517.

57. For the abolitionists on sugar protection, see *inter alia*, *Second Report of the Committee of the Society for the Mitigation and Gradual Abolition of Slavery* (London, 1825), pp. 26–33; *Anti-Slavery Reporter*, 12 (31 May 1826), pp. 185–7.

58. J. R. Ward, *British West Indian Slavery, 1750–1834: The process of amelioration* (Oxford, 1988), p. 249.

59. Green, *British Slave Emancipation*, ch. 9; Hugh Tinker, *A New System of Slavery: The export of Indian labor overseas, 1830–1920* (London, 1974); David Northrup, *Indentured Labor in the Age of Imperialism, 1834–1922* (New York, 1995); P. C. Emmer, ed., *Colonialism and Migration: Indentured labor before and after slavery* (The Hague, 1986).

60. Howard Temperley, *White Dreams, Black Africa: The antislavery expedition to the Niger, 1841–1842* (New Haven, 1991); Pieter Emmer, 'The Ideology of Free Labor and Dutch Colonial Policy, 1830–1870', in Gert Oostindie, ed., *Fifty Years Later*, pp. 207–22. The 'Cultivation System' required laborers to cultivate export crops for a certain number of days each year.

61. Davis, *Slavery and Human Progress*, pp. 179–81, 199.

62. Drescher, *Econocide*, pp. 127–9, 174–7; Howard Temperley, 'Eric Williams and Abolition: The birth of a new orthodoxy', in Solow and Engerman, *British Capitalism*, pp. 229–57.

63. See J. R. Ward, *British West Indian Slavery, 1750–1834: The process of amelioration* (Oxford, 1988), pp. 249 ff.
64. William A. Green, *British Slave Emancipation*, pp. 165, 306. Green emphasizes British anti-slavery's radicalization after Emancipation, in their placing 'highest emphasis on the protection of freedmen's liberty, not the maintenance of export levels'. 'Was British Emancipation a Success?', in *Abolition and its Aftermath: The historical context, 1790–1916*, David Richardson, ed. (London, 1985), pp. 183–202, esp. p. 199, n. 36.
65. See Howard Temperley, *British Antislavery, 1833–1870* (London, 1972), pp. 137–67; and Ruth Dudley Edwards, *The Pursuit of Reason: The Economist 1843–1993*, (London, 1993), pp. 19–20; and C. Duncan Rice, '"Humanity Sold for Sugar" The British abolitionist response to free trade in slave-grown sugar', *Historical Journal*, 13 (1970), pp. 402–18. Rice notes that sugar free traders always remained a minority in the movement (p. 416), but Temperley correctly concludes that the split depreciated the once formidable powers of popular mobilization (*British Antislavery*, p. 161).
66. *Hansard's Parliamentary Debates* 3rd ser. vol. 88, 13 August 1846, col. 662.
67. Northrup, *Indentured Labor*, p. 21, figure 2.1. In the 1850s, the British colonies received 61 per cent of indentured servants.
68. Howard Temperley, *British Antislavery*, pp. 141–51, Ward, *British West Indian Slavery*, p. 263.
69. Smith, *Wealth of Nations*, p. 400.
70. See Ian Duffield, 'From Slave Colonies to Penal Colonies: The West Indian convict transportees to Australia', *Slavery and Abolition*, 7 (1986), pp. 25–45; S. Drescher, *Capitalism and Antislavery*, ch. 6, idem., 'Cart Whip and Billy Roller' pp. 3–24; idem., 'The Ending of the Slave Trade and the Evolution of European Scientific Racism', *Social Science History*, 14 (1990), pp. 415–50; see also Chapter 9 in this volume; Jonathan A. Glickstein, *Concepts of Free Labor in Antebellum America* (New Haven, 1991). On comparative living standards in Britain and the West Indies, see Green, *British Slave Emancipation*, p. 198n., and Ward, *British West Indian Slavery*, pp. 263, 286–8.
71. See, for example, *Condition of the Slave not Preferable to that of the British Peasant, from the evidence before the Parliamentary Committees on Colonial Slavery* (London, 1833). On the historiography, see Thomas Bender, ed., *The Antislavery Debate: Capitalism and abolitionism as a problem in historical interpretation*, (Berkeley, 1992); and S. Drescher, 'The Antislavery Debate' (review essay) in *History and Theory*, 32 (1993), pp. 311–28.
72. *Anti-Slavery Reporter*, 23 (April 30 1827), p. 356. See also *the Petition and Memorial of the Planters of Demerara and Berbice on the subject of Manumission, Examined*, p. 41.
73. See, above all, Davis, *The Problem of Slavery*, chs. 8 and 9, *passim*.
74. See, *inter alia, ibid.*, esp. pp. 349–57; 453–68; Bender, *The Antislavery Debate, passim*; and Drescher, 'The Antislavery Debate', pp. 320–9. On agricultural laborers, see Peter Karsten, 'Bottomed on Justice': A reappraisal of critical legal studies scholarship concerning breaches

of labor contracts by quitting or firing in Britain and the US, 1630–1880', *American Journal of Legal History*, 34 (1990), pp. 213–61, esp. pp. 217–21; David H. Morgan, *Harvesters and Harvesting, 1840–1900: A study of the rural proletariat* (London, 1982), pp. 124–33.
75. Temperley, *British Antislavery*, pp. 93–110.
76. Merivale, *Lectures* (London, 1861), pp. 300, 353. Eric Williams invoked Merivale's economic premises to explain the rise of the British slave system in the seventeenth and eighteenth centuries (*Capitalism and Slavery*, Chapel Hill, 1944), p. 7. Based upon those same premises, however, Merivale radically rejected economic explanations for the fall of that slave system in the nineteenth century.
77. *Ibid.*, p. 303 (Merivale's emphasis) and pp. 307–8, 565. See also n. 56 above.
78. On indentured servants see Dharma Kumar, 'Colonialism, Bondage and Caste in British India', in Martin A. Klein ed., *Breaking the Chains: Slavery, bondage, and emancipation in modern Africa and Asia* (Madison, 1993), pp. 112–30, esp. p. 125. The volume of migrants from India from 1834 until the termination of indentured service in 1916, is calculated from Kingsley Davis, *The Population of India and Pakistan* (Princeton, 1951), pp. 98–9. The interhemispheric flow of Asian indentured labor (about one million) was far smaller than its African counterpart, but the flow of Asians within Asia and to Africa was also largely in the form of indentured service. As Pieter Emmer notes,

> Production of sugar and coffee in Asia and Africa for export overseas was feasible only in case labor could be subsidized or forced to work below market prices or in case the consumer market was protected.

See 'The Price of Freedom: The constraints of change in postemancipation America', in *The Meaning of Freedom: Economics, politics, and culture after slavery*, Frank McGlynn and Seymour Drescher, eds. (Pittsburgh, 1992), pp. 23–47, esp. pp. 26–8. On the implications of indentured servitude for the question of slavery's competitive viability in the Americas, see also Martin Klein, 'Slavery, the International Labour Market and the Emancipation of Slaves in the Nineteenth Century', in Paul E. Lovejoy and Nicholas Rogers, eds., *Unfree Labour in the Development of the Atlantic World* (London, 1994), pp. 197–220, esp. pp. 206–7.
79. J. E. Cairnes, *The Slave Power: Its character and probable designs* (London, 1862). Karl Marx agreed completely with Howick, Merivale and Cairnes that the terms of labor were utterly different in newly developing colonies from those in more densely populated areas. See Karl Marx, *Capital*, 1, trans. Samuel Moore and Edward Aveling (Moscow, n.d.), p. 770. Although cautious about the difficulties of comparison, in view of changing taxes and overhead costs, Thomas Holt also concluded that 'strictly speaking, it may have been cheaper to run a slave than to hire a free worker' in Jamaica (*Problem of Slavery*, pp. 124 ff.). This assessment

Free Labor vs Slave Labor 443

is consistent with the findings of economic historians of the Americas. For a recent hemispheric summary, see Laird Bergad *et al.*, *The Cuban Slave Market, 1790–1880* (New York, 1995), pp. 143–54.

80. See Alexis de Tocqueville, *Democracy in America*, 2 vols. (New York, 1945), I, pp. 376 ff.
81. *Ibid.*, pp. 336–7: 'Slave Labour (1860)'. By the end of the 1850s, British West Indian sugar exports had virtually regained their pre-emancipation levels (see Green, *British Slave Emancipation*, p. 246). Charles Buxton, recalculating from the low point of the early 1840s, viewed the post-1846 rise in exports as a vindication of the decisive success of *two* 'great' experiments, British slave emancipation and British free trade. (See Buxton 'The West Indies as They Were and Are', p. 229.) *The Edinburgh Review* illustrates the continued volatility of assessments of free vs slave labor in the 1860s. See Meadows Taylor, 'Cotton Culture in India', *Edinburgh Review*, 115 (1862), pp. 478–509; Harriet Martineau, 'The Negro Race in America', *Edinburgh Review*, 119 (1864), pp. 203–42; P. W. Clayden, 'The Reconstruction of the American Union', *ibid.*, 123 (1866), pp. 524–56. On the outcome of free labor 'experiments' by Northern capitalists and abolitionists, see Richard H. Abbott, *Cotton and Capital: Boston businessmen and antislavery reform, 1854–1868* (Amherst, 1991), pp. 87–8.
82. See Frank McGlynn and Seymour Drescher, eds., *The Meaning of Freedom: Economics, politics and culture after slavery* (Pittsburgh, 1992).
83. Merivale, *Lectures*, p. 337.
84. *Ibid.*, p. 340. From the perspective of many economic historians of the United States' South, a central theme 'remains the failure of the free-labor system to live up to the hopes of either its Republican spokesmen or the freedmen themselves'. (See Peter Kolchin, 'The Tragic Era? Interpreting Southern reconstruction in comparative perspective', in McGlynn and Drescher, *The Meaning of Freedom*, pp. 291–311, esp. pp. 293–4.)
85. The line between slave and free labor has blurred in slave historiography. See, *inter alia*, Mary Turner, ed., *From Chattel Slaves to Wage Slaves: The dynamics of labour bargaining in the Americas* (Kingston, 1995), p. 11; Mark D. Smith 'Old South Time in Comparative Perspective', *American Historical Review*, 101 (1996), pp. 1432–69. Non-economic historians now seem as skeptical about Adam Smith's view of the universal superiority of free labor as was Merivale. See, e.g., Michael Twaddle, 'Visible and Invisible Hands', in *The Wages of Slavery: From chattel slavery to wage labour in Africa, the Caribbean and England*, a special issue of *Slavery and Abolition*, 14 (1993), pp. 1–12, esp. pp. 10–11.
86. On the relation of the abolition of slavery to abolitions of other unfree labor systems see, *inter alia*, Stanley Engerman, 'Emancipations in Comparative Perspective: a long and wide view', in Oostindie, ed., *Fifty Years Later*, pp. 223–41; and Drescher, 'Reflections', in *ibid.*, pp. 243–61, esp. pp. 254–9. For an extensive overview of the complex impact of British emancipation on European consciousness, see Davis, *Slavery and Human Progress*, pp. 168–226.

Index

Abolition: arguments and motives, 1–2, 6–8, 19–24, 141, 237–40, 249, 356, 365; petitions about, 5, 15, 25–6, 28, 38–9, 43, 44–6, 52, 59–70, 72, 73, 76, 79, 80–1, 138, 168–72, 173–5, 178, 179, 181, 209, 215, 257, 284, 410, 417, 427, 428; and economic policy, 13–15, 75–8, 87–8, 120–1, 122, 125, 133; historiography, 8–9; and *laissez-faire*, 10, 13–15, 176, 367–8; and mercantilism, 10–14, 202; and humanitarianism, 15–16, 22, 28–9, 109, 199, 361–2, 364, 371; and capitalism, 18, 25–9, 170n35, 176, 196–9, 202–3, 205, 208, 213–14, 219, 221, 356, 360–2, 364, 366–7, 370–2, 383–7, 391, 434; and religion, 22–3, 37–52, 58, 68–74, 109, 146, 170, 206–7, 217, 253, 388; interest group pressures, 24–9, 59, 64–81, 160–2, 384–5; and racial ideology, 141–4, 238–41, 250–2, 275–306, 284–8. *See also* Acts, Bills, Resolutions; Parliament, abolition moves

Abolition movements (American), 15, 74, 128, 131, 217, 235–7, 254, 276–7, 289, 386; and John Brown affair, 235–8, 252; British influence on, 237–8, 257–8; and women, 258

Abolition movements (Brazilian), 117, 119–47, 158, 214, 276–7; compared with US, 120n5, 135–9, 141–2, 144–6; economic significance of, 120–1, 122, 125, 133, 141; and politics, 127–8, 131–8, 141, 144, 146–7; British influence on, 130, 131; compared with Britain, 137–40; compared with Russia, 141–3; and masses, 137–41, 145; and racial ideology, 141–4, 238–41, 250–2, 277–8

Abolition movements (British), 35–52, 88–9, 97–8, 159, 199, 237–8, 254, 275, 280–1, 303–5, 356, 400, 407, 408–13, 421; economic significance of, 8–9, 75–8, 221, 358–9, 361–2, 405–6, 411–14, 418–24; compared with France, 35–52, 60–3, 75–6, 128, 160, 161, 169–70, 181–3, 208, 280–2, 284–5; class analysis of, 57–8, 67, 71–4, 81; and masses, 51, 57–81, 128, 228, 281, 284, 300–1, 371, 385, 387–8, 417, 419, 427, 430; and reform, 72, 80; and politics, 59–67, 69, 71, 72, 75–6, 108, 284, 303, 400, 417, 421–4, 425–30, 434–5; and religion, 22–3, 37–41, 68–73, 109, 400, and women, 67, 81, 258, 390n32, 412n42; compared with Brazil, 137–40; US influence on, 237–8, 257–8; and John Brown affair, 235–43, 247–8, 249–64; and racial ideology, 284–8, 290, 291–2

Abolition movements (Cuban), 129–30, 214, 277

Abolition movements (Dutch), 117, 196–221; and politics, 205; compared with Britain, 205–11, 218–21

Abolition movements (French), 35–52, 60–3, 74, 75–6, 128–9, 159–83, 208, 217,

446   Index

Abolition movements (French) (*cont.*) 236*n*3, 281–3, compared with Britain, 35–52, 60–3, 75–6, 128, 160, 161, 169–70, 181–3, 208, 280–2, 284–5, and religion, 41–6, 170, 174; and masses, 45, 46*n*21, 48–9, 162, 178, 179–81; British influence on, 45, 59, 161–3, 166–72; and reform, 75–6, 158, 159, 160–2, 166, 169, 172–3, 175–7, 180; colonial attitudes toward, 159–60, 164–7, 175–6; and politics, 160, 163–83, 281, 284; class analysis of, 161–2, 167, 172; and women, 168, 170, 282; and racial ideology, 284–8

Abolition movements (Haiti), 127–8, 160*n*9, 163, 417*n*53

Abolition movements (Spanish empire), 129–30

Abolition movements: tactics of, 35, 37, 59, 65–6, 71, 81, 128, 138, 146, 160–3, 168–9, 236, 254–6, 280–1, 284–5, 367; newspapers, 44, 60, 65–7, 71, 73, 128, 146, 164–5, 166–8, 170, 171, 174, 179, 235–7, 240, 241, 242–8, 249–54, 257–9, 263, 285

Abolitionism: Anglo–American vs. Continental, 35–7, 117, 128–30, 162–3. *See also* Anglo–American model of abolition; Continental model of abolition

Aborigines Protection Society, 292–301

Acts, Bills, Resolutions: abolition bills, 26, 104, 128, 158, 159, 160–2, 172–3, 178*n*52, 196, 211, 237, 244, 276, 293, 364, 410, 411, 413, 417, 418, 426, 431; Anglo-French treaty (1787), 11, 12, 28; Free Port Acts (1787, 1792), 11, 12; Navigation Act (1786), 11–13, 100; Slave Carrying Act (1799), 11, 104; Somerset decision (1772), 17–19, 24, 197, 218, 282; French abolition (1794), 36, 147, 159–60, 164, 181, 218, 281; (1848), 43, 44, 117, 161–2, 181, 183, 281, 293; Reform Act (1832), 72; Golden Law of 1888 (Brazil), 119, 128, 137, 147, 158, 197; Rio Branco Law of 1871 (Brazil), 128, 135, 136; Mackau Laws (1845), 166, 169; Guadeloupe plan (1847), 175–7; Brussels Act of 1890, 213; British Emancipation Act (1833), 305–6, 355–6, 400, 419–20, 426, 430; Dutch slave emancipation (1863), 349; British Foreign Abolition Bill (1806), 362, 412

Adamson, Alan, 109

Alba, Duke of, 261

America: slave trade, 15–16, 101–4, 216, 404; slavery, 15–16, 37, 41, 43, 47, 101–2, 120–1, 122, 123, 133, 240, 400, 404–5, 407, 411, 415; Civil War, 47, 49, 59, 70, 130, 259, 260, 262, 400, 425, 430; abolition movements. *See also* Abolition movements (American)

American Anti-Slavery Society, 236

American Revolution, 10, 12, 87, 88, 89, 94, 97, 101, 104, 105, 108, 197, 201, 206, 208, 217, 218, 305, 359, 361, 363, 367–8, 383, 389, 400, 404

Amiens, Peace of (1802), 164

Amis des Noirs, 42, 45, 47, 164, 180, 181, 281, 282, 284

Anglicans, 37, 69, 70, 71

Anglo–American model of abolition, 35–7, 117, 128–30, 137–9, 147, 162–3, 168, 196–7, 400

Anglo–Dutch war (1780–4), 208–9

Anglo–French racial thought, 292–302

Anglo–French treaty of 1787, 11, 12, 28. *See also* Acts, Bills, Resolutions

Anglo–Portuguese treaty of 1810, 130
Anglo–Saxonism, 239–41, 250–2, 294–302, 306
Annales de la propagation de la foi, 44, 48
Anstey, Roger, 2, 23, 57–8, 89, 104, 108, 362, 368, 371
Anthropological Society of London, 301, 302
Anti-abolitionists, 24–9, 139n65, 214, 252, 280, 282–3, 284–5, 289–90, 415–16
Anti-slavery. *See* Abolition; Abolitionism
Antislavery Recollections, 71
Arago, Etienne, 263
Arago, François, 179
Auschwitz, 323, 326, 327, 328, 330. *See also* Holocaust

Baptists: and abolition, 38 *Fig.* 2.1, 40 *Tab.* 2.2, 69, 73, 80
Barbarism: vs. civilization, 238–40, 279–80, 294–6, 298–9, 329–30
Barham, Joseph, 412
Barker, Anthony, 285
Barracoons, 314, 319
Batavian Republic: and abolition, 211–13
Baxter, Richard, 16
Beckles, Hilary, 365, 379
Beverwijck, Johan van, 204
Bismarck, Otto von, 260
Bissette, Cyrille C.A., 164, 169, 170
Blackburn, Robin, 3, 161–2, 171–2, 207–10, 211, 213, 383, 384, 387
Blanc, Louis, 263
Blanqui, Auguste, 261
Bloncourt, Melvil, 263
Blum, Robert, 261
Bodin, Jean, 401
Brazil: slave trade, 119–23, 133–4, 349; slavery, 119–22, 133–4; abolition movements. *See also* Abolition (Brazilian)

Bright, John, 259
British Anti-Slavery Society, 169
British Emancipation Act (1833), 305–6, 355–6, 400, 419–20, 426, 430
British and Foreign Anti-Slavery Society, 254, 259
British Foreign Abolition Bill (1806), 362, 412
Broca, Paul, 302
Brogan, Denis, 361, 390
Brougham, Henry, 410
Brown, John: affair of 1859, 118, 235–64; British opinion of, 235–43, 247–8, 249–64; British media coverage of, 235–7, 240, 241, 242–8, 249–54, 257–9, 262; and religion, 253, 254, 255–6
Brown, John L., 257–8
Brown, Mary, 245
Brussels Act of 1890, 213
Buchanan, President James, 241, 252
Bugeaud, Marshal, 173–4, 178
Bunting, Jabez, 64, 69
Burnham, Forbes, 356
Buxton, Thomas Fowell, 292

Cabet, Etienne, 261
Cain, P.J., 99
Cairnes, J.E., 432–3
Canning, George, 161
Cape Colony, 101
Capitalism: and slavery, 18, 20, 25–9, 87–8, 93, 126–7, 133, 160n10, 197–8, 219n68, 305, 315–16, 323, 325, 327, 347n15, 361, 363–6, 370, 380–1, 383–4, 389–90, 403–7, 431, 434; and abolition, 18, 25–9, 170n35, 176, 196–9, 202–3, 205, 208, 213–14, 219, 221, 356, 360–2, 364, 366–7, 370–2, 383–7, 391, 434
Carlyle, Thomas, 301, 428

Carrington, Selwyn, 90, 99–102, 105–7, 379
Catholics, 63, 64, 248; and abolition, 41–9, 146, 170, 174, 206–7
Cats, Jakob, 204
Chalmers, George, 11
Civil War. *See* America: Civil War
Civilization vs. barbarism, 238–40, 279–80, 294–6, 298–9, 329–30
Clapham sect, 51, 68
Clarkson, Thomas, 1, 5, 23, 57, 68, 356, 359, 408
Cohen, William B., 283
Columbus, Christopher: voyages of, 158, 340, 341, 350
Cobbett, William, 72, 73, 357
Cobden, Richard, 259
Coffee: British imports, 102, 103 *Tab* 4.3, 104, 422
Commager, Henry Steele, 360, 361
Congregationalists, 40 *Tab*. 2.2
Conrad, Robert, 135–6, 365
Consumerism, 411–12, 416n51, 422–3
Continental model of abolition, 35–6, 128–30, 162, 163–4, 213, 304
Conversos. *See* New Christians
Corn Laws, British, 423
Costa, Emília Viotti da, 143
Cotton industry, 12, 98, 107, 425, growth of, 9, 104, 125; and slavery, 9, 125, 425; British imports, 12, 102, 103 *Tab* 4.3, 104
Coupland, Reginald, 355, 358–9, 362, 367–8
Courtet de l'Isle, Victor, 291, 293, 299–300, 301
Cromwell, Oliver, 244, 260
Cropper, James, 421
Crouzet, François, 95
Cuba: slave trade, 120, 122, 349, 381; abolition movements, 129–30, 214, 277
Curtin, Philip, 109, 289–91
Cuvier, Georges de, 289, 291

Darity, William, 379
Davis, David Brion, 2, 3, 18, 23, 57, 161, 171, 283, 304, 371, 384, 389
Davis, Ralph, 104
Deane, Phyllis, 365
Decline theory, 1–3, 7, 273; definition, 8, 87; and economic position, 76, 87–110, 196–7, 276; and slave trade, 87–90, 93–97, 104–10, 196–8, 210–11. *See also* Ragatz, Lowell; Williams, Eric
Deerr, Noel, 96, 102
Demerara, 95, 98, 101, 105
Dessalines, Jean Jacques, 243, 260, 286
Dickens, Charles, 253
Doctors: in British slave trade, 320n25, 327–8
Donnan, Elizabeth, 360, 361
Douglass, Frederick, 254–6, 258
Doyle, Arthur Conan, 196
Dupanloup, Abbé, 45, 170
Dupin, Charles, 179
Dutch: slave trade, 172n40, 200–1, 204, 210, 215, 275, 347–8, 381; economy, 202–3, 209–10; slave emancipation (1863), 349; abolition movements. *See* Abolition movements (Dutch),

Economic policy: and abolition, 13–15, 75–8, 87–8, 120–1, 122, 125, 133
Edwards, William F., 292–3
Ehrman, John, 11
Eichthal, Gustave d', 293, 294
Eltis, David, 90, 123, 126, 304
Emancipation Proclamation, 48, 70, 259, 260, 400
Emmer, Pieter, 109, 196, 381
Engels, Friedrich, 251
Engerman, Stanley, 90, 379, 382
Evangelicals: and abolition, 37–41, 51–2, 58, 68–9, 70, 71,

217, 388; and monogenism, 289–91
Exoticism, 19–22

Félice, Guillaume de, 169
Fourier, Charles, 176
France: abolition in (1794), 36, 147, 159–60, 164, 181, 218, 281; (1848), 43, 44, 117, 161–2, 181, 183, 281, 293; revolution in (1789), 41–2, 43, 75, 97, 129, 160–1, 208, 218, 281, 289, 291, 339; (1848), 44–6, 61, 78, 163, 179, 300; slave trade, 76–7, 78, 413; colonial sugar production, 97, 177; abolition. *See also* Abolition movements (French)
Frank, Anne, 331–2
Franklin, Benjamin, 404–5
Free labor, 16–18, 120–5, 132–3, 198–9, 201–2, 216, 273, 371, 390, 399–435
Free ports: effect on trade, 11–13; and slave trade, 12; Acts of 1787, 1792, 11, 12
Freedman's Aid campaign, 48–50
French Abolitionist Society, 168, 178n54
French Revolution, 41–2, 43, 75, 97, 129, 160–1, 208, 218, 281, 289, 291, 339
Frontiers, 10, 20–1, 101–2, 121, 123
Fryer, Peter, 283

Garibaldi, Giuseppe, 242, 260
Garrison, William Lloyd, 236
Gee, William, 360
Geggus, David, 107
Gemery, Henry, 197, 366
Genovese, Eugene, 387
Gladstone, John, 28
Gobineau, Arthur de, 276n1, 299, 301
Goebbels, Josef, 326
Golbéry, Silvain, 287
Golden Law of 1888 (Brazil), 119, 128, 137, 147, 158, 197. *See also* Acts, Bills, Resolutions

Goveia, Elsa, 95
Grégoire, Abbé, 42, 50, 52, 281–2, 286, 298
Grotius, Hugo, 204
Gutzmore, Cecil, 90, 108
Guadeloupe plan (1847), 175–17
Guenebault, J.H., 289

Hahner, June, 143
Haiti: abolition movements, 127–8, 160n9, 163, 417n53; revolution, 243, 250, 261, 286, 387; slave population, 416–17; sugar production, 416–17
Hargreaves, J.D., 362
Harpers Ferry, Virginia: and John Brown affair, 118, 235–47
Hartley, David, 69
Hawkesbury, Lord, 11, 12
Henriques, Duarte Dias, 345
Heine, Heinrich, 196, 213
Hilberg, Raul, 318
Hobsbawm, Eric, 365, 381
Hodgkin, Thomas, 292, 293
Hogendorn, Jan, 197, 366
Holocaust, 340; compared with Atlantic slave trade, 273, 312–32
Hopkins, A.G., 99
Holt, Thomas, 379
Höss, Rudolf, 330
Howick, Viscount Henry, 417
Hugo, Victor and abolition, 235–6, 238–9, 245, 248, 249n31, 254, 257–8, 263
Humanitarianism: and abolition, 15–16, 22, 28–9, 109, 199, 361–2, 364, 371; vs. scientific racism, 288, 290, 291–2, 300, 301–2, 303–4
Hume, David, 295, 300
Hunt, Henry, 73
Hunt, James, 301–2
Hurwitz, Edith, 68, 70

India: interest in abolition, 430
Industrial Revolution, 95, 109–10, 358, 364–5, 369, 370, 380–5, 388, 389, 429

Inikori, J.E., 104, 379, 383
Inquisition. *See* Spanish Inquisition
Irish: and abolition, 43; and nationalism, 43n13, 249n31; in US, 43, 252
Irving, Thomas, 11

Jabrun, E. de, 174
Jamaica: uprisings, 79–80, 418, 419; cost of slaves, 79; proslavery movement, 137
James, C.L.R, 1, 359, 369, 371, 387
Jardin, André, 166–7, 169
Jefferson, Thomas: Declaration of Independence, 366
Jeffrey, Francis, 80
Jenkinson, Charles. *See* Hawkesbury, Lord
Jennings, Lawrence, 162, 169, 171
Jews: persecution of, 339–41; role in slave trade, 339–51
Jollivet, Thomas, 168–9, 174, 178n53

Klingberg, Frank, 362
Knox, Robert, 299, 301
Kolchin, Peter, 122n14, 141
Kossuth, Louis, 260

Labor: free vs. slave, 16–18, 120–5, 132–3, 198–9, 201–2, 216, 399–435; as a commodity, 18–19, 77–8, 218; supply of, 120–5, 132–3
Lafayette, marquis de, 261
Laissez-faire, 10, 13–15, 99–100, 364, 368, 389, 417; and abolition, 10, 13–15, 176, 367–8; and slavery, 10, 14, 88, 361; and sugar trade, 98, 368
Lavigerie, Cardinal, 206
Lawrence, William, 290, 302
Lecky, William E.H., 1, 356
Leeward Islands, 101
Levi, Primo, 323, 326
Lincoln, Abraham, 263; Emancipation Proclamation, 48, 70, 400

Liverpool, Lord. *See* Hawkesbury, Lord
London Emancipation Committee/ Society, 259–60
Long, Edward, 282–3, 285, 289
Longfield, Montifort, 414
Lopper, Richard 109
Lorimer, Douglas A., 305

Macaulay, Thomas B., 65
Mackau, Baron, 166, 174
Mackau Laws (1845), 166, 169
Malthus, Thomas, 414–15, 416
Mansfield, Chief Justice, 18, 19, 321–2. *See also* Somerset decision (1772),
Marranos (secret Jews), 345. *See also* New Christians
Marx, Karl, 249, 251
Martineau, Harriet, 254
Martinique: uprising, 161, 181
Mathews, Father Theodore, 43
Mauritius, 101, 421
Mazzini, Giuseppe, 260
Mellor, G.R., 361
Mercantilism, 10–13, 87, 88, 99–100, 360, 361, 363, 367–8, 389; and abolition, 10–14, 202. *See also* Protectionism
Merivale, Herman, 430–3, 434
Methodists: and abolition, 38 *Fig* 2.1, 40 *Tab*. 2.2, 51, 69, 73–74, 109, 388. *See also* Wesleyans
Michelet, Jules, 293
Middle Passage, Atlantic, 314, 317, 319
Mill, John Stuart, 259
Miller, Joseph, 317
Minchinton, Walter E., 90, 107, 379
Missionaries, 40–2, 45
Monogenism, 289–91
Montebello, duc de, 177, 178n53
Montesquieu, C.L. Secondat de, 20–1, 402
Montgomery, James, 286
Morton, D.M., 293

Index

Napoleon and abolition, 163, 164, 183, 212, 291
Navigation Act of 1786, 11–13, 100. *See also* Acts, Bills, Resolutions
New Christians, 345–7
Newspapers. *See* Abolition movements
Nonconformity, 37–41, 51–2, 58, 68–70, 80
North, Lord, 5

O'Brien, Patrick, 382
O'Connell, Daniel, 43, 419
Ogé, Vincent, 261
Ouverture, Toussaint L', 287

Paris Commune, 260, 263–4; Société Ethnologique, 292–301
Parliaments (Britain), 39; abolition moves, 5–6, 25, 60, 75, 97–8, 355, 413, 417, 418; candidates, 65, 69, 72, 73
Parker, Theodore, 240
Petitions: abolitionist, 5, 15, 25–6, 28, 38–9, 43, 44–6, 52, 59–70, 72, 73, 76, 79, 80–1, 138, 168–72, 173–5, 178, 179, 181, 209, 215, 257, 284, 410, 417, 427, 428; anti-abolitionist, 26
Phillips, Wendell, 253
Philippe, Louis, 161
Pitt, William, 11, 161; and slave trade, 97
Planters, 94, 96–100, 210, 407; and abolition, 26–7, 100, 121–2, 128, 131, 133–7, 139n65, 141, 143–6, 160, 167n27, 175–7, 284, 285, 292, 367, 384, 403–4, 410, 415–16; and slavery, 418, 422, 424–5
Political economy, 10–15, 87–93, 120–21, 122, 125, 133, 164–9, 315–16, 363–4, 366–72, 379–87, 389, 399, 403–11
Polygenism, 288–9, 290–1
Poor Law, British, 427
Population: slave, 121, 123, 137n56, 216, 218n65, 317, 400, 415, 416–17, 424, 432

Portugal, 124; abolition, 124n20; slave trade, 343–5, 346–7, 381
Price, Jacob, 370
Prichard, James Cowles, 288, 292, 300, 301–2
Production. *See* Coffee; Cotton; Sugar
Profitability: slave trade, 107, 366; for planters, 94, 366
Protectionism, 10–14, 93, 95–9, 177, 420, 423–4. *See also* Mercantilism
Protestants, 37–41, 45–6, 49, 68–9, 170
Public opinion: and abolition, 24–9, 37, 57–81, 162, 178, 179–81, 251, 253, 256, 285, 371n49

Quakers: and abolition, 5, 37, 59, 68, 215, 217, 254, 292
Quatrefages, Armand de, 293, 294

Racial ideology: and abolition, 141–4, 238–41, 250–2, 275–306, 284–8; Anglo–French thought, 292–302; and slave trade, 328–30, 379–80, 400
Radetzky, Joseph, 261
Ragatz, Lowell, 88; decline theory, 1, 8, 92–4, 99, 100, 102, 107, 108, 368
Ramsay, James, 408, 421
Raynal, Abbé, 119
Re-export: of slaves, 12, 105–6, 218, 404
Reform Act (1832), 72
Réforme, La, 179, 180n60
Regulation of slave trade. *See* Acts, Bills, Resolutions
Religion: and abolitionism, 22–3, 37–52, 58, 68–74, 109, 146, 170, 206–7, 217, 253, 388
Remond, Sarah, 252, 256
Rice, Duncan, 23
Richardson, David, 104
Rio Branco Law of 1871 (Brazil), 128, 135, 136. *See also* Acts, Bills, Resolutions
Romero, Sílvio, 144

Roscoe, William, 28–9
Russia: abolition movements, 141–3

St Domingue: uprising, 80, 88, 107, 140, 158, 208, 210, 217, 218, 243, 261, 262, 281–2, 286, 287, 367
Saint-Hilaire, Geoffroy, 288, 293
Saint-Just, Louis de, 261
Saint-Simon, Henri de, 291, 293
Saint-Vincent, Bory de, 288
Say, J.-B., 414, 431
Schama, Simon, 200
Schoelcher, Victor, 52, 161, 179–81, 183, 263, 294, 296, 298–9
Scientific racism, 273, 275–306; and slavery, 273, 275–306; and humanitarianism, 288, 290, 291–2, 300, 301–2, 303–4; and polygenism, 288–9, 290–1; and Anglo–French societies, 292–300
Scott, Rebecca, 214
Seasoning: of slaves, 314, 317, 323
Semeur, Le, 171–2
Seven Years' War, 9, 102, 400; impact on British slavery, 22
Sharp, Granville, 17
Sidmouth, Lord, 70
Sierra Leone, 217, 286, 287, 411
Slave Carrying Act (1799), 11, 104. See also Acts, Bills, Resolutions
Slave system: vs. free labor, 16–18, 120–5, 132–3, 198–9, 201–2, 216, 399–435
Slave trade: and the decline theory, 1–3, 8, 76, 87–90, 93–7, 104–10, 196–8, 210–11; regulation and moves toward abolition of, 5–6, 11, 15, 25–8, 72, 104, 119, 128, 135, 158–62, 206, 211, 237, 244, 276, 409–10; and protectionism, 10–13; and laissez-faire, 10, 14, 88, 361, in America, 15–16, 101–4, 216, 404; frontier and expansion, 20–1, 121, 123; compared to other trade, 76; Britain vs. France, 76–7, 78, 413; volume, value and profits, 101–7, 120–3, 172n40, 314, 325, 341–4, 364–6, 400; in Brazil, 119–23, 133–4, 349; in Cuba, 120, 122, 349, 381; Dutch, 172n40, 200–1, 204, 210, 215, 275, 347–8, 381; compared to Holocaust, 273, 312–32, 347–9; role of Jews in, 339–51, Portuguese, 343–5, 346–7, 381; Spanish, 343–4, 381
Slavery: extent and value, 9, 16, 75–8, 95, 101–2, 120–2, 123–4, 131, 133, 240, 400, 401–2, 410, 415, 432; and sugar trade, 9, 95–9, 102–3, 104, 125, 347n15, 348, 407, 411, 431; and cotton, 9, 125, 425; in America, 15–16, 37, 41, 43, 47, 101–2 120–1, 122, 123,133, 240, 400, 404–5, 407, 411, 415; and capitalism, 18, 20, 25–9, 87–8, 93, 126–7, 133, 160n10, 197–8, 219n68, 305, 315–16, 323, 325, 327, 347n15, 361, 363–6, 370, 380–1, 383–4, 389–90, 403–7, 431, 434; in Brazil, 119–22, 133–4; and scientific racism, 273, 275–306; and racial ideology, 328–30, 379–80, 400
Slaves: cost of, 18, 78, 79, 133, 134n46, 167n28; Britain not dependent on, 18; religion of, 40, 166, uprisings, 79–80, 88, 107, 140, 158, 159, 161, 180, 181, 208, 210, 212, 217, 218, 235–64, 281–2, 286, 287, 367, 417–19; diseases of, 318–19, 320–1, 323; transit of, 319–23
Slenes, Robert, 124
Smith, Adam, 13, 88, 97, 119, 158, 198, 366, 405–7, 408, 413–15, 416, 418, 425, 426, 431, 432–3

Index 453

Société d'Anthropologie de Paris, 302
Société de la Morale Chrétienne, 45
Solow, Barbara, 95, 96–7, 379, 381, 382
Somerset decision (1772), 17–19, 24, 197, 218, 282
Spanish Empire: abolition movements, 129–30; slave trade, 343–4, 381
Spanish Inquisition, 345–6, 347
Stanley, Edward, 76
Stearns, Frank Preston, 263, 264
Stephen, George, 68, 71, 72, 73
Stephen, James, 412–13, 414, 417, 424
Steuart, James, 403–4, 405, 414
Stowe, Harriet Beecher, 258
Sugar: production, 9, 95–8, 102–3, 105, 125, 407, 415, 420–4, 426, 434; compared to cotton as profitable crop, 9, 102, 103 *Tab. 4.3*, 104; and slavery, 9, 95–9, 102–3, 104, 125, 347n15, 348, 407, 411, 431; and protectionism, 14, 93, 95–9, 177, 420, 423–4; prices and profits, 95–9, 102, 103 *Tab. 4.3*, 104, 210, 368, 420–1, 424; duties, 99–100, 420, 423; compared to coffee as profitable crop, 102, 103 *Tab. 4.3*, 104; boycotts, 412, 423

Tannenbaum, Frank, 361
Tariffs: duties on sugar, 99–100, 420, 423
Taylor, Henry, 417
Temperley, Howard, 48, 98, 359, 370, 371
Thierry, Amédée and Augustin, 292–3
Thiers, Adolphe, 167
Thirty Years' War (1648), 201
Thompson, George, 50, 66, 256, 258
Tocqueville, Alexis de, 124, 146, 175, 433
Tolstoy, Leo, 332
Tourist, The, 65, 71

Trade, British and West Indian, 76, 91 *Fig. 4.1*, 92 *Tab. 4.1*, 107, 412, 419, 420, 422–3, 434
Trevelyan, G.M., 355
Trinidad, 101, 105, 412–13
Tucker, Dean, 421
Tudesq., A.-J., 166–7, 169
Turner, Mary, 95, 97

Underground Railroad (Brazil), 139
Unitarians, 38
Univers, L', 44–5, 47, 170
Utrecht, Treaty of, 97, 106

Versailles, Treaty of, 102, 107
Vesnier, Pierre, 260–2, 263
Veuillot, Louis, 44, 47, 170
Virey, Joseph, 288, 289

Wallerstein, Immanuel, 20
Walvin, James, 71
War of the Spanish Succession (1713), 201
Ward, J.R., 94
Watson, Reverend Richard, 292, 297
Wedgwood, Josiah, 12, 209
Wesleyans: and abolition, 38 *Fig. 2.1*, 40 *Tab. 2.2*, 51, 69, 72. *See also* Methodists
West Indies: cotton production, 9, 98; sugar production, 9, 95–8; 102–3, 105, 407, 415, 420, 423, 426, 431, 434; development and growth of, 10; as frontier, 10, 20–1, 101–2; free port bills, 11, 12; and abolition, 79–80; uprisings, 140
White, Charles, 290, 302
Whitworth, Sir Charles, 90, 101
Wilberforce, William, 19, 52, 69, 70, 72, 281, 285, 286, 305, 355, 357, 360, 409, 410, 412
Wilberforce, Samuel, 424
Williams, Eric: decline theory, 1–3, 7, 8, 87–104 106–10, 197, 210–11, 273, 276; biography, 355, 357–8; *Capitalism and*

Williams, Eric (*cont.*)
   Slavery, 355–72, 379–91, 431n76
Wilmot-Horton, R.J., 414
Winterbottom, Thomas, 287
Wise, Henry, 252
Women: and abolition, 67, 81, 168, 170, 258, 282, 390n32, 412n42

Woodson, Carter G., 363
Wright, Gavin, 276

Young, Arthur, 158, 216, 402

Zong slave trade case (1781), 321–2